Praise for

THE HISTORY OF THE PELOPONNESIAN WAR

'Athenian historian (if that's what he was) Thucydides is a notoriously gritty and gristly writer. Even his fellow ancient Greeks found translating him hard going. For a happy combination of accuracy (prime Thucydidean quality), literary fluency, and interpretative skill, this new translation by super-experienced Robin Waterfield with the assistance of distinguished ancient historian Polly Low will be far more than a transient showpiece of the sort Thucydides abhorred'

Paul Cartledge, author of *Democracy: A Life*

'Robin Waterfield has a track record of marvelous translations of Herodotus, Plato, and others, and now his Thucydides is just as good—extremely readable and accessible without any dumbing down of this demanding author. It is enhanced by the introduction and notes by Polly Low, telling readers exactly what they need to know to make the most of a perpetually engrossing text'

Christopher Pelling, University of Oxford

'Waterfield's elegant, modern translation of Thucydides will serve both scholars and general readers exceptionally well, while Low's introduction and notes offer just the right amount of context and explanation, illuminating the text rather than weighing it down. In their hands Thucydides's great work shows the same "bloom of perpetual newness" that Plutarch once saw in the Parthenon'

Johanna Hanink, Brown University

'Thucydides of Athens... is a dominating author like few others. Is he a historian, or philosopher, or social scientist? The truest answer is easily all three at once. Robin Waterfield's translation of a bold and powerful writer brimming with creative ideas on matters of language and politics is crisp, readable, and true to the author's diction. Polly Low's introduction is accessible and expansive without being pedantic. Famous debates on choosing war (Athens vs. Sparta), the use and abuse of power (Athenian imperial aggressions vs. Mytilene and Melos), and descriptions of wartime suffering (Pericles's iconic funeral speech) reveal issues of war and peace, justice and law, relevant to any time. Thucydides is a writer for the ages: Waterfield and Low, his interpreters today'

Lawrence A. Tritle, Loyola Marymount University

THE HISTORY OF THE PELOPONNESIAN WAR

THUCYDIDES

Translated by
ROBIN WATERFIELD

Introduction and Notes by Polly Low

LONDON

First published in Great Britain in 2025 by Basic Books UK
An imprint of John Murray Press

1

Copyright © Robin Waterfield and Polly Low 2025

The right of Robin Waterfield and Polly Low to be identified as the Author of the Work has been asserted by them in accordance with the Copyright, Designs and Patents Act 1988.

Maps copyright © András Bereznay 2025

All rights reserved. No part of this publication may be reproduced, stored in a retrieval system, or transmitted, in any form or by any means without the prior written permission of the publisher, nor be otherwise circulated in any form of binding or cover other than that in which it is published and without a similar condition being imposed on the subsequent purchaser.

A CIP catalogue record for this title is available from the British Library

Hardback ISBN 9781399814713
Trade Paperback ISBN 9781399814720
ebook ISBN 9781399814744

Typeset in Adobe Caslon Pro

Printed and bound in Great Britain by Clays Ltd, Elcograf S.p.A.

John Murray Press policy is to use papers that are natural, renewable and recyclable products and made from wood grown in sustainable forests. The logging and manufacturing processes are expected to conform to the environmental regulations of the country of origin.

Carmelite House
50 Victoria Embankment
London EC4Y 0DZ

www.basicbooks.uk

John Murray Press, part of Hodder & Stoughton Limited
An Hachette UK company

The authorised representative in the EEA is Hachette Ireland,
8 Castlecourt Centre, Dublin 15, D15 XTP3, Ireland (email: info@hbgi.ie)

To our schoolteachers, who introduced us to Thucydides:

A. J. Bowen, Shrewsbury School

H. J. K. Usher, University College School

Merle Tong, Manchester High School for Girls

Contents

Translator's Preface	ix
List of Maps	xi
Timeline	xvii
Introduction	xix
Recommended Reading	xliii

The History of the Peloponnesian War

Book One	1
Book Two	93
Book Three	168
Book Four	244
Book Five	338
Book Six	405
Book Seven	481
Book Eight	547
Glossary	627
Notes	635
Textual Notes	681
Index of Proper Names	685

Translator's Preface

The British historian and statesman Lord Macaulay wrote in his journal for February 27, 1835, "This day I finished Thucydides, after reading him with inexpressible interest and admiration. He is the greatest historian that ever lived." Most readers of *The History of the Peloponnesian War* still come away from the book with a similar degree of excitement and respect. The prospect of translating such an important and magisterial text is therefore daunting for several reasons, not just because of the complexity of Thucydides's Greek. Despite this, however, the experience has been nothing but educational, stimulating, and enjoyable. My thanks, then, are due in the first place to Polly Low for being an equable as well as an expert collaborator. This book is designed primarily for history buffs and other general readers, as well as students, and I cannot imagine a better introduction for such an audience than the one she has written.

Two friends responded to appeals for help. Bill Murray, an expert in ancient Mediterranean ships and naval warfare, read the translation primarily to check that I had gotten those kinds of things right. And Tony Woodman, a famous scholar of ancient Greek and Roman historiography (among other things), at short notice cast his keen eye over the entire translation and suggested a great many improvements. I thank them both; the book is better for their input.

There are a number of fine translations of Thucydides in existence. Those from which I learned most are by Martin Hammond, Steven Lattimore, and Jeremy Mynott. And no translator or serious reader of the *History* can fail to have by their side the magnificent five-volume

Translator's Preface

A Historical Commentary on Thucydides by A. W. Gomme and others (1956–1981) and the equally important three-volume *A Commentary on Thucydides* by Simon Hornblower (1991–2008).

My gratitude to Lara Heimert of Basic Books extends now over several volumes of translations. Her lack of hesitation in agreeing to let me do Thucydides was extremely gratifying, not least because she gave me the opportunity to fulfill a lifelong ambition. I first started translating ancient Greek texts over forty years ago, and Thucydides has long been on my bucket list. There are too many members of the brilliant team at Basic for me to name them individually, but I thank them collectively from the bottom of my heart. And through Basic Books I was fortunate to have Katherine Streckfus once again as copyeditor and András Bereznay as cartographer. They are the best.

—*R. A. H. W.*

Maps

A. Greece — xii
B. The Athenian and Spartan Alliances — xiii
C. Sicily and Southern Italy — xiv
D. The West Coast of Asia Minor — xv
E. Acarnania and the Northwest — 147
F. Thrace — 161
G. Aetolia — 232
H. Pylos and Sphacteria — 248
I. Boeotia and the Delium Campaign — 305
J. Chalcidice — 317
K. Syracuse — 450

A. Greece

B. The Athenian and Spartan Alliances

C. Sicily and Southern Italy

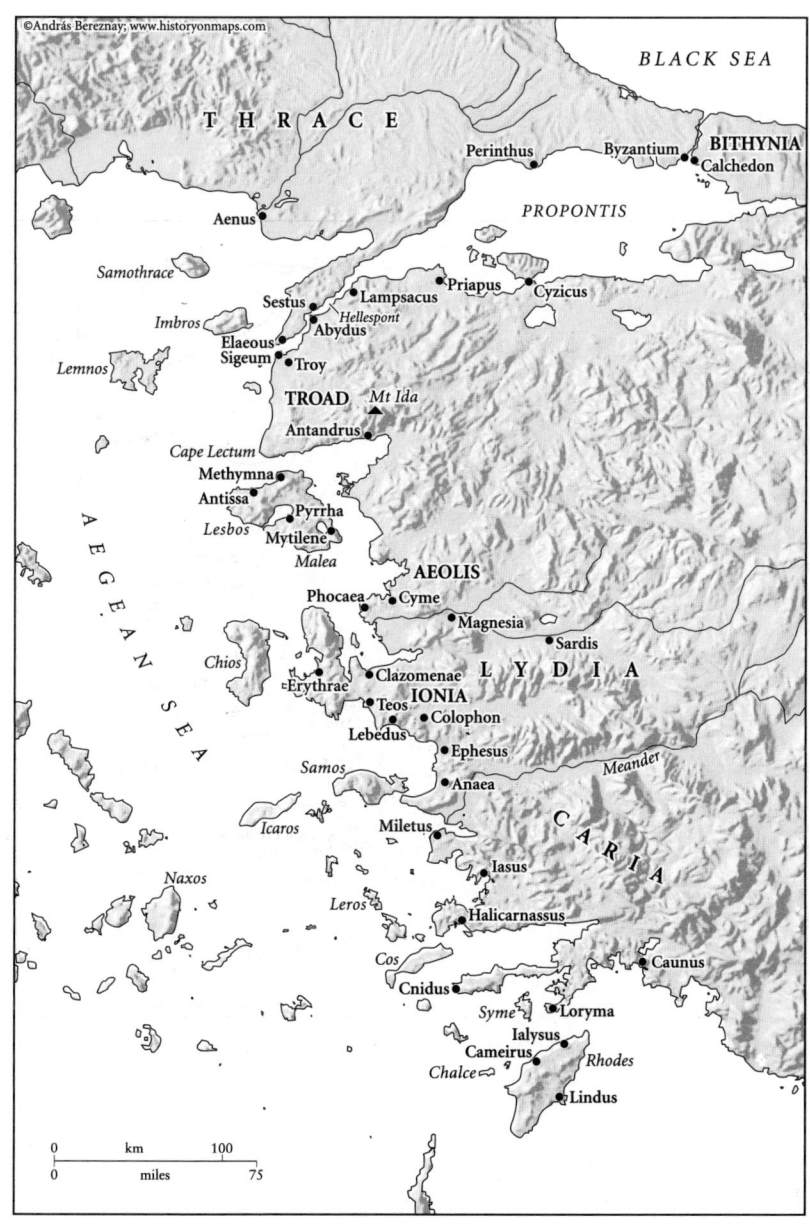

D. The West Coast of Asia Minor

Timeline

All dates are BCE

ca. 1250 (on Thucydides's chronology: 1.8.4): Trojan War
ca. 734 (on Thucydides's chronology: 6.3.1): first Greek settlements in Sicily
546–527: tyranny of Peisistratus at Athens
514: assassination of Hipparchus (brother of the Athenian tyrant Hippias) by Harmodius and Aristogeiton (1.20.2, 6.53.3–59.3)
511/510: Hippias ousted from the Athenian tyranny (6.59.4)
508/507: democratic reforms of Cleisthenes in Athens
490: first Persian invasion of mainland Greece; Battle of Marathon
480–479: second Persian invasion of mainland Greece; Battles of Thermopylae, Salamis, and Plataea
478/477: creation of the Athenian-led "Delian League" (1.96)
465: earthquake in Sparta, and revolt of the helots (1.101)
ca. 460–455: Athenian campaigns in Egypt (1.104, 1.109–110)
457: Battle of Tanagra (1.107.7–108.1); Sparta and allies defeat Athens
457: Battle of Oenophyta (1.108.3); Athenians defeat Boeotians and gain control of much of central Greece
447: Battle of Coronea (1.113.2); Boeotians defeat Athenians
ca. 450: "Peace of Callias" between Athens and Persia
446: "Thirty-Year Peace" between Athens and Sparta (and their respective allies) (1.115.1)

Timeline

440:	Samos attempts to revolt from Athens (1.115.2–117)
437:	Athenians found a settlement at Amphipolis (4.102)
431:	Peloponnesian War begins (2.2.1)
430–427:	plague in Athens (2.47–54, 2.57–58, 3.87)
429:	death of Pericles (2.65.6)
428:	Mytilene attempts to revolt from Athens (3.2–6, 8–18, 25–50)
427/426:	destruction of Plataea (3.52–68)
427/426:	civil war in Corcyra (3.69–85)
427–424:	Athenian forces in Sicily (3.86, 3.88, 3.90, 3.99, 3.103, 3.115, 4.1–2, 4.24–25, 4.58–65)
425/424:	Athenian victories at Pylos and Sphacteria (4.26–41)
424/423:	Battle of Delium (4.89–101.2); Boeotians defeat Athenians
424/423:	Spartans capture Amphipolis (4.102–108); Thucydides is exiled from Athens (5.26.5)
421:	"Peace of Nicias" between Athens and Sparta (and their respective allies) (5.18–19)
418:	Battle of Mantinea (5.65–75); Spartans (and allies) defeat Argives (and allies, including Athenians)
416/415:	Athenian attack on and destruction of Melos (5.84–116)
415:	launch of the Athenian invasion of Sicily (6.30)
413:	Spartans occupy Decelea in Attica (7.19.1–2)
413:	final defeat of the Athenians in Sicily (7.72–87)
411:	oligarchic coup in Athens (8.67)
411:	Battle of Cynossema (8.104–106); Athenians defeat Peloponnesians
411/410:	Thucydides's narrative ends
404/403:	Peloponnesian War ends

Introduction

Thucydides's *History* is the story of a war between two small communities fought in a corner of the Mediterranean more than two thousand years ago. The war was long and often brutal, but it did not dramatically change the course of history, and within a century of its conclusion both the victor (Sparta, consistently called Lacedaemon by Thucydides) and the defeated (Athens) were well on the way to political irrelevance. Even in antiquity, some wondered if this conflict really deserved to be remembered. The first-century BCE critic Dionysius of Halicarnassus, for example, thought Thucydides had made a serious error in his choice of subject matter; the Peloponnesian War, he wrote, "was neither glorious nor fortunate, but... had best never happened at all or, failing that, should have been consigned to silence and oblivion and ignored by later generations" (*Letter to Gnaeus Pompeius*, 3, trans. Stephen Usher).

Dionysius did not get his way. In fact, Thucydides is probably more widely read in the modern world than he ever was in his own time, in spite of the undeniable bleakness of his subject matter. Why? Some readers are of course genuinely interested in the conflict Thucydides recounts, and in the things we learn along the way about the politics and culture of this period, for which this work provides our fullest contemporary narrative. For others, the text's value lies in its contribution to the genre of historical writing: Thucydides developed (or claimed to develop) a novel and rigorous approach to the subject that continues to influence the historical discipline. For others again, it provides insights into political and international theory that have

Introduction

relevance far beyond Thucydides's own time. And for some, the very bleakness of the story is what makes it attractive. The novelist and politician John Buchan wrote in his memoirs of World War I that he "read and re-read Thucydides, for he also had lived among crumbling institutions" (*Memory Hold-the-Door* [*Pilgrim's Way* in the United States]). In dark times, there can be something appealing in a text that is willing to confront the realities of human behavior head-on.

Another reason the text continues to fascinate is precisely because of the diverse responses for which it allows. This introduction will offer a brief survey of this range of possible approaches to Thucydides and his work. It starts, though, with an outline of the world in which Thucydides lived and wrote, and in which the Peloponnesian War was fought.

The World of Thucydides

"Greece," in Thucydides's time, was not a single place, or even a very clearly defined one. People who thought of themselves as Greek lived in communities across the Mediterranean, not only in the area that now forms the state of Greece, but also far beyond: in Sicily and Southern Italy, in North Africa, in western Asia Minor (modern Turkey), and in the Black Sea region.

From around the eighth century BCE, these communities typically organized themselves into a distinctive form: the *polis*, which contemporary scholars often call a "city-state," and which is translated in this work as either "city" or "state." By Thucydides's time, there were over one thousand such cities in the Greek world, most of them small, some of them tiny. Most of these cities controlled a territory no larger than forty square miles (that is, around the size of Staten Island), and their populations might number in the low thousands or even hundreds. The largest one hundred cities had an average population of around thirty thousand; the remaining 90 percent were much smaller. It is important to remember the very small scale of the vast majority of these communities, not least because the two protagonists of the war—Athens and

Introduction

Sparta—were, by comparison, abnormally large. Athens, one of the largest of the city-states, had a total population of some two hundred thousand, including noncitizens and enslaved people, as well as an unusually extensive territory, covering about one thousand square miles. The territory controlled by Sparta was even larger, a consequence of aggressive expansion in the eighth and seventh centuries BCE, amounting to approximately three thousand square miles. The question of Sparta's total population, however, is hotly debated; it was perhaps in the region of one hundred thousand (again, including enslaved and noncitizen inhabitants). Even leaving a large and necessary question mark next to the exact figures, we can be confident of two things: first, that Athens and Sparta dwarfed almost every other Greek city of their own time in terms of size and resources; and second, that they remained, compared to modern nation-states (and compared to some other states of the ancient world, such as Rome), very small indeed.

All of these communities, big and small, shared some key characteristics. Perhaps the most fundamental is that not everyone who lived in a community had the same status. Some inhabitants were citizens, a status that brought greater rights (usually, some level of political participation and greater access to the law) and responsibilities (especially, for adult men, an obligation to perform military service). Criteria for citizenship varied from state to state. In Athens in this period, birth was the key factor—only someone with an Athenian mother and father could be a citizen. Many other states, including Sparta, also had a wealth requirement. Failure to fulfill the obligations of citizenship could lead to it being revoked. In some Greek communities, including Athens and Sparta, citizens were significantly outnumbered by noncitizens, who might perform important functions within the community but had either limited or—in the case of enslaved people—practically nonexistent rights.

A second distinctive characteristic of the city-state was that it was ruled by some form of constitutional government. The precise style of governance varied between states, although one consistent feature is that direct political participation was restricted to adult male citizens, and sometimes to a subset of male citizens. While tyranny, or one-man rule, was rare in this period, Thucydides makes clear (e.g., at 6.53.3) that the memory of tyrannical rule was still very present in at least some Greeks' minds. Many states were ruled by oligarchies: that is, small groups of men (in some places as few as ten, though it could be a few hundred), often selected for their ancestry or wealth. And many—especially, but not only, Athens—were democracies. In these states, sovereignty was exercised by all male citizens. Smaller committees, or even individuals, might be given responsibility for particular tasks, but these roles would typically change hands on a regular basis. Sparta's constitutional arrangements do not fit neatly into any of these categories: the city had two kings who had a limited amount of executive and military power; a ruling council of thirty elders (the Gerousia); an annually elected board of five magistrates (the "ephors," literally "overseers"), responsible for much of the day-to-day administration of the city; and a citizen assembly, which seems to have been able to ratify but not initiate decisions.

Sparta was also unusual in that its constitutional arrangements remained essentially unchanged from around the seventh century BCE until at least the end of the Classical period. Most states had more dynamic political arrangements, and complete changes of regime—from oligarchic to democratic, or vice versa—were common. These revolutions were often marked by extreme violence: Thucydides's description of the horrific civil war in Corcyra (3.81–84) has become, as the author intended, the paradigmatic account of how a change in constitution might be accompanied by temporary but dramatic social collapse. Thucydides argues that these revolutions were driven not just by internal tensions and ambitions, but also by the machinations of foreign powers. His claim (3.82.1) is that democracies, and democratic factions within cities, would naturally align with Athens, while oligarchies were backed by Sparta. This is an oversimplification of a more complicated picture, but this split between democracies and oligarchies did have an important role in shaping interstate allegiances in this period, and certainly plays a large part in Thucydides's understanding of his world.

This point leads us to another essential characteristic of the world of the Greek cities. These states, though often tiny, conceived of themselves as independent political entities, with—at least ideally—their own governments and armies, as well as their own domestic and foreign policies. But they also participated in a dense network of overlapping, and sometimes conflicting, connections with other Greek communities. One type of connection, as we have just seen, could be based on political ideologies: democrats tended to side with democrats, oligarchs with oligarchs, and both sides might sometimes privilege those affinities over loyalty to their own city—hence the many occasions in the *History* when a city is "betrayed" to the enemy by either a democratic or oligarchic faction.

Cities regularly entered into formal alliances with each other, sometimes bilateral and sometimes multilateral. The most important cases of the latter type in this period are the Spartan-led Peloponnesian League and the Athenian-led Delian League (also known as the Athenian empire). Some cities grouped themselves into regionally based federations: the Boeotian Federation (dominated in this period by the city of Thebes) is the most important example we will encounter in Thucydides's narrative. These alliances took various forms in terms of the obligations they involved and the level of equality or hierarchy they established. They had varying durations: some had an explicitly limited term (ten or thirty years was common), while some were implicitly or explicitly open-ended (the Delian League is the best example of this type). One thing they have in common is that they were, at least in theory, intended to be binding: they were ratified by civic authorities and, through the swearing of oaths, protected by divine sanction. Although, therefore, we will repeatedly find these agreements being violated during the course of the war, we should remember that such violations were not seen as trivial.

Introduction

Another, less codified, but still extremely important, form of connection between Greek communities was that based on the concept of "kinship": the belief that certain communities or groups of communities could trace their origins back to a single shared ancestor (possibly a mythical ancestor) or group of ancestors. One relatively straightforward manifestation of this phenomenon can be seen in the connection between "colonies" and "mother cities": many Greek states, especially those in Sicily, Southern Italy, and Asia Minor, believed they had been founded by settlers from communities elsewhere in the Greek world, and therefore that a particularly strong tie should exist between the two states. This might manifest in shared religious and cultural practices and in political allegiances. If a colony went on to create a further settlement, this tie of obligation could, at least in theory, extend over three generations of cities. We can find a very good example of this expectation (and, in this instance, its subversion) in the conflict between Corinth, its colony Corcyra, and Corcyra's colony Epidamnus, which forms a key part of Thucydides's explanation of the origins of the war (1.24–55).

More complex patterns of affiliation developed on the basis of shared ethnicity, though these beliefs are again founded, ultimately, on a claim to common, usually mythical, ancestry. The two most important ethnic groups we encounter in Thucydides's text are the Ionians and Dorians. The former, which included the Athenians and many communities in Asia Minor, traced their ancestry back to the mythical hero Ion; they spoke similar forms of Greek and shared some religious practices. The latter, which included the Spartans, the Cretans, and many communities in the Peloponnese and western Greece, traced their ancestry to the mythical figure Dorus; they, too, spoke a distinctive form of Greek and shared some cultural and religious affinities. It is very important to acknowledge that these ethnic groupings are, to at least some extent, artificial constructions: the mythological stories on which they were based were fluid, and we find communities emphasizing different aspects of their ethnic identity in

Introduction

different contexts. Thucydides, in fact, is notably skeptical of the real importance of many of these ethnic ties: we will repeatedly see him drawing attention to occasions when they were either deployed for cynical purposes or entirely ignored (perhaps most strikingly in his catalog of the opposing forces fighting in Sicily, at 7.57–58). But in this he is certainly pushing against the consensus of his own time, in which these sorts of ethnic links were thought to have genuine force, not just culturally but also politically.

These claims to shared kinship could be used to divide the communities of the Greek world, but in some contexts they could be used to unite them. Ion and Dorus were the founders of distinct ethnic groups, but they in turn were believed to be related: Dorus was the son and Ion the grandson (by a different father) of Hellen, the mythical ancestor of the "Hellenic" peoples—that is, of the Greeks (mentioned by Thucydides at 1.3.2). When circumstances required, therefore, it was possible for communities to draw attention to this shared aspect of their identity. As with Dorian and Ionian identities, claims based on kinship ties could be complemented by observations about shared language (although the Greeks spoke different dialects, those dialects were mutually comprehensible), shared religious beliefs, and a common style of life. They could also be based on perceived differences from (and, often, alleged superiority to) the various non-Greek "barbarian" communities that neighbored the Greek world.

The idea of shared Hellenic identity is rarely explicitly emphasized in Thucydides's narrative; the story of the Peloponnesian War is, for him, one of division between Greeks, not of unity. But being aware of the possibility of unity can help us understand why this story of division is so devastating. Indeed, Greek solidarity was not only a theoretical possibility, but something that had—albeit briefly and imperfectly—recently been achieved, in the response to the Persian invasion of 480 BCE. In the face of that threat, a number of Greek states, under the joint leadership of Athens and Sparta, had come together to inflict a memorable, implausible defeat on the vastly

Introduction

stronger Persian forces. The combined alliance of Greeks lasted only slightly longer than the campaign, and cracks in its facade were visible even before that, but the memory of the possibility of unity persisted throughout the fifth century and beyond. When the Plataeans faced the prospect of destruction at the hands of the Spartans in 427/426 BCE, for example, they repeatedly appealed to the shared experience of Plataeans and Spartans in fighting and defeating the invading Persians, invoking this as a reason why their city should be spared (3.53–59). The appeal failed: memories of past unanimity were not strong enough to withstand contemporary political exigencies. This is a characteristic feature of the political world that Thucydides describes; nevertheless, we can still detect in his account the potent place that the conflict with Persia and the solidarity it engendered still held in Greek thinking.

The memory of the Persian War could also be deployed not in order to argue for cooperation and concord between Greeks, but as a justification for the supremacy of one Greek state over others—and it is this theme that is much more visible in Thucydides's account. As Thucydides tells the story (at 1.95–97), the Athenian-led Delian League was a direct successor of the alliance of Greek states that fought against Persia. Athens took over sole leadership when the Spartans withdrew from the alliance, and then steadily increased its power and control until the alliance had evolved into an empire. Although active conflict with Persia came to an end by the middle of the fifth century (probably formalized with a peace agreement, although Thucydides does not report this), the idea that Athens's earlier hostility to Persia justified its position of leadership persisted. Thucydides tends to introduce this idea in a rather oblique way, by making characters in his history dismiss these sorts of arguments as trite or irrelevant (e.g., at 1.73.2, 5.89, and 6.83.3). But it is clear from other sources that these justifications were widespread in Athenian discourse in the fifth century (and beyond): the Athenians had saved the Greeks from the Persians and the Greeks therefore owed them something in return—namely, the right to rule

INTRODUCTION

over them. It is this Athenian accumulation of power, and the Greek (and especially the Spartan) response to it, that—for Thucydides—is the key to understanding why the Peloponnesian War broke out.

Thucydides in His World

It should already have become clear that Thucydides's interpretation of the world in which he lived seems at times to have been idiosyncratic, or at least out of line with what we can reconstruct of popular beliefs of the time. To attempt to understand how he arrived at these views, it will be helpful to look more closely at his own life, background, and intellectual affinities.

Our secure knowledge of Thucydides's life is based only on the few things he tells us in his work. (Ancient biographies of the historian exist, but these are based on a mixture of hypothesis and fabrication, and should be given no particular credence.) He was an Athenian (1.1.1), and he was present in Athens in the early years of the Peloponnesian War—something we know because he tells us he caught the plague in the great outbreak of 430 (2.48.3). In 424/423 he was one of Athens's ten generals (4.104.4), but he was sent into a twenty-year exile after his term of office ended, presumably on the basis of his poor performance (5.26.5). We do not know exactly where he spent his exile, although he does tell us in that same passage that it gave him the opportunity to talk to participants on both sides of the conflict, including Peloponnesians. We also do not know if he ever returned to Athens.

Because an Athenian had to be at least thirty years old to be eligible to serve as general, Thucydides must have been born by 454 BCE at the latest. He lived to see the end of the Peloponnesian War, though it is usually assumed (on the grounds of the unfinished state of the work, discussed further below) that he died shortly afterward, at the end of the fifth century or start of the fourth.

Thucydides's family had gold-mining interests in northeastern Greece (4.105.1), and his father's name (Olorus) was Thracian. From this, it is usually (and plausibly) inferred that he belonged to the upper socioeconomic stratum of Athenian society: it was typically the wealthiest citizens who had these sorts of international connections, not to mention involvement in highly lucrative mining operations. His service as general is also consistent with this hypothesis. The generalship was one of the few positions in democratic Athens that was chosen by election rather than by random lottery; the role therefore tended to be filled by Athenians with the connections and resources that would allow them to run a successful election campaign.

Thucydides, then, was a wealthy, politically engaged man writing about a war in which he was personally involved and in which both he and his city suffered significantly. His direct stake in this war is worth emphasizing because it is not at all prominent in the narrative he provides. Rather, the historian cultivates an air of detached objectivity, rarely giving us an explicit statement of his own political or ideological views. This stance does not, of course, mean that he had no opinions—it would be a grave mistake to treat Thucydides as an entirely dispassionate, disinterested witness to the events he narrates. But the paucity of explicit statements of opinion does leave considerable scope for disagreement about exactly what his beliefs were. They have to be pieced together from scattered comments and implications in his writing.

Thucydides does give us one clear statement about his political beliefs. On the subject of the moderate democracy that was established in Athens in 411, after the oligarchic coup of the same year, he writes, "This was the first time, at any rate in my lifetime, when the Athenians seem to have had a particularly fine political system. It was a judicious blend that took account of the interests of both the few and the many" (8.97.2). In this regime, the poorest Athenians were excluded from political participation, and a technocratic element, in the form of a committee of "legal commissioners," provided a level of control and expertise. Thucydides's approval of this system is consistent with his negative presentation of the more radical democracy that had

Introduction

run Athens since the middle of the fifth century. The democracy, and particularly the democratic assembly (which all Athenian male citizens, including the poorest, could attend), is depicted as making rash decisions, often based on insufficient knowledge, and often driven by greed or excessive ambitions. Athenian democracy (as Thucydides presents it) is also, for the most part, poorly served by its leaders, who are either too willing to pander to the whims of the masses, or too weak to properly control the people's worst instincts. However, any reconstruction of Thucydides's political views has to make space for the fact that he was clearly a great admirer of one radical democratic politician—namely, Pericles—though this might be because he saw him as not, at heart, a true democrat: "In theory there continued to be a democracy, but what was important, in fact, was that power was in the hands of the leading man" (2.65.9). In short, although Thucydides's assessment of the limitations of democracy is relatively clear, there is room for debate about what he thought was the best solution to the problem: a single talented leader, or a reformed political system. In either case, a key point for readers of the *History* to remember is that the depictions of radical democratic politics that we see in the text are deeply colored by Thucydides's skepticism about this form of government: this is a pessimist's view of democratic decision-making.

Thucydides's political views were probably not atypical among men of his class. The same might be true of his wider intellectual approach, although here we are on much less certain ground in trying to reconstruct the historian's beliefs. A recurring characteristic of his narrative is cynicism about the sincerity of religious explanations and justifications for the events he describes. He repeatedly questions the value of oracles, for example, and when he reports on states or individuals deploying religious arguments, he tends to suggest that their real motivations were more pragmatic. (We see a good example of this in his description of the exchange of accusations about ancestral curses in the immediate run-up to the outbreak of war, in 1.126–135.1.) In his own narrative, too, he prefers secular explanations over ones relying on religious custom or belief (as, for example, in his explanation for why the Spartans march into battle to the sound of pipes in 5.70.1). The evidence we have does not allow us to call Thucydides an atheist, and absolute denial of the existence or power of the gods would in any case be a very unexpected position in this period. And yet he is certainly alert to the possibility that religion could be exploited for pragmatic ends, and, unlike his great predecessor Herodotus, he is notably reluctant to give religious factors—still less the direct intervention of the gods—any causal power as a historical force.

This critical approach to conventional religious belief is compatible with a larger intellectual trend of the late fifth century with which Thucydides is often linked: that is, "sophistic" thought. The sophists were teachers of philosophy and rhetoric who are typically depicted as having a particular interest in exploring and challenging the conventional ideas of their day. This interest might manifest in various areas. One, as already noted, was questioning established religious beliefs. Another was exploring and exploiting the power of language and persuasion, and particularly the art of presenting counterintuitive or implausible positions ("making the weaker argument the stronger," as the playwright Aristophanes put it in *Clouds*). Along with many other, especially Athenian, speakers, the Athenian politician Cleon is portrayed by Thucydides as a master of these rhetorical tricks, though also as someone who (hypocritically) condemns the Athenians' susceptibility to them (3.38). Another sophistic interest, particularly important in Thucydides's work, was exploring the balance between "nature" (*phusis*) and "convention" (*nomos*). A characteristic sophistic argument was that actions based on "nature" should be privileged, because they were less likely to be clouded by hypocrisy or contingency. This argument could be applied to various spheres of behavior, but particularly to questions of justice and morality: if a society's views about right and wrong were based only on convention, rather than on any fundamental principles of nature, it might then be possible to argue that they could be ignored.

Introduction

There is no doubt that Thucydides was aware of arguments of this sort, and it is equally clear that he thought them very relevant to the story he was telling. Above all, it is the overwhelming power of the Athenian empire that provides a context for repeated exploration of the problem of justice and morality. Did the Athenians have to justify their attempt to amass as much power as they could, or was the urge to rule simply a "natural human impulse" (1.76.3), as the Athenians tell the Spartans? And, once they had acquired this power, did they have any moral obligation to restrain themselves from exercising it to the fullest extent, or was this just another piece of convention? As the Athenians at Melos argue, what nature demands is that "the strong do what they can and the weak concede them that right" (5.89). Such arguments recur in the work. However—and this is critically important—they do not appear in Thucydides's own narration, but instead are voiced by various (especially Athenian) characters in the speeches that punctuate the history. We therefore need to be very cautious about assuming that these were opinions the historian himself endorsed. Indeed, when Thucydides explores the interplay of human nature and social conventions in his narrative, as he does most compellingly in his account of the plague at Athens (2.47–54) and the civil war in Corcyra (3.81–84), the picture that emerges is more complex. There is some consistency with what we find in the speeches, inasmuch as it appears that the natural instincts of humans will tend toward self-interest and the maximization of their own power. But it is far less clear that Thucydides himself thought that was a desirable, or even an inevitable, phenomenon. This, though, is something he never says in quite so many words; rather, he provides a vivid, often horrifying description of what happens to a society when its *nomoi* start to collapse and *phusis* takes over.

Where this leaves us is with considerable space for disagreement about exactly what Thucydides's view of conventional morality was. For some readers, he is an amoralist: a man who had no time for cozy platitudes and who wanted to expose what he saw as the harsh reality of human behavior. For others, he is almost exactly the opposite: someone who saw the dangers of stripping away the conventions that allowed humans, and states, to reach some form of peaceful coexistence. Thucydides, as Buchan observed, saw the institutions around him crumbling, but it might be that this only made him more aware of the importance of those institutions.

Thucydides and (His) History

We have, so far, been skirting around an important question: Why did Thucydides write his *History*? Was it simply to preserve the story of the war? Or did he have some greater purpose in mind? Before tackling the "why" question, though, we should address the slightly more straightforward issues of "when" and "how."

Thucydides says (1.1.1) that he started writing his history at the very beginning of the war because he knew from the outset that it would be a major conflict. We need not take this claim to prescience completely at face value: while it is quite plausible that some parts of the work were composed, or at least drafted, in real time, it is also apparent that the text we have was not written in unbroken sequence from beginning to end. The scholarly attempt to reconstruct exactly when the parts were written and in what order is ongoing (and probably never-ending), but it is clear that some passages from earlier parts of the work must have been either produced or substantially revised at a later date, because they show knowledge of the end of the war (for example, 2.65.12 or 5.26).

If Thucydides revised the *History* as the war went on, that process of revision was almost certainly not completed. The narrative ends in the year 411, fully seven years before the end of the war, and breaks off in the middle of an episode, perhaps even mid-sentence; this is usually seen as the least controversial indication of the work's unfinished state. The fifth and eighth books of the work have also sometimes been thought to be earlier drafts, because Thucydides's method of reporting speeches and documentary evidence is notably different (and less complex) in these books from the one he uses elsewhere in the work: almost all speeches are reported in summary rather than written up in full, and the terms of treaties are presented as transcripts rather than incorporated into the narrative. Some have argued, however, that he might have made a deliberate decision to experiment here with a new style of presenting his material. Finally, and most subjectively, some readers find signs of inconsistency in Thucydides's explanations or interpretations over the course of the work, and think that these might best be explained as reflections of different layers of composition. If he had been able to complete a full final edit of the text (the argument goes), these glitches would have been weeded out.

A note of caution might be useful here. Discussions about composition, revision, and incompleteness can sometimes be based on an assumption that an ancient text would be "published" in a similar way to a modern one. However, while we have absolutely no explicit information about the circulation of the *History* in Thucydides's own time, we do know enough about the general literary context to be fairly certain that a model of one-off, definitive publication is unlikely. What is more probable is that smaller parts of the text would have been made available in preliminary versions, and that these parts would then have been brought together to form the whole. This might also be the appropriate place to say that the eight books into the which the work is now divided were not part of Thucydides's own scheme, but are the result of later editorial intervention.

One reason why we have to keep reminding ourselves of the potentially fluid or provisional nature of the text we have is that it runs counter to Thucydides's own insistence that his work was a meticulously crafted, definitive, and authoritative piece of writing. The emphasis on this as a written work, which comes at the very start of the *History* (1.1.1), is highly significant: this is not just a descriptive statement of Thucydides's working practices, but a programmatic declaration that the project he has undertaken is going to be quite different from what has gone before.

Introduction

To understand why this is so, we have to detour slightly into the nature of "history" in the late fifth century. Thucydides was not the first person in the Greek world to produce a written history, but he was working in a period when there were still no fixed rules, or even expectations, about what this type of work should look like. Among the areas of uncertainty was the question of how history related to the many other methods the Greeks already used in remembering and recounting the stories of their past, such as poetry, speeches, performances at festivals, and other commemorative activities. One thing these more established modes of remembering the past had in common was that they relied on orally transmitted tales, which in turn reflected a collectively agreed upon (though potentially fluid) version of a community's history. Whether or not these tales had much basis in the literal truth of earlier events was not really the key point. Rather, what was critical was that these were stories that remained meaningful and useful to the people who told and heard them. It is for this reason that the Homeric epics were often regarded by the Greeks as a sort of "historical" text—not because they report historical facts, but because they provided a mechanism for preserving a version of the past that the Greeks (or, at least, many Greeks) thought important for understanding their world. As we will see, especially in Book One, Thucydides, too, treats Homer as a historical source, and as a historical rival.

This way of reconstructing the past persists also into some of the first written histories, most notably that of Thucydides's older contemporary Herodotus. To be sure, Herodotus applies a considerable degree of critical scrutiny to the stories he reports, but he still makes collectively remembered, orally transmitted tales of past events central to much of his history. So, to come back to Thucydides, that is why his emphasis on the written nature of his work has been seen as significant: Could this be a way of signaling, from almost the first word, a move away from this world of oral history and toward a quite different way of engaging with the past?

Introduction

A few paragraphs later, Thucydides provides a more explicit statement of his intention to offer a newly rigorous method of studying the past: "Where the events and action of the war are concerned, however, my policy has been not to write down what I learned from just anyone or my personal opinions, but to do so only once I had investigated everything as meticulously as possible, whether I was present myself at the event or was informed about it by others" (1.22.2). The challenge for Thucydides's readers is to know how far he actually stuck to this methodology. This is because—unlike modern historians, and in fact also unlike some ancient historians (notably Herodotus)—Thucydides almost never gives us any indication of the sources underpinning his narrative, or the analytical decisions shaping his account of events. We therefore have to take it on trust that he has actually been as careful as he claims to have been. Perhaps he deserves this trust. There are occasions when we can corroborate from independent sources what he tells us, and the results of these comparisons are generally reassuring (the treaty he quotes at 5.47, for example, is partially preserved on a contemporary inscription, and the texts are essentially the same). But there are areas where Thucydides's take on events seems to have been quite different from that of other contemporary observers: his analysis of the causes of the Peloponnesian War is a crucial example; and the *History*'s foundational claim—that the Peloponnesian War was a single conflict lasting twenty-seven years, rather than a linked set of smaller wars—appears to have been a position that was far from universally held. When the alternative versions have survived for us to examine, then we can, of course, conduct our own historical scrutiny. But for the vast majority of Thucydides's narrative we are left reliant not just on his account of the facts but also on his interpretation of them, because he does not provide us with the information we might use to contradict him.

Leaving aside the failure to cite his sources, Thucydides's approach to researching the narrative of his history might appear quite similar to the methods of modern historiography (which is not a coincidence, because the modern discipline of history has itself been deeply influenced by Thucydides). His methodological excursus at 1.22, however, addresses an aspect of his work that can seem much more alien: that is, the inclusion of speeches. In fact, the presence of speeches was not at all unusual in Greek historiography; it is one of the features of historical writing marking its generic debt to epic poetry. What is distinctive, though, is Thucydides's attempt to define the relationship of the speeches in his work with speeches that were actually delivered: "What I have written is what I think each speaker is most likely to have needed to say about the immediate issues, while keeping as close as possible to the overall purport of the speech as actually delivered" (1.22.1). This is, even by Thucydides's often very elliptical standards, an extremely hard sentence to decode, probably because he is trying to claim two things that are not easily compatible: he wants to stick to his overall commitment to truthful reporting while still giving himself the freedom to depart from verbatim accuracy.

What is contested is how much freedom he allowed himself. Some readers of Thucydides regard the speeches as essentially authentic, barring some editing for style and length. Others see them as more or less free compositions: places where the historian gave himself space to explore the themes and problems he thought important, in terms that might never have been used by the people to whom these speeches are attributed. (Did the Athenians, for example, really describe their own empire as a "tyranny," even among themselves?) Of course, it need not be the case that the same approach was used for all the speeches in his text: some of them might be closer to what was really said; others might be more speculative (the very abstract, almost philosophical, "Melian Dialogue" of 5.84–113 fits best into the second category). Two things are, however, both clear and important. First, that Thucydides has without doubt chosen to include in his text speeches that draw attention to problems that he thought were significant. It is in the speeches that we find the fullest reflections on, for example, the nature of Athenian imperialism, the strengths and weaknesses

Introduction

of Athenian democracy, and the different characteristics of Spartan and Athenian society. The speeches, that is, are where we need to look for the core historical analysis in this work. Second, although the speeches are a forum for analysis, they cannot necessarily be taken as a statement of Thucydides's own views. This is clear not least from the fact that Thucydides often gives us a pair of opposing speeches, each offering a different perspective on the same issue. The historian's own opinions, as we have already seen, remain elusive.

The methodological excursus gives an important insight, finally, into how Thucydides intended his work to be consumed. As he put it, "The non-fabulous character of my narrative may well reduce its attractiveness.... The work has been composed as a possession for all time rather than a virtuoso performance for a single hearing" (1.22.4). Yet again, we should read this passage not so much as a statement of fact as a piece of rhetorical positioning, and one that is consistent with his opening insistence on the written status of his text. There is certainly a great deal more literary artistry in the *History* than Thucydides suggests here, not just in the crafting of individual episodes but also in the shaping of the overall structure of the narrative (for example, his decision to juxtapose his description of Athens at its best, in his account of the public funeral at 2.35–46, with Athens at its lowest ebb, in his description of the plague at 2.47–54).

What lies behind Thucydides's disavowal of the entertainment value of his work is an attempt to distance himself from other, more traditional ways of engaging with the past. Poems, songs, perhaps even other attempts at historical research (many see a dig at Herodotus in these lines), were all designed to be enjoyed as one-off performances. That mode of consumption, Thucydides suggests, does not allow for the sort of close concentration and sustained study that he is going to demand of his audience. And this, in turn, might give us a clue about the sorts of people for whom Thucydides was creating this work: not just an audience that could read, but, more specifically, those with the leisure and resources to read slowly, carefully, and critically—that is, for the people, like Thucydides, who formed the Greek world's socioeconomic elite. There is, in other words, an ideological consistency between the content and the purpose of the work. Just as Thucydides is doubtful of the ability of the masses to make good political decisions, so he sees the task of acquiring proper knowledge of the past as something that is best conducted by the few, not the many.

Thucydides and Our World

Thucydides's claim that his work should be a "possession for all time" has very commonly (and rightly) been read as something more than an instruction to his own contemporaries about how they should engage with the text. It also expresses an aspiration that the work should continue to be read long after his own day. This is a fairly common literary conceit, but readers of this text in the generations after Thucydides have tended to take it seriously because of what is said just before: "I will be content if [the *History*] is judged useful by people who want a clear view of what happened in the past—and, human nature being what it is, of what is going to happen again in the future in an approximate or closely similar way" (1.22.4).

We have already seen that Thucydides wanted to construct an accurate and authoritative account of the past. What emerges here is that he was doing this not just because he thought that past events needed to be remembered (and remembered correctly), but because the past might in some way serve as a model for understanding the future. And this, in turn, can help us understand both some distinctive characteristics of the text and some important themes in its later reception.

Thucydides does not give us a comprehensive account of every event of the Peloponnesian War (even up to 411 where his account ends). This is in some respects an obvious point: no history has ever been, or could ever be, completely exhaustive; selection and organization of a mass of material is one of the historian's basic tasks. What is distinctive about Thucydides's approach, though, is that the logic of his selection seems often to be determined precisely by his desire to identify and explain phenomena that, he thought, were "going to happen again." There are points in his work where it is quite clear that this is what he is doing. For example, he provides just one detailed narrative of an outbreak of civil war in a Greek community (in Corcyra, 3.81–84), but he notes that this sort of conflict was endemic in this period—perhaps even (he suggests) something that might happen in any period, given the consistency of human nature (3.82.2). He is sometimes explicit about the selectivity in his reporting of speeches (e.g., at 3.36.6 and 3.41). Elsewhere, though, we cannot be completely certain whether something that appears in Thucydides's narrative to be an unusual or unique event was really a one-off, or if we are intended again to extrapolate a more general pattern from this single example. The Athenian treatment of the population of Melos (5.84–116), for example, is distinctive in Thucydides's narrative for its absolute ruthlessness; modern historians of the Athenian empire, however, wonder whether this sort of behavior was really as unparalleled as Thucydides, on a superficial reading at least, makes it seem.

It is probably a reasonable assumption that Thucydides has applied this practice of focusing on (what he saw as) representative case studies throughout the work, even if not to the same extent in all parts of the work. And this leads to a question: Is Thucydides's historical agenda—his desire to create an accurate record of the war—in tension with his theoretical agenda? Might his concern to provide posterity with a repository of useful, replicable *exempla* have led him to produce an account of the war that overemphasizes some of its aspects and neglects others, perhaps even to the extent of being quite misleading? The short answer to that question is that we cannot know for sure, because we do not have any comprehensive alternative analysis of this period that we could use as a control on Thucydides's account. What we can confidently say, though, and what we should add to the growing list of things to bear in mind when reading the work, is that the simple narration of "what really happened" was not Thucydides's only, or even primary, objective. He also wanted his work to teach people lessons.

Introduction

Thucydides's wish has been granted—at least in that the *History* has become a text that many people read not because they have a particular (or even any) interest in Greek history of the fifth century BCE, but because they think they can find in it something that is applicable to their own time. This practice began in antiquity. The sixth-century CE historian Procopius, for example, included in his *History of the Wars* an account of the Justinianic plague that was closely modeled on Thucydides's narrative of the plague, and that followed its Thucydidean exemplar in using the description of the disease as a springboard for a wider exploration of social and political morality. It became very visible again in the early modern period, most famously in the work of the philosopher Thomas Hobbes, who published a translation of the *History* in 1629. Hobbes found in Thucydides's text, and particularly in the narrative, a warning for his own turbulent times: a tale of bellicose and unprincipled leaders dragging a state into an ill-advised war. He also perhaps saw in Thucydides a model for himself: a precariously positioned intellectual who could not directly criticize the political regime in which he lived, and so chose instead to offer oblique criticism through the medium of history (doubly oblique, of course, in Hobbes's case, because the history was one of a different time and place).

It was in the twentieth and twenty-first centuries, however, that the most fully fledged "theoretical" Thucydides emerged. The newly created discipline of International Relations found in the *History* both validation and inspiration for its own attempts to theorize the behavior of states, and to construct models that might be able not only to explain but also to predict and guide foreign policy decisions. For much of the second half of the twentieth century, Thucydides was co-opted above all by the "Realist" school of international theory: that is, those who argued that the sphere of foreign politics was one where moral judgments had no place, and where self-interest, power, and security should be the guiding principles. Through (often very selective) reading of Thucydides's work, and particularly its speeches, these

Introduction

theorists found what they saw as validation for their proposition that these were immutable, eternal laws of foreign politics, laws that were as applicable to the behavior of the contemporary United States and Soviet Union as they were to fifth-century BCE Athens and Sparta.

The superficial similarities between the bipolar conflict of the Cold War and the struggle between the rival Athenian and Spartan power blocs doubtless made these comparisons easier, especially because parallels could also be drawn between the (allegedly) freedom-loving democracy on one side of the conflict and the secretive, repressive regime on the other. But what is striking is that the urge to apply this Thucydides-derived model of power politics to the contemporary world has survived long beyond the fall of the Berlin Wall: its most recent application (in the shape of the so-called Thucydides Trap) takes the form of an attempt to use Thucydides's text to predict the shape of a future conflict between the United States and China. Also striking is that, as Realist theory has lost its dominant position in International Relations, Thucydides does not seem to have become any less central. Rather, he has been reappropriated in support of a whole range of different theoretical positions. In particular, he is now often enlisted in support of "Constructivist" theory, a model in which ideals and ideology are more important to understanding foreign policy than raw calculations of power and self-interest.

If Thucydides, then, were somehow observing us from the afterlife, he might be satisfied that his readers are still using his history—and have been using it for a long time—to try to obtain a "clear view" of the events of their own time. What is less certain is whether he would also be pleased that no one seems to have been able to reach a settled conclusion about what, exactly, he wanted us to see so clearly. The fact that the message of the work seems so elusive is, of course, one of the reasons it is still so compelling; but another thing that is elusive is whether Thucydides in fact ever intended anyone to be able to locate a single message in the text, or was less interested in providing the answer to the problems he described than he was in

Introduction

the process of identifying those problems. We might, indeed, wonder whether Thucydides even thought that an answer was achievable. His statement of intention at 1.22.4 promises only that readers will be able to recognize the phenomena he describes, if and when they recur, not that they will be able to do anything to change the course of events. In case we miss the point, he makes it again when introducing his meticulous description of the symptoms of the plague: "For my part, I shall simply describe what happened and explain its features so that, securely armed with this foreknowledge, people may not find themselves ignorant should it ever occur again" (2.48.3).

Equipped with Thucydides's description, we will be able to diagnose the disease from which we are suffering. But, since there is no possible cure, an agonizing death is still more or less inevitable. The only benefit of having read Thucydides, that is, is that we will know what it is that's killing us. But maybe that is enough of a reason to read the *History*: to understand rather better not just the world in which Thucydides lived, but also the endless potential of human beings to make their own worlds both worse and better.

—P. L.

Recommended Reading

A clear, balanced, and authoritative introduction to Thucydides and his *History* is S. Hornblower, *Thucydides* (Duckworth, 1987). W. R. Connor's *Thucydides* (Princeton University Press, 1984) is particularly interested in exploring Thucydides's historical and literary techniques and how the two intersect; H.-P. Stahl's *Thucydides: Man's Place in History* (Classical Press of Wales, 2003) takes a similar approach. H. D. Westlake, *Individuals in Thucydides* (Cambridge University Press, 1968), explores Thucydides's presentation of the major Athenian and Spartan characters in the *History*, and in doing so provides very useful insights into both the literary and historical techniques of the work.

More recent studies, covering a wide range of aspects of and approaches to Thucydides and his work, are assembled in three companion volumes: *Brill's Companion to Thucydides*, ed. A. Tsakmakis and A. Rengakos (Brill, 2006); *The Oxford Handbook of Thucydides*, ed. S. Forsdyke, E. Foster, and R. Balot (Oxford University Press, 2017); and *The Cambridge Companion to Thucydides*, ed. P. Low (Cambridge University Press, 2023).

Recent years have seen a particular interest in the ways in which the *History* has been understood (or misunderstood) by later readers. K. Harloe and N. Morley, eds., *Thucydides and the Modern World* (Cambridge University Press, 2012), is a stimulating collection of studies on the reception of Thucydides from the Renaissance to the early twenty-first century. Two works by political theorists offer very interesting, and quite different, perspectives on the lessons Thucydides might have for the post–Cold War world: R. N. Lebow, *The*

Recommended Reading

Tragic Vision of Politics (Cambridge University Press, 2004), and G. Hawthorn, *Thucydides on Politics* (Cambridge University Press, 2014).

R. Osborne, ed., *Classical Greece* (Oxford University Press, 2000), is a reliable introduction to the wider history of the period about which (and in which) Thucydides wrote, offering both thematic discussions of topics such as politics and warfare and a concise historical narrative of the fifth and fourth centuries BCE. J. T. Roberts, *The Plague of War* (Oxford University Press, 2017), is a more detailed narrative of the Peloponnesian War, covering much of the same ground as Thucydides's *History*, but also bringing in sources other than Thucydides and setting the war in its wider context (in particular, by taking the story down into the early fourth century). Anyone wanting a notably more positive take on the successes of Athenian democracy (and of Athens in general) than we find in Thucydides could turn to J. Ober's *The Rise and Fall of Classical Greece* (Princeton University Press, 2015).

Last and not least, one of the best ways to understand not only the background to the Peloponnesian War but also the intellectual context in which Thucydides produced his *History* is to read the work of his great predecessor and rival, Herodotus. Many English translations exist, including one by the translator of this work, Robin Waterfield, with an introduction and notes by Carolyn Dewald: Herodotus, *The Histories* (Oxford University Press, 1998).

THE HISTORY OF THE PELOPONNESIAN WAR

Book One

*The background to the war. Introduction, and early history of Greece (1.1–19); statement of methodology and aims (1.20–23.3); immediate causes of the war (**ca. 435–433/432**: 1.23.4–1.88); underlying cause of the war: the growth of Athenian power in the period after the Persian Wars (**479–ca. 440**: 1.89–118); second meeting of the Peloponnesian League at Sparta (**432**: 1.119–125); further historical background, including digressions on Cylon, Themistocles, and Pausanias (1.126–138); the final Spartan ultimatum and Pericles's reply (**432**: 1.139–146).*

1. Thucydides of Athens wrote this account of the war between the Peloponnesians and the Athenians.* He started writing as soon as hostilities began, since he anticipated not just a major conflict, but one that would be more significant than any that had gone before. He thought this because both sides came into the war when they were at the height of their powers in terms of their preparedness in every department, and he saw that the rest of the Greeks were joining one side or the other, some immediately and others planning to do so.

[2] This was certainly the greatest upheaval that had ever happened to the Greeks, and a substantial portion of the non-Greek world was

---

* An asterisk in the text refers the reader to an explanatory note (pp. 635–679).

involved as well; it is hardly an exaggeration to say that the majority of humankind was affected.* [3] For although the lapse of time made it impossible for me to find out for certain about the period before the war and the even remoter past, nevertheless the evidence that I came to trust as I looked as far back as possible led me to believe that those periods were not on as great a scale where their conflicts were concerned or in any other respect. **2.** It seems that, long ago, the land that is now called Greece was not securely settled, but in former times migration was the norm, with each group of people readily abandoning their territory every time they were overpowered by others more numerous than themselves. [2] There was no commerce, and people were wary of interacting with one another by land or sea. Each group of people sustained life from their own territory, but they produced no surplus wealth and did not cultivate the land, since they had no defensive walls and never knew when an invader might take it from them. So, because they believed that they could secure enough food for their daily livelihood wherever they might be, it was easy for them to go and live elsewhere, and hence they had no settlements of any size or any other resources to make them strong.

[3] It was especially the most fertile land that kept seeing changes of population—that is, the regions that are now called Thessaly and Boeotia, most of the Peloponnese (except for Arcadia), and the best land elsewhere. [4] In some places, the growth of power occasioned by the fertility of the land led to internal strife and destruction, and at the same time made these places more a target of intrigues by outsiders. [5] At any rate, Attica, where the soil is thin, has been free of such strife from the earliest times and has always been inhabited by the same people. [6] No slight proof of my point, that migration was responsible for the failure of the rest of Greece to develop to the same extent, is furnished by the fact that the most capable people who were driven out from other parts of Greece by war or civil strife withdrew to Athens because of its stability and, in a process that started long ago, increased the city's population by becoming citizens. In fact later

the Athenians even sent colonies to Ionia, since Attica could not support them.*

3. There is another factor that, to my mind, clearly demonstrates the weakness of the ancient Greeks. This is that before the Trojan War Greece seems never to have embarked on any collective action. [2] Nor, I think, was the country as a whole even known yet as "Greece." It seems rather to have been the case that, in the time before Hellen, the son of Deucalion,* this designation did not even exist, and places gained their names from the various peoples, especially and predominantly the Pelasgians.* But when Hellen and his sons became powerful in Phthiotis,* and their intervention was requested by other cities, one by one the peoples increasingly began to be called Greeks [*Hellēnes*] as a result of their intercourse with one another, although it took a long time for the name to supersede all others.

[3] Homer is my best witness here, because although he was born a long time after the Trojan War, he never calls the peoples as a whole "Greeks," and he reserves this name exclusively for those who served with Achilles and came from Phthiotis, who were the original Greeks. In the poems he calls them "Danaans," "Argives," and "Achaeans." Nor does he use the term "barbarian" either, and I think this is because Greeks were yet to be separated off and brought under a single competing name. [4] So the various peoples who came to be called Greeks—both those who spoke the same language and gained the name city by city and all those who were called Greeks later—were too weak before the Trojan War and had too little contact with one another for any collective action.

Even for this expedition they united only when they were more experienced mariners. **4.** The first person we hear about who had a navy was Minos.* He made himself the master of most of what is now the Greek sea—that is, he brought the Cyclades islands under his sway and was the first to colonize most of them, once he had driven out the Carians* and installed his own sons as governors. He also did his best to clear the sea of pirates, as one would expect, so as to protect his growing revenues. **5.** For long ago, as soon as traveling here and there by ship became more common, the Greeks and the barbarians who lived on the mainland coast* and on the islands took up piracy, following the lead of their most powerful men, who were motivated by personal gain and the desire to support their weaker dependents. They used to attack and plunder communities that were unwalled and made up of villages; this was, in fact, their main source of livelihood, since the enterprise did not yet carry any stigma, but was even considered quite honorable. [2] Witness some of the inhabitants of mainland Greece even today, who count success in this activity as creditable, and the old poets, who always address the same question to men arriving by sea. "Are you pirates?" they ask, on the understanding that neither would those of whom the question was asked disavow the occupation, nor would those who wanted to know hold it against them.

[3] They raided one another on land as well, and even today the old predatory ways are commonly found in Greece among the Ozolian Locrians, the Aetolians, the Acarnanians, and in that part of the mainland in general,* and as a result of their long-entrenched brigandage the habit of bearing arms has survived among these mainlanders. **6.** People used to bear arms everywhere in Greece because their settlements were unprotected and travel was dangerous; weapons were a normal part of their lives, as they are among barbarians. [2] The fact that in the regions of Greece that I mentioned people still live this way indicates that the same practice was once followed everywhere.

[3] The Athenians were the first to discard their weapons and adopt a relaxed and more graceful lifestyle. In fact, because of this taste for luxury it was only recently that well-off older Athenians stopped wearing linen tunics and binding the hair on their heads into a topknot fastened with golden grasshopper brooches. Hence, because Ionians and Athenians are kin,* this style of dress persisted for a long time among the older generation of Ionians as well. [4] The Lacedaemonians, on the other hand, were the first to adopt moderate clothing and set the current trend, and wealthier Lacedaemonians made sure

that their way of life in general was not markedly different from that of the rest of their fellow citizens. [5] They were also the first to strip naked and to rub oil into their bodies after exercising naked in public. In the old days, however, even in the Olympic games athletes used to compete with loincloths covering their genitals. The practice ended only quite recently. Among the barbarians there are still today, especially in Asia, those who wear loincloths for their boxing and wrestling contests. [6] These are far from being the only respects one could adduce in which early life in Greece resembled the way barbarians live today.

7. More recently founded cities, with plentiful wealth due to increased expertise at seafaring, were built right on the coasts with defensive walls and with each of them occupying an isthmus; that way, both trade and defense against their neighbors were facilitated. The long persistence of piracy, however, meant that older settlements, on the islands as well as the mainland, were usually built away from the coast, because the pirates used to raid not only one another but also non-seagoing coastal settlements. Still today these older settlements retain their inland locations.

8. The islanders—Carians and Phoenicians, by whom most of the islands were settled—were just as implicated in piracy.* Their ethnicity is proved by the fact that when Delos was purified by the Athenians during the current war and the graves of people who had died on the island were removed,* more than half of the dead proved to be Carians, who were identifiable by the style of the weaponry that was interred along with them and by the method of burial, which is still customary in Caria. [2] But once Minos had built his navy, sea traffic increased, because in the course of his colonization of most of the islands he expelled the criminals from them, [3] and coastal populations were able to focus more on acquiring wealth and began to live in greater security. Some of them even set about surrounding their settlements with walls, on the strength of their new prosperity. In their desire for profit, weaker peoples submitted to the domination

of the stronger, and the more powerful, with their plentiful wealth, attached smaller communities to themselves as subordinates.* [4] This process was already well advanced when, in the course of time, they launched the campaign against Troy.*

9. It seems to me, then, that it was because Agamemnon* was the most powerful man of his time that he was able to muster the expeditionary force for Troy, rather than because he was joined by the suitors of Helen, who were bound by the oaths they had sworn to Tyndareus.* [2] Those of the Peloponnesians who have received the clearest account by word of mouth from their forebears say that Pelops was the first to acquire power there, thanks to the great wealth that he brought with him from Asia to a land populated by poor people,* and that even though he was an immigrant the place was named after him. And they say that later his descendants became even greater, after the death of Eurystheus* in Attica at the hands of the Heracleidae.* When Eurystheus set out on his expedition, he entrusted Mycenae and the rest of his kingdom to Atreus because of their kinship (Atreus was his mother's brother and had been banished by his father for the killing of Chrysippus),* and when Eurystheus failed to return, Atreus became the king of Mycenae and everywhere else that Eurystheus had ruled. The Mycenaeans had no objection because they were afraid of the Heracleidae and recognized Atreus's abilities, and also because Atreus had ingratiated himself with the general populace. And so the descendants of Pelops became greater than the descendants of Perseus.

[3] In my opinion, then, it was because Agamemnon inherited this kingdom and made himself the greatest naval power that he was able to gather troops and launch the expedition, and I think this was due more to his being an object of fear than to his being the recipient of others' goodwill. After all, as Homer has stated clearly—if Homer's evidence is to be trusted—Agamemnon seems to have gone there with more ships than anyone else and to have given the Arcadians theirs as well. [4] Moreover, in the passage on the transmission of the scepter, Homer states that Agamemnon was "the lord of many islands and

all Argos."* Now, since he was a mainlander, if he lacked a navy he would not have been the ruler of any islands except local ones, and they would not have counted as "many."

[5] It is on the basis of this expedition that we are obliged to infer what earlier times were like. **10.** The fact that Mycenae was a small place, or that some other town of that era does not nowadays seem to be of any significance, is not a valid reason to doubt that the expeditionary force was as large as the poets say and as tradition claims. [2] If Sparta were deserted and all that remained were its sanctuaries and the foundations of buildings, I think that with the advance of time future generations would find it very hard to believe that its power had been as great as its fame suggested. And yet the Lacedaemonians are the masters of two of the five parts of the Peloponnese and the leaders of the Peloponnese as a whole, and have an extensive alliance outside it. Nevertheless, because the city is not a compact unit and is not equipped with sumptuous sanctuaries and buildings, but consists of separate villages in the old Greek way, it would seem inferior to its reputation. On the other hand, if the same thing happened to Athens, on the basis of its mere appearance its power would be inferred to be double what it actually is.

[3] Doubt is unwarranted, then. The most sensible course is to judge cities by their power rather than by what they look like, and it is reasonable to believe that the Trojan expedition was greater than any earlier ones, but smaller than those of today—that is, again, if we can trust Homer's account in this instance too, when he may very well have embellished and exaggerated, seeing that he was a poet. But, even so, it seems that the expedition was on a relatively small scale. [4] In Homer's account, the fleet consisted of 1,200 vessels, with the Boeotian ships crewed by 120 men and those of Philoctetes by 50. In saying this, I think he was indicating the extremes, the largest and smallest ships; at any rate, these are the only ships the size of which is given in the Catalog of Ships. That the oarsmen were also fighters he spells out in the case of Philoctetes's ships, when he says that

the rowers were all bowmen. Apart from the kings and the highest-ranking officers, it is unlikely that there were many people on the ships who were not crewmen, especially since they were going to cross the open sea with military equipment on board, and their ships were not decked but made in the old piratical style. [5] So if we look at the sizes of the largest and smallest ships, we can see that not very many men were involved, considering that it was a combined expedition from the whole of Greece.

11. The reason for this was not so much shortage of men as poverty. Because of the difficulty of obtaining supplies, they took a fairly small army, of a size that they could expect to be able to live off the land during the campaign. They won a battle on arrival—evidently, because otherwise they could not have built the defensive wall for their camp—but even then they do not seem to have made use of all the forces at their disposal, but were driven by the shortage of supplies to take up farming the Chersonese and pillage. The dispersal of their forces made it easier for the Trojans to hold their own in the struggle for ten years, since they were a match for however many soldiers were left behind at any time. [2] If the Greeks had come with plentiful supplies and had stayed all together without going out on plundering raids and without any farming—that is, if they had prosecuted the war without interruption—they would easily have won, since they held their own even with their forces divided and only some of them there at any given time; and if they had invested the city and put it under siege, it would not have taken them so long or so much effort to capture Troy. [3] But thanks to their poverty, not only were earlier expeditions feeble, but even this one, more renowned than those that went before, is shown by the facts not to live up to its reputation and the tradition about it that the poets have perpetuated.

12. Even after the Trojan War, of course, migration and settlement continued and denied Greece time for peaceful growth. [2] The long delay in the return of the Greeks from Troy was the cause of a great deal of turbulence; civil strife pervaded the cities, leading to new foundations by political exiles. [3] For instance, the present-day Boeotians were driven out of Arne* by the Thessalians in the sixtieth year after the fall of Troy and settled the land that is now called Boeotia, but was previously known as Cadmeïs.* (In fact, however, a splinter group of Boeotians had taken over this land earlier, and it was some of them who went on the expedition to Troy.) Then again, it was in the eightieth year after the fall of Troy that the Dorians and Heracleidae took possession of the Peloponnese. [4] It was far from straightforward and it required many years, but eventually Greece gained peace and security, and once such exoduses had come to an end they even sent out colonies. The Athenians founded settlements in Ionia and most of the islands, the Peloponnesians in much of Italy and Sicily, and also here and there in Greece. These foundations all postdate the Trojan War.

13. As Greece became more powerful and placed more importance on the acquisition of wealth than before, it became very common for the cities to fall under tyrannies, whereas previously there had been hereditary kingships with specified prerogatives. Their revenues were increasing and the Greeks began to equip themselves with navies and take more to the sea. [2] The Corinthians are said to have been the first to adopt something like the modern approach to shipbuilding, and Corinth is said to have been the first place in Greece where triremes were made. [3] It also seems that a Corinthian shipwright called Ameinocles made four ships for the Samians; his sojourn on Samos took place about 300 years before the end of the current war.* [4] Moreover, the earliest recorded sea battle was fought by the Corinthians against the Corcyreans; it took place about 260 years before the same date.* [5] Corinth, located as it is on the Isthmus, was a commercial center from the earliest times. In the old days, the Greeks, both those within the Peloponnese and those outside it, used to communicate with one another by land more than by sea, and since they passed through their territory the Corinthians became prosperous and powerful, as the early poets indicate by calling the place "wealthy

Corinth." Then, when the Greeks started to take more to the sea, the Corinthians equipped themselves with a navy and set about suppressing piracy. Since it was a center for trade by both land and sea, the city's revenues enabled it to remain powerful.

[6] Later, at the time of the reigns of Cyrus, the first king of the Persian empire, and his son Cambyses,* it was the Ionians who became a naval power, and during their conflict with Cyrus they were the masters of the sea in their area for a while. Polycrates, who was the tyrant of Samos when Cambyses was on the throne, used his naval strength to make some of the other islands subject to him, including Rhenea,* which he seized and dedicated to Delian Apollo. And at the time when they were founding Massalia,* the Phocaeans defeated the Carthaginians at sea.

14. These were the most powerful navies, but it seems that even they, many generations after the Trojan War, had few triremes and were still equipped with penteconters and other kinds of warships, as earlier navies had been. [2] It was only shortly before the Persian invasion and the death of Darius, the Persian king after Cambyses, that there was a good number of triremes in the navies of the Sicilian tyrants and the Corcyreans, which were the last important navies to be established in Greece before Xerxes's expedition.* [3] The Aeginetans, Athenians, and a few others had navies, but only small ones, made up mostly of penteconters. The Athenians were latecomers when, because they were at war with the Aeginetans and expecting the Persians to invade, they were persuaded by Themistocles* to build the ships they used in the war. This was before the fully decked type of warship existed.

15. That is what the Greek navies of both earlier and more recent times were like. Nevertheless, those states that took seafaring seriously became extremely strong thanks to the increase in their revenues and to their domination of others. For these states, especially those whose territories were insufficient, used to sail to the islands and make them subject to themselves. [2] But on land no conflict took place that

resulted in any significant increase in power. The only conflicts that did take place on land were disputes between some state or other and its neighbors. No distant campaigns abroad with the object of subjecting others were undertaken by the Greeks, because the greatest states had not yet formed leagues of subject allies, nor, conversely, did cities of their own accord join others as equal partners in shared campaigns; it was more the case that neighboring states fought each other one against one. [3] The exception that proves the rule is the war that was fought long ago between Chalcis and Eretria, when the rest of Greece was largely divided into alliances with one side or the other.*

16. Obstacles to growth differed from place to place. The Ionians were making good progress, but then King Cyrus and the Persians, after defeating Croesus,* campaigned against all Asia Minor between the Halys river and the sea and subjugated the cities there. And later Darius gained control of the islands as well with his Phoenician navy.* **17.** And the tyrants who ruled Greek cities cared for nothing except their own interests—their personal safety and the advancement of their own households—with the result that, by and large, they managed their cities with a view to safety. They therefore have no significant military achievements to their name and all they undertook were occasional offensives against neighbors (which, in Sicily, led to an immense increase in the tyrants' power). And so one way or another Greece was for a long time prevented from uniting and achieving anything notable, and every community was governed by unadventurous policies.

18. Eventually, the tyrants in Athens and elsewhere in Greece (which had largely been under tyrants even before Athens was) were put down by the Lacedaemonians—or at least most of them were, and this was the last generation of tyrants except in Sicily. For even though Sparta, after its foundation by the Dorians who still occupy it today, was racked by civil unrest for longer than any other state we know of, nevertheless it enjoyed good government from a very early period and was never ruled by a tyrant, because it has had the same constitution for somewhat more than four hundred years, reckoning to the end of the current war.* That is why they were in a position to settle matters in other states.

The fall of the tyrants in Greece took place not long before the Battle of Marathon between the Persians and the Athenians.* [2] Ten years later, the barbarians returned to Greece with their great armada, planning to reduce the Greeks to servitude. Given the seriousness of the impending danger, the Lacedaemonians, as the preeminent power, assumed leadership of the Greek alliance, while the Athenians decided to abandon their city as the Persians approached. They packed up their belongings, took to their ships, and became mariners. Although by working together the Greeks did succeed in repelling the barbarians, only a few years later they—not only those who had fought against him, but also Greek rebels from the King*—were split between the Athenians and the Lacedaemonians, manifestly the two greatest powers, with the Lacedaemonians strong on land and the Athenians at sea. [3] So the alliance between the Lacedaemonians and the Athenians lasted for only a few years before they fell out and, joined by their allies, went to war with each other. Other Greeks who had maintained their neutrality now began to join one side or the other. The upshot was that over the whole period from the Persian invasion to the current conflict, although there were occasional truces, they were very often fighting each other or rebellious allies, and so they became well prepared for warfare and very experienced in it by practicing in battlefield conditions.

19. Now, Sparta took no tribute from the members of the league of which it was the head, but made sure that they had oligarchic constitutions and served Lacedaemonian interests exclusively. The Athenians, by contrast, gradually took over their allies' ships (except those of Chios and Lesbos) and assigned all of them rates of tribute that they were required to pay.* So the two sides individually were more prepared for this war than they had been when they were at their strongest earlier, with their alliance against the Persians intact.

20. These, then, are my conclusions about the early history of Greece. It is difficult to trust absolutely every piece of evidence, however, because people can be counted on to accept what they are told about past events in an uncritical frame of mind, even if they concern their own country. [2] For example, most Athenians believe that Hipparchus was tyrant when he was killed by Harmodius and Aristogeiton.* What they fail to realize is that it was Hippias who was the ruler, since he was the eldest of Peisistratus's sons, and that Hipparchus and Thessalus were his younger brothers. What happened was that, on that fateful day and indeed in the nick of time, Harmodius and Aristogeiton suspected that their fellow conspirators had informed on them to Hippias, and so they left him alone, assuming he had been forewarned. But wanting to do something, however risky, before they were arrested, when they came across Hipparchus by the shrine called the Leocoreum, where he was marshaling the Panathenaic parade,* they killed him. [3] Other Greeks too have plenty of false beliefs about even the present, things not yet forgotten over the course of time; they believe, for example, where the Spartan kings are concerned, that each of them casts not one vote but two, and that the Lacedaemonian army has a Pitanate division, which never even existed.* This just goes to show how little trouble most people take to track down the truth; they would rather resort to easily available information.

21. In view of the evidence I have presented, however, it would not be a mistake to think that things happened more or less as I have related. The embellished and exaggerated versions of the poets should not be regarded as more trustworthy, nor the accounts compiled by prose-writers that are designed to please the ear rather than arrive at the truth. Their versions are unverifiable and most of them through time have won their way into the realm of the fabulous, scarcely a trustworthy source. My conclusions, however, can be regarded as sufficiently based on the most perspicuous evidence that is available for events of such antiquity. [2] It may be that it is human nature for people to judge the war they are currently fighting as the greatest there has ever been (and when it is over to be more impressed by older ones), but an impartial consideration of what actually happened will show that there really has never been a greater war than the current one.

22. As regards the speeches delivered by this person or that in the lead-up to the war or already during it, it was not easy to recall accurately the actual words that were spoken, whether I heard the speech myself or it was one that was delivered elsewhere and reported to me. What I have written is what I think each speaker is most likely to have needed to say about the immediate issues, while keeping as close as possible to the overall purport of the speech as actually delivered.* [2] Where the events and action of the war are concerned, however, my policy has been not to write down what I learned from just anyone or my personal opinions, but to do so only once I had investigated everything as meticulously as possible, whether I was present myself at the event or was informed about it by others. [3] This was a laborious form of investigation because those present at particular events gave different accounts of the same things, depending on which side they favored and how good their memory was. [4] The non-fabulous character of my narrative may well reduce its attractiveness, but I will be content if it is judged useful by people who want a clear view of what happened in the past—and, human nature being what it is, of what is going to happen again in the future in an approximate or closely similar way. The work has been composed as a possession for all time rather than a virtuoso performance for a single hearing.*

23. The greatest action of the past was the Persian invasion, yet it was swiftly decided by two battles at sea and two on land.* The current war, however, went on for a very long time and during it Greece was afflicted by worse suffering than in any comparable span of time. [2] The number of towns captured and laid waste either by barbarians or by Greeks as they fought one another was unprecedented; on their capture some were even resettled with new inhabitants. The number of people exiled or killed as a result of the war itself or internal unrest was also unprecedented. [3] Phenomena that one used to hear about but which were seldom confirmed by fact now became credible: earthquakes damaged more land than ever before and were of a greater magnitude; solar eclipses happened more frequently, judging by the records of such events in the past; some places were afflicted by severe drought and consequent famine; and then there was the most destructive thing of all, which caused the deaths of a good portion of the population—the plague.* All these calamities attacked at the same time along with the war.

[4] It was started by the Athenians and the Peloponnesians when they broke the treaty, the Thirty-Year Peace that they had entered into after the fall of Euboea.* [5] To explain why they broke it, I have prefaced my narrative with an account of their complaints and contentions, so that in the future no one will have to try to find out how the Greeks became embroiled in such a major conflict. [6] In my opinion, the truest cause, even if it was never openly stated, was the growth of Athenian power, which frightened the Lacedaemonians and made them feel that they had to go to war; but the reasons that were publicly stated by one side or the other, which led to the breaking of the treaty and the outbreak of war, were as follows.

24. The city of Epidamnus is situated on the east coast of the Adriatic; its neighbors are the barbarian Taulantians, an Illyrian people. [2] Epidamnus is a Corcyrean colony, but it was founded by Phalius, son of Eratocleides, a Corinthian of the Heracleidae clan, who was summoned from the mother city in accordance with traditional custom. There were also some Corinthians and other Dorians among the original settlers. [3] As time passed, Epidamnus became a powerful city with a sizable population, [4] but after a period of civil discord that apparently lasted for many years, they suffered terrible losses in warfare with the neighboring barbarians and their power was severely reduced. [5] In the period immediately preceding the current war, the democrats expelled the aristocrats, who then attacked with the support of the barbarians and began to send raiding parties against those in the city by land and sea. [6] Finding themselves in trouble, the Epidamnians from the city sent a delegation to Corcyra, as the mother city, asking them not to stand by while they were destroyed, but to effect a reconciliation between them and the exiles and to bring the fighting with the barbarians to an end. [7] They made this plea while seated as suppliants in the sanctuary of Hera, but the Corcyreans rejected their supplication and sent them away empty-handed.

25. The news that the Corcyreans were refusing to help them left the Epidamnians in a quandary, and they sent emissaries to Delphi to ask the god if they should entrust the city to the Corinthians, as its original founders, and try to get help in some form from them. And the god replied that they should do so—that they should place themselves under the leadership of the Corinthians. [2] The Epidamnians went to Corinth and handed the colony over as the oracle had instructed. Pointing out that their city had been founded by a Corinthian, they told the Corinthians what the oracle had said and asked them not to let them be destroyed, but to come to their aid.

[3] The Corinthians felt that it was only right for them to help and they promised to do so; they regarded Epidamnus as just as much their colony as the Corcyreans', and they were in any case angry with the Corcyreans for not treating them with the respect that was due from colonists. [4] At their joint festivals the Corcyreans were failing to grant them the customary privileges or serve a Corinthian with the first portion of a sacrificial victim as their other colonists did. This Corcyrean disdain for the Corinthians was due to the fact that, at that time, they were a match for the wealthiest Greek states in terms of their financial power and were more powerful in terms of their military resources. They boasted of the considerable superiority of their navy, occasionally even on the ground that those famous mariners, the Phaeacians, had been the original inhabitants of the island.* Motivated by this conceit, they strengthened their navy even more, until

they had real power: at the start of the war they had 120 triremes. **26.** With all these grievances, the Corinthians were happy to help Epidamnus; they encouraged volunteers to go there as settlers, and they sent a garrison made up of soldiers from Ambracia and Leucas as well as their own men. [2] They took the overland route to Apollonia, a Corinthian colony, because they were worried that the Corcyreans might make it impossible for them to get through if they went there by sea.

[3] The Corcyreans were furious when they found out that the settlers and garrison troops had reached Epidamnus and that the colony had been given over to the Corinthians. They immediately launched 25 ships, supplemented later by another squadron, and haughtily ordered the Epidamnians to dismiss the settlers and the garrison and to take back the exiles. (The exiled Epidamnians had gone to Corcyra and asked the Corcyreans to restore them to Epidamnus, bolstering their petition by pointing to their ancestors' tombs and reminding the Corcyreans of their kinship.) [4] When the Epidamnians complied with none of these demands, the Corcyreans began operations against them with a force consisting of 40 ships, as well as the exiles they were intending to restore, and the Illyrians too. [5] They took up a position close to the city and issued a proclamation to the effect that any Epidamnian who so wished could leave unharmed, and that the same went for the new arrivals too, while all those who remained would be regarded as enemies. The Epidamnians ignored this proclamation, so the Corcyreans put the city, which was situated on an isthmus, under siege.

27. When the Corinthians were told about the siege by messengers who reached them from Epidamnus, they set about raising a force to send there, as well as proclaiming the colonization of Epidamnus, and promising that all who chose to go would enjoy fair and equal rights of citizenship. If someone was reluctant to go right away but wanted to participate in the settlement program, he could deposit fifty Corinthian drachmas and remain behind. Many people either set sail for Epidamnus or put money down. [2] The Corinthians were worried that the Corcyreans might make it impossible for them to get through, and so they also asked the Megarians to provide them with ships for the fleet. Megara set about getting 8 ships ready for the Corinthians, and Pale in Cephallenia 4. Epidaurus responded to the plea with 5 ships, Hermione with 1, Troezen with 2,* Leucas with 10, and Ambracia with 8. From Thebes and Phleious they requested money, and from Elis unmanned ships and money. The Corinthians themselves were preparing a force of 30 ships and 3,000 hoplites.

28. When the Corcyreans found out about the steps the Corinthians were taking, they went to Corinth, taking with them delegates from Sparta and Sicyon, and demanded that the Corinthians withdraw not only the troops they had in Epidamnus but the new settlers, too, who had no claim to the place. [2] If the Corinthians disputed this, the Corcyreans would gladly accept arbitration in the Peloponnese by states that were acceptable to both sides, and the dispute would be settled in favor of whichever of them was adjudged to have a right to the colony. They would also be just as happy to entrust the decision to the oracle in Delphi. [3] They warned the Corinthians not to start a war. Otherwise, they said, if the Corinthians left them no choice, self-interest would compel them to look beyond their current friendships and make friends where they would prefer not to. [4] The Corinthians replied that if the Corcyreans withdrew their fleet and the barbarians from Epidamnus, they would think about how to proceed, but meanwhile arbitration was inappropriate while Epidamnus was under siege. [5] In response the Corcyreans said that if the Corinthians too withdrew their people from Epidamnus, they would comply with their demands. And finally they expressed their willingness for both sides to remain where they were with a truce in place until a decision had been reached.

29. The Corinthians would have none of it. Once they had crews for their ships and their allies had arrived, they first sent a herald ahead to declare war on the Corcyreans, and then they set out with

70 ships and 7,000 hoplites and sailed for Epidamnus and war with the Corcyreans. [2] The generals in command of the fleet were Aristeus, son of Pellichus; Callicrates, son of Callias; and Timanor, son of Timanthes; while Archetimus, son of Eurytimus, and Isarchidas, son of Isarchus, were in command of the land forces. [3] When they reached Actium—the site of the sanctuary of Apollo—which lies in the territory of Anactorium at the mouth of the Ambracian Gulf, the Corcyreans sent a herald to the Corinthians in a small boat to try to deter them from sailing against them. At the same time, they were recruiting crews for their fleet, which had been overhauled: the older ships were braced to make them seaworthy and the rest were repaired. [4] When the herald reported that the Corinthians had shown no desire for peace, and once the Corcyreans' ships were fully manned (they had 80 ships, since 40 were blockading Epidamnus), they too put to sea, deployed for battle, and engaged. [5] It was an outright victory for the Corcyreans, with 15 of the Corinthians' ships destroyed. By coincidence, this happened on the same day that their men besieging Epidamnus forced the city to come to terms, the agreement being that they could sell the new arrivals into slavery and keep the Corinthians as prisoners of war pending further decisions.

30. After the battle, the Corcyreans erected a trophy at Leucimme, a cape in their territory, and killed all their prisoners except for the Corinthians. [2] The Corinthians and their allies returned home after this defeat, leaving the Corcyreans as masters of the entire sea thereabouts. In fact, later they sailed to Leucas, a Corinthian colony, where they ravaged the farmland, and then they burned the Eleans' harbor at Cyllene, because they had given the Corinthians ships and money. [3] The Corcyreans retained their mastery at sea for a long time after the battle and launched destructive assaults by sea against Corinthian allies, until early in the summer the suffering of their allies induced the Corinthians to dispatch ships and a land army. They encamped at Actium and near Cheimerium in Thesprotis* in order to mount a guard over Leucas and the other friendly local peoples.

[4] The Corcyreans responded by making a base for their own ships and men at Leucimme. Neither fleet made a move against the other, but they spent the summer encamped opposite each other, and when winter came both sides returned home.

31. The war with the Corcyreans angered the Corinthians and they spent what was left of the year after the battle, and the following year, building ships and making ready the strongest naval force they could; the wages they offered enabled them to gather oarsmen not only from the Peloponnese itself, but from all over Greece. [2] The reports they received of the Corinthians' preparations worried the Corcyreans and, seeing that they had no treaties in place with other Greeks and had joined neither the Athenian nor the Lacedaemonian alliance, they decided to approach the Athenians for an alliance in an attempt to get their support. [3] On hearing this, the Corinthians too went to Athens to present their case. They were concerned that a combined Athenian and Corcyrean navy would make it impossible for them to settle the war in their favor. [4] An assembly was convened at which both sides made their opposing arguments, and the Corcyreans spoke somewhat as follows:

32. "It is only right, Athenians, that people who approach others with a request for help when, as is the case with us now, they have no claim on their audience as a result of having rendered some notable service or from an alliance—it is only right that they should explain, first and foremost, that what they're asking for is advantageous, or at least harmless, and, second, that their gratitude is certain. And if they fail to make this clear, they should not take it amiss if they fail to get what they asked for. [2] The Corcyreans sent us here to petition for an alliance, confident that they will be able to give you firm assurances on these points.

[3] "But there is a constant practice of ours that has turned out to be both erratic in relation to you, since now we need your support, and, given present circumstances, disadvantageous for us. [4] Never in the past have we of our own accord entered into an alliance with anyone,

yet here we are looking for outside help precisely because as a result of this practice of ours we now stand isolated in our present conflict with the Corinthians. What formerly we took to be prudence—our practice of steering clear of any external alliance, given that it could involve us in sharing the risks of another's policy—has now turned out to be folly and weakness. [5] It's true that in the battle that was fought between us we repelled the Corinthians without any help, but now they're moving against us with a larger force drawn from the Peloponnese and the rest of Greece, and it's clear to us that we cannot survive by our own strength alone and that we face a considerable risk if we succumb to them. And so we have no choice but to turn for help to you and everyone else. We deserve to be excused, then, if we now presume to contravene our previous policy of nonalignment. It's not that we are bad people; we just made a mistake.

33. "If you grant our request, it will prove good for you in a number of respects. First, you'll be helping people who are the victims, not the aggressors. Second, if you accept us as allies when our very existence is at stake, you'll be putting us in your debt in a way that we are unlikely ever to forget—and we have the greatest navy apart from yours. [2] Consider this: suppose a power that you'd have paid a very great deal to have on your side, and for which you would gladly have incurred an enormous debt of gratitude, comes to you unsolicited, offering itself to you without risk or expense; suppose in addition that it leads to your being widely admired as good people, instills a feeling of gratitude in those you'll be defending, and increases your military strength. Could any coup be more extraordinary—or more disturbing to your enemies? Throughout history few have met with this combination of benefits, and few have come seeking an alliance who are in a position to offer those from whom they are requesting help as much security and honor as they themselves will receive.

[3] "If any of you imagines that there's no war looming in which we might be of service to you, he's misguided. To think this is to fail to see that the Lacedaemonians are being driven to war by their fear of you,

and that the Corinthians, who are influential with them and hostile to you, are now trying to overpower us as a preliminary to attacking you. The point is that they don't want us to stand together in shared hostility against them, and they want to ensure that they retain the advantage in one of two ways: either by weakening us or by strengthening their own position. [4] For our part, then, our joint task is to pre-empt them—we by offering you an alliance and you by accepting the offer—and thereby to forestall their designs rather than react to them.

34. "If the Corinthians argue that it's wrong for you to accept their colonists as allies, they need to understand that all colonies honor their mother cities if they're treated well, but become estranged from them if they're wronged. Colonists are sent out on the understanding that they'll be the equals of those back home, not their slaves. [2] And there can be no doubt that the Corinthians were in the wrong, because when they were invited to submit to arbitration over Epidamnus, they chose to pursue their grievances by war rather than by fair means. [3] And the way they're treating us, their kinsmen, should warn you not to be misled by their duplicity, nor to assist them if they approach you directly with a request. It's those who have the least cause to regret doing the enemy favors who enjoy the greatest and the longest-lasting security.

35. "Nor will accepting us as allies constitute a breach of your treaty with the Lacedaemonians,* because we have an alliance in place with neither you nor them, [2] and it is stated in the treaty that any nonaligned Greek community can join whichever of the two sides it wants. [3] It would be unconscionable for the Corinthians to be allowed to recruit crews for their ships not just from fellow members of their alliance but from the rest of Greece as well—and especially from your subjects—while trying to shut us out from an available alliance and to deny us the opportunity to be helped by anyone else. They may call it unlawful if you grant our request, supposing you are persuaded to do so, [4] but we will charge you with far worse offenses if you are

not so persuaded. You'll be rejecting us even though we're in danger and even though we're not your enemies, and so far from impeding them, when they are your enemies and the aggressors, you'll be turning a blind eye to the fact that they're increasing their strength from your own empire. This is not right. You should either stop them from hiring crews in your empire or give us help too in whatever form you decide—hopefully by openly accepting us as allies and coming to our defense.

[5] "As you can now see, and as we suggested at the start, there are many advantages to our petition. But the most important point, and the firmest basis for trust, is that we have the same enemies, and these enemies are not weak but perfectly capable of making trouble for those who defect from them. It's one thing for you to turn down an offer of an alliance with a land-based power, but quite another to reject a naval power. By all means, if you can, prevent anyone else from having ships, but if that's impossible, have the strongest naval power as your friend.

36. "There may be some of you who appreciate the advantages of our request, but are still concerned that granting it will constitute a breach of the treaty. If so, they should realize that the best way to strike fear into your enemies, whatever concerns you may have, is to be strong, while being free of doubt but denying our request is a weak position and therefore less threatening to enemies who are strong. They should also realize that their deliberations today are about Athens just as much as Corcyra, and that they're failing to provide for Athens's best interests if in the face of the coming war—a war that is all but upon us—they consider only the short term and hesitate about gaining the allegiance of a place whose friendship or enmity has enormous consequences for Athens. [2] Among Corcyra's many advantages is the fact that its location on the coastal route to Italy and Sicily makes it well placed both to prevent a fleet from there joining the Peloponnesians and to help one from here on its way there.

[3] "It will take only the briefest of summaries† of both the overall situation and the particulars, as follows, to show you that we should not be abandoned. There are three navies in Greece of any significant size; they belong to you, to us, and to the Corinthians. If you do nothing to prevent two of these from uniting when the Corinthians overpower us, at sea you'll be fighting both the Corcyreans and the Peloponnesians at once. On the other hand, if you accept us as allies, you'll enter the contest against them with our ships as well as yours."

After the Corcyreans had spoken along these lines, it was the Corinthians' turn: **37.** "We have no choice. Since the Corcyreans didn't limit their remarks to the issue of your accepting them as allies, but also alleged that we are the aggressors and have no right to be making war on them, we must therefore first address these two charges before getting to the rest of what we have to say. That way, you'll have a better grasp of what we're claiming—and good grounds for rejecting their petition.

[2] "They say that they had prudential reasons for having avoided alliances with other states up until now, but in fact their reasons for pursuing this policy were iniquitous rather than virtuous. They didn't want an ally because any ally they called on for help would witness their wrongdoing and therefore cause them shame. [3] Furthermore, the self-sufficient location of their city makes it possible for them to do their own adjudicating of cases where they've harmed others rather than being bound by the terms of a treaty, because while they very rarely make voyages abroad, they very often receive visits from others, who have no choice but to put into their harbors. [4] Meanwhile, they use their specious neutrality as a cloak. It's not a way for them to avoid involvement in others' wrongdoing, as they claim, but a way for them to do wrong without anyone else's involvement. It allows them to employ force where they have the upper hand, to satisfy their greed when they can get away with it, and to feel no shame for their profiteering.

---

† An obelus in the text refers to a note in the Textual Notes (pp. 681–684).

[5] And yet, if they were the good men they claim to be, then precisely because it's unusually hard for others to bring them to account, they could have given a perfectly clear demonstration of their goodness by submitting to arbitration in these instances.

38. "But they do not demonstrate goodness in the way they treat others, and the same goes for their dealings with us. Although they're colonists of ours, they've always been rebellious and now they're openly fighting us. They weren't sent out in the first place, they say, in order to be abused, [2] and we reply that we didn't found colonies in order to be dishonored by them, but to receive the respect that is our due as their leaders. [3] At any rate, the rest of our colonies honor us; in fact, no city is held in greater affection by its colonists than Corinth. [4] Since we are acceptable to the majority and they are the only ones who find us unacceptable, they are obviously in the wrong. And it's also clear that we do not take the extraordinary step of taking offensive action against colonies unless we're being wronged to an exceptional degree. [5] Even if we were at fault, it would have been a noble gesture for them to have yielded to our anger, and it would have been disgraceful for us to have responded with violence to this restraint of theirs. [6] But, motivated by arrogance and the power of their wealth, they have wronged us in many ways. Their seizure of Epidamnus, our colony, when we came to relieve it, even though they didn't lay claim to it when it was in trouble, is only the most notable instance of their insolence. And now they retain their hold on Epidamnus by violent means.

39. "Now, they claim that they had already offered to submit to arbitration, but this should never be regarded as a meaningful offer when it comes from people who have the security of a position of superiority, as opposed to those whose words are on a par with their capability for action before they engage in hostilities. [2] But instead of making their specious offer of submitting to arbitration before they had the place under siege, the Corcyreans did so only when they anticipated our intervention. Not satisfied with being guilty themselves of crimes in Epidamnus, they've come here now wanting you to be not so much their allies as their accomplices in these crimes. Moreover, they're seeking an alliance with you because their relationship with us has broken down, [3] when properly they should have approached you when they were perfectly secure, not after we had been the victims of their aggression and they were at risk. Instead, you'll now be aiding people who didn't put their strength at your disposal then, and we will hold you equally responsible for their crimes even though you had no hand in them. If they expect you to share in the consequences, they should long ago have let you share their strength.

40. "We have established that we've come here with valid complaints, and that the Corcyreans are violent and greedy. We shall now demonstrate that it would be wrong for you to accept them as allies. [2] Even though it's stated in the treaty with Sparta that any of the states not enrolled in one or the other alliance may join either of them, this provision doesn't apply to those who join just because they want to harm another state.* It applies only to those whose request for protection doesn't entail their defection from another state, and which are not going to embroil those who accept them as allies, who would realize the consequences if they paused for thought, in war rather than peace. But that's exactly what will happen to you if you fail to heed our advice. [3] You would become not just their allies but also our enemies, where before we were fellow signatories to the treaty. Because if you join forces with them, we will have to defend ourselves against you as well as them.

[4] "And yet the right and proper thing for you to do is to stand aloof from both of us. Failing that, the alternative is to do the complete opposite and join us against them, seeing that you're already partners with us Corinthians in a peace treaty, whereas you've never even arranged a truce with the Corcyreans. Either of these alternatives would enable you to avoid establishing a principle that allows states to accept as allies defectors from other states. [5] We, too, refused to do any such thing. At the time of the Samians' rebellion,* when the

Peloponnesians were trying to decide whether to aid the rebels and the votes were tied, we voted in your favor and publicly argued that every state has the right to discipline its own allies. [6] If you're going to accept miscreants as allies and support them, you'll find that there are quite a few of your allies who will come over to our side, and the principle you'll be establishing will hurt you more than us.

41. "So much, then, for the considerations of justice that we want to impress upon you; by normal Greek standards, they are decisive on their own. Nevertheless, we also have some advice to offer and the following claim on your gratitude to mention. It seems to us that, under current circumstances, this claim should be satisfied, given that, while we're not actively harming each other, which would make us enemies, we also don't regularly rely on each other, which would make us friends. [2] Once, when you were short of warships for the conflict with Aegina just before the Persian invasion, you received twenty from the Corinthians. This favor made it possible for you to defeat Aegina, and our preventing the Peloponnesians from helping the Samians enabled you to punish Samos. And we did you these good turns at critical times, the kind of times when people at war are oblivious to everything except victory. [3] They regard anyone who is of service as a friend, even if he was formerly an enemy, and anyone who stands in their way as an enemy, even if he was a friend, since the benefits of victory are taken to outweigh the benefits of even close relationships.

42. "Do bear these favors in mind—and have the more elderly among you tell those who are younger what happened—and choose to pay us back in kind. Don't make the mistake of thinking that while there may be justice in what we're saying, in the event of war expediency may lie elsewhere. [2] Expediency is a consequence above all of making as few mistakes as possible, and although the Corcyreans are trying to frighten you into doing wrong by claiming that war is imminent, it is by no means a certainty. There's no reason to get carried away by it and earn the hatred of the Corinthians, which would not be imminent but immediate and unmistakable, when the prudent course is rather to reduce the suspicion that your treatment of the Megarians has already aroused.* [3] After all, if it arrives at an opportune moment, the most recent favor, even if it's relatively slight, has the power to annul a more substantial grievance. [4] And don't be led astray by the Corcyreans' offer of a powerful naval alliance. Not wronging one's equals is a more reliable source of strength than the risky gains to be won by an exciting but short-term prospect.

43. "We find ourselves in the same situation as the one we addressed before in Sparta, when we insisted that every state has the right to discipline its own allies, and so we expect to be allowed the same right by you. Since you were helped by our vote, we shouldn't be harmed by yours. [2] Do the same for us as we did for you, in the knowledge that the current crisis is particularly conducive to revealing who one's friends and enemies are, depending on whether they help or hinder you. [3] Heed our pleas. Don't receive these Corcyreans into your alliance, and don't assist them in their wrongdoing. [4] This is the right course of action for you, the policy that best serves your own interests."

44. Once the Corinthians had spoken along these lines and the Athenians had heard both speeches, the assembly met—twice, in fact. At the first meeting, they expressed more approval of the arguments put forward by the Corinthians, but the next day they changed their minds. While they did not make a full offensive and defensive alliance with the Corcyreans—because if the Corcyreans wanted them to take part in a joint attack on Corinth, they would be in breach of the treaty with the Peloponnesians—they did conclude a defensive alliance, committing them to helping each other if Corcyra, Athens, or their allies were attacked. [2] The Athenians believed that war with the Peloponnesians was inevitable in any case, and they did not want Corcyra, with its substantial navy, to surrender to the Corinthians. They preferred to see the two of them clash as much as possible so that, if the need arose and it came to war, all naval powers would be

weakened, not just the Corinthians. [3] And another consideration was the favorable location of the island on the coastal route to Italy and Sicily.

45. These were the considerations that led the Athenians to accept the Corcyreans as allies, and soon after the departure of the Corinthian envoys they dispatched 10 ships to help the Corcyreans. [2] The generals in charge of the fleet were Lacedaemonius, son of Cimon; Diotimus, son of Strombichus; and Proteas, son of Epicles. [3] Their instructions were not to engage with the Corinthians unless they sailed against Corcyra or any other place belonging to the Corcyreans with the intention of making a landing, in which case they were to do their best to deter them. These instructions were designed to ensure that they were not in breach of the treaty.

[4] So the Athenian flotilla went to Corcyra, **46.** but as soon as the Corinthians had completed their preparations, they sailed against Corcyra with a fleet of 150 ships. Ten of these came from Elis, 12 from Megara, 10 from Leucas, 27 from Ambracia, 1 from Anactorium, and 90 from the Corinthians themselves. [2] The contingents from each state had their own generals; the Corinthians had 5, including Xenocleides, son of Euthycles. [3] They sailed from Leucas, and when they reached the mainland opposite Corcyra they anchored at Cheimerium in Thesprotis. [4] There is a harbor there, and above it and inland, in Thesprotian Elaeatis, there is a town called Ephyra. Nearby, the Acherousian lake issues into the sea. The river Acheron, from which the lake gets its name, flows through Thesprotis and into the lake; there is another river, the Thyamis, which acts as the border between Thesprotis and Cestrine, and the Cheimerium promontory juts out between these two rivers. [5] So this is the part of the mainland where the Corinthians moored and made camp.

47. When the Corcyreans found out that they were on their way, they manned 110 ships, which were commanded by Miciades, Aesimides, and Eurybatus, and made camp on one of the Sybota islands.* The 10 Athenian ships were also there. [2] The Corcyrean land army was based at Cape Leucimme, along with a support force of 1,000 hoplites from Zacynthos. [3] The Corinthians had allies as well, in the form of a large force of barbarians, who gathered on the mainland; the mainlanders there have always been on good terms with the Corinthians.

48. Once the Corinthians had equipped themselves, they took provisions for three days and set out by night from Cheimerium to do battle. [2] At first light, as they were sailing along, they spotted the Corcyrean fleet out at sea and heading in their direction. [3] When they were within clear sight of each other, they formed up for battle. The Athenian ships were on the right wing of the Corcyrean formation and the rest of the line was held by the Corcyreans themselves, who had divided their fleet into three units, each commanded by one of the generals. [4] On the Corinthian side, the Megarian and Ambraciot ships had the right wing, the rest of the allies were distributed in separate clusters in the center, and the Corinthians themselves were on the left wing, with their fastest ships facing the Athenians and the Corcyrean right.

49. After the signal flags had been raised on both sides, they joined battle. Both the Corinthians and the Corcyreans had a great many hoplites on their decks, and numerous archers and javelineers too, because they were still relying on the clumsy old method of fighting. [2] It was a fierce battle, then, but hardly skillful: it was much like a land battle at sea. [3] When they clashed, the press of large numbers of ships all around them made it difficult for them to break away clear, and so they relied for victory more on the hoplites on the decks, who stood and fought while the ships remained motionless. There were no attempts to break through the enemy line, and the battle was fought with passion and physical strength rather than with skill. [4] Everywhere there was considerable uproar and the battle was fought in a chaotic fashion.

The role of the Athenian ships was to come up in support of any Corcyrean ships that were in trouble and thereby to intimidate the enemy, but the generals did not initiate any actual fighting for fear of transgressing their orders from the Athenians. [5] The ships on the Corinthian right wing came off particularly badly. Twenty Corcyrean ships forced them to retreat in confusion and then pursued them all the way to their camp on the mainland, where they disembarked, burned the deserted tents, and looted their property. [6] Here, then, the Corinthians and their allies got the worst of it and the Corcyreans were dominant. But where the Corinthians themselves were, on the left wing, they won a decisive victory, because the Corcyreans, who were outnumbered anyway, were missing the twenty ships that were involved in the pursuit. [7] Seeing that the Corcyreans were in trouble, the Athenians began to help in a more resolute fashion, although they held back at first from doing any ramming. But when the Corcyreans' retreat was unmistakable and the Corinthians were pushing on relentlessly, it became a free-for-all. Distinctions were no longer made, and circumstances made it impossible for the Corinthians and Athenians to avoid fighting each other.

50. After the rout, instead of taking in tow the hulls of the ships they had sunk,* the Corinthians focused on the crews. Rather than taking them alive, they sailed back and forth slaughtering them in the water, and in so doing they unwittingly killed some of their own people, because they did not know that they had been defeated on the right wing. [2] Indeed, with so many ships on both sides disposed over a large stretch of sea, once battle was joined it was not easy to tell who was winning and who was losing. Never before, in fact, had there been so many ships involved in a sea battle of Greeks against Greeks.

[3] Once the Corinthians had harried the Corcyreans onto land, they turned their attention to the wrecks and their own dead, most of whom they recovered and took to Sybota, an uninhabited cove in Thesprotis, where the barbarian land forces had gathered. Then they rallied again and sailed against the Corcyreans, [4] who, concerned to prevent the Corinthians from attempting to land in their territory, were themselves sailing into the attack with those of their ships that

were still seaworthy and their reserves, and with the Athenian ships in support. [5] By now it was late in the day. The paean had already been sung to signal the advance when the Corinthians suddenly began to back water. They had spotted twenty Athenian ships bearing down on them. These were ships that the Athenians had dispatched later to assist the first ten, because they were afraid of exactly what had happened—that the Corcyreans would lose and that their ten ships would be too few to prevent their defeat.*

51. So when the Corinthians saw these ships in the distance, they began to retreat, because they suspected that they were from Athens and that there were more yet to appear. [2] But the Corcyreans could not see the Athenian ships, which were coming up behind them, so they were astonished when the Corinthians started to back water, until some of them spotted the Athenian ships and called out that there were ships over there, coming their way. Then they too started to withdraw, since it was getting dark, and the Corinthians turned their ships around and completed their disengagement. [3] So the two sides separated and the battle came to an end at nightfall. [4] Not long after these twenty Athenian ships had been sighted (they were under the command of Glaucon, son of Leagrus, and Dracontides, son of Leogoras), they made their way through the corpses and the wreckage and arrived at the Corcyreans' camp at Leucimme. [5] It was dark and at first the Corcyreans were afraid that they were enemy ships, but then they recognized them and the ships came to anchor.

52. The next day, the thirty Athenian ships and the remaining seaworthy Corcyrean vessels set sail and made for the harbor at Sybota, which was serving as the Corinthians' anchorage, to find out if they would fight. [2] The Corinthians put to sea and took up a battle formation in open water, but then did nothing. They had no intention of deliberately starting a battle when they could see that fresh ships had arrived from Athens, and besides, they were in considerable difficulties; not only did they have to guard the prisoners, whom they had on board, but they also had no way to repair their ships in this uninhabited spot. [3] Their primary concern was how to get home; they were afraid that the Athenians might keep them from sailing away, on the ground that since the two of them had clashed, the treaty between them had been voided.

53. The Corinthians therefore decided to have some men board a small boat and go over to the Athenians without the protection of a herald's staff to test their intentions. [2] This was the gist of the message they delivered: "The wrongdoing is all yours, Athenians, because you're acting aggressively and in breach of the treaty. We are here to punish our enemies, and you take up arms against us and get in our way. If your intention is to prevent us from sailing to Corcyra or anywhere else we please—if you're breaking the treaty—here we are. We can be the first Corinthians you take captive and treat as prisoners of war." [3] All the Corcyrean soldiers who were within earshot responded to these words from the Corinthians by calling for them to be seized and put to death, but the Athenians replied to the following effect: [4] "We aren't the aggressors, Peloponnesians, nor are we in breach of the treaty; we have simply come to help our allies, the Corcyreans here. If you want to sail elsewhere, you're free to do so as far as we are concerned. But if you sail against Corcyra or any place within their territory, we'll do our best to stop you."

54. Given this response from the Athenians, the Corinthians made ready to sail home. They set up a trophy on the Sybota mainland, but the Corcyreans recovered the wrecks and the corpses that had been swept in their direction by the current and by the wind that had got up during the night and had scattered them over a wide area, and set up their own counter-trophy, as though they had been victorious, on Sybota island. [2] The two sides, each claiming victory, had the following grounds for doing so. The Corinthians set up a trophy because they had come off best in the sea battle until night had intervened, and had managed to collect most of the wrecks and the bodies of their dead; furthermore, they had at least 1,000 prisoners and had sunk about 70 ships. The Corcyreans, on the other hand, set up a trophy because they had destroyed about 30 ships; because after the arrival of the Athenians they had collected the wrecks and the bodies of their dead that had drifted in their direction; because, the day before, the Corinthians had backed water and retreated at the sight of the Athenian ships; and because after the arrival of the Athenians the Corinthians had not sailed out from Sybota against them. These were the reasons each side had for claiming victory.

55. In the course of their homeward voyage, the Corinthians took Anactorium, which is situated at the mouth of the Ambracian Gulf. It was betrayed to them by sympathizers—it had a combined Corinthian and Corcyrean population—and before returning home they installed Corinthian settlers there. As for their Corcyrean prisoners, 800 of them were slaves and were sold, but they kept 250 in captivity and treated them very well, in the hope that one day these men, who happened to be the leading and most influential men of the city, might return to Corcyra and bring the island over to their side. [2] Corcyra had survived the conflict with the Corinthians, and the Athenian ships left the island and returned home. But as far as the Corinthians were concerned, this was the first of the grievances that led to war with the Athenians—that the Athenians had fought them alongside the Corcyreans while the treaty was still in force.

56. Immediately after this, another event occurred that contributed to the rift between the Athenians and Peloponnesians and to the eventual outbreak of war between them. [2] The Corinthians were actively looking for ways to avenge themselves on the Athenians, and the Athenians, wanting to take precautions because of this hostility, made certain demands of the Potidaeans. The city is situated on the isthmus of the Pallene peninsula and is a Corinthian foundation, but it was a tribute-paying member of the Athenian alliance. The Athenians ordered them to dismantle the stretch of their wall that faced the peninsula, to hand over hostages, to dismiss the Corinthian magistrates, and from then on to refuse to accept the officers the Corinthians sent them each year. The Athenians did this because they were afraid that the Potidaeans might be persuaded by Perdiccas and the Corinthians to secede from the alliance and that they might take the rest of the Thraceward members of the alliance with them.

57. These preventive measures regarding the Potidaeans were taken by the Athenians immediately after the sea battle at Corcyra, [2] because the Corinthians were now openly at odds with them, and the Macedonian king, Perdiccas, son of Alexander, who had previously been an ally and a friend, was now an enemy. [3] This happened because the Athenians granted an alliance to his brother Philip and to Derdas, who had joined forces against him. [4] This scared Perdiccas and he turned to negotiation. He got in touch with the Lacedaemonians, hoping to foment war between the Athenians and the Peloponnesians, and he was trying to gain the backing of the Corinthians for an attempt to secure the secession of Potidaea from Athens. [5] He was also in talks with the Chalcidians of the Thraceward region and the Bottiaeans,* trying to persuade them to join Potidaea in the revolt, because he felt that it would be easier for him to make war if they were on his side as allies, since their lands bordered his own. [6] The Athenians were aware of all this and they wanted to forestall the defection of these communities. It so happened that they were in the process of sending 30 ships and 1,000 hoplites against Perdiccas's kingdom, under the command of five generals, including Archestratus, son of Lycomedes, so they told the generals in charge of this expeditionary force to demand hostages from the Potidaeans, to demolish the wall, and to be vigilant against any attempt by nearby cities to revolt.

58. The Potidaeans sent an embassy to the Athenians to try to persuade them not to make any such radical changes to their status, but they also went to Sparta, supported by a Corinthian delegation, to see if the Lacedaemonians might be willing to help them if their situation became dire. The negotiations in Athens were protracted but unproductive, and in fact the ships that were being sent north had Potidaea as their target no less than Macedon, so when the Lacedaemonian authorities promised that they would invade Attica if the Athenians attacked Potidaea, the Potidaeans saw their chance and revolted, after concluding a sworn alliance with the Chalcidians and the Bottiaeans. [2] Moreover, Perdiccas persuaded the Chalcidians to abandon and demolish their coastal settlements and move inland to Olynthus to create a single strong city there. He gave those who were displaced by this move some of his own land (in Mygdonia, near Lake Bolbe) to farm for as long as the war with Athens lasted. And so they set about razing their towns, moving inland, and gearing up for war.

59. So when the 30 Athenian ships reached the Thraceward region, they found that other places as well as Potidaea had revolted. [2] The generals thought that the forces they had were insufficient for fighting both Perdiccas and the league of rebels, so they turned toward Macedon, their original destination. Once they got there, they began to campaign with the help of Philip and Derdas's brothers, who had invaded with an army from the interior. **60.** At this point, with Potidaea in revolt and the Athenian ships off the Macedonian coast, the Corinthians, who were concerned for Potidaea and felt its danger as though it were their own, raised a force of volunteers from Corinth and hired soldiers from elsewhere in the Peloponnese, and sent it north. It consisted in total of 1,600 hoplites and 400 light-armed troops. [2] Aristeus, son of Adeimantus, a consistent supporter of the Potidaeans, was the general in command, and most of the volunteers from Corinth who served with him did so because of their affection for him. [3] They reached the Thraceward region forty days after Potidaea had revolted.

61. As soon as news of the cities' revolt reached Athens—and they had also found out that Aristeus and his men were on their way—they sent 2,000 citizen hoplites and 40 ships against the rebels, under the command of five generals, including Callias, son of Calliades. [2] Their first stop was Macedon, where they found that the 1,000 troops sent earlier had recently taken Therme and now had Pydna under siege.* [3] For a while they took up a position near Pydna and joined in the siege themselves, but then, after they had come to terms with Perdiccas and entered into an alliance, made necessary by the urgency of the situation at Potidaea and by Aristeus's arrival, they left Macedon. [4] They went to Strepsa via Brea,* and after an attempt to take Strepsa failed, they marched overland to Potidaea. The Athenian army consisted of 3,000 citizen hoplites, supplemented by many more supplied by their allies, and 600 Macedonian cavalrymen who had been with Philip and Pausanias. They were accompanied by 70 ships, which sailed along the coast. [5] They advanced in short stages and reached Gigonus* on the third day, where they made camp.

62. In anticipation of the Athenians' arrival, the Potidaeans and the Peloponnesians under the command of Aristeus made camp on the isthmus near Olynthus, and they had set up a commissary outside the city. [2] The allies chose Aristeus to command the infantry and Perdiccas the cavalry. Perdiccas had immediately broken off again from the Athenians and was now an ally of the Potidaeans, having appointed Iolaus as his viceregent at home. [3] Aristeus's plan was to keep his forces on the isthmus to guard against an Athenian offensive, while the Chalcidians, the allies from outside the Pallene peninsula, and the 200 cavalrymen provided by Perdiccas stayed at Olynthus. Then, when the Athenians moved against his men, these troops would come up and take the enemy army in the rear, trapping it between the two of them. [4] But the Athenian generals—Callias and his colleagues—sent a detachment consisting of the Macedonian cavalry and a few of the auxiliaries to Olynthus to preclude any intervention from there, while they broke camp and set out for Potidaea. [5] When they reached the isthmus and found the enemy getting ready for battle, they too formed up opposite them and soon afterward the two sides engaged. [6] Aristeus's wing and the Corinthian and other units that were with him turned the soldiers facing them and pursued them a long way beyond the battlefield, but the Potidaean and Peloponnesian contingents were defeated by the Athenians and took refuge inside the city wall.

63. When Aristeus returned from the pursuit and found that the rest of the army had been defeated, he did not know whether he should make for Olynthus or Potidaea, either option being highly dangerous. He decided to pack his troops as closely as possible and force his way into Potidaea at a run. Although he was under fire and the going was hard, he made his way through the sea alongside the breakwater. There were some casualties, but he brought most of his men through safely. [2] When the signal flags had been raised and battle was joined, the troops supporting Potidaea from Olynthus (which is about seven miles north of Potidaea, close enough to be clearly visible) advanced a short distance with the intention of coming to their assistance, and the Macedonian cavalry deployed to stop them. But the battle was quickly won by the Athenians, and once the flags had been lowered the troops from Olynthus retired back inside the city and the allied Macedonians rejoined the Athenians. Cavalry therefore played no part in the fighting. [3] After the battle, the Athenians erected a trophy and returned the bodies of the dead to the Potidaeans under a truce. The Potidaeans and their allies lost almost 300 men, and even the Athenians lost 150, including one of the generals, Callias.

64. The Athenians immediately walled off the city on the side that faced the isthmus and posted guards there. But they built no wall on the side that faced Pallene, because they did not think they had enough men both to maintain a guard at the isthmus and to send men over to Pallene to build a siege wall there; they were afraid of being attacked by the Potidaeans and their allies if they divided their forces. [2] Later, after the Athenians at home found out that Pallene had been left open to the Potidaeans, they dispatched Phormio, son of Asopius, as the general in command of a force of 1,600 citizen hoplites. When he reached Pallene, he made Aphytis* his headquarters and led his men from there toward Potidaea, advancing slowly and laying waste the farmland as he went. [3] Since no one came out from the city to offer battle, he walled off the southern side of the city. And so Potidaea was now under a solid siege on both sides, and there were also ships blockading the harbor entrance.

65. With the city walled off, Aristeus thought that all would be lost unless a relief force arrived from the Peloponnese or some miracle occurred. He suggested that all the soldiers apart from 500 should wait for a favorable wind and sail away, to allow provisions to last longer, and he expressed his willingness to be one of those who stayed behind. But this advice of his was not followed, and so, wanting also to organize matters beyond the city walls as best he could under the circumstances, he eluded the Athenian guard and sailed out. [2] He remained in the area and assisted the Chalcidians in their war in various ways, not least by decimating a force of Sermylians in an ambush near their town.* In addition, he entered into negotiations with the Peloponnesians, to see if they might be prepared to offer help in some form. [3] With Potidaea walled off, Phormio and his 1,600 men set about depredating Chalcidice and Bottice and succeeded in capturing a few small towns.

66. These were the accumulated grievances that the Athenians and Peloponnesians held against each other. The Corinthians complained that the Athenians were besieging Potidaea, a colony of theirs, and the Corinthians and Peloponnesians who were inside; the Athenians complained that the Peloponnesians had incited a state that was an ally and a tributary of theirs to revolt and had gone and openly fought alongside the Potidaeans against them. War had not yet broken out, however; the treaty still held, because the Corinthians had been acting on their own.

67. But with Potidaea under siege, the Corinthians did not let matters rest. It was not just that there were Corinthian citizens there; they were afraid of losing the place. They immediately arranged a meeting of the allies at Sparta, at which they denounced the Athenians for having broken the treaty and for injuring the Peloponnese.

[2] The Aeginetans were not openly represented at the meeting, because they did not want to provoke the Athenians, but behind the scenes they were the Corinthians' most fervent supporters in pressing for war, on the ground that they did not have the autonomy that was supposed to have been guaranteed by the treaty. [3] The Lacedaemonians also invited any of their allies and any other state that claimed to have been wronged in some way by the Athenians, and then held one of their usual citizen assemblies and told the visitors to address it. [4] Among those who stepped up one after another and voiced their complaints were the Megarians, who mentioned quite a few matters that concerned them, but the most important was their exclusion from both the harbors of the Athenian empire and the Athenian wholesale market—an exclusion that, they claimed, contravened the treaty. [5] The Corinthians stepped up last. Having let the others take the lead in stirring the Lacedaemonians to anger, they then spoke along the following lines:*

68. "Lacedaemonians, the loyalty you feel for your constitution and way of life makes you less trusting of non-Lacedaemonians when they have something to tell you. It's true that this confidence is the source of your prudence, but it means that you're far from fully informed when it comes to foreign policy. [2] A case in point: in the past we've often warned you about the potential the Athenians have for harming us, but you never learned the lessons we were trying to teach you. Instead you became suspicious of the speakers' motivations and assumed that they were talking of disputes that were of concern only to them. Hence you failed to convene this meeting of the allies before any harm was done to us, and did so only now, when we are actually being harmed.

"Of all the allies, we have the best right to speak, because we have the most serious complaints to make, in that we are being both maltreated by the Athenians and neglected by you. [3] Now, if the Athenians were covering up the wrong they're doing Greece, you might be unaware of what's going on and we'd have to explain. But as things are, what need is there for long speeches? You can see that some states have already been enslaved, that others—our allies, especially—are currently the targets of their schemes, and that for quite a while the Athenians have been taking measures in anticipation of war. [4] How else can one explain their forcible enticement of Corcyra away from us and their siege of Potidaea, when Potidaea is the best possible base for operations in the Thraceward region, and Corcyra would have supplied the Peloponnesians with an exceptionally large fleet?

69. "This is all your fault. In the first place, you let Athens grow strong after the Persian invasion, and later you connived at the construction of its Long Walls.* Second, you have so far constantly been denying freedom not just to those who've been enslaved by the Athenians, but now to your own allies as well. It's not the one who does the enslaving who denies freedom to others, but the one who could end their servitude but does nothing, and it's much more reprehensible if he has a reputation for virtue as the liberator of Greece. [2] Well, at least we are at last meeting, even if the purpose of the meeting isn't clear. The time is past when we needed to consider whether we're being wronged; now the issue is what we should do to defend ourselves. After their deliberations, men of action waste no further time before moving against their enemies while they are still undecided.

[3] "We know the Athenians' method, how they gradually encroach on others. They proceed more cautiously if they think it's just inattentiveness on your part that's allowing them to get away with it, but if they ever come to realize that you're doing nothing even though you know what they're up to, they'll press on without holding back. [4] Your quietism, Lacedaemonians, is unique in Greece. Procrastination, not force of arms, is the way you defend yourselves. Everyone else but you nips an enemy's growth in the bud, but you wait until it's increasing exponentially. [5] Yet you used to have a reputation for steadfastness—though in truth the reputation was greater than the reality. For example, all of us here know that the Persians came from the ends of the earth and had reached the Peloponnese before you

emerged and opposed them in any meaningful sense. And the situation is the same now: you're doing nothing about the Athenians, and they are a nearby people, not a remote one like the Persians. Instead of going on the offensive you prefer to defend yourselves when you're attacked, even though this entails the risk that your enemies will be far stronger by the time the contest begins. And you act like this even though you know that the Persians themselves were largely responsible for their own failure, and that so far we have repeatedly survived against the Athenians thanks to their own mistakes rather than your help. In fact, we dare say that by placing their hopes in you, some people, those who were unprepared because they trusted you to fight in their defense, have already been destroyed. [6] And please understand that we're not speaking like this out of enmity; no, this is a reprimand. Reprimands are for friends who go wrong, but enemies who do wrong meet with condemnation.

70. "In any case, we believe we have as much right as anyone to criticize our neighbors, especially since we, at any rate, think you're overlooking the fact that important differences are involved. You'll be going up against a people whose character you seem never to have analyzed, so that you don't understand how much—how completely, in fact—they differ from you. [2] The Athenians are innovators, constantly generating new ideas and quick to act on their decisions; you, on the other hand, are 'quick' to maintain the status quo and to avoid developing new policies or even taking necessary action. [3] Then again, their daring outstrips their ability, they take risks against their better judgment, and they are hopeful in the midst of danger; but your way is to act short of your ability, to doubt even certainties, and to expect never to be free of danger. [4] Or again, they are expeditious whereas you are slow off the mark; they are adventurers while you are stay-at-homes; they expect to gain from ventures abroad, whereas you expect any action you take to diminish even what you already have.

[5] "After defeating their enemies they maximize their advantage, and after being defeated they minimize the negative consequences. [6]

Moreover, although they place their bodies at the service of the state as though they weren't their own at all, their minds are very much their own and they use them to do the state good. [7] If they ever fail to see a plan through to completion, they think of that as no different from losing something they already had, while if a new endeavor of theirs enables them to gain something, they regard this success as negligible compared with the future gains to be had. If they do fail at some venture, they make good the loss by directing their hopes elsewhere. They're so quick to act on their resolutions that they're the only ones for whom hoping for something and having it are the same thing. [8] They work hard at all this throughout their lives whatever hardships and dangers are involved, and they derive very little pleasure from what they have because they are always on the lookout for more. A holiday for them is just doing what has to be done, and they regard idle leisure as more of a misfortune than tiresome employment. [9] So the best summary description of their character would be to say that they were born to have no peace themselves and to prevent others from having it either.

71. "That, then, is the character of the city that opposes you, Lacedaemonians, and yet you procrastinate. You fail to see that the people who enjoy the most enduring peace are those who use their resources for righting wrongs, but make it clear by their determination that they won't put up with being wronged themselves. Instead, your idea of fair treatment is not to provoke others and to avoid injury even in self-defense [2]—a policy the success of which is scarcely guaranteed even if you had a state little different from your own as a neighbor. But as it is, as we've just explained, your practices are old-fashioned compared with theirs; [3] yet in politics, as in the arts and crafts, new techniques must always prevail over old. When a city is at peace, unchanging institutions are best, but those with plenty of demands on their resources need plenty of innovative thinking. That's why the wider experience of the Athenians has led to far more reforms there than you've put in place here.

[4] "Let's have an end to your tardiness, then, right now. Now is the time to keep your promise and help the Potidaeans and the others by invading Attica with as little delay as possible. Otherwise, you'll be betraying to their worst enemies people who are your friends and kinfolk, and you'll be driving the rest of us, in our despair, to look for other allies. [5] And if we were to do that, neither the gods who protect oaths nor people who recognize our situation would think we were doing anything wrong. Treaties are broken not by those who in their isolation are driven to approach others, but by those who fail to defend members of their sworn alliance. [6] We won't leave you if you show a willingness to commit yourselves to our cause, because then it would be sacrilegious of us to jump ship, and besides, we'd be hard put to find other allies as congenial as you. [7] Deliberate well, taking what we've said into consideration, and try to ensure that the Peloponnese you lead is no smaller than the one your fathers handed down to you."

72. Such was the Corinthians' speech. Coincidentally, there were envoys from Athens already in Sparta who had come on other business, and after hearing the speeches they thought that they should address the meeting, not to rebut any of the charges that the cities were bringing against Athens, but to show that, given the situation as a whole, the Lacedaemonians should not come to any hasty decisions, but should prolong their inquiry. They also wanted to give them an impression of Athenian power—to remind the older people present of what they already knew, and to let the younger ones have an account of matters with which they were unfamiliar—the overall idea being that what they said would nudge the Lacedaemonians in the direction of peace rather than war. [2] So they approached the Lacedaemonians and told them that they would like to address the meeting as well, if they had no objection, and the Lacedaemonians gave them permission to go ahead. The Athenians stepped up and spoke somewhat as follows:

73. "The reason we were sent here by the people of Athens was not to respond to your allies. We had a different mission, but we've stepped up to speak because we're aware of the outcry against us, and how loud it is. We won't respond to the charges brought by the cities, because this isn't a court of law before which either we or they have to present arguments. But we want to try to make sure that your thinking about such important matters is not impaired by easy acceptance of your allies' contentions. And as for the general criticism that is leveled against us, we want to respond by proving that it's not unreasonable for us to have what we have, and that our city is not to be taken lightly.

[2] "There's no need for us to speak of the remote past, for which the evidence is hearsay rather than the personal experience of those who'll be listening to us. But there are events, such as the Persian Wars, that you do know about, and even though it's rather tiresome for us to be constantly bringing them up, we do have to talk about them. The actions we took and the danger we faced were intended to be beneficial, and since you were among the beneficiaries, we shouldn't now be denied a chance to talk about them if there's benefit in it for us. [3] What we're going to say isn't supposed to deflect criticism so much as to display the evidence that will show you the kind of city with which you'll be contending if you make a wrong decision.

[4] "Consider our record. It's not just that at Marathon we stood alone against the barbarians,* but also that when they returned later, since we were unable to mount a defense by land, we took to our ships—all of us, the entire people—and fought them at Salamis. It was this that stopped them from sailing against the Peloponnese, laying waste the land, and attacking your cities one by one—and it would have been impossible, against so many ships, for you to relieve one another. The enemy himself provided convincing proof of this, in that after the defeat of his fleet, seeing that his strength was no longer what it was, he soon withdrew the bulk of his army.

74. "This success made it perfectly clear that ships were crucial for the Greek war effort, and the three most important contributions in this context were ours: we provided the largest number of vessels, the most intelligent general, and the most steadfast commitment. Almost two-thirds of the fleet of four hundred ships were Athenian, and so was Themistocles, who as commander was chiefly responsible for the battle being fought in the narrows, which undoubtedly saved the day and was why you yourselves showed him more honor than you've ever shown any other foreigner who visited your land. [2] And never has commitment been anywhere near as courageous as ours. When there was no one to help us by land, and everyone else, right up to our borders, was already in the process of being enslaved, we abandoned our city and destroyed our property. But even then we chose not to desert the common cause of the remaining allies and we didn't want to make ourselves useless to them by dispersing, so we decided to take to our ships, whatever the risks, and not to bear a grudge against you for having failed to help us sooner.

[3] "What we're saying, then, is that we helped you more than we were helped by you. The help you provided came from cities that hadn't been abandoned and had the purpose of ensuring that they would continue to be habitable, since you were more concerned for yourselves than you were for us; at any rate, you failed to put in an appearance while our city was still intact. We, on the other hand, set out from a city that no longer existed and for which there was little hope; we accepted the risks and did our part in saving you as well as ourselves. [4] If fear for our land had by then made us capitulate to the Persians, as it had others, or if later we had believed our cause lost and hadn't courageously taken to our ships, there'd have been no point in your confronting the enemy at sea because you wouldn't have had enough ships. And the Persians' fortunes would have progressed as smoothly as they wanted.

75. "So bearing in mind our commitment then and the wisdom of our policies, do we really deserve the extreme degree of resentment

that the Greeks are displaying, at any rate as far as our possession of an empire is concerned? [2] After all, we didn't gain this empire by forceful means, but because you were reluctant to stand firm and finish the war with the Persians, and because the allies approached us and of their own accord asked us to assume leadership. [3] At first, circumstances themselves compelled us to develop our empire to its present extent; we were motivated above all by fear, but also by honor and later by self-interest. [4] And then, when hatred of us was widespread, when some of our subjects had revolted and been subdued, and when you were no longer the friends you had been, but had become suspicious and antagonistic, we decided that it was no longer safe for us to risk giving up the empire, especially because any defectors would go over to you. [5] But no one finds it objectionable if people manage their own interests well when faced with extreme danger.

76. "At any rate, you Lacedaemonians use your position of leadership to settle the affairs of the Peloponnesian cities to suit your own interests, and if at the time of which we're speaking you had stayed the course and become as unpopular in your leadership as we are, we're absolutely certain that you'd have become just as obnoxious to your allies and would have been forced either to rule with an iron fist or find yourselves in danger. [2] And by the same token we too have done nothing odd or contrary to normal human practice in accepting an empire when it was offered to us, and in hanging on to it because we were overcome by those three powerful forces—honor, fear, and self-interest. And it's not as if we were the first to do this kind of thing; it has always been the case that the weaker are controlled by the stronger. Besides, we thought we deserved our empire, and so did you until now, when calculation of what's in your best interests makes you wield the justice argument—an argument that has never dissuaded anyone proposing it from taking advantage when *they* had an opportunity to use their strength to obtain something. [3] People deserve praise if, complying with the natural human impulse to rule others, they pay greater attention to justice than is required by the power that they have. [4] In our opinion, our restraint would be best highlighted by other people, if they had what we have; but in our case, even our fairness has brought us disrepute rather than gratitude.

77. "For example, because we were finding ourselves at a disadvantage in lawsuits against our allies that arose from interstate agreements, and therefore transferred such cases to Athens to be judged under our impartial laws, we are thought to rely too much on litigation. [2] None of the allies stops to consider why imperialists from elsewhere in the world who are harder than we are on their subjects are not liable to be criticized on this score. It's because those who can employ force have no need of legal procedures. [3] Our allies have become accustomed to a relationship with us based on equality, and that's why, if they end up the slightest bit worse off than they think they deserve, owing either to a legal decision or to our exercising power as their rulers, instead of being grateful that they aren't losing more, they're more annoyed by their loss than if we had cast law aside from the start and openly gained at their expense. If we had done that, not even they would have argued that the weaker should not yield to the stronger. [4] Apparently, people resent what they perceive as legally sanctioned injustice more than the exercise of power, in the belief that the former is an unfair advantage taken by an equal, while the latter is compulsion applied by one who has superior strength. [5] At any rate, they tolerated worse treatment at the hands of the Persians, but think our empire harsh. Not that there's anything surprising in that: subjects always resent their present condition. [6] So if you overthrew us and took over the rulership of our subjects, you'd soon lose the goodwill you've gained by their fear of us—or you would if the policies you adopted resembled those of the brief period earlier when you were the leaders of the resistance to the Persians. It's not just that the customs you observe among yourselves are incompatible with those of others, but also that when any of you leaves home he abides by neither Lacedaemonian customs nor those that are observed everywhere else in Greece.*

78. "Don't rush into any decisions, then; these are weighty matters. And don't let others' opinions and complaints persuade you to make trouble for yourselves. Before you get involved in warfare, you should recognize how much of it is unpredictable. [2] The longer a war goes on, the more likely it is to turn on chances that both of us are equally unable to control, and in which both of us equally risk an uncertain outcome. [3] People embarking on a war leap into action, when that's something that should happen later, and it's only when it's going badly for them that they engage in discussion. [4] We Athenians have so far avoided this mistake ourselves, and we can see that you have too, so our advice to you is that, so long as sound decision-making is still a possibility for us both, you should not break the treaty or contravene your oaths but resolve our differences by arbitration, as stipulated in the treaty. Otherwise, we shall call to witness the gods by whom you swore your oaths and do our best to defend ourselves by responding to any hostile action you initiate."

79. Such was the Athenians' speech. Now that the Lacedaemonians had heard both the complaints of their allies against the Athenians and the Athenians' speech, they told everyone to leave and talked things over among themselves. [2] The majority inclined to the same view, that the Athenians were already culpable and that war should start as soon as possible. But Archidamus, their king, who had a reputation as an intelligent and prudent man, came forward and spoke along the following lines:

80. "Lacedaemonians, I've lived through many wars by now, and some of you are evidently as old as I am, so it can't be lack of experience, which is the most usual reason, that's making any of you eager for action, nor can it be because he thinks it a good thing to do—or risk-free: [2] a realistic assessment of the war you are now considering would show that it's bound to be a major one.

[3] "In a war against our neighbors and fellow Peloponnesians, our military resources are of the same kind as theirs and we can rapidly go

wherever we're needed. But in this instance we'd be fighting people who possess land far away, and who, moreover, are highly skilled mariners and extremely well equipped in every other respect—with both private and state wealth; with ships, horses, and weaponry; with the largest population in Greece; and with many tribute-paying allies too. Going to war with these people is hardly a matter to be taken lightly, is it? What would give us the confidence to rush in unprepared? [4] Our ships? But we're outclassed at sea, and it would take time for us to train and make ready a navy to match theirs. Our finances? But here we're even worse off, since we have no money in a state treasury and we can't readily raise it from private sources. **81.** Some might find encouragement in the thought that our superior fighting skills and greater numbers will make it possible for us to keep invading their territory and ravaging it. [2] But they have plenty of other territories in their empire and they will simply import by sea whatever they need. [3] Alternatively, we might try to get their allies to revolt, but most of them are islanders, so we'd need a navy to support them, too. [4] What sort of war shall we fight, then?

"Unless we get the better of them at sea or deprive them of the revenues that sustain their navy, we will come off worse. [5] And then we'll no longer be able to make peace on honorable terms, especially if we're thought to bear more of the responsibility for initiating the conflict. [6] At any rate, let's not be buoyed up by the hope that the war won't last long if we ravage their land. I am more afraid that we might bequeath it to our children. The point is that, in their confidence, the Athenians are hardly likely to be slaves to their land* or to be panicked by the war like novices.

82. "However, I'm certainly not suggesting that you should be indifferent—that, while our allies are being injured, you should do nothing and should not unmask Athenian scheming. But I am saying that we shouldn't yet take up arms, but should send a delegation to Athens to bring up our grievances while remaining somewhat vague about whether we plan to go to war or arbitration, and meanwhile that we should proceed with our own preparations by acquiring allies among both Greeks and barbarians, as a way of adding to our naval or financial power, and should develop our own resources as well. No one finds it offensive if those who, like us, are the objects of Athenian scheming save ourselves by gaining the friendship of barbarians as well as Greeks. [2] If the Athenians listen to our representations, all well and good. But if they don't, after two or three years have passed we shall have better protection when we go against them, if that's what we decide to do. [3] And perhaps then, when they see that we're ready for war and recognize that what we're saying implies the same level of preparedness, they'll be more inclined to back down, while their land is still undamaged and they're deliberating about property that's still theirs and as yet undestroyed. [4] Consider their land as a hostage you hold, because that's just what it is, and the more so the better it has been cultivated. We should spare it for as long as possible, and not stiffen their resistance by driving them to desperation. [5] If we're pressured by our allies' complaints into laying waste Athenian land while we're still not ready for war, we might find that the outcome is a situation that is both less honorable and more troublesome for the Peloponnese. [6] The complaints that cities and private individuals bring against one another can be resolved, but a war that a whole alliance undertakes in response to the grievances of some of its members, a war the outcome of which is impossible to predict, cannot easily be settled in a respectable manner.

83. "No one should think it cowardice if our league of cities hesitates before attacking a single city. [2] After all, they have as many allies as we do, and theirs pay tribute. Without money, weapons are useless, so war is more a matter of finance than of weaponry, and this is never more so than in a war between a land power and a sea power. [3] So let's first provide ourselves with money and not get carried away prematurely by what our allies are saying. It's we who will bear much of the responsibility for the consequences either way, so let's also be the ones to think about them calmly ahead of time.

84. "There's no need to be ashamed of the slowness and procrastination that are considered to be our chief faults. If you rush ahead, you'll find that it takes longer to finish, because you'll be taking on the enterprise while unprepared. Besides, the city we inhabit has always been free and very highly regarded, so this slowness of ours may very well be tantamount to good sense and prudence. [2] It's this quality that saves us—and we're alone in this—from arrogance when things go well or the submissiveness that's typical of others when things go badly. We're able to resist pleasure when people praise us in an attempt to urge us on to dangerous endeavors, and the same goes if anyone spurs us on by condemning us: we don't change our minds just because we're provoked.

[3] "It's thanks to this self-discipline of ours that we're both good fighters and good decision-makers—good fighters because self-respect can scarcely exist without prudence, and courage can scarcely exist without self-respect; and good decision-makers because we're brought up with too little learning to think ourselves above the laws, and with too much discipline, instilled by a strict environment, to disobey them. We lack the kind of unhelpful over-cleverness that would enable us to come up with brilliant criticisms of our enemies' plans in a speech, but fail to follow through and come up with action to suit the words. No, we regard others' plans as no worse than ours and the vagaries of fortune as unpredictable. [4] When we prepare to act against an enemy, we always do so on the assumption that we're dealing with people who are good planners, so we shouldn't base our hopes on the possibility of their making mistakes, but on ourselves and the unassailability of our own plans. It would be wrong to think that people are innately much different from one another, rather than that the strongest is the one who's brought up under the most rigorous conditions.

85. "So let's not abandon these practices; they were bequeathed to us by our fathers and adherence to them has never done us anything but good. Let's not be rushed in the brief span of a day into a decision when so many lives, so much money, so many cities, and so much honor are at stake. Let's take our time; unlike others, we can afford to, thanks to our strength. [2] Send envoys to the Athenians to discuss Potidaea and the ways in which our allies claim to have been wronged by them, especially since they're offering to submit to arbitration. When someone makes such an offer, it isn't lawful to proceed against him preemptively, as though he were guilty. At the same time, however, prepare for war. These are the measures that will put you in the strongest position and make you most feared by your enemies."

[3] That was the gist of Archidamus's speech, but Sthenelaidas, who was one of the ephors for that year, stepped up. He was the last to speak, and he addressed the Lacedaemonians as follows: **86.** "The Athenians spoke at length, but I don't understand why.* They spent a lot of time praising themselves, but they never tried to rebut the charge of wronging our allies and the Peloponnese. But surely, if they did well on that earlier occasion, against the Persians, and are now treating us badly, they deserve double the punishment, for having turned into bad people instead of good ones. [2] We, however, are the same now as we were then, and the 'prudent' course for us is not to stand idly by while our allies are being wronged. We should not put off punishing the Athenians when our allies can no longer put off their suffering. [3] Others have plenty of ships, money, and horses, but we have outstanding allies, who mustn't be betrayed to the Athenians, and the issue shouldn't be decided by legal judgments and words when we aren't being injured by words. No, we must punish the Athenians swiftly and with all our might. [4] And let no one try to convince you that the proper thing to do, while we're being wronged, is to deliberate; it is rather those who are intending to wrong us who should think long and hard. [5] So vote for war, Lacedaemonians, as your city deserves. Don't let the Athenians grow stronger and don't leave your allies in the lurch, but with the gods' help let's proceed against the wrongdoers."

87. After speaking to this effect Sthenelaidas, in his capacity as an ephor, put the vote to the assembled Lacedaemonians. [2] Now, the

Lacedaemonians vote by acclamation rather than by counting pebbles, and Sthenelaidas claimed that he could not tell whether the shout for or against war was louder. He thought he could make them more eager for war if there was no mistaking what their view was, so he said, "Lacedaemonians, those of you who think that the treaty has been broken and the Athenians are culpable, go and stand over there"—he showed them where—"and those of you who disagree, go and stand over on the other side." [3] They got to their feet and separated, and those who thought that the treaty had been broken were far more numerous. [4] They recalled their allies to the meeting and told them that they had decided that the Athenians were in the wrong, but that they wanted to convene a full meeting of the allies and put the matter to the vote, so that they could arrive at a common decision before going to war, if the decision was for war.

[5] So the allies returned home to make these arrangements, as the Athenian envoys did later as well, once they had concluded the business for which they had gone to Sparta. [6] This decision of the Lacedaemonian assembly, that the treaty had been broken, took place in the fourteenth year of the Thirty-Year Peace that followed the Euboean War and had lasted until then.* **88.** The reason the Lacedaemonians voted that the treaty had been broken and that they should go to war was not so much that they were influenced by what their allies said as that they were afraid of the further growth of Athenian power, when they could see that most of the Greeks were already under their control.*

89. What follows is an account of the circumstances that enabled the Athenians to rise to greatness.* [2] After their defeat by the Greeks at sea and on land, the Persians withdrew from Europe, and once those of them who had fled in their ships to Mycale had been destroyed, Leotychidas, the Spartan king, who had led the Greeks at Mycale, returned home with his Peloponnesian allies. The Athenians, however, and their allies from Ionia and the Hellespont (those who had by then rebelled against the King), carried on and besieged Sestus, which was in Persian hands. They spent the winter there, took the city when the barbarians abandoned it, and then sailed away from the Hellespont and went back to their various home towns.

[3] As soon as the barbarians left their territory, the Athenian people brought back their children, womenfolk, and what remained of their property from where they had been taken for safety, and set about rebuilding the city and its defensive walls. Little of the circuit wall was still standing and most houses were in ruins, but a few had survived because high-ranking Persians had used them as billets. **90.** When the Lacedaemonians heard of the Athenians' plans they sent an embassy, partly because they would have preferred a situation in which neither the Athenians nor anyone else had a wall, but mainly because their allies were putting pressure on them. The allies were alarmed by the size of the Athenian navy—which had not even existed before the war—and by the courage they had displayed in fighting the Persians. [2] Not only did the Lacedaemonians ask the Athenians to do without fortifications, but they also requested their help in demolishing any walls outside the Peloponnese that were still standing. They concealed their real intentions and suspicions, and said instead that the point was to make sure that, if the barbarians returned, they would not have a strong base of operations, such as they had recently had in Thebes. And they said that the Peloponnese could serve as a place of refuge and a base of operations for everyone.

[3] On the advice of Themistocles, the Athenians responded to the Lacedaemonians' speech by promising to send an embassy to Sparta to discuss these matters, and then promptly dismissed them. Themistocles told the Athenians to send him straight off to Sparta, but to wait before sending the other envoys who had been chosen to go with him, until the wall had been built up to the minimum height sufficient for defense. He said that the whole population of the city—men, women, and children—should work on the wall together, and that any building, private or public, that might help the project should

ruthlessly be demolished. [4] After giving them these instructions and outlining the rest of the negotiations that he would be undertaking in Sparta, he left.

[5] When he got to Sparta, he did not meet with the authorities, but kept playing for time and making excuses. Whenever someone senior asked him why he was not addressing the assembly, he told them that he was waiting for his colleagues to arrive—that they had been delayed on some other business, but he was expecting them at any moment and was surprised that they had not yet come. **91.** The Lacedaemonian officials were inclined to believe what Themistocles was saying because of their liking for him, but when some people arrived who had seen with their own eyes what was going on and stated categorically that the wall was being built and had already reached a certain height, they found it impossible to disbelieve them. [2] Realizing this, Themistocles told the Lacedaemonians not to be led astray by hearsay and suggested that, instead, they should send some trustworthy people of their own to see what was what and bring back reliable information. [3] So the Lacedaemonians dispatched their people—and Themistocles secretly forewarned the Athenians about them. He told them to detain the envoys, without making this at all obvious, and not to let them go until he and his colleagues had returned. By this time his fellow ambassadors had arrived—Habronichus, son of Lysicles, and Aristeides, son of Lysimachus—with the message that the wall was high enough, and Themistocles was afraid that once the Lacedaemonians had heard a clear report they would refuse to let them leave.

[4] The Athenians detained the Lacedaemonian envoys as instructed, and only then did Themistocles go to the Lacedaemonians and put an end to concealment. He told them that Athens now had a defensive wall and was capable of protecting its inhabitants, and that in the future, if the Lacedaemonians or their allies wanted to make representations to the Athenians, they should come knowing that they were dealing with people who knew perfectly well what was

good for themselves and for Greece as a whole. [5] When they decided that the best course was for them to abandon the city and take to their ships, they arrived at this courageous policy, the ambassadors said, unaided by the Lacedaemonians, and besides, in all their joint deliberations with the Lacedaemonians they had shown themselves to be as intelligent as anyone. [6] And now too it seemed to them that the best course was for their city to be fortified—better not just for their own citizens, but for their allies as well—[7] because it was only if there was a balance of power that they could have a comparable or equal voice at meetings where common policy was on the agenda. So, Themistocles argued, either they should all be members of a single league and no one should have walls, or the Lacedaemonians should regard the Athenians' position as correct.

92. On hearing this, the Lacedaemonians did not openly display anger toward the Athenians, because the purpose of their embassy had not been to interfere but, ostensibly, to recommend a resolution to the Athenian assembly, and also because at that time they were in fact particularly well disposed toward the Athenians because of the commitment they had brought to the war against the Persians. Nevertheless, they were secretly incensed because their will was being foiled. So the envoys on both sides returned home without any formal complaint having been lodged.

93. That is how the Athenians came to wall their city. It did not take them long, [2] and to this day, in fact, the structure shows signs of having been built in haste. The foundations are made up of all sorts of stones that have not been worked in any way so as to fit together, but put in place just as each one was when it was brought in; and many tombstones and other worked stones were incorporated. The circumference of the enclosing wall was increased in all directions, and that is why in their haste they made indiscriminate use of all available materials. [3] Themistocles also persuaded them to finish the wall around Piraeus—it had been begun previously, during his year of office as archon of the Athenians—because it struck him as a fine site, with its three natural harbors, and because he thought that their having become a seafaring people was making a major contribution toward their acquisition of power. [4] In fact, he had been the first to propose the bold strategy of making the sea theirs, and now he immediately set about laying the foundations of empire.

[5] Moreover, it was on his advice that the Piraeus wall was built with the thickness that can still be seen—wide enough for two carts traveling in opposite directions to bring up the stones. The wall was filled not with rubble or clay, but with great blocks of stone that had been squared off and fitted together, with their ends fastened to one another by clamps of iron sealed with lead. But the final height of the wall was only about half of what he had intended. [6] He wanted it to be tall and wide enough to deter hostile offensives, and, as he saw it, only a few men, drawn from those who were least fit, would be needed to guard it, while everyone else would be manning the fleet. [7] He paid particular attention to the navy, and this, I think, was because he saw that the Persian army had found it easier to attack by sea than by land. He thought that Piraeus would be more useful than the inland city, and he repeatedly advised the Athenians that, if they were ever hard pressed by land, they should move down to Piraeus and make a stand against the world at large with their navy.* [8] So this is how the Athenians came to build their walls and start preparing for war immediately after the retreat of the Persians.

94. Pausanias, son of Cleombrotus, was dispatched from Sparta as commander-in-chief of the Greek forces with twenty ships from the Peloponnese, accompanied by thirty Athenian ships and more from the rest of the allies. [2] They sailed against Cyprus,* and after subduing most of the island they went to Byzantium, which had been occupied by the Persians, and besieged it into submission. **95.** But by now Pausanias had begun to behave in an oppressive manner, and during this period of his command the rest of the Greeks became resentful of him, especially the Ionians and others who had just been liberated from the Persian empire. They approached the Athenians and asked them, as their kinsmen, to become their leaders and not to let Pausanias get away with acting in an overbearing manner. [2] The Athenians were receptive to these suggestions and they resolved not to condone Pausanias's behavior and in general to manage affairs as they thought best. [3] Meanwhile, the Lacedaemonians summoned Pausanias home so that they could question him about the reports they had been receiving. Greeks who came to Sparta were accusing him of many acts of injustice, and it looked as though he was modeling his behavior on that of a tyrant rather than acting like a general. [4] So his recall coincided with the time when the allies' dislike of him drove them (except for the forces from the Peloponnese) to transfer their allegiance to the Athenians. [5] When he arrived in Sparta, he was called to account for crimes he had committed against others as a private citizen, but he was acquitted on the most important charges—the most serious of all being that he had collaborated with the Persians, for which the evidence had been widely thought to be unambiguous.

[6] Pausanias was relieved of his command, and the Lacedaemonians instead sent out Dorcis and a few others, along with a small force, but the allies refused to accept their leadership. [7] Once this had become clear to them they left, and the Lacedaemonians subsequently sent no more replacements. They were afraid that overseas service would corrupt them, as it clearly had in Pausanias's case, and they also wanted to be relieved of the burden of the war against the Persians; they thought that the Athenians would make competent leaders, and judged them to be well disposed toward themselves at the time.

96. After the Athenians had taken over the leadership in this way, with the willing consent of the allies because of their dislike of Pausanias, they arranged for some of the cities to supply money for the war against the Persians and for others to supply ships, on the plausible ground that they were going to devastate the King's territory as a way of repaying him for their and the allies' losses. [2] This was when the Treasurers of the Greeks were first instituted as an Athenian board; it was their job to receive the tribute, as the financial contributions were called. The amount of the tribute on its first assessment was 460 talents. The treasury was on Delos,* and the meetings took place in the sanctuary there.

97. At first, the Athenians were the leaders of autonomous allies who met and deliberated collectively, and in the years between the Persian invasion and the current war they were extremely active, using warfare and their general management of affairs against the Persians, any allies of theirs who rebelled, and any Peloponnesian states that they encountered in the course of some operation or other. [2] I have recorded these events and jettisoned my original plan because this topic has been neglected by everyone before me, who wrote either about Greek history before the Persian Wars or about just the Persian Wars; because the person who did actually touch on these events in his work on Athens, Hellanicus, gave them only a brief mention and got the chronology wrong;* and also because they constitute an explanatory account of how the Athenian empire came into being.

98. The first thing they did was besiege and take Eion-on-Strymon,* a town that was occupied by the Persians, who were sold into slavery. Cimon, son of Miltiades, was the general for this campaign. [2] Next, they sold into slavery the Dolopians, who lived on the Aegean island of Scyros, which they resettled with their own people. [3] Then they fought a war with Carystus (no other place in Euboea was involved) and the Carystians eventually surrendered on terms. [4] Next they made war on the Naxians, who had seceded from the alliance, and besieged them into submission. This was the first allied state to be enslaved, contrary to Greek custom, but later the same thing happened to the others as well one by one.

99. There were various reasons why allied states rebelled. The main ones were falling behind on their tribute payments or provision of ships, and in some instances their refusal to supply troops. The Athenians were sticklers over the payments and their coercive measures made them disliked by those who were unaccustomed to suffering hardship or were displeased about doing so. [2] There were other reasons too for the increasing unpopularity of Athenian rule: they did not take part in military campaigns as equal partners, and it was easy for them to bring rebels back into line. The allies had no one to blame for this but themselves. [3] Because of their reluctance to take part in military ventures, in order to avoid leaving home most of them asked to be assessed for paying their dues in the form of money rather than ships, and so the size of the Athenian fleet grew with the help of the money the allies provided, while the allies themselves were unprepared for and inexperienced in warfare when they revolted.

100. The next events were the land and sea battles that were fought by the Athenians and their allies against the Persians at the Eurymedon river in Pamphylia. The Athenians, with Cimon, son of Miltiades, as the general in command, won both battles on a single day, and about two hundred Phoenician triremes in all were captured and destroyed. [2] Then later the Thasian revolt took place,* after they had fallen out with the Athenians over the trading posts on the Thracian mainland opposite the island and their mine workings there. The Athenians sent a fleet to Thasos, defeated them at sea, and landed troops on the island. [3] At much the same time they sent ten thousand settlers to the Strymon, drawn from their own citizens and the allies, to settle the place that was then called Nine Ways but is now known as Amphipolis.* Although they gained control of Nine Ways, a possession of the Edones, when they advanced deeper into Thrace they were annihilated at Drabescus in Edonia by the united Thracians, who regarded the founding of the colony as an act of war.

101. Defeated in battle and with their city under siege, the Thasians appealed to the Lacedaemonians and asked them to help by invading Attica. [2] Making sure that the Athenians did not hear about it, the Lacedaemonians promised to do so, and they fully intended to keep their promise, but they did not get around to it because of the earthquake that had happened, in the aftermath of which their helots and the perioeci of Thouria and Aethaea rebelled and occupied Ithome. (Most of the helots were descended from the Messenians of former times who had been enslaved back then, and so they were known collectively as "Messenians.") [3] So, with the Lacedaemonians fighting the Ithome rebels, in the third year of the siege the Thasians came to terms with the Athenians. They demolished their wall, surrendered their ships, accepted the Athenians' assessment of how much of an indemnity they were to pay right away and how much tribute they would pay in the future, and relinquished their mainland holdings and mine workings.

102. Meanwhile, the Lacedaemonians, seeing no immediate end to their war against the Ithome rebels, called for help from various of their allies, including the Athenians, who sent a small force under Cimon's command. [2] The main reason they asked for help from the Athenians was because they were supposed to be skilled at siege operations, while the length of the siege had shown their own skills in this respect to be inferior. Otherwise, they would have succeeded in taking the place by assault. [3] It was due to this campaign that the rift between the Lacedaemonians and the Athenians first came out into the open. Ithome continued to resist the assault, and the Lacedaemonians were apprehensive of the daring and revolutionary Athenian character; bearing in mind their different ethnicity, they were afraid that if the Athenians stayed on they might be persuaded by the Ithome rebels to aid their rebellion. So they sent them back home, while retaining the rest of their allies, although they concealed their suspicions and said only that they had no further need of them. [4] The Athenians realized that they were being dismissed for no better reason than Lacedaemonian mistrust, and they felt insulted. They thought it wrong for the Lacedaemonians to treat them like that, and as soon as they got home they abandoned the alliance they had made with them against the Persians and entered into an alliance with Argos, which was hostile to Sparta. And at the same oath-swearing ceremony both the Argives and the Athenians simultaneously formed an alliance with the Thessalians.

103. In the tenth year of the siege the resistance of the Ithome rebels collapsed and they came to terms with the Lacedaemonians. Under the agreement, they were to leave the Peloponnese with a guarantee of safe conduct and never set foot there again, and any of them caught doing so would become the slave of the person who caught him. [2] The Lacedaemonians also had an earlier oracle from Delphi, to the effect that they were to "release the suppliant of Zeus at Ithome." [3] So the rebels left with their families, and the Athenians took them in because of the hostility they now felt toward the Lacedaemonians. The Athenians settled them in Naupactus, which they had seized from the Ozolian Locrians, who had taken it over not long before. [4] The Megarians, too, revolted from Sparta and entered into an alliance with the Athenians because the Corinthians were defeating them in a border war. And so the Athenians gained Megara and Pegae, and they built the Megarians' Long Walls from the city to Nisaea and supplied the garrisons themselves.* This, more than anything else, was the primary cause of the Corinthians' profound hatred of the Athenians.

104. The Libyan Inaros, son of Psammetichus, who was the king of the Libyans and whose land borders Egypt, made Marea, a town south of Pharos, his headquarters and stirred most of Egypt into rebellion against Artaxerxes.* And once he had taken command of the rebellion, he brought the Athenians in as allies. [2] The Athenians, who were campaigning in Cyprus with a fleet of two hundred of their own and their allies' ships, abandoned the island and went to Egypt. They sailed from the sea into the Nile, gained control of both the river and two of the three districts of Memphis, and set about attacking the third, which was called White Fort, inside which were Persians and Medes who had fled there, and Egyptians who had not joined the rebellion.

105. Meanwhile, the Athenians landed troops at Halieis,* and a battle took place between them and the Corinthians and Epidaurians.

The Corinthians won this battle, but later the Athenians came off best in a sea battle against the Peloponnesian fleet off Cecryphalea.* [2] After this, war broke out between the Athenians and Aeginetans, and a major battle took place at sea off Aegina between the two sides, both of whom were accompanied by their allies. The Athenians won, capturing seventy Aeginetan ships, and then they landed troops and put the city under siege. Leocrates, son of Stroebus, was the general in command of this operation. [3] Subsequently, wanting to aid the Aeginetans, the Peloponnesians sent to Aegina three hundred hoplites, who had previously been helping the Corinthians and Epidaurians. Meanwhile, the Corinthians occupied the Geranea mountains* and marched down against Megara with their allies in support. Their thinking was that it would be impossible for the Athenians to come to the aid of Megara with so many of their men away on Aegina and in Egypt, and that if they did come they would have to withdraw from Aegina.

[4] The Athenians left their army on Aegina intact, but the oldest and youngest men of military age remaining in the city went to Megara with Myronides as the general in command. [5] An indecisive battle took place against the Corinthians, and the two sides separated, with neither of them thinking that they had come off worst in the action. [6] In fact, however, it was the Athenians who were the winners, and after the Corinthians had left they set up a trophy. The Corinthians were scolded by their elders in the city, and about twelve days later, once they were ready, they returned and set up their own trophy, as if they had won the battle. At this, the Athenians sallied out from Megara, and after killing the men who were setting up the trophy, they engaged the rest and defeated them. **106.** In the course of the retreat, a sizable body of the defeated Corinthians were run so hard that they lost their way and ended up on a privately owned property that was surrounded by a great ditch and offered no way out. [2] When the Athenians realized this, they posted their hoplites in front of the trapped men, to hem them in from that direction, and had their

light-armed soldiers encircle them. Then they bombarded them with stones until they were all dead. This was a traumatic incident for the Corinthians, but the main body of the army made its way home.

107. At about this time, the Athenians also began to build their Long Walls down to the sea, one leg to Phalerum and the other to Piraeus. [2] The Phocians invaded Doris, the motherland of the Lacedaemonians.* They attacked Boeum, Cytinium, and Erineus, and captured one of these towns, so the Lacedaemonians went to defend the Dorians with 1,500 of their own hoplites and 10,000 of their allies. They were commanded by Nicomedes, son of Cleombrotus, acting for the king, Pleistoanax, the son of Pausanias, who was still a child. They forced the Phocians to capitulate and surrender the town they had taken, and then they set out for home. [3] They might have wanted to go by sea and cross the Gulf of Corinth, but the Athenians had sailed around the Peloponnese with fifty ships† and were about to block that route. Nor did they judge it safe to go through the Geranea mountains, given that the Athenians were in Megara and Pegae; the passes through the mountains were difficult and the Athenians had them under constant guard, so clearly that route would be closed to them as well. [4] They decided that it would be best to wait in Boeotia and think about how to minimize the risk of crossing over to the Peloponnese. And another consideration was that some Athenians, who wanted to put an end to the democracy and the building of the Long Walls, were secretly making overtures to them.

[5] The Athenians raised a mass levy and marched out against them, along with 1,000 Argives and contingents from others of their allies, making a total force of 14,000 men. [6] They launched the expedition because they thought the Lacedaemonians were stuck, unable to get back home, and also because they had some inkling of the plot to overthrow the democracy. [7] Their numbers were augmented by some Thessalian horsemen, in accordance with the terms of their alliance, but these horsemen went over to the Lacedaemonian side mid-battle. **108.** The battle, which took place at Tanagra in Boeotia,

was won by the Lacedaemonians and their allies, with considerable loss of life on both sides. [2] The Lacedaemonians then entered the Megarid, and after mutilating their cultivated trees they returned home via Geranea and the Isthmus.

On the sixty-second day after the battle, the Athenians, led by Myronides, marched into Boeotia [3] and fought a battle at Oenophyta, in which they defeated the Boeotians and gained control of Boeotia and Phocis.* They demolished Tanagra's wall and took as hostages 100 of the wealthiest men of Opuntian Locris. They also finished their Long Walls. [4] Not only that, but next the Aeginetans came to terms with the Athenians; they demolished their walls, surrendered their navy, and agreed to pay tribute in the future. [5] After that the Athenians, under the command of the general Tolmides, son of Tolmaeus, sailed around the Peloponnese, set fire to the Lacedaemonians' shipyard, took Chalcis (a Corinthian possession), and defeated the Sicyonians after landing troops in their territory.

109. Meanwhile, the Athenians and their allies who were still in Egypt experienced warfare in all its forms. [2] At first, with the Athenians in control of Egypt, King Artaxerxes sent a Persian, Megabazus, to Sparta with money, to persuade the Peloponnesians to invade Attica as a way of drawing the Athenians out of Egypt. [3] But Megabazus was getting nowhere and the money was being spent in vain, so he and what remained of the money returned to Asia, and the King sent a large army to Egypt under the command of a Persian called Megabyxus, son of Zopirus. [4] He marched overland, and on his arrival he won a battle against the Egyptians and their allies, drove the Greeks out of Memphis, and finally trapped them on the island of Prosopitis. He besieged them there for a year and six months, until, by draining the canal and diverting the water, he left the Athenian ships high and dry and turned most of the island into mainland. At this point, he crossed over by foot and seized the island.

110. And so, after six years of warfare,* the Greek enterprise in Egypt met with calamitous defeat. A few men from the great army marched through Libya to Cyrene and were saved, but most perished. [2] Egyptians once again became subjects of the King, except for Amyrtaeus, who ruled the marshlands. The great extent of the marshes meant that he could not be caught, and moreover, the marsh-dwellers were the best fighters in Egypt. [3] Inaros, the Libyan king, the instigator of the whole Egyptian affair, was betrayed, taken prisoner, and crucified. [4] Fifty relief triremes from Athens and other allied states sailed to Egypt, completely unaware of what had happened, and put in at the Mendesian mouth of the Nile. They were attacked from the land by an army and from the sea by a Phoenician fleet, and most of the ships were destroyed. Only a few escaped and made their way home. So ended the great Egyptian expedition undertaken by the Athenians and their allies.

111. Orestes, the son of the king of Thessaly, whose name was Echecratidas, had been sent into exile, and he prevailed on the Athenians to restore him. They collected troops from Boeotia and Phocis, allies of theirs, and marched against Pharsalus in Thessaly. They gained control of as much land as they could without advancing far from their camp—the Thessalian cavalry made it impossible for them to do more—but the city did not fall to them and they failed to achieve any of the other objectives of the campaign either. So they returned home with Orestes after a futile expedition. [2] Not long after this, a force of a thousand Athenians boarded the ships at Pegae, which was currently in Athenian hands, and sailed around the coast to Sicyon. Pericles, son of Xanthippus, was the general in command.* They disembarked, fought the Sicyonians who came out to meet them, and won the battle. [3] Immediately after this, they collected some Achaeans, sailed across the gulf, and marched against Oeniadae in Acarnania. They put the place under siege, but found it impossible to take, so they returned home.

112. Three years later,* the Peloponnesians and Athenians arranged a truce for five years. [2] The Athenians accordingly refrained from warfare in Greece, but they took offensive action against Cyprus with a fleet of two hundred of their own and their allies' ships. Cimon was the general in command of this operation. [3] Sixty ships from the fleet sailed to Egypt at the request of Amyrtaeus, the ruler of the marshlands, while the rest put Citium under siege. [4] Cimon's death and a shortage of food forced them to leave Citium, however, and after they had set sail they fought a battle at sea off Salamis (the one in Cyprus) against Phoenician, Cypriot, and Cilician forces, and at the same time fought a battle on land as well. They won both battles, and then they returned home, joined by the ships from Egypt. [5] Later on, the Lacedaemonians fought the so-called Sacred War, as a result of which they gained control of the Delphic sanctuary and returned it to the Delphians. But subsequently, after the Lacedaemonians had left, the Athenians sent an army to Delphi, gained control there, and returned the sanctuary to the Phocians.

113. Sometime after this, with Boeotian exiles in possession of Orchomenus, Chaeronea, and a few other places in Boeotia, the Athenians sent an expeditionary force of a thousand of their own hoplites and various allied contingents against these enemy strongholds. Tolmides, son of Tolmaeus, was the general in command of the operation. They captured Chaeronea and sold the inhabitants into slavery, and then left after installing a garrison. [2] As they were on their way home, they were attacked at Coronea by the Boeotian exiles from Orchomenus, who were supported by some Locrians, Euboean exiles, and other sympathizers. The Athenians lost the battle, and their men were either killed or taken prisoner. [3] The Athenians then pulled out of Boeotia altogether, after arranging a truce so that they could recover their prisoners. [4] The exiled Boeotians returned and all the Boeotians regained their independence.

114. Not long after this,* Euboea seceded from the Athenian alliance, and Pericles had already crossed over to the island with an army of Athenian soldiers when he received the news that Megara had revolted and the Peloponnesians were poised to invade Attica. Apart from a few who escaped to Nisaea, the Athenian garrison at Megara had all been killed. To aid them in their rebellion, the Megarians had called in the Corinthians, Sicyonians, and Epidaurians. Pericles quickly withdrew his troops from Euboea. [2] The Peloponnesians then invaded Attica under the command of the Spartan king Pleistoanax, the son of Pausanias. They got as far as Eleusis and Thria* and laid waste the farmland there, but they advanced no farther and returned home. [3] The Athenians therefore returned to Euboea, with Pericles as the general in command, and reduced the whole island. They settled the rest of the island by agreement, but at Hestiaea they expelled the inhabitants and took their territory for themselves. **115.** The Athenians then left Euboea, and not long afterward they entered into a treaty with the Lacedaemonians and their allies that was to last for thirty years,* and returned the Peloponnesian places they had been occupying—Nisaea, Pegae, Troezen, and Achaea.

[2] Six years later, war broke out between Samos and Miletus over Priene. The Milesians were coming off worse and they went to Athens to denounce the Samians; they were joined by some Samians, acting unofficially, who wanted to bring about a regime change. [3] The Athenians therefore sailed to Samos with a fleet of forty ships, established a democracy, and took as hostages from the Samians fifty boys and the same number of men. They deposited the hostages for safekeeping in Lemnos town, installed a garrison there, and left. [4] But rather than stay on the island, some of the Samians had fled to the mainland. Once they had allied themselves with the most powerful men in the city and with Pissuthnes, son of Hystaspes, who was the governor in Sardis at the time,* they recruited a force of about six hundred mercenaries and sailed over to Samos one night. [5] The first thing they did was lead an uprising against the democrats, most of whom were taken into custody, and then, after smuggling their hostages out of Lemnos, they seceded from Athens and handed over to Pissuthnes the Athenian garrison troops and officials who were in the city. Then they set about preparing to move against Miletus. They were joined in their rebellion by the Byzantines.

116. When the Athenians found out, they sailed to Samos with a fleet of sixty ships. Sixteen of these ships were not used for the attack on Samos: some of them went to Caria to watch for the Phoenician fleet, and others went to Chios and Lesbos to summon reinforcements. So it was with forty-four ships that Pericles and his nine fellow generals fought a battle off the island of Tragia* against a Samian fleet of seventy (though twenty were troop-carriers), as it was on its way back from Miletus. The Athenians won, [2] and later, after reinforcements had arrived in the form of forty ships from Athens and twenty-five from Chios and Lesbos,* they disembarked troops, defeated the Samians on land, and blockaded the city with walls on three sides and ships at sea. [3] But Pericles detached sixty ships from the besieging force and raced off to Caunus and Caria, because news had arrived that Phoenician ships were heading their way; Stesagoras and some others had earlier taken five ships from Samos and gone to fetch the Phoenicians.

117. At this point the Samians unexpectedly launched their fleet and attacked the Athenian camp, which was unprotected by a palisade. They destroyed the sentry ships and defeated those that came out to fight them, leaving them as masters of the sea in their area, with the ability to bring things in and out as they wished. This lasted about fourteen days, [2] but then Pericles returned with his fleet and the blockade resumed. Later, additional reinforcements arrived: forty ships from Athens under the command of Thucydides, Hagnon, and Phormio; another twenty under the command of Tlepolemus and Anticles; and thirty more from Chios and Lesbos. [3] The Samians did manage a brief sea battle, but their resistance crumbled and in the ninth month of the siege they gave up and surrendered. The terms were that they should tear down their wall, give hostages, surrender their fleet, and accept an assessment of what the Athenians had spent on the war, which was to be repaid in yearly installments. The Byzantines came to terms as well and returned to their previous status as subjects.

118. A few years after this, there occurred the events I have already described—the Corcyra episode, the Potidaea affair, and the other incidents that constituted the immediate cause of the current war. [2] All the interactions I have recounted, of Greeks with Greeks and of Greeks with non-Greeks, occurred in the approximately fifty years between the departure of Xerxes and the start of the current war. In these years, the Athenians consolidated their empire and greatly increased their power. The Lacedaemonians were aware of this, but did hardly anything to stop them. They were inactive for most of the time—partly because they have always been slow to go to war unless they have absolutely no choice, and partly because they were somewhat constrained by conflicts at home—until the Athenians' power was undeniably on the rise and they were starting to encroach on the Lacedaemonians' allies. That was when they began to find the situation intolerable, and concluded that they had to commit themselves wholeheartedly to attacking and, if possible, breaking Athenian power by embarking on this war. [3] So the Lacedaemonians themselves had already decided that the treaty had been broken and that the Athenians were culpable, but they still sent a delegation to Delphi and asked the god if it would be prudent for them to go to war. And the god replied, apparently, that if they fought a forceful war victory would be theirs, and added that he would be with them, whether or not they called on him.

119. The Lacedaemonians wanted to take a vote on whether to go to war, so they summoned the allies to another meeting. The allies sent their representatives, and at the meeting each of them spoke his mind, with most of them denouncing the Athenians and calling for war. The Corinthians had already made the rounds of the cities, unofficially asking each of them to vote for war, because they were afraid that otherwise it would be too late to save Potidaea. But they also came to this meeting, and they were the last to step up and speak, along the following lines:

120. "Friends, the behavior of the Lacedaemonians is now beyond reproach: they have voted for war themselves and have convened this meeting for us to do the same. That's how leaders should behave. They must deal impartially with private interests, but they must be foremost when it comes to thinking about common interests, just as in other contexts they are foremost in the honor they receive from everyone.

[2] "Those of us who have had dealings with the Athenians in the past don't need to be told to be wary of them, but those who live farther inland and not on a sea route must understand that if they fail to fight in defense of the seaboard, it will be more difficult for them to find an external market for their agricultural produce or to receive in return the produce that the land gets from the sea. They're looking at things wrong if they think that all this talk here today has nothing to do with them. If they abandon the coastal communities to their fate, they can expect the danger to reach them one day. They are deliberating today as much about themselves as anyone else.

[3] "That's why they mustn't falter, but choose war instead of peace. It's characteristic of prudent men to live in peace as long as they are not being wronged, but it's characteristic of good men to exchange peace for war if they are wronged, and then, if there's a reasonable opportunity, to exchange war in its turn for diplomacy. Such men aren't carried away by wartime success, but they also don't submit to being wronged just because they're enjoying peace and quiet. [4] Anyone who is seduced by pleasure into hesitating will very quickly discover that doing nothing loses him the pleasant idleness that's causing him to hesitate, and anyone who overreaches himself because of wartime success is failing to realize that he's being beguiled by baseless confidence. [5] Many badly made plans have led to success because the enemy was fortunately an even worse strategist, and even more plans that were apparently well laid have ended in disgrace and failure. The point is that the degree of confidence with which we make plans is never matched when they're carried out in the real world. We do our thinking in a safe place, but plans are put into effect in conditions of fear and never fulfill their potential.

121. "We're instigating this war now because we're being wronged and we have enough grievances, and once we've avenged ourselves on the Athenians, at the appropriate time we shall bring it to an end. [2] There are a number of reasons why we will probably prevail. First, we have the advantage in terms of both numbers and military experience; second, we're all equally responsive to orders.* [3] And third, as for a navy, which is where the enemy's strength lies, we'll build one, partly from each community's individual resources and partly with the help of the money deposited at Delphi and Olympia. If we take out a loan, you see, since Athenian power relies more on hiring mercenaries than making use of their own people, we'll be able to lure their non-Athenian sailors away with the offer of better wages. Our strength, however, lies in manpower rather than money, so we're less vulnerable in this respect.

[4] "In all probability, then, it will take us only one victory at sea to finish them off. They might persist, but that will just give us more time to practice our naval skills, and once we've drawn level with them in terms of expertise, our courage will certainly enable us to overtake them. This virtue is an innate aspect of our character and not a quality they can gain by instruction, whereas with practice we can cancel out the advantage they have in skill. [5] We'll raise the money for this by making financial contributions. It would indeed be shocking if their allies put up with contributing to their own servitude, and then we fail to spend money on punishing our enemies, which is at the same time self-protection, and on making sure that they don't use these very funds to injure us once they've taken them away from us.

122. "But this isn't the only way in which we could go about the war: we could get their allies to revolt, and there would be no better way to deprive them of the revenues on which they flourish; we could build a forward operating base in their territory; and there are other measures we could take, which are unforeseeable at the moment because war is the last thing to proceed by prescribed rules, but devises its own responses to every emerging situation. And this means that the person who meets it calmly is more secure, while the one who lets it engage his emotions is more likely to fail.

[2] "Let's also bear in mind that if each of us were disputing borders with enemies of equal strength, we could cope. But that's not how things stand. The Athenians are a match for all of us at once and their strength is even more overwhelming when measured against individual states. This means that if we don't combine, people by people and state by state, and defend ourselves against them in concert—if we remain disunited, in other words—they'll have no difficulty in getting the better of us. And it may be awful to hear the words spoken, but let's be clear that defeat would lead to unqualified enslavement. [3] And to hesitate even in discussion when enslavement is at stake brings shame on the Peloponnese, as does the fact that so many cities are being made to suffer by just one. This being so, either our suffering will seem no less than we deserve, or it will look as though we're too cowardly to do something about it. And everyone will see that we're worse than our fathers. They liberated all Greece, while we're not only failing to secure liberty for ourselves, but are allowing a tyrant city to be established in Greece, despite the fact that we presume to depose sole rulers in any single city. [4] It isn't easy to see how this behavior is to be distinguished from the three greatest human defects: stupidity, weakness, and carelessness. As a result of your failure to avoid these defects, you've adopted the disdainful attitude that has been the undoing of a great many people—a sense of superiority that so commonly causes failure that its name has been changed to senselessness in recognition that no sense is involved at all.

123. "Anyway, there's nothing to be gained by criticism of the past except insofar as it helps the present. But, looking to the future, you must continue to work to defend what you have; after all, it's Peloponnesian tradition to attain to excellence through hard work. And you must not change your ways, even if these days you are slightly more wealthy and powerful, because it's wrong for qualities that were gained at a time of poverty to be lost at a time of plenty. No, you must go to war, and you have many grounds for confidence as you do so: the god promised through his oracle to be with you, and all the rest of Greece will enter the contest alongside you, out of either fear or self-interest. [2] And it won't be you who broke the treaty; in telling you to go to war, even the god considers it already broken. It's more accurate to say that what you'll be doing is coming to the treaty's aid when it has been violated. It isn't those who defend themselves who break treaties, but the original aggressors.

124. "So everything points to the propriety of your going to war, and that is also the course we're recommending for the common good, bearing in mind that the most secure bond for cities, as for individuals, is for them to have the same interests. You need not hesitate, then, to help the Potidaeans—Dorians besieged by Ionians,* when in times past it was the other way round. And don't hesitate to seek freedom for everyone else. Waiting is no longer an option. Some of us are already being harmed and it won't be long before others have the same experience, if it becomes known that we held this meeting but lacked the courage to retaliate. [2] You must see, fellow allies, that you really have no choice and that what has been said here today is for the best. Vote for war not because you're afraid of the immediate danger, but because you look forward to the lasting peace that will come from it. Peace that follows war is more stable, whereas refusing to disturb the peace and go to war is far more risky. [3] In the realization that the tyrant city that has been established in Greece is a threat to all alike, because it already exercises dominion over some Greeks and intends to do the same to the rest, let's go on the offensive and force it to capitulate. That way, we ourselves will live thereafter without fear, and we will liberate the Greeks who are presently enslaved."

125. That was the substance of the Corinthians' speech. When the Lacedaemonians had heard everyone's views, they put the vote to all the assembled allies one after another, irrespective of the sizes of their cities, and the majority voted for war. [2] They were unable to act on this decision right away, however, and launch an attack, because they were not ready, but they decided on the appropriate contributions from each of the allies and ordered the work to proceed immediately. Nevertheless, it took them almost a year to make all the necessary arrangements before they invaded Attica and embarked on open war.

126. Over the course of this period of time the Lacedaemonians sent several embassies to Athens to lodge their complaints, so that they would have the strongest justification for going to war if the Athenians ignored them. [2] The first envoys they sent demanded that the Athenians dispel Athena's curse. The story of this curse is as follows: [3] Long ago, there was an Athenian called Cylon.* He was an Olympic victor, well born and influential, and he had married the daughter of Theagenes, a Megarian who at the time was the tyrant of Megara. [4] In response to a question put by Cylon to the oracle at Delphi, the god said that he should seize the acropolis "during the greatest festival of Zeus." [5] So Cylon was given troops by Theagenes, enlisted his friends, and set in motion his bid for tyranny by seizing the acropolis. He did this at the time of the Olympic festival in the Peloponnese, since he assumed that this was the greatest festival in honor of Zeus and also that, as an Olympic victor himself, it was somehow relevant to him. [6] But he never stopped to consider whether the "greatest festival" was one that was celebrated in Athens or elsewhere, and the oracle offered no clarification. After all, the Athenians have their Diasia festival, which is known as the greatest festival in honor of Zeus the Gracious. It is held outside the city, and during it the entire population congregates to offer sacrifices, often not of regular victims but of offerings of a local kind.† But Cylon was sure that his understanding of the oracle was right and made his attempt.

[7] When the Athenians found out, they came from the countryside en masse to defend the city, and they invested the acropolis and pinned Cylon and his men there. [8] As time passed, however, the

monotony of the siege made most of the Athenians return to their homes; they left it up to the nine archons to keep watch and gave them a free hand to manage the whole matter as they thought best. In those days, most state business was the responsibility of the nine archons.

[9] Meanwhile, Cylon and the men under siege with him were suffering badly from lack of food and water. [10] Cylon and his brother managed to escape, but the rest of them were in desperate trouble, with some of them even close to death from starvation, so they seated themselves as suppliants at Athena's altar on the acropolis. [11] When the Athenians who had been tasked with keeping guard realized that people were dying in the sanctuary, they persuaded the suppliants to leave on the understanding that they would come to no harm, but then they killed them once they were outside the sanctuary. Some of them were even done away with at the altars of the Venerable Goddesses, at which they had sought protection as they were being led past. For this, the killers and their descendants were held to be accursed and offensive to the goddess. [12] So the Athenians banished these accursed men, as, later, did Cleomenes of Sparta as well, with the help of the Athenian factions that supported him;* the living were banished and the bones of the dead were dug up and thrown out of Athenian territory. They returned later, however, and their descendants still live in the city.

127. So this was the curse that the Lacedaemonians told the Athenians to dispel. On the face of it, they were motivated primarily by a desire to help the gods, but in fact it was because they knew that, through his mother, Pericles, son of Xanthippus, was implicated in the curse, and they thought that if he were banished it would be easier for them to make progress in dealing with the Athenians. [2] Nevertheless, it was not so much that they expected him to be banished as that they hoped to make him unpopular with his fellow citizens, as though the war were partly due to his being afflicted with the curse. [3] For he was the most influential person in Athens at the time and the leading figure in government, and he opposed the Lacedaemonians in everything, never letting the Athenians make any concessions but constantly urging them on to the war.

128. The Athenians retaliated by demanding that the Lacedaemonians dispel the curse of Taenarum. The Lacedaemonians had once persuaded some suppliant helots to leave the sanctuary of Poseidon at Taenarum,* and had then killed them once they were outside the sanctuary. It was this sacrilege, they believe, that was responsible for the great earthquake that struck Sparta.* [2] They also demanded that the Lacedaemonians dispel the curse of the Bronze House. Here is what happened: [3] The first time that Pausanias of Sparta was recalled by the Spartiates from his command in the Hellespont and was put on trial by them, he was acquitted of wrongdoing,* but he was no longer used in an official capacity for missions abroad. But without the Lacedaemonians' permission and on his own initiative he took a trireme from Hermione and went to the Hellespont. He made out that he was returning to prosecute the Greeks' war, but in reality he wanted to continue the intrigues with the King that he had set in motion before, since his objective was dominion over the Greeks.

[4] He had initially placed the King under an obligation and set the whole scheme in motion as follows: [5] On his first visit to the area—this was after leaving Cyprus—he took Byzantium, which was in the hands of, among other Persians, certain friends and relatives of the King, who were captured in the city when it fell. What Pausanias did was send the prisoners back to the King. He did this without the knowledge of the other allies, who were told that the prisoners had escaped. [6] His partner in this scheme was Gongylus of Eretria, the person whom Pausanias had made responsible for both Byzantium and the prisoners. Gongylus's mission to the King also included delivering a letter from Pausanias. As emerged later, the letter read as follows:*

> [7] Pausanias, the leading man in Sparta, is returning these prisoners of war to you because he wishes to do you a favor. I propose that, if you

have no objection, I should marry your daughter and make Sparta and the rest of Greece subject to you. I think I am capable of seeing this scheme through if you and I plan it together. So if you like these ideas, send a trustworthy man to the coast through whom we can communicate in the future.

129. That was the content of Pausanias's letter. Xerxes was delighted, and he sent Artabazus, son of Pharnaces, to the coast. He told him to take over the satrapy of Dascyleum (replacing the former governor, Megabates), and he entrusted him with a written reply that Artabazus was to pass on to Pausanias in Byzantium as quickly as possible, making sure that Pausanias saw the royal seal. And if Pausanias gave him any orders concerning the King's affairs, Artabazus was to carry them out to the best of his ability and as faithfully as he could. [2] When Artabazus reached Dascyleum, he carried out all his instructions, including passing the letter on to Pausanias. [3] This is what Xerxes had written in response:

> Thus says King Xerxes to Pausanias: Regarding the men whom you rescued for me from Byzantium across the sea, a record of your good deed will lie in my house forever. What you wrote pleases me. Let neither night nor day hold you back and make you pause from fulfilling any of the promises you made to me. Nor need you be inhibited by all the gold and silver you may have to spend, or by the size of the army that may be required at some point. Work confidently with Artabazus, whom I have sent to you—he is a good man—and see that both my affairs and yours prosper in ways that do both of us as much honor and good as possible.

130. After receiving this letter, Pausanias, whose standing was already high among the Greeks because of his leadership at the Battle of Plataea, became even more full of himself. He found it impossible to live in a conventional fashion: outside of Byzantium he wore Persian dress; he marched through Thrace with a bodyguard of Medes and Egyptians; he had Persian fare served at his table. His ambitions knew no limits, and in small ways he revealed in advance what he planned to do on a greater scale later. [2] He limited access to himself and kept everyone at bay, whoever they were, by his churlish treatment of them. This was one of the main reasons that the allies went over to the Athenians.

131. It was this behavior that prompted the Lacedaemonians to recall him the first time, once they became aware of it, and when he sailed off a second time on the ship from Hermione, without authorization from them, he seemed to be behaving the same way all over again. After he had been besieged into submission and driven out of Byzantium by the Athenians, he did not return to Sparta, but settled in Colonae in the Troad, and the Lacedaemonians heard that he was intriguing with the Persians and had taken up residence there for no good purpose. This was the point at which they lost their patience. The ephors sent a messenger with a coded message, telling him that either he should accompany the messenger back to Sparta, or the Spartiates would declare him a public enemy. [2] Wanting to reduce the mistrust of himself as much as possible, and certain that he could bribe his way out of the charges, Pausanias returned to Sparta for the second time. At first, he was thrown into prison by the ephors (who have the power to do this to a king), and then later, after he had negotiated his release from prison, he made himself available for examination by anyone who wanted to hold an inquiry into the case.

132. Now, neither his personal enemies nor anyone else from the citizenry as a whole could provide the Spartiates with such strong evidence that they could confidently go about punishing a man who was a member of a royal family and who was held in high honor at the time, because as cousin of the underage king, Pleistarchus, son of Leonidas, he was acting as his guardian. [2] But his misconduct and adoption of barbarian ways frequently left him open to the suspicion that he was reluctant to remain subject to the limitations of his current position. So they held a thorough inquiry into various aspects of his conduct, to see in what respects, if any, he had transgressed convention. They focused in particular on the fact that, without consulting others, he had once presumed to have inscribed on the tripod that the Greeks had dedicated at Delphi, as the first fruits of the spoils taken from the Persians, the following elegiac couplet:

When as commander of the Greeks he had destroyed the Persian army
Pausanias dedicated this memorial to Phoebus Apollo.

[3] At the time, the Lacedaemonians had quickly erased these lines from the tripod and after reinscribing it with the names of all the states that had contributed to the defeat of the Persians, they set the monument in place. But even at the time this was regarded as an unjustifiable act on Pausanias's part, and now, given his present situation, the similarities between what he had done then and his current intentions became far more noticeable.

[4] The Lacedaemonians were also informed that Pausanias was intriguing with the helots—as indeed he was, seeing that he was promising them freedom and citizenship if they joined him in an uprising and helped him attain his overall objectives. [5] But not even then, even though they believed some of what they were hearing from helot informers, did they think it right to take drastic action against him. Instead, they went about it as they invariably did when dealing with internal matters; they were always slow, where a fellow Spartiate was concerned, to make any irrevocable decisions without unequivocal evidence. But then, it is said, luckily for them, the man who was going to deliver to Artabazus the most recent letter from Pausanias to the King turned informer; this was a man from Argilus, who had once been Pausanias's boyfriend and was completely trusted by him.* He decided to betray Pausanias because he had become frightened when it occurred to him that none of the previous messengers had returned. He made a copy of the seal, so that he would not be found out if what

he was thinking was wrong, or if Pausanias should ask to make some changes to the letter, and then he opened the letter. In it he found his suspicions confirmed by exactly the postscript he had expected, in which the order was given for his death.

133. Seeing the letter made the ephors more certain of Pausanias's guilt, but they still wanted to hear him incriminate himself with their own ears, and they came up with a scheme. The informer went to Taenarum as a suppliant and built himself a hut with a secret compartment behind a partition, where some of the ephors hid. When Pausanias came to him and asked him the reason for his supplication, they heard everything perfectly. The man accused Pausanias of having ordered his death in the letter and laid everything bare in detail as he argued that in his missions to the King he had never put Pausanias at risk, and yet his reward was to be killed, as though he were not an exceptional agent. Pausanias admitted the truth of this and asked him to calm down. He assured the man that he could safely leave the sanctuary and begged him to go as quickly as possible and not to impede his activities.

134. After hearing every word the ephors went back to Sparta, and now that there was no room for doubt they planned to arrest Pausanias in the city. The story goes that just as he was about to be apprehended in the street, he spotted the face of one of the ephors approaching him and realized why he was coming for him. But another of the other ephors, a sympathizer, discreetly indicated with his head which way he should go, and Pausanias escaped arrest by running for the sanctuary of the Bronze House, which was nearby, and taking refuge there. Not wanting to be troubled by the elements, he entered a small chamber that was part of the sanctuary, and stayed still. [2] The ephors were too slow at first and missed him, but later they took the roof off the chamber and, now that they knew he was inside and cooped up there, they barricaded the doors, surrounded the chamber, and starved him out. [3] When they realized that he was about to expire where he was, in the chamber, they carried him out of the sanctuary.

He was still breathing, but he died immediately after being brought outside. [4] They were going to throw him into the Ceädas, which is where they dispose of criminals' bodies, but then they decided to bury him somewhere nearby. Later, the god at Delphi told the Lacedaemonians to move his tomb to where he had died (and that is where he lies today, at the entrance to the precinct, as the inscriptions on the stelae indicate), [5] and that since what the Lacedaemonians had done laid them under a curse, they should give two bodies to the Bronze House in requital for one. So they had two bronze statues made and set them up in the sanctuary as a substitute for Pausanias.

135. So, since the god himself had adjudged this an accursed defilement, the Athenians retaliated with the demand that the Lacedaemonians should dispel it. [2] As for Pausanias's collaboration with the Persians, the Lacedaemonians sent an embassy to Athens and accused Themistocles as well, basing the charge on what they were discovering as a result of their investigation of Pausanias's doings, and they called on the Athenians to mete out the same punishment to Themistocles that they had to Pausanias. [3] The Athenians agreed and, since Themistocles had been ostracized* and was resident in Argos (though he spent time in other parts of the Peloponnese as well), they sent men there with instructions to seize him wherever they found him and bring him to Athens. These men were accompanied by the Lacedaemonians, who were happy to take part in the hunt.

136. Themistocles was forewarned, however, and escaped from the Peloponnese to Corcyra, where he was regarded as a benefactor. But, claiming that they were afraid to harbor him and incur the hostility of the Lacedaemonians and Athenians, the Corcyreans moved him over to the mainland opposite the island. [2] Hounded by those who had been assigned to pursue him as they followed up information about his movements, he was forced by a lack of other options to seek lodging with Admetus, the king of the Molossians, who was no friend of his. [3] Admetus was not at home, but Themistocles presented himself as a suppliant to his wife, and she told him to take her and Admetus's son and go and sit by the hearth. [4] When Admetus returned home soon afterward, Themistocles revealed his identity and begged him not to take revenge on him in his fugitive status, even though he had once spoken against granting a request Admetus had made to the Athenians. He argued that, given his present circumstances, Admetus would be making a much weaker person suffer, when the noble course was for revenge to be taken on people who were peers and on an equal footing with oneself. And he pointed out that he had opposed Admetus over a request, not over a matter of life or death, whereas if Admetus were to give him up (he explained who his pursuers were and why they were after him), he would be denying him his last chance of staying alive.

137. After hearing what Themistocles had to say, Admetus raised him up along with his son, whom Themistocles was still holding, as he had been while sitting down—this is the most powerful kind of supplication—and a short while later the Lacedaemonians and Athenians arrived. They spoke at length, but Admetus refused to give Themistocles up. Instead, since Themistocles wanted to go to the King, Admetus had him escorted overland to Pydna, on the eastern coast of Alexander's kingdom.* [2] There Themistocles found a merchant ship that was sailing to Ionia and he embarked as a passenger, but a storm carried the ship to the camp of the Athenian troops who were besieging Naxos.* No one on the ship had recognized him, but Themistocles was so scared that he told the ship's captain who he was and why he was fleeing, and said that if he did not keep him safe, he would say that he had been bribed to take him on board. He also said that his safety depended on no one leaving the ship before they set sail again, and that if the captain went along with all this he could count on a handsome reward. The captain did what Themistocles was asking and, after riding at anchor off the Athenian camp for a day and a night, they finally reached Ephesus.

[3] Themistocles placated the captain by giving him money (which arrived after a while from friends in Athens and from what he had

Book One: 136–138

stored in Argos), and traveled inland with a Persian from the coast. Then he wrote to King Artaxerxes, son of Xerxes, who had recently ascended to the throne.* [4] The letter went as follows:

> I, Themistocles, have arrived in your kingdom. I did more harm to your house than any other Greek while I was forced to defend myself against your father's attacks, but the harm is outweighed by the good I did when I was safe and he was in danger during his retreat back home. The services I rendered put you in my debt [he was referring to the warning he had sent from Salamis of the impending Greek retreat and to the failure to destroy the bridges at that time,* for which he falsely took credit], and now that I am in a position to do you a great deal of good, I have been chased here by the Greeks because of my goodwill for you. Please grant me a year before I tell you in person why I have come.

138. The King is said to have admired Themistocles's plan and told him to do exactly what he had said in the letter. Themistocles spent the year of waiting becoming as fluent in the Persian language as he could and studying the customs of the land. [2] When the year was up, he went to the King and became highly influential in his court—more so than any other Greek has ever been—because of the reputation he already had, because of the hope he held out to the King of subjugating the Greeks, but above all because of his evident intelligence, which he gave the King plenty of opportunities to appreciate. [3] Themistocles's natural abilities were indeed undeniably evident, and he deserved an exceptional degree of admiration for them, more than anyone else. He needed no more than his native intelligence, without the aid of any briefing or debriefing, and very little deliberation to come up with brilliant assessments of the present, and there was no one better at conjecturing what even the remote future might hold. He had the ability to explain any business that he had in hand, and was perfectly capable of delivering competent assessments of matters outside his experience. There was also no one better at foreseeing advantages and disadvantages in a still uncertain future. In short, he was a genius at improvising the necessary response in any situation, using just his natural abilities and requiring very little preparation.

[4] He died of an illness, though some say that he took his own life by swallowing poison because he believed that there was no way to fulfill the promises he had made to the King. [5] There is a memorial to him in the agora of Magnesia in Asia, where he had been the governor of the district. The King gave him Magnesia for his bread (the place brought in fifty talents a year), Lampsacus for his wine (it was regarded as the largest producer of wine at the time), and Myous for his savories. [6] His bones, his relatives say, were taken home, in accordance with his wishes, and buried in Attica. This had to be done without the knowledge of the Athenians, because burial within Attica was forbidden for anyone who had been banished from the state for treason.

So that was how the two most illustrious men of their time, Pausanias of Sparta and Themistocles of Athens, met their ends.

139. These, then, were the demands the Lacedaemonians made on their first embassy, and the counterdemands that they met, all concerned with dispelling curses. On subsequent visits to Athens, they insisted that the Athenians should leave Potidaea and let Aegina have its independence, but above all and with particular directness they said there would be no war if the Athenians rescinded the decree that excluded the Megarians from the harbors of the Athenian empire and the Athenian agora.* [2] But the Athenians rejected all their demands and refused to rescind the decree, since they were charging the Megarians with encroaching on sacred land and on borderland that was unclaimed by either state, and with harboring runaway slaves. [3] Eventually, a final embassy arrived from Sparta, consisting of Ramphias, Melesippus, and Agesander. They made no mention at all of their usual complaints and demands, but said just this: "The Lacedaemonians want there to be peace, and there will be peace if you let the

Greeks have their freedom." The Athenians resolved to think about it and then to give the Lacedaemonians a definitive answer, so they convened an assembly and called for a general debate. [4] Plenty of people came forward to speak, and views were expressed on both sides, with some arguing for war, and others that the decree should be rescinded if it was an obstacle to peace. Then Pericles, son of Xanthippus, the most influential person in Athens at the time—there was no one more capable either as a speaker or as a man of action—stepped up and offered them the following advice:*

140. "My fellow Athenians, I haven't changed my mind. I still say that we should make no concessions to the Lacedaemonians, and I say this even though I understand that people's mood when they're listening to arguments for war isn't the same as when they're actually at war—that thinking adapts to prevailing conditions. But it's clear to me that I have to give you very much the same advice as I gave before, and I call on those of you who are persuaded by my arguments to support the decisions we make together even if we experience setbacks, or else forfeit all credit for the intelligence of those decisions if we're successful. After all, events can proceed just as waywardly as human plans; that's why we customarily attribute unexpected events to luck.

[2] "It was clear enough earlier that the Lacedaemonians were planning to fight us, and now there can be absolutely no doubt. For although it was stipulated in the treaty that if any differences arose between us, an offer of arbitration was to be accepted by the other party, and in the meantime the status quo would be maintained, they haven't yet asked us to go to arbitration, nor are they accepting our offers to do so. They'd prefer to resolve grievances by war than by discussion, and they've come here now issuing orders rather than raising their grievances. [3] They order us to leave Potidaea, to let Aegina have its independence, and to rescind the Megarian decree, and now they've come with an ultimatum, ordering us to let the Greeks have their freedom.

[4] "I wouldn't have anyone here think that we'd be going to war over a trivial matter if we refused to rescind the Megarian decree—and

this is their main proposal, that if it were revoked there would be no war—nor should there be any lingering traces of guilt in your minds that you went to war for no good reason. [5] No, this 'trivial matter' is a confirmation and test of your resolve. If you give way to them on this, you'll immediately be issued with another, more exacting order, on the assumption that out of fear you'll give way on that too. If you resist, however, you'll make it clear to them that they should really be treating you as equals. **141.** Make up your minds here and now, then, either to give in before any damage has been done, or if we go to war—which I think the better option—to do so without making concessions for any reason, great or small, and without being too afraid to keep our empire intact. It doesn't matter whether a demand, made by people of the same status as oneself, is for something completely trivial or utterly momentous: it still amounts to enslavement if it comes in the form of an order rather than being the legal verdict of a court.

[2] "As regards the war and the resources available to each side, I shall now go through them for you in some detail and you'll see that we won't be at a disadvantage. [3] The Peloponnesians are subsistence farmers, lacking both private and state funds. They therefore have no experience of protracted, overseas wars, because they're limited by their poverty to brief campaigns against one another. [4] People in this condition are in no position to man ships, because the sea is closed to them, or to keep sending out a land army, because they'd be away from their farms and using up their own personal money. [5] Wars are sustained by surplus wealth rather than by emergency taxation. Typically, farmers are more willing to commit themselves than their money to war, because they trust that they might come through safely, but they have no confidence that their money will not run out prematurely, especially if the war goes on longer than they expected, as is likely.

[6] "In a single battle, the combined Peloponnesian forces are capable of holding their own against the whole of Greece, but they're useless in a full-scale war against a power unless it has the same character

as theirs. The reason for this is that they have no single council to facilitate prompt action, and since all of them have an equal vote, individual cities, given their different ethnicities, promote their parochial interests, which means that usually nothing gets done. [7] Some of them, for instance, might want to punish an enemy with the utmost severity, while others want to minimize the damage to their property. They convene meetings only sporadically, and then they devote hardly any time to matters of common concern, and most of it to negotiating their private interests. It doesn't occur to any of them that his own negligence in this respect will have a detrimental effect, and each of them regards it as someone else's job to be diligent on his behalf. And so, with all of them thinking like this, they fail to see how destructive it is to their common interests as a whole. **142.** The critical point, however, is that they'll be held back by their lack of money; it takes them time to raise funds, and that makes them slow off the mark, but in war opportunities do not wait.

[2] "Moreover, there's no need for us to worry about their building a forward operating base in our territory or about their naval skills. [3] It's hard enough to carry out such building work against a city of equal strength† even at a time of peace, so of course it's far harder to do so in enemy territory and with our own fortifications no less of a threat to them. [4] If they do manage to build a stronghold, they'll harm only a fraction of our territory with their raids and by encouraging slaves to desert. It won't be enough to stop us from sailing to their territory and building forward operating bases there, nor will it be enough to stop us from retaliating with our navy, which is where our strength lies.

[5] "The experience of land warfare that our navy grants us is greater than the contribution their land operations make toward naval expertise. [6] It won't be easy for them to add naval expertise to their other accomplishments. [7] Even you haven't yet perfected your naval skills, and you've been in training since immediately after the Persian invasion. So how can people who are farmers and landlubbers achieve anything worthwhile, especially since we have enough ships to keep

them constantly under a blockade and unable to train? [8] Against a small blockading force their numerical superiority might make them bold, despite their lack of expertise, but if they're shut in by a large number of ships they'll do nothing. Their lack of training will make them all the more incompetent and their lack of competence will make them all the more hesitant. [9] Like anything else, seamanship requires skill and can't be practiced casually in one's spare time; it's more the case that it leaves no time for any other activity.

143. "So even if they get hold of funds from Olympia or Delphi and try to use higher wages to entice away those of our sailors who are foreigners, that would be a cause for concern only if we weren't in a position to compensate by manning our ships with ourselves and our metics, but the fact is that we *are* in such a position, and, even more importantly, our helmsmen are Athenian citizens, and we have more and better naval officers than all the rest of Greece combined. [2] In any case, a few days of higher wages aren't enough to tempt even one of our foreign crewmen to join the contest on the Lacedaemonian side, given that he'd be risking banishment from his native city and increasing his chances of defeat.

[3] "It is my opinion, at any rate, that this is very much the situation in which the Peloponnesians find themselves, whereas, as I've pointed out, we are free of their weaknesses and are better off in other important respects. [4] If they march overland against our territory, we shall sail against theirs, and the devastation of the whole of Attica wouldn't be as bad for us as the devastation of a fraction of the Peloponnese would be for them. They will have no other territory to replace it with, unless they gain some by fighting, whereas we'll still have plenty of land, both on the islands and on the mainland. That's how important mastery of the sea is. [5] Look at it this way: if we were islanders, who would be more secure than us? So what you must do now is think like islanders, as nearly as you can. Let go of your land and farmsteads, and protect the sea and the city—and do so without getting so enraged with the Peloponnesians over what you've lost that

you fight it out with them when they outnumber us by a considerable margin. After all, if we fight them and win, we'll find ourselves later fighting the same superior numbers again, and if we lose we'll also lose our allies, who are the source of our strength, since they will become restive if they see that we're incapable of mounting expeditions against them. So save your mourning for loss of life, not for loss of houses and fields. These things aren't people's owners; they are owned by people. Indeed, if I thought you'd do as I say, I'd tell you to go out to the countryside and destroy these things yourselves. That would show the Peloponnesians that you aren't going to let such things dispose you to submit.

144. "I have many other grounds for expecting us to prevail, but you must be prepared to forgo extending the empire while fighting the war, and you mustn't expose yourselves to further dangers of your own making. I'm more afraid of our own mistakes than I am of the enemy's plans. [2] But I shall explain what these grounds for optimism are in a later speech, when it's time for action. For now, let's send the envoys back home with the following response: we will allow the Megarians access to our market and harbors if the Lacedaemonians refrain from targeting us and our allies in their expulsions of foreigners, there being nothing in the treaty that forbids either the expulsions or the decree; we will let the cities have their independence if they were independent at the time the treaty was made, and when the Lacedaemonians too allow their cities to be independent as each of them chooses, rather than serving the interests of Sparta; we are willing to accept arbitration, as stipulated in the treaty, and while we will not start a war, we will defend ourselves against those who do. This response is both fair and appropriate for our city.

[3] "It's important that you understand, however, that war is inevitable, and that the more willingly we accept it, the less eager we shall find our enemies are to fight. It's also important to remember the principle that holds for both states and individuals, that the greater the danger, the greater the subsequent glory. [4] At any rate, when

our fathers stood up to the Persians, they started with fewer resources than we currently have, and they even gave up what they did have; but still, by relying on good policies rather than good luck, and on daring rather than strength, they repelled the barbarians and sowed the seeds of our current prosperity. We must live up to their example; we must do everything we can to resist our enemies, and try to pass an undiminished city on to future generations."

145. Such was Pericles's speech, and the Athenians believed that he was offering them the best advice. They voted in accordance with his recommendations and the response they made to the Lacedaemonians conformed with his point of view; they followed his advice both on particular issues and in general. That is, they told the Lacedaemonians that they would do nothing if they were ordered to do so by them, but were ready to go to arbitration, as stipulated in the treaty, in order to resolve the grievances in an equitable and fair way. So the Lacedaemonian envoys returned home, and there were no further embassies.

146. These, then, were the complaints and contentions on both sides before the war, that arose directly from events at Epidamnus and Corcyra. Nevertheless, channels of communication remained open in the midst of these recriminations, and they visited each other, without heralds but not without mistrust, because these events did in fact amount to a breach of the treaty and a justification for going to war.

Book Two

*The first three years of the war. **431/430:** outbreak of the war, and the Theban attack on Plataea (2.1–6); Spartan and Athenian preparations (2.7–17); the first Peloponnesian invasion of Attica (2.18–32); Corinthian actions in northwest Greece (2.33); the public funeral at Athens, and Pericles's funeral speech (2.34–47.1). **430/429:** second Peloponnesian invasion of Attica, and plague at Athens (2.47.2–2.54); further campaigns (2.55–58); criticism of Pericles, and his response (2.59–65); further campaigns, and the capitulation of Potidaea (2.66–70). **429/428:** the siege of Plataea (2.71–78); campaigns in northern Greece (2.79–82); Athenian naval successes in the Gulf of Corinth (2.83–92); a Spartan naval raid, and loss of nerve (2.93–94); developments in northeast and northwest Greece (2.95–103).*

1. From this point on there was war between the Athenian and Peloponnesian alliances. Communication between Athens and Sparta now took place solely by means of heralds,* and once the war had begun it went on without interruption. I have described the events of the war in the order of their occurrence, dividing my account into summers and winters.

2. The Thirty-Year Peace treaty that had been made after the fall of Euboea remained in force for fourteen years, but in the fifteenth year—when Chrysis was in the forty-eighth year of her priesthood at Argos, when Aenesias was ephor in Sparta, and when Pythodorus still had four months remaining of his archonship in Athens, in the tenth month after the Battle of Potidaea and at the start of spring*—somewhat more than three hundred armed Thebans under the command of the boeotarchs* Pythangelus, son of Phyleides, and Diemporus, son of Onetoridas, entered Plataea, a Boeotian town that was an ally of Athens, during the first watch of the night. [2] They were invited in by certain Plataeans—Naucleides and his supporters—who now opened one of the town gates, their motive being to gain power for themselves by eliminating those of their fellow citizens who were their political opponents and by aligning the city with Thebes.

[3] The arrangements were made through Eurymachus, son of Leontiades, one of the foremost men of Thebes. The Thebans could see that war was coming and they wanted to annex Plataea, which had always been at odds with them, while there was still a state of peace and before war had actually broken out.* Hence it was quite easy for them to slip in because no guard had yet been posted. [4] When they reached the agora, they halted,* but instead of following the advice of those who had invited them in—that they should immediately get to work and head straight for the houses of their enemies—they proposed to make proclamations of friendship in an attempt to settle things amicably. So the herald issued a proclamation to the effect that anyone who wanted to see the city in alliance with Thebes, in a return to the traditional constitution under which all Boeotians had once lived, should come and take a stand alongside them. They thought this would make it easy for them to bring the city over to their side.

3. When the Plataeans realized that there were Thebans inside their walls and that all of a sudden the city had been occupied, they were terrified, and, because they greatly overestimated the number of Thebans who had come in—the darkness made it impossible for them to see clearly—they came to terms and accepted the proposals without offering any resistance, especially since the Thebans were not acting violently. [2] But it seems that in the course of the negotiations they saw how few Thebans there were, and they reckoned that if they attacked they would easily overpower their opponents, since most Plataeans had no desire to break off from Athens. [3] So they decided to make the attempt. They assembled by breaking through the shared walls between their houses, to avoid being seen on the streets. They brought carts (without their draft animals) into the streets to serve as barricades and in general equipped themselves in every way that seemed likely to be of use in the present situation. [4] When everything was as ready as possible, they waited for the hour when it was still dark but dawn was imminent, and emerged from their houses to attack the Thebans. The idea was to attack not in daylight, when the Thebans would be more confident and conditions would be equal for both sides, but in darkness, when the Thebans would be more frightened and handicapped by the Plataeans' familiarity with the city. So the Plataeans launched a surprise attack and quickly became engaged in close combat.

4. When the Thebans realized that they had been tricked, they closed ranks and set about repelling the attacks wherever they occurred. [2] Two or three times they beat them back, but then the Plataeans fell on them with a terrific roar, while the women and household slaves were simultaneously screaming and yelling at them from the houses as they hurled stones and roof tiles. It had also rained heavily throughout the night, and what with one thing and another the Thebans took fright. They broke and fled through the city, but in the mud and the darkness (this was happening at the end of the month) many of them were killed. They were unacquainted with the routes through the city that would lead to safety, and they were being chased by people who were familiar with the place and could stop them from escaping. [3] Also, one of the Plataeans closed the gate by which they had entered, and which was the only one that was open, by inserting the butt of a javelin into the bar as a replacement for the bolt-pin, so that there was no way out even there.

[4] As the Thebans were chased through the city, some of them climbed up to the top of the circuit wall and threw themselves over

the edge, usually to their deaths. Others found themselves at an unguarded gate, and when a woman gave them an axe they cut through the bar without being caught and made their way out of the city; but they were soon detected, and only a few escaped this way. Others were killed here and there throughout the city. [5] But the most sizable group, which had substantially retained its coherence, burst into a large building that adjoined the city wall. The door of the building happened to be unlocked, and they thought it was a city gate that gave directly onto the outside. [6] When the Plataeans saw that the Thebans were trapped there, they were unsure whether they should set fire to the building and burn them alive or deal with them in some other way. [7] Eventually, these men, and all the other Thebans who had survived and were roaming around the city, came to terms with the Plataeans and surrendered themselves and their weapons unconditionally to them.

[8] That is how the Thebans in Plataea fared. **5.** The rest of their troops were supposed to have arrived in full force while it was still night, in case things went badly for those inside the city, and they were on their way when they heard what had happened. They set out to the rescue, [2] but the distance between Plataea and Thebes is eight miles or so and the rainfall that night slowed them down, because the Asopus river was in spate and almost unfordable. [3] They marched on through the rain and made the difficult crossing of the river, but arrived too late, after some of their comrades had been killed and the rest were being taken alive. [4] When they became aware of what had happened, they considered attacking the Plataeans who were outside the city. As is inevitable when trouble falls without warning in peacetime, there were people still out in the countryside, and equipment too. The idea was that they could use any of these people they captured in an exchange of prisoners if it turned out that some of their men had been taken alive.

[5] That was their plan, but before they had put it into effect, the Plataeans, who suspected that something of this kind would happen

and were afraid for their people outside, sent a herald to the Thebans. They said that what the Thebans had done in attempting to seize their city at a time when a treaty was in force was immoral, and warned them to harm nothing outside the walls, or else they would kill those of their men who had fallen into their hands; however, if they withdrew from their territory, they would turn the prisoners over to them. [6] This is the Theban version of the herald's message, and they say that the Plataeans swore an oath to that effect, but the Plataeans disagree.* According to them, they did not promise to hand the men over right away, but only if talks took place first and some accommodation was reached, and they deny that they swore an oath. [7] Anyway, the Thebans withdrew from Plataean territory without damaging it in any way, and the Plataeans quickly brought their things in from the countryside—and then immediately killed the prisoners. There were 180 of them, including Eurymachus, the man with whom the traitors had dealt. **6.** Then the Plataeans sent a messenger to Athens to tell them what had happened. They returned the bodies of the dead to the Thebans under a truce and organized matters in the city as they saw fit given the circumstances.

[2] The Athenians had been promptly informed about what was going on in Plataea. They immediately arrested all the Boeotians who were in Attica and sent a herald to the Plataeans, with orders to tell them to do nothing drastic with their Theban prisoners until they themselves had considered what to do with them. They had not heard that the prisoners were already dead, [3] because the first messenger had set out for Athens just as the Theban incursion began, and the second left just after the Thebans had been defeated and captured. They were completely unaware of anything that had happened subsequently, so they sent the message in ignorance, and it was only when the herald arrived that he found that the prisoners had been killed. [4] After this, the Athenians marched to Plataea, brought in provisions, installed a garrison, and evacuated the least able-bodied men along with the women and children.

7. After this action at Plataea, which was a blatant violation of the treaty, the Athenians got ready for war, as did the Lacedaemonians and their allies. Both sides were planning to send embassies to the King and to other barbarians, in the hope of securing additional help from somewhere, and both sides were trying to win alliances with Greek states that were outside their sphere of influence. [2] The Lacedaemonians also ordered the cities in Italy and Sicily that had chosen their side to build two hundred ships, with each city contributing a certain number according to its size. These ships would supplement those the Lacedaemonians already had in the Peloponnese and bring the total size of their navy up to five hundred. Each city was told to collect a specified amount of money as well, but otherwise to do nothing, and to allow the Athenians into their harbors only one ship at a time until everything was ready. [3] And the Athenians reviewed their existing alliance and made a point of sending ambassadors to the places that surrounded the Peloponnese—Corcyra, Cephallenia, Acarnania, Zacynthos—because if the friendship of these places was solid they hoped to reduce the Peloponnese by encirclement.

8. In short, there was nothing small-scale about either side's plans. Both were gripped by war fever, which should occasion no surprise because the high point of enthusiasm for a project always comes at the beginning, and at that time there were plenty of young men in both Sparta and Athens to whom war was not unwelcome because they had no experience of it. All the rest of Greece was in suspense over the clash between the two leading states. [2] Many prophecies were spoken and many oracles chanted by the priests responsible for oracular archives throughout the Greek world, not just in the cities that were going to fight. [3] Moreover, shortly before this Delos was shaken by an earthquake, when it had never experienced one before within living memory. This was declared—and was widely believed—to portend the future, and every other event of this kind was carefully scrutinized. [4] People felt far more favor for the Lacedaemonians, not least because they proclaimed their purpose to be the liberation of Greece. Every individual and every city enthusiastically did their best to support Sparta both verbally and practically, and each man thought that the cause had stalled whenever he was not assisting in person. [5] This just goes to show how widespread hostility was toward Athens, with some wanting to be free of its empire and others afraid of being absorbed by it. **9.** At the outset of the war, then, this was the state of preparation of both sides and these were their prevalent attitudes.

Each side had the following states as allies when they went to war. [2] On the Lacedaemonian side was the whole of the Peloponnese within the Isthmus* except for Argos and Achaea, both of which were neutral (the Pellenians were the only Achaeans to join the conflict on the Lacedaemonian side right away, but later they all did); outside the Isthmus, their allies were Megara, Boeotia, Locris, Phocis, Ambracia, Leucas, and Anactorium. [3] Of these states, some provided ships (Corinth, Megara, Sicyon, Pellene, Elis, Ambracia, Leucas), some provided cavalry (Boeotia, Phocis, Locris), and all the rest provided infantry. [4] That was the Lacedaemonian alliance. The Athenian allies were Chios, Lesbos, Plataea, the Messenians of Naupactus,* most of the Acarnanians, Corcyra, Zacynthos, and the tribute-paying cities in the following regions: coastal Caria, the Dorian neighbors of Caria, Ionia, the Hellespont, the Thraceward region, the islands to the east of the Peloponnese and Crete, and all the other islands except Melos and Thera. [5] Of these states, some provided ships (Chios, Lesbos, Corcyra), while the rest provided land forces and money. These were the allies and forces that each side had for the war.

10. Immediately after the Plataean episode, the Lacedaemonians sent messengers around the Peloponnese and to their allies outside, ordering them to raise an army and whatever might be needed in the way of supplies for an expedition abroad, since they intended to invade Attica. [2] When they were all set, two-thirds of each state's forces congregated at a prearranged time at the Isthmus. [3] Once the whole army had assembled, the Spartan king Archidamus, the commander-in-chief of this expedition, convened a meeting of the generals from all the states and those of the highest rank who most deserved to be present, and addressed them along the following lines:†

11. "Peloponnesians and allies, our fathers fought many campaigns in the Peloponnese itself and elsewhere, and the oldest of us here are not unfamiliar with war. Nevertheless, this is the greatest and best-equipped force with which we have ever set out. But then, even though we'll be campaigning with the largest and finest army we have ever had, we're now proceeding against a state that's at the height of its power. [2] It is our duty, therefore, to show ourselves to be no worse than our fathers and to live up to the reputation we ourselves have earned. This endeavor of ours has generated excitement throughout Greece. Everyone is watching; they wish us well because of their loathing for the Athenians, and they hope that our plans succeed.

[3] "You may think, since we're attacking with superior numbers, that there's little risk of the enemy giving battle, but despite how well prepared and equipped we are, we mustn't proceed with any less care. On the contrary, officers and soldiers from every state must constantly expect to find their contingent in danger. [4] War is an uncertain business, and attacks usually take place without warning and on impulse. Often a smaller number of men who are driven by fear fight better than a larger number, who are taken by surprise because they'd been expecting the opposition to be easy prey. [5] In enemy territory one must campaign with a bold heart, but with enough fear to take realistic precautions. That way, one is more confident in attacking the enemy and safer when being assailed.

[6] "So far from being incapable of defending itself, the state we're going against is very well prepared in every respect. We should therefore certainly expect them to give battle. If they haven't already set out, anticipating our arrival, they'll do so when they see us in their territory despoiling their land and destroying their property. [7] Fury overcomes everyone when, right before their eyes, they suddenly see themselves suffering as they've never suffered before; and it's when

they're least able to reason that they're most likely to rush impulsively into action. [8] The Athenians are even more likely than others to do this, since they think they have the right to rule others and to attack and despoil the territory of others, but they don't expect to see the same thing happening to theirs. [9] Bearing in mind, then, the strength of the city you're marching against, and understanding that the outcome will have a huge effect, for good or ill, on your own and you ancestors' reputations, follow where you are led, consider nothing more important than discipline and vigilance, and respond promptly to commands. There's nothing more beautiful, and no better defense against danger, than the sight of a large body of men acting as a single, disciplined unit."

12. That was the substance of Archidamus's speech, and after dissolving the meeting the first thing he did was send the Spartiate Melesippus, son of Diacritus, to the Athenians, to see if they might be more inclined to make concessions now that the Peloponnesians were undeniably on their way. [2] But the Athenians refused to allow Melesippus into the city, let alone into the assembly, because they had earlier been persuaded by Pericles not to receive heralds or envoys once the Peloponnesians had taken to the field. So they sent him packing without giving him a hearing. They told him to be clear of their border by the end of the day, and said that from then on, if the Peloponnesians wanted anything, they should send envoys only after pulling back to their own territory. They also had Melesippus escorted out of Attica, to make sure that he had no contact with anyone. [3] When he reached the border and was about to part from his escort, he said just this as he set off: "This day will be the beginning of much misery for the Greeks." [4] When Archidamus found out, on Melesippus's return to the camp, that the Athenians were still refusing to make any concessions, he broke camp and advanced with his army into Athenian territory. [5] The Boeotians sent their own contingent, including their cavalry, to join the Peloponnesians on this campaign, while the rest of their infantry went to Plataea and laid waste the farmland.

13. Pericles, son of Xanthippus, was one of the ten Athenian generals, and when it was clear that the invasion was imminent—that is, while the Peloponnesians were still mustering at the Isthmus and while they were on their way but had not yet reached Attica—it occurred to him that because Archidamus was a guest-friend of his,* there was a possibility that he might bypass his farms without ravaging them, either as a personal favor, or because he had been ordered to do so by the Lacedaemonians in an attempt to blacken his name, just as it had been on his account that they had earlier ordered the Athenians to dispel the curse.* He therefore told the Athenians in the assembly that although Archidamus was his guest-friend, this had never done the state any harm, and that in case the enemy excluded his farms and buildings from their general devastation of the countryside, he was giving them up and making them over to the state, so that there would be no suspicion of him on this account.

[2] For the short term, he gave them the same advice as before: they should get ready for war and bring their property in from the countryside; they should not make sorties and engage the enemy, but should remain inside the city and stand guard; and they should make ready their fleet, which was where their strength lay, and keep their allies well in hand, because, as he explained, it was the allies and the revenue they provided that made them strong. Usually, he said, success in war was a result of good judgment and reserves of money. [3] They should feel confident, therefore, because the city's average annual income from the allies was 600 talents in tribute,* not counting other sources of revenue, and he pointed out that there was still at that time 6,000 talents in coined silver remaining on the acropolis. This fund had peaked at 9,700 talents, but money had been withdrawn from it to pay for building work—the Propylaea on the acropolis and other buildings—and for the siege of Potidaea. [4] In addition, there was on the acropolis uncoined gold and silver in the form of offerings made by private individuals and the state to the gods, plus all the sacred equipment used for processions and contests, plus the spoils

taken from the Persians and other dedications of the same kind—all of which came to at least 500 talents. [5] Then he added the not inconsiderable amounts of money held by other sanctuaries, which would be available for their use, and he said that were they ever denied all other sources of income, they could use the gold plates of Athena herself. He explained that the statue* had on it pure gold weighing 40 talents, all of which was removable. They could use these treasures to protect the city, he said, but they would have to replace them later with at least the same amount.* [6] So he felt they need have no worries about their finances. As regards their military resources, he said that they had 13,000 hoplites, not counting the 16,000 who were stationed in the hill forts or manning the city's fortifications.

[7] That was how many there were on guard duty at the time of the enemy's first invasion; they consisted of the oldest and youngest men of military age, and all the metics of hoplite status. This many men were needed because the Phaleric wall* was a little over four miles long up to the city's circuit wall, five miles of the circuit wall itself was under guard (some of it, the section between the long wall and the Phaleric wall, being unguarded), and the Long Walls to Piraeus, of which the outer one was guarded, were four and a half miles long. Then the total circumference of the wall around Piraeus and Munychia* was almost seven miles, and half of that was guarded.

[8] He also reported that they had a cavalry force of 1,200 (the number included the mounted archers), 1,600 archers, and 300 seaworthy triremes. [9] These were the military resources available to Athens—and the numbers in each case are a conservative estimate—on the eve of the first Peloponnesian invasion and the start of the war. And Pericles concluded with other arguments, those he customarily used to demonstrate that they would prevail in the war. **14.** After listening to his speech, the Athenians obediently brought their families and all their household fixtures and furnishings in from the countryside; they even took the timbers from the houses. Their livestock and beasts of burden they sent over to Euboea and the offshore islands.

[2] But this upheaval was hard for them, because the majority of the population had always been accustomed to living outside the city.

15. This way of life had, from very early times, been more typical of the Athenians than of others. From the time of Cecrops and the first kings down to the reign of Theseus,* the population of Attica always lived in separate settlements, each with its own town hall and officials, and as long as there was no common danger they did not go and confer with the king, but each community managed its own affairs and deliberated on its own. In fact, they occasionally even went to war against the king, as the Eleusinians (with the help of Eumolpus) did against Erechtheus.* [2] But when Theseus became king, he used his power and intelligence to reorganize the region in various ways. In particular, he abolished the councils and offices of the rest of the towns and formed the entire population into the single state that it is today by creating a single council chamber and town hall.* Although the people lived on their own land as before, he made them regard Athens as the capital city, and since they were now making financial contributions to Athens, it became the great city that Theseus bequeathed to subsequent generations. It is because of what he did that even today the Athenians celebrate the state-funded Festival of Union in honor of Athena.

[3] Before the time of Theseus the city consisted of what is now the acropolis and the area roughly to the south of it. [4] There is good evidence for this: the sanctuaries even of other gods, let alone Athena, are either located on the acropolis itself or, if not, tend to be found close to this part of the city—for instance, the sanctuaries of Olympian Zeus, of Pythian Apollo, of Earth, and of Dionysus in the Marshes. (It is in honor of Dionysus in the Marshes that the more ancient Dionysia festival is celebrated on the twelfth day of the month Anthesterion,* which is the practice of the Ionians as well even today, since they are descendants of the Athenians.) There are also other ancient sanctuaries in this area. [5] And the spring—the one that is now called Nine Springs after it was fashioned in this way by the tyrants, but which

long ago, before the waters were enclosed, was called Fairwaters—was used in times past for the most important purposes, since it was nearby, and even today, because of this tradition, it is this water that is customarily used before weddings and for other religious ceremonies. [6] Moreover, because the acropolis was where the ancient settlement was located, even today the Athenians refer to it as "the city."

16. So living in independent settlements throughout Attica was the Athenian norm, and even after they were united the practice continued and most people were still country folk, living there with all the members of their households, not just in times long past but subsequently as well, right up to the time of the current war. That is why they found the relocation hard, and especially so because their homes had only recently recovered from the Persian invasion. [2] It was a sad and miserable experience for them to leave their homes and sanctuaries, which had always been theirs, passed down from generation to generation, thanks to the way society had been organized long ago; the prospect of changing their way of life and leaving behind what each of them felt to be the equivalent of his native city made them miserable.

17. So they came to Athens, but only a few had houses there, or friends or relatives with whom they could stay. Most people squatted in the vacant spaces of the city, or in the sanctuaries of the gods and the hero shrines, except the acropolis, the Eleusinium, and any other sanctuaries that were securely closed. Despite the fact that occupation of the Pelargicum (as this plot of land is called) under the acropolis was forbidden by a curse and proscribed by the tail end of an oracle from Delphi ("The Pelargicum is better left unworked"), in the present emergency it became home to some of the refugees. [2] And it seems to me that the oracle was fulfilled, but not at all as people might have expected. That is, the disasters that struck the city were not caused by the illegal occupation of the Pelargicum, but the occupation was made necessary because of the war, and, although the oracle does not mention war, it foresaw that someday the place would be inhabited at a time of trouble. [3] Many of the refugees even set themselves up in the towers of the city walls or wherever they could find space, because the city could not cope with the influx of all these people. Later, in fact, they parceled out the space between the Long Walls and most of Piraeus, and took up residence there. [4] At the same time, the Athenians continued to apply themselves to matters relating to the war: they mobilized some of their allies and fitted out a hundred ships for an expedition to the Peloponnese.

[5] That was the state of the Athenians' preparations, **18.** but meanwhile the Peloponnesian army was advancing. The first place they came to in Attica was Oenoe, which they intended to use as the entry point for the invasion. After making camp, they got ready to assault the wall by escalade and other means. [2] Oenoe, on the border between Attica and Boeotia, was a walled town, used by the Athenians as an outpost in times of war. So the Peloponnesians were making the preliminary arrangements for their assault and used up time there in other ways. [3] Archidamus was censured for this. He was held to have been weak during the buildup to the war and favorably disposed toward the Athenians, since he was not expressing enthusiasm about going to war. He was also maligned for the slow assembling of the army at the Isthmus and the leisurely progress of the rest of the march, but the main contributory factor was the holdup at Oenoe. [4] The Athenians used this time to bring property in from the countryside and the Peloponnesians felt that they could have attacked quickly and caught everything before it was safely inside the city, if it had not been for his tardiness. [5] So the camp seethed with anger toward Archidamus, but he continued to restrain the army, because, it is said, he was expecting that the Athenians would be unwilling to see their farmland ruined and would make some concessions while it was still intact.

19. But the assaults on Oenoe were unsuccessful, even though they tried everything, and the Athenians made no overtures to them at all, so they set out from there and invaded Attica. The invasion, with the army commanded by the Spartan king Archidamus, son of Zeuxidamus, took place about eighty days after the business at Plataea, in the summer, when the cereal crops were ripe. [2] In the first phase, they made camp and set about destroying crops near Eleusis and on the Thriasian Plain; they also routed some Athenian cavalrymen at the Rheiti lakes.* Then they advanced through Cropia,* with Mount Aegaleos to their right, until they reached Acharnae, the largest of the "demes" of Attica, as they are called. They halted there, made camp, and spent a long time destroying crops.

20. The reason Archidamus lingered at Acharnae with his forces in formation, as though they were going to fight, but did not go down to the plain during this invasion, is said to have been [2] that he hoped that the Athenians, who had an abundant stock of men of fighting age and were singularly well prepared for war, would find it impossible to do nothing while their land was ravaged and might sally out against him. [3] So since they did not offer resistance at Eleusis or the Thriasian Plain, he stationed himself at Acharnae to see if he could draw them out. [4] He found the land there suitable for encampment, and also, with three thousand citizens,† the Acharnians formed a good portion of the Athenian population,* and he thought that rather than tolerate the destruction of their property, they would rouse everyone to fight. And if the Athenians did not sally out against him during this invasion, in the future he could be less worried about depredating the plain and advancing right up to the city itself, because once the Acharnians had lost their own property they would be less inclined to face danger on behalf of everyone else's, and that would create a division in Athenian policy. [5] These were Archidamus's reasons for stationing himself at Acharnae.

21. As long as the army was at Eleusis and the Thriasian Plain, the Athenians remained hopeful that they would come no nearer. They remembered how, during the invasion of Attica fourteen years earlier by the Spartan king Pleistoanax, the son of Pausanias, he had brought his army as far as Eleusis and Thria but had stopped there and then

retreated.* (It was this retreat that led to his banishment from Sparta, because he was believed to have been bribed.) [2] But the sight of the enemy army at Acharnae, only about seven miles from the city, was more than they could endure. Not surprisingly, they found it horrible to be faced with the devastation of their land. This was outside the experience of the younger generation—and older people had witnessed it only during the Persian invasion—and they, especially the young men, felt they should go out and fight rather than let it continue. [3] Groups formed and arguments raged, with some insisting that they should go out and fight and others arguing for nonengagement. The keepers of oracular archives chanted oracles of all kinds, which people eagerly accepted, since there was something for everybody. And the Acharnians, arguing that they made up a good portion of the Athenian population and that it was their land that was being devastated, pushed particularly forcefully for engagement. So the city was in a complete and utter frenzy. The people were angry with Pericles; they remembered nothing of his earlier advice, but accused him of cowardice because he was not leading them out to battle as a general should, and held him responsible for all the bad things that were happening to them.

22. Pericles could see how difficult they were finding the situation and that they were not in the best frame of mind, but he was sure that his policy of not making sorties was the right one. So he refused to call an assembly or a military meeting, in case, when they met, anger overcame sound judgment and they went astray.* He focused on keeping the city safe and as calm as possible. [2] But he occasionally sent the cavalry out to deter advance squadrons of the Lacedaemonian army from attacking and damaging the fields near the city, and a brief cavalry engagement did take place at Phrygia,* in which one unit of Athenian horsemen and the Thessalian auxiliaries took on the Boeotian cavalry. The Athenians and Thessalians had the better of it—but then the Boeotians were reinforced by hoplites, and the Athenians and Thessalians were forced to flee, with a few lives lost. They recovered the bodies that same day, however, without the need for a truce, and the next day the Peloponnesians set up a trophy. [3] The forces that the Thessalians provided to aid the Athenians, in accordance with the long-standing treaty,* came from Larisa, Pharsalus, Peirasus, Crannon, Gyrtone, and Pherae. They were led by Polymedes and Aristonous from Larisa (each from one of the two main political factions), and by Meno from Pharsalus, but the other states also provided their own officers.

23. Faced with the Athenian refusal to come out and fight, the Peloponnesians left Acharnae and set about laying waste some other demes between Mount Parnes and Mount Brilessus.* [2] They were still there, on Athenian soil, when the Athenians dispatched the hundred ships they had been making ready, along with a thousand hoplites and four hundred archers, and sent them to raid the Peloponnese. The generals in command—Carcinus, son of Xenotimus; Proteas, son of Epicles; and Socrates, son of Antigenes—[3] set off with this force and sailed around the Peloponnesian coastline. As for the Peloponnesians, they stayed in Attica for as long as their provisions lasted and then returned home by a different route—through Boeotia—from the way they had come. As they passed Oropus,* they devastated the land known as Graea, which is farmed by the Oropians as subjects of Athens. On arriving back in the Peloponnese, the army was disbanded and they returned to their various states.

24. After the Peloponnesians had retired, the Athenians posted lookouts to watch over land and sea—a precaution they intended to maintain for the duration of the war. They also decided to create a special reserve fund of a thousand talents from the money that was stored on the acropolis; this was to be kept separate and not spent, while they drew on other funds for the war. The reserve fund was to be used solely for defending the city against a seaborne offensive by the enemy, and they prescribed the death penalty for anyone who proposed or put to the vote that it be used for any other purpose. [2] Along with this fund, they also created a reserve force of their hundred best triremes each year and selected the trierarchs for them, decreeing that this reserve fleet was only to be used along with the money and if it was required to counter the same threat.

25. The Athenians in the hundred ships that were carrying out raids in the Peloponnese were joined and aided by the Corcyreans with fifty ships and a few more of the allies from thereabouts. In the course of their voyage they caused damage in various places, and at Methone in Laconia they put men ashore and assaulted the wall, which was weak, and the town was ungarrisoned. [2] But coincidentally, the Spartiate Brasidas, son of Tellis,* was on patrol in the district, and when he was told what was going on he went to the defense of the town with a hundred hoplites. He charged through the Athenian forces, who were scattered across the countryside or facing the town wall, burst into Methone (losing a few of his men on the way), and saved the town. For this feat he became the first person in the war to receive a public commendation in Sparta.

[3] The Athenians put to sea and continued their voyage along the coast. They put in at Pheia in Elis, laid waste the land for two days, and won a battle against a force made up of three hundred elite soldiers from lowland Elis and some local Elean perioeci. [4] But then stormy winds began to blow and there was no shelter for ships where they were, so most of them went back on board and sailed around the headland—Fish Point, as it is called—to the harbor at Pheia, while the Messenians and others who had not been able to embark on the ships marched overland and took Pheia. [5] These men were subsequently picked up by the ships that had rounded the headland, and the Athenians then put to sea, abandoning Pheia, because by then the Elean army had arrived in force to secure the town. They continued to coast around the Peloponnese and wreak havoc here and there.

26. At the same time, the Athenians sent thirty ships north to raid Locris and protect Euboea. The general in command of this fleet was Cleopompus, son of Cleinias. [2] He put men ashore at several places on the coast, which were laid waste, captured Thronium and took hostages from it, and at Alope he won a battle against the Locrians who came to defend it.*

27. In the same summer the Athenians drove the Aeginetans—men, women, and children—off the island, alleging that they bore the most responsibility for the war. Besides, since Aegina is close to the Peloponnese, it seemed safer to have their own people occupy it, and indeed, before long, they sent settlers there. [2] The Lacedaemonians gave the Aeginetan refugees Thyreatis to live in and farm, not just because of their hostility to the Athenians, but because of the services the Aeginetans had rendered them at the time of the earthquake and the helot rebellion.* Thyreatis is a coastal district on the border between Argolis and Laconia. Not all the Aeginetans went to live there; some chose to go to various other places in Greece.

28. In the same summer, at the beginning of the lunar month (which seems to be the only time when this is possible), there was an eclipse of the sun in the afternoon. It was reduced to a crescent and some stars were visible, and then it became full again.* **29.** Also in the same summer, Nymphodorus, son of Pythes, an Abderite who had a great deal of influence with Sitalces (his wife was Nymphodorus's sister), was appointed by the Athenians to represent their interests in Abdera, although he had formerly been regarded as an enemy. The reason for this appointment and his summons to Athens was that the Athenians wanted to enter into an alliance with Sitalces, who was the son of Teres and a Thracian king. [2] Teres, Sitalces's father, was the first to extend the already large Odrysian kingdom farther into Thrace. For much of Thrace is occupied by independent peoples.

[3] This Teres has no connection with the Tereus who married Procne, the Athenian daughter of Pandion.* They do not even come from the same "Thrace." Tereus lived in Daulia; this is part of what we now know as Phocis, but in those days it was populated by Thracians. This is where the women lived who did what they did to Itys,* and in fact "the Daulian bird" is a common poetic name for the nightingale. Besides, it is unlikely that Pandion would have arranged a marriage

contract for his daughter—a marriage that was supposed to be of mutual benefit to both men—entailing a journey of many days to the Odrysians, rather than this shorter distance. In any case, Teres (not "Tereus") was the first really powerful Odrysian king. [4] And it was his son, Sitalces, with whom the Athenians were seeking an alliance, because they wanted him to help them gain the Thraceward region and the allegiance of Perdiccas.

[5] So after his visit to Athens, Nymphodorus negotiated the Athenian alliance with Sitalces and arranged for Sitalces's son, Sadocus, to be granted Athenian citizenship. He undertook to bring the war in Thrace to an end, and then to get Sitalces to send the Athenians a force of Thracian horsemen and peltasts. [6] He also reconciled Perdiccas with the Athenians and persuaded them to return Therme to him.* Perdiccas immediately joined forces with the Athenians and Phormio for a campaign against the Chalcidians. [7] And so the Thracian king, Sitalces, son of Teres, and the Macedonian king, Perdiccas, son of Alexander, became Athenian allies.

30. Meanwhile, the Athenians in the fleet of a hundred ships were still off the coast of the Peloponnese. They took Sollium, a small Corinthian town, and turned it and its land over to the Acarnanians of Palaerus for their exclusive use.* They also assaulted and took Astacus, where Evarchus was tyrant, and after driving him out they brought the place into their alliance. [2] Then they sailed to the island of Cephallenia, which capitulated without a fight. Cephallenia lies off Acarnania and Leucas and has four towns: Pale, Crane, Same, and Pronni. [3] Shortly after that the ships returned to Athens.

31. In the late summer of this year the Athenians raised a mass levy, metics as well as citizens, and invaded the Megarid. Pericles, son of Xanthippus, was the general in command. It so happened that the Athenians in the hundred ships who had been raiding the Peloponnese were in Aegina on their way home, and when they found out that the whole army from the city was in the Megarid they sailed over and joined them. [2] This was quite the largest army that the Athenians

ever had in the field all at once, because the city was still flourishing and had not yet suffered from the plague. There were at least ten thousand citizen hoplites (and apart from these, there were three thousand at Potidaea), who were joined for this invasion by at least three thousand metic hoplites, and then there was a considerable body of light-armed troops. After wreaking widespread havoc in the farmland, they returned to Athens. [3] Later in the war, the Athenians mounted further invasions of the Megarid every year, sometimes with cavalry and sometimes with the whole army, until they gained control of Nisaea.

32. Toward the end of the summer, the Athenians built a fortress on Atalante, a previously uninhabited island that lies off Opuntian Locris. The point was to prevent pirates from sailing from Opus and elsewhere in Locris and inflicting damage on Euboea.

These were the events of this summer after the Peloponnesian withdrawal from Attica.

33. The following winter, the Acarnanian Evarchus, wanting to get back to Astacus, persuaded the Corinthians to sail with forty ships and 1,500 hoplites to restore him to power there, and he added some mercenaries whose wages he paid himself. The expeditionary force was commanded by Euphamidas, son of Aristonymus; Timoxenus, son of Timocrates; and Eumachus, son of Chrysis, [2] and their mission was successful. There were some other places on the Acarnanian coast that they wanted to get on their side, but their attempts failed and they sailed back home. [3] As they passed Cephallenia, they landed in the territory of Crane, but the Cranians tricked them and suddenly attacked after an agreement had been made between them. The Corinthians lost a few men, but after a struggle they managed to put to sea and return home.

34. In the same winter, the Athenians held the traditional public funeral for the first to die fighting in the current war. The procedure is as follows: [2] Two days before the funeral, a tent is erected in which

the bones of the dead are put on display, and people bring what they want in the way of offerings for their loved ones. [3] On the day of the procession, chests of cypress wood are carried by carts, one chest for each tribe, with each man's bones in his tribe's chest. And a single bier, covered but empty, is included in the procession for the missing, whose bodies could not be found and collected. [4] Anyone who wants to, citizen or foreigner, can join the procession, and the womenfolk, those who are relatives of the dead, do their lamenting at the graveside. [5] The chests are destined for the national burial ground, which is in the fairest of the city's suburbs, and is where they always bury their war dead. (An exception was made for those who died in the Battle of Marathon: their bravery was judged so exceptional that they were buried on the spot.) [6] Once the remains are covered with earth, a man is chosen by the state, someone especially distinguished and judged to be highly intelligent, and he delivers a suitable eulogy for them. After that, the people depart. [7] That is how the war dead are buried, and they followed this practice throughout the war, whenever it was needed.*
[8] Anyway, for these first casualties, it was Pericles, son of Xanthippus, who was chosen to deliver the speech. At the appropriate moment, he stepped forward from the tomb, mounted a platform that had been raised so that he could be heard by as many as possible of the people who had gathered, and addressed them along the following lines:

35. "Most of those who have spoken here in the past commend the person who added this speech to the ritual, on the ground that it's good for a speech to be delivered over men who fell on the field of battle. But I should have thought that when it is by their actions that men have proved their valor we are required to show them honor by *our* actions—the kind of thing that you can see we're doing today, by laying on this public funeral for them. Then the virtues of many wouldn't be in danger of depending for their credibility on a single man, who may speak well or badly. [2] For it isn't easy to find the right balance in a speech when even people's grasp of the truth is insecure. Those of you who are aware of the facts and were well disposed to the dead might think that any demonstration falls short of what they want to hear and the truth as they know it, while those who are unacquainted with the facts might, through envy, suspect some exaggeration, if they hear of deeds that are beyond their own abilities. After all, praise of others is tolerated by people only as long as they can imagine themselves capable of doing what they're hearing about; anything that goes beyond that immediately makes them envious and skeptical. [3] But since our ancestors approved of this and thought it a noble practice, I too must follow tradition and do my best to satisfy the wishes and expectations of every one of you.

36. "I shall start with our ancestors, since it is right, as well as appropriate for an occasion like this, that they should be given the honor of being recalled to mind first. For our land has always been inhabited by the same people from one generation to another, right up to the present day,* and its freedom is the bequest to us of their virtues. [2] But they aren't the only people who deserve our praise. So do our fathers, even more so, because in addition to what they inherited, by their efforts they acquired our great empire and left it to us, the present generation. [3] Then we ourselves, who are still alive today and middle-aged or thereabouts, have substantially increased the empire and have made the city in all respects as self-sufficient as it might be for both war and peace. [4] I don't want to hold forth about matters that you all know, so I shall pass over in silence the military exploits by which our various possessions were acquired, and I won't mention the times when we or our fathers resolutely repelled the attacks of our enemies, both barbarian and Greek.* But I shall first describe the principles that enabled them to get us to where we are, and the institutions and culture that allowed our city to become great, and only then shall I go on to praise these men here. I think that such a speech is fitting for the occasion, and that everyone here, whether citizen or foreigner, will profit from hearing it.

37. "Our political system doesn't emulate the institutions of our neighbors. We are a model for others rather than imitators of them.

The system is called a democracy because it's organized in the interest not of the few but of the many, but, while every citizen is equal before the law in his private disputes, a man is preferred for public office because he's thought to deserve it for his distinction in some respect, not just because it's his turn. What counts is merit rather than social status. Nor, again, is poverty an obstacle to serving the public good: if one has some good to do the city, humble status is no bar. [2] A generous and tolerant spirit guides our lives as citizens. We don't look askance at our neighbors' daily practices, as others do, nor do we get angry with them if they do as they please; we don't even put on a disapproving face, which is hurtful even if not actually injurious. [3] In our personal interactions with one another we avoid giving offense, and in our public lives we are prevented from doing wrong above all by fear, which makes us obey the elected officials and the laws, especially those that are designed to protect the injured, but also those that may be unwritten, but which it is, by common consent, shameful to break.

38. "Moreover, we offer very many occasions to rest from our labors and refresh our spirits, such as the athletic and sacrificial festivals we put on throughout the year; and at a personal level too there are our attractive furnishings, which afford us pleasure and banish distress day after day. [2] The greatness of our city means that the produce of all the world comes into it, so that goods from other lands are just as much ours to enjoy as those that are found here.

39. "We also differ from our enemies in our approach to military matters, in the following respects: We allow our city to be open to the world; we never expel foreigners in order to prevent them from learning or observing things that, if unconcealed, an enemy would benefit from seeing. The reason is that we rely on our own courage in action more than on schemes or trickery. Consider the sphere of education as well: *they* undergo an arduous training from a very early age that's supposed to turn out real men; in our lives, however, we know nothing of such harsh restraints, but we're no less ready to face dangers as great as those they face. [2] I can prove this. First, when the

Lacedaemonians invade our land they come not unaided but with all their allies; second, when we mount an invasion, despite being unsupported by allies we generally find it easy to prevail, even though we're on foreign soil and going against people who are fighting for their homes and families. [3] Moreover, none of our enemies has yet encountered all our available forces at once, not just because we have the navy to maintain, but also because we send our land forces to many different places. Suppose a battle takes place between our enemies and a proportion of our forces: if they defeat some of us, they flatter themselves that they've repelled all of us, and if they lose they claim to have lost to our full strength. [4] And since our approach is easygoing rather than based on arduous training, and we're prepared to face danger with courage that's habitual rather than instilled by rules and regulations, the result is that we don't suffer in advance from troubles in the future, and when we're actually faced with them we turn out to be no less courageous than those whose labors have been continuous. In all these respects our city deserves to be admired—and there are more reasons besides.

40. "We are devotees of refinement with frugality and of knowledge without effeminacy. We treat wealth as something that creates opportunities for action rather than as a reason for boasting, and poverty not as something that a person need be ashamed to admit; what's shameful, rather, is not actively trying to escape it. [2] Responsibility for affairs of state is combined in the same persons with responsibility for domestic affairs, and even those whose primary focus is work still have a thorough understanding of affairs of state. In fact, we are the only people who regard a man who plays no part in public life not as apolitical but as useless, and we ourselves are capable either of formulating sound policy or at least of making sound assessments of it, since it's not discussion that we regard as detrimental to action, but failing to be informed by discussion before proceeding to appropriate action. [3] For another respect in which we differ is that we combine great courage with thinking about our undertakings; elsewhere, courage comes from ignorance and reasoning breeds hesitation. But true mental courage would rightly be attributed to those who recognize with perfect clarity what is to be feared and what is to be welcomed, and who, with the help of that knowledge, don't flinch from danger.

[4] "Our practice when it comes to doing good is also quite different from what's normal, because we make friends by doing favors, not by receiving them. A benefactor's friendship is more dependable because he keeps the feeling of gratitude alive by his kindness to the beneficiary, whereas a beneficiary, who owes gratitude in return for the favor, is less committed to the friendship, because he's aware that the good he'll be doing in return isn't a favor but the repayment of a debt. [5] And we're the only ones who fearlessly do good to others, because we do so in the confidence born of our freedom, not after working out what's expedient for us.

41. "I maintain, then, that Athens as a whole serves as an example for Greece, and it seems to me that, at an individual level, any one of us has the self-sufficiency to adapt himself to the most varied forms of action with the utmost versatility and grace. [2] And that this isn't merely boastful speaking for the occasion, but the actual truth is demonstrated by the city's power itself, because it was precisely these qualities that enabled us to acquire that power. [3] Athens is the only city today that, when tested, proves greater than its reputation. It's the only city that gives an attacking enemy no reason to feel bad because of the caliber of the people who are making him suffer, and gives the subjects of its empire no reason to reproach themselves for being ruled by unworthy people. [4] Because of the conclusive evidence that we provide, and because our power is certainly far from unwitnessed, we will be admired not just by people alive today, but by those to come as well. There'll be no need of a Homer to praise us nor of any poet whose words may give temporary pleasure, but whose interpretation of the facts will be compromised by the truth—no need, because we've compelled the entirety of sea and land to be accessible to our daring, and have everywhere established everlasting memorials of our enmity and our friendship. [5] This, then, is the character of the state for which these men here fought and died. As honorable men, they didn't think it right that it should be lost to us, and every one of us who remains should be willing to suffer on its behalf.

42. "The particular reasons why I've dwelt at length on the greatness of our city are, first, to show that there's more at stake for us in this contest than there is for those who lack these advantages, and, second, to provide unmistakable evidence to validate the eulogy that I'm giving today for these men. [2] In fact, the most important elements of my eulogy have already been mentioned, in the sense that it was the virtues of these men and of others like them that equipped the city with the qualities I've been glorifying, and there are few other Greeks for whom it would turn out to be the case, as it is for them, that their deeds measure up to what's said of them.

"In my opinion, the manner of their deaths proves that they had the virtue that is proper to men, whether this was its first manifestation or its final confirmation. [3] Even if some were flawed in other respects, we should in all fairness focus our attention on the virile courage they displayed fighting the enemy for the country of their birth. They erased the bad with the good, and the good they did collectively outweighs any harm they did as individuals. [4] Not one of these men weakened because he preferred the continued enjoyment of wealth; not one of them delayed facing danger because he hoped that one day he might escape poverty and even become rich. No, taking the punishment of our enemies to be a more desirable goal and also regarding no peril as more glorious than this, they were willing to risk their lives to be avenged on their enemies, and to regard wealth as merely an aspiration, consigning future prosperity to the dim realm of hope and expecting to rely on themselves for what was now right before their eyes in the real world. Judging that the task at hand required fighting and suffering rather than† surviving by surrendering, they ran from the disgrace of what people might say, but stood firm on the field of action with their lives on the line. And so in the briefest instant assigned them by fate, at the height of their glory but not of their fear, they surrendered their lives.

43. "That is what these men were like, a credit to their city. The rest of you should adopt an attitude toward the enemy that is no less courageous than theirs, while praying for a safer outcome. Don't consider the benefits of this attitude merely by talking about them—after all, anyone could talk to you at length about the advantages of resisting the enemy, even though you know them well enough—but make it your actual daily practice to open your eyes to the potency of the city and become its lovers. And when you are convinced of its greatness, remember that it was made so by men of courage, men who knew their duty and were determined not to shame themselves on the field of action. Even when they failed in some venture, they did not on that account think it right to deprive the city of their courage but continued to support it with the finest loan they could offer. [2] Collectively, they gave up their lives, but individually they gained ageless praise and the most conspicuous tomb—by which I don't mean the one in which they are lying, but the one in which their glory lives on, never to be forgotten, whenever an occasion arises for speech or action. [3] For the whole world is the tomb of famous men, and they are commemorated not merely by an inscription on their tombstone in their homeland, but even in lands that have no connection with them there resides in each and every person an unwritten memorial not so much of their achievements, but of their spirit.

[4] "You must now imitate these men. Judging freedom to be happiness and courage to be freedom, don't be mere spectators of war and its dangers. [5] It is not the unfortunate, those without hope of improvement, who have good reasons to be unsparing of their lives, but people for whom, as long as they live, a change for the worse is still a possibility, and who have the most to lose should they fail. [6] For a man of courage, you see, the degradation entailed by cowardice is more painful than a death that arrives unnoticed when he's at the height of his powers and filled with hope for his country.

44. "That is why to the parents of the dead who are here today I offer not commiseration but comfort. You know† that you were born into a world of change. Good fortune attends those who experience the most honorable of deaths, as these men did—or in your case the most honorable of sorrows—and for whom the period of their happiness is coextensive with their lives.† [2] I am sure that it will be hard to convince you of this, since you'll often be reminded of your sons by others' enjoyment of the good fortune that once was yours; and people don't grieve over good things they lose before they're familiar with them, but over those that are taken away after they've become used to having them. [3] Some of you are still of an age to have children and you must draw strength from the prospect of further sons, both because, at a personal level, those who come after will help you forget those who are no more, and because you'll be doing the city good. The city will benefit in two ways, by the replenishment of the population and by increased security—the latter because it's only if people are on a par with others and might possibly be risking the lives of their sons that they can contribute fairly and justly to our deliberations. [4] As for those of you who are too old to have more children, I would ask you to count as gain the greater part of your lives, the time when you enjoyed good fortune, and to bear in mind that the remaining part will not be long. Draw comfort also from the fame of your sons here. The only thing that never ages is love of honor, and it's not making money, as some say, but being honored that gladdens one's declining years.

45. "Now, it's clear to me that those of you here today who are the sons or brothers of these men are facing a great trial, because everyone tends to praise the dead, and because their supreme virtue will make it hard for you to be judged as anything but somewhat inferior, even if you deserve to be judged their equals. The living are resented as rivals, but the departed are honored with a generosity that is free from competitiveness. [2] If I am also obliged to say something to the new widows about the virtues proper to a woman, a quick word of advice will say it all: people will think best of you if you do the best you can given the limitations of your female nature and if you are talked about as little as possible by men for any reason, whether good or bad.

46. "There you have my version of the customary speech; it is as fitting a tribute as I could make it. As for action, the dead have already been honored by the act of burial, and their sons will from this day on be maintained by the state until they come of age. This is the estimable crown that the state presents both to these men and to those they leave behind as a reward for their great trials. For it is those who establish the greatest prizes for virtue who have the best men as their fellow citizens. [2] And now, do your grieving for your dead and then return to your homes."

47. That was how the public funeral was conducted this winter, and with the end of winter the first year of the war came to an end.

[2] At the very beginning of summer, the Peloponnesians and their allies, with two-thirds of their forces, as on the first occasion, invaded Attica under the command of the Spartan king Archidamus, son of Zeuxidamus. They made camp and set about ravaging the land. [3] Only a few days after their arrival in Attica, the plague made its first appearance in Athens, and although it was said to have struck many other places in Greece earlier—particularly Lemnos, but also elsewhere—there is no record from anywhere else of such a severe outbreak or of so many lives lost. [4] At first, doctors were no use because they were treating it in ignorance, and in fact they died more than others insofar as they were exposed to it more than others. No other treatment that human beings could devise was any good either. People made supplications at sanctuaries and turned to oracles and suchlike, but nothing was effective, and in the end, defeated by their troubles, they abandoned these practices.

48. It is said to have started in Ethiopia, south of Egypt, and from there it spread to Egypt and Libya, and to much of the Persian empire. [2] It struck Athens without warning. The first cases occurred in Piraeus, and people there even said that the Peloponnesians had poisoned the rainwater cisterns (there were no wells in Piraeus at the time). Later it reached Athens itself, and then the number of deaths began to rise sharply. [3] I leave it to others, whether doctors or not, to say what they think about the likely origin of the disease, and the factors that, in their view, had the capacity and power to cause such profound and disruptive changes. For my part, I shall simply describe what happened and explain its features so that, securely armed with this foreknowledge, people may not find themselves ignorant should it ever occur again.* I can do this because I myself caught the disease and witnessed other sufferers.

49. That year, it was universally agreed, was in fact particularly disease-free as far as other ailments were concerned, though any illness that anyone already had always turned into the plague. [2] In other cases there was no apparent cause, but people who were healthy suddenly started getting symptoms. They appeared first in the head, as strong feelings of heat, and redness and inflammation of the eyes, while the internal parts—the throat and tongue—very quickly became swollen with blood, and the breath turned foul and fetid. [3] This was followed by sneezing and a sore throat, and then before very long the disease would go down into the chest and cause violent coughing. Next it caused an upset stomach, whenever it settled there, and this was followed by the evacuation of every kind of bile known to the medical profession, along with a great deal of discomfort. [4] Most victims experienced empty retching that brought on violent spasms; this retching usually occurred shortly after the vomiting abated, but sometimes much later. [5] The outside of the body was neither especially hot to the touch nor pale, but reddish and livid, with outbreaks of small pustules and sores. Internally, however, there was such a burning feeling that sufferers could not endure the touch of even quite light clothing or sheets, or anything other than going naked, and what they enjoyed most was a plunge in cold water. In fact, many people who had no one to look after them actually threw themselves into cisterns, since they were in the grip of unquenchable thirst. It made no difference whether they drank much or little.

[6] Victims were afflicted with constant restlessness and sleeplessness. While the disease was at its peak, the body did not lose flesh, but withstood the ordeal better than one would have expected, so that most people died on the seventh or ninth day from the internal burning while still retaining some strength; but if they lived on, the disease descended to the bowels, where severe ulceration occurred, with attacks of acute diarrhea, and most people died later from the weakness caused by the diarrhea. [7] For the disease first settled in the head and then made its way down through all the body. Even people who survived past the most serious stages would find their extremities disfigured by the disease's attack on them. [8] It seized upon genitals, fingers, and toes, and it was common for survivors to lose these parts; some lost the use of their eyes as well. Some suffered from total memory loss immediately after their recovery; they had no idea who they were and could not recognize their friends.

50. The pathology of the disease defied explanation. Not only did it attack people with a severity that was more than human nature could endure, but it showed just how different it was from any normal disease by the following feature above all: although there were many unburied bodies, the birds and animals that prey on human corpses either kept away from them or died after taking a bite. [2] The evidence for this is that there was a noticeable lack of such birds; they were basically not to be seen, let alone seen doing anything like that. But dogs offered a better chance to observe what happened when they ate some of a corpse, because they live in close proximity to people.

51. So that was what the disease was like in general, leaving aside all the many peculiarities that marked individual cases, because it had different effects on different people. Throughout the time of the plague, the city was untroubled by any other diseases; none of the usual ones occurred, and any that did ended up as the plague. [2] People died whether they were being well cared for or were receiving no treatment. It is hardly an exaggeration to say, then, that not a single remedy was found the application of which would guarantee relief; what helped one person harmed another. [3] It became clear that no one, however strong or weak, had what it takes to resist the disease; the plague seized everyone indiscriminately, whatever regimen was being used for their treatment.

[4] The grimmest aspect of the disease was the despair that afflicted people when they realized they were sick; once they had made up their minds that there was no hope, they were well on the way to giving up without a fight. Another terrible aspect was that because people became infected as a result of caring for others, caregivers died in droves, like sheep. In fact, caring for others caused more deaths than anything else. [5] If fear made people reluctant to be near others, the victims died on their own, and many houses were emptied because no one came to look after the sick. And if they visited the sick they died. This was especially true of those who made some claim to virtue, who conscientiously showed no concern for themselves and went to friends' houses when even the relatives, defeated by the extent of their troubles, finally began to give up lamenting the dying. [6] Greater compassion, however, was displayed for the dying and the suffering by those who had survived the disease, not just because they knew from their own experience what the victims were going through, but also because they were now feeling confident, since a person did not catch the disease a second time, or at least not in a deadly form. They were congratulated by everyone else, and in the exhilaration of the moment they entertained the vain hope that in the future they would never be carried off by any other disease either.

52. The suffering was exacerbated by the crowding of people into the city from the countryside, and the new arrivals suffered worst of all. [2] There were no houses for them, they lived in shanties that were stifling in the summer heat, and they died in hellish conditions, with the bodies of the dying heaped on one another and the half-dead staggering around in the streets and at all the springs in their craving for water. [3] The sanctuaries where they camped were strewn with the bodies of those who had died there. In the face of overwhelming disaster, people lost their self-respect and began to see no point in the usual constraints, whether sacred or secular. [4] All the customary ways of managing funerals were thrown into disarray; everyone buried their dead as best they could. Many who lacked the requisites because so many of their relatives had already died resorted to shameless ways of disposing of their dead. Some put their own dead on other people's funeral pyres and lit the fire before those who had built them had made use of them; others would toss the corpse they were carrying on top of another corpse that was already being burned and run away.

53. The plague also initiated an increase in other forms of lawlessness in the city. People were more ready to go ahead and do things for which they had previously concealed their liking, since they saw how quickly fortunes could change. It was not just that people who were well off were suddenly dying, but also that their property was promptly acquired by others, who had previously been destitute. [2] People therefore saw nothing wrong with indulgently pursuing short-term satisfaction, since they regarded their lives and their property as equally fleeting. [3] No one wanted to add to their troubles by doing what seemed right, since they considered it uncertain whether they would live long enough to see it through. Anything that gave immediate pleasure or contributed to it in some way was taken to be the good and practical thing to do. [4] Fear of the gods and human laws were equally ineffective as restraints. It made no difference, as far as people could see, whether or not they respected them, since everyone was dying just the same, and no one expected to live long enough to be taken to court and pay the penalty for their wrongdoing. They felt that a far heavier sentence had already been passed and was hanging over them, and that it made sense to enjoy life a little before the sentence was carried out.*

54. That is how terribly the Athenians were suffering; they were hard put to it, with death inside the city and the depredation of the land outside. [2] It is not surprising that at this time of trouble they remembered the following verse, which older people claimed was sung in antiquity: "Dorian war will come, with pestilence as its companion." [3] A dispute arose about whether the ancients had said "pestilence" [*loimos*] or "famine" [*limos*], but given what was happening, the view prevailed that "pestilence" was correct. That was hardly surprising, since people adapt their memories to their experiences. If later they are involved in another "Dorian war" and a famine occurs, in my opinion the line will probably be recited that way. [4] Some people also recalled, if they knew of it, the oracle that the Lacedaemonians had received when, in response to their question about whether they should go to war, the god replied that if they fought a forceful war victory would be theirs, and added that he would be with them. [5] They were inclined to conjecture that what was happening matched the oracle; after all, the plague did break out just after the Peloponnesians had invaded, and the Peloponnese was not affected to any significant extent, but it made inroads in Athens above all, and then also in the most densely populated places elsewhere.* So much for what happened at the time of the plague.

55. After the Peloponnesians had ravaged the plain, they moved on to Paralus, as the coastal districts are called, and got as far as Laurium,* where the Athenians have their silver mines. They first laid waste the coastline facing the Peloponnese and then the stretch that faces Euboea and Andros. [2] Even under these circumstances, Pericles (who was one of the generals) maintained the same policy that he had advocated during the invasion of the previous year, that the Athenians should not go out and fight. **56.** While the Peloponnesians were still in the plain, however, before they went to the coastline, he had begun to make ready a hundred ships for an attack on the Peloponnese, and now that they were ready he sent them on their way. [2] There were four thousand Athenian hoplites on board, and three hundred cavalrymen in old warships that for the first time had been converted into horse-transports. The Chians and Lesbians also joined the expedition with fifty ships. [3] When these Athenian troops set out, they left the Peloponnesians behind in Attica, occupying the coastline. [4] They put in at Epidaurus in the Peloponnese, where they laid waste most of the farmland and then attacked the town, which very nearly fell to them. [5] After setting out from Epidaurus, they ravaged the farmland at Troezen, Halieis, and Hermione, which are all on the Peloponnesian seaboard. Then they set out from there and went to Prasiae, a small town on the coast of Laconia, where they laid waste the land, took the town, and sacked it.

57. All the time the Peloponnesians were in Attica and the Athenian naval expedition was under way, the plague was killing Athenians in the army and in the city. It was even said that the Peloponnesians shortened their invasion of Attica because they were afraid of the disease. They had found out from deserters that it was in the city, and they could also see that funeral rites were being performed. [2] Still, this was their longest-lasting invasion—they were in Attica for about forty days—and there was no part of the land that they left intact.

58. That same summer, Hagnon, son of Nicias, and Cleopompus, son of Cleinias, two of Pericles's fellow generals, took over the army that had been under his command and immediately set out north for a campaign against the Chalcidians of the Thraceward region and Potidaea, which was still under siege. On their arrival, they brought siege contraptions to bear against the city and tried to take it in one way or another,* [2] but they made no progress either toward capturing the city or in any other respect, or at least no progress worthy of the effort, because the plague struck and caused terrible suffering in the Athenian camp. The army was being devastated, as even the soldiers of the earlier expedition, who had previously been healthy, caught the

disease from the forces under Hagnon's command. (Phormio and his 1,600 men were no longer in the Chalcidice region.) [3] So Hagnon sailed back to Athens after a little over a quarter of his force of 4,000 hoplites had died of the disease in about forty days. The original force stayed where they were, however, and kept Potidaea under siege.

59. After the second Peloponnesian invasion, the Athenians changed their minds, since their land had been ravaged a second time and they were under attack from the plague as well as the war. [2] They now began to blame Pericles for having persuaded them to go to war and held him responsible for all their woes. They set in motion a plan to come to terms with the Lacedaemonians, and even sent an embassy to Sparta, but it was unsuccessful. In utter desperation, then, they turned on Pericles. [3] Seeing that they were reacting badly to the situation—in fact, they were behaving exactly as he had expected—he convened a meeting (he was still one of the generals) in an attempt to raise their morale, replace their anger with a gentler frame of mind, and reduce their fear. He stepped up and spoke along the following lines:

60. "I'm not surprised by your anger toward me; I recognize the reasons for it. The purpose of this assembly that I've called is to remind you of certain things and to tell you how misplaced your anger is and how wrong you are to give in to the troubles that are afflicting us.

[2] "It is my firm opinion that a state which is collectively on the right track does more good to individuals than one that's prospering as far as each of its citizens is concerned, but failing as a whole. [3] An individual may personally be faring well, but if his homeland is destroyed he still perishes along with it. On the other hand, his personal safety is far more likely to be guaranteed if he's doing badly but the state is doing well. [4] So since a state is capable of bearing individual misfortunes, but single individuals are incapable of bearing a state's misfortunes, it follows that everyone should rally to its defense—and not do what you are doing now. Terrified by your domestic misfortunes, you're neglecting our common security. You blame me for

advising you to go to war, but your acceptance of that advice makes you just as much to blame yourselves. [5] Yet your anger is directed at a man who is, I think, as good as anyone at knowing what a statesman is supposed to know and at explaining it. Moreover, I hold the city dear and am immune to bribery. [6] A person who comes up with a plan but fails to explain it clearly might as well not have had the idea in the first place, while a person who is capable in both these respects but is no friend to the city cannot speak with a proper degree of loyalty, and even if he has loyalty, if he's corruptible he would sell anything and everything for this one thing, money. [7] So if you were persuaded to go to war by me because you thought that I had these qualities even to a modest extent, while others didn't, it isn't fair for you to accuse me now of wrongdoing.

61. "It is, of course, sheer folly for those who have a choice in the matter—that is, if their situation is otherwise favorable—to go to war. But if, as was the case, one is compelled to choose between either yielding to others and then immediate subjection to them, or putting oneself at risk in order to maintain one's independence, then shunning risk is more reprehensible than confronting it. [2] I am the same person as before; I haven't changed my mind. It's you who are changing. What has happened is that you went along with my policy as long as nothing bad happened to you, and now that you're hurting you regret having done so. Now your weakened resolution judges my arguments to have been unsound, because each of you is currently feeling pain, and no one can see any sign yet of the benefits. A great change struck, with no warning, and it undermined your original intention to persevere in the decision you made. [3] After all, when something terrible suddenly happens out of the blue, something completely unpredictable, it crushes the spirit. That's what the plague did to us—the plague above all, though it was not alone.

[4] But you are citizens of a great city and were brought up to behave in ways appropriate to its greatness, and so you should also be prepared to stand firm in the face of disasters however severe they may

be, and not erase your reputation. For people think it just as right to denounce those who out of softness fail to live up to their reputation as it is to be repelled by those who presumptuously reach for a reputation they don't deserve. So after having duly mourned your personal losses, you should focus on the safety of the state as a whole.

62. "You're wrong to be afraid that our suffering in the war might be heavy and that even so we still may not win. What I've said on many other occasions should be enough to convince you of this, but I have an additional point to make, one that I think you've never acknowledged or taken to heart, nor have you seen its relevance to the greatness of your empire. I haven't addressed it either in my earlier speeches. Nor would I do so now, since it involves a rather boastful claim, if it wasn't clear to me that you're downhearted when there's no need to be. [2] You think that your empire is limited to your subject allies, but don't you see that, of the two realms that are plainly at man's service, the land and the sea, the latter is entirely under your sway? I don't mean just the amount you already control, but what you could add if you wanted to. There's no one, not the King nor any other people on earth, who can stop you from going wherever you want by sea, given the naval resources that are available to you. [3] This ability is therefore of an altogether different order from the utility of your farmsteads and land, the loss of which you're taking so hard. But feeling upset at their loss is an unreasonable reaction. It would be more reasonable to regard them as unimportant compared with your naval power—to think of your land as a mere garden and your houses as no more than the finery of wealth. You should also bear in mind that if we hold fast to our freedom and keep it safe, we will easily recover these things, whereas people who give in to others invariably find that they lose even what they had before.

"With a great deal of effort and without having inherited it from others, your fathers both gained this empire and handed it safely on to you; and it's more shameful to lose what one already has than to try to acquire something but fail in the attempt. You must prove yourselves to be as good as your fathers in both these respects, and you should engage your enemies not just with determination but with disdain. [4] Even a coward, out of ignorance of his good fortune, may think he's better than others, but disdain is an attribute of someone who has rational grounds for trusting that he is superior to his opponents—as we are. [5] Given that fortune is impartial, intelligence based on consciousness of superiority makes daring more likely to succeed. It doesn't place its trust in hope, which is valuable only in desperate situations, but in reason based on what is actually the case, which is better than hope at foreseeing the future.

63. "You're all proud of the prestige the city gains from its empire, so it's only right that you should fight in its defense. You can't avoid the suffering unless you also give up striving for the maintenance of its honor. You mustn't think that this is a single-issue contest, to decide whether you'll be enslaved or free; it's also about losing the empire and being threatened by those whose hatred your rule has incurred. [2] In case any of you, in the alarm of the moment, thinks we should make the noble gesture of giving up the empire and retiring into quietism, I tell you that this is no longer a possibility. By now, your empire is a kind of tyranny: it was arguably wrong to have taken it, but letting it go would be perilous.* [3] If people who thought like that won others over to their view, it would take hardly any time for them to ruin their city, as surely as they would if they went off and lived somewhere independently on their own. Quietists cannot survive unless they have men of action ranked alongside them. Nor is inactivity a viable policy for an imperial city, though it helps a subject city to live safely in its enslavement.

64. "If there are any of your fellow citizens who think like that, don't be led astray by them. And seeing that the decision to go to war was as much yours as mine, don't be angry with me, even though the enemy attacked—not that there was anything surprising in that given your refusal to submit—and even though on top of everything else we were struck by this plague, because that was a bolt out of the blue. In fact, out of everything that has happened, the plague is the only thing we could not have anticipated. I know that it's largely due to the plague that I'm more unpopular than I was, but that isn't fair, unless you're also prepared to attribute to me any unexpected successes you enjoy. [2] We must endure heaven-sent troubles with resignation and those that are the result of war with fortitude. That has always been the Athenian way, and it shouldn't now be brought to a halt by you. [3] You need to appreciate that Athens's reputation is second to none throughout the world because it doesn't give in when faced with misfortune, but has sacrificed more lives and expended more effort in war than any other Greek state, and has made itself more powerful than any Greek state in the past. Future generations will retain the memory of Athenian power forever, and that is so even if—since it is, after all, natural for everything to decline—we now lose some ground. They will remember that we ruled more of our fellow Greeks than anyone ever did before; that we stood up to our enemies, whether they came at us all at once or one by one, in the greatest wars ever fought; and that we lived in a city that was in all respects the wealthiest and the greatest.

[4] "It's true that a quietist might condemn all this, but people who want to make something of themselves will emulate us and powerless people will envy us. [5] To be hated for a while and judged obnoxious is the inevitable fate of all who claim the right to rule people other than themselves, so the best policy is to accept the unpopularity while pursuing the greatest goals. Hatred doesn't last long, but present splendor stays in people's memories forever as future glory. [6] Bearing in mind the glory to come in the future and the shame to be avoided in the present, commit yourselves here and now to having both the glory and the self-respect. Don't negotiate with the Lacedaemonians. Don't give any indication that your current suffering is making you downhearted. The strongest cities and the strongest individuals are those who, when faced with misfortune, in their minds suffer the least distress and in their actions offer the most resistance."

65. In speaking along these lines Pericles was trying to defuse the Athenians' anger with him and to divert their attention away from the nightmarish circumstances. [2] So far as public policy was concerned, they accepted his arguments: they stopped sending envoys to the Lacedaemonians and they redirected their energies onto the war. At an individual level, however, they were still upset by their misfortunes. Ordinary people were unhappy because they had been deprived of even the little they had started with, and powerful people because they had lost fine farms in the countryside, with their buildings and expensive furnishings. But what weighed most heavily on them was that they had war instead of peace, [3] and in fact the whole population stayed angry with Pericles until they had punished him with a fine. [4] But then not much later, as is typical of the masses,* they elected him general and made him responsible for all state business, since by then they were more inured to the pain each individual felt for his personal losses, and because they considered him the best man to see to the needs of the state as a whole.

[5] Throughout the years of peace when he was preeminent in the city, his leadership was moderate; he kept the city safe, and under his guidance it became greater than ever before. And when war broke out, it turned out that he was a good wartime leader as well, with the ability to understand in advance what the city was and was not capable of doing. [6] He died two years and six months into the war, and after his death his foresight with regard to the war became even more widely recognized.* [7] He had claimed that they would win if they avoided battle, looked after their navy, refrained from extending the empire at a time of war, and did nothing to endanger the city. But they did the opposite of all these things, and pursued policies that seemed to have more to do with personal ambition and private profit than with war, and that were bad for themselves and for their allies. They were the kind of policies where success brought honor and profit to individuals, but failure impaired the city's capacity for war. [8] The reason was that since he owed his influence to his personal distinction and intelligence, and since everyone could see that he was totally incorruptible,* he restrained the masses freely. He led them rather than being led by

them, because he did not tell them only what they wanted to hear in an improper bid for influence; his standing made it possible for him even to argue against them and provoke their anger. [9] For example, if he saw that arrogance was making them overconfident, he would give a speech that cowed them into fear, and, conversely, if he saw that they were frightened for no reason, he restored their confidence. In theory there continued to be a democracy, but what was important, in fact, was that power was in the hands of the leading man.

[10] None of his successors, however, stood out from the rest, and each of them, in his desire for political supremacy, devoted himself to surrendering even matters of policy to the whims of the masses. [11] Consequently, Athens being a great city with an empire, many mistakes were made, not the least of which was the Sicilian expedition. The problem in this case was not so much the failure to correctly size up the people against whom the expedition was directed as the failure of the people who were responsible for the expedition to make the right decisions in support of the expeditionary forces. Instead, they were too busy slandering one another in their pursuit of leadership of the people, and so they blunted the effectiveness of the army, and for the first time in the war the city was thrown into political turmoil.* [12] However, even after their failure in Sicily and the loss of all the forces they had sent (including more than half of their navy), and despite the fact that the city was now torn apart by factional strife, they still managed to hold on for eight† years, not only against their original enemies, but also against the Sicilians who had joined them, and against the majority of the allies, who had revolted. Later, Cyrus, the son of the King, became an enemy as well: he supplied the Peloponnesians with money to build ships. But the Athenians did not give in until they fell foul of one another in their internal squabbles and brought about their own ruin.* [13] This all goes to show how plentiful were the grounds that Pericles had at that time for predicting that it would not be at all difficult for the city to get the better of just the Peloponnesians in the war.

66. In the same summer, the Lacedaemonians and their allies sent a force of a hundred ships against the island of Zacynthos, which lies off Elis. The Zacynthians are colonists of the Peloponnesian Achaeans and they were allies of the Athenians. [2] There were a thousand Lacedaemonian hoplites on board under the command of the Spartiate Cnemus, who had been appointed navarch. They disembarked their troops and ravaged most of the farmland, but when the Zacynthians refused to capitulate, they sailed back home.

67. Toward the end of the summer, a Peloponnesian embassy set out for Asia for a meeting with the King, to try to persuade him to supply them with money and join the war on their side. The embassy consisted of Aristeus of Corinth; Aneristus, Nicolaus, and Pratodamus representing Sparta; Timagoras of Tegea; and Pollis of Argos, who went in an unofficial capacity. But first they went to Thrace to meet Sitalces, son of Teres, to see if they could persuade him to secede from the Athenian alliance and send a force to relieve Potidaea, where an Athenian army had the place under siege. They also wanted his help in crossing the Hellespont and realizing their chief purpose, which was reaching Pharnaces, son of Pharnabazus, who was going to have them escorted on to the King.* [2] But there happened to be Athenian ambassadors at Sitalces's court—Learchus, son of Callimachus, and Ameiniades, son of Philemon—and they persuaded Sitalces's son Sadocus, who had become an Athenian citizen, to deliver the men to them, arguing that if the Peloponnesians reached the King in Asia they would do no little harm to the city of which he was now a citizen. [3] He agreed and had them arrested as they were making their way through Thrace toward the ship on which they were intending to cross the Hellespont, before they embarked. He had provided Learchus and Ameiniades with escorts, and he had ordered these men to deliver the Peloponnesians to the Athenians. And once Learchus and Ameiniades had the Peloponnesians in their hands, they took them off to Athens.

[4] When they got there, the Athenians were afraid that Aristeus might escape and resume making trouble for them, since it was clear that earlier it had been he who was responsible for everything that had happened at Potidaea and in the Thraceward region. And so on the very day of their arrival in Athens they killed them all—without a trial and without a hearing—and threw their bodies into a ravine.* They saw nothing wrong with protecting their interests by replicating what the Lacedaemonians had been the first to do, when they seized some Athenian and allied traders who were sailing in merchant ships around the Peloponnese, put them to death, and hurled their bodies into ravines. In the early phases of the war the Lacedaemonians treated everyone they found at sea as enemies and killed them, not only those who were on the Athenian side in the war, but even those who belonged to neither side.

68. At the same time, the end of summer, the Ambraciots, accompanied by a large force of barbarians whom they had recruited, marched against Amphilochian Argos and the rest of Amphilochia. [2] Their hostility toward the Argives came about as follows: [3] Amphilochian Argos and the rest of Amphilochia were founded on the Ambracian Gulf by Amphilochus, son of Amphiaraus, when he returned home after the Trojan War and was displeased with the state of affairs there, in Peloponnesian Argos.* He named the place Argos after his homeland, [4] and it became the greatest city in Amphilochia, with the wealthiest inhabitants. [5] Many generations later, ground down by a series of catastrophes, they invited the Ambraciots, whose country bordered Amphilochia, to join them as inhabitants of Argos, and that was when for the first time the Argives began to speak Greek, as they do now, which they learned from the Ambraciots who joined them. The rest of the Amphilochians speak a non-Greek language. [6] Anyway, after a while the Ambraciots threw the Argives out and took the city for themselves. [7] When this happened, the Amphilochians placed themselves under the protection of the Acarnanians, and the two peoples called on the Athenians for additional help. The Athenians sent thirty ships, with Phormio as the general in command. When he arrived, they took Argos with their first assault and sold the Ambraciots into slavery, and the Amphilochians and Acarnanians then inhabited the city together. [8] It was after this that the Athenians and Acarnanians first formally became allies.*

[9] So the Ambraciots' hostility toward the Argives dates from their enslavement, and later, after the war had broken out, they launched this campaign with an army consisting of themselves, Chaonians, and some of their other barbarian neighbors. They went to Argos and gained control of the countryside, but although they attacked the city they failed to take it, so they returned home and each contingent went back to their own people. So much for the events that took place in the course of the summer.

69. The following winter, the Athenians dispatched twenty ships, with Phormio as the general in command, to make their way around the Peloponnese to Naupactus, which Phormio was to make his base for mounting guard over anyone sailing into or out of Corinth and the Gulf of Corinth. They also sent another six ships under the command of Melesander to Caria and Lycia to collect tribute from there and to prevent Peloponnesian pirates from making the region their base for interfering with merchant shipping from Phaselis, Phoenice, and the rest of that coastline.* [2] Melesander disembarked his men and marched into Lycia with an army made up of Athenians from the ships and some allied troops, but he lost his life and many of his men when he was defeated in a battle.

70. In the same winter, the Potidaeans found themselves no longer capable of holding out against the siege. The Peloponnesian invasions of Attica had not succeeded in forcing the Athenians to withdraw; the Potidaeans had run out of food; and, in addition to all the other sources of sustenance to which they had been compelled to resort, there had even been cases of cannibalism. Under these circumstances they made an offer of conditional capitulation to the Athenian generals who had been tasked with seeing to their downfall: Xenophon, son of Euripides; Hestiodorus, son of Aristocleides; and Phanomachus, son of Callimachus. [2] They welcomed the offer, taking into consideration the suffering of their men in the wintry northern conditions and the fact that the siege had already cost Athens two thousand talents. [3] So the Potidaeans capitulated on the following terms: They and their families, and the mercenaries, were to depart from the town with one outer garment apiece (two for women) and with a specified amount of money per person for the road. [4] They left under the protection of a truce and went to Chalcidice or wherever they could. But the Athenians thought that they could have gained control of Potidaea unconditionally, and they censured the generals for having agreed to terms without consulting them. Later, they sent some of their own people to the town as settlers and repopulated it.

[5] These were the events that took place in the course of the winter, and so ended the second year of the current war, the history of which was written by Thucydides.

71. The following summer, the combined Peloponnesian forces did not invade Attica, but marched against Plataea instead. The expedition was led by the Spartan king Archidamus, son of Zeuxidamus. He encamped his men and was ready to start laying waste the farmland, but the Plataeans lost no time in sending envoys to him, who spoke to the following effect:

[2] "Archidamus, Lacedaemonians: this attack of yours on Plataean soil is not only unjust but also unworthy of yourselves and your fathers. The fact is that after Greece had been liberated from the Persians by those Greeks who were prepared to play their part and face danger in the battle that was fought in our territory,* Pausanias, son of Cleombrotus, the leader of the army of liberation, sacrificed victims to Zeus, the god of freedom, in the agora of Plataea, and with all the allies present at his command he conceded to the Plataeans the right to occupy their land and town without interference from others. No

one was ever to campaign against us without full justification or seek to subjugate us, and if they did the allies who were present at the meeting were to strive to keep Plataea from harm. [3] This right was granted us by your own fathers in recognition of the courage and determination that we displayed in that hour of danger. But you're doing the exact opposite: you've come here, accompanied by our deadliest enemies, the Thebans, with the purpose of trying to enslave us. [4] We call to witness the gods by whom those oaths were sworn at the time, and your ancestral gods, and the gods of our land, and we call on you to end this unjust invasion of our land and not to violate your oaths, but to allow us to live in independence, just as Pausanias judged right."

72. That was the substance of the Plataeans' speech, and in response Archidamus said, "Men of Plataea, you make a fair point, if your actions match your words. By all means enjoy the right of self-determination that Pausanias allowed you, but also help us to free all the others who shared the danger then and joined you in swearing that oath, and who are now under the sway of the Athenians. That's why we've made such a great effort and gone to war—to liberate them and all other Greeks. Best of all would be for you to abide by the oath you swore and join us in this mission. Otherwise, you should do what we've already urged you to do: stay neutral and look after your own affairs without joining either side. Receive both sides in friendship, but neither side for war. Even that will satisfy us."

[2] After hearing what Archidamus said, the Plataean envoys went back into the city and delivered Archidamus's message to the popular assembly. The people replied that they could not comply with his suggestions without the approval of the Athenians, because their children and womenfolk were in Athens. Besides, they said, they were afraid for the city as a whole: after the Peloponnesian army had left, the Athenians might come and tell them that they could not be neutral, or the Thebans might come, claiming that they were included in the

Plataeans' guarantee to receive both sides, and make another attempt to seize the city. [3] Archidamus replied to this with an attempt to allay their fears. "What you should do," he said, "is turn the city and your houses over to us Lacedaemonians. Show us the boundaries of your lands, tell us how many olive trees you have and anything else that can be counted, and then leave the town and go and live elsewhere, wherever you like, for the duration of the war. When it's over, we'll give you back everything that you turned over to us, and until then we'll hold it in trust, working the land and giving you enough money to cover your needs."

73. The envoys listened to what Archidamus said and then went back once more into the city. After consulting with the people, the envoys told Archidamus that they needed first to tell the Athenians what he wanted them to do, and that if the Athenians were amenable they would comply with his demands. In the interim, they asked him to make a truce with them and not to ravage the land. Archidamus allowed a truce for the number of days the journey was likely to take and refrained from devastating the land. [2] The Plataean delegation went to Athens, discussed the matter with the Athenian people, and then returned with the following message for their fellow citizens: [3] "Men of Plataea, the Athenians say that in the past, ever since we've been allies, they have never abandoned you when you were the victims of aggression, and they won't sit idly by now but will help you with all their might. They therefore urge you, by the oaths that your fathers swore, not to do anything radical that would have implications for the alliance between you and them."

74. After the envoys had delivered this message, the Plataeans decided to stay true to the Athenians—to endure, if they had to, even the sight of the destruction of their land and whatever else fate had in store for them. They also decided that from now on no envoys would leave the city, and they gave their answer from the circuit wall—that they were unable to comply with the Lacedaemonians' demand. [2] The

very next thing King Archidamus did on hearing their answer was call to witness the gods and heroes of the land. This is what he said:

[3] "You gods and heroes of the land of Plataea, I call on you to witness that our attacking this land was not the initial wrong, but these people here were the first to break the oath. That is why we came here, to the land where our fathers defeated the Persians after praying to you, and that you made a propitious arena for the Greeks to fight in. Nor will we be doing wrong now, whatever we do, because we've made many reasonable offers without any of them being taken up. Grant that those who were the first to do wrong may be punished, and that those who are seeking to exact lawful vengeance may obtain it."

75. After making this solemn appeal to the gods, Archidamus deployed his troops for war. They first built a stockade around the town, made out of trees they had cut down, so that no sorties could be made against them. Then they began to pile earth against the city wall as a ramp, and they had so many men employed on the task that they expected the town to fall to them very quickly. [2] They brought timber they cut on Cithaeron* and reinforced both sides of the ramp with criss-cross structures made of this wood, to serve as retaining walls and to keep the soil thoroughly packed. They fetched brushwood, stones, earth, and anything else that could be thrown onto the ramp to hasten its completion. [3] With the Lacedaemonian officers responsible for the contingents of each allied city keeping the men at it, they labored continuously for [...]* days and nights on this mound, working in relays, so that some men were bringing the materials while others were sleeping and eating.

[4] In response to the rising ramp, the Plataeans erected a wall made of wooden beams on top of the stretch of wall against which the earth was being heaped up, and built into it bricks that they stripped from nearby houses. [5] The beams acted as a frame for the bricks, so that the structure would remain strong as it grew higher, and it had a screen of animal skins and hides to protect the people working on the structure and the beams from being struck by fire arrows. [6] This

greatly increased the height of the wall, but the ramp's height kept pace with it and rose up just as fast.

The Plataeans next came up with the following idea: They dug a hole through their circuit wall at the point where it abutted the earth of the ramp, and began to carry the earth away into the town. **76.** When the Peloponnesians found out, they packed clay into reed matting and threw it into the gap so that there would be nothing that could be loosened like earth and carried away. [2] Thwarted, the Plataeans called a halt to this tactic. Instead, they dug a tunnel out from the town, and when they calculated that they were under the ramp, they began once again to haul earth over to their side, this time from the bottom of the mound. For a long time the Peloponnesians on the outside were unaware of what was going on, and so they carried on adding more material but were making less progress, because earth was being drawn out from underneath and the rest of the ramp kept settling into the emptied space.

[3] However, the Plataeans were afraid that, since they were few and the enemy were many, even these tactics would not enable them to hold their own against them, so they came up with an additional ploy as well. They stopped working on the superstructure that faced the ramp, and on either side of it they began to build a curved wall off the inside of the original circuit wall and into the town, so that if the superstructure was captured there would still be this obstacle. The enemy would have to construct a whole new ramp against this semicircular wall; in order to advance inside they would have to do the same amount of work all over again and would be more vulnerable to crossfire.

[4] As well as constructing the ramp, the Peloponnesians also used siege devices in their assault on the town. One of these, that was brought to bear on the superstructure facing the ramp, battered down a large part of it, which terrified the Plataeans. Other devices were brought up against other stretches of the wall, but the Plataeans looped nooses around them and hoisted them aloft. They also fastened

long iron chains to both ends of great beams that they suspended between a pair of cranes that leaned on the wall and projected over it, with the beams horizontal to the ground. When a device was about to strike somewhere, they released their grip and let the beam fall with the chains slack, so that it crashed down onto the tip of the contraption and broke it off.

77. Seeing that the siege devices were doing them no good and that the ramp was being opposed by the counter-wall, the Peloponnesians despaired of taking the city by assault with the resources available to them at the time, so next they planned to surround it with a siege wall. [2] But first they decided to try fire—to see if, should a wind get up, they could incinerate the town, which was not large. In fact, they were constantly coming up with new ways to get the town to capitulate without the expense of a siege. [3] So they brought bundles of brushwood and started by throwing them down from the ramp into the gap between the superstructure and the earth of the ramp. The size of their workforce meant that the gap was soon filled, and then they piled up more brushwood against as much of the town as they could reach from the elevation of the ramp. Then they ignited the brushwood by tossing on lighted brands along with sulphur and pitch. [4] The blaze that ensued was the largest within living memory up to that time (or the largest man-made fire, anyway, because in the mountains, when wood rubs against wood in the wind, a flame and then a wildfire can occur without any human intervention). [5] It was a mighty conflagration, and it came very close to finishing the Plataeans, even though they had survived everything else. A large part of the city inside the wall became unapproachable, and if a wind had risen that was strong enough to drive the fire on, as their adversaries hoped, it would have been all over for them. [6] But in fact that did not happen: it is also said that a thunderstorm came on, accompanied by heavy rain that extinguished the blaze, and so the danger passed.

78. In view of this further failure, the Peloponnesians kept only a portion of their forces at Plataea, dismissed the rest, and set about surrounding the town with a wall, with each city's contingent responsible for a specific section. Trenches both inside and outside the wall provided clay for the bricks. [2] When they had finished the work, at about the time of the rising of Arcturus,* they left guards for half of the wall (the other half had Boeotian guards), withdrew the rest of their army, and went back to their various home towns. [3] The children and womenfolk of Plataea, along with the mass of those who were unfit for combat, including the elderly, had already been evacuated to Athens, and in the besieged town there remained 400 Plataeans, 80 Athenians, and 110 women to cook for them. [4] That was the total number of inhabitants when the siege began; there was no one else, slave or free, inside the town. Such were the preparations that were made for the siege of Plataea.

79. In the same summer, and at the same time as the campaign against Plataea, when the cereal crops were ripe, the Athenians sent an expeditionary force of 2,000 citizen hoplites and 200 cavalrymen against the Chalcidians of the Thraceward region and the Bottiaeans. There were three generals in command of the expedition, including Xenophon, son of Euripides. [2] When they were close to Spartolus in Bottice,* they destroyed the grain in the fields, and it even seemed likely that the town would come over to their side through the agency of certain of its citizens. But the Spartolans of the opposite persuasion sent word to Olynthus, and hoplites and other soldiers arrived to protect the place. When these troops made a sortie out of Spartolus, the Athenians joined battle with them right under the walls of the town. [3] The Chalcidian hoplites and some mercenaries who were with them were defeated by the Athenians and retreated back inside the town, but the Chalcidian cavalry and light-armed troops defeated their Athenian counterparts—[4] the Athenian light troops being a few peltasts from the district called Crousis.*

Just after the battle was over, some more peltasts arrived from Olynthus as reinforcements. [5] On seeing them, the light-armed troops in Spartolus, encouraged not just by this addition to their numbers but also by the fact that they had not been defeated earlier, launched another attack on the Athenians, along with the Chalcidian cavalry and the reinforcements. The Athenians fell back on the two companies they had left to guard the baggage train, [6] and whenever they attacked the enemy simply gave way, but when they retreated they were pressed hard and shot at by javelineers. Meanwhile, the Chalcidian horsemen kept riding up and attacking as they pleased, and it was this in particular that panicked the Athenians, who turned and ran, with the enemy cavalry in pursuit for a considerable distance. [7] The Athenians fled for safety to Potidaea, and later, after they had arranged a truce and collected the bodies of their dead, they returned to Athens with the remnants of the army; 430 men and all three generals had lost their lives. The Chalcidians and Bottiaeans erected a trophy, and once they had collected their own dead they went back to their various homes.

80. In the same summer, not long after these events, the Ambraciots and Chaonians, who wanted to conquer all of Acarnania and detach it from Athens, persuaded the Lacedaemonians to commission a fleet from their allies and to send 1,000 hoplites to Acarnania. They argued that if the Lacedaemonians joined them and launched a simultaneous attack by sea and land, so that the Acarnanians on the coast could not rally to the defense of the interior, they would easily take Acarnania and would then go on to gain control of Zacynthos and Cephallenia, which would make it impossible for the Athenians to sail around the Peloponnese as freely as before. And they held out the prospect that the Lacedaemonians might even take Naupactus as well. [2] The Lacedaemonians agreed. They dispatched their hoplites right away on a few ships under the command of Cnemus, who was still navarch, and they sent orders around to their allies to assemble a fleet and sail to Leucas as soon as they could. [3] The Corinthians were especially keen to support the Ambraciots, since Ambracia was a Corinthian

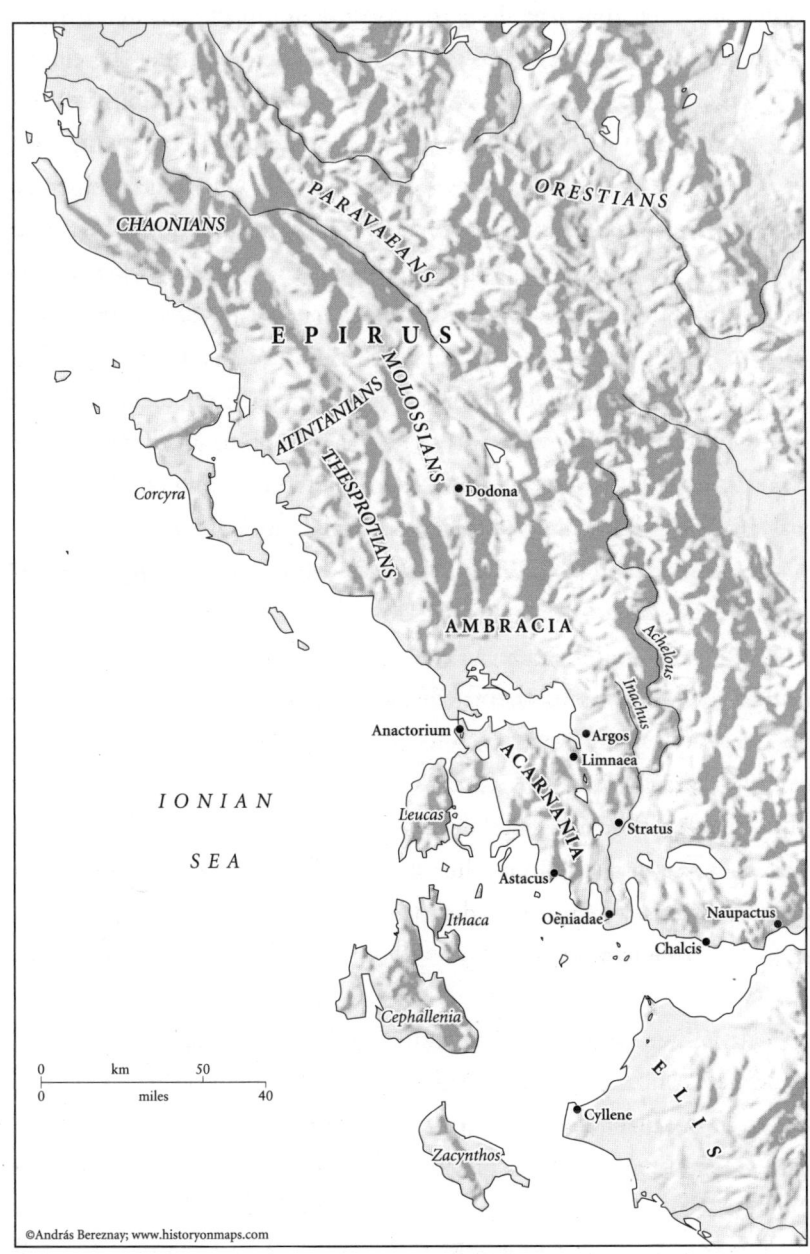

E. Acarnania and the Northwest

colony. While ships were being made ready in Corinth, Sicyon, and other places on that stretch of coastline, those from Leucas, Anactorium, and Ambracia assembled early at Leucas and waited there.

[4] Cnemus and his 1,000 hoplites sailed to Leucas without being spotted by the twenty Athenian ships that were on guard duty at Naupactus under the command of Phormio. As soon as Cnemus arrived, he immediately set the land campaign in motion. [5] He had under his command not just Greeks—Ambraciots, Anactorians, Leucadians, and the 1,000 Peloponnesians he had come with—but barbarians as well. There were, first, 1,000 Chaonians, who had no king at the time and were led by Photyus and Nicanor, members of the royal clan who were the presidents for that year. Then there were Thesprotians, who also had no king and served alongside the Chaonians. [6] There were Molossians and Atintanians, led by Sabylinthus, the guardian of the king, Tharyps, who was still underage, and Paravaeans, commanded by their king, Oroedus. There were 1,000 Orestians, who served alongside the Paravaeans, since their king, Antiochus, had entrusted them to Oroedus's leadership.* [7] And Perdiccas, without the Athenians' knowledge, sent 1,000 Macedonians, but they arrived too late.* [8] This was the army with which Cnemus set off, without waiting for the fleet from Corinth. After marching through Argolis, they sacked Limnaea, an unwalled village, and then they went to Stratus, the largest town in Acarnania. Their thinking was that if they first took Stratus the rest of Acarnania would readily capitulate.

81. When the Acarnanians found out that a sizable army had invaded by land and that an enemy fleet was also due to arrive by sea, each community took measures to protect itself, rather than going to the aid of Stratus. They sent word to Phormio, asking him to come to their defense, but he replied that he could not leave Naupactus undefended when a fleet was due to sail out from Corinth. [2] The Peloponnesians and their allies formed three divisions and advanced toward Stratus. Their plan was to make camp near the city, so that, if their words were not enough to persuade the Stratians to surrender, they could turn to action and make an attempt on the wall. [3] As they advanced toward the city, the division made up of the Chaonians and the other barbarians occupied the center; on their right were the Leucadians, the Anactorians, and those who had joined them for this campaign, and on their left was Cnemus with the Peloponnesians and Ambraciots. There was quite a distance between the three divisions, and in fact at times they could not see one another. [4] The Greeks advanced in good order, keeping a lookout, until they made camp in a suitable location. But the Chaonians, brimming with self-confidence—they had a great reputation in that part of the mainland as fighters—had no intention of making camp; they advanced at a rush along with the other barbarians, expecting to take the city without meeting any opposition and win the credit for the success.

[5] When the Stratians realized that the Chaonians were not going to halt, it occurred to them that if they could defeat them while they were on their own, the Greeks might not move against them as they had intended. They therefore laid ambushes all around the city, and when the Chaonians were close they sallied out from the city and at the same time fell on them from the ambushes. [6] The Chaonians panicked, many of them were killed, and when the other barbarians saw the Chaonians giving way, they no longer stood their ground, but turned to flight. [7] Neither of the Greek divisions knew of the fighting because the Chaonians were a long way ahead; in fact, the Greeks assumed that the reason they were pressing on was to find a site for a camp. [8] When the fleeing barbarians turned up at their camp, the Greeks took them in and, after integrating them into the army, they stayed where they were for the rest of the day and remained inactive. The Stratians did not engage them in battle because they were still waiting to be reinforced by the other Acarnanians, but they fired bullets at them from a distance with their slings, and made things very difficult for the men in the camp, who could not move without wearing armor. The Acarnanians are famously good slingers. **82.** After

nightfall, Cnemus hurried away with his army to the Anapus river, which is about nine miles from Stratus, and the next day he collected the bodies of his dead under a truce. When friendly troops from Oeniadae arrived to help him, he retreated to their territory before the Acarnanian reinforcements came. From there, the soldiers from the various contingents of his army made their way back home. For their part, the Stratians erected a trophy for their defeat of the barbarians.

83. The fleet from Corinth and the other allies on the Gulf of Corinth that was supposed to reinforce Cnemus and prevent the coastal Acarnanians from rallying to the defense of the inland never arrived. At about the same time as the fighting at Stratus, they were forced to join battle with Phormio and the twenty Athenian ships that were on guard duty at Naupactus. [2] Phormio kept an eye on them as they sailed out of the gulf along the coast, because he wanted to engage them in open water. [3] The Corinthians and the other allies had set out for Acarnania with no expectation that they would be fighting a sea battle. They had been set up more for transporting soldiers, and they did not imagine that the Athenians with twenty ships would dare to engage their forty-seven. But as they made their way along the Peloponnesian coast, they could see the Athenians sailing along the opposite coast, and when they began to sail across from Patrae in Achaea toward the mainland on the other side, on course for Acarnania, they saw the Athenians bearing down on them from Chalcis and the Evenus river.* Casting off under cover of darkness had not enabled them to get away undetected, and they were being forced to fight mid-crossing in open water. [4] The Corinthian generals were Machaon, Isocrates, and Agatharchidas, and otherwise each state that contributed ships to the fleet provided its own commanding officers.

[5] The Peloponnesians arranged their ships to form as large a circle as they could with their prows facing outward and their sterns inward, without leaving the enemy space to break through. Inside the circle were the smaller vessels that were accompanying them and their five fastest ships, which would not have far to go if they had to row

out at any point in response to an enemy attack. **84.** The Athenian ships sailed in single file around the perimeter of the Peloponnesians, whose already limited space they kept reducing by constantly sailing hard by them and giving them the impression that they were on the point of attacking. But Phormio had told them beforehand not to make the attempt until he gave the signal. [2] His hope was that the Peloponnesians would not remain in formation, as foot soldiers might on land, but that the ships would fall foul of one another and the smaller vessels would create confusion. And if, as usually happened in the early morning, the wind blew out of the gulf—which is what he was waiting for as he sailed around them—he doubted they would be able to hold steady even for a little while. He reckoned that, since he had skill on his side, it was up to him to attack whenever he chose, and that it would go best when the wind got up.

[3] When the wind started to blow, under the combined pressure of the air and the smaller craft, the Peloponnesian ships, which were already crowded together, began to lose cohesion. As one ship clashed with another, the crews tried to keep them apart with poles. With all their shouting and precautionary measures and cursing, they could not hear the rowing-masters or any other orders, and the rowers' lack of experience meant that they were unable to raise their oars out of the rough water, which made the ships less responsive to the helmsmen. At this point, Phormio saw his opportunity; he gave the signal and the Athenians attacked. They first sank one of the generals' ships and then set about disabling others as well wherever they went. The Peloponnesian ships, finding that the Athenians were making it impossible for any of them to put up a fight, turned and fled to Patrae and Dyme in Achaea. [4] The Athenians went after them and captured twelve ships, and once they had taken into captivity as many of the crews as they could, they sailed off to Molycreum. After erecting a trophy at Rhium and dedicating a ship to Poseidon, they returned to Naupactus. [5] The Peloponnesians lost no time in sailing with the remains of their fleet from Dyme and Patrae to Cyllene, the harbor of

Elis. This was also where Cnemus went when he left Leucas after the battle at Stratus with the ships from there that were supposed to have met up with the others.

85. The Lacedaemonians sent Timocrates, Brasidas, and Lycophron to the fleet to advise Cnemus, with orders to make more effective preparations for another sea battle, so that it would be impossible for a small number of ships to deny them access to the sea. [2] They were considerably surprised by what had happened, largely because this was their first experience of a naval battle. They did not think that their fleet had simply been outclassed, but that the result had been due to a lack of spirit; in other words, they had failed to factor in the contrast between the Athenians' long experience and their own brief training. So the sending of the advisory commissioners was prompted by anger. [3] On their arrival, the commissioners and Cnemus sent messages around to the allied cities ordering additional ships and began to fit out for battle those they already had.

[4] For his part, Phormio sent a message telling the Athenians of the Peloponnesians' preparations, informing them of his victory in the sea battle and urging them to send him as many ships as possible without delay, since no day passed without the possibility of an engagement. [5] They sent him twenty ships, but they also told the person bringing him the ships to go first to Crete. Nicias, a Cretan from Gortyn who represented Athenian interests there, had persuaded them to sail against Cydonia,* claiming that, although the place was hostile to Athens, they would win it over. In fact, however, he was calling them in as a favor to the people of Polichna, the neighbors of Cydonia. [6] So the Athenian commander went to Crete with the ships, where he joined the Polichnans in ravaging Cydonian farmland and was held up for quite a while by winds and rough seas.

86. While the Athenians were delayed in Crete, the Peloponnesians in Cyllene completed their preparations for battle and sailed to Panormus in Achaea, where the Peloponnesian land army had come up in support. [2] Phormio also set sail and went to Molycrian Rhium with the twenty ships with which he had fought the sea battle and anchored offshore. [3] This Rhium was on good terms with Athens, but opposite it there is another Rhium, the one in the Peloponnese. Less than a mile of sea separates the two places, and this gap forms the mouth of the Gulf of Corinth. [4] When the Peloponnesians saw the Athenians there, they moved, too, and anchored their seventy-seven ships at the Rhium in Achaea, which was not far from the encampment of their land army at Panormus.

[5] For six or seven days the two squadrons were stationed opposite each other, practicing and otherwise preparing for battle. The Peloponnesians, anxious to avoid a recurrence of the earlier defeat, had no intention of sailing beyond the two Rhiums into open water, while the Athenians, thinking that fighting in a restricted space would favor the Peloponnesians, had no intention of entering the narrows. [6] Cnemus, Brasidas, and the other Peloponnesian generals wanted to bring on an engagement soon, before reinforcements could arrive from Athens, but first they convened a meeting of their troops. They could see that most of them were frightened and demoralized by the earlier defeat, so in order to give them fresh heart the generals addressed them in the following terms:

87. "Peloponnesians, some of you may be apprehensive about the coming battle because of what happened in the last one, but there is no good ground for such fear. [2] As you know, we weren't fully prepared, and the reason we were at sea was not to fight a battle but to mount a land campaign. Then again, luck, as it turned out, was definitely not on our side, and it may even be that a degree of inexperience was a factor in our failure. It was, after all, our first sea battle. [3] So our defeat was not the result of insufficient bravery, and since our resolution has not been altogether overwhelmed but is still capable of delivering a response, it would be wrong for it to be blunted by the outcome of that event. You should appreciate that although chance may cause failure, the brave in spirit never stop being brave, and it is inconceivable that they would make inexperience an excuse for turning into cowards in any situation. [4] In any case, any disadvantage that you have because of inexperience is more than compensated for by the advantage that your bravery gives you. The chief cause of your fear is the enemy's skill. Now, skill accompanied by courage will enable soldiers in battle to remember how to put into practice what they've learned, but without courage no skill is proof against danger, because fear confounds memory so that skill without valor is no use at all. [5] So against their greater experience set your greater courage, and against the fears aroused by the defeat set the fact that you were unprepared on that earlier occasion.

[6] "You have the advantage of a large number of ships and of fighting close to friendly territory with hoplites at hand, and victory usually comes to those who have the advantage of numbers and better resources. [7] So we can't come up with a single reason for anticipating defeat. Even our earlier mistakes will now make a contribution by teaching us a lesson. [8] Be confident, then, whether helmsman or crewman, as each of you does his duty, and don't desert the post to which you've been assigned. [9] Our preparations for battle will surpass those of the previous commanders; there will be no reason for anyone to turn coward. Anyone who chooses to do so will be duly punished, but those who perform well will be suitably rewarded for their valor."

88. Such were the words of encouragement the generals spoke to the Peloponnesians. Phormio, too, was worried that his men were scared; it had come to his attention that when they gathered among themselves they expressed alarm at the number of the enemy ships. So he decided to assemble the troops in order to allay their fears and offer them some advice appropriate to the circumstances. [2] In the past, he had constantly used his speeches to condition their minds to think that there was no fleet, however great, that they could not stand up to in battle, and the crews had for a long time accepted this assessment among themselves and embraced the idea that as Athenians they did not yield to a Peloponnesian naval force. [3] But on the occasion in question he could see that their morale had been adversely affected by what they saw of the enemy, and he wanted to remind them of their former confidence. So he convened a meeting of the Athenians and spoke somewhat as follows:

89. "Men, I called this meeting because it's clear to me that you're alarmed by the enemy numbers, and because I think that things that aren't frightening shouldn't scare you. [2] In the first place, because of their earlier defeat, even the Peloponnesians themselves doubt that they are our equals, and that's why they've assembled this disproportionately large number of ships. In the second place, what about the courage that they take to be a special attribute of theirs and gives them their confidence when they attack us? Well, this confidence of theirs is based solely on the fact that on land their experience usually gives them victory, and they suppose that it will have the same effect at sea as well. [3] But if they have the advantage on land, by rights it is we who should be more confident at present, because they are no more courageous than us and each side is more confident where it is more experienced. [4] Their Lacedaemonian leaders, thinking primarily of their own reputations, are forcing most of them to take part in the battle against their wills; otherwise they would never have attempted another battle after their resounding defeat. [5] So there's no need for you to be afraid of their courage. You are far more frightening to them, and there's more to justify their fear because they've already been defeated once, and because they think you wouldn't be opposing them unless you were intending to achieve something befitting the decisive nature of that defeat.

[6] "When one side in a contest has superior numbers, as they do, it embarks on a battle relying more on strength than on judgment. But those who dare to put up a fight when they have far fewer numbers, and when they are also not being forced to it, do so because they feel perfectly secure. If the Peloponnesians are taking this into account, they'll be more afraid of us because of the unexpectedness of what we're doing than if we were facing them with commensurate forces.

[7] In the past, many armies have lost even to inferior numbers because of their inexperience, and occasionally because they were overcautious, but neither of these applies to us today.

[8] "Insofar as it's up to me, I shall avoid taking them on in the gulf or sailing into it, because, as I see it, lack of sea room is a disadvantage for a small, experienced, and fast squadron fighting a large number of inexpertly handled ships. We couldn't properly sail into the attack, because we wouldn't have the long view of the enemy that we need for a ramming run, and we wouldn't be able to back away opportunely if we were in trouble. In a restricted space, the tactic of breaking through the enemy line and turning on them is out of the question, but this is the right tactic for a fleet that has the superior seamanship. We would have to turn a sea battle into a land battle, and in that situation the side with the greater number of ships has the advantage.

[9] "So I shall be doing my best to exercise caution in this respect. Your jobs are to stay in good order by the beached ships and respond promptly to your orders, especially since the two fleets are stationed so close to each other. During the actual engagement regard nothing as more important than discipline and silence, which are valuable qualities in warfare generally and especially in a sea battle, and see that in fighting you do not fall short of your past achievements. [10] A great deal is at stake. You will either extinguish the Peloponnesians' naval hopes or make the Athenian fear of losing control of the sea a more immediate prospect. [11] Let me remind you once more that you have already beaten most of these men, and men once defeated tend not to face the same dangers a second time with the same confidence."

90. Such were the words of encouragement that Phormio in his turn spoke to his men. With the Athenians refusing to sail into the narrows of the gulf, the Peloponnesians decided to try to lure them in against their will. So at dawn they put to sea with their ships deployed in four columns, just as they had been when lying at anchor, and sailed along their own coast, heading for the interior of the gulf, with the right wing leading the way. [2] The twenty fastest ships were posted on this wing, so that if Phormio thought their objective was Naupactus and sailed in that direction himself to defend it, the Athenian ships would be unable to outdistance this wing and escape their attack, and the Peloponnesian ships would cut them off.

[3] Just as the Peloponnesians had expected, when Phormio saw them setting out he was worried about how exposed Naupactus was, and, although this was not in accord with his wishes, he hurriedly had his men board the ships and sailed along the coast, while the Messenian infantry took a parallel course on land. [4] When the Peloponnesians saw that the Athenian ships were sailing in single file, line ahead, and that they were now inside the gulf and close to the shore, which was exactly what they wanted, at a given signal they suddenly turned their ships and sailed in line abreast, but with each ship making its best speed toward the Athenians, hoping to intercept them all. [5] Eleven of the Athenian ships, however, which were in the lead, outran the Peloponnesian right wing and the turn into open water, but the other nine were caught. The Peloponnesians drove them in flight toward the land and disabled them, killing all the Athenian crewmen who could not get away from them by swimming. [6] Some of the ships they took in tow—they were all empty except for one that they had already captured along with its crew—and they were in the process of taking them away when the Messenians intervened. They plunged into the sea in full armor, climbed on board some of the ships, fought from the decks, and recovered them even as they were being towed away.

91. In this quarter, then, the Peloponnesians were victorious and disabled some of the Athenian ships, and the twenty ships from their right wing set out in pursuit of the eleven Athenian ships that had outrun their turn into open water. But all the Athenian ships except for one managed to escape and reach Naupactus safely. They took up a position by the sanctuary of Apollo with their prows facing outward and prepared to defend themselves if the Peloponnesians moved landward against them. [2] The Peloponnesians subsequently sailed up, singing a paean at the same time, as though they had already won, and one Leucadian ship was a long way ahead of the rest, in pursuit of the final Athenian ship. [3] By chance, there was a merchantman anchored out in open water, and the Athenian ship rowed around it just in time, rammed the Leucadian amidships, and sank it. [4] This was so unexpected and extraordinary that the Peloponnesians were terrified. Moreover, they had lost cohesion in the course of the pursuit, thinking that victory was theirs, and so some of the ships dug in their oars and came to a halt, since they wanted to wait for the others—an inexpedient thing to do with the enemy stationed close at hand—and others even ran aground in the shallows because of their ignorance of the area.

92. The sight of what was happening restored the Athenians' confidence, and at a single command they let out a whoop and launched an attack on the Peloponnesians. Because of the mistakes they had made and their current disarray, the Peloponnesians fought back for only a short time before turning and heading for Panormus, the place from which they had started. [2] The Athenians set out in pursuit, captured six of the ships that were closest to them, and recovered those of their own that the Peloponnesians had disabled near the shore at the beginning of the battle and had taken in tow. They killed some of the men and took a few prisoners. [3] Timocrates of Sparta had been on board the Leucadian ship that had been sunk right by the merchantman, and seeing that the ship had been disabled he killed himself. His body washed ashore at the harbor of Naupactus.

[4] On their return to Naupactus, the Athenians erected a trophy at the point from where they had sailed out to victory, and recovered all the corpses and the wrecks on their side of the gulf. Those that belonged to the enemy they returned under a truce. [5] The Peloponnesians also erected a trophy, for the victory they had won when they turned the Athenians to flight and disabled the ships by the shore, and at Rhium in Achaea, next to the trophy, they dedicated the ship they had captured. [6] After this, because they were afraid of

reinforcements arriving from Athens, all of them except for the ships from Leucas sailed under cover of darkness to Corinth and elsewhere in the Gulf of Corinth. [7] As for the twenty Athenian ships from Crete that were supposed to have joined Phormio before the battle, they reached Naupactus a short while after the fleet had returned there. And so the summer came to an end.

93. At the beginning of winter, before disbanding the fleet that had gone to Corinth and elsewhere in the Gulf of Corinth, Cnemus, Brasidas, and the other Peloponnesian commanders decided, following a suggestion by the Megarians, to make an attempt on Piraeus, the harbor of Athens. The entrance to the harbor was not guarded or closed—naturally, since the Athenians were dominant at sea. [2] It was decided that every oarsman should take his oar, his cushion, and his oar-strap and walk from Corinth to the coast on the Athenian side. Then, after they had quickly made their way to Megara, they were to launch from Nisaea, the harbor of Megara, forty ships that happened to be there, and head straight for Piraeus. [3] There was no advance guard of ships in Piraeus, nor was there any expectation that the enemy would ever launch a surprise attack like this. In fact, the Athenians believed that the Peloponnesians would not dare to attack even openly and that if they took their time over planning such an attack,† they were sure to hear about it beforehand.

[4] No sooner had the decision been taken than the Peloponnesians set out. They reached Megara at night,* launched the ships from Nisaea, and set out on their voyage—but in a change of plan they did not make for Piraeus. They had become afraid of the risks, and there was some talk later of an unfavorable wind as well. Instead, they went to the headland of Salamis that faces Megara. There was a fortress there and a guard of three ships to stop sea traffic into or out of Megara. They assaulted the fortress and towed away the three ships empty, and then they fell on the rest of Salamis, catching the inhabitants unawares, and set about plundering the land.

94. War beacons transmitted the news to Athens, and nothing that happened in the war caused a greater panic. People in the city thought the enemy had already sailed into Piraeus, while in Piraeus it was believed that Salamis had been taken and that the enemy was poised to sail against them. And that might well have happened if the Peloponnesians had kept their nerve, and no wind would have stopped them. [2] At daybreak the entire population of Athens went down to Piraeus to mount a defense. They launched ships, embarked on them hurriedly and in great confusion, and rowed to Salamis, while the infantry guarded Piraeus. [3] But as soon as the Peloponnesians, who had overrun most of Salamis, became aware that the Athenians were on their way, they sailed back to Nisaea with what they had captured—men, booty, and the three ships from the fortress at Budorum. They were also worried about their ships, which had been launched after a period of disuse and were far from watertight. After reaching Megara, they returned to Corinth on foot. [4] When the Athenians found that they had left Salamis, they too returned home, and from then on, after this episode, they began to guard Piraeus better by closing the harbors and taking other precautions.

95. At much the same time, at the beginning of winter, Sitalces, son of Teres, the king of the Odrysian Thracians, marched against Perdiccas, son of Alexander, the king of Macedon, and against the Chalcidians of the Thraceward region. He had two promises in mind: he wanted to enforce one that had been made to him and keep one that he had made himself. [2] When Perdiccas was in trouble early in the war he had promised to do Sitalces a favor, provided that Sitalces would reconcile him with the Athenians and would refuse to support the restoration and claim to the throne of his brother and enemy Philip, but he had not kept his promise. And Sitalces himself had promised the Athenians, when he had entered into alliance with them, that he would bring their war with the Thraceward Chalcidians to a conclusion. [3] So it was because of these two promises that

F. Thrace

he was going on the offensive. With him he took Amyntas, the son of Philip, with a view to placing him on the Macedonian throne; an Athenian delegation that happened to be there on this business; and Hagnon to act as commander, since the Athenians were supposed to join him against the Chalcidians with ships and as many soldiers as they could spare.

96. Setting out from Odrysian territory, he first levied troops from all the Thracians who were his subjects in an area that extended toward the coasts of both the Black Sea and the Hellespont, to the south and east of the Haemus and Rhodope ranges. Next he recruited the Getae, who live north of the Haemus mountains, and all the other peoples who live south of the Danube and in the direction of the Black Sea rather than the Hellespont. The Getae and the other peoples in this region are neighbors of the Scythians and are armed in the Scythian manner: they are all mounted archers. [2] In addition, he requested large numbers of troops from the mountain-dwelling Thracians, who were not his subjects; the weapon of choice for this people—the Dii, as they are called—is the short sword, and most of them live in the Rhodope range. Some of them he hired as mercenaries, but others went along as volunteers. [3] He levied troops also from the Agrianes, the Laeaei, and all the other Paeonian tribes that were subject to him. This was the furthest extent of his empire: it went up to the Laeaean Paeonians and the Strymon river, which rises in Mount Scombrus and flows through Agrianian and Laeaean territory, but the land west of the Strymon was inhabited by Paeonians, and from this point on they were not his subjects. [4] To the north, in the direction of the territory of the Triballi, who were not his subjects either, his empire was bounded by the Treres and the Tilataei. These peoples live to the north of Mount Scombrus, and their territory extends west as far as the Oscius river, which rises in the same mountain—a large, uninhabited mountain that forms part of the Rhodope range—as do the Nestus and the Hebrus.

97. As for the size of the Odrysian empire, its coastline went from the city of Abdera to the Black Sea and up to the Danube. With a following wind all the way this coastal voyage takes a merchantman at the very least four days and nights, while walking overland from Abdera to the Danube takes a man traveling light at least eleven days. [2] That is the extent of the coastline; the cross-country journey from Byzantium to the Laeaei and the Strymon (which is where the empire is farthest inland from the coast) takes a man traveling light thirteen days.

[3] The tribute from all the barbarian lands and the Greek cities that formed part of the empire during the reign of Seuthes, who succeeded Sitalces to the throne and increased the empire to its greatest extent, was the equivalent of about four hundred talents of silver, and came in the form of both gold and silver. At least as much again came as gifts of gold and silver, and then there were all the fabrics, both brocaded

and plain, and other household objects—gifts that were presented not just to Seuthes but even to his fellow princes and to noble Odrysians. [4] Their practice in this respect was diametrically opposed to that of the Persian empire; it involved taking rather than giving, and it was more shaming for someone to refuse to give when asked than to ask and be refused. The same system was in place throughout Thrace, but because of their wealth the Odrysians employed it more extensively—so much so that nothing was done without a gift being given. And so the kingdom grew to be great and powerful. [5] Of all the states between the Adriatic and Black seas, it was the greatest by the criterion of revenue and general prosperity, but in military strength and the size of its armed forces it fell well short of the Scythian kingdom. [6] In military terms, not only is there no comparison between the states in Europe and the Scythians, but even in Asia there is no people who could stand up to them, one for one, if they all cooperated with one another. But it also has to be said that they fall well short of others when it comes to sound decision-making and intelligent use of life's resources.

98. This was the great empire of which Sitalces was king. Once he had gathered his forces and everything was ready, he set out for Macedon. He marched first through his own kingdom, and then through the uninhabited Cercina range of mountains, which forms the border between the Sinti and the Paeonians. He traversed the mountains on the road that he himself had previously cut through woodland when he campaigned against the Paeonians. [2] As they left Odrysian territory and passed through the mountains, they had the Paeonians to the west and the Sinti and Maedi to the east. Once they were through the mountains, they arrived at Doberus in Paeonia. [3] In the course of the march, the army suffered no losses except to a certain extent through illness, and in fact its numbers increased, because many of the independent Thracians joined up of their own accord in the hope of plunder. Altogether, the army is said to have numbered at least 150,000, [4] of whom the majority were infantry, but about a third were cavalry. Most of the cavalry were Odrysians, with the Getae supplying the second largest contingent. The best fighters among the infantry were the independent Thracians who had come down from the Rhodope mountains, while the mixed rabble that made up the rest of the infantry was formidable chiefly because of its size.

99. So the army was assembling in Doberus and getting ready to descend from the heights into Lower Macedon, Perdiccas's kingdom. [2] The term "Macedonian" also includes peoples from the interior, such as the Lyncestians and Elimiotae; these peoples are allies and subjects of Lower Macedon, but have their own royal houses. [3] What is now coastal Macedon was first acquired by Perdiccas's father, Alexander, and his predecessors, who were descendants of Temenus, originally from Argos. They established their kingdom by defeating the Pierians and expelling them from Pieria, and by doing the same to the Bottiaeans in what is called Bottia. (The Pierians subsequently settled in Phagres and other places south of Mount Pangaeum and east of the Strymon, and still today the coastal waters south of Pangaeum are known as the Pierian Gulf; and the Bottiaeans are now neighbors of the Chalcidians.) [4] The Macedonians took over from the Paeonians a narrow strip of land beside the Axius river from the interior down to Pella and the sea, and once they had driven out the Edones they occupied the country called Mygdonia, which is bordered by the Axius and the Strymon rivers. [5] They also forced the Eordi out of what is still called Eordia—most of them were killed, but a small remnant settled at Physca—and the Almopes out of Almopia. [6] The Macedonians of coastal Macedon conquered other peoples as well, whose lands they still possess: Anthemus, Crestonia, Bisaltia, and much of Macedon itself. The totality of their land is called Macedon, and Perdiccas, son of Alexander, was the king there at the time of Sitalces's offensive.

100. The Lower Macedonians were unable to resist such a large army, so they took themselves off to all the defensible locations and fortresses the country held. [2] But there were few places of refuge; it was when Archelaus, Perdiccas's son, was king that the fortresses that are now to be found there were built. He also cut good, straight roads and in general developed the country's military capacity, until he had a stronger and better-equipped cavalry and infantry than all the previous eight kings of Macedon together. [3] After leaving Doberus, the Thracian army first invaded what had earlier been Philip's realm. They took Eidomene by force, but Gortynia, Atalante, and some other places capitulated and came over to their side because of their loyalty to Philip's son Amyntas, who was with Sitalces. Europus they attempted, unsuccessfully, to take by siege. [4] Next they advanced into the rest of Macedon, with Pella and Cyrrhus to their right, but instead of penetrating beyond these places into Bottiaea and Pieria they ravaged Mygdonia, Crestonia, and Anthemus. [5] The Macedonians did not even consider fighting back with their infantry, but after sending for cavalry from their allies inland they seized every opportunity to attack the Thracian army, despite being few against many. Whenever they attacked no one stood up to them—they were good horsemen and wore breastplates—but they sometimes became surrounded by large numbers of the enemy and found themselves heavily outnumbered and in serious danger, and in the end they stopped taking action altogether because they did not think there were enough of them to hazard such an unequal fight.

101. Sitalces entered into negotiations with Perdiccas about the issues that had prompted his campaign, and since the Athenians had failed to send ships—they had not believed that he would come, and had sent him merely gifts and envoys—he dispatched a division of his army against the Chalcidians and Bottiaeans, and once he had made it impossible for them to emerge from behind their defensive walls he set about despoiling the land. [2] While he was on the Chalcidic peninsula, the peoples to the south—the Thessalians, the Magnesians and the other Thessalian dependents, and the Greeks as far south as Thermopylae—became afraid that his army might come against them and began to prepare for that eventuality. [3] The same fear affected the Thracians who live on the plains beyond and to the north of the Strymon—the Panaei, Odomantes, Droi, and Dersaei, all independent peoples. [4] It was also widely believed by the Greeks in the region who were hostile to Athens that Sitalces's Thracians might be brought in by the Athenians in accordance with their alliance and march against them.

[5] But Sitalces carried on with his occupation and ravaging of Chalcidice, Bottice, and Macedon, and when he found that he was attaining none of the objectives of the invasion—and also since his men were running out of food and were suffering from the wintry conditions—he was persuaded by Seuthes, son of Sparadocus, who was his nephew and the most powerful person in the country after Sitalces, to leave and to do so sooner rather than later. Perdiccas had secretly suborned Seuthes by promising to give him his sister in marriage and a generous dowry along with her. [6] Sitalces accepted Seuthes's advice, and after staying thirty days in all, eight of them in Chalcidice, he hurried back home with his army. Later, Perdiccas kept his promise and gave Seuthes his sister Stratonice. So that is how Sitalces's expedition went.

102. Meanwhile, in the same winter, after the Peloponnesian fleet had been disbanded, the Athenians stationed at Naupactus mounted an expedition with Phormio as their leader. They sailed to Astacus, disembarked troops—four hundred Athenian hoplites from the ships and four hundred Messenians—and advanced into the interior of Acarnania. They expelled from Stratus and Coronta* men whom they judged unreliable; restored Cynes, son of Theolytus, to Coronta; and then returned to their ships. [2] Oeniadae was the only place in Acarnania to have been consistently hostile to them, but they did not think it could be attacked in winter. The problem was the Achelous river. It rises in the Pindus mountains and flows through Dolopia, Agraeis, and Amphilochia before crossing the Acarnanian plain, passing the city of Stratus in its descent from the hills. It issues into the sea by

Oeniadae, where it forms a lake around the city, so that in winter the amount of water makes it impossible to attack the place.

[3] Most of the Echinades islands lie off Oeniadae, very close to the mouths of the Achelous. This means that the river, which is a substantial one, is constantly depositing silt, until some of the islands have become joined to the mainland, and the rest are expected to do so before very long. [4] The stream is strong, deep, and muddy, and the islands, which are not far apart, act as a frame for the silt to pile up against, since they lie not in a single line but in staggered rows, so that there are no straight channels for the water to flow through and into the open sea. The islands are small and uninhabited.

[5] The story goes that when Alcmeon, the son of Amphiaraus, became a homeless outcast after murdering his mother, he was told by Apollo in an oracle to live in this land. What the god did was tell him that he would not be released from the terrors that haunted him until he found a place to live in this country that had been invisible to the sun and had not existed as earth at the time when he killed his mother, since all the rest of the earth had been polluted by him. [6] He did not know what to make of this, the story continues, until at last he noticed this depositing of silt by the Achelous and decided that, in the considerable time that he had been an outcast for killing his mother, sufficient earth would have been deposited to sustain life. So he settled in the region around Oeniadae, became its ruler, and named the land after his son, Acarnan. Anyway, that is the story that has come down to us about Alcmeon.

103. The Athenians and Phormio set out from Acarnania and returned to Naupactus. At the beginning of spring, they sailed back to Athens, taking with them the ships they had captured and those of the prisoners they had taken in the battles they had fought who were not slaves, who were exchanged for an equal number of captured Athenians. [2] So the winter came to an end and with it the third year of the current war, the history of which was written by Thucydides.

BOOK THREE

*Years four to six of the war. **428/427:** third Peloponnesian invasion of Attica (3.1); revolt of Mytilene (3.2–6); Athenian campaigns around the Peloponnesian coast and in the northwest (3.7); revolt of Mytilene continues, and the Mytileneans seek Spartan assistance (3.8–18); Athenian raid on Caria (3.19); siege of Plataea continues (3.20–24); revolt of Mytilene continues (3.25). **427/426:** fourth Peloponnesian invasion of Attica (3.26); surrender of Mytilene, and Athenian debate over Mytilene's fate (3.27–50); Athenian attack on Minoa (3.51); fall of Plataea, and debate over Plataea's fate (3.52–68); civil war in Corcyra (3.69–85); Athenian involvement in Sicily (3.86); more plague in Athens (3.87); Athenian intervention in Aetolia (3.88). **426/425:** fifth Peloponnesian invasion of Attica (3.89); Athenian activity in the west, Melos, and Boeotia (3.90–91); Spartans establish a colony at Heraclea in Trachis (3.92–93); campaigns in northwest Greece (3.94–102, 105–114); Athenian purification of Delos (3.104); further Athenian activity in the west (3.103, 115–116).*

1. The following summer, at the time when the cereal crops were ripe, the combined Peloponnesian forces invaded Attica under the leadership of the Spartan king Archidamus, son of Zeuxidamus. Once they had established themselves, they set about ravaging the land. [2] As usual, the Athenian cavalry attacked them wherever and whenever an opportunity presented itself, and they made it impossible for the main body of light-armed troops to leave the camp and damage property near the city. [3] The Peloponnesians stayed in Attica while their provisions lasted, and then they went back and dispersed to their various home states.

2. Immediately after the Peloponnesian invasion, the whole of the island of Lesbos except for Methymna defected from the Athenians.* They had wanted to do so even before the war, but the Lacedaemonians had turned down their petition for an alliance, and even now they were compelled to rebel earlier than they had intended. [2] They were building moles for their harbors, walls for their towns, and ships, and they had been waiting for all this construction work to be complete and for some necessaries they had sent for to arrive from the Black Sea, including archers and grain. [3] But the people of Tenedos, who were enemies of theirs, the Methymnaeans, and some individual Mytileneans who belonged to the opposite faction (since they represented Athenian interests in Mytilene) informed on them. They told the Athenians that the Mytileneans were trying to force the unification of the island, with Mytilene as its center, and that with the help of the Lacedaemonians and Boeotians (who were kinsmen of the Mytileneans) they were forging ahead with everything they needed to do in order to revolt. And they said that unless preventive measures were taken at once, the Athenians would lose Lesbos.

3. The Athenians were suffering badly, not just because of the plague but also because of the war, which was starting to become settled and intense, and they thought it would be a serious matter if on top of everything else they had to go to war with Lesbos, a naval power that had suffered no reduction in its strength. At first, they did not believe the allegations, largely because they did not want them to be true. But after they had sent envoys and had failed to persuade the Mytileneans to abandon the unification of the island, and to put an end to all their preparations, they became alarmed and decided they had to nip the rebellion in the bud. [2] They hurriedly dispatched forty ships that had just been fitted out for raiding in the Peloponnese, under the command of Cleippides, son of Deinias, and two other generals. [3] They sent them off in a hurry because they had been told there was a festival of Apollo Maloeis held outside the city walls in which the entire population of Mytilene took part, and they hoped that if they were quick off the mark they could take them unawares. If the attempt succeeded, well and good, but if not they were to deliver an ultimatum: the Mytileneans were to surrender their ships and demolish their walls, otherwise there would be war. [4] So the ships set off, and ten Mytilenean triremes that had come in accordance with the terms of their alliance to support the war effort were seized by the Athenians and the crews taken into custody.

[5] But the Mytileneans received advance warning. A man crossed over to Euboea from Athens and walked to Geraestus, where he found a merchant ship that was on the point of leaving; conditions for sailing were favorable, and on the third day after leaving Athens he arrived in Mytilene and told them that Athenian ships were on their way. [6] Consequently, the Mytileneans did not go out to the sanctuary of Apollo Maloeis, and they protected the unfinished sections of the walls and harbors with barricades and mounted guard over them. **4.** On their arrival a short while later, the Athenians took stock of the situation, and then the generals delivered the ultimatum as they had been instructed. The Mytileneans refused to obey, and so the Athenians declared war.

[2] The Mytileneans were unprepared for war and found themselves suddenly left with no choice in the matter. They made a halfhearted attempt, sending their ships out a short distance in front of the harbor to offer battle, but they were chased back by the Athenians. Straight after this, they opened negotiations with the generals, to see if they could find a compromise that would get the Athenian ships sent home for the time being. [3] And the Athenian generals were happy to negotiate, since they themselves were far from sure that they were strong enough to go to war with the whole of Lesbos.

[4] Once a truce was in place, the Mytileneans sent a delegation to Athens that included one of the men who had denounced them—he now regretted what he had done—to try to persuade the Athenians to withdraw their ships on the ground that they had no intention of rebelling. [5] Meanwhile, doubting that the embassy to Athens would succeed, they also sent envoys to Sparta in a trireme that got away without being spotted by the Athenian fleet, which was riding at anchor off Malea, north of Mytilene. [6] After a difficult voyage across the open sea, the envoys to Sparta entered into talks with a view to obtaining help in some form. **5.** But the other delegation returned from Athens without having achieved anything, and so the Mytileneans and the rest of Lesbos except for Methymna went to war. The Methymnaeans were on the Athenian side, as were the Imbrians, the Lemnians, and a few other allied states in the region.

[2] The Mytileneans raised a mass levy and made a sortie against the Athenian camp. They came off best in the ensuing battle, but then they withdrew, since they lacked the confidence to camp for the night on the battlefield. [3] After that they took no action, because they did not want to risk battle without the support of whatever additional forces might come from the Peloponnese. [4] And in fact Meleas of Laconia and a Theban called Hermaeondas did turn up. They had been dispatched before the rebellion, but had failed to get there before the arrival of the Athenian expeditionary force. Later, however, after the battle, they slipped in on a trireme. Their advice was that the Mytileneans should send another trireme back with them to Sparta carrying envoys, and that is what the Mytileneans did.

6. The Athenians were considerably heartened by the inactivity of the Mytileneans. They called for support from their allies, and the allies came all the more quickly because the Lesbians were not giving any indication of strength. The Athenians brought some of their ships round to anchor south of Mytilene; constructed two fortified camps, one on each side of the city; and established blockades on both harbors. [2] But although they denied the Mytileneans the use of the sea, the rest of the island was under the control of the Mytileneans and the other Lesbians, who had by now sided with the Mytileneans. On land, the Athenians controlled only a small area immediately around their camps and Malea, which was the main base for their fleet and where they had their commissary. That was how the Mytilenean war was going.

7. This summer, at about the same time, the Athenians also sent thirty ships around the Peloponnese. The general in command was Asopius, son of Phormio, since the Acarnanians had specifically asked for a son or relative of Phormio as commander. [2] In the course of their journey the ships ravaged the coastal parts of Laconia, [3] but after that Asopius sent most of the fleet back home, retaining twelve ships, with which he went on to Naupactus. [4] Then later he mobilized the Acarnanians and campaigned with all his forces against Oeniadae, sailing up to the city on the Achelous river while the land army laid waste the farmland.* [5] The people of Oeniadae refused to submit, however, so Asopius dismissed his land forces and sailed to Leucas. He landed troops at Nericus,* but as they were returning to the ships, he himself and a fair number of his men were killed by a force made up of local inhabitants who had rallied in defense and a few garrison troops. [6] The Athenians later sailed away after recovering their dead from the Leucadians under a truce.

8. The Mytilenean envoys who had been sent on the first ship were told by the Lacedaemonians to go to Olympia so that the rest of the allies could hear what they had to say and decide what to do. So they went to Olympia—this was the Olympic festival at which Dorieus of Rhodes was victorious for the second time—[2] and at the conference that was convened after the festival they spoke in this fashion:*

9. "Lacedaemonians and allies, we are well aware of what's normal in Greece when people revolt at a time of war and leave their former alliance: those who accept them as allies welcome them insofar as they are useful, but think badly of them as traitors to their previous friends. [2] This assessment is not unfair if the rebels and the people from whom they are separating have the same ideology and intentions,† if they are evenly matched in terms of their military capacity and strength, and if there's no reasonable excuse for the rebellion. But that's not the case with us and the Athenians, and no one should think the worse of us for deserting them in their hour of danger after being valued by them in peacetime.

10. "We shall first address the issues of justice and honor, especially since we're asking you for an alliance, because we know that there's no permanence to either friendship between individuals or cooperation between states unless each party judges the other to be behaving with sincerity—and also unless they are fundamentally like-minded, because a difference of outlook leads to disagreement about what action to take.

[2] "The alliance between us and the Athenians dates from the time when you withdrew from the war with the Persians and it was the Athenians who stayed on to finish the job. [3] The purpose of the alliance, however, was not the subjugation of the Greeks by Athens, but the liberation of the Greeks from Persia. [4] They were our leaders, and as long as they treated us as equals we were happy to follow. However, when we saw that they were not only easing up on their hostility toward the Persians, but were also intent on enslaving their allies, we became extremely concerned. [5] Because of the large number of conflicting points of view, the allies were unable to unite and defend themselves, and so they were all enslaved except for us and the Chians. We cooperated with the Athenians in their campaigns as people who were nominally free and autonomous. [6] But, judging by what had already happened, we could no longer trust the Athenians as leaders. It was hardly likely that, after subjugating states that were fellow members of the alliance with us, they would refrain from doing the same, if they ever felt strong enough, to those of us who were left.

11. "If we had all remained independent, we'd have been more confident that they'd do nothing to disturb the status quo. But since they had subjugated most of our fellow allies, while our relationship with them was still one of equality, it was bound to make them increasingly irritated to see the majority already yielding and us the only ones still claiming equal status, especially since they were gaining in strength all the time and we were becoming increasingly isolated. Equality of fear is the only reliable basis for an alliance, because then if one party wants to break the treaty, they are deterred by the realization that they wouldn't be attacking from a position of advantage. [2] In short, the only reason we were left independent was that they thought their imperialistic goals could be achieved in our case by specious argument and policy rather than by armed aggression. [3] At the same time, we were useful to them as evidence for their contention that people with the same voting power as them would not be fighting alongside them willingly† unless those who were being attacked were in the wrong. Moreover, they also started by bringing in the strongest states against the weaker ones, leaving the stronger ones until last, since they would be sure to find them weaker once all the rest had been removed. If they had started with us, at a time when collectively the allies were still strong and had a rallying point, the process of subjugation wouldn't have been so easy for them. [4] Then again, our navy gave them reason to fear that at some point it might be united and joined to yours or someone else's, and so threaten Athens. [5] And another factor in our ability to hold our own was our cultivation of the Athenian people and their various leaders. [6] All the same, judging by the way they treated others, we wouldn't have survived for very long, in our opinion, if the current war hadn't broken out.

12. "What kind of 'friendship' or 'freedom' was this proving to be? How could we trust them, when our tolerance of each other was insincere—when they curried our favor in wartime out of fear and we did the same to them in peacetime? Trust in such cases is usually guaranteed by mutual goodwill, but in our case it was secured by fear.

It was fear rather than friendship that maintained the alliance, and whichever of us was the first to be emboldened by a sense of security would also be the first to break the treaty. [2] So if anyone thinks that it's wrong of us to be going ahead and rebelling while the threat that they pose to us is still potential rather than actual—if anyone thinks that we should wait and see if the threat becomes real—he's not looking at the matter right. [3] After all, if we had the ability to plot against them just as they do against us, and to postpone acting against them just as they do against us, we'd be their equals and there'd be no need for us to be their subjects. But since they always have the option of attacking us, we should have the option of taking precautions.

13. "These, Lacedaemonians and allies, were the reasons and grievances that prompted our revolt. They are clear enough to convince anyone who listens to us of the reasonableness of our action, and strong enough to frighten us into trying to find a source of safety. We wanted to revolt long ago; we approached you about it before the outbreak of war, but your refusal to accept us as allies quashed the impetus for the time being. But now, when the Boeotians proposed it, we immediately did as they suggested. In fact, we regarded it as a double secession—from the Greeks, so that we wouldn't have to join the Athenians in harming them but would help to liberate them, and from the Athenians, so that we would preempt any future attempt on their part to destroy us. [2] However, our rebellion has taken place too soon; we're still not well enough prepared. This makes it all the more important that you accept us as allies and send help quickly, so that at one stroke you're both harming your enemies and showing yourselves to be ready to defend those who need defending.

[3] "This is a unique opportunity. The Athenians have been crippled by plague and by all their expenses, and their ships are either cruising off your coast or have been deployed against us. [4] It's unlikely that they have many ships in reserve, and if you launch a second invasion of Attica this summer by sea as well as by land, they'll either be unable to resist your fleet or they'll withdraw their ships from both

the Peloponnese and Lesbos. [5] Moreover, it would be wrong for any of you to think that you'd be risking your lives for a land that isn't your concern. Lesbos may seem far away, but it will be close by when help is needed, because the critical fighting will take place not in Attica, as is generally thought, but in the territories on which Attica depends for support. [6] The Athenians' income consists of the money paid by their allies, and it will become even greater if they overcome us, because no other state will dare to revolt and there'll be additional income from us—and we'll be treated far worse than those who were enslaved earlier. [7] But if you commit yourselves to aiding us, you'll gain a state with a sizable navy—and there's nothing you need more—and it will be easier for you to defeat the Athenians because you'll be detaching their allies from them, since every one of them will be emboldened to come over to you. Moreover, you'll eradicate the charge that has been brought against you of failing to support those who secede from the Athenians. If you're seen to be liberators, your victory in the war will be more certain.

14. "The Greeks are looking to you for a better future, and we are asking you to respect that. Respect also Olympian Zeus: we're no different from suppliants, here in his sanctuary. Accept the Mytileneans as allies and come to their rescue. Don't let us down when our very lives are at stake, and when there will be widespread profit if we succeed, but the harm that will ensue if you reject our petition and we fail will be even more widespread. Prove yourselves men of the kind that the Greeks expect and our fears desire."

15. After listening to this speech by the Mytileneans, the Lacedaemonians and their allies accepted their petition and entered into an alliance with them. As for the suggested invasion of Attica, they told the allies who were present to make their way with all speed to the Isthmus with the usual two-thirds levy so that they could proceed with it. The Lacedaemonians themselves were the first to arrive, and they set about readying slipways for the ships at the Isthmus, so that, once they had hauled them over from Corinth to the sea on the Athenian side,* they could launch a simultaneous attack by sea and land. [2] But while the Lacedaemonians were determinedly going about this work, the rest of their allies were slow to assemble, because they were busy with their harvests and far from enthusiastic about the campaign.

16. The Athenians realized that all these preparations were being undertaken because they were judged to be weak, and they wanted to show that this assessment was wrong and that they were perfectly capable of repelling the attack from the Peloponnese without moving the fleet that was stationed at Lesbos. So they manned 100 ships, embarked both citizens (excluding the two wealthiest classes) and metics, and set out past the Isthmus, giving proof of strength and making armed landings wherever they wished.† [2] The Lacedaemonians were taken aback by this and they began to think that what the Lesbians had told them was untrue. The situation seemed hopeless: their allies had not yet arrived, and they also received a report that the 30 ships that were cruising off the Peloponnese were ravaging their dependent territory. And so they returned home. [3] Later, they did get a fleet ready to send to Lesbos: they sent orders to the cities for a total of 40 ships, and Alcidas, who had been appointed navarch, was to sail with them. But for the time being they returned home, and at this the Athenians did the same with their 100 ships.

17. While these 100 ships were at sea, the Athenians had more ships on active service and elsewhere than ever before, about the same number or even more than at the start of the war. [2] They had 100 ships protecting Attica, Euboea, and Salamis; another 100 off the Peloponnese; and in addition there were those at Potidaea and elsewhere, so that they had a total of 250 ships on active service in a single summer. [3] Along with Potidaea, it was the navy above all that consumed their money. The men serving at Potidaea were two-drachma hoplites, each receiving one drachma a day for himself and one for his attendant, and there were 3,000 of them at first, and no fewer at the end of the siege. Phormio brought 1,600 more hoplites, but they left before the end. And all the many crewmen were paid a drachma a day as well.* [4] These were the Athenians' main expenses early in the war, and the 100 ships meant that they had more ships manned than ever before.*

18. During the same period of time, while the Lacedaemonians were at the Isthmus, the Mytileneans marched overland against Methymna, in the belief that it would be betrayed to them by their sympathizers, with a force consisting of their own citizens and mercenaries. Their assault on the town did not go as expected, however, and they left. They went to Antissa, Pyrrha, and Eresus; consolidated their hold on these places; strengthened their walls; and then hurried back home. [2] After they had left, the Methymnaeans in their turn launched a campaign against Antissa. But they were badly mauled by the Antissans and their auxiliaries, who sallied out against them; many Methymnaean lives were lost and the remainder beat a hasty retreat. [3] After the Athenians discovered how things were—that the countryside was under Mytilenean control and that they did not have enough soldiers there to do anything about it—early in the autumn they sent 1,000 citizen hoplites under the command of the general Paches, son of Epicurus. [4] The hoplites themselves rowed the ships on which they sailed, and when they arrived they surrounded Mytilene with a single wall that had towers built into it here and there at key locations. [5] So Mytilene was now firmly excluded from both the land and the sea, and summer came to an end.

19. The Athenians were short of money for the siege of Mytilene, even though this was when for the first time a special property tax was paid that raised two hundred talents. So they sent twelve ships to collect tribute from the allies, under the command of Lysicles and four other generals, [2] and they sailed around collecting money from various places. In Caria, Lysicles marched inland from Myous across the plain of the Meander river as far as the hill of Sandius,* where he was attacked by the Carians and Anaeans. Lysicles himself and many of his men were killed.

20. In the same winter, the Plataeans came up with a desperate scheme. They were still besieged by the Peloponnesians and Boeotians, they were suffering badly from lack of food, there was no hope of a relief force arriving from Athens, and there was no prospect of their being saved in any other way. So they and those Athenians who were enduring the siege along with them came up with a plan. In its original version, as proposed by Theaenetus, son of Tolmides, who was a seer, and Eupompides, son of Daimachus, who was one of the Plataean generals, all of them were to break out and try to force their way over the enemy's wall. [2] But half of them got cold feet, thinking that it was too much of a risk, and there remained 220 men in all who were committed to the escape plan. Here is how they went about it: [3] They constructed ladders that were exactly the same length as the height of the enemy's wall, basing their calculations on the number of courses of bricks, where the wall facing them had not been plastered. Many people at once counted the courses, so that, even if some made mistakes, the majority would arrive at the correct figure, especially since they made repeated counts, and the wall, which was not too far away, was sufficiently visible for their purposes. [4] So that is how they found how long the ladders should be, by basing their estimate of the required length on the standard thickness of a brick.

21. The structure of the Peloponnesians' wall was as follows: It had two circuits, one facing Plataea and the other in case there was an Athenian attack from the outside; these two circuit walls were some sixteen feet apart. [2] In the space between them, quarters had been built and allocated to the guards, and these quarters filled the space so that there appeared to be a single thick wall with battlements on both sides. [3] At intervals of ten battlements there were tall towers that were equal in width to the wall, which is to say that they extended as far as both the inside and the outside faces of the wall, so that there was no way past a tower, and the guards had to walk through the middle of them. [4] Whenever there was heavy rainfall at night, therefore, the guards abandoned the battlements and kept watch from the towers, since they were not too far apart and had roofs. That was what the wall was like that kept the Plataeans under blockade.

22. When everything was ready, the Plataeans waited for a stormy night with rain, wind, and no moon, and then set out. They were led by the men who had first suggested the attempt. After crossing the surrounding ditch, they reached the enemy's wall undetected by the guards, because they were invisible in the dark and the sound of their approach was drowned out by the howling of the wind. [2] Also, they were very spread out in case their weapons clashed and gave them away. They were lightly armed and had shoes only on their left feet, so that they could have sure footing in the mud.* [3] They approached the battlements at a section of wall between towers, because they knew that it would be unguarded. First came the men carrying the ladders, which they propped against the wall. Next, twelve men, lightly armed with daggers and corselets, climbed up; their leader was Ammeas, son of Coroebus, who was the first to make the ascent. The rest followed him up, with six men going to each of the two towers. After them came more lightly armed men with spears, and to make it easier for them to climb up, their shields were carried by others behind them, to be handed to them when they were close to the enemy.

[4] The guards in the towers discovered the Plataeans when one of them, in taking hold of the battlements, dislodged a tile, which fell with a crash, but by then most of them were up on the wall. [5] At once a shout went up, and the main army rushed toward the wall, with no idea what the threat was because of the storm and the darkness of the night. At the same time, the Plataeans who had stayed behind in the town emerged and attacked the Peloponnesians' wall on the opposite side from where their comrades were scaling it, to distract the enemy's attention from them as much as possible. [6] So the enemy soldiers became confused and stayed where they were; none of them

dared to leave his post and help his comrades, and they had no idea what was happening. [7] The Peloponnesian company of three hundred who had the job of providing support in emergencies was also on its way around the outside of the wall toward where the first shouts had arisen. War beacons were lit to alert Thebes, but the Plataeans had prepared for this: they had beacons of their own on the city walls that they now lit, to confuse the message the enemy beacons were trying to convey. The Thebans would misread what was happening, and the Plataeans who were breaking out would have escaped and reached safety by the time they came.

23. Meanwhile, the first squad of the Plataeans who were scaling the wall had reached the top and had taken control of the two towers by killing the guards. They occupied the corridors through the towers and guarded them to prevent reinforcements from passing through. Others set ladders against the towers from the wall, and quite a few men climbed up on them. Then, while these men were hurling missiles from the towers to deter the enemy troops, who were coming up both at ground level and along the wall, the rest of their comrades, the majority, were engaged in putting large numbers of ladders in place, toppling the battlements, and getting over the outside wall. [2] After climbing down, each man took up a position on the lip of the outer ditch and shot arrows and javelins from there at anyone coming up along the wall to prevent the rest from crossing.

[3] When almost everyone had crossed the wall, the last of them—the men from the towers—climbed down with some difficulty and made their way to the ditch. Just then the three hundred bore down on them with torches in their hands. [4] The Plataeans, standing on the lip of the ditch, could see them quite well out of the darkness, and they aimed their arrows and javelins at the unprotected parts of their bodies, while they themselves were too far away for the enemy's torches to pierce the gloom and make them visible. Consequently, even the last of the Plataeans managed to cross the ditch without being caught, although it was far from easy and they had to force their

way across. [5] Ice had formed on the surface of the ditch water, not firm enough walk on, but more the semiliquid kind that is formed when the wind is from the east or the north, and the snow that had fallen in the night, driven by just such a wind, had raised the level of water in the ditch until they could hardly keep their heads above it as they crossed. But it was precisely the violence of the storm that was the main factor in the success of their escape.

24. Setting out from the ditch and keeping close together, the Plataeans took the road toward Thebes, with the shrine of the hero Androcrates to their right. Their thinking was that they were hardly likely to be suspected of taking a road that led in the direction of the enemy. Besides, they could see that the Peloponnesians were hunting for them on the road that went to Athens via Cithaeron and Dryoscephalae. [2] They stayed on the Thebes road for less than a mile before turning back and taking the road that leads to Cithaeron via Erythrae and Hysiae, and after reaching the mountains they made it safely through to Athens. There were 212 of them, but there had been more: a few had turned back to the town before scaling the wall, and one of them, an archer, had been captured at the outer ditch. [3] In any case, the Peloponnesians called off the pursuit and returned to their stations. The Plataeans in the city knew nothing of what had happened, and the men who had turned back told them there were no survivors, so the next day they sent a herald to request a truce so that they could recover the bodies, but once they learned the truth they canceled the request. So this is how the men from Plataea got over the wall and escaped.

25. Toward the end of the same winter, Salaethus, a Lacedaemonian, was sent to Mytilene in a trireme. By landing at Pyrrha and walking from there along the bed of a stream to a place where the Athenians' siege wall was scalable, he entered Mytilene without being spotted.* He told the magistrates that an invasion of Attica would take place and that the forty ships that were supposed to help them would arrive as well; this was why he had been sent on ahead, he said, and he would be taking overall charge. [2] The boost to their confidence made the Mytileneans less inclined to come to terms with the Athenians. So this winter came to an end and with it the fourth year of the current war, the history of which was written by Thucydides.

26. The following summer, the Peloponnesians first dispatched the forty promised ships to Mytilene, giving the command to Alcidas, their navarch, and then the Lacedaemonians and their allies invaded Attica, the idea being that by making trouble for the Athenians on both fronts they would be less able to send a force against the ships that were on their way to Mytilene. [2] This invasion was led by Cleomenes, who was standing in for his nephew Pausanias, the son of Pleistoanax, who was the king but still a minor. [3] They destroyed anything that had regrown in the parts of Attica that they had laid waste before and expanded their depredation to all the parts they had previously omitted. This was the invasion that the Athenians found the most distressing after the second one. [4] The Peloponnesians were constantly waiting for news from Lesbos of what their ships had achieved, on the assumption that they had already reached the island, and they extended their ravaging of Attica while they waited. But when nothing happened as they had expected and their food had run out, they went back to the Peloponnese and returned to their various home towns.

27. Meanwhile, the Mytileneans were forced to come to terms with the Athenians, because the ships from the Peloponnese were taking their time and had not arrived, and because their food had run out. [2] What happened was that when even Salaethus gave up expecting the ships to arrive, he issued hoplite arms and armor to the general populace, who had previously not had proper weaponry, because he planned to make a sortie against the Athenians. [3] But once the people were armed, they stopped obeying the civil authorities. They convened themselves as an assembly and told the aristocrats that if they did not bring out all the food from where it was stored and distribute it to everyone, they would come to terms with the Athenians by themselves and surrender the city.

28. The authorities realized that they were powerless to stop this from happening and that they would be in danger if they were excluded from the agreement, so they joined with the others in coming to terms with Paches and the army. According to the agreement, the Athenians had the right to deal with the Mytileneans as they wished, their troops were to be admitted into the city, and the Mytileneans were to send representatives to Athens to plead their case. Pending the return of these representatives, Paches was not to imprison, sell into slavery, or execute any Mytilenean. [2] These were the terms of the agreement, but the foremost members of the pro-Lacedaemonian faction were terrified, and when the army entered the city their fear got the better of them, and despite the terms of the agreement they went and sat as suppliants at the altars. Paches persuaded them to leave the sanctuaries with a guarantee of safety, and he deposited them in Tenedos town until the Athenians had decided what to do. [3] He also sent triremes to Antissa and won that place back as well, and in general arranged military matters as he saw fit.

29. The Peloponnesians in the forty ships, who were supposed to have arrived quickly, took their time even while they were still sailing around the Peloponnese, and then failed to pick up the pace for the rest of their voyage. The Athenians at home were unaware of their activity until they put in at Delos, and it was when the Peloponnesians left Delos and reached Icaros and Myconos that they first heard that Mytilene had fallen. [2] They wanted to get more precise information, so they sailed to Embatum, near Erythrae,* which they reached on about the seventh day after the fall of Mytilene. Once they had precise information, they met to try to decide what action to take given the circumstances, and a man from Elis called Teutiaplus spoke to them as follows:

30. "Alcidas and fellow Peloponnesian army commanders, in my opinion we should sail to Mytilene at once, before we're detected by the enemy. [2] In all probability, we shall find plenty of gaps in their defenses; this is usual when men have only just occupied a city. This will certainly be the case at sea, because they never expect an enemy to launch a seaborne attack, and because it's at sea that our strength lies in this instance. But it is also likely that, because they assume that they've already won, their land forces will have been billeted in a disorganized and careless fashion throughout the city. [3] So if we fall on them suddenly and by night, I feel sure that, with the help of our remaining friends inside, we'll manage to seize control. [4] Let us not shrink from the danger, but bear in mind that it's just this kind of thing that makes warfare unpredictable, and that the most successful general is the one who guards against such carelessness in himself and attacks when he sees it in an enemy."

31. That was the substance of Teutiaplus's speech, but Alcidas was not convinced that he was right. Some of the others who were there, exiles from Ionia and Lesbians who had joined the expedition, had some advice for him as well. Since he thought Teutiaplus's plan too risky, they said, he should seize one of the Ionian cities, or Cyme in Aeolis. With such a base they could detach Ionia from Athens—and the prospects of success were good, since they had been welcomed by everyone—and deprive the Athenians of their greatest source of income. Furthermore, the Athenians would have to bear the expense of any naval blockade they imposed. And they added that they thought they could persuade Pissuthnes* to support them militarily. [2] But Alcidas did not like this idea either. Since it was too late to save Mytilene, his plan consisted mainly of getting back to the Peloponnese as quickly as possible.

32. He set out from Embatum along the coast, and at Myonnesus in the territory of Teos* he slaughtered most of the prisoners he had taken in the course of his voyage. [2] When he put in at Ephesus, a deputation of Samians from Anaea came to him.* They told him that killing men who had not lifted a hand against him and were not his enemies, but had been forced into the Athenian alliance, was not the right way to liberate Greece. If he carried on, they said, he would turn few of his enemies into friends and would find that far more of his friends became enemies. [3] He saw that they were right and released the prisoners he still held from Chios and some of the others. For people had made no attempt at flight when they saw his ships, but had come up to them, taking them to be Athenian; they had never expected to see Peloponnesian ships on their side of the Aegean while the Athenians had mastery of the sea.

33. When Alcidas left Ephesus, it was with some haste. In fact he was fleeing, because when he was lying at anchor off Clarus he had been spotted by the *Salaminia* and the *Paralus*,* which happened to be in the area on a mission from Athens. Afraid of being pursued, he took to the open sea; he intended not to make land anywhere, if he could help it, before the Peloponnese. [2] Reports about the Peloponnesian fleet reached Paches and the Athenians from Erythrae and indeed from everywhere. The Ionian cities had no defensive walls, so there was widespread fear that as they sailed along the coast the Peloponnesians would fall on the cities and sack them—that is, assuming they had no intention of making their stay permanent. Then the *Paralus* and the *Salaminia* supplied Paches with a firsthand report of the sighting of Alcidas at Clarus. [3] He hastily set out in pursuit. He kept it up as far as the island of Patmos, but when it became clear that Alcidas was out of reach, he returned to Mytilene. He would have preferred to encounter the Peloponnesians in open water, but since that had not happened, he considered it fortunate that they had not been trapped somewhere and forced to construct a camp, because he would then have had to detail ships to watch them and set up a blockade.

34. As he was on his way back along the coast, he stopped at Notium, the harbor of Colophon,* where the Colophonians had settled after the upper city had fallen to a Persian force commanded by Itamanes, whose intervention had been solicited by one of the factions at a time of civil unrest. This had happened at about the time of the

second Peloponnesian invasion of Attica. [2] The fugitives from Colophon who had taken up residence in Notium were once again at one another's throats. One faction had requested and been given Arcadian and barbarian mercenaries by Pissuthnes and were living in a walled-off sector of the town, where pro-Persian Colophonians from the upper city who had come to join them were also living as citizens. The other faction had been forced out, and it was these outcasts who called in Paches. [3] Paches invited Hippias, the leader of the Arcadians in the walled-off sector, to a conference, on the understanding that he would return him to his fortress safe and sound if Hippias found Paches's terms not to his liking. So Hippias came out to meet him, but Paches took him into custody, without actually binding him, and launched a surprise attack on the walled-off sector, taking the enemy unawares. After capturing the fort, he killed all the Arcadians and barbarians who were inside. Later he returned Hippias to the fort, as he had promised, and once he was inside he seized him and had him executed by bowmen. [4] He handed Notium over to the Colophonians, excluding those who had espoused the Persian cause. Later the Athenians sent out men to refound the town and settled it under Athenian laws, populating it also with all the Colophonians they could find living elsewhere.

35. After returning to Mytilene, Paches saw to the submission of Pyrrha and Eresus. The Lacedaemonian Salaethus had been hiding in the city, but Paches found him and sent him off to Athens along with the Mytileneans he had deposited in Tenedos and anyone else whom he judged to bear responsibility for the rebellion. [2] He also sent most of his troops back home, while he stayed on with the rest and arranged matters in Mytilene and the rest of Lesbos as he saw fit.

36. When Salaethus and the others arrived in Athens, the Athenians immediately executed Salaethus, even though he offered, among other things, to get the Peloponnesians to leave Plataea, which they were still besieging. [2] There were various proposals as to what to do with the others, but in the end, motivated by anger, they decided to kill not just the prisoners who had been brought to Athens, but all adult male Mytileneans, and to sell the women and children into slavery. They were furious about the revolt in general, because the Mytileneans had rebelled despite not having the same subject status as the other allies, and their fury was further exacerbated by the fact that the Peloponnesian ships had dared to venture to Ionia to help them. This was held to be evidence that the revolt had long been premeditated. [3] They therefore quickly sent a trireme to inform Paches of this decision of theirs and ordered him to kill the Mytileneans.

[4] The very next day, however, there was something of a change of heart. They now saw their decision as brutal and thought they had gone too far in voting to destroy a whole city rather than just those of its citizens who were guilty. [5] When the Mytilenean envoys who were in Athens and their Athenian supporters learned of this change of heart, they worked on the authorities to reopen the debate. It was all the easier for them to get their way because it was clear to the authorities too that the majority of the citizens wanted to have a chance to reconsider the matter. [6] An assembly was swiftly convened and various views were expressed. One of the speakers was Cleon, son of Cleaenetus, the person who had prevailed in the previous assembly with his proposal to condemn the Mytileneans to death. He was in general the most violent person in Athens, and at that time he was the speaker the people found the most persuasive by a wide margin. He came forward again and spoke along the following lines:

37. "I've often come to realize that a democracy is incapable of ruling over others; this is not the first time, but the realization was particularly driven home to me by your present change of heart about the Mytileneans. [2] The fact that in your daily relations with one another there's no element of fear or intrigue leads you to relate to your allies in the same way. You don't see that every mistake you make is a result of being won over by their arguments, and every time you give in to them out of pity, your weakness endangers you and doesn't win you their gratitude either. You're failing to take account of the fact

that your empire is a tyranny, imposed on unwilling subjects who, for their part, intrigue against you.* You don't win their obedience by making concessions that do you harm, nor are they obedient because of any feelings of loyalty toward you. They obey you because you are stronger than they are.

[3] "Most alarming of all is the prospect of inconstancy in our decision-making. You need to appreciate that a city that relies on laws that go unchallenged, even if they're imperfect, is stronger than one that relies on laws that are fine in themselves, but are unenforced; that unsophisticated self-discipline is more practical than undisciplined cleverness; and that ordinary people can generally manage their cities better than their intellectual superiors can. [4] Clever people want to appear wiser than the laws and to win every public debate, knowing that there's no more important field in which they might display their intelligence, and the outcome of this kind of behavior is that they invariably bring about their cities' ruin. But people who doubt their own intelligence do not consider themselves smart enough to judge the laws or competent enough to criticize a speech delivered by a fine speaker, and since they're impartial judges and aren't competing with others they usually come to the right conclusions. [5] We speakers must similarly not get so carried away by the eloquence and intellectual rivalry that we offer you, the Athenian people, advice that goes against what we really think.

38. "For my part, I haven't changed my mind, and I'm surprised at those who've reopened the debate about Mytilene. They've made the passage of time a factor, and that always works to the advantage of wrongdoers, because as time passes the injured party calms down and goes after the perpetrator with less intensity. If the punishment is to fit the crime it must be exacted as soon as possible after the injury.† I also wonder who's going to take the opposite position and claim to show that the Mytileneans' wrongdoing is good for us and that our misfortunes harm our allies. [2] Clearly he must either be confident enough in his abilities as a speaker to contend that your firm decision was no decision at all, or he's been bribed to try to mislead you with elaborate and specious arguments. [3] In these kinds of competitions, the state hands out prizes to speakers[†] while incurring the risks itself.

[4] "It's you who are responsible for all this, because you perversely turn speakers' orations into a contest. You have the habit of being spectators of speeches and hearers of action. Your assessment of the feasibility of action in the future depends on the eloquence of the speechmakers, and when it comes to assessing actions that have already taken place, you don't regard a deed that you've witnessed as more deserving of trust than one that you've merely heard about from clever critics. [5] What you're best at is being taken in by every newfangled argument, while refusing to go along with any that are tried and tested. You're under the spell of anything unusual, and mistrustful of what's familiar. [6] Most of all, every one of you wants to be a good speaker himself, or at least to rival good speakers by showing himself capable of keeping up with their trains of thought. You applaud points speakers are making before they've finished making them; you're as quick to anticipate what's being said as you are slow to anticipate its consequences. [7] It's almost as though you were looking for a different world from the one we live in and ignoring the facts before you. In short, the pleasure of listening to speeches overwhelms you, and you behave like spectators attending a sophistic display rather than people taking thought for what's best for their city.

39. "I don't want you to fall back on these habitual responses, and so I tell you plainly that no single city has ever done you as much wrong as Mytilene. [2] Personally, I can make allowances for people who rebelled because they found your rule intolerable or because they were forced to do so by the enemy. But what about people who occupy an island and a walled city, and therefore have no reason to fear our enemies except by sea, where with their own fleet of triremes they are scarcely defenseless? People who are self-governing and treated by us with particular respect? Under these circumstances, we can't call what they did a rebellion, because the term applies only to people who are suffering some form of oppression. No, this is a case of intrigue and insurrection, and they sided with our bitterest enemies in an attempt to destroy us. And that is more dangerous for us than if they had made war on us on their own in an attempt to increase their own power.

[3] "They learned nothing from seeing what happened to others, despite the fact that we've crushed all those who revolted from us in the past; nor did the risk to their current prosperity deter them from embarking on this dangerous course of action. Overconfident about the future, and with hopes that outran their abilities but not their desires, they committed themselves to war, preferring might to right. At a time that they imagined would give them a chance of success, they attacked us without the slightest justification for doing so. [4] It's not uncommon for states that meet most fully and swiftly with unexpected good fortune to become arrogant. It's usually the case that success is less perilous for people when it's expected than when it's unforeseen; it's almost easier for people to keep misfortune at bay than it is for them to keep prosperity intact. [5] The Mytileneans should long ago have received no better treatment from us than the other allies, and then they wouldn't have become so arrogant. After all, generally speaking, it's natural for people to despise those who placate them and respect those who stand up to them.

[6] "Even now we must punish them as their wrongdoing deserves. And we shouldn't pin the blame on the oligarchs while pardoning the general populace. They all joined together in attacking you, though the commoners could have turned to us, in which case by now they'd have recovered control of their city. But, judging it less of a risk to side with the oligarchs, they joined the revolt. [7] Look at it this way. If you impose the same punishment on allies who were forced by the enemy to defect as on those who deliberately chose to do so, do you imagine that there are any who won't seize on the slightest pretext for defecting, when the reward for success is freedom and the penalty for failure is tolerable? [8] And every city that revolts will thereby seriously endanger our money and our lives. If we're successful, we'll

recover a ruined city, and from then on you'll be deprived of further revenue from it, and revenue is the source of our strength; if we fail, we'll have added another enemy to those we already have, and the time that should be spent defending ourselves against our current enemies will be spent fighting our own allies.

40. "So we shouldn't hold out any hope, whether secured by eloquence or bought by bribes, that they will be pardoned on the ground that they simply made a mistake, as people do. The harm they did us was not involuntary; they plotted against us knowing full well what they were doing, but only involuntary actions are forgivable. [2] I fought earlier as well, at the first debate, for the decision you made, and now I'm fighting for you not to reconsider what's already been decided, and not to be led astray by the three things that are particularly detrimental to imperial power: compassion, the charm of speeches, and forbearance. [3] There's nothing wrong with mutual sympathy between people who are on the same side, but feeling compassion for people who won't return it and who are bound to be our perpetual enemies is misplaced. Speakers who have a charming way with words can compete in less important arenas, not one in which the brief pleasure they give will be followed by great harm to the city, while they themselves reap the rewards of their eloquence. And forbearance is properly shown to those who are going to be our friends in the future as well, not to those who will consistently remain just as much our enemies as before.

[4] "I have only one point to make, then, in summing up. If you follow my advice you'll be treating the Mytileneans as they deserve and at the same time doing what's best for Athens, whereas if you decide otherwise you won't be winning their gratitude so much as passing sentence on yourselves. For if they were right to revolt you must be wrong to have an empire. But if, despite its being wrong, you still expect to have an empire, then it's in your interest to punish these people—even, believe me, if it's an unreasonable thing to do; otherwise, you must give up your empire and do the virtuous thing,

since virtue will then no longer be the dangerous option. [5] Choose to defend yourselves by punishing them as they would have punished you. Just because you survived their scheming, don't prove yourselves to be more charitable than the schemers, but bear in mind what in all likelihood they'd have done to you if they'd won, especially since they were the aggressors. [6] For it's primarily those who make trouble for others when they have no good reason for doing so who carry aggression to the point of annihilation. They do so because they're concerned about the danger if any of their enemies remain. After all, someone who suffers unwarranted harm and survives is more dangerous than an enemy in a fair fight.

[7] "So don't be traitors to yourselves. Recall as exactly as you can how you felt before—how you thought it all-important to crush them. Now is the time to pay them back. Don't let their present plight sap your resolve, and don't forget the danger that once hung over you. [8] Punish them as they deserve. Make it perfectly plain to the other allies that rebellion will be punished with death. If they understand this, there'll be less need for you to neglect your enemies and fight your own allies."

41. The next speaker, after Cleon had spoken in this vein, was Diodotus, son of Eucrates. It had been Diodotus who had also argued most forcefully at the previous assembly against killing the Mytileneans. He came forward on this occasion too and spoke in the following vein:

42. "I have no criticism of those who've given us this opportunity to revisit the decision we made about the Mytileneans, and I do not applaud those who tell us off for debating crucial issues more than once. Haste and emotion are the two major obstacles to good decision-making—emotion because it tends to be accompanied by folly, and haste because it tends to be accompanied by narrow-mindedness and superficiality of judgment. [2] And anyone who insists that speeches are not the way to clarify matters is either stupid or has some personal interest in the matter. He's stupid if he thinks there's any other way to elucidate the obscurities of the future, and he's self-interested if his aim is to push through a disgraceful proposal—in which case, recognizing that he can't give a good speech in a bad cause, he thinks that if he does a good enough job of defamation, he'll cow both the opposition and the audience into submission.

[3] "But people who anticipate the words of their adversary and accuse him of putting on a rhetorical performance for money are the most difficult to deal with. If a speaker charged merely with ignorance fails to make his case, he steps down with a reputation for being more stupid than dishonest, but when the charge is dishonesty even a speaker who wins his case becomes suspect, and if he fails he's thought to be dishonest as well as stupid. [4] The city is the loser in such a case, because fear robs it of its advisers. Indeed, Athens would be more successful if these obnoxious citizens were incompetent speakers, because then we wouldn't make the mistakes consequent on being so often persuaded by them. [5] A good citizen should prove himself the better speaker by fair debate, not by scaring off his opponents. And while a sensible city shouldn't reduce the honor already enjoyed by a speaker whose advice is generally good, it also shouldn't keep conferring honors on him; and not only should it not punish a speaker for failing to win assent, but it shouldn't dishonor him either. [6] Thus a sensible city would minimize the likelihood that a successful speaker, with his eye on yet higher honors, might promote policies with which he doesn't really agree in order to make himself popular, or that an unsuccessful speaker might resort to similar flattery in his turn in an attempt to win the people over.

43. "But this isn't our practice at all, and what's more, the slightest suspicion that someone might be speaking for gain, however excellent his advice, is enough to make us deprive the city of the evident benefit he has to offer, out of indignation at the unsubstantiated suspicion that he might have been bribed. [2] It has become normal for straightforwardly given good advice to be no less suspect than bad advice—so normal that just as someone whose aim is to get the most appalling policies adopted has to rely on deceit to win the general populace over, so a speaker whose proposals are good also has to bend the truth in order to be believed. [3] Thanks to this overthinking, Athens is the only state that can't be benefited openly, without recourse to guile, because anyone who openly gives good advice is thought to be expecting to make a stealthy profit from it somehow.

[4] "On issues of the greatest importance to the city and in situations like the present one, it ought to be assumed that we speakers think further ahead than you, with your focus on short-term results, especially since, as advisers, we are accountable, but as listeners you are not. [5] If both the persuasive speaker and the persuaded listener were equally liable to penalization, you'd be more sober in your decisions. But as things are, there are times when, in the heat of the moment, when things go wrong, you punish one man, the one who persuaded you, for his misjudgment, and not yourselves for your mistake, even though you were collectively responsible for it.

44. "I'm not here either to defend the Mytileneans or to denounce them. The issue for us today, if we're sensible, isn't whether they've done wrong, but whether we're making decisions that are right for us. [2] Suppose I prove them to be guilty of serious wrongdoing: it doesn't follow that I'm also going to recommend that they be killed, unless that would be expedient for the city; nor, if I demonstrate that they deserve pardon, does it follow that I'd let them off,† unless there's some clear benefit in that for the city. [3] We should be deliberating about the future, not the present, don't you think? Cleon forcefully insists that the imposition of the death penalty will prove to be advantageous in the future, in the sense that it will discourage rebellion, and I too base my view on what will be good for us in the future—but I push with equal forcefulness for the opposite conclusion, which I am sure is the right course. [4] I urge you not to reject the practical advantages of my proposal because of the apparent reasonableness of his. You might be attracted to his proposal; it might seem more just in view of the anger you currently feel for the Mytileneans. But we're not engaged in a legal dispute with them, and so there's no need for arguments about right and wrong. We're trying to decide how they might best serve our interests.

45. "Now, throughout Greece, the death penalty is prescribed for many offenses, even some that are relatively insignificant compared to the one at issue today, but people still accept the risk because they're carried away by hope. No one has ever embarked on a hazardous enterprise convinced that he's going to fail. [2] By the same token, what rebel city has ever made its move believing that the resources available to it from itself or its allies were inadequate? [3] Mistakes, both personal and collective, are inevitable, given human nature, and there's no legal means of preventing them, even though every imaginable way of penalizing criminals to reduce the harm they do to society has been prescribed and tried out. Long ago the penalties for the worst crimes were probably less severe, but over the course of time, as infractions were still taking place, most of them have ended up as the death penalty. But even so, the infractions continue.

[4] "So either something that people fear more than death has to be found, or we're left just with death. But death is no deterrent, because poverty makes people bold through sheer necessity, and affluence fills them with presumptuous pride that makes them always want more, and every other condition of life entails its own dominant passion that induces people to take risks. However people are placed, they can be gripped by some irresistible and overpowering force. [5] In short, there's no situation in which hope and desire fail to do immense damage—the one leading and the other following, the one devising schemes and the other holding out the prospect of good chances of success. Precisely because they're invisible, they prove stronger than dangers that can be seen. [6] And then on top of hope and desire there's good fortune, which is just as powerful a factor in deluding people, because when it comes out of the blue, as it sometimes does, it leads people to take risks even if their resources are inadequate. It has the same effect on cities, too, insofar as when the most important

issues are at stake, such as freedom or being ruled by others, every individual joins all his fellow citizens in irrationally overestimating his abilities. [7] In a word, when human nature has a strong impulse to do something, it's impossible for it to be deterred, either by force of law or by any other object of fear. It would be really naive to think otherwise.

46. "It follows, then, that we mustn't allow trust in the effectiveness of the death penalty to skew our decision-making; nor should we put it beyond the reach of rebels' hope that they could repent and bring their mistake to an end in the shortest possible time. [2] You need to bear in mind that, as things are at present, any state that revolts and then realizes that it's going to fail can come to terms with us, because it's still capable of covering our expenses and paying tribute in the future. But don't you see that in the alternative scenario every rebel state will prepare better than they do now and will hold out to the bitter end under siege, if the outcome is the same whether it comes to terms slowly or quickly? [3] Isn't it bound to hurt us if the consequence of denying them the chance to come to terms is an expensive siege? And suppose the city falls to us: that's no good for us either, because what we recover is a ruin; we'll lose the revenue from it, and revenue is the source of our strength against our enemies.

[4] "So when we pass sentence on rebellious cities we shouldn't harm ourselves by being sticklers for the law. It would be better for us to see how, by punishing them moderately, we can keep them strong and continue to have them as a source of revenue. We should choose to base our security not on the threat of our laws, but on the vigilance of our actions. [5] At the moment, we do the opposite: if a free state, an unwilling subject, revolts, in an attempt to regain its right of self-government, which is not an unnatural thing for it to do, and we subdue it, we feel obliged to punish it severely. [6] The way we should treat free men is not with extreme punishment at the time of their rebellion, but with extreme vigilance before they rebel, and by trying to ensure in advance that it never occurs to them to do so. And if they do rebel, we should lay the blame on the smallest possible number of people.

47. "There's another aspect that you need to consider as well, to see how badly wrong you'd be to find Cleon's proposal acceptable. [2] As things are at present, the common people of all the allied cities are well disposed toward you. Either they refuse to join the oligarchs in rebellion, or, if they're forced to do so, the men who instigated the rebellion have an enemy in their midst and when you go to war with the renegade city you have the people as an ally. [3] If you destroy the common people of Mytilene when they played no part in the rebellion, and when they voluntarily surrendered the city to you as soon as they were armed, in the first place you'll be committing the crime of killing your benefactors, and in the second place you'll bring about exactly the situation the oligarchs want. That is, when they get the cities to secede, they'll have the people as allies in their midst, because you'll already have made it clear that the same punishment awaits the guilty and the innocent alike. [4] Even if the people were guilty, you should act as though they weren't, in order not to make enemies of our only remaining allies. [5] For the preservation of our empire, voluntary submission to injustice seems to me far more expedient than destroying in the name of justice those it would be better to spare. Cleon claims that punishment combines justice and expediency, but I've shown that no such combination is possible in this instance.

48. "Be persuaded by me, then, because you recognize that my proposal is the better one. Don't be swayed too much by pity or moderation; I, no more than Cleon, would not have such emotions influence you. Base your decision only on the strength of my suggestions. In a calm and collected fashion, try the Mytileneans whom Paches considered guilty and sent here, but let the rest form a government. [2] That will not only be good for us in the future, but it will make our enemies afraid right now, because, from an enemy's point of view, a person is strengthened more by good decisions than by mindless aggression and brute force."

49. That was the substance of Diodotus's speech. It was extremely hard to tell which of these policies was better, and despite their change of heart the Athenians struggled to reach a decision. The show of hands was very close, but Diodotus's view prevailed. [2] A second trireme was immediately and hastily dispatched in the hope that they would not find that the first one—which had a lead of about a day and a night—had already arrived and that Mytilene had been destroyed. [3] The Mytilenean envoys supplied the ship with wine and barley-meal, and promised generous rewards if they got there on time. The sense of urgency was so great that the rowers remained at their oars as they ate their barley-meal mixed with wine and olive oil, and they slept and rowed in shifts. [4] Luckily, there was no contrary wind, and the first ship was not hurrying on its disagreeable mission, while the second one was pressing ahead with such speed. But the first ship beat them to it. Paches read the decree and was just about to put the Athenian people's decision into effect when the second ship put into port and prevented the massacre. That was how close Mytilene came to destruction.

50. The other men—those whom Paches had sent to Athens because he considered them the prime movers of the rebellion—were executed by the Athenians on the motion of Cleon. There were slightly more than a thousand of them. The Athenians also demolished the walls of Mytilene and took over its ships. [2] Later, instead of assessing the Lesbians for tribute payment, they divided the land (except for what belonged to the Methymnaeans) into three thousand allotments, and apart from three hundred that were reserved for the gods, they gave the rest to cleruchs, who were selected by lot from their own citizens and sent out to the island. The Lesbians agreed to pay two minas a year for each allotment and then farmed the land themselves. [3] The Athenians also took possession of the towns on the mainland that Mytilene had controlled, and from then on they were subjects of Athens. That is how things turned out for Lesbos.

51. In the same summer, after the fall of Lesbos, the Athenians sent an expeditionary force under the command of the general Nicias, son of Niceratus, against the island of Minoa, which lies off Megara. The

Megarians had built a tower there and were using it as a fortified outpost. [2] Nicias wanted it, rather than Budorum and Salamis, to become the Athenians' base for watching over Megara, because it was closer. The idea was to make it impossible for the Peloponnesians to use Megara as a place from which to launch stealthy naval expeditions with either state triremes (as had happened before)* or privateers, and at the same time to prevent shipping from getting through to Megara. [3] First, he captured by escalade from the sea two towers that jutted out from the side facing Nisaea. Having thus opened the channel between the island and the coast, he also walled off the mainland side of the island at a point where it was close to the coast, and where relief could have been brought in by means of a bridge across shallows. [4] This work was finished in a few days, and afterward Nicias built a fortress on the island itself, left a garrison there, and returned home with the rest of his forces.

52. This summer, at about the same time, the Plataeans, too, who had run out of food and could no longer endure being besieged, came to terms with the Peloponnesians. This is how it came about:* [2] The Peloponnesians assaulted the city wall, and the Plataeans were finding it impossible to repel the attack. This made the Lacedaemonian commander realize how weak the Plataeans were, but he held back from taking the city by military means, as he had instructions from Sparta not to do so. The Lacedaemonians' thinking was that if at some point there was a peace treaty in place with Athens, and by the terms of the agreement each side was to return to the other the places it had taken during the war, Plataea would not have to be returned, because it had come over to the Peloponnesian side voluntarily. So he sent a herald, who told the Plataeans that if they were prepared to surrender the city to the Lacedaemonians voluntarily and accept them as judges, they would treat no one unjustly and would punish only the guilty.

[3] After the herald had delivered this message, the Plataeans, who were now desperately weak, surrendered the city. The Peloponnesians

supplied the Plataeans with food for several days, pending the arrival from Sparta of the five men appointed as judges. [4] When they arrived, no formal accusation was brought forward, but the Plataeans were summoned to a meeting at which they were asked just one question: whether they had been of service in any respect to the Lacedaemonians and their allies during the current war. [5] In response, the Plataeans asked to be allowed to speak at some length. They chose as their spokesmen Astymachus, son of Asopolaus, and Lacon, son of Aeimnestus, who represented Lacedaemonian interests in Plataea, and these men came forward and spoke somewhat as follows:

53. "Lacedaemonians, we surrendered our city to you because we trusted you. We didn't expect to undergo this kind of trial but a more conventional procedure, and we agreed not to go to arbitration but to be tried, as we are, by no other judges than the five chosen by you, because we felt sure that we'd receive fair treatment from them. [2] But now we're afraid that we might have been mistaken on both counts, because we have good grounds for suspecting that the most dire of fates is at stake in this trial and that you'll turn out not to be impartial. We infer this from two facts: first, you issued no preliminary statement of the charges against which we were to defend ourselves—in fact, we had to ask for permission to speak—and, second, your question to us was curt, and one to which a truthful answer would result in adverse consequences for us, while a false answer would simply be challenged. [3] So, given that our position is completely hopeless, we have no choice but to risk saying something, and this also seems the safer course, since otherwise, given our situation, we might well be charged with having left unspoken the very words that, if spoken, would have saved us. [4] But the attempt to persuade you raises further difficulties, on top of those we already have. If we had no knowledge of each other, we could do ourselves good by introducing evidence of which you were unaware. But as things are, whatever we say will be addressed to people who are already fully aware of it, and what we're afraid of isn't that, in accusing us, you've decided that we're worse people than you, but that as a favor to others the cause that we plead has already been prejudged.

54. "Nevertheless, by presenting arguments proving not only that we're in the right where our dispute with the Thebans is concerned, but also that we've done right by you and the rest of the Greeks, we shall remind you of all the good we've done and try to get you to see the validity of our argument. [2] To your question—your curt question—whether we've been of service in any respect to the Lacedaemonians and their allies during the current war, we reply as follows: if you're asking the question because you take us to be enemies, then you weren't wronged if you received no benefit from us; but if you regard us as friends, it's you, not we, who are in the wrong, because it's you who've taken up arms against us. [3] We've proved our worth not only in peacetime, but also against the Persians: we weren't the first to break the peace now, and we were then the only Boeotians to take part in the fight for the freedom of Greece.* [4] Despite being mainlanders, we fought in the naval battle at Artemisium, and we joined you and Pausanias for the battle that took place on our soil. On every other occasion, too, when the Greeks were threatened at that time, we played a part that was out of all proportion to our strength. [5] And we've been of help to you, in particular, Lacedaemonians: at the time when the rebel helots occupied Ithome after the earthquake and you were terrified as never before or since, we sent a relief force of a third of our fighting men.* These are things that should not be forgotten.

55. "That was how we chose to behave on those critical occasions in the past. Later, we became enemies, but that was your fault. When the Thebans attacked us,* we asked you for an alliance, but you turned us down and told us to approach the Athenians, because they lived nearby, while you were far away. [2] Still, we didn't act at all unusually toward you in that war, nor were we ever likely to. [3] We refused to secede from the Athenian alliance when you pushed us to do so, but that wasn't wrong of us, because they helped us against the Thebans when you held back, and it would therefore have been wrong for us to betray them. This is especially so given that we'd been well treated by them, and it was at our request that we were accepted into the alliance and even granted Athenian citizenship. It was only right, then, for us to respond readily to their orders. [4] Besides, when you or the Athenians order your allies to do something, it isn't the followers who are responsible if right is transgressed, but those who are leading them astray.

56. "There are many other instances of wrongs that the Thebans have done us, and you yourselves are well aware of their most recent act of aggression, which is the cause of our present troubles. [2] They attempted to seize our city at a time of peace and, moreover, on a holy day.* There was nothing wrong, then, in our getting even with them; we were acting in conformity with the universally established principle that it's a sacred right to resist a hostile offensive, and it would therefore be preposterous for us to come to harm now because of what we did to them. [3] If you're going to base your notion of justice on your short-term interest and on the Thebans' current hostility, you'll show yourselves to be no true judges of right and wrong but people who pander to expediency.

[4] "They may seem useful to you now, but consider how much more useful we and all the Greeks except them were on that earlier occasion, when the danger you faced was greater. Nowadays it's you who attack others and are objects of fear, but at the time we're talking about the barbarians were threatening you and everyone else with servitude, and these Thebans sided with them. [5] In all fairness, our present offense—if that's the correct description of anything we've done—should be offset by our past commitment to your cause. You'll find that the lesser is outweighed by the greater, and that at that critical time, when it was rare for any Greek to pit his courage against the might of Xerxes, praise was won not by those who looked to their own security, and in the face of the invasion tried to arrange things to their own advantage, but by those who were willing to risk their lives boldly, doing what was right. [6] We were of that number

and we were especially honored, but now we're afraid that the same standards that guided us then might be our undoing now, since we did what was right and chose Athens, rather than doing what was advantageous and choosing you. [7] Yet you should make it clear that you judge the same things consistently in the same way, and you should see that your advantage lies precisely in safeguarding what you take to be your short-term interests while displaying unwavering gratitude toward honorable allies.

57. "You should bear in mind that at present most Greeks regard you as paragons of virtue. This case that you're judging will not pass unnoticed, as you're well thought of and we're blameless, and so if the decision you reach is inappropriate, you'd better be careful: despite your superior virtue, the Greeks might find it unacceptable for you to have passed such a judgment on good men, and they might not tolerate the dedication in their common shrines of spoils ripped from our dead bodies, when we were the benefactors of Greece. [2] The sacking of Plataea by Lacedaemonians will horrify them, as will the fact that you wiped the whole city off the face of Greece, buildings and all, in order to gratify Thebans, when your fathers inscribed our city on the tripod at Delphi* because of our courage. [3] See how awful things have got for us! Our city was on the verge of destruction during the Persian conquest, and now you, who previously valued our friendship extremely highly, consider us less important to you than the Thebans and have put us through two terrible ordeals: first, the prospect of being starved to death if we refused to surrender our city, and now the prospect of being condemned to death by you. [4] We Plataeans, whose commitment to the Greek cause was out of proportion to our strength, have been rejected on all sides; we're all alone with no one to protect us. None of our former allies is helping us; you were our only hope, Lacedaemonians, but unfortunately we fear that we can't trust you.

58. "Yet we feel we have the right to ask you, in the name of the gods who sanctified our alliance then,*† and in view of our honorable conduct in the service of Greece, to be flexible and to reconsider everything of which you've been persuaded by the Thebans. Ask them for a concession in return—that you should not have to kill people whose deaths would dishonor you, and that you should earn gratitude for restrained rather than shameful conduct. Don't make trouble for yourselves by giving pleasure to others. [2] Hardly any time is needed for taking our lives, but long, hard work will be required to efface the infamy resulting from it. For we aren't enemies whom you might reasonably punish, but sympathizers who had no choice but to go to war. [3] So in all conscience you should deliver a verdict that spares our lives and takes account of the fact that we surrendered to you of our own free will and with hands outstretched for mercy—and Greek law prohibits the killing of suppliants. And you should also acknowledge that we've never done you anything but good.

[4] "Look at the graves of your fathers, who were killed by the Persians and buried here in our land. Every year we regularly honor them with clothing and all the customary offerings, paid for by the state, and we bring them the first fruits of all the produce of our land in its season. We do this as sympathizers from a friendly country and as allies of those who were once our comrades in arms. If you were to reach the wrong verdict in our case, you'd be undoing all of this. [5] Don't you see? Pausanias had them buried here because he thought he was laying them in friendly soil and among friendly people. But if you kill us and turn Plataea into Theban territory, you'll be leaving your fathers and relatives in enemy soil and among their murderers,* deprived of the honors that they now receive. Isn't that exactly what you'd be doing? What's more, you'll reduce to servitude the land where the Greeks won their freedom, make desolate the sanctuaries of the gods to whom they prayed before defeating the Persians, and deny those who established and founded the rites to your fathers the right to perform them.

59. "Such behavior does not sit well with your reputation, Lacedaemonians. You're violating the common customs of the Greeks and

bent on sinning against your forefathers. You'd be destroying us, your benefactors, not because you've been wronged yourselves, but because of the hostility of others. It would be better to let your hearts be moved and to spare us. Bring prudent compassion to bear on our case and take into consideration not only the horror of our fate, but also what kind of people would be suffering it—what kind of people we are. Bear in mind, too, that even people who don't deserve it can meet with disaster, which is an unpredictable thing. [2] As is fitting for us and as our need compels us, we invoke the gods of all the Greeks, worshipped at our common altars, and beg you to find what we're saying acceptable. Citing the oaths that your fathers swore never to forget, we are suppliants at your fathers' tombs, and we call on the dead not to let us be subjected to Thebes, and not to let their best friends be betrayed to their worst enemies. We remind you of that day when in company with your fathers we achieved the most glorious of victories—and now here we are today facing the possibility of the most terrible of fates.

[3] "We have to bring our speech to an end now, but that's a tough thing for people in our position to do, because to end the speech is to bring the danger to our lives closer. But this is what we say now in conclusion: we didn't surrender the city to the Thebans—we'd have preferred death by starvation, the foulest kind of death—but we approached you because we trusted you, and if we fail to convince you, in all justice you should restore us to the condition we were in before and let us choose for ourselves which of the dangers that come our way we confront. [4] At the same time, we insist that as Plataeans, the most committed supporters of the Greek cause, and as suppliants, we shouldn't be delivered out of your hands and your protection to the Thebans, our bitterest enemies. We urge you instead to be our saviors and not to be the agents of our destruction when you're the liberators of all other Greeks."

60. After this speech by the Plataeans, the Thebans were afraid that the Lacedaemonians might be moved to make concessions, so they stepped up and said that they too would like to speak, since, although in their opinion it was a mistake, the Plataeans had been allowed to give a long speech rather than just an answer to the question that had been put to them. Once the Lacedaemonians had given them permission, they spoke somewhat as follows:

61. "We wouldn't have asked to speak if the Plataeans had given a brief answer to the question that was put to them. But instead they chose to focus on us, to make an irrelevant and lengthy defense when they've not even been accused of anything, and to praise themselves when no one has criticized them. So now we have to respond to their accusations and refute their self-praise, in order to make sure that they're helped by neither our bad name nor their good one, and that you reach a verdict after hearing the truth on both counts.

[2] "This is how our dispute with the Plataeans began. We were the founders of the city (this was later than the foundation of the rest of Boeotia) and along with it some other places that we took over after driving out their various populations. But contrary to our original arrangement, the Plataeans disdained to accept our leadership, and they separated themselves off from the rest of Boeotia, in contravention of tradition. Then, when we tried to apply force, they went over to the Athenians and joined them in making a great deal of trouble for us, for which they too have suffered in return.

62. "They say that at the time of the Persian invasion they were the only Boeotians who didn't collaborate with the enemy; this is something on which they particularly pride themselves and with which they reproach us. [2] But we claim that the reason they didn't side with the Persians was that the Athenians didn't either. By the same token, when the Athenians later attacked the Greeks, they were the only Boeotians to side with the Athenians for this, too. [3] But you need to consider the conditions under which each of us did what we did. Our city was then governed neither by an oligarchy that granted equal rights to all, nor by a democracy. The city's affairs were in the hands of a narrow oligarchy—a form of government that's directly opposed to the rule of law and the ideal of moderate administration; in fact, it's close to being a tyranny. [4] These men hoped to strengthen their position even more if the Persian side won, so they used force to suppress the common people and made the barbarians welcome. The city as a whole, then, was not fully responsible for its actions on this occasion, and it isn't fair to blame it for any mistakes made when it wasn't under the rule of law. [5] At any rate, you should take into account what happened after the Persians left and the city gained lawful government. Sometime later the Athenians launched their offensive on the rest of Greece and tried to make Boeotia subject to their rule.* Actually, they had already taken possession of most of it thanks to civil discord within our cities—but we fought them at Coronea and defeated them,* and then we went on to liberate Boeotia, and now we're playing a resolute part in the liberation of everyone else by providing more cavalrymen† and a larger force than any of the other allies.

63. "So much for our defense against the charge of collaborating with the Persians. We shall now try to demonstrate that you Plataeans have wronged the Greeks more than we have and that it's therefore you who are more deserving of punishment in any shape or form. [2] You claim to have become Athenian allies and citizens in order to protect yourselves against us, but if that were true you should have asked them to intervene only against us instead of joining them in attacking others. You had the possibility of refusing if at any point you were unwilling to follow the Athenians' lead, since your alliance with the Lacedaemonians here—the alliance of which you make so much in your defense—was already in place.* That alliance was strong enough to deter us from taking offensive action against you and, most importantly, to give you the security to make your own decisions. No, you acted willingly; you weren't coerced into preferring to side with the Athenians.

[3] "You say that it would have been wrong for you to betray your benefactors, but the thorough betrayal of the entire community of

Greeks, with whom you had a sworn agreement,* is far more wrong and far more unjustifiable than the betrayal of just the Athenians, when they are enslaving Greece and the rest of us are trying to liberate it. [4] The debt of gratitude you paid the Athenians was disproportionate, and you can't escape the dishonor of it; you say that you invited them in because you were the victims of wrongdoing, but you became their accomplices in wronging others. And yet, in an exchange of favors, what's dishonorable is the failure to repay like with like; there's no dishonor in failing to repay a justly incurred debt of gratitude if repaying it leads to injustice.

64. "You've made it perfectly clear that it wasn't because you were concerned for the Greeks that you were the only Boeotians at the time not to collaborate with the Persians, but because the Athenians didn't either, and you wanted to do the same as them and the opposite of the rest of us. [2] And now you expect to benefit from this 'virtuous behavior' of yours when it was prompted by others. That's unreasonable: you chose the Athenians, so you continue to share their fortunes. Don't cite the sworn alliance of the past as something that should save you now. [3] You deserted it, and you violated it by assisting rather than resisting the enslavement of the Aeginetans and other members of the alliance. Moreover, you did all this of your own free will, enjoying the same constitution that you have now; you weren't coerced into taking sides, as we were. And you spurned the final offer we made before the siege, that we'd leave you in peace as long as you became neutral. [4] Is there anyone, then, who's more deserving of the hatred of all Greeks than you, since you displayed courage in the cause of doing them harm? You've proven that you're no longer entitled to the credit that you claim for your past actions, and your true nature and motives have now been revealed. For when the Athenians embarked on the path of injustice, you went along with them.

[5] "So much, then, for our demonstration that our collaboration with the Persians was involuntary, while your collaboration with the Athenians was the opposite. **65.** As for the most recent wrong you

claim to have suffered, that we made an unlawful attack on your city at a time of peace and during a sacrosanct festival season, we believe that here, too, the fault is less ours than yours. [2] If the attack on the city had been our initiative, and we fought you and ravaged your land as enemies, we did wrong. But if your leading men—men of the greatest wealth and the highest birth—invited us in of their own free will because they wanted to detach you from your alliance with outsiders and restore you to the traditional ways shared by all Boeotians, in what sense did we do wrong? After all, in a criminal venture, it's the leaders rather than the followers who are culpable. [3] But it's our considered opinion that neither they nor we did wrong. They were Plataeans, just like you, and in fact they had a greater stake in the state than you did.* They opened a gate in the wall and brought us into their city as friends, not as enemies, because they wanted to stop the worse elements of the citizen body from deteriorating even further, and they wanted the better elements to have what they deserved. They saw themselves as moderators of your policies and your conduct, and their intention was not to make the city an alien place for you to live, but to reconnect you with your kindred. They didn't want you to break your peaceful relations with any state, but to be at peace with all alike.

66. "We can prove that we didn't act as enemies. We harmed no one, and we issued a proclamation to the effect that anyone who wanted to be governed in accordance with the traditional ways of all Boeotians should come and join us. [2] And you were happy to do that; you agreed to our terms and at first you did nothing. But later you realized how few of us there were, and even though we might indeed be thought to have done something rather unacceptable, in entering the city without the approval of the majority, you didn't repay like with like by abstaining from violence and relying on diplomacy to get us to leave. No, you violated the agreement by attacking us, and some of our men you killed in hand-to-hand fighting (which doesn't upset us so much, because they died in a fair fight), while others, with their hands reaching out for mercy, you took alive. And later, although you had assured us that you wouldn't kill these prisoners, you did just that in defiance of every law. Were these not terrible things to have done? [3] In doing all this you committed three crimes in a short space of time: the violation of the agreement, the subsequent killing of the prisoners, and your lying promise to us that you wouldn't kill them if we left your rural properties alone. And yet you still claim that we were the ones who acted unlawfully and that you've done nothing that deserves punishment. [4] No, not if these judges reach the correct decision: you'll be punished for all your crimes.

67. "Lacedaemonians, we've presented the facts in such detail both for your sake and for ours. You need to know that you'll be right to find them guilty, and we need to know that our desire to punish them was fully justified. [2] Don't let your hearts be moved by their talk of their past virtues, if that's what they were. An honorable past record should help people who are the victims of injustice, but it should entail double the penalty for people who act dishonorably, because their action conflicts with what would be expected of them. Nor should they be helped by their lamentations and pleas for compassion, or by invoking your fathers' tombs and the desolation of their city. [3] To this we respond by pointing to the far worse fate they meted out to our slaughtered youth. These young men had fathers too; some of them had died at Coronea in the process of bringing Boeotia over to your side, and those who survived into old age and their empty houses have far more right to beg you to punish these men. [4] People who've suffered undeserved misfortune should meet with compassion, while the suffering of people who deserve it—like these Plataeans—is, on the contrary, a cause for rejoicing. [5] In any case, the desolation of Plataea is their fault, because they deliberately rejected those who would have made better allies. Their unlawful actions weren't a response to any suffering we caused them; their decision was motivated by hatred rather than justice. Whatever repayment they make now would still not be adequate compensation for what they did, because their suffering will be legally sanctioned; they aren't reaching out their hands in a plea for mercy after a battle, as they claim, but submitting to a legal procedure to which they agreed.

[6] "So, Lacedaemonians, we're asking you to defend Greek law, violated by these people, and to show us, in return for our unlawful suffering, the gratitude we deserve for our commitment to your cause. Don't let us be displaced from your favor by their words. Give the Greeks an example so that they know that in your courts you'll introduce contests not of words but of deeds. Good deeds need no more than a brief account, while speeches embellished with fine phrases are screens for wrongdoing. [7] But if leaders do what you're doing today and rely only on the essential points in every decision they make, people will be less inclined to look for clever ways to describe their unjust actions."

68. After the Thebans had spoken to this effect, the Lacedaemonian judges felt that the original question to the Plataeans, whether the Lacedaemonians had in any way been well served by them in the war, still required an answer. They contended that they had of course all along wanted the Plataeans to stay out of the war, in accordance with the original treaty made by Pausanias after the Persian invasion,* and that subsequently, before the siege, they had offered them the opportunity to be neutral in accordance with the terms of the treaty. Since the Plataeans had refused the offer, the Lacedaemonians felt that they had now been released from the treaty by their own good intentions and regarded themselves as having been badly served by the Plataeans. So they again had the Plataeans brought up before them, this time one by one, and asked each of them the same question—whether they had been of service in any respect to the Lacedaemonians and their allies in the war—and they took away and killed those who admitted that they hadn't, making no exceptions. [2] They killed at least two hundred Plataeans and twenty-five of the Athenians who had been under siege with them. The women they sold into slavery.

[3] For about a year the Lacedaemonians let the city be home to some men from Megara who had been sent into exile as a result of

an internal political dispute,* along with those of their sympathizers among the Plataeans who had survived. But then they razed the entire city to the ground, foundations and all, and next to the sanctuary of Hera they built a guesthouse, two hundred feet square, with rooms occupying two stories on all four sides of the courtyard. They reused the Plataeans' roofing and doors for the building; they converted the rest of the bronze and iron fittings from inside the city into couches that they dedicated to Hera; and they also built for her a one-hundred-foot stone temple. The land they confiscated and leased out for periods of ten years to Theban tenants. [4] The Lacedaemonian aversion to Plataea was motivated almost entirely by a desire to please the Thebans, whom they regarded as useful allies in the war that by then was becoming a settled fact. [5] That was how Plataea met its end in the ninety-third year of its alliance with Athens.*

69. The forty Peloponnesian ships whose mission had been to go to the aid of Lesbos, and which had then fled across the open sea with the Athenians in pursuit, were caught in a storm off Crete and were forced to straggle back to the Peloponnese. At Cyllene they found thirteen Leucadian and Ambraciot triremes as well as Brasidas, son of Tellis, who had been sent to advise Alcidas. [2] After their failure at Lesbos, the Lacedaemonians planned to increase the size of their fleet and sail to Corcyra, where there was a schism along political lines. The Athenian presence at Naupactus consisted of only twelve ships, and the Lacedaemonians wanted to get to Corcyra first, before a larger force came from Athens. So Brasidas and Alcidas set about making the preliminary arrangements for this expedition.

70. Corcyra had been in a state of unrest ever since the prisoners who had been taken in the battles for Epidamnus were released by the Corinthians and returned home. On the face of it, they were released on the payment of bail of eight hundred talents by the Corcyrean representatives in Corinth, but in fact it was because they had agreed to win Corcyra over to the Corinthian side. On their return, they set to work and began to solicit other Corcyreans one by one with the aim of getting the city to defect from the Athenians. [2] A ship arrived from Athens and another from Corinth, each of them bringing envoys, and a debate was held, as a result of which the Corcyreans voted to continue as allies of Athens on the same terms as before, but also to be on good terms with the Peloponnesians, as they had been in the past.

[3] A man called Peithias, who was a self-appointed representative of Athens in Corcyra and the person the people looked to for leadership, was taken to court by the oligarchs on the charge of subjecting Corcyra to Athens. [4] After his acquittal, he in turn took the wealthiest five of the oligarchs to court, claiming that they had been cutting down vine props in the sanctuary of Zeus and Alcinous, an offense for which the penalty was one stater per stake. [5] They were found guilty, and the fine was so large that they went and sat in the sanctuaries as suppliants, hoping to come to some arrangement over the payment, but Peithias (who was also a member of the council) persuaded the Corcyreans to enforce the law. [6] Constrained by this ruling, and at the same time because they found out that Peithias was intending, during his term as councilor, to persuade the popular assembly to enter into a full offensive and defensive alliance with Athens, the oligarchs banded together, burst into the council meeting with daggers drawn, and killed Peithias and about sixty others, both councilors and private citizens. A few of those who shared Peithias's views escaped to the Athenian trireme, which had not yet sailed.

71. After this coup, the oligarchs convened a meeting of the Corcyreans. They assured them that what had happened would prove to be for the best, in the sense that Corcyra was now scarcely likely to be enslaved by the Athenians, and they suggested that from then on they should receive neither Athenians nor Peloponnesians unless they came in a single ship and in peace, and should regard any larger number as hostile. At the end of their speech, they induced the assembled people to ratify this policy. [2] They also immediately sent envoys to Athens to explain that what had happened was to everyone's advantage and to persuade those who had taken refuge there to do nothing rash that might lead to reprisals. **72.** But on their arrival the Athenians arrested the envoys on a charge of sedition, as well as everyone who agreed with them, and deposited them in Aegina.

[2] Meanwhile, after the arrival of a Corinthian trireme with Lacedaemonian envoys on board, those who held the reins of power in Corcyra attacked the democrats and defeated them in battle. [3] When night fell, the democrats fled to the higher parts of the city, including the acropolis, where they gathered their forces and established themselves, and they also occupied the Hyllaic harbor. The oligarchs seized the agora, where most of them lived, and the harbor close to the agora that faces inland. **73.** The next day there was a little skirmishing, and both sides sent messengers out to the countryside, calling on the slaves to join them with the promise of freedom. Most of the domestic slaves had joined the democrats, and the oligarchs were reinforced by eight hundred mercenaries from the mainland.

74. The fighting resumed two days later, and the democrats, who had the stronger positions and outnumbered the oligarchs, were victorious; they also had the courageous support of their womenfolk, who hurled roof tiles down on the enemy from the houses and braved the turmoil with a courage that belied their gender. [2] The oligarchs were routed late in the afternoon, and they became afraid that the democrats would proceed against the shipyard, gain control of it without a struggle, and cut off their last chance of escape. So they set fire to the houses and the tenements around the agora to make it impossible for the democrats to get through. They did not spare their own houses, let alone those belonging to others, and in the end a great deal of merchandise was reduced to ashes. In fact, the city might well have been totally destroyed if a wind had got up and blown the flames into it. [3] Once the fighting was over, the two sides spent a quiet night on guard. Since the democrats had won, the Corinthian ship slunk away, and most of the mercenaries got away to the mainland without being intercepted.

75. The next day, the Athenian general Nicostratus, son of Dieitrephes, came to the relief of the city from Naupactus with twelve ships and five hundred Messenian hoplites. He set about negotiating an accommodation and gained the consent of both factions that only the ten ringleaders should be put on trial (but they had already fled), that an agreement should be drawn up to allow everyone else to live together in peace, and that they should enter into a full offensive and defensive alliance with Athens. [2] Once these negotiations were completed, he was going to sail back home, but the leading democrats persuaded him to leave five of his ships with them, to make it less likely that their opponents would try anything, while they would man five of their own ships to join his flotilla.

[3] Nicostratus agreed, and the people began conscripting their enemies to crew the ships, but these men were afraid that they would end up in Athens, so they went and sat as suppliants in the sanctuary of the Dioscuri. [4] Nicostratus tried to reassure them and get them to leave the sanctuary, but they refused. The democrats seized on this refusal as a reason to arm themselves, regarding their opponents' suspicions about sailing with Nicostratus as proof of their nefarious intentions. They confiscated the weapons from their opponents' houses and would have killed any of the oligarchs they met if Nicostratus had not prevented it. [5] Seeing what was happening, the other members of the oligarchic faction, numbering four hundred or more, went and sat in the sanctuary of Hera as suppliants. But the democrats were afraid they might attempt another coup, so they persuaded them to leave the sanctuary, transported them across to the island that lies opposite the sanctuary, and arranged for provisions to be taken over to them there.

76. This was the state of the civil war when, on the fourth or fifth day after the men had been taken across to the island, the Peloponnesian ships arrived from Cyllene, where they had been berthed after their voyage from Ionia. There were fifty-three of them and they were commanded, as before, by Alcidas, with Brasidas also on board as

his adviser. They moored at Sybota, a harbor on the mainland, and at daybreak they sailed against Corcyra. **77.** The Corcyreans, in considerable disarray, and fearful not just about the Peloponnesian offensive but also about the situation in the city, tried to make ready sixty ships all at once and kept sending them out against the enemy as soon as they were manned, ignoring the Athenians' advice to let *them* sail out first, with the Corcyreans following later with all their ships at once. [2] As a result of this uncoordinated approach to the enemy, two of the Corcyrean ships immediately went over to the other side, and on some other ships the crews fought among themselves. It was complete chaos. [3] Seeing the confusion, the Peloponnesians formed up for battle with twenty of their ships against the Corcyreans, and with the rest against the twelve Athenian ships, which included the *Salaminia* and the *Paralus*.

78. The Corcyreans, who were making futile attacks with only a few ships at a time, were in trouble in their sector. The Athenians, alarmed at the number of ships that confronted them and afraid of being surrounded, held off engaging the main body of enemy ships or those that occupied the center against them, and instead attacked on the flank and sank one ship. After that, the Peloponnesians on that wing formed a circle, while the Athenians sailed around it and tried to make them lose cohesion. [2] When the Peloponnesians facing the Corcyreans realized what was happening, they became afraid of a repetition of what had happened at Naupactus;* they went to support their comrades, and the combined fleet made a concerted attack on the Athenians. [3] At this, the Athenians began to retreat by backing water, the idea being also to give the Corcyreans as much time as possible to escape ahead of them, while they slowly retired and the enemy ships were drawn up against them. [4] That was how the battle went; it ended at sunset.

79. The Corcyreans now became afraid that the enemy, assuming victory, would sail against the city, or pick up the prisoners from the island, or do something equally momentous, so they brought the men back from the island to the sanctuary of Hera and kept the city under guard. [2] But despite their victory, the Peloponnesians did not have the stomach for an attack on the city, and instead, with thirteen Corcyrean ships in tow, they sailed back to their base on the mainland. [3] The next day they still refrained from assaulting the city, even though the Corcyreans were frightened and in disarray, and even though this was apparently Brasidas's advice to Alcidas. But Alcidas outranked him. Instead, they landed at Cape Leucimme and proceeded to ravage the farmland.

80. The Corcyrean democrats, meanwhile, had become terrified by the possibility of a seaborne attack, so they conferred with the suppliants and the other oligarchs to see how the city might be saved, and they persuaded some of them to embark on the ships—for in spite of all the confusion, they managed to man thirty ships to await the expected attack. [2] The Peloponnesians carried on ravaging the land until midday and then sailed back to the mainland. At nightfall, they received signals by beacon fires informing them that sixty Athenian ships were on their way from the direction of Leucas. The Athenians had dispatched this fleet, under the command of the general Eurymedon, son of Thoucles, when they found out about the civil war and the imminent departure for Corcyra of the ships commanded by Alcidas. **81.** The Peloponnesians therefore lost no time, but set out quickly for home that same night, keeping close to land. They made sure of their escape by hauling their ships across the isthmus of Leucas,* because they were afraid of being spotted if they sailed around the island.

[2] When the Corcyreans learned of the approach of the Athenian ships and the departure of the enemy, they brought the Messenians into the city—they had previously been outside—and ordered the ships they had manned to sail around to the Hyllaic harbor. While the ships were on their way, they killed any of the enemy they found in the city, and when the ships arrived they took off them the men whom they had persuaded to embark and did away with them. Then they went to the sanctuary of Hera. They persuaded about fifty of the

suppliants to stand trial and condemned them all to death. [3] When they saw what was happening, most of the suppliants—those who had not agreed to stand trial—proceeded to kill one another right there in the sanctuary. Others hanged themselves from trees, or took their own lives in whatever way they could. [4] After Eurymedon had arrived with his sixty ships he stayed for seven days, and the Corcyreans spent this time slaughtering any of their fellow citizens whom they judged to be their enemies. They accused them of subverting the democracy, but some were killed because of personal feuds and others by people who owed them money. [5] Death came in every shape and form; everything that one might expect to happen in such circumstances happened, and then more. Fathers killed sons; people were dragged from the sanctuaries and killed right next to them; some even died after being walled up inside the sanctuary of Dionysus.

82. Civil discord thus escalated into savagery, and the conflict seemed even worse than it was because there were few or no precedents.* Later, almost all the Greek world was convulsed; in city after city the democratic leaders and the oligarchs fell out with one another, with the former wanting the Athenians to intervene and the latter the Lacedaemonians. At a time of peace there would have been no reason to appeal to them and no desire to do so, but with these two states at war, and with alliances available to the disputants on either side that would enable them to injure their opponents and correspondingly to strengthen their own position, opportunities for calling them in were readily on hand for those who wanted to bring about political change. [2] Thanks to civil discord, states were afflicted with many horrors, of the kind that happen and will always happen as long as human nature remains the same, but differing in intensity and form according to the differing circumstances. At a time of peace and in favorable conditions states and individuals alike are guided by better policies, because they are not subject to forces beyond their control. But war is a teacher of violence: it makes the necessities of life scarce and in most people elicits emotions that reflect their circumstances.

[3] So civil strife became a feature of political life, and in later cases, because the people involved were aware of what had taken place earlier, they went much farther down the path of excess, both in the ingenuity of their enterprises and in the horrendous forms their revenge took. [4] The customary verbal evaluations of deeds were exchanged for new ones when people wanted to justify their behavior: reckless daring was regarded as courage and as displaying loyalty to one's political group, and prudent hesitation as specious cowardice; moderation was considered a screen for lack of courage; applying intelligence to everything was judged an excuse for doing nothing. Impulsive rashness was added to the notion of manliness; and if anyone thought things over in an attempt to ensure safety, he was taken to be giving a plausible pretext for his inaction. [5] An angry person was deemed trustworthy, and anyone who contradicted him was suspect. A successful schemer was intelligent, but not as clever as a person who detected a scheme. Anyone who thought ahead in an attempt to avoid either option was undermining his political group and had been panicked by his opponents. A person was praised, then, both for anticipating someone who was intending to do harm and doing it first, and for encouraging someone to do harm who previously had no intention of doing so.

[6] Moreover, ties to one's political comrades became stronger than ties to one's family, because comrades were more ready to act boldly and without demur. After all, political associations of this kind are not formed for the purpose of working with the established laws to help the general public, but to subvert conventional standards for selfish reasons. And their pledges of loyalty to one another were reinforced not by divine law but by collaborating in breaking the law. [7] If political opponents came up with an excellent proposal, the other side, if they had the upper hand, accepted it not in a spirit of generosity, but only with practical self-defensive precautions. Taking revenge on someone was more important than not being harmed in the first place. Any oaths of reconciliation that were actually sworn by members of

opposite factions were administered to meet some current difficulty, and so remained in force only as long as they had nothing else to rely on. When an opportunity arose to catch an enemy off-guard because of his trust in the oaths, the one who first dared to do this found his vengeance sweeter than he would have if he had not acted in an underhand fashion, because he took into account not just that his preemptive strike involved no risk to himself, but also that by getting the better of his opponent by deceit he won the prize for intelligence. In general, people are happier to be called clever crooks than stupid paragons of virtue; they are ashamed of the latter label, but proud of the former.

[8] The cause of all these evils was the pursuit of political power motivated by greed and ambition, and the consequent fanaticism of those competing for power. Rival political leaders deployed specious slogans, with one side championing popular equality before the law and the other the prudence of aristocratic government. They claimed to be serving the public good, but in reality they just wanted to defeat their opponents, and in this no-holds-barred competition to get the better of one another they committed the most terrible atrocities and pushed for even worse punishments, imposing penalties that went way beyond what was required by justice and the good of the city; the limit was set only by what would please their side at the time. They were ready to satisfy their immediate ambitions by means of an unjust vote of condemnation or by using force to gain power. The actions of neither side were motivated by religious considerations, and greater regard was given to those who managed to achieve something abhorrent by means of specious argument. Citizens who belonged to neither side were destroyed by both, whether for refusing to join or out of resentment at their survival.

83. So it was thanks to civil strife that every form of wickedness became confirmed throughout Greece. Simple decency, a major constituent of integrity, was mocked until it vanished; division into groups, wary of one another and opposed in their thinking, was widely prevalent. [2] No argument was potent enough and no oath terrible enough to reconcile them; all power-possessors reckoned that there was no chance of security anyway, and so were more concerned to avoid harm than they were able to trust others. [3] The less intelligent among them were more commonly the survivors, because, being anxiously aware of their own shortcomings and of the intelligence of their opponents, and certain that they would come off worse in any battle of words, and that they would be caught unawares thanks to the versatility of their opponents' minds, they proceeded boldly to action. [4] The others, superciliously trusting their prescience and assuming that they did not need to act where they could use their intelligence, were more likely to be caught off-guard and destroyed.

[84. But, to resume, it was in Corcyra that most of these horrors were perpetrated for the first time—all the things that people do when they retaliate against leaders who have been ruling them with more arrogance than moderation, if those leaders give them the opportunity for revenge; all the immoral strategies that people adopt when, wishing to escape their daily poverty—a wish that is exacerbated by suffering—they covet their neighbors' property; and the savage and implacable attacks carried out by those who, not for gain but largely in a coarse outburst of anger, turn on others who are more or less their equals. [2] At this time of crisis for the city, with civic life in meltdown, human nature, which in any case habitually does wrong even if that involves breaking the law, triumphed over the laws and relished showing itself to be impotent against passion, too strong for justice, and hostile to superiority in any shape or form. For people would not have preferred revenge to piety, or gain to the avoidance of injustice, were it not for the destructive power of envy. [3] In seeking to avenge themselves on others, they chose to overturn the universal laws about such things—laws that offer the hope of salvation to people in trouble—and did not leave them in place against a time of danger when they would be needed.]*

85. These, then, were the terrible consequences of the fury that the citizens of Corcyra felt for one another. It was the first time such a thing had happened. Eurymedon and the Athenians then left in

their ships. [2] But about five hundred Corcyreans had escaped the slaughter, and later these exiles occupied fortresses on the mainland opposite the island, gained control of Corcyrean territory there, and used it as a base from which to raid the island. These raids were very effective, and there came to be a severe shortage of food in the city. [3] These oligarchs also sent envoys to Sparta and Corinth to negotiate their reinstatement in Corcyra, but that got them nowhere. Later they equipped themselves with boats and mercenaries, and a force numbering about six hundred sailed over to the island. [4] Once they were there, they burned their boats so that their only hope would be to become masters of the island. They built themselves a fortress up on Mount Istone and set about trying to destroy the Corcyreans in the city and gain control of the land.

86. Toward the end of the summer, the Athenians sent twenty ships to Sicily under the command of the generals Laches, son of Melanopus, and Charoeades, son of Euphiletus, [2] because Syracuse and Leontini were at war. All the other Dorian states in Sicily except Camarina were allies of Syracuse and had been included in the Lacedaemonian alliance since the very beginning of the war, but they had not actually taken part in the fighting. Leontini had as allies the Chalcidian cities* and Camarina. In Italy, Locri was on the Syracusan side and Rhegium was with Leontini because of the kinship between the two peoples. [3] The Leontinian alliance sent a delegation to Athens, not just because they had long been allies, but also because they were Ionians, to try to persuade the Athenians to send them ships, since they were being denied access to both sea and land by the Syracusans. [4] And the Athenians did send the ships, ostensibly because of their kinship as Ionians, but in fact because they wanted no grain to be brought into the Peloponnese from there, and to test the waters to see if it might be possible for them to bring Sicily under their control.* [5] So they established their base at Rhegium in Italy and supported their allies in the war. And so the summer came to an end.

87. The following winter, the plague struck Athens for the second time; it had never altogether left, but there had been a break. [2] This second attack lasted for a little over a year, whereas the first one had lasted a full two years, and there was nothing that oppressed the Athenians more than this or more seriously degraded their capacity for war. [3] No fewer than 4,400 serving hoplites died, as well as 300 cavalrymen, and the number of deaths among the general population was beyond reckoning. [4] There were also at that time many earthquakes in Athens, Euboea, and Boeotia, with the most severe at Orchomenus in Boeotia.

88. In the same winter, the Athenians in Sicily and the Rhegians campaigned with a fleet of thirty ships against the Islands of Aeolus, as they are called.* It was impossible to do so in the summer because of the shortage of water. [2] The islands are inhabited by the Liparians, who were colonists from Cnidus. They live on just one of the islands, of no great size, called Lipara, and set out from there to farm the others, which are called Didyme, Strongyle, and Hiera. [3] The islanders believe that Hephaestus has his forge on Hiera, because it can be seen sending up a great deal of fire at night and smoke in the daytime. The islands are situated opposite the territory of the Sicels and that of Messina, and were in alliance with Syracuse. [4] The Athenians ravaged the land, but failed to get them to defect, and so they returned to Rhegium. So the winter came to an end and with it the fifth year of the current war, the history of which was written by Thucydides.

89. The following summer the combined Peloponnesian forces, under the command of the Spartan king Agis, son of Archidamus, got as far as the Isthmus with the intention of invading Attica, but many earthquakes occurred, and they canceled the invasion and turned back.* [2] At about the same time as these earthquakes, at Orobiae in Euboea, the sea withdrew from the land as it was then and returned in the form of a wave that inundated a considerable part of the town. The water level then subsided, but some of the flood remained, so that what had formerly been land was now sea. Everyone who could not run to safety on high ground died. [3] The island of Atalante off Opuntian Locris was similarly flooded, and the water destroyed part of the Athenian fortress* and smashed one of the two ships that had been hauled ashore there. [4] The withdrawal of the sea happened at Peparethos, too,* but without any subsequent flooding, and an earthquake caused the collapse of part of the city wall, the town hall, and a few other buildings. [5] I believe that the cause of this phenomenon is that at the point where the earthquake is most violent, it pushes the sea back, and then when the water is suddenly pulled back† again with greater force than usual, flooding results. I do not think that such a thing could happen in the absence of an earthquake.

90. In the same summer, various campaigns were fought in Sicily under various conditions; some pitted Sicilian Greeks against one another, while others involved the Athenians and their allies. I shall mention only the most important actions, those in which the Athenians and their allies either acted together or were attacked by their enemies. [2] The Athenian general Charoeades had already died fighting the Syracusans, leaving Laches in sole command of the fleet. Together with his allies, he mounted an expedition against Mylae, a dependency of Messina that was garrisoned by two regiments of Messinians. The Messinians made an attempt at ambushing the men from the ships, [3] but the Athenians and their allies routed the ambushers, taking many lives in the process. They then assaulted the wall and forced the inhabitants to come to terms, surrender their acropolis, and join them in offensive action against Messina. [4] And when the Athenians and their allies subsequently attacked Messina, the Messinians too went over to them, after giving hostages and providing the other usual guarantees of good faith.

91. In the same summer, the Athenians sent thirty ships around the Peloponnese under the command of the generals Demosthenes, son of Alcisthenes, and Procles, son of Theodorus, and sixty ships and two thousand hoplites to Melos, under the command of the general Nicias, son of Niceratus. [2] The Melians were islanders, but they had no desire to be subject to Athens or even to become their allies, and the purpose of the expedition was to bring them into the Athenian alliance. [3] Even with their land being ravaged, the Melians refused to be won over, so the Athenians left Melos and went to Oropus in Graea.* They made land at night, and the hoplites from the ships set out right away on foot for Tanagra in Boeotia. [4] Responding to a prearranged signal, all the available men from Athens marched overland and joined them there, commanded by the generals Hipponicus, son of Callias, and Eurymedon, son of Thoucles. [5] They made camp, laid waste the land during the daylight hours, and spent the night in their camp. The next day they fought a battle against a combined force of Tanagrans who had come out against them and Thebans who had come to help the Tanagrans. The Athenians won and seized some of the enemy's weapons, and after setting up a trophy some of them returned to Athens while others went to the ships. [6] Nicias then sailed along the coast of Locris with his sixty ships, laid waste the farmland, and returned home.

92. It was at about this time that the Lacedaemonians founded their colony at Heraclea in Trachis.* They did so for the following reasons: [2] All Malians belong to one or another of three territorial groups: the Paralians, the Irians, and the Trachinians. The Trachinians had suffered badly in a war with their neighbors, the Oetaeans, and at first they intended to attach themselves to the Athenians, but they doubted their reliability, so they sent a delegation to Sparta instead, with Teisamenus as their chosen envoy. [3] The Trachinians were joined by representatives of Doris, the motherland of the

Lacedaemonians,* who were also asking for help, because they, too, were being harassed by the Oetaeans. [4] After listening to their petition, the Lacedaemonians decided to send out the colonists, partly because they wanted to help the Trachinians and the Dorians, but partly also because they thought that the foundation of the town would serve them well in the conflict with Athens. They could fit out a fleet there for use against Euboea, which was only a short voyage distant, and the town would lie usefully on the route to the Thraceward region. All in all, they were very eager to establish a foundation there. [5] The first thing they did, then, was consult the god in Delphi, and at his urging they sent out the settlers, perioeci as well as Spartiates, and invited any other Greeks to join them, unless they were Ionians, Achaeans, and certain other peoples. The founders, who led the settlers, were three Spartiates: Leon, Alcidas, and Damagon. [6] Once the town had been founded, they rebuilt its defensive wall, and it is now known as Heraclea; it lies about four and a half miles from Thermopylae and a little over two from the sea. They went on to build shipyards, and they barred the approach on the side toward Thermopylae by building a wall in the pass itself, to make protecting the place easier.

93. The Athenians' first reaction to the foundation of the town was fear. They considered it primarily a threat to Euboea, since the crossing to Cape Cenaeum in Euboea was so short. But the future turned out to confound this expectation, because they never had any trouble from Heraclea. [2] The reason for this was that the Thessalians (who were dominant in that region) and the peoples whose territories were threatened by the foundation dreaded the prospect of such powerful neighbors. They relentlessly harassed and fought the new arrivals until they wore them down, even though at first they were very numerous indeed, because since it was the Lacedaemonians who were founding the city everyone had gone there confidently, believing that it would be a safe place to live. [3] In fact, though, it was above all the governors sent there by Sparta who did the most to ruin the place and reduce its population; they frightened off a great many people with their harsh and occasionally unfair administration, which made it all the easier for their neighbors to have the upper hand.

94. That summer, at about the same time that the Athenians were being checked on Melos, the Athenians on the thirty ships that were sailing around the Peloponnese first killed some lookouts who had set a trap for them at Ellomenus in Leucadian territory on the mainland, and then attacked Leucas, with their forces supplemented by a full levy of all the Acarnanians (except for the people of Oeniadae), by the Zacynthians and Cephallenians, and by fifteen ships from Corcyra. [2] With their land being devastated on both sides of the isthmus—on the mainland and on the island, where the city of Leucas and the sanctuary of Apollo are located—the Leucadians, who were greatly outnumbered, took no action. The Acarnanians urged Demosthenes, the Athenian general, to wall off the city, because they thought it would be easy to blockade it into submission and hoped to be rid of a city that had always been hostile to them.
[3] Just then, however, Demosthenes was persuaded by the Messenians that with such a large force assembled he had a good opportunity to attack the Aetolians, who were a constant threat to Naupactus; and if he defeated the Aetolians, they said, it would be easy for him to bring the rest of the mainland over to the Athenian side. [4] They said that although the Aetolians were a populous and warlike people, they lived in unwalled and widely separated villages, and used only light arms; so, they argued, it would not be difficult to overcome them before they could combine. [5] They suggested that he should first move against the Apodoti, then the Ophiones, and then the Eurytanes (who constitute the largest of the Aetolian tribes, speak an incomprehensible version of Greek, and were believed to eat their meat raw). Once he had conquered these three tribes, they said, it would be easy to win over the rest.

95. Demosthenes agreed with the Messenians in order to keep them happy, but especially because he thought that with his mainland allies bolstered by the Aetolians he would be able to move against the Boeotians by land, without being reinforced from Athens. He would march through Ozolian Locris to Cytinium in Doris, with Mount Parnassus on his right, and then down into Phocis.* Since the Phocians had always been on good terms with Athens, Demosthenes thought they would voluntarily take part in the offensive, or could be won over by force—and Phocis and Boeotia are immediate neighbors. So, against the wishes of the Acarnanians, he set out from Leucas with his entire army and sailed to Sollium.* [2] He communicated his plan to the Acarnanians, but they refused to support him because of his failure to blockade Leucas, so he launched his campaign against the Aetolians with the rest of his army: the Cephallenians, the Messenians, the Zacynthians, and the three hundred Athenian marines from his own ships—the fifteen Corcyrean ships having already left. [3] He made Oeneum in Locris his base; these Ozolian Locrians were allies and they were to bring the full quota of their forces to meet the Athenians in the interior. Since they were neighbors of the Aetolians and similarly equipped, he thought it would help a great deal to have them on his side because of their familiarity with Aetolian tactics and the region.

96. He had his army spend the night at the sanctuary of Nemean Zeus, where the poet Hesiod* is said by the local inhabitants to have been killed (thus fulfilling an oracle he had received that he would die "in Nemea"), and at daybreak he set out and marched into Aetolia. [2] Potidania fell to him on the first day, Crocyleum on the second, and Teichium on the third, where he paused and sent the booty to Eupalium in Locris. His plan was to continue with these conquests all the way up to the Ophiones, and if they refused to come to terms, he would return to Naupactus and march against them later. [3] The Aetolians, however, had been aware that this invasion was in the offing from the moment the plan was made, and when it took place they rallied in large numbers; all of them came to help, even the most remote of the Ophiones, the Bomians and the Callians, whose land extends to the Malian Gulf.*

97. However, the Messenians' advice to Demosthenes was much the same as it had been from the start: they assured him that it would not be difficult to conquer Aetolia and urged him to move as quickly as possible against the villages; he should not give the Aetolians time to gather all their forces and organize resistance, but try to take the villages one by one as they lay in his path. [2] He thought this was good advice, and his successes had made him optimistic because he was meeting with no opposition. So without waiting for the Locrians who were supposed to join him (he was critically short of light-armed javelineers), he advanced against Aegitium,* attacked, and took it with his first assault, because the inhabitants had fled and taken to the hills above the village, which was situated on high ground about nine miles from the sea. [3] But the Aetolians had already rallied to the defense of Aegitium, and they attacked the Athenians and their allies by charging down the hillsides from all directions and pelting them with javelins. Whenever the Athenians advanced against them, the Aetolians gave way, and whenever the Athenians withdrew, they attacked. That was how the fighting went for a long time, with advances followed by retreats, and the Athenians came off worse in both maneuvers.

98. As long as their archers had arrows and were able to fire them, the Athenians held their own, since the Aetolians, being light-armed, were driven back under fire. But then the archers lost cohesion after their captain was killed, and the Athenians, worn out by their long and repeated efforts, and under constant pressure from the Aetolians and their javelins, turned and fled. They died as they stumbled into gullies from which there was no way out; they died because they were on unfamiliar terrain, and their guide, a Messenian called Chromon, had been killed. [2] The Aetolians, who were fleet of foot and not burdened by heavy arms and armor, were hard on their heels during the rout, and many of the Athenians were caught and cut down on the spot by their javelins. Most of them missed the roads and ended up in trackless woodland, and the Aetolians brought fire and burned the wood around them. [3] The Athenian soldiers attempted every form of escape and met with every form of death, and the survivors barely managed to make it safely back to the coast and to Oeneum in Locris, from where they had started. [4] Many of the allies and about 120 of the Athenian hoplites were killed. So many hoplites died, all in the prime of their lives; they were undoubtedly the best men that Athens lost in the current war. Procles, one of the two generals, also lost his life. [5] The Athenians recovered the bodies of the dead from the Aetolians under a truce, and then they withdrew to Naupactus and later sailed back to Athens. But Demosthenes remained in and around Naupactus, because he was afraid of the Athenians' reaction to what had happened.

99. At more or less the same time, the Athenians who were in Sicily sailed to Locri. They made an armed landing, defeated the Locrians who came to give battle, and captured a frontier post on the bank of the Halex river.

100. In the same summer, the Aetolian envoys who had earlier been sent to Corinth and Sparta—Tolophus of the Ophiones, Boriades of the Eurytanes, and Teisander of the Apodoti—received a positive response to their request that an expeditionary force be sent against Naupactus, to pay the Messenians back for having brought in the Athenians. [2] In the autumn, then, the Lacedaemonians sent three thousand allied hoplites, of whom five hundred were from Heraclea in Trachis, which had just recently been founded. The force was commanded by Eurylochus, a Spartiate, and he was accompanied by two other Spartiates, Macarius and Menedaius.

The History of the Peloponnesian War

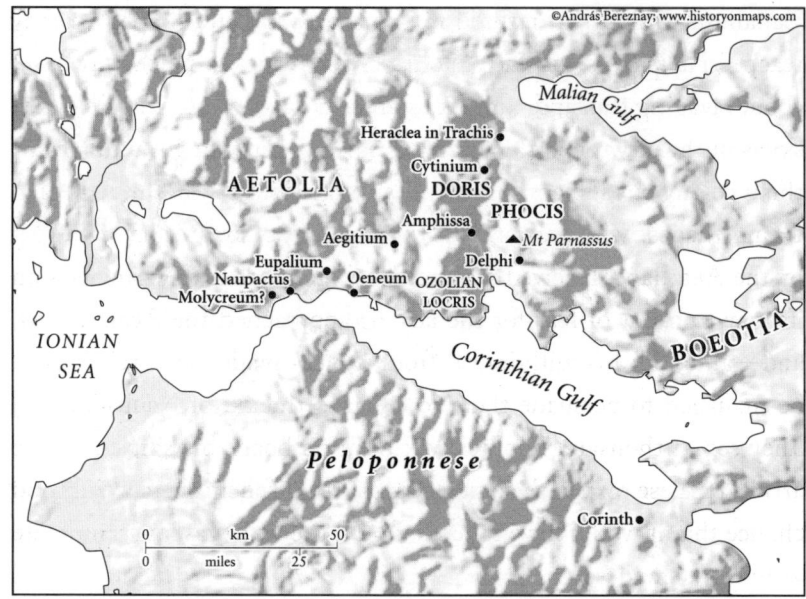

G. Aetolia

101. The army assembled at Delphi, and Eurylochus made overtures to the Ozolian Locrians because he would have to pass through their territory to get to Naupactus, and also because he wanted to detach them from the Athenians. [2] The most cooperative of the Locrians were those from Amphissa, because they wanted protection from their enemies, the Phocians. They were the first to give hostages, and they persuaded the others, who were afraid of the approaching army, to do the same. Of these others, the first to give hostages were the neighbors of the Amphissans, the Myoneans, who live in the most inaccessible part of Locris; then the Myoneans were followed by the Hypnians, Messapians, Triteans, Chaleians, Tolophonians, Isians, and Oeanthians, who all took part in the campaign. The Alpaeans gave hostages, but did not take part, and the Hyaei only gave hostages after a village of theirs called Polis had been seized.

102. When everything was ready and Eurylochus had deposited the hostages at Cytinium in Doris, he set out with his army for Naupactus. As he marched through Locris he took Oeneum and

Eupalium, which had refused to come over to him. [2] When they reached Naupactus and the Aetolians had arrived in support, they set about ravaging the land, and they gained control of the unwalled outskirts of the city. Then they went to Molycreum, which was a Corinthian colony but subject to Athens, and captured it. [3] The Athenian Demosthenes, who was still in the Naupactus area after his defeat by the Aetolians, received advance intelligence that the army was on its way, and out of fear for the city he approached the Acarnanians, and—although his withdrawal from Leucas made them reluctant—he managed to persuade them to come to the aid of Naupactus. [4] They sent a thousand hoplites with him on board his ships, and the arrival of these men at the city saved it; without them there was a good chance that it would have fallen, because the wall was long and there were few defenders.

[5] When Eurylochus and his troops learned that the Acarnanians were inside the city and that it would be impossible for them to take the place by force, they withdrew, but not in the direction of the Peloponnese. They went to the district that is now known as Aeolis—that is, to Calydon, Pleuron, and other places thereabouts—and to Proschium in Aetolia.* [6] The reason they did this is that the Ambraciots had approached them and asked them to join their own troops in an attack on Amphilochian Argos and Amphilochia as a whole, and Acarnania too. They argued that, if they gained control of these places, the whole of the mainland would be on the Lacedaemonian side. [7] Eurylochus found their argument persuasive. He dismissed the Aetolians and remained quietly in the district, taking no action and waiting for the time when he would be needed to support the Ambraciots in their campaign against Argos. And so the summer ended.

103. The following winter, the Athenians in Sicily marched against the Sicel town of Inessa, where the acropolis was garrisoned by Syracusans. They were joined by their Greek allies and by those of the

Sicels who were unwilling subjects and allies of Syracuse and had revolted, so that they were now fighting on the Athenian side. They assaulted the town but retired after finding it impossible to take. [2] As they were retreating, the Syracusans from the citadel attacked the allies who were in the rear, behind the Athenians. They charged at them and routed a section of the army, taking quite a few lives in the process. [3] Laches and the Athenians next made a number of incursions from their ships into the territory of Locri. A force of about three hundred Locrians, under the command of Proxenus, son of Caparon, came to give battle at the Caicinus river. The Athenians won and then withdrew, taking with them some weaponry that they had captured.

104. In the same winter, in response to an oracle, the Athenians purified Delos.* It had earlier been purified by the tyrant Peisistratus as well, though he had not purged the whole island, but only as much of it as was visible from the sanctuary. But now the whole island was purified. This is how it was done. [2] They removed all the tombs on Delos of those who had died, and issued an edict that from then on no one was to die or give birth on the island, but should be taken over to Rhenea. The distance between Rhenea and Delos is so short that when Rhenea was annexed by Polycrates, the tyrant of Samos, who had mastery of the sea for a while and ruled the other islands, he dedicated the island to Delian Apollo by linking it to Delos with a chain. On the occasion in question, after the purification the Athenians celebrated the quadrennial Delia festival for the first time.

[3] Long ago there used to be a great concourse on Delos of the Ionians and inhabitants of the surrounding islands. They would come as pilgrims along with their wives and children, just as the Ionians flock nowadays to the Ephesia festival; the cities brought choruses, and athletic and musical contests were held. [4] The best indication of what the ancient festival was like is given by Homer in the following lines from the *Hymn to Apollo*:*

> *O Phoebus, since it is Delos that most delights your heart,*
> *Where the Ionians with their trailing robes gather*
> *With their children and wives on your avenue;*
> *Where they please you with boxing and dancing and song*
> *Whenever they hold these contests in your honor.*

[5] Further lines from the same hymn make it clear that there was a musical contest as well and that the Ionians went there to compete in it. For instance, he concludes his praise of the female Delian chorus with the following lines, in which he also mentions himself:

> *But come in kindness, Apollo and Artemis! And hail*
> *All you maidens! Remember me in later years*
> *When some other earth-dwelling mortal*
> *Arrives here, long-suffering, and asks you:*
> *"O maidens, what man comes here as the sweetest singer*
> *And pleases you most?" And you answer all together*
> *With one voice: "A blind man from rugged Chios."*

[6] Thus Homer bears witness to the fact that long ago there was a great concourse and festival on Delos. Later the islanders and the Athenians carried on sending choruses and sacrificial offerings, but most of the rites and the contests fell into disuse—which was not surprising, since it was a result of catastrophic events in Ionia*—until the Athenians revived the contests on this occasion, and added a horse race, which had not been a feature of the festival before.

105. In the same winter, the Ambraciots kept the promise they had made to Eurylochus when they detained his army, by taking to the field with three thousand hoplites against Amphilochian Argos. They entered Argive territory and took Olpae, a strongly built fortress on a hill by the sea that had formerly been fortified by the Acarnanians, and that they had used for judicial inquests in cases affecting both Acarnanians and Amphilochians. The city of Argos lies just short of three miles away, on the coast. [2] Some of the Acarnanians rallied to the defense of Argos, while others took up a position at a place in Amphilochia called Crenae, where they could mount guard and try to stop Eurylochus and his Peloponnesians from crossing the border undetected to link up with the Ambraciots.* [3] They also sent messengers to fetch Demosthenes, the general who had led the Athenian forces in the invasion of Aetolia, whom they wanted to be their leader, and to the twenty Athenian ships that were off the Peloponnese, commanded by Aristoteles, son of Timocrates, and Hierophon, son of Antimnestus. [4] And the Ambraciots at Olpae sent a message back to their city, telling them to raise a mass levy and come to help them, because they were afraid that Eurylochus and his men would be unable to get past the Acarnanians, in which case either they would have to fight on their own or, if they chose to retreat, it would be dangerous for them to do so.

106. When the Peloponnesians under Eurylochus heard that the Ambraciots had reached Olpae, they quickly set out from Proschium to reinforce them. They crossed the Achelous river and marched through the Acarnanian countryside, which was undefended because of the reinforcements sent to Argos. To the east was the city of Stratus and its garrison, and to the west the rest of Acarnania. [2] After passing through the territory of Stratus they proceeded through Phytia, then along the border between Phytia and Medeon, and then through Limnaea. Then they left Acarnania and entered the territory of the Agraei, who were on their side. [3] Finally, after reaching Mount Thyamus, which is in Agraean territory, they crossed it and descended after dark into Argive land. They passed undetected between Argos and the Acarnanian guard at Crenae and joined the Ambraciots at Olpae. **107.** With their forces united, at daybreak they established themselves at a place called Metropolis and made camp.

Before long the twenty Athenian ships reached the Ambracian Gulf to assist the Argives, and Demosthenes also arrived, with two hundred Messenian hoplites and sixty Athenian archers. [2] The ships anchored off Olpae and blockaded the hill from the sea, while the Acarnanians and a few Amphilochians—only a few because most of them were forcibly prevented from leaving by the Ambraciots—had already joined forces at Argos and were getting ready to give battle to the enemy. They chose Demosthenes as the overall commander of the allied force, supported by their own generals. [3] He moved his men up and made camp not far from Olpae, with a great ravine separating the two armies.

For five days the two sides remained inactive, but on the sixth they formed up for battle. The Peloponnesians outnumbered and outflanked Demosthenes's troops, so, fearing encirclement, he had about four hundred of his men, hoplites and light-armed troops together, lie in ambush on a sunken path that was overgrown with bushes. At the precise moment when the two armies engaged, they were to rise up and take the enemy's projecting wing in the rear. [4] When both sides were ready, the armies drew close to each other. Demosthenes held the right wing with the Messenians and the few Athenians, and the rest of the line was made up of the various contingents of Acarnanians and the Amphilochian javelineers who had managed to get through. The Peloponnesians and Ambraciots were all mixed up together, except for the Mantineans, who formed a single unit on the left wing but not at the very end, while Eurylochus and his men held the far left and faced Demosthenes and the Messenians.

108. When they were at close quarters, the Peloponnesians on the left wing, which extended beyond their opponents' right wing, initiated an encircling maneuver. But the Acarnanians suddenly emerged from where they had been hiding, fell on them in the rear, and routed them so completely that they had no chance to stand their ground and fight back. Moreover, their fear spread until most of the rest of the army turned to flight, because when the others saw the destruction of the section of their line where Eurylochus and the best men in the army were, they became absolutely terrified. It was the Messenians, who were with Demosthenes in that part of the field, who bore the brunt of the action. [2] But the Ambraciots, the most warlike people in that part of Greece, and the others on the right wing defeated the contingents opposite them and chased them off the field to Argos. [3] On their return to the battlefield, however, they saw that most of the army had been defeated, and then they came under attack from the rest of the Acarnanians, so they made their escape to Olpae. It was tough going and many of them lost their lives, since they were rushing forward out of formation and with no discipline. The Mantineans were the exception; as they retreated they kept formation better than the rest of the army.

It was late in the day when the battle came to an end, **109.** and the next day, with Eurylochus and Macarius dead, Menedaius assumed command. The scale of the defeat was so great that he did not know what to do. If he stayed in Olpae he doubted he could withstand a siege, since he was now cut off by land as well as by the Athenian ships at sea, and he thought withdrawal would be hazardous. So he approached Demosthenes and the Acarnanian generals requesting a truce that would allow him to withdraw and to collect the bodies of his dead. [2] Permission to collect the bodies was granted, and the Acarnanians set up a trophy and collected the bodies of the dead from their side, who numbered about three hundred. But they expressly refused to make a truce that would allow the entire enemy army to withdraw. However, Demosthenes and his Acarnanian colleagues made a secret truce to allow the Mantineans, Menedaius, and the other Peloponnesian officers and notables to beat a hasty retreat. In part, Demosthenes's intention was to isolate the Ambraciots and their mercenary contingent, but mainly he wanted to tarnish the reputation of the Lacedaemonians and Peloponnesians among the Greeks of that region as people who betrayed their allies and put their own interests first. [3] So the Peloponnesians collected their dead and quickly buried them as best they could, and those who had permission to do so covertly began to plan their withdrawal.

110. Demosthenes and the Acarnanians received information that the Ambraciots had raised a mass levy of troops from the city (as requested in the first message from Olpae) and were marching through Amphilochia on their way to help their fellow countrymen. Their intention was to join up with them at Olpae, but they were completely unaware of what had happened. [2] Demosthenes immediately sent a division of the army to lie in wait on their route and to occupy the key positions before the Ambraciots arrived, and he also got ready to take the field against them.

111. Meanwhile, the Mantineans and the others who had been granted a truce left Olpae on the pretext of foraging for greens and firewood. They left stealthily and in small groups, gathering what they had ostensibly gone out for, but once they were some distance away from Olpae they sped up. [2] The Ambraciots and the others who had stayed in Olpae emerged from the fortress in a body when they realized what was going on, and themselves set out at a run as well, in an attempt to catch up with the escapees. [3] At first, the Acarnanians thought the entire army was leaving, despite the fact that no truce had been arranged, and they set off after the Peloponnesians. When some of their generals ordered them to stop and explained that there was a truce protecting the Peloponnesians, one of the Acarnanians threw his javelin at the generals, as he considered this a betrayal. Subsequently, however, they allowed the Mantineans and the Peloponnesians to go, but set about killing the Ambraciots. [4] In fact, however, there was a great deal of argument and uncertainty about whether any given person was Ambraciot or Peloponnesian. Roughly two hundred of them were killed, and the rest escaped to Agraeis, where they were taken in by Salynthius, the king of the Agraei, who was on their side.

112. Meanwhile, the Ambraciots from Ambracia reached Idomene,* which consists of two lofty hills. The taller of these hills was occupied by the men sent ahead from the main body by Demosthenes, who got there first after nightfall without being spotted, while the Ambraciots had already ascended the lower of the hills and bivouacked there for the night.† [2] Demosthenes and the rest of his men set out as soon as it was dark and they had eaten a meal, and while he led half of his forces toward the pass, the other half marched through the mountains of Amphilochia. [3] Just before dawn he attacked the Ambraciots, who were still in their beds and completely unaware of what had happened over the previous days. At first, in fact, the prevalent view was that they were being approached by some of their own men. [4] Demosthenes had deliberately posted the Messenians in front and had told them to greet the Ambraciots in the Dorian dialect, so as to lull the sentries into a false sense of security, while they could not be seen because it was still dark.

[5] So Demosthenes fell on the Ambraciot army and routed it. Most of the Ambraciots were killed on the spot, while the rest set out for the mountains in an attempt to escape. [6] But the roads had already been occupied, and besides, the Amphilochians were in their own familiar territory and were light-armed soldiers fighting hoplites, while the Ambraciots had no local knowledge and no idea where to turn. So they stumbled into gullies and into the ambushes that had been laid for them and were killed. [7] Every means of escape was tried. Some even headed for the sea, which was not far away. Coincidentally, the Athenians' ships happened to be sailing by while the battle on land was raging, and when the Ambraciots saw them they swam over to them, thinking in the panic of the moment that, if they had to die, it would be better for them to be killed by the men in the ships than by the Amphilochians, who were barbarians and their worst enemies. [8] So this is how the Ambraciots met with disaster, and few out of many made it safely back to Ambracia. The Acarnanians stripped the corpses of their arms and armor, and after they had set up a trophy they returned to Argos.

113. The next day, a herald came to the Acarnanians from the Ambraciots who had escaped from Olpae to Agraeis, to ask permission to collect the bodies of their men who had been killed by the Acarnanians after the first battle, when they tried to escape from Olpae without the protection of a truce along with the Mantineans and the others who had received a guarantee of safe conduct. [2] The herald could see the arms and armor of the Ambraciots who had come from Ambracia, and the quantity surprised him because, being unaware of the calamity, he assumed that they must have belonged to his comrades. [3] Someone asked him why he was surprised and how many of his men had died, because in his turn the questioner mistakenly supposed that the herald had come from the Ambraciots who had been at Idomene.

"About two hundred," said the herald.

[4] "These are clearly not the arms and armor of two hundred men," retorted the questioner, "but of more than a thousand."

"You mean they didn't belong to our comrades in the battle?" said the herald.

"Yes, they did," said the man, "if you were involved in the battle yesterday at Idomene."

"But we didn't fight anyone yesterday. It was the day before, in the course of our withdrawal."

"Well, I can assure you that these men were our opponents yesterday. They came as reinforcements from Ambracia."

[5] When the herald heard this and realized that the relief force from Ambracia had been annihilated, he cried out loud in his grief. Stunned by the magnitude of the defeat that had taken place, he left right away without completing his business or staying to ask for the dead. [6] And in fact of all the disasters that occurred in the course of the current war, this was the worst to strike any single Greek state in such a short space of time. I have not given the number of the dead, because the total said to have perished is unbelievable, when account is taken of the size of the city. What I am certain of, however, is that if the Acarnanians and Amphilochians had followed the advice of the Athenians and Demosthenes and attacked Ambracia, they would have taken it without a struggle. But in fact they were afraid that if the Athenians occupied Ambracia they would be more troublesome neighbors for them than the Ambraciots were.

114. The Acarnanians next gave a third of the spoils to the Athenians and distributed the rest among their towns. The Athenians' share was stolen from them in the course of their voyage, and the spoils that are today dedicated in the Athenian sanctuaries are three hundred *panoplies* that were set aside for Demosthenes and that he brought with him when he sailed back to Athens. He had fewer misgivings about returning home now, despite his defeat in Aetolia, because of this successful outcome. [2] The Athenians in the twenty ships also left and went to Naupactus.

After the departure of the Athenians and Demosthenes, the Acarnanians and Amphilochians made a truce with the Ambraciots and Peloponnesians who had taken refuge with Salynthius and the Agraei, to allow them to leave Oeniadae, where they had retired after leaving Salynthius, in safety. [3] For the future, the Acarnanians and Amphilochians entered into a one-hundred-year treaty of alliance with the Ambraciots on the following terms: the Ambraciots were not required to join the Acarnanians in a campaign against the Peloponnesians, nor were the Acarnanians required to join the Ambraciots against the Athenians, but otherwise they were to come to each other's aid in the event of an attack on either of their lands; and the Ambraciots were to return any Amphilochian territory or hostages they held, and not support Anactorium in its hostility toward the Acarnanians. Once these terms had been agreed, they brought their war to an end. [4] Subsequently, the Corinthians supplied Ambracia with a garrison of three hundred of their hoplites commanded by Xenocleides, son of Euthycles, who had a troublesome journey overland but did eventually get there. So much for events in Ambracia.

115. In the same winter, the Athenians in Sicily made an armed landing from their ships in the territory of Himera; they had the support of the Sicels, who invaded the Himeran hinterland from the interior. They also sailed against the Islands of Aeolus. [2] On returning to Rhegium, they found there the Athenian general Pythodorus, son of

Isolochus, who had been sent to take over Laches's command. [3] The Athenian allies in Sicily had gone to Athens and persuaded the Athenians to send more ships to support them. They did so because, even if their land was controlled by the Syracusans, they were being denied access to the sea by only a few ships, and so they were assembling and preparing a fleet to do something about this. [4] The Athenians proposed to man forty ships to send them, not just because they thought this would bring the fighting there to an end more quickly, but also because they wanted their fleet to be in practice. [5] So they sent one of their generals, Pythodorus, with just a few ships, and planned later to send Sophocles, son of Sostratides, and Eurymedon, son of Thoucles, with the bulk of the ships. [6] At the end of winter, Pythodorus, who by then had the command of Laches's ships, sailed against the Locrian fort that had earlier been captured by Laches, but he was defeated in battle and returned to Rhegium.

116. Just at the turn of winter and spring, a stream of fiery lava issued from Mount Etna, as had happened before. It destroyed some of the land of the people of Catana, who live at the base of Etna, which is the largest mountain in Sicily. [2] This eruption apparently took place in the fiftieth year after the previous one, and altogether, it is said, there have been three eruptions since the Greek settlement of Sicily.

[3] These were the events that took place over the winter, and so ended the sixth year of the current war, the history of which was written by Thucydides.

Book Four

The seventh, eighth, and ninth years of the war. **425/424:** *more Athenian activity in the west, and sixth Peloponnesian invasion of Attica (4.1–2.3); Demosthenes establishes an Athenian outpost at Pylos (4.2.4–6); Athenian activity in Thrace (4.7); further developments at Pylos (4.8–23); Athens in the west (4.24–25); Athenian victory, and Spartan surrender, at Pylos (4.26–41); Athenian campaigns around Corinth (4.42–45); civil war in Corcyra (4.46–48.5); more Athenian activity in the west and northwest (4.48.6–49); Spartan and Athenian attempts to negotiate with Persia (4.50); Athenian suspicions of Chios (4.51).* **424/423:** *developments on Lesbos (4.52); Athenian campaigns in Cythera and Laconia (4.53–57); developments in Sicily (4.58–65); Athenian and Spartan interventions at Megara (4.66–74); Athenian activities in the northeast and Boeotia (4.75–77); Brasidas leads a Spartan force north (4.78–88); Athenian defeat at Delium (4.89–101.4); more Spartan victories and Athenian losses in the north (4.101.5–116).* **423/422:** *a one-year truce (4.117–119); Brasidas continues to campaign in the north (4.120–129, 135); Athenian countermeasures (4.130–133); conflict between Mantineans and Tegeans (4.134).*

1. The following summer, at the time when the grain was coming into ear, ten Syracusan and the same number of Locrian ships sailed to Messina in Sicily and took control of it. They did so at the invitation of the Messinians themselves, and the city seceded from Athens. [2] The main reason the Syracusans had for doing this was that the place was obviously a key entry point into Sicily, and they were afraid the Athenians might make it a base of operations and move against them sometime with a larger force than they currently had. The Locrians, however, were motivated by hostility toward Rhegium and wanted to reduce the city by attacking it from both land and sea. [3] The Locrians had also launched a full-scale invasion of Rhegium, to make it impossible for the Rhegians to go to the aid of the Messinians, and because some political exiles from Rhegium who were being sheltered in Locri asked for their intervention. Rhegium had long been riven by political discord, which made it impossible for them to defend themselves at that time against the Locrians, who were therefore all the more eager to attack them. [4] After laying waste their land, the Locrians withdrew their land army, while their ships remained on guard at Messina. Other ships, for which crews were currently being found, were to join them at the anchorage there, and then the Locrians would make Messina a base from which to prosecute the war against Rhegium.

2. At about the same time in the spring, before the cereal crops were ripe, the combined Peloponnesian forces invaded Attica under the command of the Spartan king Agis, son of Archidamus. They encamped and set about ravaging the land. [2] The Athenians dispatched to Sicily the forty ships they had been making ready, along with the two remaining generals, Eurymedon and Sophocles; a third general, Pythodorus, had been sent on ahead and was already in Sicily. [3] Their instructions were also to put in at Corcyra as they sailed past,* to see what they could do for the Corcyreans in the city, who were being harassed by the exiles on the mountain. Moreover, sixty Peloponnesian ships had been sent to Corcyra to help the men on the mountain, and since there was a serious shortage of food in the city they foresaw little difficulty in seizing control. [4] Demosthenes held no command after his return from Acarnania, but the Athenians gave

him permission, in response to his own request, to make use of these ships at his discretion for operations on the Peloponnesian coast.

3. When the ships reached the coast of Laconia in the course of their voyage, they found out that the Peloponnesians had already reached Corcyra. Eurymedon and Sophocles were in favor of pushing on for Corcyra, but Demosthenes told them first to stop off at Pylos and to continue their voyage once they had done what was necessary. They argued against him, but by chance a storm arose that carried them into Pylos anyway. [2] Demosthenes immediately demanded that they fortify the place, saying that this was why he had embarked with them. He pointed out that there was plenty of wood and stone, and that despite being a natural strongpoint, the place was undefended, as was the land around it for quite a distance. For Pylos is some forty-six miles from Sparta and is situated in the territory that was formerly Messenia;* its local name is Coryphasium. [3] Eurymedon and Sophocles replied by saying that there were many uninhabited headlands in the Peloponnese that he could occupy if he wanted to squander public money. But in Demosthenes's opinion Pylos had certain advantages over anywhere else. It had an adjacent bay that could act as a harbor, and he thought that if the Messenians, whose roots were there and who spoke the same dialect as the Lacedaemonians, made it their base of operations, they would be able to make a great deal of trouble for the Lacedaemonians, and would at the same time be a reliable garrison for the place.*

4. Demosthenes failed to persuade either the generals or, later (when he told the taxiarchs as well what he wanted to do), the troops,† but the army was kept idle by unfavorable sailing conditions, and eventually the soldiers, having nothing better to do, were moved to go around the site and fortify it. [2] They took the matter in hand and set about the work. They had no iron tools for working stone, so they selected suitable rocks, brought them to the site, and fitted them together according to each one's shape. If clay was needed anywhere, for lack of containers they carried it on their backs, bent over forward so as to lose as little as possible, and with their hands clasped behind them. [3] One way and another, then, they pushed on and tried to finish working on the most assailable parts before the Lacedaemonians came and attacked the place. Most of the site was naturally strong and had no need of a wall. **5.** But the Lacedaemonians happened to be celebrating a festival, and besides, they made light of the news when they heard it, because they felt sure that when they took to the field, either the Athenians would offer no resistance or they would easily be overwhelmed and captured. In any case, they were also somewhat stymied by the fact that their army was still in Attica. [2] It took the Athenians six days to fortify the parts of the site that faced land and the other vulnerable parts, and then the bulk of the fleet hastened away for Corcyra and Sicily, leaving Demosthenes with five ships to protect the place.

6. The Peloponnesians who were in Attica hurried home when they found out about the occupation of Pylos, which the Lacedaemonians and King Agis regarded as their own. Besides, since they had invaded early and the grain was not yet ripe, there was a severe shortage of food in the army. Moreover, the men were suffering from the unseasonably cold, wet weather. [2] So there were many reasons for them to return home early, and this turned out to be the shortest of their invasions: they stayed in Attica for only fifteen days.

7. At the same time, Simonides, one of the Athenian generals, went to Eion (the one in the Thraceward region),* which, despite being a colony of Mende, had sided with the Peloponnesians. He collected a few Athenians from the garrison posts, along with a larger force of local Athenian allies, and took the town when it was betrayed to him by sympathizers. But the Chalcidians and Bottiaeans immediately rallied to the town's defense, and Simonides was driven out with considerable loss of life.

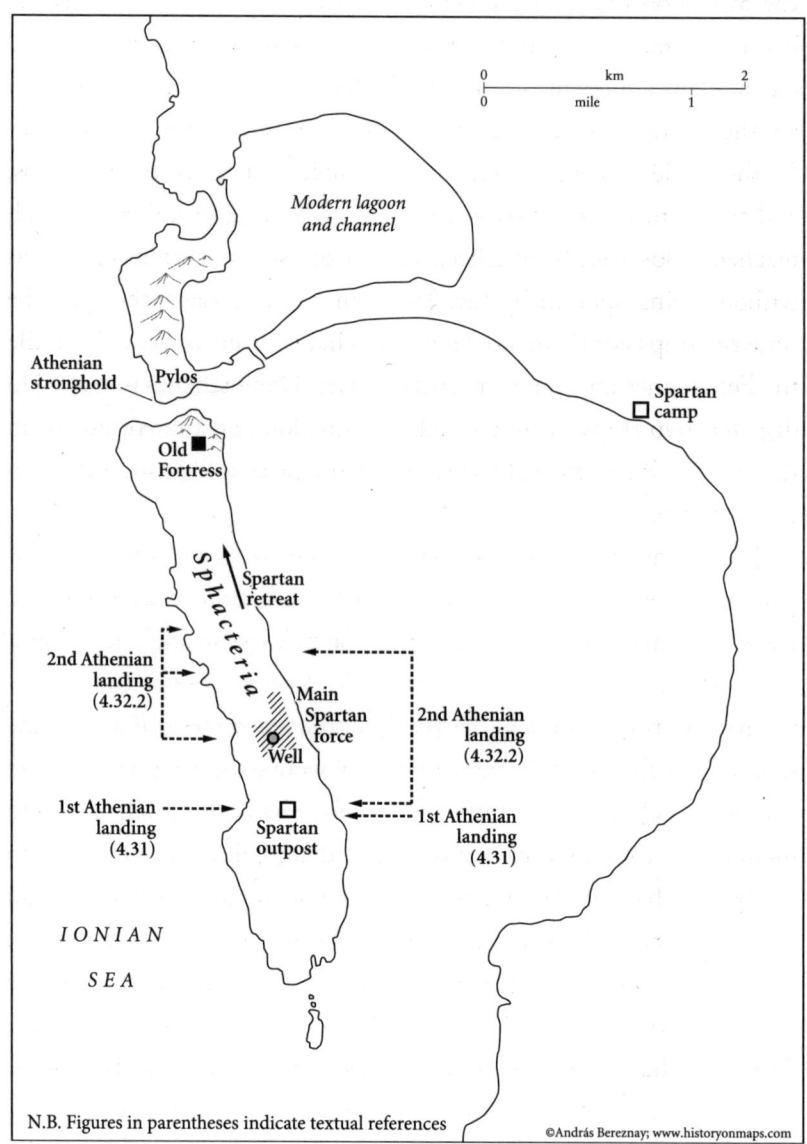

H. Pylos and Sphacteria

8. Once the Peloponnesian army had returned home from Attica, the Spartiates (without the helots) and the perioeci from the nearest towns immediately set out to attack Pylos, while the rest of the Lacedaemonians approached more slowly, having only just returned from another campaign. [2] They also sent word around the Peloponnese for their allies to come as quickly as possible to support them at Pylos, and they sent the same message to the sixty ships at Corcyra, which reached Pylos after having been hauled across the isthmus of Leucas without being spotted by the Athenian ships at Zacynthos. By the time the ships got there, the land forces had arrived as well. [3] While the Peloponnesian ships were still en route, Demosthenes managed to dispatch two ships in time to tell Eurymedon and the Athenians in the ships at Zacynthos of the threat to the place and to urge them to come at once.

[4] So the Athenian ships were making their way toward Pylos with all speed in response to Demosthenes's urgent request, and the Lacedaemonians were getting ready to attack the stronghold by both land and sea. They foresaw no difficulty in taking the place, because the fortifications had been hastily built and there were few men inside. [5] As for the Athenian ships they were expecting, which were coming to help from Zacynthos, if the place had not actually fallen to them by the time they arrived they intended to block the entrances to the bay so that the Athenians could not anchor there. [6] The island called Sphacteria extends right across the mouth of the bay so that each end of it is close to the mainland, which makes the bay a safe haven and the entrances to it narrow; the one by Pylos, where the Athenians had their stronghold, is wide enough for the passage of two ships, and the one by the mainland at the other end for eight or nine ships. The entire island is wooded and pathless because of being uninhabited, and is almost three miles long.† [7] So they planned to block the entrances to the bay with ships packed close together, prows facing outward.

They were also worried that the Athenians might use Sphacteria as a base from which to carry out operations against them, so they ferried hoplites over to it and posted others along the coast of the mainland. [8] Then, not only would the island be hostile to the Athenians, but so would the mainland; they would have no opportunity to disembark there, since the coastline of Pylos itself, facing the open sea beyond the northern entrance to the harbor, had no bays, and therefore no place from which they could set out to support their men in Pylos. The Lacedaemonians also thought they would probably be able to take the stronghold without having to fight at sea and that it would be a risk-free venture for them, since the place had been occupied on the spur of the moment and the men inside had no food. [9] Having decided on this plan, they cast lots to select hoplites from each of the companies and began to ferry them over to the island. Earlier units went over to the island and returned in rotation, but the last unit, the one that was caught there, consisted of 420 hoplites with their helot orderlies under the command of Epitadas, son of Molobrus.

9. Demosthenes could see that the Lacedaemonians were going to attack simultaneously by land and sea, so he, too, made his preparations. The triremes he still had from those that had been left behind by Eurymedon he hauled onto the shore under the lee of the stronghold and surrounded with a stockade, and he equipped their crews with shields—albeit ones that were mostly poor and made of wicker. There was no way for him to get hold of proper weaponry in an uninhabited place, and even these shields were seized from a 30-oared Messenian privateer and a dispatch boat that happened to have put in there. About 40 of these Messenians were armed as hoplites, and he put them to work alongside the others. [2] Most of his men, whether armed or not, he posted to the best-fortified and strongest parts of the site facing inland, and their job was to defend the place in the event of an infantry attack. He himself selected from the whole force 60 hoplites and a few archers, and he led them outside the stronghold to the stretch of coast where he thought it most likely that the

Lacedaemonian ships would try to force a landing. The terrain there, facing the sea, was rugged and rocky, but as their wall was weakest at that point, he thought that was where the Lacedaemonians would commit to forcing their way inside the stronghold.[†] [3] The Athenians had not made the wall strong there because they never expected to be weaker at sea, but if the Lacedaemonians forced their way ashore, the chances were that the stronghold would be taken. [4] So Demosthenes went right down to the edge of the sea at this point, and after deploying the hoplites for his attempt to prevent an enemy landing, he encouraged them along the following lines:

10. "Men, my comrades in this risky enterprise, in a critical situation such as this I hope none of you wants to be thought smart by calculating how great the peril is that we face. No, I would have each and every one of you engage the enemy with unreflective optimism, confident that he will survive even this. What holds true for every critical situation is true for us today: there's no time for calculation, but only the necessity of meeting the danger without the slightest irresolution.

[2] "In fact, as far as I can see, the situation actually largely favors us, if we resolve to stand our ground and not be panicked by their numbers into throwing away the advantages we have. [3] What I'm getting at is this. The ruggedness of the place I consider to be to our advantage, and if we stand firm it will help us in our fight, but if we fall back, despite the difficulty of the terrain it will be easy going for them if there's no one to stop them. Then we'll find ourselves facing a more formidable enemy, since it won't be easy for him to withdraw again if he's hard pressed by us. It will be easiest for us to repel them when they're on their ships, but once they've disembarked they'll be on equal terms with us. [4] Nor should we be particularly alarmed by their numbers. They may be many, but it will be so difficult for their ships to come to anchor that only a few of them will be fighting at any one time. We're up against a larger force, but they're not fighting us on land, where conditions for both sides are equal. No, they'll be fighting

from ships, and at sea there are many factors that need to coincide if the outcome is to be favorable. [5] In my opinion, then, the difficulties they face offset the fact that we're fewer in number. Besides, you're Athenians, and you know from experience what disembarking from ships is like when the enemy fights back—I mean, that it's never possible to force a landing if the defenders stand firm and don't fall back out of fear of the noise and menace of the approaching ships—and so I call on you to stand your ground, to repel the enemy right at the shoreline, and thereby to save both yourselves and our stronghold."

11. These words of encouragement by Demosthenes boosted the Athenians' confidence, and they went down and formed up at the water's edge. [2] Meanwhile, the Lacedaemonians had set out, and as well as attacking the stronghold by land with their army, they also brought their ships into play. Forty-three ships were involved in the assault, and on board was their navarch, the Spartiate Thrasymelidas, son of Cratesicles. He was attacking exactly where Demosthenes had expected it. [3] So the Athenians were trying to repel attacks by both land and sea. The Lacedaemonians divided their fleet into relays of a few ships, because it was impossible for larger numbers to approach the shore, and they took it in turns to hang back and attack, filled with determination and urging one another on in their attempt to force their way ashore and take the Athenian fortress.

[4] None of them was more conspicuous than Brasidas, who was in command of one of the triremes. He could see that the difficulty of the place was making the captains and helmsmen hesitate out of fear of staving in their ships, even when there was a chance of making land, so he called out to them. It made no sense, he said, for them to be sparing mere timbers while letting the enemy get away with having built a fortress in their territory. He ordered them to force a landing even if that meant breaking their ships, and he told the allies that it was wrong to repay the Lacedaemonians for all the benefits they had received by shrinking back from danger, and that they should donate their ships to Sparta at this time of the city's need by

running aground; one way or another they should make a landing and overpower the men and the stronghold. **12.** As well as urging the others on in this way, he compelled his own helmsman to run his ship aground and walked out onto the gangplank. He tried to get ashore but was beaten back by the Athenians, and then he lost consciousness as a result of all the wounds he sustained. As he fell into the outrigger his shield slipped off into the sea and was washed ashore, and later the Athenians recovered it and made it part of the trophy that they set up for this attack.

[2] However determined the others were, they were unable to make a landing because of the difficulty of the terrain and because the Athenians resolutely stood their ground. [3] Things were so back to front that the Athenians were fighting on land, and indeed Laconian land, against a seaborne attack by the Lacedaemonians, and against Athenian resistance the Lacedaemonians were trying to disembark from ships onto land that belonged to them but was now in enemy hands—even though, at the time, the Lacedaemonians' reputation consisted largely in their being a quintessential land-based people and supreme at land warfare, while the Athenians' lay in their being seafarers and excelling at naval warfare.

13. All this day and for a good part of the next the Lacedaemonians kept up their assaults on the fort, but then they gave up. On the third day they sent some of their ships to Asine to fetch wood to make siege contraptions, thinking that, although the stretch of wall by the harbor was quite high, it was the best place to make a landing, and they could take it with the help of such devices. [2] At this juncture the Athenian ships from Zacynthos arrived, fifty in number, because they had been joined by some of the guard ships from Naupactus and four Chian triremes. [3] When they saw that both the mainland and the island were thronging with hoplites, and that the Lacedaemonian ships were keeping to the bay without coming out to give battle, they were not sure where they could find anchorage, but then they went to Prote, an uninhabited island not far distant, and made camp there. The next day they prepared for battle and put to sea, ready to fight the enemy in the open sea if they chose to come out against them, or otherwise intending to sail into the bay themselves and attack them there.

[4] The Lacedaemonians did not put out to sea to give battle, but, as it happened, neither had they carried out their plan of blocking the entrances to the bay. Instead, as there was no action on land that day, they were arranging crews for their ships and preparing to fight in the bay, which was far from small, if there was an incursion there. **14.** Seeing this, the Athenians moved into the attack at both entrances. They fell on the major portion of the Lacedaemonian ships, which were already clear of the shore and lined up with prows opposed, and turned them to flight. Since only a short distance separated the two fleets, the Athenians pursued them closely, and they disabled a large number of ships and captured five, one of them with its crew. The rest, which had escaped to the shore, they proceeded to ram, and moreover they set about battering some ships even while the crews were going aboard, before they put to sea. They also attached ropes to some empty ships—the crews had turned to flight—and began to tow them away.

[2] When they saw what was happening, the Lacedaemonians were extremely perturbed, because their men on the island were about to be cut off, and they ran to the rescue. They waded into the sea in full armor, seized hold of the ships, and tried to pull them back, and each man thought the attempt had stalled whenever he was not assisting in person. [3] In short, it was utter pandemonium, with both sides reversing their normal way of fighting: what the Lacedaemonians were doing, in their determination and excitement, can perhaps best be described as fighting a sea battle from land, while the Athenians, who were winning and wanted to make the most of their success, were fighting a land battle from their ships. [4] Each side made the other suffer, and many were injured, but by the time they separated the Lacedaemonians had saved their empty ships, apart from those that had first been captured. [5] The two sides retired to their respective

camps, and as soon as the Athenians had erected a trophy, returned the bodies of the enemy dead, and secured the wrecks, they began to patrol and surveil the island, now that the men there were cut off. The Peloponnesians on the mainland, who were now at full strength, stayed in position, maintaining their threat against Pylos.

15. When news of what had happened at Pylos reached Sparta, they regarded it as a calamity and decided that the authorities should go to the camp at once, assess the situation for themselves, and determine what needed to be done. [2] When they saw that there was no way for them to help their men on the island, and because they did not want them to come to grief as a result of shortage of food, or be overwhelmed by superior numbers and taken prisoner, both of which were distinct possibilities, they decided to see if the Athenian generals would agree to a truce at Pylos while they sent envoys to Athens to discuss a permanent settlement and try to recover their men in as short a time as possible.

16. The generals accepted their proposal and a truce was made on the following terms: The Lacedaemonians were to surrender the ships that had been involved in the battle, were to bring every other warship they had in Laconia to Pylos and hand them over to the Athenians, and were not to bear arms against the stronghold either by land or sea; the Athenians were to allow the Lacedaemonians on the mainland to send a specified amount of prepared food over to the men on the island (two Attic quarts of barley-meal per hoplite, along with a pint of wine and some meat, and for each of their attendants half of these rations),* and these provisions were to be sent over under Athenian supervision, with no unsupervised visits to the island allowed; and, despite this clause, the Athenians would maintain their guard over the island, short of landing on it, and were not to bear arms against the Peloponnesians by land or sea. [2] If either side infringed these conditions in any way, the agreement would immediately be null and void, and the truce was to last until the Lacedaemonian envoys returned from Athens. The Athenians were to convey the envoys to and from Athens in a trireme, and on their return this truce would be terminated; the Athenians would return the Lacedaemonian ships in exactly the same condition they were in when they received them. [3] So a truce was agreed on these terms, the ships (about sixty in number) were handed over, and the envoys were sent on their way. When they arrived in Athens they spoke to the following effect:

17. "Athenians, the Lacedaemonians sent us here to negotiate a settlement in the matter of our men on the island—one that will prove acceptable to you because of the advantages it offers, and at the same time will be as conducive to our honor as current circumstances allow in view of our misfortune. [2] In speaking at some length, we won't be departing from our normal practice, because, while it's customary in our country not to use many words where few suffice, it's also customary for us to use more words when the occasion requires us to rely on speech to explain something important and accomplish what needs to be done.* [3] Please don't listen to what we say in a hostile frame of mind, and please don't feel that we're trying to explain matters to you as though you were unintelligent. Consider what we say to be a reminder of good policy addressed to people who have the ability to recognize it as such.

[4] "You have the opportunity to turn your current success to good account. You can retain what you've won, gain honor and glory as well, and avoid what invariably happens to people when something good unexpectedly comes their way: because they're currently enjoying greater success than they ever expected, they bullishly thirst after more. [5] On the other hand, those who have frequently experienced the ups and downs of life have good reason to be particularly distrustful even when fortune smiles on them; and in all likelihood that is the prevalent attitude here in Athens, thanks to your experiences, as it is among us thanks to ours.

18. "You may also know the truth of what we're saying by considering our present situation: we, the people with the greatest reputation in Greece, have been reduced to coming here, though in the past we thought that it was us who had the authority, more than anyone else, to grant the kind of request that we've now come to ask of you. [2] And yet we've not been brought to this because our strength is less than it was, nor because an increase in our strength led us arrogantly to overreach ourselves. No, we had the resources that we always have, but we made an error in judging what we could accomplish with them, and that's something to which no one is immune.

[3] "So it would be unreasonable of you to think, just because your state and its allies are currently strong, that you will always have fortune on your side. [4] Prudent people are those who make a safe investment of their gains in view of their uncertainty (and these same people would also cope more intelligently with setbacks), and who think of war not as something that can be restricted to whatever limited involvement one might wish to have, but as something that must follow the course determined by its vicissitudes. Moreover, it's people who understand this who are least likely to stumble, because they aren't carried away by trust in their military successes, and are most likely to bring the fighting to an end at a time when fortune is smiling on them. [5] And that, Athenians, is exactly the right course for you in our case. But if you ignore our advice and come to grief, which is always a possibility, beware, as it might later be thought that you won even your present successes by luck, when it was possible for you to leave to posterity a secure reputation for strength and intelligence.

19. "The Lacedaemonians are inviting you to enter into a treaty that will end the war. They're offering you peace and alliance, and suggesting besides that we should essentially be on good and friendly terms with each other. In return, they're asking you for the men on the island, and they think that granting this request will be better for both of us, because otherwise there's the possibility that they might force their way off the island when a chance to escape presents itself, or they might be even further reduced and fall into your hands. [2] In short, we don't believe that great enmities are very likely to be brought to a secure end if one side seeks to retaliate against the other, and if, when it substantially has the upper hand, it binds its opponents with oaths and forcibly imposes an unfair settlement on them. No, enduring peace results when it's in the victors' power to impose a harsh settlement, but instead they act decently and make peace on moderate terms, surprising their adversary by conquering him in goodness as well. [3] For when an adversary is under an obligation to repay goodness in kind—when he no longer feels that he has to retaliate because he was coerced into coming to terms—his conscience makes him readier to abide by the terms to which he has agreed. [4] And people are more likely to act like this toward their major enemies than they are toward those with whom their breach is no more than slight. It's a fact of human nature that while people are glad to make counter-concessions to those who give ground of their own accord, they're ready to risk life and limb even contrary to their better judgment when faced with overweening arrogance.

20. "There's no better time than now for us to be reconciled, before something irreparable comes between us and makes it inevitable that you'll have our undying hostility, personal as well as official, and lose all the benefits that we're now inviting you to enjoy. [2] While matters are still undecided, while you stand to gain glory and our friendship, and while we have the chance of avoiding dishonor and gaining a reasonable settlement following our setback, let's be reconciled. Let's choose peace instead of war and relieve the suffering of the rest of Greece. Moreover, the Greeks will consider you more responsible for the peace than we are. They're caught up in a war without knowing which of us started it, but if there's a settlement, which is now largely up to you, it's you who will gain their gratitude. [3] And if you decide to accept our proposals, you can secure the friendship of the Lacedaemonians, because they issued the invitation and found themselves treated with favor rather than force. [4] Consider all the advantages that are likely to ensue: if Sparta and Athens see eye to eye, you can be certain that the rest of the Greek world, being weaker than us, will show us every possible mark of honor."

21. Implicit in this speech by the Lacedaemonians was their belief that the Athenians had been desiring peace for some time, but had been prevented from getting their way by Lacedaemonian opposition; so if peace was offered, they thought, the Athenians would leap at the chance and return the men. [2] But the Athenians reckoned that, with the men on the island in their power, the treaty with the Lacedaemonians would now be waiting for them whenever they wanted it, and they thirsted after more. [3] It was above all Cleon, son of Cleaenetus, who encouraged them in this belief; he was one of the populist leaders at that time and was the speaker the general populace found the most persuasive. He convinced them to respond to the Lacedaemonian proposal by saying that the men on the island should first surrender their weaponry and themselves and be brought to Athens, and that once they had arrived the Lacedaemonians should return Nisaea, Pegae, Troezen, and Achaea, places that had not been taken in war but in consequence of a previous treaty, to which the Athenians had agreed when they had experienced a serious setback and had a particular need at the time for a treaty.* Once the Lacedaemonians had done that, he said, they could have their men back and make a treaty to last as many years as both sides wanted.

22. The Lacedaemonians did not directly respond to this, but asked the Athenians to appoint a committee to discuss the matter with them in detail and at leisure until they came up with terms to which both sides agreed. [2] At this, Cleon inveighed strongly against them. He had known all along, he said, that the Lacedaemonians were up to no good, and they had now made this clear by their unwillingness to speak openly before the people and their preference for conferring with just a few men. If they had any sound proposals to make, they should let everyone hear them. [3] But as far as the Lacedaemonians were concerned, there was no way they could speak in public about any concessions they might decide to make in view of their misfortune, because if they offered a concession and it was turned down, they would lose face before their allies. And since they could also see that the Athenians were not going to do as they suggested and accept moderate terms, they left Athens without having achieved anything.

23. On their return to Pylos, the truce immediately came to an end and the Lacedaemonians asked for their ships to be returned to them, as had been agreed. But the Athenians refused to give them back, citing as grounds of complaint an attack on the stronghold in breach of the truce and some other seemingly trivial matters. They insisted that, according to the terms of the truce, it was voided by any infringement. The Lacedaemonians argued back, accusing the Athenians of making a serious mistake in not returning the ships, and then they left and prepared to fight. [2] So the fighting resumed at Pylos, with both sides sparing no effort. The Athenians had two ships constantly sailing in opposite directions around the island by day, and at night the whole fleet anchored around the island, except on the side facing the sea when it was windy. Twenty ships arrived from Athens to join them in the blockade, so that they now had seventy ships in all.* The Peloponnesians who were encamped on the mainland kept assaulting the Athenian fort, while watching for any opportunity that might allow them to rescue their men.

24. Meanwhile, in Sicily, the Syracusans and their allies had brought the other ships they had been preparing to Messina, to join those that were on guard there, and made Messina a base from which to prosecute the war. [2] It was above all the Locrians who had been urging them to do this, because of their hostility toward Rhegium, and they had launched a full-scale invasion of the territory of Rhegium. [3] The Syracusans wanted to try a battle at sea, since they could see that the Athenians had only a few ships on hand, and had found out that the larger fleet that had been due to arrive was engaged in the siege of Sphacteria. [4] If they defeated the Athenian fleet, they could blockade Rhegium by land and sea, and they felt sure that they would easily subdue it. Then they would be in a very strong position, because, since the cape on the Italian coast on which Rhegium is located and

Messina in Sicily are very close to each other, the Athenians would not be able to lie off Rhegium and control the strait. [5] The strait between Rhegium and Messina consists of a stretch of sea where Sicily and Italy are at their closest; it is the so-called Charybdis through which Odysseus is supposed to have sailed.* Because of the narrowness of the strait and because the water rushes into it from two great seas, the Tyrrhenian and the Sicilian, it has strong currents and is rightly regarded as hazardous.

25. It was in this strait that the Syracusans and their allies were forced to fight late one day to defend a boat that was passing through it. They put to sea with just over thirty ships against sixteen Athenian ships and eight from Rhegium. [2] The Athenians won, and the Syracusans and their allies beat a hasty retreat as best they could back to their own camps, with the loss of one ship. Nightfall put an end to any further fighting.

[3] After this, the Locrians withdrew from Rhegium, while the fleets of the Syracusans and their allies assembled and anchored near Messina at Cape Pelorus, where they were joined by their land army. [4] The Athenians and Rhegians sailed up and attacked when they saw that the ships were unmanned, but they lost one ship to a grappling iron, though the crew managed to swim away. [5] Then the Syracusans embarked on their ships and set out along the coast in the direction of Messina with the captured ship under tow. The Athenians attacked again, but the Syracusans turned their prows away from the shore and struck the first blow, and the Athenians lost another ship. [6] So the Syracusans had come out on top during their voyage along the coast as well as in the earlier battle, such as it was, and they brought their ships into the harbor of Messina.

[7] Information reached the Athenians that Camarina was to be betrayed to the Syracusans by Archias and his supporters,* so they sailed there at once. The Messinians seized the opportunity and launched a full-scale campaign by land and sea against nearby Naxos, a Chalcidian city. [8] On the first day, they confined the Naxians

within their walls while they ravaged the land, and on the next they sailed south and laid waste the farmland near the Acesines river while their land forces made an assault on the city. [9] But then the Sicels from beyond the hill country came down in large numbers to support the Naxians against the Messinians. The sight of them raised the Naxians' morale, and, encouraging one another by saying that the Leontinians and their other Greek allies were on their way, they suddenly charged out of the city and fell on the enemy. The Messinians turned to flight and over a thousand of them were killed, while the rest had a hard time as they made for home. They were attacked on the roads by the Sicels and most of them lost their lives. [10] The fleet returned to Messina later and the various contingents dispersed to their various homes.

The Leontinians and their allies, joined by the Athenians, immediately attacked Messina, thinking that it had been badly weakened. While the Athenians made an attempt by sea on the harbor, the land forces attacked the city. [11] But the Messinians, and Demoteles with his unit of Locrians, who had been left in the city as a garrison after the defeat at Naxos, made a sortie against them. Much of the Leontinian army turned and ran at this unexpected attack, and many were killed, but when the Athenians saw what was happening they disembarked from their ships and intervened. They caught the Messinians out of formation and chased them back inside the city. Then, after erecting a trophy, they returned to Rhegium, [12] and subsequently the Sicilian Greeks carried out land campaigns against one another without Athenian involvement.

26. Meanwhile, at Pylos, the Athenians still had the Lacedaemonians on the island under siege, and the Peloponnesian forces on the mainland were still where they had been. [2] Maintaining a watch on the island was hard on the Athenians, because there was little food or water. There was no spring except for one right up on the acropolis of Pylos, and that was not abundant. The men usually made scratch-holes

in the shingle on the beach and drank the kind of water that could be expected there. [3] Moreover, conditions were cramped because there had not been much space for them to make camp, and since there was no proper anchorage for the ships, the crews took turns to eat on land while the rest lay at anchor out at sea. [4] They also became very demoralized by the length of the siege, which was unexpected. They had thought that it would take only a few days to besiege the men into submission, seeing that they were on an uninhabited island and had only brackish water to drink.

[5] The reason why the men were able to hold out was that the Lacedaemonians had called for volunteers to take provisions to the island, in the form of milled grain, wine, cheese, and any other foodstuffs that men under siege could use. They offered a substantial reward and promised freedom for any helot who managed to get food onto the island. [6] And most of those who braved the danger and got food onto the island were helots, setting out from wherever they were in the Peloponnese and sailing under cover of darkness to the seaward side of the island. [7] They looked most of all for an opportunity to be driven ashore by the wind; it was easier for them to get to the island without being noticed by the triremes on guard when the wind was blowing in from the sea, because that made it impossible for the Athenians to anchor their ships on both sides of the island. The helots sailed in quite recklessly because they had agreed with the Lacedaemonians what the monetary value was of the boats they drove ashore, and Lacedaemonian hoplites were guarding the island's landing-places. But all those who ran the risk when it was calm were caught. [8] There were also divers, who swam underwater to the island across the bay, towing on a cord honeyed poppy-seed and pounded linseed in leather sacks. At first these divers escaped detection, but later the Athenians were on the lookout for them. [9] One way or another, then, both sides exercised their ingenuity, the Lacedaemonians in finding ways to get food onto the island and the Athenians in trying to make sure that they did not get away with it.

27. When the Athenians in Athens heard that the army was in a bad way and that food was finding its way onto the island, they did not know what to do, and they were afraid that their blockade might be overtaken by winter. It was obviously going to be impossible for them to transport supplies around the Peloponnese—the place was so isolated that even in the summer they had not been able to send an adequate quantity of supplies—and it was clear that maintaining the blockade when the place had no harbors would not be practicable. The men on the island would either be saved when the blockade was called off, or they might wait for bad weather and use the boats that were bringing them food to escape. [2] What worried the Athenians most was the Lacedaemonians; they thought they must be in a strong position to have stopped negotiating with them, and they regretted their rejection of the peace treaty.

[3] Cleon, realizing that they thought him less trustworthy because he had wrecked the peace negotiations, claimed that the men who brought the news of Pylos were not telling the truth. So the messengers suggested that, if they did not believe them, the Athenians should send some observers—and Cleon himself was chosen by the Athenians as one of the observers, along with Theagenes. [4] When Cleon realized his dilemma—that either he would have to give the same report as the messengers he was maligning, or contradict them and be caught in a lie—he advised the Athenians, since he could see that on balance public opinion was now also in favor of taking military action, not to bother with sending observers; that would be a waste of time and an opportunity missed, he said. Instead they should sail against the men on the island, if they thought the reports they were receiving were true. [5] With a pointed allusion to Nicias, son of Niceratus, who was one of the generals and a political enemy of his, he said it was a shame that the generals were not real men, because it was easy to get an expeditionary force ready, sail to Pylos, and make prisoners of the men on the island. If he were general, he said, that is what he would do.

28. The Athenians' response to this was to ask Cleon, in a rather rowdy fashion, why he was not already on his way to Pylos, if it seemed so easy to him. Seeing this, and at the same time because Cleon was obviously alluding to him, Nicias told him that as far as he and his fellow generals were concerned, he could take any troops he liked and make the attempt. [2] At first Cleon thought Nicias was bluffing and was not really ready to let him go, but when he realized that he was genuinely willing to give him the command, he backtracked, saying it was Nicias who was the general, not him. He was frightened now, even though he did not think that Nicias would go so far as to resign his command. [3] But Nicias repeated what he had said and continued to offer to resign his command at Pylos, calling on the Athenians to act as witnesses. And, with behavior that is typical of a crowd, the more Cleon tried to evade the expedition and to retract what he had said, the more the Athenians persisted in urging Nicias to surrender his command and called on Cleon to sail.* [4] In the end, since under the circumstances he could not escape the consequences of his words, he accepted command of the expedition. He stepped up and said he was not afraid of the Lacedaemonians and would take no citizen soldiers to Pylos, but only the Lemnians and Imbrians who were there in Athens, the peltasts who had come to help from Aenus and elsewhere,* and four hundred archers. With these men added to the army already at Pylos, he said, within twenty days he would either bring the Lacedaemonians alive to Athens or kill them there. [5] The Athenians burst into laughter at his boast, but the more sober elements of the population were pleased, because they reckoned that there were two possible outcomes, both of them good: either they would be rid of Cleon—this was the possibility they thought more likely—or, if they were wrong about this, he would deliver the Lacedaemonians to them as their prisoners.

29. Once he had completed his business in the assembly and the Athenians had formally voted to entrust the expedition to him, Cleon chose one of the generals at Pylos, Demosthenes, as his colleague, and hurriedly got ready to leave. [2] He chose Demosthenes because he had found out that he was planning to make a landing on the island himself, in view of the fact that the troops were eager to chance it; they were suffering from the barrenness of the place and were more besieged than besiegers.

[3] A fire on the island had increased Demosthenes's confidence. Most of it was wooded and pathless because of never having been inhabited, and previously this had concerned Demosthenes, since he considered it to be to the advantage of the enemy, in the sense that if a force of any size landed there, the Lacedaemonians could attack from hidden positions and make them suffer. The Lacedaemonians' failings and forces would not be so visible to the Athenians because of the trees and shrubs, but they would easily be able to see all the Athenian soldiers' weaknesses, and, since the initiative would be theirs, they could launch surprise attacks on them wherever they chose. [4] Then again, if he had his men push their way into the thickets to fight at close quarters, he thought that even though the Lacedaemonians were outnumbered, their familiarity with the terrain would enable them to prevail, since his men's ignorance of it would count for more than their numbers. However many men he had, they would be wiped out without realizing it was happening, because they would not be able to see where to go to help one another. **30.** These thoughts were particularly ready to occur to him because of what had happened in Aetolia, where the woods had been largely to blame for his defeat.*

[2] But the cramped conditions on the island meant that for their midday meal the Athenians were forced to land at its tip and prepare their food there (while keeping a lookout), and one of them had accidentally set fire to a small area of woodland. Then a wind had got up, and before anything could be done about it most of the trees and shrubs had been burned. [3] Now that he had a better view of the Lacedaemonians, Demosthenes could see that there were more of them than he had thought; he had previously underestimated their numbers, judging by the amount of food that was being sent over

there.† At this point, then, the Athenians began to take the idea of an assault on the island more seriously, as something that might deliver significant results, and as the island was now easier to disembark on, Demosthenes laid the groundwork for the attempt. One of the measures he took was to summon reinforcements from the nearby Athenian allies.

[4] Cleon had earlier written to Demosthenes telling him to expect his arrival, and now he reached Pylos with the troops he had requested. After he and Demosthenes conferred, the first thing they did was send a herald to the Lacedaemonian camp on the mainland to give them the opportunity, if they chose to take it, to tell the men on the island that they would come to no harm if they surrendered their weapons and themselves to the Athenians, on the understanding that they would be kept in custody, but in reasonable conditions, until an agreement had been reached on the broader issue. **31.** The Lacedaemonians rejected the offer, so the Athenians waited for one day, and then the next day they put to sea after boarding all their hoplites on just a few ships at night, and a little before dawn they disembarked on both sides of the island, the side facing the open sea and the side on the bay. There were approximately eight hundred hoplites, and they advanced at a run against the first of the Lacedaemonians' guardposts.

[2] The Lacedaemonians were deployed as follows: This first guardpost was manned by about thirty hoplites; in the second of the three guardposts, which was on the flattest part of the island and near the water source, were most of the Lacedaemonians and the commanding officer, Epitadas; and only a few soldiers were guarding the very end of the island, facing Pylos, which rose steeply from the sea and was extremely difficult to attack from the land, because there was also an old fortress there, made out of unworked stones, which might prove of use to them, the Lacedaemonians thought, if they were particularly hard pressed and had to retreat. That was the disposition of the Lacedaemonian troops.

32. The Athenians ran to the first post and it took them hardly any time to kill the guards, who were still in their beds, groping for their weapons. They had no idea that the Athenians had made a landing; they had thought that the ships were sailing as usual to take up their nighttime posts. [2] At daybreak, the rest of the Athenian forces landed on the island as well; this landing party was made up of all the men from seventy-plus ships (excluding only the oarsmen from the lowest level),* variously equipped; eight hundred archers and at least as many peltasts; the Messenians who had come to help; and all the others who were stationed at Pylos, except for those who were guarding the stronghold. [3] Demosthenes organized them into separate units of two hundred, give or take a few, and they occupied all the highest points of the island so as to make things as difficult as possible for the enemy, who would be completely surrounded. There was no single point where they could launch a counteroffensive, and, given the Athenians' superior numbers, they were exposed to attack from all sides. If they went for the men in front of them, they would be fired on from behind; if they went for the men on their flanks, they would be fired on by the troops deployed on one or the other side of them. [4] Wherever they went, the enemy was always going to be behind them—and these were light-armed troops, who are the most difficult to cope with, because their arrows, javelins, stones, and slings are effective at a distance. It was impossible for the Lacedaemonians even to draw near them: they could run away faster and they moved into the attack whenever the Lacedaemonians fell back. That was Demosthenes's original plan for the landing, and it was this plan that he now put into effect with the disposition of his forces.

33. When Epitadas and his soldiers—that is to say, the main body of the men on the island—saw that the first guardpost had been wiped out and that the Athenians were advancing on them, they fell into line and advanced against the Athenian hoplites, wanting to make it a close-quarters fight. The hoplites were directly in front of them, while the light-armed troops were on their flanks and behind them. [2] But they were prevented from engaging the hoplites or putting their experience to use by the missiles of the light-armed troops, which were coming at them from every direction, and also because the Athenian hoplites did not counter their advance with one of their own but stayed where they were. The Lacedaemonians succeeded in forcing the light-armed troops to turn and flee whenever they ran up into the attack, but then they would turn around in mid-flight and fight back; they were lightly equipped and easily opened up a gap between themselves and the Lacedaemonians, and because of the difficulty and roughness of the terrain, owing to its having previously been an uninhabited wasteland, it was impossible for the heavily armed Lacedaemonians to pursue them over it.

34. The two sides skirmished with each other like this for a short while, but eventually the Lacedaemonians became too tired to run out promptly in response to an attack. When the light-armed troops realized that the Lacedaemonian defense was falling off, their confidence soared. They could see that they greatly outnumbered the Lacedaemonians, and as they became more accustomed to them, they became less frightened of them, because they had not immediately suffered as much as they had expected to. At first, when they had disembarked on the island, they had been overawed by the thought that they were going up against Lacedaemonians, but they no longer saw them as a threat, and with one voice they gave a sudden yell, charged at them, and began to ply them with stones, arrows, and javelins—whatever each man had to hand. [2] The combined yell and charge disconcerted the Lacedaemonians, who were not used to this kind of fighting. Dust from the recently burned woodland rose high into the air, and it was difficult for them to see what they were facing when, along with the dust, they were being bombarded with arrows and stones from so many men. [3] Now they found themselves in real trouble. Their felt helmets were no protection against the arrows, javelins broke off in them as they struck home, and there was nothing they could do to help themselves. With their vision inhibited, they had no way of knowing what was coming, and their opponents were shouting too loudly for them to hear the orders coming from within their own ranks. There was nothing but danger on every side, and they began to doubt that there was any way for them to defend themselves and get through the ordeal safely.

35. Eventually, with the numbers of wounded now increasing because all they could do was turn and turn about in the same restricted space, they closed ranks and fell back on the old fortress at the tip of the island, which was not far away and was manned by some of their comrades. [2] No sooner had they given ground when the light-armed soldiers, greatly encouraged, attacked with an even more ferocious yell. During the retreat, some of the Lacedaemonians were cut off and killed, but most of them managed to reach the safety of the fortress, and they joined the guards there in organizing themselves to put up a defense at every point where it could be attacked. [3] The Athenians were right behind them, but the place was such a strongpoint that they were unable to surround and encircle it, so they made a direct, frontal assault in an attempt to dislodge them. [4] For a long time—for most of the day, in fact—both sides held out, despite the toll taken on them by the fighting, their thirst, and the heat of the sun, with one side trying to dislodge their adversaries from the hill and the other trying to hold their ground. It was easier for the Lacedaemonians to defend themselves now than it had been before, because there was no enemy on their flanks.

36. There was no end in sight, so the Messenian general approached Cleon and Demosthenes and said the men were exhausting themselves pointlessly. If they would let him take some of the archers and light-armed troops and find a way round behind the enemy, he thought he could force his way into the fortress. [2] They gave him the men he requested and, setting out from a concealed spot to prevent the enemy from seeing him, he made his approach as best he could by way of the precipitous face of the island, where the Lacedaemonians had not posted guards, because they trusted in the natural inaccessibility of the place. It was far from easy, and he barely made it, but he was not seen by the Lacedaemonians as he made his way around, so that when he suddenly appeared on the hill in their rear, his arrival was so unexpected that they panicked, while the Athenians were reinvigorated by the sight of what they had been waiting for. [3] And so the Lacedaemonians were now under attack from both sides and found themselves—to compare small with great—in the same situation as at Thermopylae.* On that occasion, they were annihilated when the Persians took the path and came around behind them, and now these Lacedaemonians were exposed to being attacked from both front and rear. They were no longer able to offer resistance. Because they were few and their opponents many, and because they had been weakened by their inadequate diet, they began to give ground—and the Athenians were now in control of all the approaches.

37. When Cleon and Demosthenes realized that the Lacedaemonians would be wiped out by their men if they gave way even a little more, they called a halt to the fighting and restrained their men. They wanted to take the Lacedaemonians alive to Athens and hoped that when they heard the herald's offer their determination would crumble and they would submit, given the perilous situation in which they found themselves. [2] So they had the herald proclaim that if they wanted they could surrender their arms and themselves to the Athenians, and let the Athenians decide what to do with them. **38.** On hearing this offer, most of the Lacedaemonians lowered their shields and waved their hands in the air to indicate their compliance. Then, with the truce in force, Cleon and Demosthenes, and for the Lacedaemonians Styphon, son of Pharax, began to negotiate. Of the earlier commanders, the first, Epitadas, had been killed, and the next man to be appointed, Hippagretas, was still alive, but was lying among the corpses, because he was thought to be dead. In accordance with Lacedaemonian custom, Styphon had been nominated as the third in line, should something happen to the others. [2] Styphon and his associates said they would like to communicate with the Lacedaemonians on the mainland to find out what they should do. [3] The Athenians refused to let any of them go, but invited heralds to come from the mainland. After two or three consultations, the last man to sail over to the island from the Lacedaemonians on the mainland delivered the following message: "The Lacedaemonians command you to decide for yourselves what you should do, provided it is nothing dishonorable." And after talking things over among themselves, they formally surrendered their arms and themselves to the Athenians.

[4] The Athenians kept them under guard for the rest of the day and the following night, and then the next day they erected a trophy on the island and in general got themselves ready for the voyage home, which included distributing the prisoners among the trierarchs for safekeeping; and the Lacedaemonians sent a herald and fetched their dead over to the mainland. [5] The numbers of those killed on the island and taken prisoner were as follows: 420 hoplites in all had gone across; of these, 292 were taken to Athens alive and the rest were dead. Among the prisoners were about 120 Spartiates. Not many men on the Athenian side were killed, because there had been no close-quarters fighting.

39. The men were blockaded on the island for seventy-two days in all, from the time of the battle in the bay to the time of the battle on the island. [2] For about twenty of these days, while the envoys were away seeking a peace treaty, they were being supplied with provisions, but for the rest of the time they were maintained by what was smuggled in by boat. In fact, there was still some grain on the island and some other foodstuffs that were left behind, because Epitadas, the commanding officer, had given each of his men less than what was possible. [3] The Athenians and Peloponnesians then withdrew their forces from Pylos and returned to their respective homes. For all its madness, Cleon had kept his promise: he brought the men to Athens within twenty days, just as he had undertaken to do.

40. Nothing that happened in the war caused greater astonishment in Greece. No one expected the Lacedaemonians to surrender because of hunger or any other exigency; they thought they would hold on to their weapons and die fighting as best they could. [2] People refused to believe that the men who had surrendered were of the same caliber as those who had died. Sometime later, one of the Athenian allies confrontationally asked one of the prisoners from the island whether it was those of his comrades who had fallen who had been truly good men, and he replied that it would indeed be a valuable spindle (by which he meant "arrow") that could tell good men from bad—his point being that it was a matter of chance who was struck and killed by stones and arrows.*

41. After the captives had been brought to Athens, the Athenians decided to keep them bound and imprisoned until an agreement had been reached, and if the Peloponnesians invaded Attica before then, they would bring them out and kill them. [2] They garrisoned Pylos, and the Messenians from Naupactus sent the most suitable of their men there; it was, after all, their homeland, because Pylos is in what used to be Messenia. These Messenians carried out plundering raids in Laconia and caused a great deal of trouble, since they spoke the local dialect. [3] It was the Lacedaemonians' first experience of guerrilla warfare, and when helots started deserting they became afraid that they might face a more widespread domestic rebellion. So it was a difficult time for them, and although they did not want the Athenians to know how worried they were, they kept sending envoys to them, trying to recover both Pylos and their men. [4] But the Athenians thirsted after more, and however many times the Lacedaemonians came, they sent them away empty-handed. So much for events at Pylos.

42. In the same summer, immediately after this, the Athenians attacked Corinthia with a force consisting of eighty ships, two thousand citizen hoplites, and two hundred cavalrymen in horse-transports. They were accompanied also by some of their allies from Miletus, Andros, and Carystus, and the force was commanded by three generals, including Nicias, son of Niceratus. [2] They put to sea and at dawn they came ashore at the beach between the Chersonesus headland and the Rheitus streambed, where the shoreline is overlooked by the Solygea hill. This hill is where long ago the Dorians encamped and made war on the Corinthians in the city, who were Aeolians; today it is the location of a village called Solygea. The beach where the ships came ashore is less than a mile and a half from the village, about seven miles from Corinth, and three miles from the Isthmus. [3] But the Corinthians had received advance information from Argos about the Athenian attack and had already gone to defend the Isthmus with all their forces, except those who lived beyond the Isthmus and five hundred men who were away in Ambracia and Leucas on garrison duty. The rest of them were all to a man watching out for where the Athenians would come ashore. [4] They failed to spot the Athenians, however, because they sailed in under cover of darkness, but when they were alerted by beacons they left half of their men at Cenchreae, in case the Athenians moved against Crommyon,* and hurried away to fight back.

43. Battus, one of the two Corinthian generals who were involved in the battle, took one company and went to protect the village of Solygea, which was unfortified, while Lycophron went to engage the Athenians with the rest. [2] The Athenians had only just disembarked when the Corinthians attacked. They first attacked the Athenian right wing, which was in front of the Chersonesus headland, and then the rest of the army as well. The fighting was intense and entirely at close quarters. [3] The right wing, made up of Athenians and Carystians (who had been posted at the far end of the wing), withstood the Corinthian attack and pushed their opponents back, though with difficulty. The terrain there sloped steeply uphill, and the Corinthians retreated to a dry-stone wall and began to rain stones down on the Athenians from above. Then, after chanting a paean, they attacked once more, and again the Athenians withstood their charge and close-quarters fighting resumed. [4] Then one of the Corinthian companies came to support their left wing, and the Athenian right wing was routed and driven back to the sea. But when they reached their ships, the Athenians and Carystians rallied once more. [5] Meanwhile, the rest of the two armies had been fighting continuously, especially the Corinthian right wing, which was led by Lycophron and was putting up a strong resistance against the Athenian left, because they expected the Athenians to make an attempt on the village of Solygea.

44. Both sides held out for a long time, neither giving way to the other. But eventually the Corinthians were routed, as the Athenians had the valuable support of their cavalry while they had none. They retreated to the top of the hill and halted there, without coming down to resume the fight. [2] Most of the Corinthian losses were sustained on the right wing during this rout, and the general, Lycophron, was one of the casualties. And the rest of the Corinthian army did much the same;† they were not hard pressed and did not have to flee in haste when they were forced back, but they retreated to the high ground and took up a position there. [3] Since the Corinthians were no longer advancing and offering battle, the Athenians set about stripping the corpses of their arms and armor and recovering their own dead, and then before very long they erected a trophy.

[4] The other half of the Corinthian army, which was stationed on guard at Cenchreae in case the Athenians sailed against Crommyon, had not been able to see the battle because Mount Oneum was in the way, but when they saw the dust and realized what it meant they immediately set out to help. And when the older Corinthians in the city became aware of what had happened, they, too, set out to play their part. [5] Seeing this large force advancing on them, and also because they thought that a relief force was on its way from nearby Peloponnesian towns, the Athenians hastily withdrew to their ships with their spoils and the bodies of their dead, apart from two, whom they had left on the field because they had not been able to find them. [6] Once they had embarked on their ships, they went over to the offshore islands, and from there they sent a herald and arranged a truce so that

they could recover the two bodies they had left behind. The Corinthians lost 212 men in the fighting and the Athenians just under 50.

45. The Athenians set out from the islands that same day and sailed to Crommyon in Corinthia, which is some fourteen miles from Corinth itself. They anchored there, laid waste the land, and bivouacked for the night. [2] The next day they first sailed along the coast to the territory of Epidaurus and made a landing there, and then they went to Methana (the one between Epidaurus and Troezen). They built a wall to cut off the isthmus of the peninsula where† Methana is situated from the mainland, installed a garrison, and then plundered the farmland of Troezen, Halieis, and Epidaurus. When they had finished fortifying the place they sailed back home.

46. While all this was going on, Eurymedon and Sophocles, who had left Pylos for Sicily with [...]* Athenian ships, arrived in Corcyra and joined the men from the city in an expedition against the Corcyreans who had established themselves on Mount Istone. These oligarchs had earlier crossed over to the island from the mainland, after the period of civil unrest, and they were still in control of the countryside and doing a great deal of harm.* [2] The Athenians took their fortress by assault, and the oligarchs fled in a body to a hill. They agreed to surrender the mercenaries they had hired and, as for themselves, to hand over their weapons and let the Athenian people decide their fate. [3] Eurymedon and Sophocles had them taken over to the island of Ptychia to be guarded there, with their safety guaranteed by a truce, until they could be sent to Athens, on the understanding that if even one of them was caught trying to escape, the truce would come to an end for all of them.

[4] But the leading democrats in Corcyra were not convinced that the Athenians would put the men to death when they reached Athens, and they came up with the following scheme: [5] They managed to dupe a few of the men on Ptychia by surreptitiously sending over friends of theirs, who were instructed to pretend that they had the

oligarchs' best interests at heart and to tell them that it would be best for them to escape as soon as possible—they would get a boat ready for them—because the Athenian generals were intending to hand them over to the Corcyrean democrats. **47.** The men believed this tale and were caught trying to sail away on the boat that had been contrived for them, and so the truce came to an end and all the oligarchs were handed over to the Corcyreans. [2] The Athenian generals contributed not a little to this outcome. What gave the story circumstantial plausibility, and made those who came up with the scheme more confident about putting it in hand, was that everyone knew the generals would be unhappy if the men were taken to Athens by anyone other than themselves; they did not want others to gain the credit for taking them there just because they were on their way to Sicily.

[3] So the Corcyreans took the men in charge and imprisoned them in a large building. Later they brought them out, twenty at a time, and had them pass between two lines of hoplites posted on either side. The men were bound to one another, and were beaten and stabbed by any of the hoplites who recognized a personal enemy among them. Men with whips walked alongside them and forced any of them who were dragging their feet to pick up the pace. **48.** By taking them out of the building in this way the Corcyreans killed sixty of them in all, while the prisoners inside the building had no idea what was going on and thought they were being moved to another location. But when someone told them what was happening and they learned the truth, they appealed to the Athenians and told them that, if they wanted them dead, they should kill them themselves. They said that from then on they would not leave the building and would do their best not to let anyone else in.

[2] But the Corcyreans had as little intention of forcing their way in through the door as the oligarchs had of opening it. They climbed up onto the roof of the building, made holes through the roofing material, and began to hurl tiles and shoot arrows down inside. [3] The oligarchs protected themselves as best they could, but at the same

time most of them set about killing themselves, either by driving into their throats the arrows their enemies had shot at them, or by hanging themselves with cords taken from some beds that happened to be in the building or with strips torn from their clothing. Night fell while the tragedy was still unfolding, and for most of it the killing went on, as they died by their own hands or were killed by the missiles shot at them by their enemies on the roof.

[4] The next day, the Corcyreans stacked the bodies one across the other on carts and took them out of the city. All the women they had captured in the fortress were sold into slavery. [5] So this is how the Corcyreans from the mountains met their deaths at the hands of the democrats and how the strife that had afflicted the state so severely came to an end—or at least there were no more outbreaks during the current war, because there was no significant element remaining of the nondemocratic faction. And the Athenians sailed away to Sicily, their original destination, and supported their allies in the fighting there.

49. As summer was drawing to a close, the Athenians in Naupactus and the Acarnanians campaigned against Anactorium, a Corinthian town lying at the mouth of the Ambracian Gulf, and took it with help from inside. Once the Acarnanians had expelled the Corinthians, they occupied the place themselves with settlers drawn from all over Acarnania. And so the summer came to an end.

50. The following winter, in Eion (the one on the Strymon), Aristeides, son of Archippus, one of the generals in command of the Athenian ships that had been sent out to the allies to collect tribute, arrested a Persian called Artaphernes who was on his way from the King to Sparta. [2] He was taken to Athens, and the Athenians had the King's letter, which was written in Assyrian script, translated and read.* The letter was long, but the gist of it was that the King did not understand what it was that the Lacedaemonians wanted, because none of the many envoys who had come to his court said the same thing. If they wished to make themselves clear, he wrote, they should send men to him with Artaphernes. [3] The Athenians subsequently put Artaphernes on a trireme and sent him to Ephesus along with their envoys, but when they got there they found out that the King—Artaxerxes, son of Xerxes—had recently died (it had happened during the time when Artaphernes was in Athens), and so they returned home.

51. In the same winter, the Chians tore down their newly built wall on the orders of the Athenians, who suspected them of some rebellious design against themselves. But they first obtained pledges from the Athenians and as firm a promise as they could extract from them that they would not devise any policies that would change the status quo on Chios. So the winter came to an end and with it the seventh year of the current war, the history of which was written by Thucydides.

52. At the very beginning of the following summer, there was a partial solar eclipse at the time of the new moon, and early in the same month there was an earthquake.* [2] The exiles from Mytilene and the other Lesbian towns, or most of them at any rate, set out from their bases on the mainland and took control of Rhoeteum,* with the help of mercenaries they had hired from the Peloponnese and others they had gathered locally; but once they had been given two thousand Phocaean staters they returned the town unscathed. [3] Next they marched against Antandrus* and took it with the help of their sympathizers inside the town. Gaining Antandrus was the essential first stage of their plan to liberate all the rest of the towns in the region, the Coastal Towns, as they are known, which had previously been dependencies of Mytilene and were now Athenian possessions. With Antandrus in their hands, where timber was available locally and from nearby Mount Ida, they would have a ready source of supplies for all kinds of preparatory work, including shipbuilding, and then, with it as their base, it would be easy for them to make trouble for Lesbos, which was not far away, and to subjugate the Aeolian towns on the mainland. This was the plan they were intending to put into effect.

53. In the same summer, the Athenians campaigned against Cythera with a fleet of sixty ships, two thousand hoplites, a small cavalry force, and some of their allies from Miletus and elsewhere. The generals in command of the army were Nicias, son of Niceratus; Nicostratus, son of Dieitrephes; and Autocles, son of Tolmaeus. [2] The island of Cythera lies off Laconia, south of Cape Malea, and is inhabited by Lacedaemonian perioeci. Each year an officer called the commissioner for Cythera used to cross over to the island from Sparta, and the Lacedaemonians regularly sent hoplites there as a garrison. In short, they kept a close eye on the island, [3] not just because it was a port of call for merchant ships on their way to the Peloponnese from Egypt and Libya, but also because their presence there made it more difficult for pirates to raid Laconia from the sea. Laconia, all the coastline of which juts out toward the Sicilian or Cretan seas, is vulnerable to depredation only from the sea.

54. After reaching the island, the Athenians detailed ten ships and two thousand* Milesian hoplites to take the coastal town called Scandea. Meanwhile, the rest of the soldiers disembarked on the side of the island that faces Cape Malea, and no sooner had they set out toward Cythera town than they found the full levy of enemy troops in the field. [2] In the ensuing battle, the Cytherans stood their ground for only a short while before turning and fleeing inland to their town. Later, they came to an agreement with Nicias and his fellow commanders whereby they were not to be killed, but otherwise they would leave it up to the Athenians to decide what to do with them. [3] In fact, Nicias had earlier been in communication with some of the Cytherans, which speeded up the completion of the agreement in the short term and ensured subsequently that its terms were more favorable to them. Otherwise the Athenians would have expelled the Cytherans, because they were Lacedaemonians and because the island lay so close to Laconia. [4] Once the agreement was in place, the Athenians took over Scandea, the harbor town, and installed garrisons on the island. Then they sailed to Asine, Helos, and a great many other coastal settlements, where for about seven days they made landings, encamped when and where they had the opportunity to do so, and ravaged the land.

55. The Athenians' occupation of Cythera led the Lacedaemonians to expect them to make similar incursions elsewhere in their territory, so they did not concentrate all their forces at any one point, but sent out garrisons here and there throughout their territory, with each garrison made up of however many hoplites were needed for that particular location. All in all they were on high alert, and given the circumstances—the terrible, unforeseen disaster on Sphacteria, Pylos and Cythera in enemy hands, and war coming at them from so many directions and so rapidly that it was impossible to guard against—they were afraid of rebellion threatening the status quo. [2] There were several consequences. First, contrary to their usual practice, they raised a force of four hundred cavalrymen and an archery unit; second, for the first time in Lacedaemonian history they became reluctant to fight, because they were engaged in a contest where the crucial element was the sea, for which the kind of military forces they had were unsuited—and, moreover, their opponents were the Athenians, who always felt that not to attempt a thing was to fall short of what they expected to achieve. [3] Third, the run of bad luck they had experienced over a short stretch of time had shocked them to the core with its unexpectedness, and they were afraid they might meet with some fresh setback as disastrous as the one on Sphacteria. [4] All this sapped their confidence for battle, and they thought that any action they took would end in failure, because their morale, which was based on their previous inexperience of setbacks, had been undermined.

56. So the Athenians who were now laying waste the coastline met with hardly any opposition. Whenever they made a landing against any given garrison, the troops' morale was so low that they considered

themselves to be outnumbered. The soldiers from one garrison, however, based near Cotyrta and Aphroditia, did fight back; they charged the disordered mob of light-armed troops and panicked them, but withdrew again when the hoplites offered resistance. A few of them were killed and their arms and armor were seized, and after erecting a trophy the Athenians sailed back to Cythera. [2] From there they sailed around Cape Malea to Epidaurus Limera, and after laying waste some of the land they went to Thyreatis, which is part of the district known as Cynouria, on the border between Argolis and Laconia. It belongs to Sparta, but they had given it to the Aeginetan refugees because of the services the Aeginetans had rendered them at the time of the great earthquake and the helot rebellion, and because despite being subject to Athens they had always inclined to the Lacedaemonian cause.

57. While the Athenians were still on their way to Thyreatis, the Aeginetans abandoned the fortress they were in the process of building on the coast and retreated inland to their main town, which is just over a mile from the sea. [2] They were being assisted in the building work by soldiers from one of the Lacedaemonian garrisons in the area, but when the Aeginetans asked the soldiers to join them in the town, they refused, because they thought it would be dangerous for them to be shut up inside. Instead they retreated to a hill and played no part in the action, judging themselves to be no match for the Athenians. [3] Just then the Athenians made land, advanced with all their men into Thyreatis, and gained control of it. They burned the town to the ground, looted its contents, and took with them back to Athens all the Aeginetans who had survived the fighting, along with the resident Lacedaemonian governor, Tantalus, son of Patrocles, who had fallen into their hands after being wounded. [4] They also took with them a few men from Cythera, who they thought would pose a danger if left on the island. The Athenians decided to deposit these men on the Aegean islands, but they let the rest of the Cytherans remain in their homeland on payment of tribute of four talents a year. And they decided to kill all the Aeginetan prisoners, because of their long-standing hostility toward Athens, and to imprison Tantalus along with the other Lacedaemonians, the ones captured on Sphacteria.

58. In the same summer, in Sicily, the peoples of Camarina and Gela made a truce, in the first instance just with each other. Then representatives from all the other Sicilian Greek states met in Gela for a conference to discuss the possibility of a general peace. Many opinions were expressed both for and against, as the representatives argued with one another and urged their respective claims when they thought they were coming off worst in the discussion. One of those who spoke was a Syracusan, Hermocrates, son of Hermon, and he was the one whom the assembled representatives found particularly persuasive. He addressed the assembled delegations as follows:

59. "Fellow Sicilian Greeks, I'm going to speak even though the city I represent is larger than most and isn't suffering from the fighting as much as others. Despite this, I want to tell the meeting what, in my opinion, the best policy is for Sicily as a whole. [2] There's no need for me to list and go on at length about all the negative aspects of the war: you already know them. I mean, no one is forced into war by ignorance, any more than he's deterred by fear if he thinks he'll gain from fighting. No, the fact is that some people think that what they'll gain from war more than compensates for its dangers, while others are prepared to accept the risks rather than suffer a short-term loss. [3] But if in these cases neither side in a war is in fact doing what's best for it, then encouragement to reconcile can only help them. [4] And it will be of inestimable value to us in our present situation if we see the truth of this, in view of the fact that it was, of course, because each state wanted a favorable resolution of its own concerns that war broke out among us in the first place—and in view of the fact that, even though we're now using the back and forth of discussion to try to be reconciled with one another, if the outcome of the conference is that none of us has obtained what he feels to be fair, war will resume.

60. "If we have any sense, however, we should appreciate that the issue for this conference isn't going to be just our particular concerns, but whether it's too late for us to save Sicily as a whole from the Athenians, who, if I'm any judge of the matter, have designs on it. As regards our particular interests, we should regard the Athenians as far more compelling peacemakers than any argument I could come up with. There's no stronger power in the Greek world than the Athenians. They've come here, with just a few ships at present, to observe our mistakes, and by making specious use of the lawful name 'alliance' they're trying to turn the natural enmity that exists between us to their own advantage. [2] I mean, if we engage in war and ask for their intervention (and these are people who are perfectly willing to intrude their forces on others even without having been asked), and if we spend our money on weakening ourselves (which is to say, on paving the way for their dominion), when they see that we're exhausted, the odds are that they'll come back at some point with a more substantial force and try to subjugate the whole island.

61. "If we have any sense, however, any of us should only ever call in allies, with all the attendant risks, if doing so enables us to add to our possessions, rather than when it subtracts from what we already have. And we should recognize that there's nothing more destructive of our cities and of Sicily than internal quarreling; all of us together, all the inhabitants of Sicily, are the objects of Athenian scheming, and yet we're divided among ourselves, city against city. [2] It's crucial that we realize this and make peace with one another, as both individuals and states; we must unite in order to try to save Sicily as a whole. Let no one think that while those of us who are Dorians are the enemies of Athens, those of Chalcidian stock are safe thanks to their kinship with the Athenians as Ionians.* [3] The Athenians are meddling in Sicily not because there are two ethnic groups here and they hate one of them, but because they long to possess *all* the goods that Sicily provides, which belong to all of us in common. [4] They gave themselves away just recently when the ethnically Chalcidian cities appealed to them to intervene: even though these cities have never of their own accord supported any Athenian enterprise, as they were supposed to by the terms of their alliance, yet the Athenians fairly leaped at the chance to abide by the terms of the treaty.

[5] "It's easy to forgive the Athenians for their rapacity and forward planning; I have no blame for those who want to rule but only for those who are too ready to submit. It's a constant trait of human nature to dominate anyone who yields and to defend oneself against anyone who attacks. [6] But if we recognize all this and still fail to take appropriate precautions, and if any of us here today considers it not to be of paramount importance that we should unite to deal appropriately with the common threat, it's we who are in the wrong. [7] And the swiftest way to right the wrong would be for us to settle our differences, because the Athenian base of operations isn't their own territory, but the territory of those who invited them here. [8] If we do this, the war will be brought to an end, not by fighting but by peace. Our quarrels will be brought to a trouble-free conclusion, and the villains who were invited here for plausible reasons will have no reason not to leave without having achieved any of their goals.

62. "As far as the Athenians are concerned, then, you can see how great the benefits are of making the right decision. [2] When everyone in the world agrees that peace is best, why shouldn't we, too, make peace among ourselves? Suppose one person is doing well and another person isn't: Don't you think that it's peace rather than war that would put an end to the latter's lack of success and help to preserve the former's flourishing? Don't you think that peace has honors and distinctions of its own, which can be won without danger, and has numerous other advantages that could be listed at length alongside the many disadvantages of war? This is what you should bear in mind, and rather than make light of my warnings, each of you should make use of them for his own salvation. [3] If anyone here thinks that the justice of his cause guarantees that he'll gain his objectives, or that violence is the way to do so, he should prepare for disappointment and not take it too hard if he fails. He should recognize that many people in the past, who pursued wrongdoers with retribution, not only failed to right the wrong but failed even to survive; and that others, who hoped to use force to gain an advantage, have often ended up not increasing their holdings but losing what they already had. [4] The fact that retribution is a response to injustice is no guarantee that it will succeed even though in all justice it should, and the fact that physical force inspires confidence doesn't make it a sure way to get what one wants. The uncertainty of the future is usually the most important factor in events, and although there's nothing more treacherous, it nevertheless seems also to play a very useful role, because if we all equally fear the future, we're more likely to think twice before moving against one another.

63. "So in fact we have two reasons to be alarmed: our vague dread of an uncertain future, and the fearsome reality of the Athenians in our land. And our failure to see our plans through and achieve the targets we set ourselves as individuals should be attributed to the effective constraint of these two factors. So let's banish from our land these enemies who are threatening us, and above all let's be reconciled for all time, or at least let's make a truce that will last as long as possible and postpone our private quarrels until later. [2] In short, let's recognize that, if we do as I'm suggesting, each of us will keep his city free, and then, as free agents, we shall be able to pay back anyone who does us good or harm honorably and on equal terms. But if we fall under the dominion of others, which will be the consequence of failing to do as I'm suggesting, paying people back will be out of the question, and the best-case scenario will remain one in which we'd be forced to become the friends of our worst enemies and the enemies of those who should be our friends.

64. "Now, as I said at the beginning, I represent the greatest city in Sicily, so I'm more likely to be an assailant than a defender. But my awareness of what the future might hold leads me to think that compromise is the right course. There's no point in my harming my enemies if the outcome of that is that I suffer worse harm myself, and it would be stupid if my desire to get the better of others led me to believe that I have full mastery not only over my own policies but also over fortune, which is beyond my control. It would be better for me to make all reasonable concessions. [2] And I think it right for the rest of you to do the same as me, and to accept this not because you've been forced to do so by your enemies, but of your own free will. [3] There's no disgrace in making concessions to one's own people; Dorians meet other Dorians halfway, and Chalcidians do the same with their kin. We are one another's neighbors; we call the same sea-girt country our home; we are known by the same name, 'Sicilian Greeks.' I suppose that we'll fight one another in the future and that we'll come to terms again by conferring among ourselves. [4] But whenever we're faced with an attack from abroad, if we have any sense we'll always unite in defense, since the weakening of any one of us endangers all of us together. And in the future we shall never invite others in as allies or as peacemakers. [5] If we adopt this policy now, in the present circumstances, there are two benefits that we'll be securing for Sicily: we shall be rid of the Athenians and of internal war, and hereafter we shall live by ourselves in a land that is free and less vulnerable to others' schemes."

65. The Sicilian Greeks were won over by Hermocrates's speech. They agreed on a resolution that the fighting would come to an end with each city keeping what it currently had, except for Camarina, which would gain Morgantina on payment of a stipulated sum of money to Syracuse. [2] The allies of the Athenians asked for a meeting with the Athenian leaders and explained that they were going to make peace and that the treaty would affect the Athenians as well. Once they had gained the Athenians' assent, the agreement came into force, and after a while the Athenians left Sicily. [3] But when they got back to Athens, the Athenian people punished the generals. Two of them, Pythodorus and Sophocles, were sent into exile, and the third, Eurymedon, had to pay a fine. The charge was that the generals had had the opportunity to conquer the Sicilian states and had been bribed to withdraw. [4] The war was going so well for them that they did not expect to meet any obstacles; they expected to achieve everything they set out to do, whether it was possible or impracticable, and whether they had a large or an inadequate force in the field. The reason for this was that their hopes and expectations had been fueled by the fact that, contrary to their expectations, they had been successful more often than not.

66. In the same summer, the Megarians were being hard pressed by the war. It was not just that the Athenians were invading their territory in full force twice a year,* but that they were also suffering from the raids of their own exiles, who had been banished from the state by the democrats after a period of civil discord and had made Pegae their base.* So they started debating among themselves whether they should let the exiles return, so that the state would not be facing destruction on two fronts. [2] When all this muttering came to the attention of the friends of the outlaws, they, too, began to insist, more openly than before, that this was exactly what the city should do. [3] But the democratic leaders were frightened, because they recognized that the people were suffering too much to be able to continue supporting them for very long. They approached the Athenian generals Hippocrates, son of Ariphron, and Demosthenes, son of Alcisthenes, with a view to handing the city over to them, because they thought that, for themselves personally, this was a less risky option than the restoration of men whom they had banished. [4] The plan was that the Athenians should first take the Long Walls (which ran for somewhat less than a mile from the city to the Megarians' port town, Nisaea) to forestall any resistance by the Peloponnesians in Nisaea (this was the only place a garrison had been installed to safeguard Megara), and that then the democratic leaders would try to deliver the city to them. In their opinion, it would immediately become easier for the Megarians to accede to this after the first part of the plan had been carried out.

67. So once both parties had decided what they would do and say, the Athenians sailed by night to the Megarian island of Minoa. Six hundred hoplites under the command of Hippocrates stationed themselves close to the Long Walls in a trench from which the bricks for the walls had been dug. [2] The troops under the command of Demosthenes, the other general, who were light-armed Plataeans, and also some Athenian frontier guards, lay in wait at the sanctuary of Enyalius, which was closer to the walls. No one knew they were there except the men whose business it was to know what was going on that night. [3] Not long before dawn, these Megarians, the would-be traitors, put the following plan into effect: They had a rowboat, and for quite some time now, pretending they were going on smuggling expeditions, they had been arranging for the gate to be opened and, with the permission of the officer in command of the Peloponnesian garrison, had been taking the boat on a cart by night through the ditch to the shore and rowing off; and then before daybreak they would bring the boat back on the cart and take it inside the walls through the gate. Their professed reason for doing this was that they wanted their excursion† to go unnoticed by the Athenians, as there would be no boat to be seen in the harbor.

[4] So when the time came, the cart was already in the gateway, and the gate had been opened as usual, ostensibly to readmit the rowboat. This whole setup had been prearranged, and when the Athenians saw that the gate was open they dashed from their hiding places, because they needed to reach it before it was shut again and while the cart was still between the two doors of the gate to prevent it from being closed. At the same time, the pro-Athenian Megarians killed the soldiers who were guarding the gate. [5] The Plataeans and the frontier guards in Demosthenes's unit were the first to run through the gate (to where the trophy now stands), and when they were just inside they engaged the Peloponnesians, some of whom had realized what was happening—they had not been far away—and were coming up to offer resistance. The Plataeans defeated these Peloponnesians and made the

gate secure for the approaching Athenian hoplites, **68.** and then, as each of the hoplites got through the gate, he made straight for the city wall.

[2] A few of the Peloponnesian garrison troops fought back for a while, some of them at the cost of their lives, but the majority turned and fled. They were frightened by this nighttime attack, and, seeing that the Megarians who were trying to betray the city to the Athenians were among those fighting against them, they came to think that *all* the Megarians had turned against them. [3] The reason for this was that, coincidentally, the Athenians' herald, acting on his own initiative, had called out an invitation for Megarian volunteers to come and fight alongside the Athenians. When the Peloponnesians heard this, they waited no longer and fled back to Nisaea, certain that they were facing a concerted attack.

[4] By dawn, the Long Walls were in Athenian hands and the city was in turmoil. The Megarians who had intrigued with the Athenians, joined by a great many others who were in the know, declared that they should open the gate and go out to give battle. [5] The arrangement they had made was that as soon as the gate was open the Athenians would rush in, and that they would be distinguishable, and hence would avoid injury, because they would have coated their bodies with olive oil.* They felt even safer now in opening the gate because four thousand Athenian hoplites and six hundred cavalrymen had also arrived, as arranged, after an overnight march from Eleusis. [6] So there they were, daubed with oil and standing ready by the gate, when one of the conspirators revealed the plot to the other faction. These oligarchs closed ranks, went to the gate in a body, and argued that they should not go out to fight—that this was something they had never felt brave enough to do in the past, when they were stronger, and that it would be stupid to fight when the risk to the city was plain to see. If anyone disobeyed them, they warned, the fighting would take place right where they were, in the city. They gave no indication that they knew what was really going on, and simply insisted that theirs was the best policy. But at the same time they stayed on

guard by the gate, to make sure that the plotters had no chance to put their scheme into effect.

69. As soon as the Athenian generals realized that there had been a setback of some kind and that they would not be able to take the city by force, they set in motion a plan to surround Nisaea with a wall. Their thinking was that if they could take Nisaea before a relief force arrived, Megara, too, would be more ready to capitulate. [2] Iron was quickly brought from Athens, along with stonemasons and everything else they needed. They started the work from the walls that were in their hands and built a cross-wall facing Megara. Then, with separate divisions of the army either digging the ditch or working on the walls, and making use of stones and bricks taken from houses outside the city, they built walls from the cross-wall down to the sea on both sides of Nisaea. Wherever a palisade was needed, they built one out of trees, both cultivated and wild, that they cut down for this purpose; and the outlying houses received battlements, so that they formed part of the fortifications.

[3] This work occupied the whole of that day, and by the afternoon of the following day the wall was all but finished. At this, the soldiers in Nisaea became frightened: they were short of food, because food had been brought to them daily from Megara; they did not think that a relief force would arrive soon from the Peloponnese; and as far as they knew the Megarians were now their enemies. So they reached an accommodation with the Athenians, the terms being that once each of them had surrendered his arms, he would be allowed to leave on payment of a specified sum of money, and that the Athenians could deal at their discretion with the Lacedaemonian garrison commander and any other Lacedaemonians in Nisaea. [4] Once they had agreed to these terms, they left, and the Athenians demolished the Long Walls at the point where they joined the city of Megara, took possession of Nisaea, and proceeded with their other arrangements.

70. It so happened, however, that the Lacedaemonian Brasidas, son of Tellis, who was preparing for an expedition to the Thraceward region, was in the neighborhood of Sicyon and Corinth at the time. The news that the Megarians' Long Walls had been captured made him afraid for the Peloponnesians in Nisaea and worried that Megara might fall. He therefore sent a message to the Boeotians telling them to come as quickly as possible with an army and meet him at Tripodiscus (this is the name of a village in the Megarid that lies at the foot of Mount Geranea), and he went there himself with a force of 2,700 Corinthian hoplites, 400 from Phleious, 600 from Sicyon, and all the rest of his expeditionary force that had already assembled, hoping to reach Nisaea before it fell. [2] He had set out at night for Tripodiscus, so he did not at first know that Nisaea had fallen, and when he found out he took a select force of 300 from his army and, before his presence became known, reached Megara without being spotted by the Athenians, who were down on the coast. In principle—and in actuality, if it were possible—he wanted to make an attempt on Nisaea, but above all he wanted to enter Megara and make it secure. So he requested admittance for him and his men, saying that he hoped to recover Nisaea.

71. However, both the factions in Megara had reasons for fear. The democrats were afraid that Brasidas might banish them after bringing back the people they had exiled, and the oligarchs were afraid that the democrats, fearful of this very possibility, might attack them, and that the city would be destroyed by internal fighting while the Athenians were lying in wait nearby. So they refused to admit him, and both sides chose to do nothing and wait to see what happened. [2] Both the democrats and the oligarchs expected a battle to take place between the Athenians and the relief force, and they therefore thought it would be safer for them to join their friends once they had actually won. Having been refused entry, Brasidas rejoined his army.

72. The Boeotians reached Tripodiscus at dawn. Even before Brasidas's message they had been planning to relieve Megara, since they regarded a threat to Megara as a threat to themselves, and a full complement of their forces had got as far as Plataea. But spurred on even more by the arrival of Brasidas's messenger, they sent 2,200 hoplites and 600 cavalry, while their main force returned home. [2] In all, the army that Brasidas now had with him amounted to at least 6,000 hoplites. As for the Athenians, their hoplites were standing to arms by Nisaea and the coast, while their light-armed troops were dispersed over the plain. The Boeotian cavalry fell on the light-armed troops—this came completely out of the blue, because it was the first time the Megarians had ever received help from anywhere*—and they turned and fled toward the coast. [3] The Athenian cavalry countered by charging out against the Boeotians and engaging them at close quarters; the battle was prolonged and neither side thought they had come off worse. [4] The Athenians did succeed in killing the Boeotian cavalry commander and a few of his men as they drove for Nisaea itself; they stripped the bodies of their arms and armor, and since they had possession of these corpses they returned them under a truce and set up a trophy. But in fact, considering the action as a whole, by the time they separated neither side had secured a decisive result, and so the Boeotians returned to their own men and the Athenians to Nisaea.

73. Brasidas and his army next moved closer to the sea and Megara. They found an advantageous position and formed up for battle, but they took no action because they expected the Athenians to attack them. They knew that the Megarians were waiting to see which side won, [2] and they thought they were well placed in two respects. First, it would not be they who initiated the fighting and chose to bring on the danger of battle, and, second, since they had made it clear that they were ready to defend themselves, it would be fair for victory to be assigned to them even if no dust were raised, as it were.*† At the same time, they felt that things were turning out well for them with regard to Megara, too, [3] because if they had failed to show up they would have had no chance of victory, and they would clearly have lost the city right away, just as if they had been defeated in battle. But as things were, there was even a chance that the Athenians would refuse battle, with the result that they would prevail without a fight over those they had come to confront.

[4] And that is exactly what happened. The Athenians took no action either, since they were not being attacked, though they did emerge and form up against the Long Walls, but because the generals judged that they had more to lose by fighting, they held back for a while. The generals reasoned that their mission had largely been successful, and that if they initiated a battle against superior numbers they might win and take Megara, but if they lost they would severely weaken the Athenians' hoplite effectiveness, whereas Brasidas was naturally ready to take the bolder course and risk losing some of the men there with him, because they constituted only a fraction of the whole Peloponnesian army.[†] Then, as nothing was being attempted by either side, first the Athenians returned to Nisaea, and then later the Peloponnesians set out to go back to their original position. So the Megarians who were friends of the exiles received a boost to their confidence from the assumption that Brasidas had won and that the Athenians had finally declined battle, and they opened the gate to Brasidas and the commanders of the various Peloponnesian contingents. And once they had let them in—to the consternation of those who had been working with the Athenians—they discussed the future of the city with them.

74. Later, after his allies had disbanded and returned to their various cities, Brasidas left as well; he went back to Corinth, where he continued to prepare for his expedition to the Thraceward region, which had been his original destination. [2] As soon as the Athenians returned home, the Megarians in the city who were most deeply implicated in the conspiracy with the Athenians stealthily slipped away, realizing that they had been found out. But the other members of their faction, after consultations with the friends of the outlaws, let these exiles return from Pegae, once they had given their word and solemnly promised not to harbor any grudges, but to advocate only what was in the best interests of the state. [3] But when these men were in office, they held a military review of the hoplites, assembling the various companies in different parts of the city, and singled out both their personal enemies and the hundred or so men who they thought had been foremost in intriguing with the Athenians. They then forced the people to decide in an open ballot what to do with them, and once they had been condemned, they executed them and set up an extreme oligarchy in the state. [4] And no regime change that originated in civil strife and was carried out by so few people has ever lasted such a long time.*

75. In the same summer, when the Mytilenean exiles were on the point of realizing their plan of fortifying Antandrus,* Demodocus and Aristeides, the generals in charge of the Athenian tribute-collecting ships, were in the Hellespont (a third general, Lamachus, had taken ten ships into the Black Sea). When they heard about the work that was going on at Antandrus, they were concerned that the place might become just as much of a threat to Lesbos as Anaea was to Samos. (Anaea was where the Samian exiles had settled; they were helping the Peloponnesians in naval matters by providing helmsmen, they disrupted normal life in the city of Samos, and they were taking in people who left the city.) So Demodocus and Aristeides assembled an army from the local Athenian allies and sailed to Antandrus. The enemy made a sortie out of the town to fight them, but the Athenians won and recovered the place. [2] Shortly after this, Lamachus, on his arrival in the Black Sea, anchored in the territory of Heraclea at the Cales river and lost his ships when rainfall in the highlands caused a flash flood. He and his men traveled by foot through the land of the Bithynian Thracians, which is the part of Asia that lies just beyond Europe, and reached Calchedon, the Megarian colony at the mouth of the Black Sea.

76. Also in the same summer, immediately after his return from the Megarid, the Athenian general Demosthenes took a fleet of forty ships to Naupactus. [2] He and Hippocrates had been intriguing with some men from the Boeotian cities who wanted to overthrow the constitution and turn it into an Athenian-style democracy.* The person who was chiefly responsible for the idea was Ptoeodorus, an exile from Thebes, and the plan was as follows: [3] Some men were to betray Siphae, a coastal town on the Gulf of Corinth in the territory of Thespiae, while others were to hand over Chaeronea, a dependency of Boeotian Orchomenus (or "Minyan" Orchomenus,* as it used to be called). It was the exiles from Orchomenus who were the most active conspirators, and they were currently hiring mercenaries from the Peloponnese; Chaeronea lies at the edge of Boeotia, near Phanotis in Phocis, and some Phocians were also among the conspirators. [4] The Athenians, for their part, were to occupy Delium, a sanctuary of Apollo in the territory of Tanagra that faces Euboea, and all this was to happen at the same time on a stated day so that the Boeotians would not all go to the defense of Delium, but separate divisions of their army would have to go to whichever trouble spot was closest to them. [5] If the attempt went well and Delium was fortified, they had good grounds for confidence. Even if there was no immediate constitutional revolution throughout Boeotia, once Siphae, Chaeronea, and Delium were in their hands, and Boeotian farmland was being raided, and there was a refuge for any disaffected Boeotians near at hand, it was likely that the whole region would be destabilized; and when the time was ripe for the Athenians to move to support the rebels, they expected, given that the Boeotian forces would not be united, to find it easy to settle matters as they wanted.

77. That was the plan. When the time came, it was Hippocrates who was going to lead an army into Boeotia from Athens, and he sent Demosthenes on ahead with the forty ships to Naupactus so that he could gather an army from the Acarnanians and the other local allies and sail to Siphae to receive its betrayal. And they fixed the day on which everything was to go ahead simultaneously. [2] On his arrival at Naupactus, Demosthenes found that Oeniadae had been forced

into the Athenian alliance by a concerted effort of the Acarnanians, and he recruited from all the local allies an army that he used first for an attack on Salynthius and the Agraei. Once they had capitulated, he went ahead with all the other arrangements to ensure that he would get to Siphae when he was supposed to.

78. This summer, at about the same time, Brasidas set out with 1,700 hoplites for the Thraceward region. When he reached Heraclea in Trachis he sent a messenger to Pharsalus, where he had friends, asking them to escort him and his army through Thessaly, and after he had been joined at Melitea in Achaea by Panaerus, Dorus, Hippolochidas, Torylaus, and Strophacus (who represented Chalcidian interests in Pharsalus), he continued on his way. [2] He was escorted by other Thessalians as well, including Niconidas, who was on good terms with Perdiccas. It was never easy to pass unescorted through Thessaly, especially with an army, and in fact all Greeks feel the same and look askance at anyone who passes through another's country without permission. Moreover, most Thessalians had always been well disposed toward Athens, [3] so if it had been the Thessalian way to have a form of government that granted equal rights to all—if they had not traditionally been governed by narrow oligarchies—Brasidas would have been stopped in his tracks. Even as things were he was confronted at the Enipeus river by some Thessalians of the opposite persuasion to his friends, who tried to stop him and said he had no right to proceed without the consent of the whole Thessalian community. [4] His escorts replied that they would not act as his guides if there were any objections, that Brasidas's arrival had been unexpected, and that in escorting him they were only doing their duty as his guest-friends. And Brasidas himself said he had come as a friend to the land of Thessaly and to themselves; that he was bearing arms against the Athenians, not the Thessalians; and that as far as he knew there was no hostility between the Thessalians and the Lacedaemonians such that they could not set foot on each other's land. He assured them that he would not now advance if the Thessalians objected to it (nor, in fact, would he have been able to), but he was asking them not to stand in his way.

[5] After listening to what he said, the Thessalians left. At the urging of his escorts, Brasidas set off at the double, before a larger body of men could be assembled to stop him. In fact, on that day he set out from Melitea and ended his journey at Pharsalus, where he halted by the Apidanus river; the next day he reached Phacium, and on the next he crossed the border into Perrhaebia. [6] At this point his Thessalian escorts left him, and the Perrhaebians, who are subjects of the Thessalians, brought him to Dium, which was within Perdiccas's realm.* Dium is a Macedonian town that is overlooked by Mount Olympus and is situated in the south of Macedon.

79. So Brasidas raced through Thessaly before anyone could make the arrangements needed to stop him, and then he made his way to Perdiccas and Chalcidice. [2] Frightened by recent Athenian successes, Perdiccas and the cities in the Thraceward region that had seceded from Athens had asked for the army that he brought. The Chalcidians thought the Athenians would move against them first, and nearby towns that had not rebelled were also secretly joining the Chalcidians in asking for help. And Perdiccas, although not an open enemy of the Athenians, was afraid as well, because he had a history of being at odds with them—but his primary motivation was that he wanted to subjugate Arrhabaeus, the king of the Lyncestians.

[3] What made it easier for them to have an army sent from the Peloponnese was the Lacedaemonians' current run of misfortune. **80.** With the Athenians attacking the Peloponnese and focusing in particular on their home territory, they hoped that the best way to deter them would be to retaliate and make trouble for them by sending an expeditionary force against their northern allies,* especially since these allies had offered to pay their expenses, and the reason they had asked for their intervention was so that they could rebel. [2] Besides, the Lacedaemonians were happy to have a pretext for sending some

helots away, as they were worried that, with Pylos taken, they might be induced by current circumstances to revolt.

[3] The Lacedaemonians were so afraid of the helots' confidence† and their numbers that they once even carried out the following measure (by and large, the primary consideration for the Lacedaemonians in their relations with the helots has always been self-protection): They announced that any helots who considered that they had done the Lacedaemonians outstanding military service should present themselves to be selected for emancipation. This was a test. They thought that the individuals who first came forward expecting to be freed would be those who most probably had enough self-esteem to attack them. [4] They selected about two thousand, who crowned themselves with garlands and paraded around the temples in celebration of their freedom—but shortly afterward the Lacedaemonians made away with them, and no one knew how any of them met their deaths. [5] So now they had no hesitation in sending seven hundred helots, armed as hoplites, to serve with Brasidas, and the rest of the force he took were Peloponnesians he hired as mercenaries.

81. As for Brasidas himself, the Lacedaemonians chose him for this mission because he was very eager to go and the Chalcidians were eager to have him. His reputation in Sparta was that of a man who achieved whatever he set out to do, and every time he was sent on a mission he demonstrated what an invaluable asset he was to the city. [2] His present mission was a case in point: he was so fair and moderate in his dealings with the cities that defection from Athens became very widespread and he was able to take other places by treachery. This meant that when the Lacedaemonians wanted to come to terms, as they subsequently did, they had places they could offer in exchange for those held by the Athenians, and in the meantime the Peloponnese gained some relief from the pressure of war. Then again, later, after the war in Sicily, Brasidas's honorable and intelligent behavior, which some had experienced and others believed in from hearsay, was a major factor in making the Athenian allies turn readily to Sparta.

[3] He was the first to be sent out to them, and because they found him to be a man of thorough integrity, he left them with the firm hope that the others who came after him would be cut from the same cloth.* 82. So at the time in question, when the Athenians heard of his arrival in the Thraceward region they declared a state of enmity between themselves and Perdiccas, whom they held responsible for Brasidas's going there, and they began to keep a closer watch on their allies in the region.

83. As soon as Brasidas had arrived, Perdiccas took him and his army, along with his own forces, and marched against Arrhabaeus, son of Bromerus, who was the king of the Lyncestian Macedonians, a neighboring people. Perdiccas had a quarrel with him and wanted to reduce him to vassalage. [2] But when he arrived at the pass into Lyncus, and Brasidas got there as well with his army, Brasidas said that, before it came to fighting, he wanted to parley with Arrhabaeus to see if he could persuade him to become an ally of Sparta. [3] Arrhabaeus himself had in fact been making overtures of a kind, to the effect that he was prepared to entrust the dispute between himself and Perdiccas to Brasidas as an impartial arbitrator, and at the same time the Chalcidian envoys who were accompanying them were trying to persuade Brasidas that he must leave Perdiccas something to fear, so that they would find him a more committed ally and be able to use him for their own purposes. [4] Besides, when Perdiccas's envoys had been in Sparta they had said much the same, that he would bring many of his neighbors into alliance with Sparta, and consequently Brasidas felt that he had more of a right to negotiate with Arrhabaeus on behalf of the state. [5] Perdiccas, however, said he had not brought Brasidas north to arbitrate his disputes, but to destroy all those whom he identified as enemies, and that it would be wrong of him to meet with Arrhabaeus when he was covering the expenses of half of Brasidas's army. [6] Nevertheless, despite Perdiccas's objections and anger, Brasidas did meet with Arrhabaeus, and Arrhabaeus prevailed on him to withdraw his troops without invading his country. But Perdiccas

resented this and afterward paid only a third instead of half of the army's expenses.

84. Immediately after this episode, in the same summer and shortly before the vintage, Brasidas and the Chalcidians marched against Acanthus, a colony of Andros. [2] The Acanthians were divided among themselves about whether or not to let him in. One faction had joined the Chalcidians in inviting him north and on the other side there were the democrats. But because the commoners were worried about their grapes, which had not yet been gathered in, they were persuaded by Brasidas to let him in on his own and decide what to do once they had heard what he had to say. So they let him in, and he came before the popular assembly—he was in fact a pretty competent speaker for a Lacedaemonian—and spoke along the following lines:*

85. "The fact that the Lacedaemonians sent me and my army on this mission, Acanthians, proves the truth of the proclamation we made at the beginning of the war: that we were going to fight the Athenians in order to liberate Greece. [2] No one should reproach us for having taken so long to come north. We simply made a mistake about the war in the south, where we hoped to overthrow the Athenians quickly and without any danger to you. But now that the opportunity has arisen, we've come, and with your help we shall try to bring about their defeat.

[3] "I'm surprised that you closed your gates against me and that my arrival didn't make you rejoice. [4] In Sparta—that is, before we actually came here—we thought we'd find people who were already our allies, in spirit at least, and that our coming would meet a need. That's why we ran the great risk of making a journey of many days through foreign lands and why we've shown such total commitment. [5] But if your goals are different, if you choose to take a stand against your own liberty and that of the Greeks in general, the consequences could be disastrous. [6] The point is that it's not just a matter of your own resistance. It's also that those whom I approach subsequently will

be less likely to come over to my side, because it will trouble them that you, the people I went to first, who represent a notable city and have a reputation for intelligence, turned me down. And I shall have no credible explanation to give for that. They'll think either that there's something wrong with the freedom I'm offering, or that I've come here lacking the strength and ability to protect them in the event of an Athenian attack. [7] But the army I have here now is the same one that I had with me when I went to help Nisaea, and even though the Athenians had superior numbers on that occasion they refused to engage. And they're hardly likely to send against you an army even of that size, given that it would have to come by sea.

86. "My purpose in coming here is not to harm the Greeks but to liberate them, and I bound the authorities in Sparta with the most solemn oaths to respect the independence of any cities I might win over as allies. We don't want to force or trick you into becoming our allies; far from it, we want to support you in your fight to free yourselves from enslavement by the Athenians. [2] I maintain, then, that since I'm giving you unequivocal guarantees, there's no reason for you to doubt what I say, and that I shouldn't be regarded as a powerless protector. You should set aside your doubts and join our side in the war.

[3] "If any of you is reluctant because he has a personal fear of another man and is worried that I might hand the city over to this or that faction, he should absolutely trust me on that score. [4] I've not come here to support any faction, nor, in my opinion, would I be bringing real freedom if I were to set aside Lacedaemonian tradition and enslave the majority to the few or the minority to the general populace. [5] That would be a harsher imposition than foreign rule, and we wouldn't earn gratitude for our efforts; we would deserve censure rather than honor and glory. We ourselves would incur, for all to see, the charges that constituted our reason for going to war with the Athenians, and we would be more loathed for incurring them precisely because we had tried to make it seem that we were acting with integrity. [6] After all, it's more disgraceful for people with a

reputation for probity to gain their ends by hypocrisy and deceit than by open force. A person who employs force can justify his aggression by the fact that fortune endowed him with superior strength, but one who employs deceit is deliberately putting into effect an unjustifiable scheme. 87. So, as you can see, we Lacedaemonians give very careful consideration to the things that matter most to us, and in addition to the oaths I mentioned before, you could have no greater confirmation of sincerity than one that comes from men whose deeds, viewed in the light of their words, are bound to demonstrate that they mean what they say because it coincides with their own interest.

[2] "If you say that you're unable to accept what I'm offering, but still bear us goodwill and shouldn't be made to suffer for this rejection—if freedom seems to you to be not without its dangers, and you regard it as right for me to offer it to those who are able to accept it, but wrong to force it on anyone who doesn't want it—I shall first call on the gods and heroes of your land to witness that although I came to do you good I failed to persuade you, and then I shall turn to despoiling your farmland and more forceful methods. [3] And under the circumstances I won't think that what I'm doing is wrong, but indeed that I'm perfectly justified, for two compelling reasons: first, if you're not on our side, I need to protect the Lacedaemonians from your 'goodwill' toward them, so that they aren't harmed by the tribute you pay to the Athenians; and second, I need to make sure that the Greeks aren't prevented by you from being freed from servitude. [4] Otherwise it would indeed be unreasonable for us to act like this; we Lacedaemonians wouldn't feel obliged to free those who don't want to be freed unless the common good of all Greeks was at stake. [5] To put this another way, we don't want an empire; what we want is to put an end to the Athenians' empire, and we'd be acting against the interests of the majority if in our attempt to provide autonomy for everyone we let you get away with your opposition.

[6] "Deliberate well, therefore, and strive to be the first to strike a blow for Greek freedom. That way you'll earn everlasting glory, no

harm will come to any individual's property, and you'll bestow on your city as a whole the fairest of names."

88. That was the substance of Brasidas's speech. The Acanthians first argued at length both for and against the proposal and then held a secret ballot. Because they found what Brasidas had said encouraging—and because they were frightened for their grape harvest—the majority decided to secede from the Athenians. After getting Brasidas to pledge fidelity to the oaths the Lacedaemonian authorities had sworn when they sent him north, that any cities he won over as allies would be autonomous, they let his army in. [2] And shortly after this, Stagirus,* a colony of Andros, also seceded.

These were the events that took place in the course of this summer.

89. Right at the start of the following winter, the Athenian generals Hippocrates and Demosthenes were due to have Boeotia betrayed to them. Demosthenes was supposed to sail to Siphae while Hippocrates marched to Delium, but a mistake was made about the days on which each of them was supposed to set out with his forces. Demosthenes sailed to Siphae too soon, and although he had on board the Acarnanians and many other allies from that part of Greece, he achieved nothing, because the plot had been disclosed by Nicomachus, a Phocian from Phanotis, who told the Lacedaemonians, and they told the Boeotians. [2] Forces came up in support from all over Boeotia—Hippocrates had not yet arrived in Boeotia to create a diversion—and both Siphae and Chaeronea were in their hands before the Athenians got there. And when the pro-Athenian Boeotians realized that a mistake had been made, they abandoned their plan to stir up rebellion in the cities.

90. Hippocrates raised a mass levy of the Athenian forces, consisting of citizens, metics, and foreigners who were in town, but he reached Delium too late, when the Boeotians had already withdrawn from Siphae. He encamped his army and set about fortifying Delium.* [2] His men dug a ditch around the sanctuary and the temple,

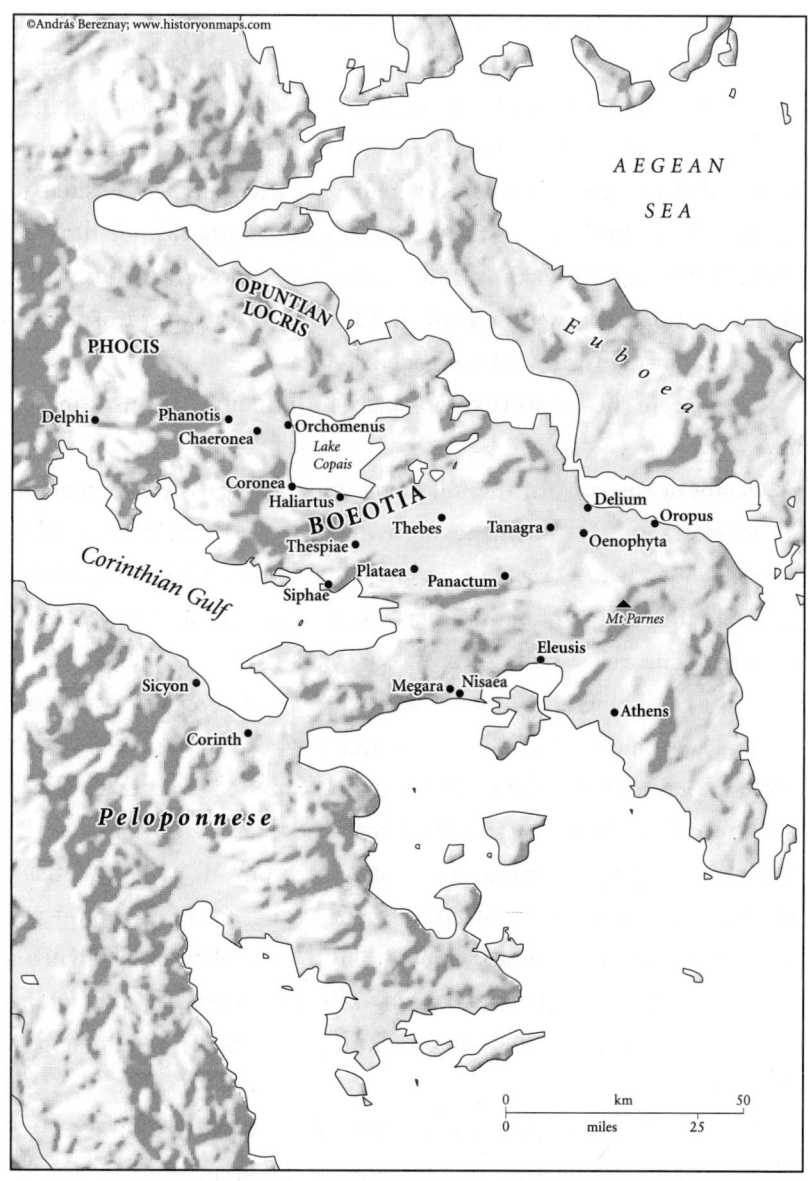

I. Boeotia and the Delium Campaign

heaped up the earth from the ditch to serve as a rampart, and drove stakes into the ground alongside the earthworks. Then they cut down the vines that were growing around the sanctuary and added them to the embankment, along with stones and bricks that they took from nearby building plots, and in short did everything they could to raise the height of the earthworks. They set up wooden towers where necessary and where there was no sanctuary building—for instance, where a stoa had collapsed. [3] They started on the third day after setting out from Athens, spent that day and the next on the work, and finished on the morning of the fifth day. [4] Then, since the work was largely finished, the main force left Delium and went about a mile in the direction of home. At this point the hoplites halted and rested, but most of the light-armed troops carried straight on. Meanwhile, Hippocrates, who had stayed behind in Delium, posted guards and saw to the completion of any unfinished aspects of the fortifications.

91. Over the course of these days the Boeotians were mustering at Tanagra, and by the time they found out that the Athenians were already heading home, the contingents had assembled from all the cities. Most of the boeotarchs (there were eleven in all) were against fighting, considering that the Athenians were no longer in Boeotia—they were right on the borders of Oropus when they halted—but the senior officer, Pagondas, son of Aeoladas, one of the two boeotarchs from Thebes (the other was Arianthidas, son of Lysimachidas), judged the risk worth taking and wanted to fight. He convened the troops, one company at a time so that they would not all be away from their weapon stands at once, and tried to win the Boeotians over to the idea of advancing on the Athenians and precipitating the contest. He spoke to the following effect:

92. "Boeotians, it's wrong for any of us commanders to have entertained the thought that we should fight the Athenians only if we find them on Boeotian soil. After all, they crossed the border and built a stronghold for themselves here with the intention of destroying Boeotia, and so there can be no doubt that they're our enemies, whether we find them elsewhere or in the land from which they set out to make war on us. [2] And if any of the commanders considered it a less dangerous option not to fight, I call on him now to think again. The time for a man to calculate and think about the possible consequences to his own land isn't when he's been attacked, but when, with his own possessions secure, he wants more and chooses to attack someone else. The two cases are completely different. [3] Besides, it's your tradition to resist a foreigner's attack, whether it takes place in your own or another's territory. And it's far more important for you to resist the Athenians, since, apart from anything else, they share a border with us. [4] When dealing with neighbors, it's always the case that freedom depends on holding one's own. With the Athenians in particular, people who set out to enslave not only their neighbors but far distant peoples, how could we not be obliged to fight to the bitter end? Just look at what happened to the Euboeans across the water there,* and at the way the Athenians treat most of the rest of Greece. You have to appreciate that while in other cases neighbors fight over the borders of their lands, in our case, if we're defeated, a single, undisputed boundary stone will be planted in the ground, encompassing the entirety of Boeotia, because they'll invade in force and take it all over. [5] That's how much more dangerous they are as neighbors than others.

"It's characteristic of those who are emboldened by their power—like the Athenians in our times—to campaign with fewer misgivings against anyone who passively puts up a fight only in his own territory. But they're less ready to grapple with someone who advances beyond his borders to confront them and initiates the fighting if the opportunity presents itself. [6] We have firsthand experience of this in the case of the Athenians, because it was our victory over them at Coronea, at a time when, as a result of our internal dissension, our land was in their hands, that enabled us to establish the considerable freedom from fear that we've enjoyed in Boeotia up until now.* [7] This is worth bearing in mind. The older ones among us must match their earlier deeds, while the younger ones, sons of the fathers who proved their valor then, must do their best not to bring shame on the virtues that are their heritage. Trusting that we shall have the support of the god whose sanctuary they have sacrilegiously fortified and are occupying, and trusting the favorable omens that we received when we performed the sacrifices, let's engage these Athenians and show them that while they might achieve their objectives by attacking people who don't fight back, when they meet people who have a noble tradition of fighting to liberate their land and who have too strong a sense of justice to enslave others' land, they won't get away without meeting opposition."

93. With such words of encouragement to the Boeotians, Pagondas persuaded them to move against the Athenians. It was already late in the day, so he quickly broke camp and led his forces off. Once he drew near to the Athenians, he halted at a place where an intervening hill made it impossible for either side to see the other, formed up his troops, and got them ready for combat. [2] When Hippocrates, who was still at Delium, heard of the Boeotian advance, he sent a message to the army, ordering it to form up in line, and not long afterward he arrived in person. He left three hundred cavalrymen at Delium, to act as guards in case of an attack and to watch out for an opportunity in the course of the fighting to attack the Boeotians. [3] The Boeotians in their turn detailed some men to defend against these Athenian cavalrymen, and then, when everything was in order, they appeared over the hill and halted in the formation they had planned for the battle. The army was made up of about seven thousand hoplites, over ten thousand light-armed troops, a thousand cavalrymen, and five hundred peltasts. [4] The Thebans and their confederates held the right wing; the center was occupied by the contingents from Haliartus, Coronea, Copae, and the other lakeside towns; the contingents from Thespiae, Tanagra, and Orchomenus were on the left wing; and cavalry and light-armed troops were posted on both wings. The Thebans marshaled twenty-five ranks deep; elsewhere the depth varied. [5] So much for the composition and disposition of the Boeotian forces.

94. The Athenians had the same number of hoplites as the Boeotians; they were formed up eight deep along the whole line with cavalry on both wings. They had no regular light-armed troops for this battle, nor indeed did the city have any such unit. The light-armed troops who had taken part in the invasion greatly outnumbered their Boeotian counterparts, but most of them had gone along without weapons, since the army consisted of the full levy of resident foreigners and citizens; in any case, they had been the first to set out for home, and so there were not many of them present for the battle. [2] When they were all in formation and battle was about to be joined, the general, Hippocrates, passed along the line and tried to encourage them by speaking somewhat as follows:

95. "Athenians, I don't have much to say, but a brief speech is as good as a long one for men of courage, and acts more as a reminder than as a set of fresh instructions. [2] None of you should suppose that we're incurring such great danger on foreign soil where we have no business; we may be in Boeotian territory, but what's at stake in this contest is our own land. If we win, the Peloponnesians will be deprived of the Boeotians' cavalry and you'll never find them invading your land again. With a single battle, you'll both gain this country and make great strides toward freeing your own. [3] Advance against them, then, in a manner worthy of Athens—the fatherland whose leadership of the Greek world makes each of us proud—and worthy of your fathers, who under the command of Myronides defeated these men you see before you in battle at Oenophyta and who once possessed their land."*

96. Hippocrates got as far as the middle of the army with this exhortation, but no further, because the Boeotians (who had themselves been urged on by a hurried speech also delivered on the field by Pagondas) chanted a paean and advanced from the hill. The Athenians in their turn advanced and met the Boeotians at a run. [2] The soldiers at the extreme right and left of the two armies all had the same experience that prevented them from engaging: they were foiled by streambeds. But the rest closed in a fierce battle, with men shoving at one another with their shields. [3] The Boeotian left wing, all the way up to the center of the line, was being beaten by the Athenians, who pressed hard on the enemy at this point. The Thespians suffered in particular, because the line on either side of them gave way, so that they became surrounded by the Athenians in a confined space and were cut to pieces in hand-to-hand fighting, trying to defend themselves. The Athenians sustained losses as well, including some who were killed by their own men when, in the confusion caused by the encircling movement, they failed to recognize one another. [4] So in this part of the field the Boeotians were coming off worse, and they fled to join the fighting elsewhere, but their right wing, where the Thebans were, was getting the better of the Athenians. They pushed them back, gradually at first, harrying them all the way.

[5] But Pagondas had two squadrons of his cavalry hidden behind the hill, and at this point he ordered them up to ease the pressure on his left wing; and when they suddenly appeared over the hill the victorious Athenian wing panicked, thinking that another army was advancing against them. [6] So now, what with this panic on their right wing and with the left being harried and having its cohesion broken by the Thebans, the entire Athenian army turned to flight. [7] They headed variously toward Delium and the coast, or Oropus, or Mount Parnes, or simply wherever individuals thought they might be safe. [8] But the Boeotians—especially their cavalry and the Locrians, who arrived to support the Boeotians just as the rout was starting—were hard on their heels and killed them, until nightfall intervened and made it easier for most of the fugitives to reach safety. [9] And the next day, the Athenians at Oropus and Delium (which remained in their hands despite the defeat) left garrisons and were taken home by sea. **97.** The Boeotians erected a trophy, collected the bodies of their dead, and stripped the Athenian dead of their arms and armor. They then retired to Tanagra, leaving a guard at the battlefield, and began to make plans for attacking Delium.

[2] A herald who was on his way from Athens to ask permission to recover the dead met a Boeotian herald on the road, who turned him back, telling him that nothing was going to happen until he himself had returned to Boeotia from Athens.* He appeared before the Athenians and delivered his message from the Boeotians. He charged the Athenians with aggression and violating Greek norms, [3] in that it was established Greek custom for invaders of others' territory to spare the territory's sanctuaries. The Athenians, however, had fortified Delium, made it their home, and all the things that people do on unhallowed ground were taking place there. Water that the Boeotians were forbidden to touch except for sacred rituals was being drawn from the spring, carried away, and used for washing. [4] So on behalf of the god and themselves, the Boeotians, invoking Apollo and the other deities whose sanctuary it was, were proclaiming that only after the Athenians had left the sanctuary could they take their dead back home.

98. After the herald had delivered this message, the Athenians sent their own herald to the Boeotians. They denied that they had treated the sanctuary sacrilegiously in any respect and promised not to intentionally damage it in the future either. That was not why they had entered it in the first place, they said; they had done so to make it a base for retaliating against the aggressors. [2] It was Greek custom that whoever had the mastery of any piece of land, large or small, always took possession of the sanctuaries as well and looked after them in ways that were as close as they could manage to what was traditional. [3] And in fact all Greeks who inhabit a tract of land from which they had forcibly expelled others—and that was most Greeks, including the Boeotians—attacked what were originally others' sanctuaries and now possess them as their own. [4] If the Athenians had been able to gain mastery of more Boeotian land, it would be theirs, and so, the situation being as it was, they were refusing to leave the bit they occupied, because they regarded it as their own. [5] As for interfering with the water, this had been a matter of necessity, and the necessity was not of their own sacrilegious making. No, they had been forced to make use of the water in the course of defending themselves against the Boeotians, who had taken the first step by targeting Athenian land.

[6] Any action carried out in wartime or at a time of danger of any kind would surely meet with forgiveness, they argued, even from the god. After all, altars are a place of refuge for people who do wrong involuntarily, and it is people who do wrong when they are under no compulsion to whom the term "lawbreaking" is applied, not those who are driven by circumstances to take bold defensive action. [7] As for the dead, those who presume to give them back in exchange for sanctuaries are acting with far greater impiety than those who refuse to use sanctuaries as bargaining counters in order to recover what's rightly theirs. [8] Finally, the Athenians told the Boeotians to affirm, without adding any qualifications, that they could recover their dead, not on condition of their leaving Boeotian land (for the land they were on was no longer Boeotian land but their own, won by the spear), but under a truce, as was traditional.

99. The Boeotians replied that if the Athenians were in Boeotia, they could, on leaving it, take their dead back home, but that if they were on Athenian soil it was up to them to decide what to do. They said this because they thought that Oropus (where the bodies were actually lying, since the battle had been fought on its borders) was Athenian, because of its subject status, and yet that the Athenians could not take possession of the bodies if they, the Boeotians, chose to prevent them. In other words, they were pretending to be unwilling to make a truce over land that was not theirs, and so "If you leave our land you'll also recover what you're asking for" was the right response to make.

After hearing this reply of theirs, the Athenian herald left without having achieved anything. **100.** The Boeotians immediately sent for javelineers and slingers from the Malian Gulf, and after the battle further reinforcements had arrived: two thousand Corinthian hoplites, the Peloponnesians who had been garrisoning Nisaea before they were forced out, and the Megarians as well. So they marched against Delium and attacked the Athenian stronghold. They went about the attempt in various ways, but finally succeeded in capturing the place by bringing up a contraption that had the following design:

[2] They sawed a large log in two lengthwise, hollowed all of it out, and then fitted it tightly together again, so that it was like a pipe; at one end of the beam they hung a cauldron on chains, into which a curved iron nozzle was bent down, and much of the wood of the beam was plated with iron as well. [3] They brought this device on carts from a considerable distance up to the wall at a point where it had been largely made out of vines and sticks, and when it was close, they inserted a great bellows into their end of the beam and pumped it. [4] The blast of air passed through the airtight beam and into the cauldron, which contained lighted coals, sulphur, and pitch, and so produced a great flame that set the wall on fire, making it impossible for anyone to stay on it. The Athenians abandoned the wall and fled, and that is how the wall was taken. [5] Some of the defenders were killed and two hundred were captured, but most of the rest got on board the ships and were transported back home.

101. Delium fell on the seventeenth day after the battle, and not long afterward, in ignorance of what had happened, the herald from Athens arrived again on the matter of collecting the bodies of the dead. This time, the Boeotians stopped repeating their earlier answer and let the bodies be collected. [2] Just under five hundred Boeotians lost their lives in the battle, while the Athenians lost not quite a thousand hoplites, including the general, Hippocrates, and a large number of light-armed troops and people from the baggage train.

[3] Not long after this battle, Demosthenes, who had earlier set sail for Siphae only to find that the plan to have the town betrayed to him had miscarried, took his army of Acarnanians, Agraei, and four hundred Athenian hoplites and made a landing at Sicyon. [4] But before all the ships had made land the Sicyonians came up. They routed the men who had already disembarked and chased them back to the

ships, taking some lives and capturing some prisoners in the process. Then they erected a trophy and granted a truce so that the bodies of the dead could be collected.

[5] Another thing that happened during the days of these events at Delium was the death of Sitalces, the king of the Odrysians. He launched a campaign against the Triballi but was defeated in battle. Sitalces's nephew Seuthes, son of Sparadocus, became king of the Odrysians, and also ruled over as much of the rest of Thrace as had formed part of Sitalces's realm as well.

102. In the same winter, Brasidas and his allies from the Thraceward region campaigned against Amphipolis, the Athenian foundation on the Strymon river. [2] Aristagoras of Miletus was the first to try to found a settlement where Amphipolis now lies, when he was in flight from King Darius, but he was driven out by the Edones.* Then thirty-two years later the Athenians also tried: they sent ten thousand settlers (both Athenians and volunteers from other places), but they were annihilated at Drabescus by the Thracians. [3] The Athenians returned twenty-nine years later under the leadership of Hagnon, son of Nicias, who was the designated founder; they drove out the Edones and founded Amphipolis on the site that had formerly been known as Nine Ways. [4] They set out from Eion, a seaport and trading station of theirs at the mouth of the river that was a little under three miles from the current city of Amphipolis—so named by Hagnon because the Strymon flows around two of its sides. Hagnon provided for the place's security by constructing a long wall that matched the bend of the river, and he made the town conspicuously visible from sea and land.*

103. This was the place that Brasidas marched against with his army, setting out from Arnae in Chalcidice. By afternoon he had reached Aulon and Bormiscus, where Lake Bolbe issues into the sea, and after his men had eaten he carried on through the night. [2] It was winter and a light snow was falling, so he picked up the pace, but that was also because he wanted to avoid being seen by people in Amphipolis—except by those who were going to betray the city to him. [3] His accomplices in the city were some people from Argilus (a colony of Andros) who had taken up residence there, and some others who had been won over by Perdiccas or the Chalcidians. [4] The town of Argilus is not far from Amphipolis, and the Argilians had always been viewed with suspicion by the Athenians. They were the prime movers of the conspiracy, as soon as Brasidas's arrival in the region created the opportunity, and for quite a while they had been plotting with the Argilians who were citizens of Amphipolis for the betrayal of the city. So now they welcomed Brasidas into Argilus, declared their secession from Athens that same night, and before daybreak brought his army to the bridge over the river. [5] Amphipolis is some distance from the crossing point, and there were no walls extending down as there are today, but a small guardpost had been established there. Brasidas easily overcame the guards, partly because there were traitors among them and partly because it was winter and they were not expecting to be attacked. He crossed the bridge, and hardly any time passed before he was in possession of the rural estates of the Amphipolitans, who had residences throughout the entire district.

104. His crossing of the river had taken the people in the city by surprise, and many of those who lived outside were captured, though some fled for refuge within the walls. The city was in an uproar, exacerbated by the Amphipolitans' suspicions of one another. [2] In fact, if Brasidas had marched straight for the city instead of choosing to let his men turn to looting, he would probably have taken it, or so people say. [3] But in fact he had his army make camp, and since he had already overrun the land outside the city, and there was no sign of the response he had been expecting from his collaborators inside, he remained inactive. [4] The enemies of the would-be traitors were numerous enough to make sure that the gates remained closed for the time being, and with the consent of Eucles, the Athenian general who was with them in Amphipolis to see to the place's protection, they sent a message to the other general who was in the Thraceward region, Thucydides, son of Olorus, the author of this history. He was on Thasos—the island, a colony of Paros, is about half a day's voyage by sea from Amphipolis—and they urged him to come and help them.* [5] On receiving the message he set sail as quickly as he could with seven ships that happened to be there with him. His main goal was to get to Amphipolis before it was handed over to Brasidas, and if he was too late he planned to occupy Eion before the enemy could.

105. Meanwhile, Brasidas urgently wanted to secure the city before Thucydides got there, if he could. The probability of this naval force arriving from Thasos worried him, and he was also concerned about the influence that Thucydides had among the leading men of the mainland, as a result of his having acquired the right to work the gold mines in that part of Thrace. He thought it likely that his chance of getting the people of Amphipolis to capitulate would vanish once Thucydides arrived, because they would be expecting him to assemble a force of Athenian allies from the islands and Thrace and save them. [2] He therefore drew up a moderate agreement and made a proclamation to the effect that any of the Amphipolitans and the Athenians who were in the city who wished to stay would keep their property and enjoy fair and equal political rights, while anyone who did not wish to stay could leave within five days, taking his belongings with him.

106. Most of the Amphipolitans began to change their minds as a result of this offer by Brasidas, especially as only a few citizens were Athenians while the majority were of mixed origins, and there were many inside who were friends and relatives of those who had been captured outside. Contrary to what they had feared, they found the proclamation to be fair—the Athenians because they would be glad to leave, since they considered themselves to be more at risk than anyone else and because they were not expecting help to arrive anytime soon, while the two factors that weighed equally with the rest of the

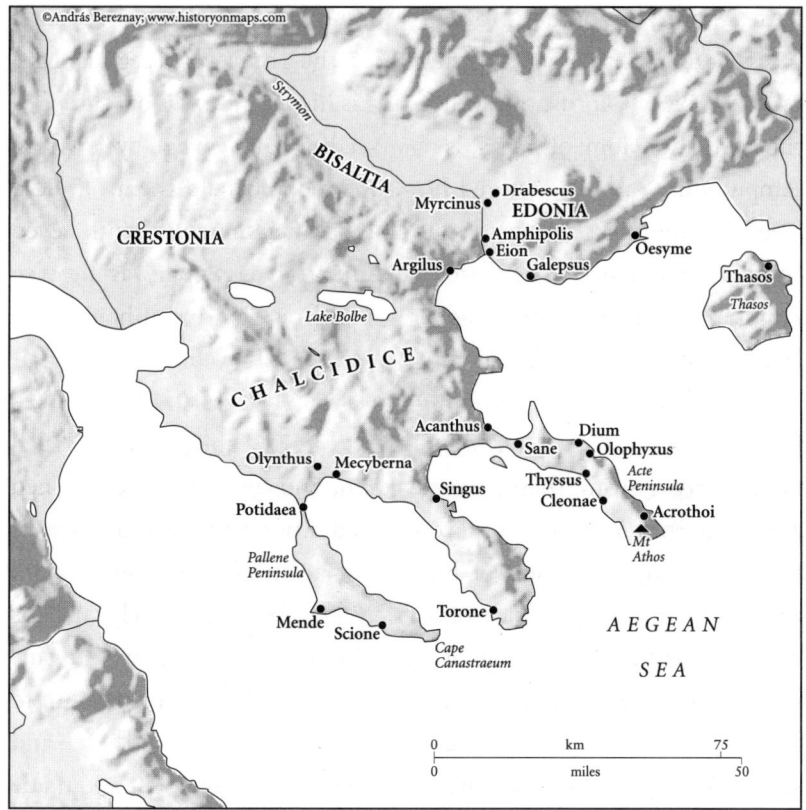

J. Chalcidice

population were that they would retain their rights as citizens and, contrary to their expectations, would be freed from danger. [2] The upshot was that the partisans of Brasidas also now began to speak openly in defense of the offer, since they could see that the general populace had been converted and was no longer listening to the Athenian general in the city. The agreement was therefore put into effect, and they let Brasidas into the city on the terms he had announced in the proclamation. [3] So the Amphipolitans surrendered the city, but in the evening of the same day Thucydides came sailing into Eion with his seven ships. [4] Brasidas had just gained Amphipolis and he came within a night of taking Eion, because if these Athenian ships had not come to help so rapidly it would have fallen to him at first light the next day.

107. After this, Thucydides arranged matters in Eion to ensure that it would be safe both in the short term, in case of an attack by Brasidas, and in the longer term, and he admitted into the town those who, under the terms of the agreement, wanted to leave Amphipolis and join him there. [2] Meanwhile, Brasidas suddenly set off down the river with a large number of boats to attack Eion. His intention was to seize the headland that projects from the wall and thereby gain control of the entrance to the town, and at the same time he made an attempt on it by land as well. But he was repulsed on both fronts, and he turned to seeing that Amphipolis was furnished with everything it needed for its defense. [3] Myrcinus, an Edonian town, also came over to his side, because Pittacus, the Edonian king, had been assassinated by the children of Goaxis and by his own wife, Brauro.* A short while later, Galepsus and Oesyme (both colonies of Thasos) did the same as well. Perdiccas arrived very soon after the fall of Amphipolis and helped Brasidas put these places in order.

108. The enemy's possession of Amphipolis alarmed the Athenians a great deal, not least because the city had been useful to them in two respects: it supplied them with timber for building ships, and it was a good source of financial revenue. They were also alarmed because, although the Lacedaemonians had previously been able to reach Athenian allies as far as the Strymon (provided that the Thessalians gave them passage through their land), as long as they lacked control of the bridge their advance ended there, as farther upstream the river formed a great, long marsh, and in the direction of Eion it was patrolled by triremes. But now, the Athenians were thinking, they could easily do just that.

They were also afraid of their allies defecting. [2] In everything he did, Brasidas presented himself as a moderate man, and whenever he gave a speech he made it clear that his mission was to liberate the Greeks. [3] And the cities that were subject to Athens were particularly encouraged to rebel when they heard about the fall of Amphipolis and the offer he had made there—which is to say when they heard about his leniency. In fact, they secretly approached him, asking for his aid, and each of them wished to be the first to secede. [4] It seemed to them that they had nothing to fear, first because they underestimated Athenian power (which later turned out to be just as great as the mistake they made in their estimate of it), and second because they were largely judging the situation by nebulous optimism rather than by cautious prudence. People invariably entrust their desires to unconsidered hope, and if something is not to their liking they reject it through reasoning they take to be absolutely compelling. [5] Furthermore, the Athenians had recently taken a beating in Boeotia, and Brasidas was saying things that were seductive and untrue—that the Athenians had refused to engage him when he had attacked[†] Nisaea even though his army was unsupported—and all this gave them confidence and inclined them to believe that the Athenians would not send an expeditionary force against them. [6] But above all they were altogether ready to take the risk because of the immediate thrill of rebellion and because this would be a first test of Lacedaemonian determination.

The Athenians were not unaware of what was going on, and, insofar as they could at short notice and in winter, they sent garrisons to be installed in each of their subject cities. Brasidas, meanwhile, sent an urgent message to Sparta, asking for more soldiers, and on his own initiative he was getting ready to build triremes on the Strymon. [7] But the Lacedaemonians did not do as Brasidas had asked, partly because the most influential men among them were envious of him, and partly because their overriding wish was to recover the men from Sphacteria and bring the war to an end.

109. In the same winter, the Megarians took back the Long Walls, which had been in Athenian hands, and razed them to the ground, and Brasidas followed up his taking of Amphipolis with a campaign, along with his allies, against the peninsula called Acte. [2] This peninsula runs down from the King's canal,[*] and lofty Mount Athos forms its extremity in the Aegean Sea. [3] There are several towns on it: Sane, a colony of Andros, which is right by the canal and faces the sea toward Euboea; and then Thyssus, Cleonae, Acrothoi, Olophyxus, and Dium. [4] These towns are inhabited by a mixed population of barbarians, who speak Greek as well as their own language. There is a little Chalcidian stock as well, but most of them are Pelasgians* (descendants of the Etruscans who once inhabited Lemnos and Athens), along with Bisaltians, Crestonians, and Edones. These are not large places. [5] Most of them went over to Brasidas, but Sane and Dium held out, so he and his army lingered in their territories and laid them waste.

110. As soon as it became clear that they were not going to give in, he marched instead against Chalcidian Torone, an Athenian possession. A small group of citizens had invited him to come and were ready to betray the town to him. He got there around dawn, when it was still dark, and had his army make camp near the sanctuary of the Dioscuri, which is about a third of a mile from the town. [2] The rest of the citizens of Torone and the Athenian garrison were unaware of his presence, but his supporters were sure that he would come, and a few of them had surreptitiously left the town to watch for his approach. When they saw that he had arrived, they took with them into the town seven of his light-armed soldiers, armed with daggers. Twenty men had originally been detailed for this assignment, but only these seven, who were led by Lysistratus of Olynthus, had the courage to enter the town. They slipped through a gap in the seaward wall and without being spotted climbed up to the highest guardpost (the town is situated on a sloping hill) and killed the guards. Then they began to break through the postern gate on the side of the town facing Cape Canastraeum.

111. Brasidas and his army advanced a little way, but he took no further action for the time being apart from sending a hundred peltasts on ahead. The idea was that, when some gates had been opened and the agreed signal had been given, they would be the first to dash into the town. [2] To their surprise, however, nothing happened for a while, but they gradually moved closer to the town. The pro-Lacedaemonian Toroneans inside, along with the seven men who had entered, were making things ready for the attack, and when they had broken through the postern gate and had opened the gate near the agora by cutting through the bar, they first brought some of the peltasts around and had them enter by the postern gate. Their job was to take the unsuspecting citizens in the rear, so that they would be thrown into a panic by being suddenly attacked from both sides at once. Then the conspirators gave the agreed fire signal and let the rest of the peltasts in through the gate near the agora.

112. When Brasidas saw the signal he set off at a run, rousing his troops into action, and they gave a concerted yell that terrified the citizens of Torone. [2] Some of his men immediately rushed in through the main gate, while others gained entry by means of planks that happened to be leaning against a collapsed section of wall that was being rebuilt, to make it easier to haul stones up. [3] Brasidas and most of his men immediately turned inland toward the upper parts of the town, because he wanted to make a thorough and secure job of taking it, while the rest of his forces scattered here and there throughout the place.

113. The response of most of the Toroneans to this attempt on their town was bemusement, since they had no idea what was going on, but Brasidas's supporters and others who approved of the attempt immediately joined the attackers. [2] When the Athenians became aware of the attack—there were about fifty Athenian hoplites in the agora, where they slept—a few of them were killed in hand-to-hand fighting. The rest fled either on foot or on the two ships that were on guard, and made it safely to the fort at Lecythus (a projection of the city into the sea, isolated on a narrow isthmus), which the Athenians had taken over and occupied. [3] The pro-Athenian Toroneans also took refuge there with them.

114. By the time it was light the town was securely in Brasidas's hands. He issued a proclamation to the Toroneans who had taken refuge with the Athenians that, if they wanted, they could leave the fort, return to their own homes, and exercise their rights as citizens without fear. But to the Athenians he sent a herald ordering them to evacuate Lecythus, since it belonged to the Chalcidians; they could leave safely, he said, with a sworn guarantee of safe conduct, and could take their property with them. [2] The Athenians refused to leave, but they asked him to let them have a truce for a day to recover their dead. Brasidas granted them a two-day truce, and he spent this time fortifying the houses near the fort, while the Athenians strengthened their position.

[3] Brasidas convened a meeting of the Toroneans and gave a speech that was more or less identical to the one he had given at Acanthus. He said it would be wrong to regard his collaborators in the capture of the city as bad men or as traitors, because their goal had not been enslavement and they had not been bribed, but had acted for the good of the town and for its freedom. And it would be equally wrong, he said, for those who had not taken part in the conspiracy to think they would be treated differently from those who had, because he had not come either to destroy the town or to take any individual's life. [4] That was why he had made the proclamation to those who had taken refuge with the Athenians; he wanted them to know that he thought no worse of them for their sympathy with the Athenian cause. And he was sure that, once they had some experience of the Lacedaemonians and saw that their treatment of them was more just than that of the Athenians, they would feel more, not less, well disposed toward them; it was only their lack of experience of the Lacedaemonians that made them afraid at the moment. [5] And so he called on all the citizens to be ready to be loyal allies, and he warned them that from then on they would be held responsible for any lapses. As for the past, the way to think of it was not that the Lacedaemonians had been wronged by the Toroneans, but that the Toroneans had been wronged by others stronger than themselves, so that they were not to blame if they had opposed the Lacedaemonians in any way.

115. After he had reassured them with this speech, and once the truce had expired, he began the assault on Lecythus. The Athenians fought back from the fort, such as it was, and from houses they had fortified with battlements, and on the first day they managed to repel the Lacedaemonians. [2] But the next day, when the Lacedaemonians were about to bring up a contraption with which they planned to shoot fire at the wooden breastworks and were already approaching in force, as a countermeasure the Athenians erected a wooden tower on top of a building at the point where they thought it most likely that the Lacedaemonians would bring the contraption to bear, and which was particularly vulnerable to attack. Not only did they carry up numerous amphoras and storage jars filled with water, and some hefty rocks, but many men also climbed up into the tower. [3] But this was too much weight for the building and it suddenly collapsed with a terrific crash. Those Athenians who were nearby and saw what had happened were more dismayed than frightened, but those who were farther away, and especially those farthest away, inferred from the noise that the place had already fallen, and set off in flight to the coast and the ships. **116.** When Brasidas saw what was happening and realized that they were abandoning the battlements, he ordered his men forward. The fort fell to him right away and he killed everyone he found there. [2] After their hasty departure from the place, the Athenians sailed over to the Pallene peninsula in their boats and ships.

At Lecythus there is a sanctuary of Athena, and when he was on the point of attacking, Brasidas had announced that he would give thirty minas of silver to the first man to scale the wall. But now he thought that more than human agency had been involved in the capture of the place, so he paid the thirty minas to the goddess for her sanctuary. He demolished the buildings at Lecythus, cleared away all the rubble, and dedicated the whole site as sacred ground. [3] He then spent what was left of the winter organizing the places that he held and intriguing against the rest, and with the end of winter the eighth year of the war came to an end.

117. At the very beginning of the spring of the following year, the Lacedaemonians and the Athenians agreed to a truce for a year. The Athenians thought this would stop Brasidas from causing any further defections among their allies and that it would give them time to organize countermeasures; and they also thought that, if things went well for them, they could make a proper peace later. The Lacedaemonians correctly assessed what the Athenians were frightened of and thought that once they experienced a respite from trouble and hardship they would be more eager to reconcile, and would therefore return the men they had captured on Sphacteria and make peace for a longer period of time. [2] They attached more importance to getting their men back while Brasidas's good fortune lasted <than to anything else>.† And yet if he carried his successes further and brought about parity between the two sides, they would still not have the prisoners, and if they were defending themselves on equal terms there was no certainty that they would in fact win. [3] So they arranged a truce for themselves and their allies on the following terms:

118. "Concerning the sanctuary and oracle of Pythian Apollo:* we think it right that anyone should be able to consult the oracle according to traditional practice without deceit or fear. [2] This is resolved by the Lacedaemonians and their allies here present, and they affirm that they will send heralds to the Boeotians and Phocians and do their best to persuade them, too, that this is right. [3] Concerning the god's valuables:* we resolve to take steps to discover the culprits, going about it in a right and proper fashion and in accordance with traditional practice, along with you and anyone else who wishes to join in, all acting in accordance with traditional practice. [4] Where these two issues are concerned, these are the resolutions of the Lacedaemonians and their allies.

"The following was resolved by the Lacedaemonians and their allies if the Athenians agree to a peace treaty: each party shall keep to its own territory and retain what it now holds. The Athenians at

Coryphasium* are not to go beyond Bouphras or Tomeus; there shall be no contact between those on Cythera and members of our alliance, whichever party initiates the contact; those at Nisaea and Minoa are not to cross the road that leads from the gateway of the shrine of Nisus to the sanctuary of Poseidon and from the sanctuary of Poseidon up to the bridge to Minoa, nor are the Megarians and their allies to cross this road, and the Athenians are to retain possession of the island they captured,* with neither side communicating with the other; and the Athenians are to retain what they now possess in the territory of Troezen, in accordance with the agreement between the Troezenians and the Athenians. [5] As for access to the sea, the Lacedaemonians and their allies may sail off their own coasts and those of their allies, not in warships, but in any other kind of oared vessel with a capacity of up to five hundred talents.* [6] Heralds and envoys (and their attendants, however many of them may be thought necessary) who are involved in negotiations designed to bring the war to an end or in arbitration are to have their safety guaranteed on land and sea as they travel to and from the Peloponnese and Athens. [7] While the truce is in force, deserters, whether free or enslaved, are not to be taken in by either you or us. [8] Both you and we are to submit our disputes to arbitration in accordance with traditional practice, settling them by due legal process, not by warfare. [9] This is resolved by the Lacedaemonians and their allies. If any of your resolutions are better or more equitable than ours, come to Sparta and inform us. Any equitable proposal that you make will be taken seriously by both the Lacedaemonians and their allies. [10] Those who come are to have been granted the same full authority to make decisions that you requested of us. The truce shall last for one year.

[11] "Resolved by the people.* The tribe Acamantis was the prytany, with Phaenippus the secretary and Niciades the chairman. Laches moved that for the good fortune of the Athenians they should conclude the truce on the terms agreed by the Lacedaemonians and their allies and approved by the Athenian people: [12] The truce is

to last for one year, starting from this day, the fourteenth day of the month Elaphebolion.* [13] During this period, envoys and heralds are to travel between the two parties and discuss the terms for bringing the war to an end. [14] The generals and the prytaneis are first to convene the assembly on the matter of the proposed peace <at which>† the Athenians are to discuss whatever proposals the embassy might make for bringing the war to an end. And the embassies here present are forthwith to swear before the people to abide by the truce for the stipulated period of one year.

119. "This was agreed by the Lacedaemonians and their allies with the Athenians and their allies on the twelfth day of the Lacedaemonian month Gerastios. [2] Those who made the agreement and ratified the truce were the following. For the Lacedaemonians: Taurus, son of Echetimidas, Athenaeus, son of Periclidas, and Philocharidas, son of Eryxilaidas; for the Corinthians: Aeneas, son of Ocytus, and Euphamidas, son of Aristonymus; for the Sicyonians: Damotimus, son of Naucrates, and Onasimus, son of Megacles; for the Megarians: Nicasus, son of Cecalus, and Menecrates, son of Amphidorus; for the Epidaurians: Amphias, son of Eupaidas; for the Athenians: the generals Nicostratus, son of Dieitrephes, Nicias, son of Niceratus, and Autocles, son of Tolmaeus."

[3] So the truce came into effect on these terms, and discussions about a more lasting peace were held continuously throughout the year of its being in force.

120. At about the same time that the Athenians and Lacedaemonians were approaching <their allies to officially announce the truce>,† Scione, a city on the Pallene peninsula, defected from the Athenians to Brasidas. (The legend in Scione is that they were originally from Pellene in the Peloponnese, and that as their founders were returning from Troy they were driven ashore at this place by the great storm that struck the Achaean fleet and settled there.) [2] After their defection, Brasidas sailed over to Scione by night with one of his triremes going on ahead while he followed behind in a small boat. The reason for this was that if he encountered a vessel larger than his dispatch boat, the trireme would defend him, and if another trireme turned up, a hostile one, he thought it would not turn against the relatively small boat, but against the ship, which would thereby keep him safe. [3] After he had made the crossing, he convened a general meeting of the Scioneans and repeated the speech he had delivered at Acanthus and Torone, adding that they deserved the highest praise because, with Pallene cut off at the isthmus by the Athenian possession of Potidaea, making them effectively islanders, they had of their own free will joined the cause of freedom without waiting timidly for what was evidently in their best interests to be forced upon them by others.* This proved that in the future they would also have the courage to withstand anything else, however difficult, and if things went according to plan, he would regard them as truly the most faithful of the friends of Sparta and would accord them unqualified respect.

121. His words filled the Scioneans with a sense of purpose. All alike were inspired, even those who had previously disapproved of what was happening, and they resolved to endure whatever the war brought without complaining. They received Brasidas warmly and, apart from other tokens of honor, they crowned him at state expense with a golden crown as the liberator of Greece, and individuals wreathed him with ribbons and treated him as they would a successful athlete. [2] He installed a garrison in the town as a temporary expedient and then sailed back over to Torone, but he soon sent a more substantial army to Scione, because he wanted to make attempts on Mende and Potidaea with the Scioneans' help. He expected the Athenians to send a force, treating the peninsula as though it were an island,* and he wanted to forestall them. In fact, he had also embarked on intrigues with people inside these two cities with a view to having them betrayed to him.

122. Brasidas was about to move against Mende and Potidaea when the men who were traveling around bringing news of the truce reached him; the Athenians were represented by Aristonymus and the Lacedaemonians by Athenaeus. [2] So the army returned to Torone while they briefed Brasidas about the pact, and all the new Lacedaemonian allies in the Thraceward region accepted the decision. [3] Aristonymus agreed to everything else, but when he counted the days and realized that the Scioneans had defected after the truce had come into effect, he said they were not covered by the terms of the agreement. Brasidas, however, repeatedly claimed they had defected in time and said he would not give the place up.

[4] When Aristonymus's report about this reached Athens, the Athenians were immediately ready to launch a campaign against Scione, but the Lacedaemonians sent envoys and argued that this would be a breach of the truce. They trusted Brasidas, they said; the town was theirs and they were ready to submit to arbitration about it. [5] But the Athenians considered arbitration risky; they wanted to take offensive action against Scione as quickly as possible, and they were furious that even those who were now effectively islanders were choosing to defect from them, trusting in the Lacedaemonians' strength on land, which would be of no help. [6] In fact, the truth of Scione's defection was as the Athenians claimed: the town had defected two days after the conclusion of the truce. The Athenians immediately enacted a decree, on the motion of Cleon, to reduce the town and kill the Scioneans. Preparing for this expedition was their sole focus; they did nothing else.

123. At this point, Mende (a colony of Eretria on the Pallene peninsula) defected from Athens. Brasidas accepted them, too, as allies and felt justified in doing so, despite the fact that they had clearly come over to him while the truce was in force, because he was himself accusing the Athenians of violating the truce in certain respects. [2] It was Brasidas's resolute spirit that tipped the scales and made the Mendeans feel capable of this bold move, and the fact that he was refusing to give up Scione was another factor that helped them make up their minds. Besides, the supporters of Brasidas in Mende were few in number, and once they had embarked on this course they could no longer let it go; out of fear for their lives if their negotiations with him were found out, they had coerced a reluctant general populace into agreeing to the defection. [3] As soon as the Athenians learned that Mende had rebelled, they became even more enraged and began making the preliminary arrangements for moving against it as well as Scione. [4] Expecting their arrival by sea, Brasidas transported the children and womenfolk of the two towns to safety in Olynthus, and sent over to Pallene a force made up of five hundred Peloponnesian hoplites and three hundred Chalcidian peltasts, all under the command of Polydamidas. And they all worked together to prepare themselves for the impending arrival of the Athenians.

124. Brasidas and Perdiccas, meanwhile, launched a joint campaign for a second time against Arrhabaeus in Lyncus. Perdiccas's forces consisted of Macedonians from his kingdom and hoplites from the Greek cities there, while in addition to the rest of his Peloponnesian troops Brasidas had Chalcidians, Acanthians, and soldiers from other allied towns according to their strength. There were about three thousand Greek hoplites all told, and they were accompanied by altogether almost a thousand Macedonian and Chalcidian cavalrymen, and then a large body of barbarians. [2] On entering Arrhabaeus's kingdom they found the Lyncestians ready for battle, and they took up their own position facing them. [3] Each side's infantry occupied one of two hills with level ground in between, and the first engagement took place between the cavalry units of both armies when they charged down into this plain. The first infantry to advance from their hill and offer battle were the Lyncestian hoplites—they set out at the same time as the cavalry—so Brasidas and Perdiccas led out their own infantry against them. They engaged the Lyncestians, routed them, and killed a considerable number of them. The survivors escaped to high ground and abandoned the fight.

[4] Next, after erecting a trophy, Brasidas and Perdiccas rested for two or three days pending the arrival of the Illyrians who were supposed to be joining Perdiccas as mercenaries. Then Perdiccas became

restless and wanted to proceed against the villages of Arrhabaeus's realm, but Brasidas was anxious about Mende, in case the Athenians attacked by sea before he could get back and made it suffer, and since the Illyrians had also not arrived he was unenthusiastic about Perdiccas's plan and was more in favor of withdrawing from Lyncus. **125.** Just then, while they were arguing, they received information that the Illyrians had deserted Perdiccas and sided with Arrhabaeus. The upshot of this was that now both of them thought it better to withdraw, because they were afraid of the Illyrians, a warlike people. As a result of their disagreement, however, no firm decision was made as to exactly when they should set out, but as soon as darkness fell that night the Macedonians and the mass of barbarians were seized with one of those mysterious panics to which large armies are liable. Thinking that the approaching army was many times larger than it actually was and would arrive momentarily, all at once they turned to flight and headed for home. By the time Perdiccas found out—at first he had not realized what was going on—his men had left him no choice but to leave before he had met with Brasidas, the two camps being quite a long way from each other.

[2] At daybreak, when Brasidas saw that the Macedonians had already gone and that the Illyrians and Arrhabaeus were about to attack, he planned his own withdrawal. He formed his hoplites into a compact square, with the light-armed soldiers inside, [3] and gave his youngest soldiers the job of charging out and skirmishing with the enemy wherever they attacked. He himself intended to form a rearguard during the withdrawal with three hundred handpicked men, and to resist and repel the enemy's frontline troops. And to give them heart, before the enemy drew close he quickly encouraged them by speaking along the following lines:

126. "Peloponnesians, if I didn't suspect that you were frightened because you've been left isolated and are facing an attack from a sizable horde of barbarians, I would just be encouraging you, without also feeling that I had to explain things to you. But in view of the defection of our allies and the large numbers of the enemy, I shall try to make you understand what's really important by offering a few words that will serve as reminders and encouragement. [2] What I'm getting at is that valor in war is to be expected of you whenever it's called for; it has nothing to do with the presence or absence of allies, but is due simply to your own native excellence. Nor should large numbers of soldiers on the other side be frightening for men like you, seeing that the states from which you come aren't like theirs, in which it isn't the many who rule the few, but the minority who rule the majority, having acquired dominion solely through victory in battle.

[3] "At the moment you're frightened of these barbarians because you haven't encountered them before, but if you think about the engagement you've already fought with those of them who are Macedonians,* and if you accept my estimate of them and what I feel certain of from having heard them described by others, you should conclude that there'll be nothing to fear. [4] When the respects in which an enemy is actually weak but gives an impression of strength are exposed for what they are, they serve to banish fear and embolden their opponents—the reverse of the situation where an enemy really does have a certain advantage, and an opponent who's unaware of it attacks with unwarranted confidence.

[5] "The prospect of fighting these barbarians is frightening to people who have no experience of them: their numbers are a terrifying sight, the loudness of their war cries is unbearable, and the way they pointlessly brandish their weapons makes them seem threatening. But when it comes to the actual engagement, those who aren't unnerved by the spectacle and the yelling and the brandishing find them to be quite different. The fact that they don't fight in formation makes it impossible for them to feel shame if they give ground under pressure, and since it makes no difference to their honor whether they are moving into the attack or away from it, their courage is never really tested. There's nothing better than a battle in which no soldier is answerable to anyone else for offering him an excuse to save his life without

dishonor. And they regard intimidating you while not taking risks as a more reliable way of winning than hand-to-hand fighting; otherwise, they'd rely on the latter rather than the former.

[6] "From what I've said, you can now see clearly that everything that seems terrifying about them in advance is very slight when it comes to action; it's no more than a nuisance to eye and ear. If you're not fazed by its forcefulness, and if, when the time comes, you conduct yourselves in an orderly fashion and remain in formation as we retreat, you'll soon reach safety. And in the future you'll know that rabbles such as this one, when they're up against men who stand unyielding against their first charge, boast of their courage by shouting threats from a distance of what they intend to do; but when men give way to them, they leap at the chance to make a safe display of courage as they follow hard on their heels."

127. After these encouraging words, Brasidas and his army began to retreat. When the barbarians saw this they moved into the attack, yelling at the tops of their voices and making a terrific din; they expected the Greeks to turn to flight and thought they would then catch up with them and wipe them out. [2] But the skirmishers ran out to confront them wherever they charged up, and Brasidas and his elite unit held out against their attacks. Contrary to the barbarians' expectations, then, the Greeks were not routed by their first assault, and from then on they continued to withstand every subsequent attack and to fight back; and whenever the barbarians were not attacking they carried on with their withdrawal. When Brasidas and his troops reached open country, most of the barbarians kept their distance; they left some of their men to continue the pursuit and the attacks, but the rest set off at a run in the direction taken by the fleeing Macedonians, killing those they caught up with, and when they reached the narrow pass from Macedon to Arrhabaeus's kingdom, where the road ran between two hills, they occupied it, knowing that there was no other route Brasidas could take. And as he approached the most difficult stretch of the pass they began an encircling movement in an attempt to cut him off.

128. But Brasidas realized what was happening, and he told the three hundred men who were with him to run to the hill that he thought they stood a chance of taking—not in formation, but with each man running as fast as he could—and to try to dislodge the barbarians who were already on it before more of those who were encircling them got there. [2] Brasidas's task force fell on the barbarians who were occupying the hill and defeated them, and then it was easier for the bulk of the Greek army to make its way up the hill, because the barbarians were terrified by the fact that they had been forced off the high ground there. In fact, they called off their close pursuit of the Greeks, judging that now they had reached the border and made good their escape. [3] With the heights occupied by his men, Brasidas carried on in greater safety and arrived that same day at Arnisa, the first town in Perdiccas's realm.

[4] The Greek soldiers were furious about the early withdrawal of the Macedonians, and whenever they came across one of their ox-carts on the road, or some baggage that had fallen off, as inevitably happens when frightened men are retreating by night, they unyoked the oxen and slaughtered them, and appropriated the baggage for themselves. [5] As a result, Perdiccas considered Brasidas an enemy, and from then on he nursed in his heart a hatred for the Peloponnesians that was abnormal for him given his poor relations with the Athenians; and disregarding the demands of self-interest he did all he could to come to an agreement with the Athenians as soon as possible and break off with the Peloponnesians.

129. On leaving Macedon and returning to Torone, Brasidas found that Mende was already in Athenian hands. He stayed where he was and did nothing because he considered that under the circumstances it was impossible for him to sail over and bring help to Pallene, but he kept Torone under guard. [2] For at about the same time as the operations in Lyncus, the Athenians had dispatched the expeditionary force they had been preparing against Mende and Scione. It consisted of 50 ships (10 of them Chian), 1,000 of their own hoplites, 600 archers, 1,000 Thracian mercenaries, and other peltasts from their allies in the northern Aegean. The generals in command were Nicias, son of Niceratus, and Nicostratus, son of Dieitrephes. [3] They set out with the fleet from Potidaea, put in near the sanctuary of Poseidon, and advanced against Mende. The Mendeans, along with 300 Scioneans who had come to help and the mercenaries from the Peloponnese, making a total of 700 <peltasts and...> hoplites,† under the command of Polydamidas, had already taken up a position on an easily defensible hill outside the city. [4] Nicias tried to get to them by means of a path up the hill with a force of 120 light-armed soldiers from Methone, 60 handpicked Athenian hoplites, and all the archers, but he suffered casualties and was unable to force the position. There were very few ways to get up the hill, and Nicostratus, meanwhile, attacked it with the rest of the army by a less direct route, but the result was complete chaos and the entire Athenian army came very close to defeat. [5] In view of the stubborn resistance by the Mendeans and their allies, the Athenians withdrew and made camp that day, and after nightfall the Mendeans returned to their city.

130. The next day the Athenians sailed round the headland to the side of Mende that faces Scione. They took over the outskirts of the city and spent the whole day ravaging the farmland. No sortie was made against them because of political discord among the Mendeans, and that night the 300 Scioneans returned home. [2] The next day, Nicias took half the army and marched as far as the border between Mende and Scione, laying waste the land as he went, while Nicostratus with the rest of their troops took up a position at the upper gate of the city, on the road to Potidaea. [3] This happened to be where the Mendeans and their allies had their weapons stacked, just inside the wall, so Polydamidas marshaled his troops and urged them to go out and fight. [4] One of those on the democratic side of their factional dispute objected, saying that they would not make a sortie and that in fact there was no need for fighting, and just as he had finished speaking Polydamidas grabbed him by the arm and shook him. At this the people immediately seized their weapons and turned in a rage on the Peloponnesians and their anti-democratic accomplices. [5] They fell on their opponents, who turned and fled, shocked by the suddenness with which fighting had broken out, and frightened of the gates being opened for the Athenians, because they took this attempt on their lives to be part of a prearranged plan.

[6] Those of the Peloponnesians who were not killed right away escaped to the acropolis, which they had held since their arrival, and the whole Athenian army—by now Nicias had returned and was close at hand—burst into the city. Since the gates had not been opened to them by prior agreement, they looted it as though it were an enemy city they had taken by storm, and it was only with difficulty that the generals stopped their men from slaughtering the inhabitants as well. [7] When it was all over, the Athenian generals told the Mendeans to keep their constitution unchanged, and that they should pass judgment among themselves on those whom they took to be responsible for the rebellion. The Peloponnesians on the acropolis they walled in by building a wall on both sides down to the coast, and they posted guards on the wall. So with Mende now under their control, the Athenians proceeded against Scione.

131. The Scioneans and the Peloponnesians came out to give battle and took up a position on a steep hill in front of the town, which the Athenians needed to take if they were to surround the city with a siege wall. [2] They launched an all-out attack on the hill and in the ensuing battle they succeeded in dislodging their opponents from it. They then made camp, erected a trophy, and got ready to build a siege wall around the town. [3] Not long afterward, when they were already engaged in this work, the mercenaries who were under siege on the acropolis of Mende overcame the guard by the sea and reached Scione under cover of darkness. Most of them got safely past the army camped outside and entered the town.

132. While the wall was being built around Scione, Perdiccas made overtures to the Athenian generals and entered into a pact with the Athenians. He was motivated to do so by his hatred of Brasidas, arising out of the retreat from Lyncus, and in fact he had started to negotiate with the Athenians immediately after that episode. [2] It so happened that Ischagoras of Sparta was intending to bring an army overland to Brasidas, so Perdiccas—partly because Nicias was telling him to give the Athenians clear proof of his reliability now that he had entered into the pact, and partly because he himself no longer wanted any Peloponnesians in his kingdom—worked on his guest-friends in Thessaly (he was always on familiar terms with the leading men there) and was so successful in halting the progress of the army and its equipment that Ischagoras did not even bother to ask the Thessalians for passage. [3] However, Ischagoras, Ameinias, and Aristeus, who had been sent by the Lacedaemonians to supervise affairs, did manage to reach Brasidas by their own efforts, and they illegally brought him from Sparta some young men to be installed as governors of the cities, so as not to leave such appointments to chance.* And so he made Clearidas, son of Cleonymus, the governor of Amphipolis, and Pasitelidas, son of Hegesander, the governor of Torone.

133. In the same summer, the Thebans demolished the Thespians' wall, accusing them of collaborating with the Athenians. This was something they had long wanted to do, and now they had their opportunity, because the flower of the Thespian army had been cut down in the battle with the Athenians.* [2] Also in this summer the temple of Hera at Argos burned down; the priestess, Chrysis, had gone to bed after putting a lighted lamp near the garlands, so that everything was on fire and had burned to the ground before she became aware of it. [3] Afraid of the Argives' reaction, Chrysis fled that very night to Phleious. In accordance with their established practice, the Argives appointed another priestess, whose name was Phäeinis. Chrysis's term as priestess covered eight full years of the current war, and the ninth was halfway through when she fled. [4] By the end of the summer Scione had been completely surrounded by a siege wall, and the Athenians left a garrison there and returned home with the rest of their army.

134. During the following winter the truce kept the peace between the Athenians and Lacedaemonians, but at Laodoceum in Oresthis the Mantineans and their allies fought a battle against the Tegeans and their allies. It was not clear who won, because both the Mantineans and the Tegeans turned the wing opposite them, and they both erected trophies and sent spoils to Delphi. [2] But after an evenly balanced battle in which many lives were lost on both sides, and once darkness had cut short the action, the Tegeans spent the night there and erected a trophy right away, whereas the Mantineans withdrew to Bucolion and erected their trophy later.

135. Another thing that happened, right at the end of winter when it was almost spring, was that Brasidas made an attempt on Potidaea. He approached under cover of darkness and set up a ladder, without being detected because it was the interval after the bell had been passed on and before the man passing it on had returned to his post.* However, in no time at all they were found out, before anyone had climbed up the ladder, and Brasidas quickly led his army back again without waiting for daylight.

[2] So the winter came to an end and with it the ninth year of the current war, the history of which was written by Thucydides.

Book Five

The tenth to sixteenth years of the war. ***422/421:*** *further purification of Delos (5.1); more campaigns in the north, and the deaths of Cleon and Brasidas (5.2–12); the Peace of Nicias (5.13–25).* ***421/420–420/419:*** *the "second preface" (5.26); diplomatic intrigues (5.27–50); troubles for Sparta at Heraclea in Trachis (5.51–52.1).* ***419/418:*** *conflict between Argos and Epidaurus (5.52.2–56).* ***418/417:*** *conflict escalates to involve Athens and Sparta (5.57–64); Spartan victory at the Battle of Mantinea (5.65–75); peace between Sparta and Argos (5.76–81).* ***417/416:*** *tensions between Sparta and Argos resume (5.82–83).* ***416/415:*** *Athenian expedition against Melos, the "Melian Dialogue," and the fate of Melos (5.84–116).*

1. The following summer, the truce remained in effect until the time of the Pythian games.* While it was still in force the Athenians evicted the Delians from Delos, on the grounds that at the time of their consecration they had been polluted by some ancient offense, and also because they thought their purification of the island (which, as I explained earlier, they thought they had properly carried out by removing the tombs of the dead) had been defective in allowing the inhabitants to remain.* The Delians set out, with each man making his own way, and settled in Atramyttium in Asia, which Pharnaces gave them.*

2. After the truce was over, Cleon persuaded the Athenians to send him to the Thraceward region with 1,200 Athenian hoplites, 300

Athenian cavalrymen, a larger number of allied troops, and thirty ships. [2] He first put in at Scione, which was still under siege. From there he added some of the hoplites from the garrison to his force, and then he sailed to Cophus Bay, which is close to Torone. [3] Since he had found out from deserters that Brasidas was not there, and also that the garrison was no match for his troops, he advanced on the town with his land forces and sent ten ships around into the harbor. [4] But first he came to the wall with which Brasidas had surrounded the town; he had made Torone a single city by demolishing part of the old wall and including the suburbs within the new wall.

3. Pasitelidas, the Lacedaemonian governor, and the garrison troops he had with him came out to defend the wall and fought back against the Athenian assault. Since they were having a hard time of it, and the ships that Cleon had sent to the harbor were on their way as well, Pasitelidas became afraid that the ships would reach the town before he had time to get back and, finding it undefended, would capture it—and then, with the new wall in Athenian hands, he would be caught between a rock and a hard place. So he raced back into the town, [2] but it was too late. It had already fallen to the Athenians from the ships, and the Athenian infantry, who were hard on his heels, poured into the town without meeting any opposition through the section of the old wall that had been demolished. In hand-to-hand fighting, they killed some of the Peloponnesians and Toroneans, but took others alive, including Pasitelidas, the governor.

[3] Brasidas was heading back to Torone to help, but he retreated when he found out on the road that the town had fallen. He had been within five miles of reaching the place in time. [4] Cleon and the Athenians erected two trophies, one at the harbor and the other at the new wall. He sold the women and children of Torone into slavery, but the men, about 700 in all—Toroneans, Peloponnesians, and a few Chalcidians—he sent off to Athens. The Peloponnesians later left Athens, once the peace treaty had been concluded,* while the others were taken in by the Olynthians in a one-for-one exchange of prisoners. [5]

At much the same time, Panactum, an Athenian border fortress, was betrayed to the Boeotians. [6] After installing a garrison in Torone, Cleon left and sailed around Mount Athos, heading for Amphipolis.

4. Meanwhile, Phaeax, son of Erasistratus, and two others were sent by the Athenians with two ships on a diplomatic mission to Italy and Sicily. [2] Following the departure of the Athenians from Sicily after the peace treaty,* the Leontinians had enrolled a large number of men as citizens, and the democrats were contemplating a redistribution of the land. [3] This did not go unnoticed by the Leontinian aristocrats; they summoned Syracusan help and expelled the commoners, who roamed the countryside, each man fending for himself, while the aristocrats came to an arrangement with the Syracusans whereby they abandoned Leontini, leaving it empty, and settled in Syracuse as citizens. [4] Later, some of them, dissatisfied with their new situation, left Syracuse again and took over a part of Leontini called Phoceae, as well as Bricinniae, a fortress in Leontinian territory. They were joined by most of the people who had previously been expelled, and once they were settled they made war on Syracuse from these two strongholds.

[5] It was when word of all this reached the Athenians that they dispatched Phaeax on his mission, to see if they could prevail upon their own allies there, and, if possible, the other Sicilian Greeks, to unite and mount a campaign against the Syracusans on the ground that they were becoming dangerously powerful, and thereby save the people of Leontini. [6] On his arrival, Phaeax succeeded in winning over the Camarinaeans and Acragantines, but at Gela things did not go his way, and he did not bother to visit the rest of the cities because it was clear that they would not be receptive to his proposal. So he withdrew through Sicel lands to Catana, and as he was passing he visited Bricinniae, where he encouraged them to keep up the good work. Then he sailed for home.

5. On his voyage out to Sicily and then again on his way back, he also engaged in negotiations with some of the Italian cities, in an attempt to get them to favor Athens. He happened to come across some Locrian settlers as well, who had been expelled from Messina. They had been sent as settlers to Messina after the Sicilian Greek peace treaty when there was political discord in the city and one of the two factions had invited them in; in fact, for a while Messina had been Locrian. [2] Phaeax encountered them as they were on their way back to Locri, but he did them no harm because the Locrians had already assented to his proposal that they should enter into a treaty with the Athenians. [3] Locri had been the only state of those allied with the Sicilian Greeks that had not made a treaty with the Athenians during the negotiations that led to the Sicilian Greek reconciliation—nor would they have done so then if they had not been involved in a war against Hipponium and Medma, neighboring states that were colonies of theirs. And so later Phaeax arrived back in Athens.

6. Cleon had by now left Torone and sailed against Amphipolis. With Eion as his base, he attacked Stagirus, a colony of Andros, but failed to take it; however, he did assault and take Galepsus,* a colony of Thasos. [2] He also sent envoys to Perdiccas, telling him to come with an army in compliance with the terms of their alliance, and he sent other envoys to Polles in Thrace, the king of the Odomantes, asking him to supply him with as many Thracian mercenaries as he could. Then he remained inactive in Eion, pending the arrival of these reinforcements. [3] When Brasidas was informed of all this, he took up a counter-position at Cerdylium. This Argilian village is on high ground west of the river, not far from Amphipolis, and all the surrounding countryside is visible from it, so that he would know when Cleon set out with his army. That is what he expected him to do—to regard the Lacedaemonians as no threat, given their numbers, and to march inland against Amphipolis with the forces he already had. [4] At the same time, Brasidas was also assembling a battalion of 1,500 Thracian mercenaries and requesting from the Edones a full levy of peltasts and cavalry. And he had 1,000 peltasts from Myrcinus and

Olynthus, in addition to those in Amphipolis. [5] The hoplite force he had assembled numbered approximately 2,000, and there were 300 Greek cavalrymen. Brasidas had about 1,500 of these soldiers under his own command at Cerdylium, while the rest had been posted to Amphipolis under the command of Clearidas.

7. For a while, Cleon remained inactive, but then he was forced to do what Brasidas had expected him to do. His men were chafing at their idleness and reflecting on his leadership, comparing his ineptitude and irresolution with Brasidas's expertise and boldness, and saying how reluctant they had been to leave home and join him. [2] So when these mutterings came to his attention, in order to alleviate their boredom at being stuck in one place he mustered them and took to the field. [3] He acted in the same confident spirit that had brought him success at Pylos and had convinced him of his wisdom, because he expected no counterattack by the troops inside the city. In fact, he claimed to be going merely to reconnoiter the place. He said he was waiting† for the reinforcements not to ensure a safe margin of superiority in case of trouble, but because he planned to surround the city with men and take it by storm. [4] When he arrived he had his army encamp on an easily defensible hill right in front of Amphipolis, while he went and surveyed the marshes of the Strymon and how the city was placed in relation to Thrace. [5] He had no doubt that he would be able to leave the hill whenever he wanted without having to fight, because there was no one to be seen on the wall and no one was emerging from the gates, either, all of which were closed. He even concluded that it had been a mistake not to bring siege contraptions with him, because he thought it would have been easy to take the city, undefended as it was.

8. As soon as Brasidas had seen that the Athenians were on the move, he had come down from Cerdylium and entered Amphipolis. [2] He did not lead his men out and deploy them in response to the Athenians, because he had misgivings about his forces. He thought them inferior not in numbers—the two sides were more or less evenly matched in that respect—but in quality, because the Athenian expeditionary force was unadulterated by foreigners, and supported by the best of the Lemnians and Imbrians. So he planned to attack them with the help of a trick. [3] He thought that letting his opponents see how many men he had and their makeshift equipment would reduce his chances of success, and that he would be better off if he attacked before they had time to observe his forces, and before they had any real grounds for thinking him no threat. [4] So he selected 150 hoplites, assigning the rest of his forces to Clearidas, and proposed to make a surprise attack on the Athenians before they left. His thinking was that there would never be a better opportunity for him to catch them on their own, before their reinforcements arrived. So he called together all his troops, and in order to motivate them and explain his strategy he spoke in the following vein:

9. "Peloponnesians, you hardly need a long speech from me to explain the kind of land from which we hail, that courage has always kept it free, and that you are Dorians about to fight Ionians, whom you invariably defeat. [2] What I want to do, rather, is tell you my plan of action, so that you won't be discouraged by the fact that we're taking the risk of attacking not with all our forces at once, but with a small detachment that might seem unequal to the task. [3] My guess is that our adversaries have come here because they consider us no threat. In the belief that no one will come out and fight them, they've climbed that hill and are now spending their time out of formation in reconnaissance, underestimating the danger we pose. [4] The most successful general is the one who clearly recognizes when his opponents are making this kind of mistake and at the same time takes action that's based on a true assessment of his own capability. He doesn't necessarily reveal his intentions by having his men adopt a counter-formation to theirs; he does whatever it takes to gain an advantage given the situation with which he's faced. [5] The most glorious stratagems are those that best deceive the enemy and most benefit one's friends.

[6] "So while they're still unprepared and confident, while their intention, by the look of things, is to slip away rather than to stand up to us, and while they're in this nonchalant and unfocused state of mind, I and my task force will take them by surprise, hopefully, with a rapidly executed charge into the heart of their army. [7] As for you, Clearidas, after a while, when you see that I'm giving them a hard time, and, I expect, cause for concern, take the Amphipolitans and the rest of our allies, throw open the gate, race out of the city into the attack, and make haste to engage them as quickly as possible. [8] I'm confident that this in particular will cause them to panic, because the second wave of an attack is always more frightening to an enemy than the troops who are already there and fighting.

[9] "So, Clearidas, for your part, display the valor we expect of a Spartiate. And as for you men, our allies, follow his lead without yielding to fear. Bear in mind that the three elements of successful fighting are willpower, self-respect, and obedience to officers, and that today either you'll gain your freedom and the right to be called allies of Sparta, if you acquit yourselves well, or you'll be known as slaves of Athens, if you're lucky enough to avoid being killed or put up for sale in the slave market, and your servitude will be harsher than it was before. Moreover, you'll impede the liberation of the rest of the Greeks. [10] So now that you're aware how much is at stake in this contest, prove yourselves true men, and for my part I shall make it clear that I'm not the kind of person who offers advice to others without putting it into practice himself."

10. After making this speech, Brasidas got ready for his own sortie and stationed Clearidas and the rest of his men at the so-called Thracian Gate, so that they could sally out and attack as instructed. [2] His descent from Cerdylium had not gone unnoticed, however, and, since the interior of the city was perfectly visible from outside, he was seen sacrificing in the sanctuary of Athena and making his arrangements. Cleon, who had earlier gone ahead to do some reconnoitering, was told that the whole enemy army could be seen inside the city, and the hoofs of many horses and the feet of many men were visible under the gates, so that it looked as though they were on the point of making a sortie. [3] On hearing this news, he went to see for himself. Since he did not want to fight a decisive battle before the arrival of the auxiliaries and he thought he had time to get away, he ordered the signal for withdrawal to be given and at the same time instructed the army to pull back in the direction of Eion with the left wing leading the way, which was in fact the only possibility. [4] But the maneuver seemed to him to be taking too long, so he started to lead the army away himself by having the right wing execute a quarter turn, thus exposing his men's unshielded side to the enemy.

[5] Brasidas instantly saw his chance. At the sight of the Athenian army on the move, he spoke to his companions and the men of his task force. "They're not going to stand up to us," he said. "That's obvious from the way they keep moving their spears and their heads. That's generally a sign of men who are disinclined to stand up to an attack. Get someone to open the gate for me—the gate I specified—and let's go out and fight as quickly as possible and with high confidence."

[6] He himself sallied out of the gate by the stockade, which was the first in the long wall as it was at the time, and charged up the main road leading from this gate. This is where the trophy now stands as one passes the steepest part of the hill. He attacked the center of the army, and the Athenians, terrified by their lack of cohesion and shocked by his boldness, turned and ran. [7] At the same time, Clearidas, obedient to his orders, sallied out by the Thracian Gate and bore down on the enemy. The upshot was that the Athenians were thrown into confusion by being unexpectedly and suddenly attacked at two points. [8] Their left wing, the one closest to Eion, had already gone some way ahead, and now it immediately broke away and continued its flight. Since this wing was already retreating, Brasidas started to make his way over to the right wing, but he was wounded as he did so. The Athenians failed to notice that he had fallen, but some of his companions picked him up and carried him off the field.

[9] The Athenian right wing was putting up more of a resistance, and Cleon, whose original plan had been to avoid a fight, turned immediately to flight, but a peltast from Myrcinus caught up with him and killed him. The hoplites closed ranks there on the hill and fought off Clearidas's attacks two or three times; they gave way only when they were surrounded by the cavalry from Myrcinus and Olynthus and by the peltasts, and were turned to flight by their javelins. [10] So now the whole Athenian army was in flight. Many were killed in the hand-to-hand fighting or by the Chalcidian cavalry and the peltasts, and the survivors struggled to get back to Eion, taking many different routes through the hills. [11] The men who had rescued Brasidas and carried him from the field of battle took him into the city. He was still breathing at this point and he understood that his men had won the battle, but he died shortly afterward. [12] When the rest of the army returned with Clearidas from their pursuit of the fleeing Athenians, they stripped the dead of their arms and armor and erected a trophy.

11. Somewhat later, all the allies processed in full armor and buried Brasidas at public expense inside the city, just off what is now the agora. The Amphipolitans fenced off his tomb, and to this day they shed the blood of sacrificial victims to him as a hero and have awarded him games and annual sacrifices in his honor. They also designated him the founder of the town, once they had demolished the buildings that honored Hagnon as founder and obliterated all concrete reminders of his founding. They did this not just because they regarded Brasidas as their savior (and because, given the circumstances, fear of Athens induced them to flatter their Lacedaemonian allies), but also because, since they were now enemies of Athens, they regarded it as inappropriate and offensive to honor Hagnon as they had before.*

[2] They gave the Athenians permission to collect the bodies of their dead. Roughly six hundred Athenians died, but only seven of their opponents. This was due to the kind of battle it was, not a pitched one but a random and panic-stricken affair. [3] Once they had collected the bodies, the Athenians sailed back home, while Clearidas

and his colleagues turned their attention to the political reorganization of Amphipolis.

12. At about the same time, as summer was coming to an end, Ramphias, Autocharidas, and Epicydidas, who were on their way from Sparta to the Thraceward region with a supporting force of nine hundred hoplites, stopped at Heraclea in Trachis and remedied everything that struck them as procedurally defective. [2] They were still there when the battle took place at Amphipolis and the summer came to an end.

13. Very early in the following winter, Ramphias and his colleagues marched through Thessaly and got as far as Pierium,* but since the Thessalians had not granted them permission to pass through their land, and especially since Brasidas, to whom they were taking the hoplites, had died, they turned back and headed for home. There did not seem to be any point in carrying on, given that the Athenians had left after their defeat and they did not have the competence to carry out any of Brasidas's plans. [2] But the main reason they turned back was that they knew, when they had set out, that the Lacedaemonians had been leaning more toward peace than war.

14. In fact, immediately after the battle at Amphipolis and Ramphias's withdrawal from Thessaly, both the Athenians and the Lacedaemonians brought their military operations to an end and favored peace rather than war. The Athenians felt this way because they had been defeated twice in fairly rapid succession, at Delium and then at Amphipolis. They no longer had the confidence in their strength that had led them to reject previous offers of peace, in the belief that they could count on their good fortune to bring them victory. [2] They were also worried that these defeats would foster more widespread defection among their allies, and they regretted that they had not seized the excellent opportunity they had had after Pylos to make peace. [3] As for the Lacedaemonians, the war was turning out to be quite different from what they had expected when they had imagined that it would take them only a few years to overthrow the Athenians by ravaging their farmland. Then they had met with defeat on Sphacteria—defeat of a kind that was unprecedented in Lacedaemonian history—and their land was being raided from Pylos and Cythera.* Moreover, their helots were deserting, and they were constantly worried that those who remained in Laconia would be induced by current circumstances to revolt (as they had before)* with the help of those who had left. [4] Then again, the Thirty-Year Peace between them and the Argives was on the point of expiring,* and the Argives were refusing to enter into another treaty unless Cynouria* was returned to them—and the Lacedaemonians thought that war with both Argos and Athens at the same time would be beyond them. Besides, they suspected that some of the Peloponnesian cities would change sides from them to Argos, which is exactly what happened.

15. With these considerations in mind, then, both sides were inclined to come to terms, and especially the Lacedaemonians, because of their desire to recover the men from Sphacteria, some of whom were Spartiates, men of high rank and relatives of others of similarly high status. [2] They had started to negotiate straight after these men had been taken prisoner, but the Athenians were doing so well at the time that they had refused to make peace on equal terms. But after the Athenian defeat at Delium the Lacedaemonians were quick to realize that they would be more receptive to the notion of peace, and so they had concluded the one-year truce, during which the two sides were to meet and discuss a more lasting peace.

16. But it was the second Athenian defeat at Amphipolis and the deaths of Cleon and Brasidas that tipped the scales. These two men had both been vehemently opposed to peace—Brasidas because of the success and honor that war brought him, and Cleon because he thought that if there was no action it would be harder for him to conceal his crookedness, and he would be less credible when he disparaged others. At this point, then, the current main aspirants for political leadership in each city—the Spartan king Pleistoanax, son of Pausanias, and Nicias, son of Niceratus, who was the most successful

Athenian general at the time—became far more determined to end the war. Nicias wanted to keep his good fortune intact before he met with defeat and his reputation suffered. In the short term he wanted to be rid of hardship himself and to end it for his fellow citizens, and in the future he wanted to be remembered as one who throughout his career had done his city nothing but good. He believed that being remembered for this is a consequence of not taking risks and comes to people who entrust themselves to luck as little as possible, and that it is peace that makes it possible to avoid taking risks. And Pleistoanax wanted peace because he was being slandered by his political enemies about his return from exile; they were constantly playing on the Lacedaemonians' religious scruples by bringing up his name every time they suffered a setback, and claiming that it was because of his unlawful return that these things were happening to them.*

[2] They were accusing him of having collaborated with Aristocles of Delphi† to bribe the prophetess in Delphi to give the following reply, over and over again, to any Lacedaemonian delegates who came to consult the oracle: that they were to bring the seed of the Zeus-born hero back from abroad to their land, and that if they failed to do so they would plow with a silver plowshare.* [3] And eventually, his accusers said, she persuaded the Lacedaemonians to restore Pleistoanax and to mark his restoration with the same dances and sacrifices as when Sparta had first been founded and the dual kingship instituted.* He had been banished because he was suspected of having been bribed to withdraw from Attica,* and he had spent the time—he was restored in the nineteenth year of his exile—living on Mount Lycaeum,* in a house half of which lay in the sanctuary of Zeus, because he was afraid of the Lacedaemonians. **17.** So the reason he was eager for peace was that he was chafing under these slanderous accusations, and he thought that if there was peace—if the Lacedaemonians were suffering no setbacks and were recovering the prisoners—he would be unassailable, whereas in wartime it is inevitable that prominent people are always blamed for defeats.

[2] They met for discussions throughout the winter, and when it was almost spring, in order to make the Athenians more compliant, the Lacedaemonians made a threatening gesture, by sending word around the Peloponnesian cities to get ready to build a forward operating base in Attica. As a result of the meetings, at which many claims were presented by both sides, it was finally agreed that they would conclude a peace treaty on the understanding that each side was to return what it had taken in war, except that the Athenians would keep Nisaea. This exception was made because, when the Athenians demanded the return of Plataea, the Thebans said they were not holding on to the place by coercion but with the consent of the Plataeans, who had come over to their side by agreement, rather than because Theban sympathizers had betrayed the city. And the Athenians had responded to this by saying that they had gained Nisaea in the same way. With these terms agreed, the Lacedaemonians summoned their allies to a meeting, and they all voted for peace except for the Boeotians, Corinthians, Eleans, and Megarians, who were dissatisfied with the whole business. The treaty was then concluded and peace was made between the Athenians and the Lacedaemonians, with both sides swearing to abide by the following terms:*

18. "The Athenians, and the Lacedaemonians and their allies, entered into a treaty on the following terms, and swore to it city by city: [2] Where the common sanctuaries of the Greeks are concerned, in accordance with traditional practice anyone may perform sacrifices, consult oracles, and act as an official delegate, and he is to travel without fear by land and by sea. Apollo's sanctuary and temple in Delphi are to be self-determining, in accordance with traditional practice, in respect of their legislation, taxation, and jurisdiction, as they apply to themselves and their territory. [3] The treaty is to last for fifty years for the Athenians and the allies of the Athenians, and for the Lacedaemonians and the allies of the Lacedaemonians, without deceit or damage, by land and by sea. [4] It shall not be permitted for them to bear arms against each other with harmful intent, neither the Lacedaemonians and their allies against the Athenians and their allies, nor the Athenians and their allies against the Lacedaemonians and their allies, by any means or contrivance. They are to settle any disputes that arise between them by legal procedures and oaths, in whatever way may be agreeable to both parties. [5] The Lacedaemonians and their allies are to return Amphipolis to the Athenians. Inhabitants of the cities handed over to the Athenians by the Lacedaemonians are to be permitted to leave and go wherever they wish, themselves and their belongings. The following† cities that pay tribute to the Athenians, as stipulated in the time of Aristeides,* are to be autonomous, and once the treaty is in force, it shall not be permitted for the Athenians and their allies to bear arms against them with harmful intent, provided that they pay the tribute. The cities are: Argilus, Stagirus, Acanthus, Stolus, Olynthus, and Spartolus.* They are to be allies of neither party, neither the Lacedaemonians nor the Athenians, but if the Athenians persuade them and they are willing, it shall be permitted for the Athenians to make them allies. [6] The peoples of Mecyberna, Sane, and Singus* are to inhabit their cities on the same terms as the people of Olynthus and Acanthus. [7] The Lacedaemonians and their allies are to return Panactum* to the Athenians. The Athenians are to return to the Lacedaemonians and their allies Coryphasium, Cythera, Methana, Pteleum, and Atalante, and also any Lacedaemonians who are imprisoned in Athens or anywhere else that is subject to the Athenians.* And the Peloponnesians who are under siege in Scione are to be released, as are all the other Lacedaemonian allies who are in Scione and all those sent into the city by Brasidas, and any allies of the Lacedaemonians who are imprisoned in Athens or anywhere else that is subject to the Athenians. Equally, the Lacedaemonians and their allies are to release any Athenians they are holding. [8] Regarding Scione, Torone, Sermylia, and any other city that is in Athenian hands, the Athenians shall decide as they see fit about them and the other cities. [9] The Athenians are to swear oaths to the Lacedaemonians and their allies, city by city. Seventeen men from each city are to swear the oath in the most binding fashion recognized by each city. The oath shall be as follows: 'I shall abide by this agreement and treaty justly and without deceit.' The Lacedaemonians and their allies are to swear the same oath in Athens, and both parties are to reaffirm the oath every year. [10] Stelae inscribed with the treaty are to be set up at Olympia, Delphi, the Isthmus, on the acropolis at Athens, and in the Amyclaeum* in Sparta. [11] If either party finds that some matter or issue has been overlooked, it is no violation of the oaths for the two parties, the Athenians and the Lacedaemonians, to hold fair and proper discussions and to make alterations as they see fit. **19.** The treaty comes into force in the ephorate of Pleistolas on the twenty-seventh day of the month Artemision, and in Athens in the archonship of Alcaeus on the twenty-fifth day of the month Elaphebolion.* The following people swore the oaths and poured the libations: For the Lacedaemonians, Pleistoanax, Agis, Pleistolas, Damagetus, Chionis, Metagenes, Acanthus, Daithus, Ischagoras, Philocharidas, Zeuxidas, Antippus, Tellis, Alcinadas, Empedias, Menas, and Daphilus. And for the Athenians, Lampon, Isthmionicus, Nicias, Laches, Euthydemus, Procles, Pythodorus, Hagnon, Myrtilus, Thrasycles, Theagenes, Aristocrates, Iolcius, Timocrates, Leon, Lamachus, and Demosthenes."

20. This treaty was concluded as winter was turning into spring, right after the City Dionysia festival, when exactly ten years had passed, plus a few days, since the beginning of the current war.† [2] The way to assess the length of the war is by the passage of time; one should not rely on the lists of archons or other officials of this or that place whose names are used to date past events. This is not an accurate method, because an event might have occurred at the beginning or in the middle or at any point in their terms of office. [3] But the method of counting by summers and winters, as adopted in this work, shows, since each of these seasons is equivalent to half a year, that there were ten summers and ten winters in this first war.

21. Lots were drawn and it fell to the Lacedaemonians to be the first to return what they held. They immediately released the men they held as prisoners and sent Ischagoras, Menas, and Philocharidas as envoys to the Thraceward region to order Clearidas to hand Amphipolis over to the Athenians and to tell everyone else to comply with the terms of the treaty as they applied to them. [2] But their allies regarded the treaty as not in their best interests and refused to comply with it, and because he wanted to remain on good terms with the Chalcidians Clearidas refused to surrender Amphipolis, arguing that he could not do so without their consent. [3] But he quickly left Amphipolis with the envoys and went to Sparta to defend himself in person, in case Ischagoras and his colleagues should accuse him of disobedience, and also because he wanted to know if the agreement was still alterable. But he found that the Lacedaemonians were bound by their oaths, and when they sent him back again with orders to surrender the place, or at least to pull out all the Peloponnesians who were in it, he set off right away.

22. It so happened that the allies were in Sparta again, and the Lacedaemonians ordered those of them who found the treaty unacceptable to implement it. But the allies gave the same reason for rejecting it as before and said they could only agree to a treaty that was less unjust than this one. [2] Faced with their intransigence, the Lacedaemonians dismissed them and entered into an alliance with the Athenians by themselves. Their thinking was that the Argives were highly unlikely to renew the treaty with them,* since they had already refused when Ampelidas and Lichas had gone as envoys to Argos; that the Argives without the Athenians were no real threat; and that, since the rest of the Peloponnesians would turn to the Athenians for help if the opportunity arose, this alliance would guarantee that they did nothing of the sort. [3] So when envoys had come from Athens and discussions had taken place, they entered into an agreement and swore oaths of alliance as follows:

23. "The Lacedaemonians and the Athenians shall be allies for fifty years on the following terms: If hostile forces enter Lacedaemonian territory and harm the Lacedaemonians, the Athenians are to aid the Lacedaemonians in whatever way they can, employing all the strength

at their command. If the invader departs, leaving the land ravaged, the city in question shall be the enemy of the Lacedaemonians and the Athenians and shall be made to suffer by both, and the two of them shall end hostilities at the same time. They shall act throughout with justice and determination and without deceit. [2] If any enemy enters Athenian territory and harms the Athenians, the Lacedaemonians are to aid the Athenians in whatever way they can, employing all the strength at their command. If the invader departs, leaving the land ravaged, the city in question shall be the enemy of the Lacedaemonians and the Athenians and shall be made to suffer by both, and the two of them shall end hostilities at the same time. They shall act together with justice and determination and without deceit. [3] If the enslaved population rises up in revolt,* the Athenians are to assist the Lacedaemonians with all the strength at their command. [4] On each side, the same people shall swear to these things who swore to the other treaty. The oath is to be reaffirmed every year when the Lacedaemonians go to Athens for the Dionysia and the Athenians go to Sparta for the Hyacinthia. [5] Each party is to place a stele inscribed with the terms of the alliance, the one in Sparta by the temple of Apollo in the Amyclaeum and the one in Athens by the temple of Athena on the acropolis. [6] If the Athenians and the Lacedaemonians decide that anything needs to be added to or deleted from the terms of the alliance, whatever they decide shall be no violation of the oaths for either party. **24.** The oath was sworn by the following Lacedaemonians: Pleistoanax, Agis, Pleistolas, Damagetus, Chionis, Metagenes, Acanthus, Daithus, Ischagoras, Philocharidas, Zeuxidas, Antippus, Alcinadas, Tellis, Empedias, Menas, and Daphilus. And by the following Athenians: Lampon, Isthmionicus, Laches, Nicias, Euthydemus, Procles, Pythodorus, Hagnon, Myrtilus, Thrasycles, Theagenes, Aristocrates, Iolcius, Timocrates, Leon, Lamachus, and Demosthenes."

[2] This alliance was made not long after the peace treaty, and the Athenians returned the prisoners they held from Sphacteria to the Lacedaemonians. This was at the beginning of the summer of the

eleventh year of the war. Here ends my account of the first war, which went on continuously for these ten years.

25. Following the peace treaty and the alliance between the Lacedaemonians and the Athenians, which were entered into after the ten-year war, in the ephorate of Pleistolas in Sparta and the archonship of Alcaeus in Athens, those who accepted the treaty were at peace, but the Corinthians and some of the Peloponnesian cities were trying to sabotage the arrangements, and this immediately led to further turbulence between Sparta and its allies. [2] Moreover, as time went on, the Athenians came to mistrust the Lacedaemonians because they were failing to implement some of the provisions of the agreement. [3] And although they refrained from attacking each other's land for six years and ten months, elsewhere the suspension of hostilities was insecure, and they made as much trouble for each other as they could. And eventually they were in fact compelled to break the treaty that had brought the ten-year war to an end and there was a resumption of open war.

26. The following account of events, also written by Thucydides of Athens, goes in chronological order, with the narrative divided into summers and winters, up to the time when the Lacedaemonians and their allies brought the Athenian empire to an end and captured the Long Walls and Piraeus.* This moment arrived after a total of twenty-seven years of warfare. [2] It would be quite wrong for anyone to claim that the intervening stretch of time while the peace treaty was in force was not one of warfare. Anyone who wants to say this should look at what actually distinguishes peace from war, and he will find it implausible to think of this period as one of peace, when the two sides neither returned nor received everything that had been agreed in the treaty, and when, apart from this, they violated the treaty in the Mantinean and Epidaurian wars, and in other respects as well; the allies in the Thraceward region were as hostile as ever toward Athens; and the truce that the Boeotians observed was one that had to be renewed every ten days. [3] So anyone who adds up the actual periods of time will find that the total of the first war, the ten-year one, and the dubious peace that followed it, and the later war after that, is indeed twenty-seven years, plus a few days. And he will also find that this was the only time when people who confidently assert something on the strength of oracles were to be trusted, [4] because I remember that throughout the war, from beginning to end, there were many who prophesied that it was bound to last for "thrice nine years."

[5] I lived through the whole war. I was old enough to be in full possession of my faculties, and I paid close attention to make sure that I would have precise knowledge of every detail. In fact, I was banished from my country for twenty years after my generalship at Amphipolis, and so I was able to acquaint myself with the affairs of both sides (especially those of the Peloponnesians, given that I was in exile from Athens) and to regard them calmly and collectedly.* [6] So I shall now give an account of the dispute that arose after the ten-year war and the breach of the peace treaty, and then the subsequent course of the war.

27. After the conclusion of the fifty-year peace and the subsequent alliance, the delegates from the Peloponnese who had been summoned to the negotiations left Sparta. [2] The others went straight back home, but the Corinthian delegates turned aside to visit Argos first. They met with some of the city's leading politicians and argued that since the Lacedaemonians had entered into a treaty and alliance with their former bitter enemies, the Athenians, and had done so not for any good purpose but in order to enslave the Peloponnese, it was up to the Argives to see to its salvation. They should pass a resolution, the Corinthians suggested, to the effect that any independent Greek city that was prepared to submit to a fair and impartial judgment on the matter could, if it so wished, enter into a defensive alliance with the Argives; and they should appoint just a few commissioners with full authority to manage the business without having to consult the people, because if the people were involved, and they rejected a city's application, the fact that the city had applied for an alliance would be public knowledge. And they claimed that hatred of

the Lacedaemonians was so widespread that many cities would want to join. [3] Once the Corinthians had made these recommendations, they went back home.

28. In response to the Corinthians' arguments, the Argives to whom they had spoken referred the proposal to their council and popular assembly, and the Argives passed the resolution and chose twelve men with whom any of the Greeks who so wished could negotiate with a view to forming an alliance, apart from Athens and Sparta, neither of which was allowed to join the prospective league without the consent of the Argive people. [2] The Argives were more ready to accept the proposal because it was clear that there was going to be war with Sparta anyway, since their treaty with them was on the point of expiring, and also because they hoped to become the leading state in the Peloponnese. At this time Sparta had a very poor reputation, and its reverses had made it an object of contempt, while Argos was in excellent condition in all respects, because it had not taken part in the Athenian War,* and had reaped the benefits of having a treaty in place with both the Lacedaemonians and the Athenians. [3] So the Argives were ready to receive into their alliance any of the Greek states that so wished.

29. The Mantineans and their allies were the first to go over to them, out of fear of the Lacedaemonians. The reason for this fear was that, while the war with Athens was still ongoing, the Mantineans had forcibly subjected a part of Arcadia, and they thought that, since the Lacedaemonians now had nothing else going on, they would not tolerate their rule there. So they were glad to turn to Argos, which they considered a great city and a constant enemy of Sparta, and which had a democratic constitution, just as they did. [2] After the defection of the Mantineans, there was muttering in the rest of the Peloponnesian cities as well that they should do likewise. They thought the Mantineans had changed sides because they had special knowledge of some kind, and at the same time they were angry with the Lacedaemonians, not least because it was stated in the treaty of alliance with Athens that it was no violation of the oaths for the Lacedaemonians and the Athenians to add something to the treaty or delete something from it, if they saw fit to do so. [3] The Peloponnesians found this clause particularly disturbing; it led them to suspect that the Lacedaemonians might want to enslave them with Athenian help, because, in all justice, the clause should have read that any amendment was to be agreed by all the allies, not just the Lacedaemonians and Athenians. [4] So out of fear most of them were attracted to the idea of following the Mantineans' example and making individual alliances with Argos.

30. When all this muttering in the Peloponnese came to the Lacedaemonians' attention, and they found out that the Corinthians had not only suggested this course of action, but were intending to enter into a treaty with Argos themselves, they sent envoys to Corinth to see if they could nip the movement in the bud. They accused them of being the instigators of the whole business and said that if they deserted Sparta and became allies of Argos they would be in breach of their oaths. They said their refusal to accept the treaty with Athens already put them in the wrong, since the terms of their alliance with Sparta included the clause that a majority vote of the allies was binding, unless there was some impediment from gods or heroes.

[2] The Corinthians, in the presence of all the other allies who, like them, did not accept the treaty (the Corinthians had summoned them earlier), argued back against the Lacedaemonians. They did not openly state their real grievances—that the Lacedaemonians had not recovered Sollium or Anactorium from the Athenians for them, and that there were other respects in which they considered themselves to have been left at a disadvantage—but offered the pretext that they would not betray their friends in the Thraceward region. When these friends of theirs had first joined Potidaea in rebellion, the Corinthians had concluded individual treaties with each of them, and later they had made other commitments under oath as well. [3] They therefore denied that their refusal to be included in the treaty with the Athenians constituted a transgression of their oaths to the allies, on the grounds that they had given pledges, sworn in the name of the gods,

to these allies of theirs and would not violate and betray these oaths. The wording was "unless there is some impediment from gods or heroes," and this seemed to them to be precisely a case of an impediment from the gods. [4] That was what they had to say about those long-standing oaths of theirs; as for an alliance with Argos, they would consult with their friends and decide what it was right for them to do. [5] So the Lacedaemonian envoys returned home. There were envoys from Argos also in Corinth, who urged the Corinthians to enter into the alliance with them without delay, and the Corinthians told them to be sure to come to the next meeting in Corinth.

31. A delegation also promptly came from Elis. They first made an alliance with the Corinthians, and then they went from Corinth to Argos, as they had been instructed, and became allies of the Argives. The Eleans and the Lacedaemonians had fallen out over Lepreum.* [2] Sometime in the past there had been a war between Lepreum and some of the Arcadians, and the Lepreates had asked the Eleans for an alliance on the understanding that they would be given half of their territory if they won. Once they had brought the war to an end, the Eleans allowed the Lepreates to cultivate the designated land themselves and fixed a rent of a talent a year to be paid to Olympian Zeus. [3] The Lepreates paid this rent up until the start of the war with Athens, but then they used the war as an excuse to stop, and when the Eleans applied pressure the Lepreates turned to the Lacedaemonians. When the matter was submitted to the Lacedaemonians for arbitration, the Eleans, suspecting that they would not get a fair hearing, gave up on arbitration and began to ravage the Lepreates' land. [4] But the Lacedaemonians still ruled that the Lepreates were an autonomous people and that the Eleans were in the wrong, and when the Eleans refused to abide by this verdict, the Lacedaemonians installed a hoplite garrison in Lepreum. [5] The Eleans took the view that the Lacedaemonians had accepted as allies a state that had defected from them, and they referred to the clause in the treaty stipulating that what any people held at the start of the Athenian War they were to hold at the end as well; and so, alleging that they were being unfairly treated, they defected to the Argives, and they, too, entered into an alliance with them in the prescribed manner. [6] The Corinthians joined the Argive alliance straight after them, and so did the Chalcidians from the Thraceward region. The Boeotians and the Megarians, however, agreed between themselves not to get involved; they wanted to see what the Lacedaemonians would do, and they thought that, as they had oligarchic constitutions, the Argive democracy was a worse fit for them than the Lacedaemonians' form of government.

32. This summer, at about the same time, the Athenians brought their siege of Scione to a successful conclusion. They put all the adult males to death, sold the children and women into slavery, and gave the Plataeans the land to occupy. They also allowed the Delians to return to Delos, because they were seriously concerned about their military setbacks, and the god in Delphi had so instructed them in an oracle. [2] And the Phocians and Locrians went to war with each other.

[3] Now that the Corinthians and Argives were allies, they went to Tegea to try to get it to defect from Sparta. Bearing in mind that it possessed a sizable portion of the Peloponnese, they thought that, if it came over to their side, they would be well on their way to gaining all of it. [4] But the Tegeans said they would do nothing to oppose the Lacedaemonians. At this point, the Corinthians, who up until then had been determinedly pushing ahead with the negotiations, eased up on their contentiousness and became afraid that none of the others would come over to their side. [5] Nevertheless, they went to the Boeotians and asked them to become allies of themselves and the Argives and in general to act in concert with them. They also asked the Boeotians to form a joint mission with them to Athens, and to arrange for them the same kind of truce that the Boeotians had with the Athenians, the kind that had to be renewed every ten days, which the Athenians and Boeotians had concluded with each other shortly

after the fifty-year treaty had come into force. And the Corinthians asked the Boeotians to renounce their truce with the Athenians if the Athenians rejected the proposal, and from then on to make no treaties without their own involvement. [6] In response to the Corinthians' pleas, the Boeotians told them to defer the matter of the alliance with Argos, but they did accompany them to Athens. They failed to obtain the ten-day truce for them, however; the Athenians told the Corinthians that they already had a truce with them—that is, if they were allies of the Lacedaemonians. [7] But the Boeotians still did not renounce their ten-day truce, although the Corinthians begged them to and protested that they had agreed to do so. So the Corinthians had no more than a de facto truce with the Athenians.

33. In the same summer, the Lacedaemonians marched at full strength, under the command of their king Pleistoanax, son of Pausanias, against the Parrasians in Arcadia, who were subjects of the Mantineans. Their help had been requested by a faction of the Parrasians, and they also hoped to destroy the fortress at Cypsela. This fortress, built and garrisoned by the Mantineans, was situated in Parrasian territory and commanded the Sciritis region of Laconia. [2] The Lacedaemonians laid waste Parrasian farmland, and the Mantineans left their city garrisoned by Argives while they protected the territory of their allies. But they withdrew when it proved impossible for them to save either the Cypsela fortress or the Parrasian villages. [3] The Lacedaemonians gave the Parrasians the right of self-government, and after demolishing the fortress they returned home.

34. In the same summer, on the return to Sparta from Thrace of the soldiers who had gone there with Brasidas—they had been brought back by Clearidas after the peace treaty—the Lacedaemonians voted that the helots who had fought under Brasidas were to be free and could live wherever they chose. And shortly afterward, since they were now at odds with the Eleans, they settled them along with some freedmen at Lepreum, on the border between Laconia and Elis.

[2] They also dealt with the men from Sphacteria who had surrendered their weapons and been taken alive. The Lacedaemonians were afraid that these men, expecting their status to be reduced, might stir up trouble while they were still full citizens, so they disenfranchised them, even though some of them were in office. As noncitizens, they could neither hold office nor be the principals in any commercial transaction. Later, however, they became full citizens again.

35. And another thing that happened this summer is that the people of Dium took over Thyssus, a town on the Athos peninsula that was an ally of Athens.

[2] Throughout the summer there were diplomatic exchanges between the Athenians and the Peloponnesians, but no sooner was the treaty in place than both sides became suspicious of each other over the non-return of the places stipulated in the treaty. [3] The Lacedaemonians had drawn the lot to be the first to return what they held, but they had not given back Amphipolis and the other places. Furthermore, they were not inducing their allies in the Thraceward region, the Boeotians, or the Corinthians to accept the treaty, despite the fact that they were constantly saying they would ask for Athenian help in forcing the holdouts to accept it; and they proposed—though without committing themselves in writing—time limits, after which those who were refusing to be included in the treaty were to be declared enemies of both themselves and the Athenians. [4] So when the Athenians saw that none of this was actually happening, they began to suspect that the Lacedaemonians had no intention of doing what was right, and they refused to return Pylos when the Lacedaemonians demanded it. They even began to regret that they had returned the prisoners from Sphacteria, and they hung on to the other places while waiting for the Lacedaemonians to keep their promises.

[5] The Lacedaemonians, for their part, claimed to have done all they could. They had returned the Athenian prisoners they held, had withdrawn their troops from the Thraceward region, and had done

everything else that it was in their power to do. They claimed that the return of Amphipolis was out of their hands, but that they would do their best to get the Boeotians and Corinthians to include themselves in the treaty, and would try to get Panactum back and to recover all the Athenian prisoners who were in Boeotian hands. [6] But they demanded the return of Pylos, or at least the evacuation of the Messenians and helots from the place, as a quid pro quo for their evacuation of their troops from Thrace, and said that the Athenians could garrison the place themselves if they wanted. [7] And after frequent meetings and much discussion during the summer, they succeeded in persuading the Athenians to withdraw from Pylos the Messenians and the others, helots and deserters from Laconia. [8] The Athenians settled these people in Crane in Cephallenia.* So there was no warlike activity this summer and no attacks by one side against the other.

36. The following winter, however, there was a fresh board of ephors in Sparta, since the term of office of those who had made the treaty had come to an end—and some of the new ephors were actually opposed to it. Envoys from the Lacedaemonian allies arrived for a meeting in Sparta, at which there were also present delegates from Athens, Boeotia, and Corinth. A great deal of discussion took place but no terms were agreed, and when they were leaving for home, Cleoboulus and Xenares, the two ephors who particularly wanted to sabotage the treaty, held private talks with the Boeotians and the Corinthians. They advised them to coordinate their policies as much as possible, and they urged the Boeotians first to ally themselves with the Argives, and then with the help of the Corinthians to get the Lacedaemonians to become allies of the Argives. If that happened, they thought, it would reduce to a minimum the pressure on the Boeotians to enter into an alliance with the Athenians. And given a choice, they said, the Lacedaemonians would choose to have the Argives as their friends and allies even if the consequences were the hostility of the Athenians and the dissolution of the treaty. The two ephors knew that friendship

with Argos on fair and honorable terms was something the Lacedaemonians always desired, because it would make it less risky for them to make war outside the Peloponnese. [2] However, they urged the Boeotians to hand Panactum over to the Lacedaemonians,† so that the Lacedaemonians stood a chance of getting Pylos back in exchange for it, which would put them in a better position to renew the war with Athens.

37. Having been given these instructions by Xenares, Cleoboulus, and the ephors' supporters in Sparta, the Boeotians and Corinthians left Sparta to deliver their reports to their respective communities. [2] But two of the highest officers of Argos were watching out for them on the road as they left. These two Argives joined them and discussed with them the possibility that the Boeotians might join the Corinthians, Eleans, and Mantineans in becoming allies of Argos. In their opinion, they said, if this went ahead and they followed the same policy, it would be easy for them to make war or peace even with Sparta, if they wanted, and with any other state if the need arose. [3] The Boeotian envoys were delighted to hear this, because, by happy coincidence, it meshed perfectly with what their friends in Sparta had told them to do. When the two Argives saw that they were open to the idea, they left, saying they would send envoys to the Boeotians. [4] When the Boeotian envoys got back home, they gave the boeotarchs a report of the discussion in Sparta and the discussion they had had with the Argives they had met. The boeotarchs were delighted and became all the more committed to their plans, because it had turned out that not only were their friends in Sparta asking for the same things that they wanted, but the Argives were also pursuing the same goal. [5] And before long, envoys arrived from Argos with the proposals mentioned above. The boeotarchs thanked them for their offer and sent them away after promising to dispatch envoys to Argos to negotiate the alliance.

38. At this point, the boeotarchs, the Corinthians, the Megarians, and the envoys from Thrace agreed among themselves that they would first swear oaths to the effect that they would come to the defense

BOOK FIVE: 36-39

of one another as the need arose, and would not go to war or make peace with any state unless they all agreed to do so, and that once this covenant was in place the Boeotians and Megarians (who were working together) would join the Argive alliance. [2] But before this agreement had been ratified by oaths, the boeotarchs briefed the four councils of the Boeotians about it—these councils are the supreme authority in Boeotia*—and recommended that a pact be made with any state that wanted to join them in a sworn pledge of mutual assistance. [3] But the Boeotian councilors rejected the proposal because they were afraid of going against the Lacedaemonians by making a pact with the Corinthians who had defected from them. This happened because the boeotarchs did not brief the councils about what had happened in Sparta—that the ephors Cleoboulus and Xenares, and their supporters, had advised them first to form an alliance with Argos and Corinth and then to do the same with the Lacedaemonians themselves—because they believed that even without this information the councils would not vote for a course of action other than what the boeotarchs had already decided on and were recommending. [4] And so the project was frustrated. The Corinthians and the envoys from Thrace left empty-handed, and the boeotarchs, who had previously been intending to try to arrange an alliance with Argos if they had won over the councilors, stopped bringing proposals about Argos before the councils and did not send the envoys to Argos as they had promised. The whole issue became subject to indifference and deferral.

39. In this same winter, the Olynthians launched a sudden attack on Mecyberna, which was garrisoned by Athenians, and captured it.* [2] Talks went on continually between the Athenians and Lacedaemonians about the places each held that belonged to the other, and the Lacedaemonians came to hope that if the Athenians got Panactum back from the Boeotians, they themselves would recover Pylos. So they sent envoys to the Boeotians and asked them to hand over both Panactum and the Athenians they had in captivity, so that they could recover Pylos in exchange for them. [3] But the Boeotians refused to do this unless the Lacedaemonians entered into a separate alliance with them, as they had with the Athenians. The Lacedaemonians knew that this would put them in the wrong with the Athenians, because it was stipulated in their treaty that neither of them was to make peace with or war on anyone without the other's consent. But because they wanted to take over Panactum, in order to exchange it for Pylos, and also because those who were pushing for the annulment of the treaty were committed to the arrangements with the Boeotians, they did make the alliance—this happened as winter was turning into spring—and the demolition of Panactum was immediately put in hand.* And so the eleventh year of the war came to an end.

40. Very early the following summer, the Argives had reasons for concern. The promised Boeotian envoys had not come, and they found out that Panactum was being demolished, and that there was now a separate alliance in place between the Boeotians and the Lacedaemonians, so they became afraid that all their allies would go over to the Lacedaemonians, leaving them isolated. [2] They thought that it was the Lacedaemonians who had persuaded the Boeotians to demolish Panactum and to be included in the treaty with Athens, and that the Athenians knew this, which meant that it would no longer be possible for them to enter into an alliance even with the Athenians. Previously, as a result of the antagonism between the Athenians and Lacedaemonians, they had hoped that if their treaty with the Lacedaemonians was not renewed they would at least have the Athenians as allies. [3] So with that avenue closed to them, and because they were afraid of facing simultaneous war from the Lacedaemonians, Tegeans, Boeotians, and Athenians, the Argives—who had previously rejected the treaty with the Lacedaemonians, and had entertained the proud hope of becoming the leading state in the Peloponnese—lost no time in sending envoys to Sparta. They sent people they thought the Lacedaemonians would find particularly congenial—Eustrophus and Aeson—because it seemed to them that the best course open to them in the circumstances was to secure a treaty with the Lacedaemonians on whatever terms could be agreed and then to remain inactive.

41. On their arrival, the Argive envoys began discussing with the Lacedaemonians the terms on which a treaty might be made. [2] At first, the Argives requested an arbitrator—either a city or an individual person—to settle the matter of Cynouria, which was a constant bone of contention because it was on the border between them. (Cynouria contains the Thyreatis district and the town of Anthene, and was occupied by the Lacedaemonians.) But then, although the Lacedaemonians refused to allow the matter to be raised, but indicated their willingness, if the Argives so wished, to make a treaty on the same terms as the previous one, the Argive envoys nevertheless induced the Lacedaemonians to agree to the following terms: that for the time being they should enter into a peace treaty for fifty years, but that it was open to either side, after having declared its intention and provided that neither Sparta nor Argos was suffering from plague or war, to decide the issue of Cynouria by warfare (as they had previously, when each of them had claimed victory),* but with no pursuit allowed of the defeated side beyond the border of either Argos or Sparta. [3] At first, the Lacedaemonians considered this a ludicrous notion, but because they really wanted the Argives as friends, they subsequently agreed to the terms the Argives were demanding and had the treaty drawn up in draft form. But they told the envoys that, before it was all finalized, they should first return to Argos and show the document to the assembled people, and if they were happy with it the Argives should send envoys to the Hyacinthia festival for the exchange of oaths. And so the envoys left.

42. While the Argives were going about this business, the Lacedaemonian envoys Andromedes, Phaedimus, and Antimenidas, who had been tasked with recovering Panactum and the prisoners from the Boeotians and returning them to the Athenians, found that Panactum had been demolished by the Boeotians on their own initiative. The reason the Boeotians gave was that long ago, after a dispute had arisen between them and the Athenians over the place, the two parties had sworn that neither of them should occupy it, but they were to make use of the land together. But the Boeotians did release the Athenian prisoners they held, and Andromedes and his colleagues conveyed them to Athens and handed them over. They also told the Athenians about the demolition of Panactum, thinking that they were handing it back too, in the sense that it would no longer be occupied by an enemy of Athens. [2] But the Athenians took this news very badly. In their opinion, they had been wronged by the Lacedaemonians, not just because of the demolition of Panactum, which was supposed to be returned to them intact, but also because they found out that the Lacedaemonians had entered into a separate alliance with the Boeotians, despite the fact that they had earlier promised to join the Athenians in coercing those who were refusing to accept the treaty. Then they started considering all the other ways in which the Lacedaemonians had defaulted on the agreement and began to regard themselves as the victims of deceit, and the upshot was that they replied angrily to the envoys and sent them packing.

43. With the Lacedaemonians and the Athenians at odds over this, those in Athens, too, who wanted the treaty to be annulled immediately began to press their case. [2] One of these warmongers was Alcibiades, son of Cleinias.* In any other city, he would have been regarded as still a young man at the time, but in Athens he was respected for the dignity of his ancestry. He certainly believed that it was better for the Athenians to look to Argos rather than Sparta, but nevertheless his opposition was also due to personal pride and his longing for supremacy. He resented the fact that the Lacedaemonians had negotiated the treaty through Nicias and Laches and had overlooked him because of his youth, rather than giving him the honor in keeping with his family's long-standing tradition of representing Lacedaemonian interests in Athens. His grandfather had renounced this office, but Alcibiades intended to revive it by seeing that the Lacedaemonian prisoners from Sphacteria were well treated. [3] One way and another, then, he felt that he was being slighted, and he opposed the treaty right from the start. He said that the Lacedaemonians were not to be trusted, but had made the treaty with Athens in order to crush the Argives with the help of their new treaty partners, and then renew their attacks on a now isolated Athens. So at the time in question, as soon as the Athenians and Lacedaemonians had fallen out, he got in touch with the Argives of his own accord, telling them to come to Athens as soon as possible to propose an alliance, and to bring the Mantineans and Eleans as well. He said that this was a golden opportunity and that he himself would do all he could to help them.

44. After hearing Alcibiades's offer, and because they now knew that the Athenians had not been involved in the negotiations leading to the Lacedaemonian alliance with the Boeotians, and that there was in fact a high level of tension between the Athenians and the Lacedaemonians, the Argives began to care less about their envoys in Sparta, who were there to negotiate a treaty, and to incline more toward Athens. They took the view that the Athenians had been their friends for a long time, that they had a democratic constitution like themselves, and that, given their great power at sea, they would be valuable allies if war broke out. [2] So they immediately sent envoys to Athens to discuss an alliance, and their envoys were joined by representatives of the Eleans and Mantineans.

[3] But envoys arrived in haste from Sparta as well. The delegation consisted of men who the Lacedaemonians thought would be most acceptable to the Athenians—Philocharidas, Leon, and Endius. The Lacedaemonians were worried that the Athenians would conclude the alliance with the Argives in a fit of anger, and the envoys were also to ask for the return of Pylos in exchange for Panactum, and to defend the Lacedaemonian alliance with the Boeotians on the ground that it meant no harm to the Athenians. 45. They addressed the council on these matters and explained that they had come with full authority to settle all the disputes between them. This worried Alcibiades. He thought that if they repeated in the popular assembly what they had

told the council, they would win over the people and the alliance with Argos would be rejected. [2] So he employed the following trick to dupe the Lacedaemonian envoys. By assuring them of his trustworthiness, he got them to believe that if, when they addressed the assembly, they made no mention of the fact that they had come with full authority, he would see that Pylos was returned to them; he would win the Athenians over as effectively as he was currently opposing them on this issue, and he would bring about a reconciliation on all the other outstanding matters as well. [3] He had two reasons for doing this: he wanted to distance the envoys from Nicias, and he thought that if he could discredit them in the eyes of the Athenian people, as men who had no honest intentions and were utterly inconsistent in what they said, he could bring about the alliance with the Argives, Eleans, and Mantineans. [4] And that is exactly what happened. When the Lacedaemonian envoys came before the people and were questioned, they contradicted what they had said in the council and denied that they had come with full authority. At this, the Athenians lost patience with them, and when Alcibiades denounced the Lacedaemonians even more forcefully than before, they hung on his words and were ready to invite the Argives and their partners into the assembly and make them allies on the spot. But an earthquake occurred before the alliance could be ratified, and this assembly was postponed.

46. At the assembly the next day, although Nicias, too, had been taken in by the trick that had actually been designed to dupe the Lacedaemonians and had led them to deny that they had come with full powers, he still claimed that it was best for them to be on good terms with the Lacedaemonians, and he proposed that they should defer the issue of their relationship with Argos and send another embassy to the Lacedaemonians to find out what their intentions were. He argued that the continued avoidance of war was good for Athens, because, since the city was thriving, it was in its best interests to preserve this prosperity as long as possible, but did not suit the Lacedaemonians, who were in a bad way, and for whom, therefore, any excuse to risk all through warfare would be a godsend. [2] In short, he persuaded the Athenians to send an embassy to Sparta, consisting of himself and others, with the job of telling the Lacedaemonians that if their intentions were honest, they should return to them both Panactum, with the fortress rebuilt, and Amphipolis, and should annul the alliance with the Boeotians if the Boeotians continued to refuse to be included in the treaty, in compliance with the stipulation that neither of them was to enter into a treaty with anyone else without the other's consent. [3] The Athenians also told the envoys to say that if they, the Athenians, had wanted to violate the agreement, they would by now have entered into an alliance with the Argives, who were in Athens for precisely that purpose. So they sent Nicias and his fellow envoys off to Sparta with thorough instructions as to what to say about this matter and the other complaints they had.

[4] The envoys arrived in Sparta and delivered their message. They concluded by saying that, in the event that the Boeotians continued to refuse to be included in the treaty, if the Lacedaemonians did not annul their alliance with them the Athenians would enter into an alliance with the Argives and their partners. The Lacedaemonians, prevailed upon by the ephor Xenares and his supporters, refused to annul the alliance with the Boeotians, but at Nicias's request they did reaffirm their oaths. Nicias was afraid that if he returned home completely empty-handed he would be vilified—as indeed he was—because he was held to have been responsible for the treaty with the Lacedaemonians. [5] And on his return, when the Athenians heard of his complete failure in Sparta, they became furious with him. They judged that they had been wronged by the Lacedaemonians, and when Alcibiades introduced the Argives and their allies into the assembly they made a treaty of alliance with them as follows:

47. "A treaty was made for a hundred years between the Athenians and the Argives, Mantineans, and Eleans on behalf of themselves and each party's subject allies, without deceit or damage, by land and by sea. [2] It shall not be permitted for them to bear arms against each other with harmful intent, neither the Argives, Eleans, Mantineans, and their allies against the Athenians and their subject allies, nor the Athenians and their allies against the Argives, Eleans, Mantineans, and their allies, by any means or contrivance. [3] On the following terms the Athenians, and the Argives, Eleans, and Mantineans, are to be allies for a hundred years: If hostile forces attack Athenian territory, the Argives, Eleans, and Mantineans are to go to Athens to help, following a request by the Athenians, in whatever way they can, employing all the strength at their command. If the invader departs, leaving the land ravaged, the city in question shall be the enemy of the Argives, Mantineans, Eleans, and Athenians, and shall be made to suffer by all these states. It shall not be permitted for any of these states to bring the war against the city in question to an end unless it is so agreed by all of them. [4] And the Athenians are to go to help Argos, Mantinea, and Elis if hostile forces attack the territory of the Eleans or the Mantineans or the Argives, following a request by these states, in whatever way they can, employing all the strength at their command. If the invader departs, leaving the land ravaged, the city in question shall be the enemy of the Athenians, and of the Argives, Mantineans, and Eleans, and shall be made to suffer by all these states. It shall not be permitted for any of these states to bring the war against the city in question to an end unless it is so agreed by all of them. [5] They shall not allow armed men to pass for the purpose of war through their own territory or that of their respective subject allies, nor by sea, unless all the states—the Athenians, Argives, Mantineans, and Eleans—have voted to allow the passage. [6] The state that sends troops to the aid of another is to provide a maintenance allowance for up to thirty days from the time of† their arrival at the city that requested help, and shall likewise provide for their return. If the troops are needed for a longer time, the city that summoned them is to maintain them. It shall provide every hoplite, light-armed soldier, and archer with three Aeginetan obols a day, and every cavalryman with one Aeginetan drachma. [7] The city that summoned help is to have the leadership of the army when the fighting is in its own territory. If all four states decide on a joint campaign, they are all to share equally in the command. [8] The Athenians are to swear to the treaty on behalf of themselves and their allies, and the Argives, Mantineans, Eleans, and their allies are to swear city by city. The oath is to be sworn over unblemished sacrificial victims in the most binding fashion recognized by each city. The oath is to be as follows: 'I shall abide by this treaty of alliance, complying with its terms justly and without deceit, and I shall not transgress it by any means or contrivance.' [9] In Athens the oath is to be sworn by the council and the home authorities, and administered by the prytaneis. In Argos, it is to be sworn by the council and the Eighty and the Coordinators, and administered by the Eighty. In Mantinea, it is to be sworn by the Ministers of the People and the council and the other officers, and administered by the members of the Sacred College and the War Leaders. In Elis, it is to be sworn by the Ministers of the People and the holders of political offices and the Six Hundred, and administered by the Ministers of the People and the Guardians of the Laws. [10] The oath is to be reaffirmed by the Athenians going to Elis, Mantinea, and Argos thirty days before the Olympic festival, and by the Argives, Eleans, and Mantineans going to Athens ten days before the Great Panathenaea. [11] The Athenians are to inscribe the terms of the agreement that pertain to the treaty, the oaths, and the alliance on a stone stele on the acropolis.* The Argives are to do the same in the sanctuary of Apollo in the agora, and the Mantineans in the sanctuary of Zeus in the agora. All the states together are to erect a bronze stele in Olympia during this year's Olympic festival. [12] If all the states together decide that some improvement needs to be added to the terms of this agreement, whatever they all decide after deliberating together shall be authoritative."

48. These were the terms of the treaty of alliance. This treaty, however, did not lead to a renunciation by the Lacedaemonians and the Athenians of the treaty between them. [2] But the Corinthians, despite being allies of the Argives, did not include themselves in this new alliance, nor had they joined an alliance that the Eleans, Argives, and Mantineans had earlier made with one another when they swore to treat the same states as enemies or friends. They said they were satisfied with the original defensive alliance, whereby the parties swore to help one another if they were attacked, but would not join them in campaigning against others. [3] So the Corinthians distanced themselves from their allies and began to incline once more toward Sparta.

49. The Olympic festival took place this summer—this was the one at which Androsthenes of Arcadia was victorious in the pancratium for the first time—and the Lacedaemonians were excluded from the sanctuary by the Eleans, which meant they could not take part in the sacrifices or compete in the games. The exclusion was for nonpayment of the fine the Eleans had imposed on the Lacedaemonians in accordance with Olympic law, claiming that they had attacked the fortress of Phyrcus and had sent hoplites into Lepreum, an Elean possession, during the Olympic truce.* The fine was two thousand minas—that is, two minas for each hoplite, as prescribed by the law.

[2] The Lacedaemonians sent representatives and argued that the guilty verdict was unfair, because the truce had not yet been proclaimed in Sparta when they sent in the hoplites. [3] But the Eleans said that the truce was already in force in Elis† (which is the first place where it is proclaimed), and that consequently this act of aggression had taken them unawares, since they were at peace and off their guard, as is normal at a time when a treaty is in force. [4] In response to this the Lacedaemonians said that the Eleans should not have proclaimed the truce in Sparta if they already thought it had been transgressed; the fact that they did so showed they did not think they had been wronged, and they pointed out that after the proclamation they had not attacked them anywhere. [5] The Eleans stuck to their original argument and refused to be persuaded of the Lacedaemonians' innocence; but, they said, if the Lacedaemonians were willing to return Lepreum to them, they would waive the part of the fine that was owed to them, and they themselves would pay on behalf of the Lacedaemonians what was due to the god.

50. When the Lacedaemonians rejected this offer, the Eleans next suggested that if the Lacedaemonians did not wish to return Lepreum, what they could do instead, since they were so keen on having access to the sanctuary, was ascend the altar of Zeus at Olympia and swear in the presence of the Greeks that they would pay the fine at a later date. [2] But since the Lacedaemonians also rejected this offer, they were excluded from the sanctuary† and did their sacrificing at home, while the rest of the Greeks, except for the people of Lepreum, sent their delegates to the festival. [3] But the Eleans were still afraid that the Lacedaemonians might force their way into the festival, so they had some of their young men stand guard under arms, and these troops were joined by a thousand from each of Argos and Mantinea, and some Athenian cavalrymen, who had all been waiting at Harpine for the festival to start. [4] Nevertheless, the festival-goers were terrified that the Lacedaemonians might make an armed incursion, especially when a Lacedaemonian—Lichas, son of Arcesilas—was flogged by the umpires in the arena. His winning chariot had been entered as belonging to the Boeotian state because of his debarment from the games, but then, wanting to make clear that the chariot was his, he strode into the arena and crowned the charioteer.* The upshot of this incident was that everyone became much more afraid and expected a drastic response from the Lacedaemonians. But they did nothing and the festival came to a peaceful end.

[5] After the Olympic festival the Argives and their allies went to Corinth to ask them to join their alliance. Envoys from Sparta happened to be there too and there was much discussion, but nothing was resolved, because after an earthquake they all dispersed to their respective homes. And so the summer came to an end.

51. The following winter, a battle took place between the people of Heraclea in Trachis and the Aenianians, Dolopians, Malians, and some Thessalians. [2] These neighboring peoples were hostile to Heraclea because the sole reason the place had been fortified was to pose a threat to their lands.* They were hostile to Heraclea from the moment it came into existence and did their best to destroy it. On the occasion in question, they won the battle against the Heracleots and killed the commanding officer, the Lacedaemonian Xenares, son of Cnidis, along with some Heracleots. So the winter came to an end, and with it the twelfth year of the war.

52. Right at the start of the following summer the Boeotians took over Heraclea—it was in a very bad way after the battle—and dismissed the Lacedaemonian Agesippidas for misgovernment. They took the place over because they were afraid that the Athenians might seize it while the situation in the Peloponnese had the Lacedaemonians reeling. But the Lacedaemonians were enraged by what the Boeotians had done.

[2] In the same summer, with the cooperation of the Argives and their allies, Alcibiades, son of Cleinias, who was one of the Athenian generals for the year, entered the Peloponnese with a small force of Athenian hoplites and archers, which was supplemented by men provided by Athens's allies from thereabouts. He marched through the Peloponnese with this force, settling various matters relating to the alliance as he went. One of the things he did was persuade the people of Patrae to extend their walls down to the sea. He himself was intending to build further fortifications at Rhium (the one in Achaea), but the Corinthians, Sicyonians, and others in whose interests it was that the place not be fortified came up and stopped him.

53. In the same summer war broke out between the Epidaurians and the Argives. The pretext had to do with the sacrificial offering to Apollo Pythaeus, for whose sanctuary the Argives had overall responsibility. The Epidaurians had an obligation to bring a sacrificial victim to the festival in atonement for their butchering of oxen, but they had failed to do so. But even apart from this ground for complaint,

Alcibiades and the Argives wanted to see if they could bring Epidaurus into the Argive alliance. That would keep the Corinthians quiet, and the Athenians would have a shorter route by which to bring help from Aegina to Argos than by sailing around Scyllaeus.* So the Argives, making out that they were doing so on their own initiative, were getting ready to invade Epidaurus in order to enforce the delivery of the sacrificial offering.

54. At much the same time, the Lacedaemonians took to the field at full strength under the command of King Agis, son of Archidamus, and went to Leuctra, which lies on their own border in the direction of Mount Lycaeum.* No one knew what their destination was, not even the cities that supplied troops. [2] But since the border-crossing sacrifices were inauspicious, they returned home and sent word around to their allies to prepare for a campaign after the coming month, which was Carneios,* a sacred month for Dorians. [3] After their withdrawal the Argives set out on the twenty-seventh of the month before Carneios and, counting the whole period of the expedition as that day, the twenty-seventh, they invaded the territory of Epidaurus and laid it waste.* [4] The Epidaurians asked for help from their allies, but some of them used the sacredness of the month as an excuse, while others came up to the border with Epidaurus but took no further action.

55. While the Argives were in Epidaurus, at the invitation of the Athenians envoys from the cities gathered in Mantinea. After some discussion, Euphamidas of Corinth said there was a mismatch between their words and their deeds. Here they were, he said, meeting and talking about peace, while the Epidaurians and their allies and the Argives were under arms and confronting one another; they should first go and get both armies to disband, and then they could resume talking about peace. [2] His proposal met with agreement, and they went and brought the Argives out of Epidaurian territory. Later, however, after the delegates convened again but were still unable to reach an accommodation, the Argives invaded Epidaurus again and laid it waste. [3] The Lacedaemonians also took to the field and went to Caryae,* but since there, too, their border-crossing sacrifices turned out to be unfavorable, they went back home. [4] The Argives ravaged about a third of the territory of Epidaurus and then returned home. They were reinforced by a thousand Athenian hoplites, under the command of the general Alcibiades, who had found out that the Lacedaemonians had taken to the field, but once they were no longer needed they went back to Athens. And so the summer passed.

56. The following winter, undetected by the Athenians, the Lacedaemonians sent a garrison of three hundred under the command of Agesippidas by sea into Epidaurus. [2] The Argives went to Athens and complained that although there was a clause in their treaty to the effect that none of the parties to the treaty was to allow enemies to pass through its own territory, the Athenians had allowed the Lacedaemonians to pass along the coast. They said that unless the Athenians in their turn reinstalled the Messenians and helots in Pylos to harass the Lacedaemonians, they would consider themselves to have been wronged. [3] The Athenians were persuaded by Alcibiades to add at the end of the inscription recording their treaty with Sparta that the Lacedaemonians had not honored their oaths, and they installed the helots from Crane* in Pylos to carry out plundering raids, but otherwise they remained inactive. [4] Throughout the winter no pitched battle took place between the warring Argives and Epidaurians, only ambushes and raids, with some loss of life on both sides. [5] And as winter was turning into spring, the Argives went to Epidaurus with scaling ladders, expecting to find it empty of troops because of the war and therefore capable of being taken by assault, but they failed to achieve their objective and left. So the winter came to an end, and with it the thirteenth year of the war.

57. In the middle of the following summer, the Lacedaemonians marched at full strength against Argos with a force made up of citizens and helots, and commanded by the Spartan king Agis, son of

Archidamus. The Epidaurians, who were allies of theirs, were in trouble, while some of the Peloponnesian states had defected from them and others were disgruntled, so they reckoned that if they did not take preemptive action, and do so quickly, matters would go from bad to worse. [2] The Tegeans and all their other Arcadian allies marched with them, while their allies from the rest of the Peloponnese and beyond mustered at Phleious.* The Boeotians contributed five thousand hoplites, the same number of light-armed troops, and five hundred cavalrymen, each supported by a foot soldier; the Corinthians contributed two thousand hoplites; each of the other states contributed what it could; and the Phleiasians contributed their full levy because the fighting was to take place in their territory.

58. The Argives, however, knew what was going on from the moment the Lacedaemonians began to prepare for the expedition, and when the Lacedaemonians set out to join the rest of their forces at Phleious they took to the field themselves. They were reinforced by the Mantineans, who also brought their own allies, and the Eleans came with three thousand hoplites. [2] They advanced and met the Lacedaemonians at Methydrium in Arcadia,* and each of the two armies occupied a hill. The Argives began to organize themselves to fight the Lacedaemonians while they were on their own, but Agis moved his army during the night, and, without being detected by the Argives, he went to Phleious and linked up with his allies. [3] At daybreak, the Argives realized what had happened. They set out and went first to Argos, but then they took the road toward Nemea, because this was the route they expected the Lacedaemonians and their allies to take down into the plain. [4] Agis, however, did not come by the route the Argives expected him to take. He ordered the Lacedaemonians, Arcadians, and Epidaurians to follow his lead on an alternate route, a difficult one, down into the Argive plain. And the Corinthians, Pellenians, and Phleiasians went by yet another steep route. The Boeotians, Megarians, and Sicyonians, however, were ordered to take the road toward Nemea, where the Argives had taken up a position, so that if the Argives went into the plain and attacked Agis's division, they could pursue and harass them with their cavalry. [5] After making these dispositions, Agis entered the plain and laid waste the farmland of Saminthus and elsewhere.

59. When it was daylight and the Argives found out about these movements, they started back from Nemea to defend the plain. They encountered the Phleiasian and Corinthian forces, and, although they killed a few of the Phleiasians, they themselves lost a greater number—though not much greater—to the Corinthians. [2] The division of Agis's army consisting of the Boeotians, Megarians, and Sicyonians proceeded, as ordered, toward Nemea and found that the Argives were no longer there, but had gone down into the plain when they saw their land being ravaged. In fact, they were forming up for battle, and the Lacedaemonians were lining up opposite them. [3] The Argives were hemmed in on all sides: they were cut off from Argos in the plain by the Lacedaemonians and the contingents with them; they were cut off from the hills by the Corinthians, Phleiasians, and Pellenians; and they were cut off from the route to Nemea by the Boeotians, Sicyonians, and Megarians. Nor did they have any cavalry, because the Athenians were their only allies who had yet to arrive.

[4] However, most of the Argives and their allies did not consider the situation especially dangerous, and they even thought the battle would take place under circumstances that were favorable to them. In their opinion, it was the Lacedaemonians who were cut off, since they were in Argive territory and close to the city. [5] But two Argives—Thrasyllus, who was one of the five generals, and Alciphron, who represented Lacedaemonian interests in Argos—approached Agis just as the armies were about to engage and discussed with him the possibility of avoiding battle. They claimed that the Argives were ready to offer and accept arbitration leading to a fair and equal settlement of any grievances the Lacedaemonians had against them, and were prepared to make a treaty and live on peaceful terms with them from then on.
60. The Argives who made this offer did so on their own initiative;

they had been given no such instructions by the people. And in accepting the offer, Agis too acted on his own, without the consent of the majority and without consulting others; all he did was communicate his decision to just one man, a Lacedaemonian official who was accompanying the expedition. Agis agreed to a truce of four months' duration to give the Argives time to carry out what they had undertaken to do, and then he immediately led his division of the army away without issuing orders to any of the other allies. [2] Agis was their lawful leader, so the Lacedaemonians and their allies followed him, but among themselves they criticized him severely. They thought they had had a chance to engage the enemy under circumstances that were favorable to them—an enemy who was cut off on all sides by both infantry and cavalry—and that they were leaving without anything to show for all the effort that had gone into the expedition.

[3] This was in fact the finest army of Greeks there had ever been. It was seen at its best while it was assembled at Nemea, before it had separated into divisions, when it consisted of the Lacedaemonians at full strength, the Arcadians, Boeotians, Corinthians, Sicyonians, Pellenians, Phleiasians, and Megarians. Every contingent was made up of elite soldiers from each city, and they felt that the army as a whole was a match not just for the Argive alliance but for any other alliance as well that might be added to it. [4] On their way back, then, Agis came in for criticism along these lines from the army, but then the various contingents dispersed and went back to their homes.

[5] For their part, too, the Argives were critical of those who had made the truce without the consent of the people—far more critical than the Lacedaemonians were of Agis. They, too, felt that they had been presented with a unique opportunity, and that the Lacedaemonians had been allowed to escape, because the contest would have taken place when their own city was close at hand, and they had the sterling support of many allies. [6] So after they returned home they began to stone Thrasyllus in the Ravine, which is where the legal scrutiny of campaigns takes place before generals are allowed back

into the city. Thrasyllus escaped death by fleeing to the altar, but they confiscated his property.

61. After this, the Athenian force of a thousand hoplites and three hundred cavalrymen arrived under the command of the generals Laches and Nicostratus. But the Argives still shrank from breaking the truce with Sparta, so they asked the Athenians to leave and balked at the idea of introducing them into the popular assembly, where they wanted to present their case, until they caved in to the pleas of the Mantineans and Eleans, who were still in Argos. [2] The Athenians—through Alcibiades, who had come to Argos as their representative—repeated what they had said to the council: that the Argives had no right to make the truce without consulting their allies, and that now, given the opportunity afforded by their arrival in Argos, they should resume the war. [3] The allies found this argument persuasive, and they immediately set out to attack Orchomenus in Arcadia. All of them went except the Argives; they had been no less persuaded by Alcibiades's arguments, but they stayed behind for a while before later proceeding to Orchomenus as well.

[4] The whole allied force stationed itself close to Orchomenus, put it under siege, and launched repeated assaults. They were motivated by the desire to add the city to their alliance, and by the fact that hostages from Arcadia had been placed there by the Lacedaemonians. [5] The Orchomenians were worried about the weakness of their wall and about the size of the force attacking them, and so, since there was no sign of anyone coming to their aid and they were frightened of being annihilated before help arrived, they agreed to terms whereby they joined the alliance, gave hostages of their own to the Mantineans, and handed over those that the Lacedaemonians had left with them.

62. Now that they had Orchomenus, the allies next discussed which of the remaining places they should attack first. The Eleans wanted it to be Lepreum and the Mantineans Tegea, and the Argives and Athenians voted with the Mantineans. [2] The Eleans were angry that the vote had gone against attacking Lepreum and went back home, but the rest of the allies stayed in Mantinea and got ready to go against Tegea. And there were also some people within Tegea itself who wanted to betray the city to them.

63. When the Lacedaemonians returned home from Argos after the four-month truce had been concluded, Agis came in for severe criticism for not having conquered Argos for them when he had what they considered a unique opportunity. After all, they said, it was not easy to assemble so many allies of such caliber. [2] And when they heard of the fall of Orchomenus, they were even angrier with him; in fact, they were so furious—which was very out of character—that they decided to raze his house to the ground and fine him 100,000 drachmas. [3] He begged them not to, saying that he would redeem the charge against him with an honorable military achievement, and that if he failed to do so, then they could do what they wanted. [4] So they postponed the fine and the razing of his house and passed what was for Sparta an unprecedented decree: they chose ten Spartiates to be his advisers, and said that he had no authority to lead an army away from enemy territory† without their consent.*

64. At this point, a message reached the Lacedaemonians from their friends in Tegea saying that if they did not come soon, Tegea would defect from them to the Argive alliance, and that they had almost done so already. [2] The Lacedaemonians reacted to this with unprecedented speed and sent a full levy of both citizens and helots. [3] They went first to Orestheum in Maenalia* and ordered their Arcadian allies to form themselves into a single contingent and come hard on their heels to Tegea. Although the full levy of Lacedaemonians had gone as far as Orestheum, they sent home from there a sixth of their forces, including the oldest and the youngest men of military age, to stand guard at home, and then the rest of the army went to Tegea. Before long their Arcadian allies arrived. [4] The Lacedaemonians also sent emissaries to Corinth, the Boeotians, the Phocians, and the Locrians, ordering them to send reinforcements to Mantinea as quickly as they could. Even though the order arrived without much notice, and it was not easy for them to pass through the intervening enemy territory unless they formed themselves into a single unit—which meant waiting for one another—they still carried out their orders with all speed. [5] Meanwhile, the Lacedaemonians, along with the Arcadian allies who were with them, invaded Mantinean territory, made camp by the sanctuary of Heracles, and set about ravaging the land.

65. When the Argives and their allies saw the Lacedaemonians, they occupied a steep and easily defensible hill and took up battle formation. [2] The Lacedaemonians immediately advanced against them until they were within range of the Argives' stones and javelins—at which point one of the older men in the army, seeing the strength of the position they were attacking, called out to Agis that he was proposing to cure one evil with another. By this he meant that Agis was wanting his present inopportune determination to be a means of making amends for his discreditable withdrawal from Argos. [3] And Agis—perhaps because of what the man had shouted out, or perhaps because some other thought, or even the same one, had suddenly occurred to him as well—lost no time in leading his army back before it engaged the enemy. [4] When he reached the territory of Tegea, he set about diverting into Mantinean territory the water that commonly leads to fighting between the Mantineans and Tegeans, since it damages the land of one or the other of them, depending on the direction in which it flows. He wanted to force the men off the hill by their need to do something about the diversion of the water when they found out about it, and he wanted the battle to take place on level ground. [5] So he stayed there by the water for the rest of the day, seeing to its diversion.

The initial reaction on the part of the Argives and their allies to the Lacedaemonians' sudden and unexpected withdrawal was astonishment; they could not guess what had caused it. But then, when the Lacedaemonians continued to withdraw and disappeared from view, and they themselves remained inactive, with no pursuit of the enemy taking place, they started once more to criticize their generals, not just for the earlier occasion, when they had let the Lacedaemonians off the hook near Argos, even though they had them at a disadvantage, but also because now the Lacedaemonians were escaping and no one was setting out after them; they felt that this inactivity was a lifeline for the Lacedaemonians and a betrayal of themselves. [6] And after the generals had recovered from their initial shock at the Lacedaemonians' retreat, they led their men off the hill and advanced onto level ground, where they encamped with the intention of proceeding against the enemy.

66. The next day, the Argives and their allies formed ranks in the order in which they were intending to fight if they made contact with the enemy. As the Lacedaemonians were making their way back from the water to their original encampment at the sanctuary of Heracles, they suddenly saw the enemy only a short distance away, all of them already off the hill and in battle formation. [2] Never, as far back as memory went, had there ever been an occasion that frightened the Lacedaemonians more than this one, because they had hardly any time to prepare. They immediately fell to and hastily formed themselves up in their turn, with King Agis giving all the orders. This was his legal right: [3] When a king is at the head of an army he is in complete command. He personally tells the generals what is to be done; they tell the company commanders; the company commanders tell the officers in charge of platoons; they in their turn tell the section leaders; and the section leaders pass the orders on to the men in their sections. [4] Any verbal orders that are needed are handed down through the same chain of command, and they quickly reach their destination, because, with a few exceptions, almost all the Lacedaemonian army is made up of officers subordinate to other officers, so that many men are involved in making sure that things happen as they should.

67. On this occasion, the Sciritae made up the left wing, a position that is always reserved exclusively for these Lacedaemonians;* next to them were the Brasidean troops from Thrace along with the freedmen; then came the Lacedaemonians themselves, arranged in order company by company; next to them were the Heraeans from Arcadia; and then the Maenalians. The Tegeans were on the right wing, with a few Lacedaemonians at the extreme end of the line, and there was cavalry on both wings. [2] That was the disposition on the Lacedaemonian side. As for their opponents, the Mantineans had the right wing, because the action was taking place in their territory; next to them were the Arcadian members of the alliance; then the thousand elite Argives (the unit had long been provided with training in warfare by the city at public expense); next to them were the rest of the Argives; then came their allies from Cleonae and Orneae; and then finally the Athenians held the left wing, along with their own cavalry.

68. That was how the two sides deployed their forces in preparation for battle. It looked as though the Lacedaemonians had a numerical advantage. [2] I could not come up with a precise figure for the numbers of soldiers in individual contingents on the two sides, nor for each army overall.* The secretiveness of the Lacedaemonians about their state affairs made it impossible to know their numbers, and on the other side the figure was suspect because of the natural human tendency to exaggerate their own numbers. However, the following calculation makes it possible to see how many Lacedaemonians were present that day. [3] Leaving aside the Sciritae, who numbered 600, seven companies took part in the battle, and in each company there were four platoons, and in each platoon there were four sections. In a section, four men fought in the front rank, but they did not all have the same depth. This varied according to the wishes of the company commander, but generally speaking they formed eight ranks. So, discounting the Sciritae, along the whole line the front rank was made up of 448 men.

69. Just before the two armies engaged, each contingent was addressed by its own general as follows: the Mantineans were reminded that they would be fighting for their homeland and that what was at stake was the retention of self-rule, which they had now experienced, and the avoidance of servitude, which they did not want to experience again; the Argives were told that they should no longer tolerate the persistent loss of their ancient hegemony and of the former equal distribution of power in the Peloponnese—that they would be fighting to recover these and also to avenge the many wrongs perpetrated by men who were their enemies and neighbors; and the Athenians were told how good it would be, when fighting alongside so many brave allies, to prove themselves second to none of them, and it was explained to them that by defeating the Lacedaemonians in the Peloponnese they would make their empire more secure and extensive, and moreover that they would never again have to suffer another invasion of their land. [2] Such were the addresses delivered by the generals to the Argives and their allies. As for the Lacedaemonians, unit by unit and accompanied by their war-songs, they exhorted one another, their trusty comrades, to draw on their expertise, knowing that long practical training is a more certain guarantee of safety than brief encouragement, however well expressed.

70. After this, battle was joined. The Argives and their allies advanced with purposeful fury, while the Lacedaemonians marched at a measured pace and to the accompaniment of many pipers, who were, as usual, stationed among them, not for religious reasons, but to make sure that by marching in step their pace was uniform and their formation did not break apart, as tends to happen to large armies when they advance into battle.*

71. While the two sides were still closing on each other, King Agis decided on the following maneuver: There is a particular phenomenon that happens to all armies. As they approach the enemy, their line becomes extended on the right wing, so that the right of both sides projects beyond the left of their opponents. This happens because the soldiers are afraid, and each of them tucks his exposed side as much as possible behind the shield of the man positioned on his right, thinking that the closer the contact, the better the protection.* It is the end man of the right wing who is primarily responsible, since he urgently wants to keep his undefended side away from the enemy at all times, and then everyone else as well, impelled by the same fear, follows his lead. [2] On the occasion in question, in fact, the Mantineans projected well beyond the wing held by the Sciritae, and the Lacedaemonians and Tegeans projected even farther beyond the Athenian wing, by virtue of the fact that they had the larger army. [3] Agis was worried that the Mantineans were overlapping them so much that his left wing would be outflanked, so he signaled the Sciritae and the Brasideans to extend their line until they were level with the Mantineans. He then ordered the generals Hipponoidas and Aristocles to go over with two companies from the right and fill the gap that this move had created by inserting them into it. His thinking was that his own right would still have superior strength, while with this arrangement the wing facing the Mantineans would be more secure.

72. Anyway, what actually happened was that because Agis gave the order at short notice, while the advance was already under way, Aristocles and Hipponoidas refused to go over—an offense for which they were later charged with cowardice and banished from Sparta. Then the enemy engaged, and although Agis ordered the Sciritae to close back up again, since the companies had not gone over to them, they too were no longer able to plug the gap. [2] However, despite the Lacedaemonians' decided inferiority in tactical skill on this occasion, they showed beyond the shadow of a doubt that they made up for it by their superiority in courage.

[3] When the hand-to-hand fighting began, the Mantineans on the right wing routed the Sciritae and the Brasideans, and the Mantineans, their allies, and the thousand-strong elite Argive unit burst into the gap and began to wreak havoc among the Lacedaemonians. They surrounded them, forced them to retreat, and pushed them all the way back to their wagons, killing some of the older men stationed there. [4] In this part of the field, then, the Lacedaemonians were coming off worse, but it was a different story for the rest of the army, especially in the center, where King Agis and his guard of three hundred so-called Knights* were. They fell on the older Argive troops (those known as the Five Companies), the contingents from Cleonae and Orneae, and the Athenians who were stationed next to them and forced them to retreat. In fact, most of their opponents did not even stand their ground

and fight back, but gave way as soon as the Lacedaemonians attacked. Some were even trampled underfoot in the rush to avoid being caught.

73. The collapse of the army of the Argives and their allies in the center made it likely that both wings would begin to break up as well. Moreover, the Lacedaemonians and Tegeans on the right wing were starting to encircle the Athenians with their projecting flank, so that the Athenians were in danger left and right: they were being encircled on their left, and they were exposed on their right where their comrades had already been defeated, and if their cavalry had not been there to help they would have suffered more losses than any other contingent in the army. [2] But luckily, when Agis saw that his left wing, which faced the Mantineans and the thousand Argives, was in trouble, he ordered the entire army to go to the part of the field where he was facing defeat. [3] As soon as this happened—that is, when the army ignored them and turned aside from them—the Athenians and those of the Argives who had not been defeated had time to escape. But the Mantineans and their allies, and the elite corps of Argives, were too dispirited to continue to attack their opponents; when they saw that the others had been defeated and that the Lacedaemonians were bearing down on them, they turned to flight. [4] Many Mantinean lives were lost, but most of the elite Argives escaped. They were not hard pressed as they fled, however, nor was it a lengthy retreat: the Lacedaemonians fight for as long as it takes and stand their ground stubbornly until they have turned the enemy to flight, but once that has happened they do not pursue the fugitives far or for long.

74. That, or something very like it, was how the battle went. It was certainly the greatest all-Greek battle that had taken place for a very long time, and the combatants were the most important states in Greece. [2] The Lacedaemonians made a display of the shields of the enemy dead and then immediately erected a trophy and set about despoiling the corpses. Then they collected the bodies of their own dead, took them away to Tegea, where they were buried, and returned the bodies of the dead to the enemy under a truce. [3] There were seven hundred dead from Argos, Orneae, and Cleonae; two hundred from Mantinea; and the Athenians and Aeginetans together lost two hundred soldiers and both generals. The allies of the Lacedaemonians suffered too few losses to be worth mentioning, and although it is hard to know the truth about the Lacedaemonians themselves, it was said that approximately three hundred of them died.

75. When the battle was imminent, the other Spartan king, Pleistoanax, set out to help with the oldest and youngest men of military age, but when he reached Tegea he learned that the battle had been won and went back to Sparta. [2] The Lacedaemonians sent word to their allies from Corinth and beyond the Isthmus to turn back, and they themselves went back to Sparta, where they dismissed their allies and turned to celebration, since it was time for the Carneia festival. [3] And this single achievement of theirs put an end to the disparagement of them that was then current in Greece—that the catastrophe on Sphacteria had exposed their weakness, and that they were fundamentally indecisive and slow off the mark. It now seemed that it had been bad luck that caused them to be maligned, while their spirit remained the same as ever.

[4] The day before the battle, since the main Argive army was absent, the Epidaurians mounted a full-scale invasion of Argos and killed many of the men the Argives had left to protect their land when they marched out. [5] After the battle, as soon as three thousand Elean hoplites had come to help the Mantineans, and the Athenians had been reinforced by a further thousand hoplites, all these allies marched against Epidaurus during the Lacedaemonian celebration of the Carneia and began to wall off the city, with each contingent working on a different section of the wall. [6] Although the rest of them gave up, the Athenians promptly completed their assigned task, the fortification of the Heraeum headland, and then all the allies contributed men for the garrison of the fortress before returning to their various homelands. And so the summer ended.

76. Very early in the following winter, after they had celebrated the Carneia, the Lacedaemonians took to the field, and once they had reached Tegea they sent envoys on ahead to Argos with an offer of peace. [2] Even before the battle there had been men in Argos who were well disposed to them and who wanted to overthrow the democracy, and after the battle it was far easier for them to persuade the general populace to come to terms with Sparta. They wanted first to make peace with the Lacedaemonians again and then to conclude an alliance with them—and then to launch an attack on the democrats. [3] Lichas, son of Arcesilas, who represented Argive interests in Sparta, was one of the Lacedaemonian envoys. He brought two proposals, one if they wanted war and the other if they wanted peace. After much argument for and against—coincidentally, Alcibiades was there—the partisans of Sparta, who were now emboldened to act openly, persuaded the Argives to accept the offer of peace. The agreement read as follows:*

77. "It is resolved by the Lacedaemonian assembly to make peace with the Argives on the following terms: The Argives are to return to the Orchomenians the children of theirs whom they hold as hostages, and to the Maenalians their men, and to the Lacedaemonians the men they hold in Mantinea, and they are to withdraw from Epidaurus and demolish the fortifications there. [2] If the Athenians do not withdraw from Epidaurus, they are to be the enemies of the Argives and the Lacedaemonians, and of the allies of the Lacedaemonians and the allies of the Argives. [3] All the children that the Lacedaemonians hold as hostages are to be restored to their cities. [4] Concerning the sacrificial victim owed to the god, the Argives, if they so wish, shall tender an oath to the Epidaurians, but if they do not so wish, they shall swear one themselves.* [5] The Peloponnesian cities, both great and small, are all to be self-governing in the traditional way. [6] But if any state outside the Peloponnese invades the Peloponnese with harmful intent, they are to repel it after having deliberated together to decide on the course of action that is most equitable for the Peloponnesians. [7] The allies of the Lacedaemonians from outside the Peloponnese are to be included in the treaty on the same terms as the Lacedaemonians themselves, and the allies of the Argives are to be included in the treaty on the same terms as the Argives themselves, with the right to keep and control their own territories. [8] The Lacedaemonians and the Argives are not to make peace before showing this document to their allies for their approval, and if the allies have any observations to make, they are to refer them to their home authorities."

78. The Argives accepted this wording and the Lacedaemonian army returned home from Tegea. But subsequently further diplomatic exchanges between them took place, and not long after concluding the peace treaty the same negotiators arranged for the Argives to abandon their alliance with the Mantineans, Eleans, and Athenians, and to enter into a treaty of alliance with the Lacedaemonians. The treaty read as follows:

79. "It has been resolved by the Lacedaemonians and the Argives that there shall be a treaty of alliance between them for fifty years on the following terms: Any legal disputes are to settled by fair and impartial means in the traditional way. The other Peloponnesian states may participate in the treaty of alliance as independent and self-governing entities, controlling their own territory as they traditionally have done, and settling legal disputes by fair and impartial means. [2] The allies of the Lacedaemonians from outside the Peloponnese are to be included in the treaty on the same terms as the Lacedaemonians themselves, and the allies of the Argives are to be included in the treaty on the same terms as the Argives themselves, with the right to keep and control their own territories. [3] If the need arises for a joint military expedition anywhere, the Lacedaemonians and Argives are to deliberate to decide on the course of action that is most equitable for the allies. [4] If any of the cities, whether within or outside the Peloponnese, is involved in a dispute, whatever the issue, be it borders or anything else, they are to settle it themselves;† but any quarrel between one of the allied cities and another is to be referred for arbitration to any city that they both agree will be impartial. But private persons are to be judged in the traditional ways."

80. After this treaty of alliance had come into force, the two sides returned to each other any possessions they had taken in war and resolved all other outstanding matters. They now began to follow common policies, and they voted not to receive any herald or embassy from the Athenians unless they abandoned their fortresses and left the Peloponnese, and not to come to terms with or make war on any state unless they did so together. [2] They acted with passionate determination in all they did, especially when they sent a joint embassy to the Thraceward region and to Perdiccas, and managed to persuade Perdiccas to join their alliance. (He did not immediately abandon his alliance with the Athenians, however, but he was contemplating doing so, because he saw that the Argives had seceded and he himself was ancestrally Argive.)* Not only that, but they reaffirmed their former oaths with the Chalcidians and made fresh pledges as well. [3] The Argives also sent envoys to the Athenians, ordering them to evacuate the fort at Epidaurus. And since the Athenians could see that their men were few, compared to the numbers of the others in the garrison, they sent Demosthenes to extract them. But when he got there he pretended to arrange an athletic competition outside the fort, and when the non-Athenian elements of the garrison troops went outside he closed the gates against them. But later, after reaffirming their treaty with the Epidaurians, the Athenians returned the fortress of their own accord.

81. After the defection of the Argives from the alliance, the Mantineans held out for a while, but then, finding they could not manage without the Argives, they too came to an agreement with the Lacedaemonians and relinquished control of their subject cities. [2] Moreover, a force made up of a thousand Lacedaemonians and a thousand Argives took to the field. First the Lacedaemonians on their own went to Sicyon and established a narrower oligarchic regime there, and then both of them together overthrew the democracy in Argos, and an oligarchy that was acceptable to Sparta seized power. All this happened when winter was coming to an end and it was almost spring, and so the fourteenth year of the war came to an end.

82. The following summer, the people of Dium (the one on the Athos peninsula) seceded from Athens and went over to the Chalcidians, and the Lacedaemonians reorganized any matters in the Achaean cities that they had previously found unacceptable.

[2] The democrats in Argos gradually regrouped and recovered their courage. They waited for the very day of the Gymnopaediae festival in Sparta and attacked the oligarchs. There was fighting in the city, which the democrats won, and they killed or banished the oligarchs. [3] The Lacedaemonians, who for some time had been turning down the requests of their friends in Argos to come and support them, postponed the Gymnopaediae and went to help. When they reached Tegea and found out that the oligarchs had been beaten, they refused to go any farther, despite the pleas of the exiled oligarchs. Instead, they returned home and celebrated the Gymnopaediae.

[4] Later, a meeting took place in Sparta at which both the Argives in the city and those who had been banished were represented, and their allies, too, sent delegations. After many speeches from both sides, the Lacedaemonians concluded that the Argives in the city were in the wrong and resolved to march against Argos, but there were postponements and delays. [5] Meanwhile, however, the Argive democrats, out of fear of the Lacedaemonians, took the view that their best hope lay with the Athenians and secured a renewal of their former alliance. They began to build Long Walls down to the sea so that, if they were denied access to their farmland, they would be able to sustain themselves by importing supplies by sea with Athenian help. [6] Some of the Peloponnesian cities, too, were complicit in the building of the walls. The entire population of Argos—men, women,

and slaves—took part in the work, and joiners and stonemasons came from Athens to help them. And so the summer came to an end.

83. The following winter, when the Lacedaemonians heard about the building of the Long Walls at Argos, they marched there along with their allies, apart from the Corinthians. Present also were some of their partisans from Argos itself. The army was led by the Spartan king Agis, son of Archidamus. [2] The support they had expected to find from within the city never materialized, but they gained control of the unfinished walls and tore them down. They also seized Hysiae, an Argive village, and killed all the free men they found there. Then they withdrew and dispersed to their various cities. [3] Next the Argives in their turn invaded the territory of Phleious, in retaliation for the fact that they had taken in the men who had been banished; in fact, most of the exiles had been allowed to take up residence there. They ravaged the land and then went back home.

[4] In the same winter the Athenians set up a blockade of Macedon. Their grievances against Perdiccas were, first, that he had joined the Argive and Lacedaemonian alliance, and, second, that when they had been getting ready to lead an army against the Chalcidians of the Thraceward region and against Amphipolis, under the command of the general Nicias, son of Niceratus, he had betrayed his alliance with them and the army had been disbanded largely because of his defection.† The Athenians therefore now considered him an enemy. And so the winter came to an end, and with it the fifteenth year of the war.

84. The following summer, Alcibiades took a fleet of twenty ships to Argos. He seized 300 men—those who still seemed untrustworthy and sympathetic to Sparta—and the Athenians deposited them on the islands that lay close to Athens and were under their control.

The Athenians also launched an expedition against the island of Melos with a fleet made up of thirty of their own ships, six from Chios, and two from Lesbos, and with 1,200 of their own hoplites,

300 archers, and 20 mounted archers, accompanied by about 1,500 hoplites supplied by their allies and the islanders. [2] The Melians, colonists of Sparta, were refusing to submit to Athens as the other islanders had. Early in the war they had remained neutral and inactive, but after the Athenians tried to coerce them by ravaging their land they became openly hostile.* [3] So this was the army with which the generals Cleomedes, son of Lycomedes, and Teisias, son of Teisimachus, invaded the island. They encamped there, but before doing any harm to the land, they sent envoys to negotiate with the Melians, who denied them access to the people and told them to state their business to the authorities and the ruling oligarchs.*

85. The Athenian envoys began in the following vein: "So we're not to address the people because you're worried that they might be taken in if we presented our case all at once in a continuous speech of plausible arguments, without there being an opportunity for them to be challenged. We know this is why you've brought us before just the few oligarchs. So why don't you, the forward guard, mitigate the risk even further? Why don't you avoid set speeches as well, and address the issues point by point, responding immediately to anything we say that strikes you as unacceptable, and make up your minds like that? And to start with, why don't you tell us if you approve of this proposal?"

86. In reply, the Melian commissioners said, "We have no problem with a calm exchange of views, but it seems to be at odds with the fact that you have an army here right now, and are not merely threatening war in the future. It looks to us as though you've come with your minds already made up, whatever we say. Presumably, then, if we win the argument thanks to the justice of our case, and therefore do not give in, the outcome will be war, and if we agree with what you say the outcome will be servitude."

87. Athenians: "Well, if you're going to give weight to conjectures about the future—if you've met with us for any purpose other than considering how your city may survive given current circumstances and what's right before your eyes—there's no point in our carrying on. But if we're meeting to consider how your city may survive, we can speak."

88. Melians: "It's natural and understandable for people in our situation to explore many angles in our arguments and thinking. You're quite right that this conference is about our survival, so let the discussion proceed—and in the manner you propose, if you like."

89. Athenians: "Well then, for our part we won't rely on fancy claims. We won't argue that we have a right to our empire because we defeated the Persians, or that we're attacking you now because of wrongs you've done us: a speech along those lines would be both long and unpersuasive. And by the same token we expect you not to imagine that you'll win us over by arguing that even though you're colonists of the Lacedaemonians, you didn't join them for any of their campaigns, or that you've never done us any wrong. No, we think you should negotiate realistically, basing yourselves on the intentions each of us really has, since you know as well as we do that when people stop to think, they see that justice is a consideration only between those who have an equal ability to coerce, while the strong do what they can and the weak concede them that right."

90. Melians: "We think, then, that it's in your interest (and we have to argue like this, since you're obliging us to talk about expediency rather than justice) that you do not abolish the common good whereby for anyone who is ever in danger, what is reasonable is also what is just—in other words, that such people should be allowed to use and be helped even by arguments that fall short of perfect precision. And this principle is in your interest as much as anyone else's, because your own fall would bring the most terrible vengeance down on your heads and make you an example to all."

91. Athenians: "Actually, even the prospect of our empire coming to an end doesn't worry us. It's not those who rule others—as the Lacedaemonians do, no less than us (not that the Lacedaemonians are at issue today)—who deal severely with people they've conquered. What's dangerous is if the subjects of an empire attack their former rulers and defeat them. [2] And insofar as this is a possibility, you should leave it to us to run the risk. What we'll do now is demonstrate that we're not just here to benefit our empire; what we'll be saying today is also supposed to enable your city to survive. We don't want it to be hard for us to rule you, and we want you to survive because it's in both of our interests."

92. Melians: "And how is servitude as advantageous for us as ruling is for you?"

93. Athenians: "Because you'd be submitting before you suffered the worst of fates, and it's in our interest not to destroy you."

94. Melians: "So wouldn't you find it acceptable for us to stay out of the war, as friends rather than enemies, but allies of neither side?"

95. Athenians: "No, because it's not so much that your hostility harms us as that your friendship is taken by our subjects to be proof of our weakness, whereas your hatred is taken to be proof of our power."

96. Melians: "Do your subjects really consider what you're doing to be reasonable, when you make no distinction between people with whom you have no connection and those who in most cases are your colonists, and who in some cases have been subdued after rebelling from you?"

97. Athenians: "As far as right and wrong are concerned, they don't think there's anything to tell between these two categories of people—but they do think that those who refuse to succumb do so because they're strong, and that if we fail to attack them, the reason is that we're afraid of them. It follows that, even apart from the increase to the size of our empire, subduing you will also make us more secure; and it's especially because we're masters of the seas and you're islanders, and relatively weak ones, that you should succumb to us."

98. Melians: "What about if we remain neutral? Don't you think you'd be secure then? Here we go again: just as you didn't allow us to talk of justice and are trying to persuade us to defer to your interests, so we have to try to persuade you by explaining that what's to our advantage might also be to your advantage. After all, how are you going

to avoid making enemies of all those states that are currently allied to neither side, when they look at what you're doing here and conclude that one day you'll attack them as well? What you're doing, surely, is increasing the number of your enemies and inviting the hostility of people who neither intended nor wished to be your enemies."

99. Athenians: "No. The people who pose a particular threat to us aren't those who live here and there on the mainland, who, thanks to their freedom, will be slow in taking precautions against us, but the islanders—both those who,† like you, aren't our subjects, and those who are already enraged by our empire and the restrictions it imposes on them. These are the people who are most likely to succumb to recklessness and involve both themselves and us in danger that could have been foreseen."

100. Melians: "But if you're prepared to go to such desperate lengths to hang on to your empire, and those you've already enslaved are prepared to do the same to be free of it, surely we, who are still free, would be thoroughly craven and cowardly if we failed to do whatever it takes, however extreme, to avoid becoming enslaved."

101. Athenians: "Not if you look at the situation with prudent eyes. This is not an evenly matched contest to test your courage and see whether you can avoid incurring shame; you should be thinking, rather, about how to survive, and that means not resisting those whose strength is far greater than yours."

102. Melians: "But we know that in war fortune is sometimes more impartial than one might expect from the numerical disparity of the two sides. If we give in to you we immediately abandon hope altogether, but if we take action there's still hope that we may not be mowed down."

103. Athenians: "Hope is a source of comfort at times of danger, and the damage she does to those who rely on her isn't fatal, provided they have further resources to draw on. But hope is costly, and those who stake their all on a roll of the dice understand this only when they're ruined and it's no longer possible for them to act on that understanding and protect themselves against her. [2] You are weak and your survival is hanging in the balance, so don't let this happen to you. And don't behave as the masses do either. When they're hard pressed and have been let down by lucid hopes, although they could still save themselves by human means they resort to murky ones—prophecies, oracles, and the like, all of which cause harm by giving people hope."

104. Melians: "You can be sure that we, too, see the difficulty of contending against your strength *and* against a non-impartial fortune. Nevertheless, we believe that with the help of divine fortune we won't be defeated, because we're making a stand as righteous men against aggressors, and we trust that our deficiency in strength will be remedied by our alliance with the Lacedaemonians—an alliance that makes them honor-bound to come to our aid, because of the claims of kinship, if for no other reason. Under these circumstances, our confidence is far from reckless."

105. Athenians: "Well, we too don't think that we'll prove to lack the favor of the gods, because there's nothing in what we're claiming or doing that departs either from what people believe about the gods, or from normal human intentions toward one another. [2] We maintain that it's an inescapable law of nature that both gods and human beings always rule others wherever they have power; we believe this to be true of the gods and we know it to be true of men.* We didn't make this law, nor were we the first to act on it after it was made.† We found it in existence and we shall leave it to exist forever after us; and we act upon it in the knowledge that you and anyone else who became as powerful as us would do the same. [3] As far as the gods are concerned, then, it would be unreasonable for us to fear that we'll be at a disadvantage. As for what you say about the Lacedaemonians—that you trust that they'll feel themselves honor-bound to come to your aid—we consider you blessed in your naïvety, but we don't envy your folly. [4] There's no one more virtuous than the Lacedaemonians in their dealings with one another and their obedience to their local laws and customs. Where outsiders are concerned, however...well, one could go on at length about how they behave, but in brief, one might best clarify their conduct by saying that they're the most conspicuous example we've encountered of people who regard what gratifies themselves as the honorable thing to do, and what is to their advantage as the just thing to do. But, of course, this description doesn't support the irrational hope you expressed just now of being rescued by them."

106. Melians: "But that's exactly why we're absolutely convinced now that, in their own interests, they won't want to betray us, their colonists, because that would make them mistrusted by the Greeks who are well disposed to them and would be of service to their enemies."

107. Athenians: "Are you forgetting that self-interest and self-preservation go together, and that doing the right and honorable thing is risky? And there's no one who has less stomach for taking risks than the Lacedaemonians."

108. Melians: "But in our opinion, even though it may be dangerous for them, they're likely to accept the risk for our sake. We think they'll consider it less risky to help us than others, because our position close to the Peloponnese makes it easier for them to act, and because the similarity of our outlook as their kin makes us more to be trusted than others."

109. Athenians: "But when people are contemplating aiding others in their struggle, they don't see their security as dependent on those others being well disposed toward them, but on a considerable prevalence of real power. The Lacedaemonians take this into consideration even more than others—or so we judge by the fact that when they attack others, they don't have confidence in their own forces but are always accompanied by large numbers of their allies. So they're hardly likely to sail over to an island when we are masters of the sea."

110. Melians: "But they could send others as well. The Cretan Sea is large, and interception is more difficult for those who control it than survival is for those who want to evade them. [2] And even if they fail in this respect, the Lacedaemonians would turn against your land, and against the remaining allies of yours that Brasidas didn't approach. And then your efforts will be directed not toward land that has nothing to do with you, but toward what is more properly yours."†

111. Athenians: "Yes, something like this may happen in your case as it has in others; such diversionary tactics are not unfamiliar. But you should also appreciate that the Athenians have never yet retired from a siege through fear of others. [2] We can't help noticing, however, that although you said you'd be giving thought to your survival, you've said nothing so far, in all the time we've been talking, that would give anyone the confidence to think that you'd be saved. Your strongest grounds are no more than hopes for the future, but your actual resources are meager in comparison with those that are currently arrayed against you. In short, you're displaying a distinct lack of rationality in your thinking, though you could still send us out of the chamber and come up with another plan, less reckless than those you've presented so far. [3] At any rate, you surely won't put your trust in the sense of shame that has so often been the undoing of people who are confronted with a threat to their honor at a time of unmistakable danger. The attractive power of the concept of what is called 'honor' has frequently induced men, even when they can foresee the consequences, to be overcome by a mere word, so that of their own free will they fall victims to irremediable disasters and, thanks to their folly, earn worse dishonor than chance would have accorded them. [4] If you're sensible, you'll make sure that you avoid this mistake, and you won't think it unseemly to give in when the greatest of cities invites you to become an ally on moderate terms, such that you can keep your own land and merely pay tribute; nor will you think it unseemly, when you're offered a choice between war and survival, to avoid stubbornly choosing the worse option. People are most commonly successful when they refuse to yield to equals, behave with due deference to superiors, and are moderate toward inferiors. [5] Think things over carefully, then, even after we've left the chamber, and keep reminding yourselves that you're deliberating about your homeland;

you have just the one homeland, and its success or failure will depend on just the one decision."

112. The Athenians then withdrew from the conference, and the Melians, left to themselves, decided to uphold pretty much the same position they had held during the debate. So they replied to the Athenians as follows: [2] "Our decision is still the same as it was at the beginning, Athenians: we're not suddenly going to deprive our city of its freedom, seven hundred years after its foundation. Instead, placing our trust in the divine fortune that has preserved our land until now and in the human help of the Lacedaemonians, we shall endeavor to survive. [3] But we call on you to let us be your friends, enemies of neither side, and to withdraw from our land after making a pact with us on terms that seem acceptable to both parties."

113. Once the Athenians had received this response from the Melians, they refused to discuss the matter further and said, "It seems to us, if these decisions of yours are any guide, that you are unique in judging the future to be clearer than what's right before your eyes, and in regarding uncertainties as present realities. Since you've staked so much on placing your trust† in the Lacedaemonians, in fortune, and in hope, your downfall will be that much greater."

114. The Athenian envoys returned to the camp, and faced with the Melians' refusal to submit, their generals turned straight to war. They divided their forces among the various Melian towns and surrounded Melos itself with a wall. [2] Then, after leaving some of their own men and some of their allies to mount guard by land and sea, the bulk of the Athenian army withdrew, while those they had left behind stayed on the island and maintained the siege.

115. At much the same time, the Argives invaded the territory of Phleious and lost about eighty men in an ambush by the Phleiasians and their own exiles. [2] And the Athenians based in Pylos seized a major haul of booty from the Lacedaemonians, to which the Lacedaemonians responded with a proclamation. Even now they did not want to break the truce and restart the war, but they had their heralds proclaim that any Laconian who so wished could plunder the Athenians. [3] And the Corinthians, who had a number of ongoing private disputes with the Athenians, declared war on them, but the rest of the Peloponnesians refused to support them.

[4] A night sortie by the Melians gained them the section of the Athenian siege wall where the Athenians had their commissary, with some loss of life on the Athenian side. Then they withdrew, taking with them into the city grain and as many other useful items as they could carry, and took no further action. After this incident, the Athenians tightened their guard. And so the summer came to an end.

116. The following winter, the Lacedaemonians undertook their long-delayed expedition against Argos, but withdrew when the border-crossing sacrifices were inauspicious. But since it was clear that the Lacedaemonians had intended to attack, the Argives became suspicious of certain men in the city, and they took some into custody while others escaped.

[2] Meanwhile, the Melians succeeded once more in capturing a section of the wall the Athenians had built around the city, a different section this time, which was inadequately guarded. [3] As a result of these Melian successes, the Athenians sent more soldiers, under the command of Philocrates, son of Demeas. Now under heavy siege, and also because of some treachery from within,† they chose to come to terms with the Athenians, agreeing that the Athenians could deal with them as they wished. [4] And the Athenians killed all the young adult males of Melos that they could find, and sold the children and women into slavery. Later they sent out five hundred settlers and populated the island themselves.

Book Six

*The seventeenth and eighteenth years of the war. Introduction to Sicily (6.1–5). **416/415–415/414**: Athenian preparations for the invasion of Sicily (6.6–26). **415/414**: mutilation of the herms at Athens, and related accusations of sacrilege against Alcibiades (6.27–29); the Athenian invasion force departs, reactions in Sicily (6.30–41); the Athenians reach Corcyra and Italy (6.42–52); Alcibiades is recalled to Athens, and Thucydides digresses to discuss the fall of the sixth-century Athenian tyrants (6.53–59); the Athenians complete their inquiry into the herms affair, Alcibiades is convicted but escapes (6.60–61); campaigns in Sicily (6.62–88.8); Alcibiades advises the Spartans (6.88.9–93). **414/413**: further campaigns in Sicily (6.94–104); fighting in the Peloponnese (6.105).*

1. In the same winter, the Athenians revived their desire to mount an expedition against Sicily—this time with a larger force than the one that had gone with Laches and Eurymedon*—to see if they could conquer it. Few in Athens had any sense of the size of the island or of how many people, both Greeks and barbarians, lived there, and they did not appreciate that they would be undertaking a war that would be hardly less demanding than the one against the Peloponnesians.* [2] After all, it takes almost eight days for a merchant ship to circumnavigate Sicily, and yet despite its size it is separated from the mainland by only two and a quarter miles of sea.

2. Here is how the island was originally settled, and what follows is a full tally of the peoples who lived there. The oldest settlers of any part of the island are said to have been the Cyclopes and the Laestrygonians,* but I for one am unable to say what their race was, where they came from, or where they went after leaving the island; all there is to go on are the tales of the poets and what this person or that claims to know about them. [2] It seems clear that the Sicanians were the next to have settled there. Their own story is that they were the original inhabitants, since they claim to be indigenous, but it turns out that in fact they were Iberians who were driven from the Sicanus river in Iberia by Ligurians. At that time the island was called "Sicania" after them (whereas earlier it had been called "Trinacria"), and even today the Sicanians still live in the western part of Sicily.

[3] During the fall of Troy, some Trojans escaped the Greeks in their ships and ended up in Sicily.* They became the neighbors of the Sicanians and were known collectively as "Elymians," and their cities were Eryx and Egesta. Subsequently, some Phocians who had been at Troy joined the Elymians in their settlements once they reached Sicily; at first they were driven by stormy weather to Libya. [4] As for the Sicels, they originally lived in Italy, but they crossed over to Sicily to escape from the Opici. The story that they crossed the strait on rafts is not implausible—they could have waited for a favorable wind to rise that would enable them to make the crossing—but perhaps they reached the island by some other means. Even today there are still Sicels in Italy, and it was a Sicel king called Italus who gave his name to the country.

[5] The Sicels arrived in Sicily in large numbers, and after defeating the Sicanians they displaced them into its southern and western parts, and consequently the island became known as "Sicily" [*Sikelia*] instead of "Sicania." After their arrival in Sicily the Sicels occupied and lived in the most fertile parts of the land for close to three hundred years before the arrival of Greeks in the island, and even now the central and northern parts of the island are theirs. [6] There were also Phoenician settlements throughout Sicily; they occupied the coastal headlands

and the small offshore islands in order to trade with the Sicels. But when the Greeks began to arrive in large numbers by sea, the Phoenicians abandoned most of their settlements and lived together in three cities—Motya, Soloeis, and Panormus—near the Elymians, because they had a solid alliance in place with them, and because this was the part of the island that was the shortest distance from Carthage.*

So that is the tally of the various barbarians who settled in Sicily and those were the circumstances of their arrival. **3.** The first Greek settlers came from Chalcis in Euboea under the leadership of Thoucles; they founded Naxos and built the altar of Apollo the Founder that still stands outside the town and at which the delegates sacrifice before leaving Sicily on a mission to a sacred site.* [2] The following year saw the foundation of Syracuse by Archias, a Corinthian of the Heracleidae clan, once he had first driven the Sicels off the island on which the inner city stands (which is no longer surrounded by water). In later years, once the outer city, too, had gained walls, Syracuse became very populous. [3] In the fifth year after the foundation of Syracuse, Thoucles and the Chalcidians from Naxos took to the field and, once they had expelled the Sicels by force of arms, founded Leontini and then Catana. The Catanaeans, however, chose their own founder, Evarchus.

4. At about the same time, Lamis too came to Sicily from Megara with a band of settlers and founded a place called Trotilus on the river Pantacyas. Later he left Trotilus and for a short while joined the Chalcidians in Leontini, but after they threw him out he founded Thapsus. Lamis died, but the rest of his companions, after being forced to leave Thapsus, founded Megara Hyblaea, named for the Sicel king Hyblon, who let them have the land† and led them to it. [2] After living there for 245 years, they were forced to leave the city and its land by Gelon, the tyrant of Syracuse.* But before this episode, 100 years after they had founded Megara Hyblaea itself, they sent for† Pammilus, who came from Megara, the mother city, and helped them found Selinous.

[3] Gela was founded jointly by Antiphemus of Rhodes and Entimus of Crete, who introduced settlers there 45 years after the

foundation of Syracuse. The city was named after the Gelas river, but the place where the acropolis is today, which was the first part to be fortified, is known as Lindii. The institutions appointed for the new settlement were Dorian. [4] Almost 108 years after the foundation of Gela, the Geloans founded Acragas, which they named after the Acragas river. They chose Aristonous and Pystilus as the founders and modeled its institutions after those of Gela.

[5] Zancle was originally settled when raiders went there from Cumae, the Chalcidian city in Opicia, but later a large number of people came from Chalcis and elsewhere in Euboea and were granted plots of land. The founders of Zancle were Perieres of Cumae and Crataemenes of Chalcis. (It was the Sicels who first called the place Zancle, because it is shaped like a sickle—a *zanklon* in the Sicel language.) Later the inhabitants were driven out by the Samians and other Ionians who landed on Sicily in the course of their flight from the Persians, [6] but not many years later Anaxilas, the tyrant of Rhegium, expelled the Samians, founded it himself as a city with a mixed population, and renamed it Messina after his ancestral homeland, Messenia.

5. Himera was founded as a colony of Zancle by Eucleides, Simus, and Sacon. Most of the first settlers were Chalcidians, but they were joined by the Myletidae, as they are called—Syracusan exiles who had been defeated in a civil war. The dialect spoken there was a cross between Chalcidian and Dorian, but the institutions were predominantly Chalcidian. [2] Acrae and Casmenae were founded by Syracusans—Acrae 70 years after the foundation of Syracuse, and Casmenae about 20 years after Acrae. [3] Camarina was originally founded by Syracusans about 135 years after the foundation of Syracuse; its founders were Dascon and Menecolus. But the Camarinaeans were evicted from the city after losing a war against Syracuse, from which they had defected, and then later Hippocrates, the tyrant of Gela, turned founder. He had been given the territory of Camarina as ransom for Syracusan prisoners, and he refounded the city. He in his turn was driven out by Gelon, and then later the city was founded for the third time by the Geloans.†

6. These are the Greek and barbarian peoples of Sicily, and this is the size of the island against which the Athenians had become eager to campaign. The truest cause* of the expedition was that they aimed to rule the entire island, but they also wanted to make themselves look good by helping their kinsmen and the allies they had acquired there.† [2] There were present in Athens envoys from Egesta, and it was they in particular who spurred on the Athenians with their passionate appeals. The reason the envoys were there was that they were at war with the neighboring city of Selinous—the issues were intermarriage rights and disputed land—and since the Selinountians had called in the Syracusans, their allies, the Egestans were hard pressed on land and at sea.

So the Egestans were reminding the Athenians of the treaty of alliance they had concluded with Leontini at the time of Laches's generalship and the earlier war,* and were asking them to send help in the form of a fleet. They came up with many arguments for this, but the main one was that if the Syracusans got away scot-free with their expulsion of the Leontinians* and destroyed the Athenians' remaining Sicilian allies, they would have supreme power in Sicily; then there was a good chance that at some point they would send a substantial force to help the Peloponnesians—as Dorians helping their Dorian kin and as colonists helping their Peloponnesian mother cities—and it was likely that this combined Dorian army would overthrow even the might of Athens. It would therefore be sensible, they said, for the Athenians, with the help of their remaining Sicilian allies, to resist the Syracusans, not least because they themselves would provide enough money to fund the war. [3] After hearing these arguments again and again at meetings of the assembly, from the Egestans and those who were speaking in their support, the Athenians voted, as a first step, to send envoys to Egesta to check whether they really had the money they claimed to have in the state treasury and the sanctuaries, and also to find out what the current situation was in the war between Egesta and Selinous.

7. So the Athenian envoys were dispatched to Sicily. Meanwhile, in the same winter, the Lacedaemonians and their allies (except for the Corinthians) attacked Argolis. They laid waste the land, though not much of it, and carried off grain on carts they had brought with them. Once they had arranged for the Argive exiles to be settled in Orneae* and left a few of their soldiers there, they arranged a temporary truce during which the Orneatae and the Argives were not to damage each other's land, and then they returned home with their forces. [2] Shortly afterward, however, when the Athenians came with thirty ships and six hundred hoplites, the Argives took to the field at full strength and set about besieging Orneae along with the Athenians. But during the night after the first day of the siege, with the army bivouacked at quite a distance from the town, the Orneatae fled. The next day, when the Argives realized what had happened, they razed Orneae to the ground and then withdrew, and later the Athenians sailed for home.

[3] The Athenians also transported a force made up of some of their own cavalry and that of the Macedonian exiles who were being sheltered in Athens to Methone (the one on Macedon's border), and they set about depredating farmland belonging to Perdiccas. [4] The Lacedaemonians sent word to the Chalcidians of the Thraceward region, who had ten-day truces in place with the Athenians, ordering them to provide military support to Perdiccas, but they refused. And so the winter came to an end, and with it the sixteenth year of the current war, the history of which was written by Thucydides.

8. Right at the beginning of the following summer the Athenian envoys returned from Sicily accompanied by the Egestans, who brought sixty talents of uncoined silver, or, in other words, a month's pay for sixty ships, which was how many they were going to ask the Athenians to send. [2] The Athenians convened an assembly to hear what the Egestans and their own envoys had to say; and what they heard was a number of statements that were promising and untrue—in particular, that there was plenty of money available in the sanctuaries and the state treasury. So they voted to send sixty ships to Sicily, under the command of the generals Alcibiades, son of Cleinias; Nicias, son of Niceratus; and Lamachus, son of Xenophanes. Out in the field the generals would not be answerable to anyone else, and they were tasked with helping Egesta against Selinous; with assisting the Leontinians in reestablishing Leontini; and, in general, if the war went well for them, with arranging affairs in Sicily in ways that they judged to be in the best interests of Athens.

[3] The assembly met again four days later to decide how to get the ships ready as quickly as possible and to grant the generals any additional supplies they might need for the expedition. [4] Now, Nicias had not wanted to be chosen as one of the commanders; he thought that the Athenians' decision was a mistake and that the grounds on which they were basing their aim of conquering the whole of Sicily, a massive undertaking, were inadequate and specious. He wished to talk them out of it, and so he stepped up and offered the Athenians the following advice:

9. "The topic before this assembly today is how to go about preparing for the expedition to Sicily. But in my opinion, this begs the very question we should still be asking: whether it's advisable for us to be undertaking the expedition. Perhaps we shouldn't be persuaded by foreigners to commit ourselves to a war that has nothing to do with us; perhaps we should give further thought to such an important matter. [2] And yet I owe my high standing in Athens to warfare; fear of losing my life is a factor that weighs with me less than with others. I'm not saying that a man who takes his personal safety and his property into account isn't just as good a citizen as others. After all, more than anyone else, such a man would have self-interested reasons for wanting the city to be guided to success. But just as in the past I've never sought honor and high office by saying anything other than what I truly believe, so now I shall speak as I judge best for the city. [3] Given the major features of the Athenian character, it would get me nowhere to advise you to preserve what you have and not to risk what's at hand for what's uncertain and no more than a future prospect. What I propose to do instead is explain that this isn't the time for haste and that the place you're targeting is likely to prove ungovernable.

10. "It's my contention that your† desiring to sail there amounts to inviting further enemies over here in addition to those we'd leave behind. [2] Perhaps you imagine that the recent treaty* provides some security. But while it's true that as long as you make no move it will remain in force—even if only in name: certain men from both here and the other side have seen to that—if we suffer a significant defeat anywhere our enemies will rapidly respond by attacking us. After all, in the first place, the agreement was forced on them by the setbacks they had experienced, so that it was less honorable for them than for us, and in the second place, even with the treaty concluded there are many issues still in dispute. [3] Some of our enemies—and not the weakest of them—have yet to accept the treaty, and some of these holdouts are openly at war with us, while others are inhibited by ten-day truces, but only because the Lacedaemonians are still observing the peace. [4] It's more or less a certainty that if they found us with our forces divided—which is exactly what we're rushing to do now—they'd seize the opportunity to attack us with the help of the Sicilian Greeks, whom in the past they'd have valued immensely as allies.

[5] "All this has to be taken into consideration. We shouldn't choose to endanger the city when it's in a precarious position, and we shouldn't chase after a new empire before we've secured the one we have.* I mean, the Chalcidians of the Thraceward region, who've been in rebellion against us for so long, remain unsubdued, and there are other mainlanders whose allegiance is suspect. We're promptly helping the Egestans because they're our allies and they've been wronged, but we have yet to pay back these rebels for the wrongs that we ourselves have long been suffering at their hands.

11. "There's a critical difference involved here: if we subdued the rebels we'd also be able to keep them subdued, but even if we did manage to get the better of the Sicilian Greeks, the distance involved and their numbers would make it hard for us to govern them. But it makes no sense to attack people when it will prove impossible to keep them down if you defeat them, and when, if you fail to defeat them, you'll be worse off than before you made the attempt. [2] It seems to me that the Sicilian Greeks, at any rate as they are now, would be considerably less of a threat to us if they were ruled by the Syracusans, for all that this is the prospect the Egestans are making out to be such a great threat. [3] I mean, as things are at present, they might perhaps come against us one by one as a way of gratifying the Lacedaemonians, but if they were ruled by Syracuse it's unlikely that one empire would pit itself against another, because the means they'd employ to strip us of our empire—that is, cooperation with the Peloponnesians—are likely to be employed by the Peloponnesians to destroy their empire in its turn.

[4] "The Greeks there would be most frightened of us if we stayed away, and secondarily if we made a brief display of our power and then left. We all know that the farther away a power is, and the less it puts its reputation to the test, the more it's an object of awe. But if we were to suffer any kind of setback they'd immediately consider us less of a threat and join with their friends here to attack us. [5] Your own experience with the Lacedaemonians and their allies bears this out, Athenians: it's because you got the better of them when your initial fear of them led you to think success an unlikely outcome that you now feel you can ignore them and set your sights on Sicily. [6] But you shouldn't get overexcited by your enemies' misfortunes; you should feel confident only when you defeat them by superior strategy. You must understand that the only thing that's on the Lacedaemonians' minds, because of their shame, is how even now they might defeat us, and thus reach a satisfactory resolution of their disgrace, especially since above all else and for the longest time they've been cultivating a reputation for military prowess. [7] So if we have any sense, the issue for us is not the barbarian Egestans in Sicily, but how to protect ourselves expeditiously against the oligarchical schemes of Sparta.

12. "We should also bear in mind that we've only recently, and far from fully, recovered from a terrible plague and a war; we've only just started to rebuild our stocks of money and men. And what's right for us is to draw on these stocks here at home—for our own good, not that of these outcasts begging for help. It's in their interest to come up with plausible lies and to involve others in danger while they themselves supply nothing but words. If the enterprise succeeds, there's no way they could express their gratitude that would match our efforts, and if it happens to fail they'll implicate their friends in their destruction. [2] So if a certain person,* who's delighted to have been chosen as one of the commanders, advises you to commit to the expedition, and does so, especially since he's still rather young for command, for purely self-interested reasons—so that, while being admired for his stable of horses, he may also get a little something from his command to offset his extravagant lifestyle—don't provide him with the opportunity to gain personal distinction at the cost of endangering Athens. No, try to see that people like him deplete state funds and squander their own, and that the affair is too important to be decided and hastily taken in hand by a relatively young man.

13. "It scares me to see these people sitting here today offering this man encouragement, and in response I urge those of you who are older not to feel ashamed of being thought a coward if you vote against war, even if you're sitting next to one of these people. I urge you also not to succumb, as they may prove to have done, to an obsessive lust for what you don't have, but to realize that success is hardly ever the outcome of desire, but almost always of forethought. No, for the sake of your homeland, which is now in greater danger, I dare say, than ever before, raise your hands in opposition. The borders between us and Sicily have proven their effectiveness: the Ionian Sea for voyages along the coast, and the Sicilian Sea for voyages across open water. Vote that these borders remain in place and that the Sicilian Greeks may be left to themselves, inhabiting their own land and making their own treaties among themselves too. [2] And I encourage you to tell the Egestans, in particular, that since they started the war against the Selinountians without us, they should also finish it by themselves. And I recommend that in the future we stop forming alliances as we have been accustomed to in the past, with peoples to whose defense we come when they're in trouble but from whom we get no help ourselves when we need it.*

14. "And you, honorable chairman, if you see it as your job to care for the city and you want to be a good citizen, put the matter to the vote and allow the Athenians to renew the debate. If you're worried about putting it to the vote a second time, you may be sure that with so many witnesses present you won't be accused of setting an illegitimate precedent. You'll be curing the city of a bad decision it has reached, and that's exactly what constitutes the proper use of office: it enables a man to help his homeland as best he can, or at any rate to avoid doing it deliberate harm."

15. That was the substance of Nicias's speech, but most of the Athenians who stepped forward after him spoke in favor of the expedition and against revoking the earlier decision; only a few speakers put the opposite case. [2] The one who pushed most vigorously for the expedition was Alcibiades, son of Cleinias, partly because he wanted to oppose Nicias, who was invariably his political enemy and who had referred to him disparagingly in his speech, but especially because he really wanted this command, in the hope that he would be responsible for the capture of both Sicily and Carthage, and that success would benefit him personally by enriching him and enhancing his reputation. [3] For in order to maintain his prestige in Athens, he was indulging his desire for horse-breeding and other expensive pursuits beyond what he could afford. It was this extravagance of his, in fact, that was chiefly responsible later for the defeat of Athens, [4] in the sense that most people became alarmed at the extent to which he was prepared to flout convention in order to satisfy his dissolute lifestyle, and at the scale of his ambitions whenever he became involved in any enterprise. So they turned against him, thinking that he was aiming to make himself tyrant, and although where state affairs were concerned his conduct of the war was outstandingly good,† at a personal level people came to resent his way of life; they therefore placed themselves in others' hands, and before long they had brought about the downfall of the city. [5] Anyway, on the occasion in question he stepped up and addressed the Athenians along the following lines:

16. "Athenians, I have more of a right to command than others—I have to make this my starting point because Nicias attacked me on this issue—and at the same time I believe that I deserve it. The things for which I'm criticized certainly confer glory on my ancestors and myself, but that's not to say that they aren't also good for Athens. [2] There was a time when the Greeks thought that Athens had been ground down by the war, but the magnificent display I put on when I represented our city at the Olympic festival altered their perception of it for the better, even to the extent that they exaggerated its power. What I did was something that no individual has ever done before: I entered seven chariots and came first, second, and fourth, and all my other arrangements for the festival were in keeping with my victory.

"My points are, first, that it's customary for a man who does this kind of thing to be honored, and second, that the very doing of such things leads others to suppose that we are a powerful people. [3] Given all the ways I distinguish myself in the city—the choruses I fund and so on—it's natural for my fellow citizens to become envious, but, again, my distinctiveness also lets the outside world know that we're strong. And it can hardly be described as useless folly when the money a man spends benefits not only himself but also the city. [4] But by the same token, it isn't wrong for such a high-minded man to expect special treatment. After all, there's no question of equal shares when someone's doing badly; his trials and tribulations aren't shared with anyone. So just as any failures among us are ignored by others, people should accept the fact that successful men are going to be superior to them—or they should grant equality to the unfortunate before claiming equality with the successful.

[5] "I know that although such a man—in fact, anyone who stands out for his distinction in any field—is resented during his lifetime, especially by his peers, but also by his contemporaries in general, yet the legacy he leaves behind him is that people claim kinship with him even when the claim is unfounded, and the country of his birth—and this goes for every country in the world—doesn't treat him as an outsider, or as someone who went astray, but as one of their own and as someone to be honored for his achievements. [6] Fame of this kind has been my goal, and that's why I've been criticized for my lifestyle, but consider my management of state affairs and see whether it has been worse than anyone else's. Without endangering you to any significant extent, and without great expense, I brought the most powerful Peloponnesian states together and forced the Lacedaemonians to stake everything on the outcome of a single day at Mantinea.* They may have come off best in the battle, but even now their morale has yet to recover.

17. "And so you can see that my youth and allegedly insane folly came up with effective diplomacy for countering the might of the Peloponnesians; it was precisely my passion that made my words convincing and won people over. So there's no need now to be afraid of my character. As long as I'm still at the height of my youthful powers, and as long as Nicias seems to be blessed by fortune, make use of what the two of us have to offer. [2] And don't change your minds about the expedition to Sicily on the ground that we'd be sailing against a great power. The cities there may be populous, but their populations are made up of rabbles drawn from here and there, since the citizen bodies are very changeable and liable to new intakes. [3] And as a result, no one feels himself to be living in a place to which he owes loyalty, and they haven't equipped themselves with weaponry for their personal safety or with the usual farmsteads in the countryside. Instead, either by persuasive oratory or as a result of factional disputes, and taking the view that if they fail to make a go of it where they are they can relocate elsewhere, individuals take what they can from public funds and make that their source of income. [4] It's hardly likely that this kind of rabble listens with one mind to proposals or is capable of cooperation when it comes to action. It's more likely that states would come over to our side one by one, if what we tell them is attractive enough, especially if they're at odds with one another, as our information leads us to believe.

[5] "Moreover, although they brag about their hoplites, they don't have even as many of these as they claim. Remember how throughout Greece there turned out to be fewer hoplites than each state had reckoned it possessed; in fact, finding that they'd been greatly deceived about their number, the Greeks struggled to come up with adequate forces of hoplites for the current war. [6] That, or so I've heard, is how things stand in Sicily, and there's also yet another factor that will smooth the way for us even more: we'll be joined by many barbarians, who'll support our attack on the Syracusans because they hate them. Nor will the situation here in Greece be an impediment, if you look at it right. [7] After all, our fathers had the same enemies as those we're now being told we'd leave behind if we sailed against Sicily, and they had the Persians as enemies as well, and yet they acquired our empire without any advantage other than their strength at sea. [8] In any case, the Peloponnesians have never been more defeatist when facing us than they are today, and even if their confidence were high, they have the capacity only to invade Attica (which they can do even if we don't sail for Sicily), but they can't make trouble for us with their fleet, because the ships we'll have left behind will be a match for them at sea.

18. "So what plausible reason could we have for hesitating? What reason could we come up with for not going to help our allies there? We have an obligation to defend them since, after all, we exchanged oaths with them to that effect, and we also shouldn't excuse ourselves by arguing that they didn't help us. The reason we included them in our alliance was not to make it possible for them to come here and help us in our struggles, but so that they might make trouble for our enemies there, and so prevent them from coming here and attacking us. [2] That's how we acquired our empire—and the same goes for all imperialists, not just us: we unhesitatingly responded to pleas for help as they arrived, whether they came from barbarians or Greeks. After all, if we were to do absolutely nothing or were to distinguish on ethnic lines whom we should and shouldn't help, we'd hardly add to the empire at all. In fact, we'd risk losing it altogether, because, faced with a superior power, people don't just defend themselves against it when it attacks, but take steps to ensure that no attack occurs in the first place. [3] It isn't up to us to regulate the extent to which we'd like to be rulers; given the position we occupy, we have no choice but to intrigue against some of our subjects and keep a tight grip on the rest, because if we aren't the rulers of others, the chances are that we'll be ruled by others ourselves. A policy of inaction must mean something different to you than it does to others, unless you change your ways to resemble theirs.

[4] "Our conclusion, then, can only be that by attacking our enemies there we'll improve our situation here—and that being so, let's undertake the expedition. We'll stamp out Peloponnesian pride if they see us scorning the torpor by which everyone is gripped and sailing against Sicily of all places. Moreover, there are two possible outcomes: either—and this is most likely—once we've added the cities there to our alliance, we'll be the effective rulers of all Greece, or we will at least weaken the Syracusans, which will be good for us and for our allies. [5] Our ships will make it safe for us to stay, if things are going well, or leave, because as masters of the seas we'll contain the Sicilian Greeks, even all of them at once. [6] And don't be put off by Nicias, with his talk of nonintervention, and his attempt to set the younger generation at variance with the older. No, relying on your usual orderly system—the one employed by our fathers, too, who when young raised the city to the pinnacle it now occupies by conferring with their elders—try likewise not to impede the city's advance. Take the view that youth and age are helpless without each other, and that the city is at its strongest when it's a blend of everyone together, whether their abilities are third-rate, average, or first-rate, and that it will degenerate, just as anything does, if it's idle, and all its expertise

will wither. On the other hand, if it keeps contending, it will gain additional experience, and will become further accustomed to defending itself by action rather than mere words. [7] All in all, I'd state my view as being that a city which is accustomed to activity would very quickly be ruined by a change to inactivity, and that the people who live in the greatest security are those who deviate as little as possible, in the conduct of their political lives, from their existing customs and systems, even if these customs and systems aren't ideal."

19. The effect of this speech by Alcibiades, along with those of the Egestans and the exiled Leontinians—who stepped up, reminded the Athenians of the oaths they had sworn, and requested help by formally supplicating them—was to make the Athenians far more committed to the expedition than they had been before. [2] Nicias realized that the time had passed when he might have dissuaded them with the same arguments he had used before, but he thought he might be able to get them to change their minds if he stressed the scale of the armament that would be required and just how great it would have to be. So he stepped up and delivered another speech, along the following lines:

20. "Athenians, it's obvious that you're utterly determined to undertake this expedition, and I pray that it will turn out as well as we hope, but given the circumstances I shall continue to speak my mind. [2] On my understanding of the information I've received, these are sizable cities that we're intending to attack, and it's not the case that some are subject to others, or that they're in need of regime change of a kind that they might welcome, such as a move from enforced servitude to a less oppressive form of government; nor are they likely to thank us for replacing their freedom with subjection to our empire. And their numbers are another factor: there are many Greek cities there, considering that it's just one island. [3] Not counting Naxos and Catana, which I expect to side with us because of their kinship with the Leontinians, there are seven other Greek cities. Their resources are in all respects on a par with ours, and this goes above all for the two cities against which we're sailing, Selinous and Syracuse. [4] What

I mean is that they have plenty of hoplites, archers, and javelineers, and plenty of triremes and a host of people to man them. They have money, some of it in private hands, and some also in the sanctuaries of Selinous, and in addition the Syracusans are paid a tithe in tribute by some of the barbarian Sicilians. But the chief ways in which they have the advantage over us are that they have plenty of cavalry and their grain is homegrown rather than imported.*

21. "Against this kind of might what's needed is not just a fleet and an ordinary army, but a fleet with large numbers of land forces on board—that is, if we want to make good our plans and not be excluded from land operations by their numerous cavalry. And we'll need this large land army especially if the cities are sufficiently frightened of us to join forces, and if we fail to make any friends (except the Egestans) who might supply us with cavalry for our defense in numbers that match the enemy's. [2] It would be disgraceful for us to be forced off the island or to send for reinforcements later just because we hadn't thought things through carefully enough in the first place. The initial force that we send against the island must be large enough for the job at hand, and it must reflect the recognition that we're planning to launch an expedition far from our own country, and that this won't be the same kind of campaign as when you attacked someone to support your subjects in this part of the world.† Here there's friendly territory from which you can easily be supplied with necessaries, but for this expedition you'll be leaving home far behind and going to an altogether foreign country, from which it's not easy for a messenger to return, even within four months, during the winter.

22. "So in my opinion, in order to hold our own against the enemy cavalry, we should take a large force of hoplites and large numbers of archers and slingers. There should be both Athenian hoplites and allied hoplites from our subject states and from any of our Peloponnesian allies that we can persuade or hire to join us. We must have clear superiority at sea to facilitate supplying our forces, but we must also take grain with us from here in cargo ships, in the form of wheat and

roasted barley, and bakers as well, who are to be withdrawn proportionately from the mills and pressed into paid service. That way, even if unfavorable sailing weather makes it impossible for supply ships to get through, the army will still have food—the point being that it will be so large that few of the cities there will be able to accommodate it. And we must get everything else ready as best we can and avoid becoming dependent on others; above all, there must be as much money as possible available from here. It would be better to regard the Egestan money, which we're told is ready there, as being ready only in theory.

23. "My point is this: If we go there ourselves, equipped not only with a corps of hoplites that is a match for them (except when compared with their overall fighting strength), but actually surpassing them in every point, even so it will be difficult for us to conquer Sicily or indeed to extricate ourselves safely. [2] We should think of ourselves as an expeditionary force going to found a city among hostile foreigners, in the sense that such people have to gain control of the land on the first day, as soon as they come ashore, because they know that if they fail in that the whole country will be up in arms against them. [3] This is exactly the possibility that I'm afraid of, and I'm therefore aware that, while we're sorely in need of good planning, we're even more in need of good luck. But since luck is by definition fickle, I want to entrust myself to it as little as possible on this expedition and to rely for my safety—insofar as one can reasonably be sure of such a thing—on armament. [4] That, in my opinion, is the way to guarantee safety for Athens as a whole as well as for us, the soldiers of the expeditionary force. And I'm prepared to resign my command in favor of anyone who thinks otherwise."

24. With these words Nicias hoped either to dissuade the Athenians from undertaking the expedition, by giving them an idea of the scale of what was needed, or, if he was compelled to embark on the campaign, to at least be able to do so with forces that would make it as safe as possible. [2] But far from becoming disenchanted with the expedition because of the effort required to prepare for it, the Athenians became even more enthusiastic. Nicias's plan completely backfired: they thought his advice was good and that if they followed it they would minimize the risk. [3] Everyone alike was consumed by lust for the expedition: the older men because they believed either that they would overwhelm the places they were sailing against, or at least that nothing disastrous could happen to such a mighty force; the younger generation because they longed for adventure in distant lands and were confident that they would come to no harm; and the mass of ordinary soldiers and sailors because they believed they would profit in the short term and that the increase in Athenian power would bring them endless pay in the future. [4] And the outcome of this excessive enthusiasm by the majority was that dissenters were so afraid of being thought unpatriotic if they voted against the expedition that they did nothing.

25. Eventually, an Athenian stepped up and appealed to Nicias. He said he should stop prevaricating and procrastinating, and should state there and then, in front of everyone, what resources the Athenians should vote to approve for him. [2] But Nicias was unwilling to do that. He said he would prefer to discuss this question unhurriedly with the other commanders, but that as far as he could judge there and then they would need to sail with at least a hundred of their own triremes, some of which (the precise number to be decided) should be troop-carriers, and that they should requisition other ships from their allies. As for the total number of Athenian and allied troops, he said there should be at least five thousand, and more if possible, and that the rest of the forces which they should get ready and take with them—archers from Athens and Crete, slingers, and any other kinds of soldiers that seemed appropriate—should be commensurate with these numbers.

26. Immediately after this speech, the Athenians voted that the generals were to have full powers to decide about the size of the expeditionary force and all the arrangements for sailing, and should do whatever they judged best for Athens. [2] After this they went ahead with the preparations, which is to say that they sent the allies their instructions and drew up lists of those who were to be drafted in Athens. There were factors that made it easier for them to furnish themselves with everything: the city had recently recovered from the plague and the years of relentless warfare, there was a plentiful new crop of young men, and the lack of warfare had enabled them to accumulate funds.

But while they were busy with these arrangements, **27.** in a single night almost all the stone herms in Athens (the familiar ones with the rectangular form that is typical of Athenian herms), of which there were many standing before the doorways of private homes and in sanctuaries, had their faces mutilated.* [2] The perpetrators were unknown, but the state offered substantial rewards for information in an attempt to track them down, and in addition they passed a decree granting immunity to anyone—citizen, foreigner, or slave—who chose to apprise the authorities about any other sacrilegious act of which they knew. [3] They took the matter more seriously than they otherwise might, because it was widely regarded as a bad omen for the expedition* and also as the work of a revolutionary conspiracy to overthrow the democracy.*

28. Information was duly received from some metics and their attendants, but it had nothing to do with the herms; it concerned earlier occasions when other statues had been mutilated by drunken young men as a prank, and they also told of mock celebrations of the Mysteries that had taken place in private houses.* Alcibiades was one of those who was accused of this sacrilege. [2] The fact that Alcibiades was implicated was seized on by those who particularly resented him because he stood in the way of their ambition to be the undisputed champions of the people. They thought that if they could get him exiled they would be the city's leading politicians, so they made a great deal of the affair. They loudly insisted that the motive for both the profanation of the Mysteries and the mutilation of the herms had been to overthrow the democracy, and that none of this had been done without his involvement, citing as evidence his general lawlessness and elitist way of life.

29. At first, Alcibiades tried to defend himself against the charges. Despite the fact that by now everything that was needed for the expedition was ready, he said that before setting sail he was willing to stand trial to resolve the question of whether he was guilty as charged, and to pay the penalty if he was found guilty of any of the charges, but he insisted that he should retain his command if he was found not guilty. [2] He begged the Athenians not to listen to scurrilous talk about him while he was absent, but to put him to death right away if they found him guilty, and he argued that it would be more prudent for them not to send him off on such an important campaign with a charge of this kind unresolved. [3] But his enemies were afraid that if he stood trial right away he would have the soldiers and sailors of the expeditionary force rooting for him, and that the people might weaken and take his part because it was thanks to him that the Argives and some of the Mantineans were joining the expedition. So they set about persuading the Athenians that his trial should be postponed, and deterring them from holding it right away by putting forward yet more speakers to argue that the departure of the expeditionary force should not be delayed; Alcibiades should sail immediately, they said, but should return and stand trial within a specified number of days. What they wanted to do was come up with even more serious charges against him—which would be easier if he was absent—before sending for him and bringing him back to stand trial. And the Athenians decided that Alcibiades should set sail.

30. After this—by which time it was midsummer—the expeditionary force left Athens for Sicily. Most of the allies, the grain-transports, the warships, and all the rest of the supporting force had earlier been ordered to assemble at Corcyra, and from there they were to sail together across the Ionian Sea to Cape Iapygia. The Athenians themselves and some of the allies who were in Athens went down to Piraeus at daybreak on the appointed day and manned the ships for departure. [2] It is hardly an exaggeration to say that all the rest of the residents of Athens, both citizens and foreigners, also accompanied them down to Piraeus. Every Athenian was sending on their way those they held dear—friends, relatives, sons—and as they went their mood was a combination of hope and misery: the prospect of extending the empire gave them hope, but the possibility that this might be the last time they saw their loved ones, bearing in mind how far from home they were being sent, elicited cries of grief. **31.** Since the time had come for them to separate from one another in perilous circumstances, the dangers occurred to them more than when they had voted for the expedition, but they were still encouraged by the immediate show of strength—by the sheer quantity of all the various assets they could see before their eyes. As for the foreigners and the rest of the crowd, they came to view the execution of a remarkable, extraordinary plan, because this initial force was the most costly and magnificent ever to have been dispatched by a single Greek city at the height of its powers.

[2] The number of ships and hoplites that made up the force sent against Epidaurus under Pericles* (which was the same force that was then sent under Hagnon against Potidaea) was about the same: on that occasion, Athens alone contributed four thousand hoplites, three hundred cavalrymen, and a hundred triremes, and then there were fifty triremes from Lesbos and Chios, and all the many allied troops who were included in the expedition. [3] But they had only a short way to go to reach their destination and their equipment was unexceptional, whereas this expeditionary force expected to be away for a long time and had the ships and land forces to deal with contingencies both at sea and on land. Great and extremely costly pains had been taken over the fleet by the trierarchs and the city: the state was paying every oarsman a drachma a day and had supplied the hulls of sixty warships,† forty troop-carriers, and first-class officers for them, while the trierarchs contributed extra pay, on top of what the state was providing, for the upper bench of oarsmen and the officers,* and spent money freely on the figureheads and other fittings with which they were expected to furnish the ships. Each of the trierarchs went to the greatest lengths to ensure that his own ship stood out as much as possible from the rest

for its magnificence and speed, and there was keen competition among the infantrymen (who had been selected from the best of the call-up lists)* over the quality of their weaponry and personal equipment.

[4] Given the mutual rivalry among men assigned the same functions in the expeditionary force, it all looked more like a display of Athenian might and power designed to impress the Greeks at large than a force that was going to fight a war. [5] If the amount of money the state spent on the expedition, and the amount that individual soldiers spent, too, had been added up, it would have been found that altogether a vast amount of money was being taken out of Athens. The state's expenses included not just what it had already spent, but the funds it was sending out with the generals, and individuals' expenses included not just what they had spent on their personal equipment, and, if they were trierarchs, what they had spent on their ships, and would spend in the future, but also, even apart from his state pay, the amount that every man was likely to have brought as travel money, on the assumption that this was going to be a protracted campaign, and all that individual soldiers or merchants were taking on board for trading purposes. [6] In fact, the expeditionary force attracted just as much attention for its astonishing audacity and brilliant appearance as for its superiority in military terms over those it was going against; and then there were also the facts that this was the longest voyage from home ever attempted by such a force, and that it was undertaken with the highest hopes for the future, based on its resources.

32. When the ships had their full complement of crews and everything they intended to take with them had been stowed on board, the trumpet sounded the signal for silence and they spoke the prayers that are customary before putting to sea, but they all did so at once, conducted by a herald, rather than one ship at a time. Then wine was mixed with water in great jars, and on every ship the marines and the commanding officers poured libations from gold and silver cups. [2] And all the onlookers on land, both Athenian citizens and others present who wished Athens well, joined in the prayers. After they had chanted a paean and all the libations had been poured, they put to sea. At first they went in single file, but then they raced one another as far as Aegina, and from there they set out with all due speed for Corcyra, which was where the rest of their allies were assembling.

[3] Meanwhile, rumors about the expedition were reaching Syracuse from all quarters, but for a long time they were dismissed as utterly incredible. An assembly was convened, but even then the people who spoke were divided (as the following speeches illustrate) between those who trusted the information about the Athenian campaign and those who thought the opposite. One of those who spoke was Hermocrates, son of Hermon. Believing that he had clear knowledge of the facts, he stepped up to address the Syracusans and offered the following advice:

33. "I imagine that you'll disbelieve me, as you have others, too, when I tell you the truth about the Athenians' expedition, and I'm well aware that people who deliver either a speech or a report that seems to defy belief not only fail to persuade their listeners but are also taken to be foolish. All the same, seeing that the city is at risk, I'm not going to let such concerns hold me back, since I'm sure in my own mind that what I have to say is based on clearer knowledge of the facts than anyone else's. [2] For all that you find it astonishing, the Athenians have indeed set out against you with a substantial force of both ships and men. They claim to be coming to Sicily to aid their allies, the Egestans, and to restore Leontini, but the truth is that they want to possess Sicily, and especially our city, because they think that if Syracuse is theirs the rest of the island will easily fall to them. [3] So since you can safely assume that they'll be here before long, you need to see how to make the best use of your resources to defend against them. It would be a mistake to think them no threat, because then you'll be taken off your guard, and it would be a mistake to disbelieve what I'm saying, because then you'll fail to take any steps at all to protect the city.

[4] "But even if you believe what I'm saying, there's no reason to be dismayed by their audacity and their power. We'll be able to give as good as we get, and the fact that they're coming with a substantial army

actually plays into our hands. They'll be doing us a considerable favor where all the other Sicilian Greeks are concerned, who out of fear will be more willing to fight alongside us, and whether we defeat them or repel them before they've done what they came to do—for I have no doubt that, one way or another, their expectations will be frustrated—we'll end up with a glorious achievement to our name. And I fully expect this outcome, [5] because it's a rare expeditionary force, whether Greek or barbarian, that's been successful a long way from home. First, they arrive in lesser numbers than the native inhabitants and their neighbors, who are all frightened into joining forces; second, they might fail from lack of supplies on foreign soil—but even then they bequeath renown to the people they planned to subdue, even when the failure is largely their own fault.* [6] By the same token, when, contrary to expectations, the Persians suffered a massive defeat, these same Athenians were acclaimed, because it was Athens that the Persians had come to attack. It wouldn't be surprising if the same thing happened in our case.

34. "So let's make our preparations in a spirit of confidence. We need to send envoys to the Sicels to consolidate our relationship with some and try to get on good terms with others, to make them our allies. And let's send envoys to the rest of Sicily to explain that they're in as much danger as we are, and to Italy with a view to entering into alliances with the cities there or at least making sure that they won't receive the Athenians. [2] In fact, I think we ought to send envoys even to Carthage. The situation won't surprise them, because the possibility of an Athenian attack on their city is a constant concern of theirs; since they're likely, then, to think that if they do nothing to help Sicily they'll be laying up trouble for themselves, they'll probably be willing to help us, either secretly or openly—or somehow, at any rate. If they choose to do so, there's no one with greater resources than them nowadays; they have more gold and silver than anyone else, and it's money that ensures success in war and in everything else. [3] Let's also send a delegation to Sparta and Corinth to ask them to send help here right away and to revive the war there.

[4] "There's another measure—one that I think the circumstances particularly call for—but your habitual lack of enterprise will make you reluctant to agree to it. Still, here goes. If all the Sicilian Greeks, or at least as many as will join us, launched all the ships we have with provisions for two months and confronted the Athenians at Taras and Cape Iapygia, leaving them in no doubt that the contest will be about crossing the Ionian Sea before it's about Sicily, nothing would unnerve them more. We'd force them to calculate that while we're protecting Sicily from a friendly base—Taras being on good terms with us—they have a lot of sea to get across with all their armament. They'd realize that the length of the voyage will make it hard for them to stay in formation, and that therefore, since they could only engage us in a sluggish and piecemeal fashion, they'll be vulnerable to being attacked by us. [5] Alternatively, they might leave the heavier ships behind and come at us with their fastest ships in close formation. Well, if they've been using oars, we'll be attacking exhausted men, and if we decide not to attack, we also have the possibility of retiring to Taras. In the latter case, they—now with little in the way of provisions, because they crossed the sea expecting to fight—would find themselves on an uninhabited stretch of coastline and wouldn't know what to do with themselves. If they found somewhere to stay, we'd box them in, and if they tried sailing along the coast they'd abandon the rest of their fleet, and their morale would be sapped by the uncertainty of knowing how the cities stood, and whether any of them would give them shelter.

[6] "Speaking for myself, then, I am convinced that these calculations will check them and they won't even move from Corcyra. Either they'll spend time talking things over and gathering intelligence about our numbers and our dispositions, and then they'll be overtaken by winter, or they'll be so shocked by this unexpected turn of events that they'll disband the expeditionary force. And this latter possibility is all the more likely because my information is that the most experienced of their generals is in command against his will and would be delighted to have an excuse to give up if he were faced

with some significant action on our part. [7] Our numbers would be exaggerated in the reports they received, of that I'm quite certain, and it's human nature for the mind to be swayed by what it hears. It's also human nature to be more frightened of people who attack first, or at least leave the attackers in no doubt that they'll resist, because that makes the attackers realize that they're in as much danger as their opponents. [8] This is exactly what the Athenians must be feeling at the moment. They're attacking us on the assumption that we won't put up a fight, and their low opinion of us is justified because we didn't join the Lacedaemonians and see to their destruction. But if, contrary to their expectations, they see us taking bold action, they'll be more frightened by the surprise than by our true power.

[9] "I hope above all that I can persuade you to take this bold course, but failing that I hope to persuade you to get everything ready for war as quickly as possible. Everyone here should be aware that although contempt for attackers is demonstrated by valor in the field, the most expedient course for us now would be to consider preparations made in fear to be safest and to act as though we were in immediate danger. The Athenians are coming. In fact, I have not the slightest doubt that they're already at sea and are almost here."

35. That was the substance of Hermocrates's speech, but the Syracusans still held various conflicting views. Some believed that there was no way the Athenians would come and that Hermocrates was mistaken; others maintained that even if they did come, what they could do to the Syracusans was less than what the Syracusans could do to them; yet others belittled the whole business and turned it into a joke. There were only a few who believed Hermocrates and were fearful of what the future might bring. [2] The next person who stepped up to speak was Athenagoras, a demagogue who at the time was the speaker the people found the most persuasive. He spoke somewhat as follows:

36. "Anyone who doesn't want the Athenians to be deluded enough to come here and fall into our hands is either a coward or unpatriotic. I'm not surprised by the audacity of those who perpetuate such rumors and try to scare us out of our wits, but I'm astonished at their stupidity if they think their motives aren't transparent. [2] It's because they have personal reasons for being afraid that they want to reduce the city to panic; that way, they think, they can use the general fear as a screen for their own activities. And that's exactly the effect of the rumors they've been spreading. After all, these rumors didn't appear out of thin air: they're man-made, and the men who made them are those who never stop stirring things up here. [3] You'd be well advised to work out what's likely to be true by focusing your inquiries not on the reports delivered by these men, but on what clever and experienced people would do—people such as I take the Athenians to be. [4] They're hardly likely to leave the Peloponnesians behind when the peace there is still fragile and undertake another war just as great as the one in Greece.* In fact, in my opinion, given the number and size of our cities, they're happy it's not *we* who are attacking *them*.

37. "But suppose the reports are correct and the Athenians were to come. In my opinion, Sicily has more resources for carrying on a war than the Peloponnese does: it's better equipped in all respects, and our city on its own is far stronger than the army that's supposed to be on its way, even were it twice as large. In any case, I'm sure the Athenians aren't bringing any cavalrymen with them—and they won't be able to gain any from here either, apart from a few from Egesta—nor are their hoplites as numerous as ours. The reason for this is that they're coming by sea. I mean, it would be a major achievement for them to complete the long voyage here with just unladen ships, and they'll have all the rest of the equipment, hardly an insignificant amount, that they need for an attack on a city as great as ours. [2] It follows—and I have no hesitation in saying this—that even if they brought with them another city as great as Syracuse, settled on our border, and made war on us, they'd surely struggle to avoid complete destruction. And their destruction will be all the more likely given that all Sicily will unite and fight them, and that their base will be a camp hastily assembled on landing; they'll have nothing beyond their mere tents and a bare minimum of supplies, while our cavalry will prevent them from going out on extended foraging expeditions. In short, I very much doubt that they'd be able even to establish themselves on land; that's how much stronger I consider our forces to be.

38. "But, as I say, I'm sure that since the Athenians are well aware of the difficulty of attacking us, they're safeguarding their empire as it stands, and that men here are making up stories that are and always would be impossibilities. [2] This isn't the first time I've known what these men are up to; I've never doubted that their intention is to terrify you, the people of Syracuse, as a way to gain political power in the city themselves. This is why they perpetuate rumors like these or even more pernicious ones, and it also underlies what they do. What I'm truly afraid of is that these constant efforts of theirs may bring them success; we're bad both at taking precautions before we suffer and at doing anything about it when we realize what's going on. [3] That is why the city is rarely at peace. That is why it frequently brings more dissension and conflict upon itself than on its enemies, and why we're sometimes afflicted by tyrannies and narrow oligarchies that trample on people's rights.

[4] "If you allow me to lead the way, I shall do my best to make sure that none of these evils occurs in our time. I shall persuade you, the majority, to punish those who contrive such schemes, not just when they're caught in the act (which is not an easy thing to do), but also for what they would do if they could. The point is that it's essential to forestall not just an enemy's actions but his intentions, inasmuch as the person who's the first to suffer is the one who fails to take precautions. And as for the few, the oligarchs, I shall challenge them, keep a close watch on them, try to get them to mend their ways. I think that's the best way to head off their nefarious schemes. [5] And then I've often asked myself: What actually is it that you young men want? To hold high office already? But that's illegal, under a law that was established not to keep people out of office if they have the competence, but because you aren't ready for it. Or is it that you don't want to be on

a footing of equality with the general populace? But how can it be fair for members of the same citizen body not to enjoy the same rights?

39. "It may be objected that democracy is neither intelligent nor fair, and that men of property also make the best and most competent political leaders. But to this I reply that democracy is the name of the system that involves the community as a whole, whereas oligarchy involves only a fraction of it; that rich people are best at protecting state assets and intelligent people at offering advice, but the common people are best at assessing the advice they've been given; and that in a democracy these three groups, severally and all together, have an equal share. [2] Oligarchs, however, pass risks on to ordinary people while not merely demanding more than their fair share of the benefits, but denying them to others and keeping them all for themselves. That's what you rich young men want, but in a great city such ambitions will always be thwarted.*

40. "You utter fools: If you don't understand that you're promoting measures that are bad for the city, there are two alternatives. Either you're less intelligent than any Greek I've ever heard of, or you're less just, if you recognize the perniciousness of your measures but persist in pushing them. But even now it's not too late. Either because of some new insight or because you've changed your ways, promote the interests of the state, interests that are shared by all its citizens, in the realization that if you do this you can have a fair share—and the best of you a greater share—of the benefits enjoyed by the general populace, but that if you follow a different course the chances are that you'll lose everything. And let's have no more of these reports and rumors; recognize that the people you're addressing know what you're up to and won't let you get away with it. [2] The point is that even if the Athenians are on their way, this city of ours will put up a defense in keeping with its greatness; we have generals who'll see to that. And if, as I believe, none of these reports is true, the city won't be terrified by your words into choosing you as its leaders and thereby imposing self-inflicted enslavement on itself. No, it will consider your words objectively as though they were equivalent to deeds, and rather than being robbed of its existing freedom on the basis of your rumors, it will try to remain free by taking practical steps to make sure that it remains out of your hands."

41. After Athenagoras had spoken in this vein, one of the generals got to his feet and suggested that there was no need for any more speeches. He himself responded to the situation by speaking along the following lines: [2] "It's pointless for speakers to make personal attacks on one another and for the audience to listen to such things. What we should be doing, in view of the reports that keep coming in, is seeing how each and every one of us, and the city as a whole, can best get ready to repel the attackers. [3] Even if the effort turns out to be unnecessary, there's nothing lost by enhancing the glory of the state with all the accoutrements in which war exults, such as horses and weaponry. [4] We generals will see that this happens and oversee the proceedings. We'll also make sure that men are sent around the cities for reconnaissance and for any other purposes that seem appropriate. We have in fact already taken some such steps, and anything we discover will be brought promptly to your attention." After this speech by the general, the Syracusans dissolved the assembly.

42. By then the Athenians and their allies had all assembled at Corcyra. The first thing the generals did was carry out a final review of the army and organize the anchorages for the ships and the campsites for the troops. They formed the army into three divisions, with each general assigned one division by lot, first so that they could stagger the times when they were at sea and avoid a shortage of water, anchorages, and supplies at the places where they put in; and second because, with the generals assigned separate divisions, the army would be more orderly and manageable. [2] Then they sent three ships on ahead to Italy and Sicily to find out which cities would give them shelter, with instructions also to meet them ahead of time so that they knew where to go.

43. The Athenians then set out from Corcyra for Sicily with their forces, which were as follows: a total of 135 triremes (100 from Athens, of which 60 were fast sailers and the rest troop-carriers, with the

Chians and other allies supplying the remainder) and 2 pentecouters from Rhodes; a total of 5,100 hoplites (of whom 1,500 were Athenians from the call-up lists, 600 were thetes serving on board the ships as marines,* and the rest were auxiliaries supplied by the allies, some of them Athenian subjects, but also 500 Argives and 250 Mantinean and other mercenaries); a total of 480 archers (80 of whom were from Crete); 700 Rhodian slingers; 120 Megarian exiles serving as light-armed troops; and a cavalry squadron of 30 men on board a single horse-transport.

44. This was the size of the initial force that was sailing over to Sicily for the war. Their supplies and provisions were carried by 30 grain-transports, which also had on board bakers, stonemasons, joiners, and tools for wall-building, and along with these cargo ships there were another 100 vessels that had been conscripted for the expedition. Many other ships and merchant vessels also accompanied the fleet of their own free will for commercial reasons, and they all set out at this time across the Ionian Sea from Corcyra. [2] The whole force made land at Cape Iapygia and Taras, or wherever they could, and then sailed along the Italian coast until they reached Rhegium on the toe of Italy. But on the way no city granted them more than water and anchorage—and Taras and Locri not even these—while refusing them access to a market or even entry into the town.

[3] While they were assembling at Rhegium, they made camp outside the town—they did not have permission to go inside—at the sanctuary of Artemis, and the Rhegians provided them with a market there. After beaching the ships they took no further action. They entered into discussions with the Rhegians, arguing that, as Chalcidians, they should support the Chalcidian Leontinians,* but the Rhegians said they would remain neutral and would do whatever the other Italian Greeks collectively decided to do. [4] The Athenians started to think about the best way to conduct their campaign in Sicily, and at the same time they were waiting for the ships they had sent on ahead to return from Egesta, because they wanted to know if the money the messengers had mentioned in Athens actually existed.

45. Meanwhile, the Syracusans had been receiving undeniable reports from all kinds of sources, not least their scouts, that the Athenian fleet was at Rhegium, and under these circumstances they could no longer be in any doubt and set about their preparations with a will. Among other measures, they sent men to the Sicels—garrison troops in some cases, envoys in others—and manned the frontier posts in their own territory. Within the city itself, they checked the weaponry and horses to make sure that they were up to the mark, and did whatever else they needed to do for a war that was rapidly approaching and was in fact almost upon them.

46. The three ships that had been sent on ahead returned from Egesta and rejoined the Athenians at Rhegium; they reported that the rest of the money the Egestans had promised did not exist and that thirty talents was all that was forthcoming. [2] The generals' confidence plummeted at this early setback on top of the refusal of the Rhegians to fight alongside them; it was not just that the Rhegians had been the first people they had tried to win over, but that they had had a better chance of success with them than anyone else, because they were allies of the Leontinians and had always been well disposed toward Athens. As for the Egestans, although Nicias had expected this outcome, it came as a shock to the other two generals.

[3] The scheme the Egestans devised to fool the Athenians was as follows: When the first Athenian envoys had come to inspect their resources, they had taken them to the sanctuary of Aphrodite at Eryx and shown them the dedications; there were a great many objects—goblets, ladles, censers, and so on—and they were all of silver, so their impressive appearance effectively disguised the reality of their meager financial resources. And when they entertained the Athenian crews in private homes, they not only collected the gold and silver drinking-vessels from Egesta itself, but borrowed more from the nearby towns as well, both Carthaginian and Greek, and whenever entertainment was being laid on, these vessels were brought into the house and passed off as the host's own. [4] So, since everyone was using pretty

much the same vessels, and wherever the Athenians from the triremes went they saw many valuable items, they were dazzled, and when they returned to Athens they reported that they had seen evidence of a great deal of wealth. [5] And when word got around that the Egestans did not have the money, those who had been taken in themselves and who had then convinced others came in for heavy criticism from the troops. But the generals turned to deliberating about how to proceed given the realities of their situation.

47. Nicias's proposal was that they should use the entire army for an attack on Selinous, which was after all the primary objective of their mission. If the Egestans came up with money for the whole army, they should rethink their plans, but if not they should at least demand that they provide upkeep for the sixty ships they had asked for, and stand fast until they had brought their war with the Selinountians to an end either by force of arms or diplomacy. Then, after sailing past the other cities, letting them see the might of Athens and demonstrating their commitment to their friends and allies, they should sail for home, unless they were able briefly and unexpectedly to help the Leontinians or bring any of the other cities over to their side. At any rate, he said, they should not endanger Athens by squandering Athenian money.

48. Alcibiades said that with such a large army at their disposal it would be shameful to leave and return home without having achieved anything. What they should do is approach all the Greek cities other than Selinous and Syracuse, and befriend the Sicels as well or get those who were subjects of Syracuse to defect. Then the Sicels would supply them with grain and men. But the first step, he said, was to win over the Messinians, because Messina was situated exactly where ships make land after crossing over from Italy, and could act both as a safe harbor and as a base of operations that had the capacity for their forces. Only once they had won over the cities and knew who would be fighting on whose side should they attack Syracuse and Selinous, unless the Selinountians came to terms with the Egestans and the Syracusans allowed the Athenians to resettle Leontini.

49. Lamachus said they should attack nowhere else but Syracuse and should lose no time in bringing the Syracusans to battle close to the city, before they had time to prepare and while they were still in as much of a panic as they ever would be. [2] Every army, he argued, is at its most formidable at the beginning, whereas if it wastes time before putting in an appearance people's courage revives, and they're more likely to think it no threat when they actually see it. But if they were to attack suddenly, while the Syracusans were still frightened by the prospect of their coming, success would almost be guaranteed, and everything would work in their favor to terrify the Syracusans: the sight of them (because now was the time when they would appear at their most numerous), the Syracusans' anticipation of future suffering, and especially the threat of imminent battle. [3] In all probability, he went on, because the Syracusans were in denial about the Athenian expedition there would still be plenty of people outside the city in the fields, and while they were moving themselves and their belongings into the city there would be rich pickings for the army, if they took up a dominant position close to the city. [4] Under these circumstances, the rest of the Sicilian Greeks were unlikely to ally themselves with the Syracusans and would come over to them without waiting to see which side won. And he said that they should leave Rhegium and make Megara Hyblaea their anchorage and base of operations, as it was deserted* and was not far from Syracuse by either sea or land.

50. Despite submitting these proposals, when it came to making a decision Lamachus threw his weight behind Alcibiades's plan, so next Alcibiades went to Messina on his own ship and raised the prospect of an alliance. The Messinians refused to entertain the idea, however, and Alcibiades returned to Rhegium with their response: that they would provide the Athenians with a market outside the city, but they were not allowed inside. [2] Immediately after his return, the generals manned and provisioned sixty ships, selected from all three divisions, and sailed to Naxos, leaving the rest of the army in Rhegium with one of the generals. [3] Once the Naxians had given them access to the town, they sailed on to Catana, but they were turned away thanks to the Syracusan sympathizers there, and they moved on to the Terias river. After spending the night there, the next day they headed for Syracuse in single file with the remainder of the squadron. [4] Ten ships were sent ahead to the Great Harbor of Syracuse to see if the Syracusan fleet had put to sea, and to sail up close and proclaim from the decks of the ships that the Athenians had come in accordance with their alliance and kinship with the Leontinians to restore them to their homeland, and that accordingly any Leontinians in Syracuse could leave without fear, knowing that they were going to join their friends and benefactors, the Athenians. [5] Having issued this proclamation and surveyed the city, its harbors, and the lay of the land outside the city that would act as their base for the fighting, they returned to Catana.

51. The Catanaeans convened a general meeting of the citizens, and although they still refused to give shelter to the army, they invited the generals to enter the town and explain what it was they wanted from them. While Alcibiades was speaking and the citizens were focused on the assembly, Athenian soldiers broke through an ill-fitting postern gate without being spotted, entered the city, and set about purchasing supplies. [2] The sight of these soldiers inside the town terrified those of the Catanaeans who were Syracusan sympathizers, and a few of them slipped away, while everyone else voted in favor of an alliance with Athens and invited the entire army to come from Rhegium. [3] So the Athenians returned to Rhegium and then set out for Catana, this time with all their forces, and on their arrival they began setting up camp.

52. A message arrived from Camarina saying that if they went there the city would go over to them, and they also heard that the Syracusans were manning their fleet. They put to sea with all their forces and went first to Syracuse, but since they saw no sign of a fleet being manned they carried on toward Camarina. After making land at the beach they entered into negotiations with the town. But the Camarinaeans refused them shelter, because they had sworn to allow only one Athenian ship at a time into their harbor unless they came at the Camarinaeans' own request. [2] So the Athenians sailed away empty-handed. They landed men at a certain point in Syracusan territory and plundered the farmland, and after the Syracusan cavalry came to offer resistance and killed some of the light-armed soldiers, who were scattered here and there over the countryside, they returned to Catana.

53. At Catana, they found that the *Salaminia* had come from Athens to fetch Alcibiades, with orders that he was to return to Athens to defend himself against the charges the state was bringing against him. They were also to fetch some other men from the army as well, those whom the informers had named as involved in the impious mocking of the Mysteries along with Alcibiades, and some others who were to be charged for desecrating the herms.

[2] The Athenians had not slackened their efforts, after the departure of the expeditionary force, to get to the bottom of what had happened in the affairs of the Mysteries and the herms, but they did so without testing the reliability of the informers. They were so suspicious that they believed everything they were told, and the trust they placed in bad men led to the arrest and imprisonment of some truly good men. They thought that interrogation and inquisition would serve them better than having someone get away without being investigated, even if he was a man known for his goodness and the informer was a man of bad character. [3] For the general populace was well aware from anecdotes they had heard that in its final years the tyranny of Peisistratus and his sons had been oppressive, and moreover that it had been overthrown not by themselves and Harmodius, but by the Lacedaemonians, so they were in a constant state of fear and treated everything with suspicion.

54. Aristogeiton and Harmodius's exploit was in fact no more than a fortuitous consequence of a love affair. I shall describe the incident at some length in order to show that even the Athenians, let alone anyone else, are unaware of the facts where their own tyrants are concerned and are ignorant about this incident.* [2] When Peisistratus died of old age while still tyrant, it was not Hipparchus, as most people believe, but Hippias who, as the eldest son, became the ruler. Now, Harmodius, a famously beautiful youth, was loved by and was the partner of Aristogeiton, a citizen of the middle class. [3] But Peisistratus's son Hipparchus propositioned Harmodius, who spurned him and then told Aristogeiton what had happened. Aristogeiton was profoundly upset, as any lover would be, and was afraid that Hipparchus might use his power to steal Harmodius away from him, so he immediately began to scheme to overthrow the tyranny, insofar as someone of his rank could hope to do so. [4] Meanwhile, Hipparchus had propositioned Harmodius again, with equally little success, and although Hipparchus did not want to do Harmodius any violence, he did want to humiliate him, and he arranged to do so in a subtle way, as though it had nothing to do with this business.

[5] On the whole, the tyranny was not oppressive, and the tyrants' rule was not resented. In fact, there was nothing more important to them than the cultivation of excellence and intellectual pursuits. They instituted a mere 5 percent income tax on Athenian citizens, made the city a thing of beauty, successfully waged its wars, and performed the requisite sacrifices at the sanctuaries. [6] In general, the same laws obtained in the city as before, except that the tyrants made sure that the highest offices always went to one of their people. Among those who held the annual archonship in Athens was Peisistratus, son of Hippias (this was after Hippias had become tyrant), who had the same name as his grandfather; it was he who, during his archonship, dedicated the altar of the Twelve Gods in the agora and the altar of Apollo in the Pythian sanctuary. [7] When the Athenian people later extended the altar in the agora, the inscription was erased, but the one in the Pythian sanctuary is still legible, though the letters are faint. It reads as follows:

This memorial of his archonship Peisistratus, son of Hippias,
Dedicated in the precinct of Pythian Apollo.

55. I am quite certain it was the eldest son, Hippias, who became the ruler, and if I insist on this point that is because I have more accurate information than others, but the same conclusion would be reached by anyone who took the following facts into consideration: First, Hippias is the only one of the legitimate brothers who appears to have had children. This is indicated not just by the Pythian altar but also by the stele on the Athenian acropolis that lists the injustices of the tyrants. Unlike the five children of Hippias (their mother was Hippias's wife Myrrhine, daughter of Callias, son of Hyperochides), no child of Thessalus or Hipparchus is mentioned on this stele. The point here is that it would have been natural for the eldest son to have been the first to marry. [2] Second, on the same stele his name is written immediately after that of his father, and this, too, must surely be because he was the eldest son and succeeded to the tyranny. [3] Nor, thirdly, do I think that Hippias would have taken over the tyranny easily and promptly if Hipparchus had been in office at the time of his death, and Hippias had tried to establish himself as tyrant that very day. But because the citizens were already accustomed to living in fear, and his mercenaries had been meticulously trained, he maintained control without coming close to being in danger; he did not flounder, as would a younger brother who had no prior continuous familiarity with the exercise of power. [4] Hipparchus is the one whose name is widely known, however, because of his unfortunate end, and so he has been supposed by future generations to have been the tyrant.

56. Be that as it may, Hipparchus found a way to carry out his plan of humiliating Harmodius for having spurned his advances. After promising that his sister, an unmarried young woman, would take part in a certain procession as a basket-carrier, the tyrants dismissed her, saying that she was unworthy of the position and denying that they had even offered it to her.* [2] This made Harmodius furious, and for his sake Aristogeiton, too, became far more incensed than he had been. All the practical arrangements with their fellow conspirators were in place, and they were just waiting for the Great Panathenaea, because this was the only day in the year when it was not suspicious for citizens—those who were to take part in the parade—to assemble under arms. The plan was for Harmodius and Aristogeiton to strike the first blow, and for their fellow conspirators immediately to join in and help to defend them against the tyrant's bodyguards. [3] For the sake of safety there were only a few people in on the plot, but they expected that, however few they were, their bold stroke would encourage even people who had not previously been aware of the plot to join them on the spur of the moment, seeing that they were already armed, in the attempt to win their freedom.

57. On the day of the festival, Hippias was outside the city walls in the district called the Potters' Quarter; he was accompanied by his bodyguards and was seeing to the procedural details of the parade. Harmodius and Aristogeiton, who had by now armed themselves with daggers, set to work. [2] But when they saw one of their fellow conspirators chatting familiarly with Hippias (who was not aloof, but could be approached by anyone), they became afraid; they thought they were being informed on and expected to be arrested at any moment. [3] So they decided to see if before being arrested they could at least avenge themselves on the man who had hurt them and because of whom they had taken so many risks. With no further ado they rushed inside the city gates and found Hipparchus by the shrine called the Leocoreum. They immediately and unhesitatingly fell on him—the one motivated by a lover's anger, the other because he had been insulted—and stabbed him to death. [4] One of them, Aristogeiton, briefly escaped the bodyguards when a crowd of people ran up, but he was captured later and brutally treated. Harmodius was killed on the spot.

58. When news reached Hippias in the Potters' Quarter, he immediately made his way not to the site of the incident but to the hoplites who were taking part in the procession. They were some distance away, and he wanted to get to them before they found out. He composed his features so as not to betray what had happened and told them to shed their military gear and make their way to a certain place that he indicated. [2] They did as they were told, thinking that he had something to tell them, but he ordered his mercenaries to collect their arms and armor, and then he immediately picked out the men he held responsible, along with any others who were found to have daggers, when it was the custom for only shields and spears to be carried in the parade.

59. It should now be clear, then, that the plot originated in a lover's resentment and that it was a sudden failure of nerve that led to Harmodius and Aristogeiton's reckless stroke.* [2] After this incident, the Athenians suffered much more under the tyranny. Hippias was now more fearful than he had been before and put many of his fellow citizens to death, while at the same time he was constantly turning his thoughts toward foreign lands to see if he could discern anywhere a safe refuge for himself in the event of revolution. [3] At any rate, even though he was an Athenian, he subsequently gave his daughter Archedice to a man from Lampsacus, Aeantides, the son of Hippoclus (the tyrant of Lampsacus), because he had become aware that these two had a great deal of influence with King Darius. On Archedice's tomb in Lampsacus there is inscribed the following epigram:

This dust here conceals Archedice, daughter of Hippias,
  The best man in Greece of his generation.
Though father, husband, brothers, and sons were tyrants,
  Never was she beguiled into presumption.

[4] After having ruled Athens as tyrant for three years, Hippias was deposed in the fourth year of his reign by the Lacedaemonians and the Alcmeonidae in exile.* He made his way with a sworn guarantee of safe conduct to Sigeum and to Aeantides in Lampsacus. From there he went to King Darius—and from there twenty years later, by which time he was an old man, he set out along with the Persian army to Marathon.*

60. At the time in question, then, as a result of reflecting on this episode and calling to mind what they had gathered about it by hearsay, the Athenian people were angry and mistrustful of the men who had been accused in the affair of the Mysteries. It was widely believed that everything that had happened was part of an oligarchic and tyrannical conspiracy. [2] Because of their suspicion and anger, many notable men had already been imprisoned, and rather than there being an end in sight, every day they grew more vicious and more arrests were made. So at this point one of the prisoners, the man who was widely believed to be the most guilty of them all, was persuaded by a fellow prisoner to turn informer, whether or not what he said was true.* Opinions are divided, but neither then nor later was anyone able to say for certain who had been involved in the business. [3] He was persuaded by the argument that, even if he was innocent, he should claim the promised immunity from prosecution and so both save himself and put an end to the mistrust that was pervading the city—because it would be less risky for him to confess his guilt with a guarantee of immunity than to profess his innocence and be taken to court. [4] So he informed against himself and others in the matter of the herms, and the Athenian people happily accepted what they took to be the truth, because previously they had been worried that they might never know the identities of the conspirators who were seeking to overthrow the democracy. So they immediately released the informer and those fellow prisoners of his whom he had not implicated, while they put those he had denounced on trial. Some of these men, those they had in custody, they executed, while those who fled were condemned to death and a price was put on their heads. [5] In all this no one knew for certain whether or not the victims had deserved their punishment, but the short-term benefit to the city as a whole was unmistakable.

61. As for Alcibiades, his enemies persisted in the attacks they had started even before he set out for Sicily and the Athenians began to think badly of him. Since they imagined that they now knew the facts in the matter of the herms, they grew ever more certain that the profanation of the Mysteries, in which he was implicated, had the same purpose as the mutilation of the herms—that is, that it was a conspiracy to overthrow the democracy. [2] And as a matter of fact, right in the midst of all this commotion a Lacedaemonian army marched as far as the Isthmus. It was not a large army, and they had something to attend to that related to the Boeotians, but it was widely believed in Athens that this had been Alcibiades's doing—that the Lacedaemonian expedition had been prearranged and had nothing to do with the Boeotians, and that if they had not already acted on the information they had received and arrested the men, the city would have been betrayed to the Lacedaemonians. In fact, they even spent one night under arms in the city sanctuary of Theseus. [3] Moreover, during the same period of time Alcibiades's friends in Argos had become suspected of plotting to overthrow the democracy, and at this juncture the Athenians removed the Argive hostages from the islands where they had been deposited and handed them over to the democrats in Argos to be put to death for the same crime.

[4] There were multiple reasons, then, why Alcibiades had fallen under a cloud of suspicion, and the upshot was that the Athenians wanted to put him on trial and execute him. So they sent the *Salaminia* to Sicily to fetch him and others who had been named by the informers. [5] The officers of the *Salaminia* had been told to order Alcibiades to follow them home to defend himself against the charges, but not to arrest him, taking care not to disturb the soldiers in Sicily, whether their own or the enemy's. Above all, they wanted the soldiers from Mantinea and Argos, whom they considered to have been persuaded to join the expedition by Alcibiades, to stay. [6] So Alcibiades and his fellow suspects left Sicily on board Alcibiades's personal ship, along with the *Salaminia*, with Athens as their destination. But when they reached Thurii they broke away; they jumped ship and disappeared, because they were afraid of returning home to face trials when popular opinion was prejudiced against them. [7] The crew of the *Salaminia* searched for Alcibiades and his companions for a while, but finding no trace of them anywhere they left and set out for home. Not long afterward, Alcibiades, now an outcast, sailed over

to the Peloponnese from Thurii, and the Athenians condemned him and his companions to death in their absence.

62. Next, the remaining Athenian generals in Sicily divided the army into two and cast lots to see which division each of them would command. Then they set sail with both divisions toward Selinous and Egesta. They wanted to find out whether the Egestans were going to give them the promised money, to assess the situation in Selinous, and to come to some understanding of the causes of the friction between Selinous and Egesta. [2] They sailed west along the north coast of Sicily, the part that faces the Tyrrhenian Sea, and put in at Himera, which is the only Greek city in that part of Sicily. But they were not made welcome in Himera, so they carried on. [3] In the course of their voyage they took Hyccara, a Sicanian coastal town that had sided against Egesta. After enslaving the inhabitants, they handed the town over to the Egestans, whose cavalry had joined them, and their land forces marched back through Sicel territory all the way to Catana, while the fleet sailed around the coastline with the people they had enslaved. [4] Nicias, however, headed straight for Egesta from Hyccara and rejoined the army once he had completed his business there, which included the receipt of 30 talents. The Athenians then sold the slaves, which brought in 120 talents. [5] They sent messengers around their Sicel allies with orders to send troops and attacked Hybla Geleatis, a town that was hostile to them, but failed to capture it. And so the summer ended.

63. At the very beginning of the following winter the Athenians began to get ready to attack Syracuse, but the Syracusans were doing the same, preparing to move against the Athenians. [2] At first they had feared and expected an immediate Athenian attack, but as each day passed without that happening, their morale rose. And then it turned out that the Athenian fleet was carrying out operations on the opposite side of Sicily, far from Syracuse, and after the failure of the Athenian attempt to take Hybla by main force the Syracusans came to think less of the danger they posed, and, as a mob is inclined to do when it is confident, they kept demanding that their generals lead them against the Athenians in Catana, since the Athenians were not coming to them. [3] Moreover, the Syracusan cavalry out on reconnaissance kept riding up to the Athenian army and taunting them, especially by saying that it looked as though they had come to settle on alien soil as their neighbors, rather than to resettle the Leontinians on their native soil.

64. Aware of the growing Syracusan contempt for their abilities, the Athenian generals decided to try to draw the entire enemy army as far as possible away from the city. Meanwhile, they would use the time gained to sail under cover of darkness and occupy some suitable site for a camp without interference by the Syracusans. They were sure that in this way the successful establishment of a position would be easier for them than if they were disembarking from ships against an enemy who was ready to receive them, or if they were known to be making their way by land, because they had no cavalry and the plentiful Syracusan cavalry would wreak havoc among their light-armed troops and camp followers; but in this way they could occupy a place where they would be relatively safe from the Syracusan cavalry. And Syracusan exiles who were accompanying them told them about the place they did in fact occupy, near the sanctuary of Olympian Zeus. So the Athenian generals came up with the following plan to realize their aims:

[2] They gave the mission to a man who was loyal to them but whom the Syracusan generals would take to be on their side. He was a citizen of Catana, and he claimed to have come from men in Catana whose names were known to the Syracusan generals and whom they knew to be among their remaining friends in the city. [3] He told them that the Athenians spent the nights in the city, at some distance from the camp where their arms and armor were stored, and that if it suited the Syracusans they could launch an attack at dawn on a specified day with all their forces. Their sympathizers in Catana would close the gates against those who were in the city and set fire to the Athenian ships, and it would be easy for the Syracusans to attack the stockade

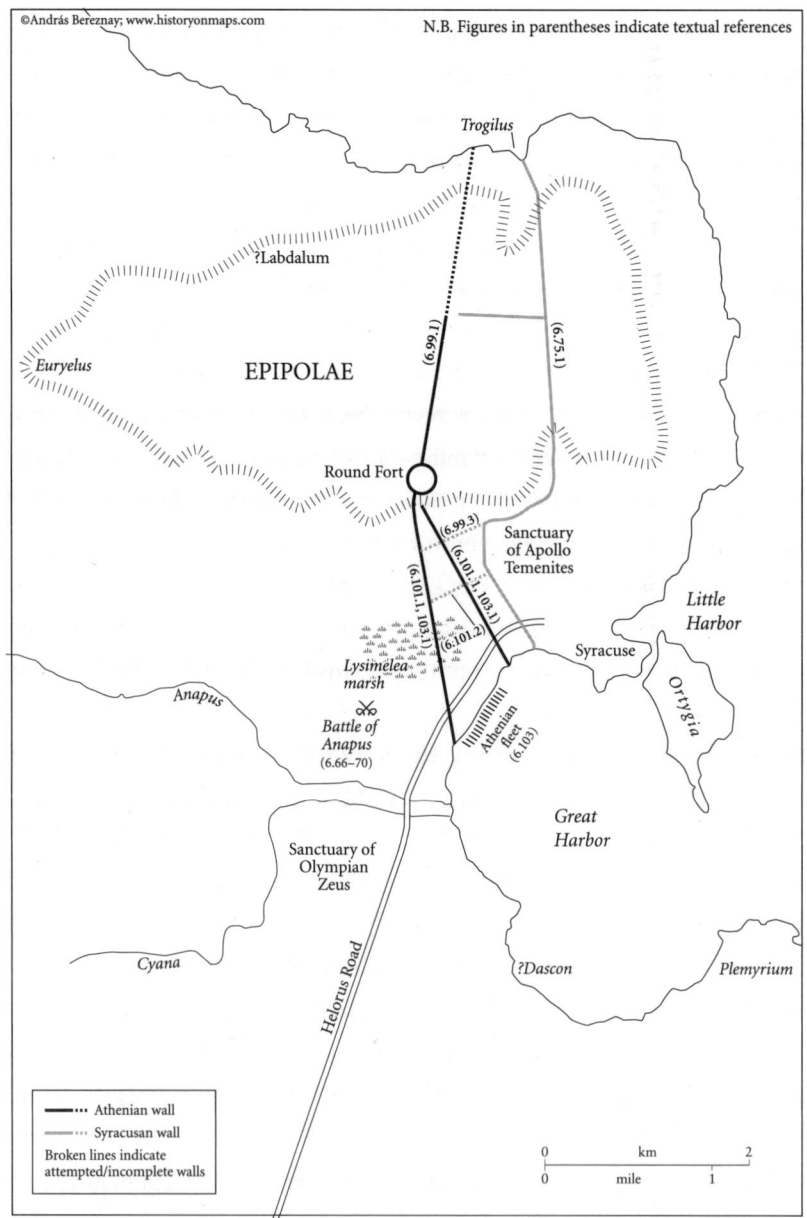

K. Syracuse

and capture the camp. And he said that many Catanaeans would join in and that the men who had sent him were ready and waiting.

65. The Syracusan generals, who already felt that they had grounds for confidence and had been planning to attack Catana even in the absence of any such ruse, gave the man's story far less thought than they should have done and fell for it. They immediately chose a day for their arrival and sent the man back to Catana. By then some of their allies had arrived—the Selinountians and others—so the generals ordered a full levy of Syracusans to take to the field. Once the forces were ready and the time appointed for their arrival was at hand, they marched toward Catana and spent the night at the Simaethus river in Leontinian territory. [2] When the Athenians heard that they were on their way, they collected their entire army, including some Sicels and others who had joined them, embarked them on the warships and transport vessels, and sailed under cover of darkness to Syracuse. [3] At dawn the Athenians began disembarking men in the Great Harbor, not far from the sanctuary of Olympian Zeus, in order to stake out a site for their camp, and the Syracusan cavalry, who had ridden ahead and were the first to enter Catana, found that the entire Athenian army had left by sea. They wheeled around and told the infantry what had happened, and then cavalry and infantry together turned back to defend Syracuse.

66. Meanwhile, since the Syracusans had a long journey ahead of them, the Athenians had plenty of time to establish their forces in a favorable location, where they were likely to be able to initiate the fighting at a time of their choosing and where the Syracusan cavalry would find it virtually impossible to injure them, either during an engagement or beforehand. On one side the cavalry would be kept at bay by low walls, buildings, trees, and marshland, and on the other side there were cliffs. [2] The Athenians cut down the trees nearest to their campsite, carried them down to the shore, and built a stockade to protect the ships, and at Dascon, which was where the enemy could most easily come at them, they hastily erected a barricade made of timbers and unworked stones they collected, and destroyed the bridge

over the Anapus. [3] During these preparations of theirs, no soldiers sallied out of the city to try to stop them; the first to confront them was the Syracusan cavalry, and then later all the infantry as well, once it had assembled. At first they approached the Athenian camp, but the Athenians refused to advance against them, so they pulled back across the Helorus road and bivouacked for the night.

67. The next day the Athenians and their allies got ready for battle, with their forces drawn up as follows: on the right wing, the Argives and Mantineans; in the center the Athenians; and on the other wing the rest of the allies. Half of the army was posted forward and marshaled eight ranks deep, and the other half, also eight deep, was deployed near the tents in a hollow square, with orders to stand by and watch out for where the army was in particular trouble. The baggage train was placed inside the square formed by these reserves. [2] The Syracusans formed their hoplites into ranks sixteen deep, with no reserves; these hoplites consisted of the full levy of Syracusan citizens and the allies who had come to support them. These auxiliaries were mainly from Selinous, but there was also a squadron of about 200 cavalrymen from Gela, and about 20 horsemen and 50 archers from Camarina. They posted their cavalry, numbering at least 1,200, on the right wing with the javelineers next to them. [3] The Athenians were intending to initiate the fighting, and just before they did so, Nicias passed along the line, addressing words of encouragement to each of the various peoples who made up the army and thus to the army as a whole, along the following lines:

68. "I can keep this brief, men, seeing that there's no doubt about the trial of strength in which we've come to compete, and because our preparedness alone will, I believe, do a better job of inspiring us with confidence than the fine words that are needed for a weak army. [2] After all, given that we are Argives, Mantineans, Athenians, and the best of the islanders—given that men of such quality are fighting side by side in such numbers—how could any of us fail to have high hopes of victory? Especially when what we're up against is a mass levy, which is to say that they aren't the elite force that we are. Besides, they're Sicilian Greeks, people who may look down on us but won't stand up to us, because they lack the skill to shore up their courage. [3] Each of you should also bear in mind that we're far from home and that there's no friendly land nearby except any that you might win yourselves in battle. What I'm reminding you of is the opposite of what I'm sure the Syracusans are telling themselves by way of encouragement. They're reminding themselves that the contest will be for their homeland, but I'm pointing out that since you're not in your homeland you have to win or face a difficult retreat, under attack from their numerous cavalrymen. [4] So, bearing in mind your caliber, you need have no hesitation in attacking the enemy. You must see that you have less to fear from them than from the demands and difficulties of your current situation."

69. As soon as he had delivered this address, Nicias began to lead his men forward. It was bad timing for the Syracusans: they had not been expecting to fight so soon, and in fact some of them had left and gone into the city, since it was nearby. They hurriedly ran up to support their comrades, but as they were late they fell in and joined the bulk of the army wherever they could. For the Syracusans were not lacking in commitment or bravery, either in this battle or in the others that followed. They were no less courageous than their opponents as long as skill sustained their resistance, and it was only when it let them down that, despite themselves, they failed to fulfill their good intentions. They had not expected the Athenians to be the first to attack, and they were forced to defend themselves at short notice, but despite this, as soon as they had armed themselves they advanced to meet the oncoming enemy.

[2] Preliminary outfighting took place between each side's stone-throwers, slingers, and archers, and as tends to happen with light-armed troops, each side put the other to flight. Then the diviners brought forward the customary sacrificial victims and the trumpeters gave the signal for the hoplites to engage. [3] The hoplite units on each side advanced toward each other. It was not just their homeland

that was at stake for the Syracusans in the battle; each individual was fighting in the short term for his life and in the longer term for his freedom. As for their opponents: the Athenians were fighting to appropriate land that belonged to others and to avoid the harm that would come to Athens if they were defeated; the Argives and the rest of the allies who were not Athenian subjects were fighting to help the Athenians gain their objectives and to see their own homelands once more if they returned victorious; and while the subject allies were motivated above all by their own immediate survival, which was likely to depend on victory, a secondary motivation was the possibility that if they helped the Athenians subdue others, they might find their own subjection to Athens less arduous.

70. For a long time after the two sides had clashed in hand-to-hand fighting they held out against each other. It so happened that in the midst of the fighting a storm broke, with heavy rain and a certain amount of thunder and lightning, and this turned out to be another factor that contributed to the fear of those who had minimal acquaintance with warfare and who had never been in battle before.* Their more experienced comrades, however, attributed the storm to the season of the year, and felt that their opponents were a far graver concern as long as they remained undefeated. [2] The Argives were the first to push back their opponents on the Syracusan left, then the Athenians did the same to their opposite numbers, and at this point the rest of the Syracusan line broke and turned to flight. [3] The Athenians did not chase them far because the Syracusan cavalry, which was both numerous and undefeated, made that impossible; they charged up at any hoplites they saw breaking out in pursuit and forced them back. But they pursued them in a body as far as it was safe to do so and then withdrew and set up a trophy. [4] After the Syracusans had reassembled on the Helorus road and formed themselves up as best they could under the circumstances, despite their defeat they divided their forces, sending some of their men to protect the sanctuary of Olympian Zeus, because they thought the Athenians might steal the valuables that were housed there. The rest of them then retreated back inside the city.

71. The Athenians left the sanctuary alone, however, and settled down for the night where they were, after collecting their dead and laying them on a pyre. The next day they granted the Syracusans a truce so they could recover their dead, gathered up the bones of their own dead for burial, and sailed back to Catana with the spoils. The Syracusans and their allies had lost some 260 men, the Athenians and their allies about 50. [2] They sailed away not just because it was now winter, but also because they decided it was no longer feasible to carry on the war where they were until they had sent for cavalry from Athens and gathered more from their local allies, so that they would no longer be entirely dominated by the Syracusan cavalry. They also wanted to wait until they had collected money from their friends in Sicily and more had come from Athens; until they had gained the allegiance of some of the Greek cities, which they hoped would be more inclined to submit after the battle; and until they had provided themselves with everything else they would need, including grain, for another attempt on Syracuse in the spring.

72. With this plan in mind the Athenians sailed away to winter quarters at Naxos and Catana, while the Syracusans buried their dead and then held an assembly. [2] Hermocrates, son of Hermon, came forward to speak, a man who was second to none in intelligence whatever the issue; he had also proved himself an experienced and competent military leader and was known for his remarkable bravery. He used his speech to boost the Syracusans' morale and to stop them from being overwhelmed by what had happened. [3] He argued that their spirit had not been defeated; what had harmed them was their lack of discipline. All the same, they had not been as thoroughly outclassed as might have been expected, particularly given that they were, so to speak, amateurs who had gone up against the foremost craftsmen of war in the Greek world.

[4] And two other things that did them a great deal of harm, he claimed, were the number of the generals, or, in other words, their divided command (they had fifteen generals), and the undisciplined lawlessness of the rank and file. If there were fewer generals and they were all experienced men, he said, and if they spent the winter preparing the hoplite division and making it as large as possible, by supplying arms and armor to those who had none and by putting them through a rigorous course of training, they were almost certain to defeat the enemy. They already had the courage to do so, and all they needed in addition was discipline on the field of battle. They could expect both courage and discipline to improve by themselves, he argued, because discipline is honed by danger, and courage automatically gains in confidence when it is combined with trust in skill. [5] As for the generals, they should choose just a few, and they should be given full powers of command, supported by an oath sworn by the people to the effect that they would be allowed to command at their own discretion. Then matters that ought to be kept secret were more likely to remain secret, and all their other preparations would go ahead in an orderly fashion and without being questioned.

73. After listening to Hermocrates's speech, the Syracusans voted to adopt all his proposals and chose him as one of just three generals along with Heracleides, son of Lysimachus, and Sicanus, son of Execestus. [2] They also sent envoys to Corinth and Sparta to ask them, as their allies, for aid and to persuade the Lacedaemonians to support them by prosecuting the war with Athens more resolutely and openly, so that the Athenians would either have to withdraw their forces from Sicily or would be less able to send reinforcements to their army in Sicily.

74. Almost as soon as the Athenian army arrived in Catana they sailed to Messina, which they had been told would be betrayed to them. The scheme came to nothing, however, because of Alcibiades. When he was relieved of his command and summoned back to Athens he expected to be banished from the city, so he used his knowledge of the Athenians' plans to warn the friends of Syracuse in Messina. By the time the Athenians came, the pro-Syracusans in Messina had killed the men Alcibiades had told them about, and now that they were the dominant faction they armed themselves and prevailed on the city to bow to their wishes and refuse to admit the Athenians. [2] The Athenians stayed for some thirteen days, but the weather was bad, supplies were failing, and they were getting nowhere, so they returned to Naxos. They laid out their camp, surrounded it with a stockade, and spent the winter there. They also dispatched a trireme to Athens to ask for money and cavalry, to arrive at the beginning of spring.

75. The Syracusans spent the winter on building work. They extended the city's walls to encompass the Temenites sanctuary* and along the whole area that faces Epipolae, so that if they suffered a setback, and an attempt was made to wall off the city, the Athenians would be faced with the challenge of building at greater length; and they turned Megara Hyblaea into a fortified outpost and fortified the sanctuary of Olympian Zeus as well. They also planted stakes on the shoreline wherever there were landing-places. [2] And knowing that the Athenians were spending the winter in Naxos, they marched with all their forces against Catana. They ravaged some of the farmland there, set fire to the Athenian tents and camp, and then returned home.

[3] When the Syracusans heard that the Athenians were sending envoys to Camarina on the strength of the alliance that had been made in Laches's time,* to see if they could bring the city in on their side, they responded by sending envoys of their own. They were uncertain of the Camarinaeans' loyalty; they thought they had been half-hearted in supplying the men they had sent for the first battle, and they suspected that in the future, in view of the Athenians' success in the battle, they would refuse them any further help and would be persuaded by their earlier friendship with Athens to change sides. [4] When Hermocrates and the rest of the delegates from Syracuse arrived in Camarina, joining Euphemus and his colleagues for the Athenians, a meeting was convened of the Camarinaeans, and

Hermocrates, who wanted to prejudice them against the Athenians, spoke somewhat as follows:

76. "We envoys haven't come here, Camarinaeans, because we're afraid that you might be intimidated by the Athenians' current strength, but rather to make sure you're not won over by the arguments they're going to present before you've heard what we have to say as well. [2] You know their pretext for coming to Sicily, but the real reason is exactly what we all suspect: as I see it, they don't want to restore the Leontinians to their homeland so much as to evict us from ours. I mean, it doesn't make sense for them to depopulate cities over there in Greece and found new settlements here—to look out for the interests of the Leontinians because they're Chalcidians and kin, but to keep the Chalcidians in Euboea in a state of servitude,* when the former are colonists of the latter. [3] The same method they used to acquire an empire there they are now trying out here. What happened there was that the Ionians and others who were Athenian colonists voluntarily accepted their leadership as a way of avenging themselves on the Persians, but then the Athenians subjugated them all, accusing some of refusing to supply troops, others of campaigning against one another, and others of whatever specious wrong they could make to fit a given case. [4] The issue wasn't freedom, then. The point of resisting the Persians wasn't, for the Athenians, the liberation of the Greeks, nor was it, for the Greeks, their own freedom. Athens's purpose was the enslavement of the Greeks to itself rather than to Persia, and the Greeks' purpose was to change their master to one no less wily, but who used his wiles for evil purposes.

77. "It's not difficult to find charges to bring against the Athenians, but we haven't come here today to demonstrate the many wrongs they've committed. You already know of them. What I want to do, rather, is point out the mistake all of us Sicilian Greeks are making. Although we know how the Greeks over there became enslaved because they failed to come to one another's defense, and although we're faced now with the same deceptions being used against us—I mean, their claim that they've come to restore their kin, the Leontinians, and to help their allies, the Egestans—we're unwilling to unite and show them in no uncertain terms that there are no Ionians here, no Hellespontians, no islanders who are slaves now of the Persian king and now of some other master, but that Sicily is inhabited by Dorians, a free people originating in an independent Peloponnese. [2] Or are we waiting to fall to them city by city, although we know that this is the only way we could fall and although their tactics are plain to see? Sometimes they use diplomacy to try to foster disunity among us; sometimes they set us to fight among ourselves by holding out the prospect of having them as allies; and sometimes they do what damage they can with comforting words tailored to individual cases. Faced with the destruction of our comrades in other parts of the island, do we imagine that the horror will somehow pass us by? Do we imagine that the first to suffer will suffer alone?

78. "And if anyone thinks that it isn't himself but me, the Syracusan, who's the enemy of the Athenians, and finds abhorrent the idea of facing danger on behalf of my land, he should realize that what's at stake isn't just my land. No, he'll be fighting on mine, but no less at stake will be his also, and he'll be all the safer since Syracuse won't already have fallen, and with me as his ally he won't be fighting unsupported. And he should bear in mind that what the Athenians want is not to punish the Syracusans for their hostility, but rather to use Syracuse as a pretext for securing his friendship. [2] Then again, if anyone is envious or afraid—both of which are possible responses to our greatness—and therefore wants Syracuse to be weakened so that it learns moderation, but to survive for the sake of his own security, he's hoping and wishing for something that isn't humanly possible. It's impossible for any individual to regulate fortune to suit his desires.

[3] "Besides, if he's wrong, then once he's been reduced to a lamentable state by his troubles he might well wish for another opportunity to envy my prosperity! But that's never going to happen if he abandons me and refuses to accept the risks, which in reality are the same for both of us, however they're described. What I mean is that he may

think that he's securing our power, but in fact he's securing his own safety. [4] Camarinaeans, you above all should have foreseen all this, because you're our immediate neighbors and will therefore be the next to be threatened. So stop behaving like half-hearted allies, as you are at present. If the Athenians had arrived first in Camarinaean territory, you'd have requested and appealed for our help; by the same token, you should now openly be urging us not to give in at all. But up until now, at any rate, neither you nor any of the other Sicilian Greeks have taken this step.

79. "Perhaps—though this would be a cowardly move—you'll labor the issue of justice as it applies to both us and the invaders, and point out that you have an alliance in place with the Athenians. That's true, but you didn't enter into it to the detriment of your friends. You did so in case an enemy attacked you and of course to help the Athenians—but when they're the victims, not when they're the aggressors, as they are now. Look, even the Rhegians, who are Chalcidians, are refusing to help them resettle their fellow Chalcidians, the Leontinians. [2] They're holding back when on the face of it they have no good reason for doing so, because they suspect the reality behind the Athenians' fine appeal to justice. This makes it all the more shocking to find you relying on a specious excuse to justify the fact that you're willing to help your natural enemies and destroy your kin, whose natural claim on you is far stronger, by joining forces with their worst enemies. [3] There's no justice in this; justice requires that you defend your kin without succumbing to fear of the Athenian forces. If we all stand together there's nothing to fear in their forces; they're dangerous only if the opposite happens and we're divided among ourselves, which is exactly their objective. Even when they attacked us when we were on our own and carried the day, they failed to achieve their goals; all they did was hurry away.

80. "As long as we stick together, then, there's no reason to lose heart—but there's every reason for you to fight alongside us more wholeheartedly, especially since help is on its way from the Peloponnese—in other words, from people who utterly outclass the Athenians at warfare. And let no one think that the caution that inclines you to help neither side, on the ground that you're allies of both, is either fair to us or safe for you. [2] Considerations of justice might make it seem fair, but in fact it isn't. Why? Because if the result of your not supporting us by military means is defeat for the victim and triumph for the victor, all you've achieved by your absence is a double failure: a failure to protect and safeguard the former, and a failure to prevent the latter's iniquities. The better course, obviously, is to protect the welfare of Sicily as a whole and prevent the wrongdoing of your 'friends,' the Athenians, by allying yourselves with those who are being wronged and are also kin.

[3] "To summarize what we Syracusans are saying: First, there's clearly as little need to explain the situation to you as to anyone else, because you know it as well as anyone; what we're doing instead is appealing to you, and protesting that if you don't do as we ask we'll find ourselves betrayed by our fellow Dorians and plotted against by our perpetual enemies the Ionians. [4] Second, we're saying that if the Athenians subdue us, they'll owe their victory to your policies (though of course they'll take all the credit for themselves), and that the victory prize they'll gain will be none other than the people who enabled their victory. And on the alternative scenario, if we turn out to be the winners, it will still be you who'll suffer, when we punish you for endangering us. [5] Think carefully, then. You've to choose now between two courses: one involves no risk but leads immediately to servitude; the other has you siding with us and holds out the possibility that, if we win, you'll avoid the disgrace of accepting these people as your masters and avert our enmity, which would not soon wane."

81. After Hermocrates had spoken in this vein, Euphemus, the Athenian envoy, spoke along the following lines: **82.** "We came here to renew the earlier treaty of alliance, but in view of the Syracusan's slanders we also have to explain why it's reasonable for us to possess our empire. [2] He himself mentioned the most important piece of evidence—that there's perpetual hostility between Ionians and Dorians. Quite so, and as Ionians our concern was to find a way to secure as much independence from the Dorian Peloponnesians as we could, seeing that they're more numerous than us and are our near neighbors.

[3] "After the Persian War, thanks to our possession of a fleet we were able to detach ourselves from the Lacedaemonian empire and Lacedaemonian leadership. The only thing that gave them the right to command us rather than the other way around was that at the time they were stronger than us. We govern the places that were previously subject to Persia and that chose us as their leaders, because it seemed to us that the best way to avoid subjection to the Peloponnesians was to have the power to defend ourselves. And however much the Syracusans accuse us of enslaving our kin, strictly speaking we did not in fact do wrong in subjugating the Ionians and the islanders, [4] because they had joined the Persians in attacking us, their mother city.* They didn't have the courage to rebel against Persian rule and suffer the loss of their property, as we did when we abandoned our city. No, they chose servitude for themselves, and they wanted to inflict it on us as well.

83. "This, then, is why we have an empire: not just because we deserve it as compensation for providing the Greek forces with the largest number of ships and unswerving commitment, and for the harm the Ionians and islanders did us by unhesitatingly aiding the Persians, but also because we were aiming to strengthen ourselves against the Peloponnesians. [2] And we're not making any fancy claims along the lines that we deserve our empire because we single-handedly defeated the Persians, or that we put ourselves in danger to secure the freedom of these subjects of ours rather than that of all Greeks, including ourselves.

"No one finds it objectionable if someone tries to secure his own safety. And it's concern for our own safety that has brought us here now, but it also seems clear to us that your interests and ours coincide. [3] We will demonstrate this by means of the very charges the

Syracusans are bringing against us and by the suspicions you harbor, rather too fearfully. For we know that people who are suspicious and frightened may be temporarily mollified by words, but later, when it comes to action, they do what's in their best interests. [4] My point is that it's fear, as we've told you, that motivates our imperialism over there, and it's fear that has prompted us to come here, too, to join with our friends in settling the island so as to secure our safety. We're not interested in enslaving anyone but in making sure that we don't suffer enslavement.

84. "No one should suppose that protecting you is none of our business. If you're safe, you see, and capable of offering robust resistance to the Syracusans, there's less chance of their sending a force to help the Peloponnesians, which would be very bad for us. That's why what happens to you is now of the greatest concern to us. [2] It also explains why it makes good sense for us, once we've restored the Leontinians, not to have them as our subjects, like their kinsmen in Euboea, but as strong as possible, so that they can threaten the Syracusans for us from their own land, which borders theirs. [3] As far as Greece is concerned, we're capable of dealing with our enemies even by ourselves, and the Chalcidians, whose enslavement they say sits awkwardly with our attempt to free the Greeks here, serve our interests by having no military capability and supplying only money. But as far as Sicily is concerned, what serves our interests is for the Leontinians and our other friends to be fully autonomous.

85. "For a tyrant or an imperial state* no course of action is irrational if it conduces to his or its interest, and only the trustworthy count as kin. Whether hostility or friendship is the appropriate response must be decided case by case. And what's good for us here isn't to weaken our friends, but to have them strong enough to make our enemies incapable of effective action. [2] There's no reason to doubt what I'm saying: we manage even our allies over there so that each of them is useful to us in his own way. The Chians and Methymnaeans are self-governing, provided they supply us with ships; the majority have somewhat less freedom and pay us tribute; and despite the fact that they're islanders and it would be easy for us to take them over, we allow others of our allies to be completely free, because they occupy strategic locations around the Peloponnese.* [3] It's only reasonable to suppose, then, that the way we arrange matters here, too, will serve our interests and, as we're saying, be a response to our fear of the Syracusans. The point is that their aim is to rule over you. They want to use mistrust of us as a means of getting you Sicilian Greeks to join them, and then to rule Sicily themselves, whether that takes force or simply follows from the fact that, once we've failed and left the island, there'll be no one here to help you. And their dominion is inevitable if you join them, because we'd find it virtually impossible to tackle such a large combined force, and they'd be strong enough to deal with you once we were gone.

86. "Anyone who disagrees with what I'm saying is refuted by the following fact: when you invited us over here on that earlier occasion,* the threat you dangled before us was precisely that if we did nothing while you were subjugated by the Syracusans we ourselves would be at risk. [2] So it's not right for you to have reservations now about exactly the same argument that you expected to win us over then, and it's not right for us to be mistrusted because we've come this time in greater strength to confront Syracusan might. They're the ones you should mistrust.

[3] "There's no way, you see, that we can stay here unless you join us, and even if we turned bad and conquered you, the length of the voyage and the difficulty of garrisoning large cities equipped with land-based forces would make it impossible for us to keep you in our power. The Syracusans, however, live threateningly close to you, not in a military camp like us but in a city whose population outnumbers the forces we have here. They never stop plotting against you and they seize every opportunity they can find; there have been plenty of cases by now that prove this, with their treatment of Leontini the prime example. [4] And now they have the temerity to treat you as though you were too obtuse to see what they're up to, by inviting you to help them against

those who are trying to frustrate their schemes and who have so far prevented Sicily from falling under their sway. [5] Our response to this is to invite you to enjoy a far more authentic kind of security, by asking you not to jettison the real safety that each of us affords the other, and to appreciate that, given their superior numbers, they're always in a position to proceed against you, even without allies, while you have a unique opportunity to resist them with substantial outside help. If you give way to your mistrust and let this force leave before it's achieved anything, or even after it's suffered a reversal, a time will come when you'll wish you could see even a fraction of it, but by then it will no longer be able to do anything for you even if it did come.

87. "Camarinaeans, neither you nor anyone else should be influenced by the negative things the Syracusans say about us. We've given you a completely frank explanation of why we're objects of suspicion, and we're now going to recapitulate the key points of what we've been saying. We think you should find them persuasive. [2] Our claims, then, are that we rule our subjects over there to ensure that we're not subject to anyone else; that we're liberating the Greeks here to ensure that they don't make trouble for us; that the number of times we have to intervene in others' affairs reflects the number of times we have to protect ourselves against danger; and that we are now here not unbidden, but, as before, in response to the invitation of those of you who are being wronged, in order to fight alongside you. [3] Don't take on the role of judges or correctors of what we're doing, and don't try to get us to change course, which would be difficult at this stage, but insofar as there's any aspect of our interventionism—of our character, I might say—that does you good, too, separate it out from the rest and make the most of it, in the realization that what we do doesn't harm everyone alike but even benefits the great majority of the Greeks. [4] For throughout the Greek world, even in places where we have no presence, we're on everyone's minds. Anyone who expects to be victimized anticipates our help, and every mischief-maker anticipates the distinct possibility that he'll be in danger if we come. We make it inevitable that the latter will restrain himself, reluctant though he may be, and that the former will live in trouble-free safety. [5] So don't reject this gift of safety, which is freely available to anyone who asks for it and today is yours for the taking, but join with us in reducing the Syracusans† to the same level as the other states, and instead of constantly being on your guard against them, choose the ability even to have designs on them one day as their equals."

88. After this speech by Euphemus, the Camarinaeans found themselves in a quandary. On the one hand, they were well disposed toward the Athenians (except insofar as they thought they would enslave Sicily), and the Syracusans were their perpetual enemies, since they shared a border. But, on the other hand, this was offset by their fear, given the proximity of the Syracusans, that they might come out on top without Camarinaean help: that was why they sent those few horsemen in the first place, and why they decided to increase the amount of practical support for the Syracusans in the future, though as little as they could get away with. So, under the circumstances, not wanting to give the Athenians the impression that they thought less of them, especially since they had won the battle, they decided to give the same answer to both sides. [2] As a result of their deliberations, then, the answer they gave was that since the two parties, both of them their allies, were at war with each other, they thought that, given the situation, the only way they could remain true to their oaths was to be neutral. And so the Athenian and Syracusan envoys left.

[3] The Syracusans continued to gear up for war, while the Athenians, encamped at Naxos, approached the Sicels to try to win as many of them as they could over to their side. [4] Only a few of the Sicels who lived on the coastal plains and were subjects of Syracuse had defected, but almost all of those who lived inland, whose communities had always been self-governing, joined the Athenians and sent food and in some cases money down to the army on the coast. [5] The Athenians attacked those who were refusing to come over to their side and forced some of them to join, but they could not get to the rest

because the Syracusans were sending help in the form of garrisons for the towns. After moving their anchorage from Naxos to Catana for the winter and rebuilding the camp the Syracusans had burned down, they made it their winter quarters. [6] They sent a trireme to Carthage on a goodwill mission to see if they could get help from there; they sent envoys to Etruria, where some of the towns were even coming forward of their own accord with offers of military support; and they dispatched messengers around the Sicel towns and to Egesta, asking them to send as many horses as possible. And they continued to get everything ready for the circumvallation of Syracuse—brick-making equipment, iron, and whatever else they might need—so that they would be ready for war at the beginning of spring.

[7] As the Syracusan envoys who had been sent to Corinth and Sparta were sailing along the southern Italian coast, they tried to persuade the Greek cities there not to turn a blind eye to what the Athenians were doing, arguing that they were just as much targets of Athenian schemes as their Sicilian compatriots; then, when they reached Corinth, they delivered a speech asking them to send help on the strength of their kinship. [8] The Corinthians needed no further incentive and immediately voted to do all they could to help the Syracusans. They also sent their own representatives to Sparta along with the Syracusan delegation to help them persuade the Lacedaemonians to wage war in Greece against the Athenians more openly and to send help in some form to Sicily.

[9] The Corinthian envoys were not the only visitors to Sparta: Alcibiades was there too, with the men who had accompanied him into exile. He had originally sailed on a merchantman straight from Thurii to Cyllene, but then later he had gone to Sparta at the Lacedaemonians' own request—with a guarantee of safe conduct, because he was uncertain how they felt about his involvement in the Mantinean business.* [10] And what happened was that when addressing the Lacedaemonian assembly, both the Corinthians and the Syracusans made the same request as Alcibiades and prevailed on the Lacedaemonians

to do as they asked. The ephors and the other Lacedaemonian authorities had already been intending to send envoys to Syracuse to ask them not to come to terms with the Athenians, but they had not committed themselves to helping them in military terms. But then Alcibiades stepped up and roused the Lacedaemonians with a stirring speech, somewhat as follows:

89. "I first need to address the negative things that people are saying about me so that you won't let suspicion prejudice you against me as I raise matters that concern us all. [2] Now, my family's representation of your interests in Athens was given up by my forefathers because of some complaint or other, but I revived it on my own initiative and performed various services for you, not least in relation to the defeat at Pylos. I never wavered in my commitment, but when you were in the process of making peace with the Athenians, you conferred power on my political enemies and brought dishonor on me by negotiating the treaty through them. [3] That's why I was justified in making trouble for you by supporting Mantinea and Argos and by opposing your interests in a number of other ways.

"While you were actually suffering at the time, some of you became excessively angry with me; if this applies to anyone here, I would ask him to reconsider once he's heard the truth, and to be open to changing his mind. Or again, some of you may have thought the worse of me because, in addition to opposing you, I associated with democrats, but you must see that it's not right to hold even this against me. [4] All forms of opposition to dynastic power are called 'democracy,' and my family has always been opposed to tyranny.* That's why the leadership of the people remained firmly in our hands. Given the democratic regime in Athens, however, it was also necessary to conform to current conditions in a great many respects. [5] In our political interventions, we tried to toe a more moderate line than the prevailing irresponsibility, but nowadays (not that it's a new phenomenon) there are people who lead the masses in pernicious directions—the same people who saw to my banishment. [6] But that was not our way. We acted as leaders of the city as a whole, because we thought it our duty to help preserve the form of government we had inherited, under which Athens rose to a pinnacle of power and called no one master. As for democracy, anyone with any sense recognized it for what it was, and because I've been wronged by it more than anyone, I could list its flaws as well as anyone—but there's nothing new to be said about a system the folly of which is undeniable. However, we didn't think it safe for us to see to a change of regime in Athens when you, our enemies, were encamped nearby.

90. "So much for the context of the allegations against me. But now I need to tell you about certain matters that you'll want to take into consideration and that I should bring to your attention, insofar as I have information that's new to you. [2] Our primary objective in sending an expeditionary force to Sicily was to try to subjugate the Sicilian Greeks—but then we planned to subjugate the Italian Greeks as well, and then to make an attempt on the Carthaginian empire and Carthage itself.* [3] If all or most of this went well, our next target was to be the Peloponnese. We'd bring from the west an army composed of all the Greeks who had recently joined our side, and we'd hire in large numbers barbarians, both Iberians and others from the non-Greek peoples there who are recognized as being the best fighters. We'd use the abundant timber of Italy to greatly increase the size of our navy, and with these ships encircling and blockading the Peloponnese and a simultaneous assault by our land forces we'd win some cities in battle and others by circumvallation. In all probability, the Peloponnese would fall to us easily, and then the whole of the Greek world would be included in our empire. [4] As for money and grain in quantities sufficient to make all this go smoothly, the newly added territories there would supply us with enough without touching our revenues here.

91. "You've now heard what our intentions were for the expedition that's under way—and who should know them better than I? The generals who remain will carry out the same plan if they can. But I must also tell you that Sicily will fall unless you send help there. [2] Despite being more or less amateurs at war, the Sicilian Greeks might still prevail even now if they united and cooperated. But fighting alone the Syracusans have already lost a battle despite deploying their entire fighting force, and since they're now hemmed in by sea they'll be unable to withstand the forces the Athenians currently have there. [3] Now, if Syracuse falls, all Sicily will follow, and Italy shortly afterward. Then before long the danger from there that I've just warned you about will descend on you. [4] None of you should imagine, therefore, that your deliberations concern only Sicily; the Peloponnese is threatened too, unless you do the following and do so without delay: You must embark on ships an army consisting of men who will get themselves there as oarsmen and then immediately be ready to serve as hoplites as well. And—an even more useful suggestion, I think—you must give the command to a Spartiate, tasked with organizing the forces he already has and putting pressure on those who are reluctant to join up. The presence of a Spartiate will boost the morale of the friends you already have there and will reduce the concerns the undecided have about joining.

[5] "At the same time you must wage war more visibly here in Greece. This will have two consequences: the Syracusans will be more likely to hold out once they see that you're concerned for them, and the Athenians will be less likely to send reinforcements for their forces. [6] What you must do is fortify Decelea in Attica.* This has always been the Athenians' worst nightmare; dealing with such a forward operating base is the only aspect of warfare that they consider to be outside their past experience. And the surest way to injure an enemy is to get accurate information as to what it is that he most fears and then inflict it on him. I mean, people become afraid, surely, when they recognize their particular weaknesses, which they know better than anyone. [7] I'll pass over many of the ways in which the establishment of such a base will do you good and constrain your opponents, and just highlight the most important. First, you'll appropriate most of the property that's to be found in the countryside, and you won't always have

to seize it: some of it will come to you on its own.* Second, Athens will immediately lose its revenues from the silver mines of Laurium, and individuals will lose the income they currently gain from the land and the lawcourts.* Above all, there'll be less revenue coming in from their allies, who will neglect their obligations once they see that you're now prosecuting the war with determination. 92. Lacedaemonians, it's up to you whether and how quickly and resolutely any of these proposals are put into effect. I'm perfectly confident that they're feasible, and I don't think you'll find that they're misguided.

[2] "It would be wrong, I believe, for any of you to think the worse of me, whom you once took to be a staunch Athenian, for cooperating with Athens's greatest enemies to do it as much harm as I can, and it would be wrong for you to mistrust what I'm saying as no more than the fervor that is typical of exiles. [3] I am a fugitive from the iniquity of those who sent me into exile, but not, if you accept what I'm saying, from being of service to you. The true enemies of my country are, surely, not those like you who injure it in some respect, but those who compel its friends to become its enemies. [4] In short, the Athens to which I'm loyal isn't the city that's now wronging me, but the one in which it wasn't dangerous for me to exercise my rights as a citizen; in fact, I don't see what I'm doing now as attacking a place that's still my country, but rather as trying to recover a place that used to be my country. The true patriot isn't the man who refrains from attacking his city when he's been unjustly deprived of it, but the one whose loyalty is so ardent that he does all he can to get it back.

[5] "So you need have no doubts or worries about me. You should rely on me in every dangerous situation and ordeal, recognizing the truth of the saying that's on everyone's lips, that if I did you substantial harm as an enemy, I'd be considerably useful to you as a friend, given that I know the Athenians' intentions but was only guessing at yours. And I call on you now to appreciate that you're deliberating about issues that are of supreme importance to you, and not to shrink from campaigning in both Sicily and Attica. A small fraction of your

forces supporting the struggle in Sicily will safeguard your considerable interests there, and you'll destroy Athenian power once and for all. Then you yourselves will live in safety, and you'll be the leaders of all Greeks everywhere, who will follow you willingly, not because they're being coerced but because you've won their loyalty."

93. This speech by Alcibiades energized the Lacedaemonians. They had already been planning, on their own initiative, to march against Athens, but they had been procrastinating and awaiting developments. However, his detailed recommendations fired them up and they told themselves that the speech had been delivered by the one man who had the greatest insight into the state of affairs. [2] So now they began to give some thought to fortifying Decelea and, more immediately, to sending help in some form to Sicily. They appointed Gylippus, son of Cleandridas, to the Syracusan command, with orders to consult with the Syracusans and the Corinthians and to do whatever it took under the circumstances to see that the Sicilians received help as effectively and quickly as possible. [3] Gylippus now told the Corinthians to send two ships to him at Asine and to fit out the rest of the ships they were planning to send so that they would be ready for sailing when the time came. With these arrangements in place, the envoys left Sparta. [4] Meanwhile, the Athenian trireme that the generals had dispatched from Sicily to fetch money and cavalry arrived in Athens, and after hearing their news the Athenians voted to send both the money for the troops' maintenance and the cavalrymen. And so the winter came to an end, and with it the seventeenth year of the current war, the history of which was written by Thucydides.

94. The following year, right at the beginning of summer, the Athenians in Sicily set out from Catana against Megara (the one in Sicily), where the Syracusans had been in possession of the land ever since, as I mentioned earlier, they had evicted the inhabitants during the reign of the tyrant Gelon. [2] The Athenians disembarked, ravaged the countryside, attacked a fortress garrisoned by Syracusans, and then, when they failed to take it, both the land army and the ships followed the coast to the Terias river. Then they marched inland, laid waste the plain, and burned the grain. They encountered a small body of Syracusans, killed a few of them, and then returned to their ships after setting up a trophy. [3] After returning to Catana and stocking up on provisions there, the whole army marched against Centoripa, a Sicel town, which entered into a pact of friendship and came over to them. Then they returned to Catana, burning the grain in the fields of Inessa and Hybla as they went. [4] Back in Catana, they found that the cavalrymen, 250 in all, had arrived from Athens; they brought their tack but no horses, on the assumption that they would get them locally. The ships also brought 30 mounted archers and 300 talents of silver.

95. In the same spring the Lacedaemonians marched against Argos, but they got no farther than Cleonae when an earthquake occurred and they returned home.* After this the Argives invaded neighboring Thyreatis and gained a massive haul of booty from the Lacedaemonians, which raised at least 25 talents when sold. [2] Not long after this, during the same summer, in Thespiae the democrats attempted a coup, but they failed because the Thebans sent help. Some of the democrats were taken into custody, while others fled to Athens.

96. In the summer of this year, when the Syracusans found out that the Athenian cavalry had arrived and that they were now planning to attack them, they judged that it would be difficult for the Athenians to wall them off even if they prevailed in battle unless they gained control of Epipolae, a steep-sided plateau situated directly above the city. Their plan, therefore, was to guard the access points to Epipolae so they would not be caught unawares if the enemy tried to enter by these routes. These were the only possible approaches to Epipolae. [2] The rest of the plateau slopes steeply down to the city, and all of it is visible looking inland from the city. The Syracusans called it "Epipolae" because it is higher than [*epipolēs*] the rest of the place.

[3] Hermocrates and his fellow generals had just recently taken up their appointments, and at daybreak the entire Syracusan army went out to the meadow beside the Anapus and a review was conducted of their troops in full armor. But first they created an elite company of 600 handpicked hoplites who were to guard Epipolae and respond rapidly as a unit if they were needed for some other assignment. They were commanded by Diomilus, an exile from Andros.

97. But during the night before the day of the Syracusans' review, the Athenians, now with their entire army, left Catana and landed, without being detected, at a place called Leon, about three-quarters of a mile from Epipolae. After disembarking their land forces the ships anchored at Thapsus, which is on a peninsula projecting into the sea from a narrow neck of land, not far from Syracuse either by land or sea. [2] After erecting a barricade across the isthmus, the Athenian naval force in Thapsus remained inactive, but their land forces immediately raced off to Epipolae and reached the plateau by way of Euryelus before the Syracusans, once they realized what was happening, could get there from the meadow where the review was taking place.

[3] All the Syracusans set out to confront the Athenians as fast as they could, including Diomilus's 600, but Epipolae was at least three miles away from the meadow. [4] This meant they were rather disordered when they attacked the Athenians, and the battle for Epipolae was an Athenian victory. The Syracusans lost about 300 men, including Diomilus, and retreated back to the city. [5] After the battle, the Athenians set up a trophy and granted the Syracusans a truce so they could collect their dead. The next day they marched down from Epipolae right up to the city, and when the Syracusans remained inside they pulled back and built a fort at Labdalum (which faces Megara Hyblaea on the edge of the cliffs of Epipolae), so they would have somewhere to store their equipment and valuables when they moved forward either to fight or to build walls.

98. Before long, their forces were supplemented by 300 cavalrymen from Egesta and about 100 more supplied by the Sicels, Naxos, and elsewhere. They already had the 250 Athenians, who had by then either bought horses or been given them by Egesta and Catana, so that in all they had a cavalry troop of 650. [2] After installing a garrison in the fort at Labdalum, the Athenians moved on to the fig tree, where they took up a position and quickly built the Round Fort. The Syracusans were alarmed and came out of the city determined to give battle and not just passively to let things happen. [3] But as the two armies were lining up opposite each other, the Syracusan generals noticed that their men were disorganized and finding it difficult to form up, so they led them back into the city, leaving behind only some of the cavalry, who had the job of trying to prevent the Athenians from fetching stones and straying farther afield. [4] But this Syracusan squadron was attacked and routed by the Athenian cavalry troop, working in combination with a single regiment of Athenian hoplites. Several Syracusans lost their lives, and the Athenians erected a trophy for their victory in this engagement.

99. The next day, some of the Athenians made a start on building the wall that was to extend northward from the Round Fort, while others brought stones and timber and laid them on the ground all the way to the place called Trogilus, which was the endpoint of the shortest line for the wall from the Great Harbor to the sea on the other side. [2] The Syracusans were no longer prepared to risk their forces in a general battle against the Athenians, and following a recommendation of the generals, especially Hermocrates, they decided it would be better to build a counter-wall to intercept the line of the Athenian wall, the idea being that if they succeeded in building their wall first, it would make it impossible for the Athenians to complete theirs. Moreover, in case the Athenians attacked them during the building work, they decided to send a division of their army to counter this possibility and to forestall an Athenian assault by erecting a stockade and occupying the approaches. They hoped to force the Athenians to call a halt to their building work and turn their attention to them. [3] So they came out of the city and set about building this counter-wall, which involved cutting down some of the olive trees in the Temenites precinct. The wall, below the Round Fort, ran at a right angle from the city wall to the Athenians' wall and was furnished with wooden towers. [4] The Athenian ships had not yet sailed into the Great Harbor from Thapsus; the Syracusans still controlled the coast, and the Athenians were being supplied from Thapsus by land.

100. Having divided their forces, the Athenians were afraid the Syracusans would find them less of a challenge, and they were also in a hurry to complete their own wall, so they made no move to hinder the Syracusans at their work. Once the Syracusans reckoned that they had made sufficient progress with the palisade and the counter-wall, they left one regiment to guard their building work and returned to the city.

The Athenians, for their part, destroyed the underground pipes that brought some of Syracuse's drinking water into the city, and waited until they could see that most of the Syracusans had retired to their shelters at midday—some of them even went back inside the city—and that the guards of the palisade were inattentive. Then they sent forward 300 of their best men, along with a select body of mobile troops armed as hoplites. Their orders were to make a sudden charge toward the counter-wall while the rest of the army, in two divisions, each under the command of one of the two generals, advanced, respectively, toward the city, in case the Syracusans sent help, and toward the stretch of palisade that ran past the pyramid.† [2] The 300 attacked and took the palisade, and the Syracusan guards abandoned it and fled back to the outworks at the Temenites sanctuary. Their pursuers burst inside the forts along with the fugitive Syracusans, but once inside they were forcibly thrown back out, and some of the Argives and a few Athenians were killed there. [3] Then the entire army pulled back from its various positions. They destroyed the counter-wall, uprooted the palisade, carried off the stakes for their own use, and erected a trophy.

101. The next day, starting from the Round Fort, the Athenians began building a wall on the cliff above the marsh—the cliff on this side of Epipolae faces the Great Harbor—on the shortest line for the wall down over the level ground and the marshland to the harbor. [2] At this, the Syracusans came out of the city and set about building their own wall, with the object of preventing the Athenians from running theirs down to the sea; starting, as before, from the city wall, they built a palisade through the middle of the marshland, and also dug a trench alongside it. [3] When the Athenians had completed the wall that abutted the cliff, they launched an attack, similar to that of the day before, on the Syracusans' palisade and ditch. They ordered the ships to come from Thapsus to the Great Harbor of Syracuse, and at first light they descended from Epipolae to the level ground and crossed the marsh where it was muddy and the surface was as firm as it gets, by laying down doors and planks and walking over them. As the sun rose they captured almost all the palisade and the ditch, and later they also gained the missing stretch.

[4] The ensuing battle went the Athenians' way. After the Syracusans turned and fled, the soldiers on their right wing headed for the city, while those on the left made for the river. Wanting to prevent them from crossing the river, the 300 elite Athenians pushed on at a run toward the bridge. [5] This worried the Syracusans, and since they had most of their cavalry with them they engaged the 300, turned them to flight, and drove into the Athenians' right wing. This attack caused the regiment occupying the front line of the wing to be infected by the panic of the 300, [6] and when Lamachus saw this he moved over from the left wing in support. He had with him a small body of archers and the Argives, but after crossing a ditch he and a few men who had crossed with him were cut off, and he was killed along with five or six of his companions. The Syracusans were quick off the mark and they immediately snatched up the bodies before the Athenians could retrieve them, and took them across the river to a

place of safety. Then they, too, retreated as the rest of the Athenian army bore down on them.

102. Meanwhile, the Syracusans who had originally fled toward the city regained their confidence at this turn of events. They doubled back from the city in good order to resist the Athenians who were confronting them, and they also sent a detachment of their men to the Round Fort on Epipolae, thinking that they would find it undefended and take it. [2] They succeeded in taking the thousand-foot stretch of Athenian outworks, which they left in ruins, but Nicias, who happened to have been left behind there because he was ill, prevented the loss of the Round Fort itself. He ordered the hoplites' attendants to set fire to the equipment and to all the timbers that were lying on the ground in front of the wall, since he realized this was the only way for them to save their lives, given that they had no one to defend them. [3] He turned out to be quite right: the fire made the Syracusans break off their advance. In fact, they pulled back toward the city, because by then the Athenians lower down had chased their opponents off the field, and a relieving force was on its way back to the Round Fort, and also because the Athenian ships from Thapsus were sailing as ordered into the Great Harbor. [4] In view of all this, the Syracusans up on Epipolae quickly left, and the entire army went back inside the city, believing that they currently lacked the resources to prevent the Athenians from running their wall down to the coast.

103. The Athenians next erected a trophy and granted the Syracusans a truce so they could collect their dead, while they recovered the bodies of Lamachus and those who had fallen with him. Since the whole expeditionary force was now present, both the fleet and the land army, they set about walling off the Syracusans with a pair of walls from Epipolae and the cliffs. [2] The army was being supplied from all over Italy, many Sicels who had not previously committed themselves came to support them, and three pentecounters arrived from Etruria. In short, matters in general were progressing toward the fulfillment of their hopes. [3] The Syracusans were no longer sure that they would prevail in the war, not least because no help had come from the Peloponnese in any form, and they began to talk among themselves about coming to terms and approached Nicias—who was now the sole general, on Lamachus's death—to negotiate a settlement. [4] No final decision was reached, however, but, as one might expect from people who were desperate and facing a more thorough siege than before, a number of different overtures were made to Nicias, and the talk in the city was even less consistent. Part of the problem was that their current woes were making them somewhat suspicious of one another, and they sacked the generals on whose watch this situation had come about, on the ground that, if their suffering was not due to bad luck, it was due to the generals' treachery. The three new generals they appointed were Heracleides, Eucles, and Tellias.

104. Meanwhile, Gylippus of Sparta and the Corinthian ships, intent on relieving Sicily, had reached Leucas. But the news that kept arriving there was bleak and always included false information to the same effect—that Syracuse was already completely blockaded—so Gylippus gave up on Sicily. But he still wanted to keep Italy safe, so he and Python of Corinth took two Lacedaemonian and two Corinthian ships and sailed as quickly as they could across the Ionian Sea to Taras. The Corinthians were to follow later, once they had found crews for two ships from Leucas and three from Ambracia in addition to their ten. [2] From Taras Gylippus sent envoys first to Thurii, in acknowledgment of the citizenship that had once been granted his father,* but he was unable to win them over, so he set out along the Italian coast. But when the wind blows steadily from the north into the Gulf of Terina it blows strongly, and Gylippus was caught by it. He was driven out into the open sea and reached Taras again only after enduring the most dreadful weather. He had the ships, which had taken a terrible beating in the storm, hauled ashore and repaired. [3] When Nicias learned of his approach and heard how few ships he had, he was supremely unconcerned, as the Thurians had been as well. He regarded this more as a piratical enterprise than anything more serious and put off taking precautions.

105. This summer, at much the same time, the Lacedaemonians and their allies invaded Argos and ravaged most of the farmland. The Athenians sent thirty ships to support the Argives—an act that constituted an absolutely blatant violation of their treaty with Sparta. [2] Previously they had been supporting the Argives and Mantineans in their conflict with Sparta by carrying out raids from Pylos and around the Peloponnesian coast, but they had never actually made landfall in Laconia; the Argives had repeatedly asked them to make at least a token armed landing in Laconia and then to leave after helping them to ravage a tiny part of it, but they had always refused. But now, under the command of Pythodorus, Laispodias, and Demaratus, they came ashore and laid waste land at Epidaurus Limera,* Prasiae, and elsewhere, so that now the Lacedaemonians had a more plausible reason for retaliation. [3] After the Athenians sailed back home from Argos and the Lacedaemonians left as well, the Argives invaded Phleiasian territory and devastated some of the land before returning home.

BOOK SEVEN

*Years eighteen and nineteen of the war. **414/413**: Spartan forces arrive in Sicily (7.1–8); Athenian activity in northern Greece (7.9); Athens decides to send reinforcements to Sicily (7.10–17); Sparta invades Attica and establishes a base at Decelea (7.18–19.2). **413/412**: fighting in Sicily continues (7.19.3–26); Athenian financial worries (7.27–28); the massacre at Mycalessus (7.29–30); further engagements in Sicily (7.31–56); catalog of the forces present in Sicily (7.57–59.1), before the final and decisive naval battle (7.59.2–71); Athenian retreat across Sicily and final defeat (7.72–87).*

1. After repairing their ships, Gylippus and Python sailed from Taras to Locri. By now they had better information about the situation in Syracuse—that the walling-off of the city was incomplete, so that it was still possible for them to arrive with an army and enter by way of Epipolae—and for a while they were undecided whether they should travel down the east coast of Sicily and take the risk of sailing into Syracuse, or go first to Himera along the north coast, gain an army made up of the Himerans themselves and any others they could persuade to join, and approach Syracuse by land. [2] Their eventual decision was to head for Himera, not least because the four Athenian ships (that, despite his original neglect, Nicias had dispatched when he learned that Gylippus and Python were at Locri) had not yet reached Rhegium. They crossed the strait before this guarding force was in place and reached Himera via Rhegium and Messina.

[3] Once they were there, they persuaded the Himerans to support their campaign by both supplying troops and arming any men from their ships who lacked weaponry—they had beached their ships at Himera—and they sent word to the Selinountians to send a full levy of their troops to meet them at a particular location. [4] The Geloans too promised to send men, though not many, and so did some of the Sicels, who were much more ready to join them now than they had been before, for two reasons: the recent death of Archonides (a man of considerable power who had been the ruler of some of the Sicels in the region and had supported the Athenians), and because Gylippus had come from Sparta and seemed to be in earnest. [5] And so Gylippus set out for Syracuse, taking with him an army made up of those of his ships' crews and marines who were armed, who numbered about seven hundred; from Himera a total of a thousand hoplites and light-armed troops and a hundred cavalrymen; some Selinountian light-armed troops and cavalry; a small contingent of Geloans; and about a thousand Sicels in all.

2. Meanwhile, the Corinthians were bringing help from Leucas as fast as they could in the form of the rest of the ships; Gongylus, one of the Corinthian commanders, was the last to set out on his single ship, but the first to reach Syracuse. He arrived shortly before Gylippus and, finding the Syracusans on the point of holding a general meeting with a view to bringing the war to an end, he checked them from doing so and cheered them up by telling them that more ships were on their way and that Gylippus, son of Cleandridas, was in command, having been entrusted with the mission by the Lacedaemonians. [2] The Syracusans took heart at the news and immediately marched out at full strength to link up with Gylippus, since they found out that he was now actually quite close. [3] Meanwhile, Gylippus captured Ietae, a Sicel fortress that was on his route, and then he reached Epipolae with his men in battle array. He ascended to the plateau by way of Euryelus (the same route the Athenians had originally taken) and marched with the Syracusans against the Athenian fortifications.

[4] He happened to come at the critical moment when the Athenians had completed almost a mile of the double wall to the Great Harbor and were still working on the remaining short stretch that would take the wall down to the sea. As for the other wall, the one bound for Trogilus and the sea on the other side, stones had already been laid on the ground along most of its length, and some stretches of it had been left half-finished while others had been completed. That was how close Syracuse came to destruction.

3. The Athenians were at first thrown into confusion by the sudden approach of Gylippus and the Syracusans, but they managed to form up in ranks. After halting nearby, Gylippus sent a herald to them with the message that if they would agree to leave Sicily within five days, taking with them all their belongings and equipment, he was ready to enter into a truce. [2] But the Athenians slighted the herald, sending him back without a response, and then both sides began to get ready to fight. [3] But Gylippus saw that there was some confusion in the Syracusan ranks and they were finding it difficult to form up, so he led the army back to more open ground. Nicias did not have the Athenians advance against the enemy, but stayed by their wall without doing anything, and when Gylippus realized that he was not going to be attacked he led his army back to the high point called Temenitis and spent the night there.

[4] The next day, Gylippus took most of his men and had them form up facing the Athenian walls, preventing the Athenians from sending reinforcements elsewhere. Meanwhile, the Labdalum fort, which could not be seen by the Athenians, fell to the detachment Gylippus sent against it, and all those found inside were killed. [5] And on the same day an Athenian trireme that had been stationed near the Little Harbor was captured by the Syracusans.

4. Next the Syracusans and their allies began to build a single wall up across Epipolae from the city at a right angle to the Athenian wall; if the Athenians were unable to prevent the building of this cross-wall, it would become impossible for them to wall off the city.

[2] The Athenians had just gone up to Epipolae after completing the wall down to the sea, but one stretch of the wall was vulnerable and Gylippus advanced against it with his army. He attacked under cover of darkness, [3] but the Athenians were bivouacked outside it, and when they realized that Gylippus was approaching they countered his advance with one of their own. When Gylippus saw them coming, he quickly led his men back again, and the Athenians increased the height of the wall. They guarded this section themselves, and they now sent some allied companies here and there along the rest of the wall to mount guard.

[4] Nicias thought it would be a good idea to fortify Plemyrium, as it is called—a headland opposite the city that juts out into the Great Harbor and makes its mouth narrow. It seemed to him that if it were fortified it would be easier to bring in supplies, because his ships would be moored closer to the Little Harbor and would not have to put to sea from a remote corner of the Great Harbor to counter any move against his supply ships by the Syracusan fleet. By now, in fact, Nicias was more inclined to focus on the war at sea, seeing that since Gylippus's arrival the situation on land had become rather less encouraging. [5] He therefore brought some men and the ships over to Plemyrium and built three forts in which were deposited the bulk of their stores, and the place now became the anchorage for both the transports and the warships. [6] This move turned out to be the major cause of the first phase of the degradation of the ships' crews. There was little water available, and it was not close at hand, so whenever the sailors went out—to gather firewood as well—lives were lost to the Syracusan cavalry, who controlled the countryside. A third of the Syracusan cavalry had been stationed in the village at the sanctuary of Olympian Zeus, precisely to prevent the soldiers in Plemyrium from going out and causing damage. [7] At the same time, Nicias also found out that the remaining Corinthian ships were on their way. He sent twenty ships to guard against them, with instructions to lie in wait for them at Locri, Rhegium, and the approach to Sicily.

5. Gylippus continued to build the wall across Epipolae, using the stones that the Athenians had laid out earlier for their own use, and he also had his men maintain a permanent presence in battle formation out in front of the wall. The Athenians responded by forming up for battle themselves and confronting Gylippus's troops. [2] At what he took to be the opportune moment, Gylippus initiated the fighting. The two sides came to close quarters and the battle was fought between the walls, where it was impossible to make use of the Syracusan cavalry. [3] The Syracusans and their allies lost the battle; they collected their dead under a truce and the Athenians erected a trophy. Gylippus† convened an army assembly and told them that the defeat was his fault, not theirs, because he had deployed them too far within the walls and so had lost the benefit of the cavalry and javelineers. He would lead them again into battle, he said, [4] and he urged them to think positively. They were at least as strong as the Athenians in terms of their forces, and, as far as their mental strength was concerned, it would be unthinkable for them, as Peloponnesians and Dorians, not to expect to get the better of Ionians, islanders, and other trash and drive them out of the country.

6. Later, at the opportune moment, he again led them forward. Nicias and the Athenians held the view that even if the enemy were reluctant to initiate the fighting, it was still imperative for them to react to the Syracusans' counter-wall, because by then it had almost passed the end of their wall, and if it got past it, it would make no difference whether they fought and won every battle or did not fight at all.† So they responded by moving forward in their turn against the Syracusans. [2] Gylippus advanced with his hoplites outside the walls rather than inside as before, and stationed his cavalry and javelineers on the Athenian flank in the open ground where the construction of both walls ceased. And so battle was joined. [3] In the course of the fighting the cavalry attacked the Athenian left wing, which was facing them, and turned it to flight. This led to the defeat by the Syracusans of the rest of the army as well, and the Athenians were driven in rout back inside their fortifications. [4] And that night the Syracusans preempted the Athenians by continuing their building work and getting past the Athenians' wall. And so they were past the point where they could be impeded by the Athenians, and the Athenians had altogether lost the ability, even if they defeated them in battle, to wall off the city.

7. Next the twelve remaining Corinthian, Ambraciot, and Leucadian ships, under the command of Thrasonides, a Corinthian, reached Syracuse—they had evaded the Athenian guard without being spotted—and helped the Syracusans complete the cross-wall. [2] Meanwhile, Gylippus had traveled around the rest of Sicily gathering recruits for both his fleet and his army, and at the same time winning over communities that had either shown little enthusiasm or had so far refused to play any part in the war. [3] Moreover, Syracusan and Corinthian envoys were dispatched to Sparta and Corinth to see if it might be possible for troops to be brought over somehow, perhaps in cargo ships or other boats, because the Athenians had also sent for reinforcements. [4] The Syracusans spent the time enlisting crews for their ships and practicing maneuvers so they could mount operations at sea as well as on land, and overall their confidence was high.

8. When all this came to the attention of Nicias, and since he could see that the enemy's strength and his own problems were increasing day by day, he, too, dispatched messengers, sending them to Athens to bring them up to date. He had often done this before as well, to keep them informed of everything as it happened, but he felt it was particularly important then given the direness of the situation as he saw it. It was his opinion that if the Athenians did not either recall the army or send substantial reinforcements, all would be lost. [2] But he was worried that the messengers might be such poor speakers, or even so forgetful, that they would deliver an inaccurate report; they might also say what the rabble wanted to hear rather than the truth. So he put his report in writing, thinking that this would be the best way for him to inform the Athenians of his views without their being distorted by anyone delivering the message, so that they would be in a position to come to a decision on the basis of the facts. [3] So his chosen envoys left with his letter and full instructions as to what to say, while he turned his attention to the army, which he now maintained in a defensive posture rather than choosing to take risks.

9. Toward the end of the summer, the Athenian general Euetion joined forces with Perdiccas for a campaign against Amphipolis.* Despite his large force of Thracians, he failed to take the city by land, so he took his triremes around to the Strymon and began to besiege the city from the river, with Himeraeum as his base. And so the summer came to an end.

10. The following winter, the men sent by Nicias arrived in Athens. They repeated what he had orally instructed them to say, answered any questions that arose, and handed over the written report. The city secretary stepped up and read the letter to the Athenians, which went somewhat as follows: **11.** "Athenians, in the past I have sent you many other letters to keep you informed about events here, and it is no less critical now for you to understand our situation and decide what to do. [2] As you know, then, we won most of our battles against the Syracusans, whom we were sent to fight, and we built the fortifications that we are currently occupying. But then Gylippus came to Syracuse from Sparta with an army made up of Peloponnesian troops and also soldiers from some of the Sicilian towns. He lost the first battle he fought against us, but the next day we were overwhelmed by his large cavalry contingent and his javelineers and we retreated to our fortifications. [3] So now we have left off the circumvallation of the city, and the enemy's superior numbers are forcing us to remain inactive—I should explain that guarding the fortifications is absorbing so much of our hoplite force that we don't have the whole army available—and they have built a single wall past ours, making circumvallation of the city impossible unless this counter-wall of theirs were to be attacked and taken, which would require a sizable force. [4] In short, the upshot is that although we are supposed to be besieging them, we are actually under siege ourselves, on land at any rate, because their cavalry is making it impossible for us to venture far into the countryside.

12. "They have also sent envoys to the Peloponnese to request reinforcements, and Gylippus has gone to the Sicilian towns to persuade those who are currently uninvolved to fight for him, and to see if from the others he can recruit even more troops for both the army and the ships. [2] My information is that they plan to use their land forces for an attempt on our fortifications and to launch a simultaneous attack by sea. [3] And let none of you think it strange that I say 'by sea.' Although our fleet was at first in peak condition in terms of the dryness of the hulls and the integrity of the crews, yet now, as the enemy has learned, the ships have been at sea for so long that they have become waterlogged, and the crews have been whittled down. [4] It is impossible for us to beach the ships and dry them out because the enemy's fleet is at least a match for us—in numbers, at any rate, and it may even outnumber us—and so keeps us constantly on the alert for an attack. [5] They practice their maneuvers in plain sight, they have the initiative when it comes to attacking, and it is easier for them to dry out their ships because they are not maintaining a blockade.

13. "This would hardly be the case if our fleet greatly outnumbered theirs and we were not forced, as we are now, to use all our ships for guard duties. But if we relax our vigilance even for a moment our supplies will not get through; even now we have to bring them in past the enemy city, which is far from easy. [2] As for the crews, we have lost men and we are still losing men even now. How? Because when our sailors forage far and wide for firewood, food, and water they are killed by the enemy cavalry, and because our slaves are deserting now that we no longer outmatch the enemy. At the same time, those of the foreign crewmen who were pressed into service leave the moment they find an opportunity to do so and return to their various cities. Others, those who are being paid, who were initially motivated by the high rate of pay and came to make money rather than fight, did not expect to find the enemy resisting with his fleet and all his other resources, and they either leave on the pretense of searching for deserters or just seize opportunities to make themselves scarce, Sicily being a large island. Then there are others who blunt the effectiveness of the fleet by putting their money to use: they corrupt the trierarchs and have enslaved Hyccarans* join the crews in their stead.

14. "You do not need me to tell you that a crew is not at peak efficiency for long, and that there are few sailors who can set a ship moving and row in time. [2] But the most frustrating aspects of the situation are that there is nothing I, as general, can do to stop this from happening—you are, after all, not an easy people to control—and that there is nowhere for us to replenish our crews, whereas our enemies can do so all over the place. In our case, however, both the men we have and the men we lose necessarily come from those we brought out with us, given that our current allies, Naxos and Catana, are unable to help in this respect. [3] All the enemy needs is a single development—that the places in Italy that currently supply us, seeing our situation and your refusal to send reinforcements, go over to their side—and they will win the war without any further fighting by starving us into submission.

[4] "I could have written you a different letter, one that may have been more pleasant to hear, but such a letter would have been less useful, as it is imperative that you know the facts of the situation here in order to decide what to do. In any case, I know what you are like: you want to hear pleasing words, and then later you find fault if the outcome of such words fails to be equally pleasing. And so I thought it safer to tell you the truth.

15. "As far as the original purpose of the expedition is concerned, no blame is to be attached to the conduct of either the rank-and-file soldiers or the officers; you can take my word for this. But since all Sicily is united and they are expecting a fresh army from the Peloponnese, and the forces we have here are incapable of withstanding even those they already face, you must decide here and now either to recall them or to send another army. If you decide to send another army, it must be at least as large as the first one and made up of both land and naval forces, and you must also send a great deal of money and someone to replace me. I have a problem with my kidneys that makes it impossible for me to stay on. [2] I think you ought to do this for me, seeing that when I was healthy I often served you well in positions of command. But whatever you intend to do, do it now, right at the beginning of spring. Do not procrastinate over this, but understand that it will not be long before the enemy's resources are supplemented from within Sicily, and that although the reinforcements from the Peloponnese will take longer to arrive, nevertheless, if you are careless, they will evade your guard as they did before and will get here before you."

16. That was what Nicias wrote in his letter. After the Athenians had heard what he had to say, they did not grant his request to be relieved of his command, but appointed two temporary commanders, Menander and Euthydemus, from among the men who were on the spot there in Sicily. They were to share the command with Nicias until other generals were appointed and sent out to join him. That way, he would not have to endure the stress alone while he was ill. Moreover, they voted to send a fresh army consisting of both land and naval forces drawn from Athenians on the call-up lists and from the allies. [2] And they appointed Demosthenes, son of Alcisthenes, and Eurymedon, son of Thoucles, as Nicias's co-commanders. Eurymedon was sent off to Sicily right away, around the time of the winter solstice, with ten ships and 120 talents of silver; he was also to inform the troops there that help was on the way and that their needs would be met. **17.** Demosthenes stayed behind and got everything ready for the expedition, which was to leave at the beginning of spring, by ordering up forces from the allies and arranging for money, ships, and hoplites from Athens itself.

[2] In addition, the Athenians sent twenty ships around the Peloponnese to guard against any attempt to sail over to Sicily from

Corinth and the Peloponnese. [3] The Corinthians had been greatly encouraged by the report their envoys brought back about the improvement of the situation in Sicily. Their earlier dispatch of ships had been timely, they felt, and now they were preparing to send hoplites off to Sicily in cargo ships, while the Lacedaemonians were planning to use the same method to send troops from the rest of the Peloponnese. [4] The Corinthians were also manning twenty-five ships that were to bring to battle the Athenian ships on guard at Naupactus; this would make it harder for the Athenians there to prevent the Corinthian cargo ships from setting out, since they would have to protect themselves against the triremes deployed against them. 18. The Lacedaemonians were making preparations as well, getting ready for the invasion of Attica they had previously decided to mount, which the Syracusans and Corinthians were urging them to undertake. They had learned that the Athenians were going to send reinforcements to Sicily, and they thought an invasion might stop them from doing so. And Alcibiades was pressing his case, arguing that they should fortify Decelea* and not slacken their efforts in the war.

[2] A critical factor was that Lacedaemonian confidence had increased. There were two reasons for this. They thought it would be easier for them to win now that the Athenians were fighting on two fronts, against both themselves and the Sicilian Greeks, and they reckoned that the Athenians had been the first to break the treaty. They felt that in the earlier phase of the war it had been chiefly they who had been on the wrong side of the law.* In the first place, the Thebans had entered Plataea at a time when there was supposed to be peace,* and in the second place they had refused to submit to arbitration when the Athenians had called on them to do so, even though it was stipulated in the earlier treaty that no one should bear arms with hostile intent if the other side was willing to go to arbitration.* This had led them to believe that their ill fortune had been deserved, and they took to heart the defeat at Pylos and the other setbacks they had experienced. [3] But since the Athenians had used the thirty ships

based at Argos to ravage some of the farmland of Epidaurus Limera, Prasiae, and elsewhere, and were also carrying out raids from Pylos, and since every time there had been an altercation about one of the disputed clauses of the treaty, the Athenians had refused to submit to arbitration when the Lacedaemonians had called on them to do so, the Lacedaemonians had become convinced that the transgression they had been guilty of earlier had now been committed in exactly the same form by the Athenians in their turn, and so they had become eager for war. [4] Accordingly, during the winter they sent messages around to their allies ordering supplies of iron and got ready all the material and tools they would need to establish the forward operating base, and at the same time they were raising the auxiliary force to be sent off to Sicily in the cargo ships, and requiring the rest of the Peloponnesians to do the same. And so the winter came to an end and with it the eighteenth year of the current war, the history of which was written by Thucydides.

19. Right at the beginning of the spring of the following year, earlier than ever before, the Lacedaemonians and their allies invaded Attica under the command of the Spartan king Agis, son of Archidamus. First they set about laying waste the land around the plain and then they fortified Decelea, assigning different aspects of the work to different states. [2] Decelea is some fourteen miles from Athens and about the same distance, or a little farther, from Boeotia. The fortifications were built overlooking and commanding the plain and the best of the farmland, and were visible from as far away as Athens. [3] While the Peloponnesians in Attica and their allies were building this fortress, those in the Peloponnese were occupied with the dispatch of the hoplites to Sicily in the cargo ships. The Lacedaemonians picked the best of the helots and the freedmen and made up a contingent of about 600 hoplites from these two groups, with Eccritus, a Spartiate, as their commander, and the Boeotians supplied 300 hoplites under the command of Xenon and Nicon of Thebes and Hegesander of Thespiae. [4] These soldiers made up the first batch to put to sea from Taenarum in Laconia, but not long afterward the Corinthians sent off a contingent of 500 hoplites, made up partly of Corinthians themselves and partly of Arcadians who had been hired as mercenaries, with Alexarchus, a Corinthian, appointed to the command. The Sicyonians also contributed men, sending 200 hoplites along with the Corinthians, under the command of a Sicyonian called Sagreus. [5] The twenty-five Corinthian ships for which crews had been found during the winter remained in a confrontational position near the twenty Athenian ships in Naupactus until the hoplites had set out from the Peloponnese in the cargo ships. This was precisely the job for which they had been manned in the first place, to divert the Athenians' attention from the cargo ships to these triremes.

20. Meanwhile, at the same time as the fortification of Decelea, right at the beginning of spring, the Athenians took action as well, sending thirty ships around the Peloponnese under the command of Charicles, son of Apollodorus. Charicles's orders included stopping at Argos and asking the Argives to embark on his ships the hoplites they were obliged to provide by the terms of their alliance with Athens. [2] They also sent Demosthenes on his way to Sicily, as planned, with sixty Athenian ships and five from Chios, 1,200 Athenian hoplites drawn from the call-up lists, and as many men as could be pressed into service from each of the islands, and they collected from the rest of their subject allies whatever they could provide that would be useful for the war. The first thing Demosthenes was instructed to do, while he was sailing around the coast, was to support Charicles in his operations in Laconia, [3] so he sailed to Aegina and waited there for any missing elements of his expeditionary force to arrive and for Charicles to pick up the Argive hoplites.

21. In Sicily, at about the same time in the spring, Gylippus arrived in Syracuse, bringing as many men as he had been able to raise from each of the cities he had prevailed upon. [2] He told the Syracusans, at a meeting he convened, that they should man all their seaworthy ships and try their luck in a sea battle, and he expressed his hope that this would lead to an outcome that in military terms made the risk worthwhile. [3] He received especially strong support from Hermocrates, who tried to get the Syracusans to see that they should approach such an attempt on the Athenians at sea with confidence. He argued that even the Athenians' naval expertise was not innate or something they had possessed forever, but they were landsmen, more so than the Syracusans, and it was the Persians who had forced them to acquire naval skills. He said that in any confrontation with people as daring as the Athenians it was those who matched them in daring who would prove to give them the most trouble, and that the Syracusans could have the same effect on their enemies as the Athenians did by imitating the way the Athenians cowed others by the boldness of their attack even when they had no numerical advantage. [4] He had no doubt, he said, that by unexpectedly daring to stand up to their fleet, the Syracusans would panic the Athenians, and that the advantage they would thereby gain would more than compensate for any harm the Athenians could inflict with their skill on Syracusan inexperience. Accordingly, he urged them to try their luck with their fleet and to hold their nerve. [5] So the Syracusans, persuaded by Gylippus, Hermocrates, and others, committed themselves to fighting the Athenians at sea and began to enlist crews for their ships.

22. When the fleet had been made ready, Gylippus led out all his land forces under cover of darkness. The plan was that he would attack the forts at Plemyrium by land while at the same time and at a prearranged signal the Syracusan triremes went to work. Thirty-five of them sailed into the attack from the Great Harbor and the other forty-five sailed around from the Little Harbor (where the Syracusans also had their shipyard), the idea being that they would link up with those inside the Great Harbor and together attack Plemyrium from the sea. Then the Athenians would be thrown into confusion on both fronts. [2] The Athenians responded rapidly by manning sixty ships.

With twenty-five of these they took on the thirty-five Syracusan ships that were in the Great Harbor, while the rest, which went to meet those that were sailing around from the shipyard, were immediately embroiled in a battle just outside the entrance of the Great Harbor. For a long time the two sides held out against each other, with the Syracusans trying to force their way into the harbor and the Athenians trying to stop them.

23. Meanwhile, since the Athenians at Plemyrium had gone down to the shore and were focused on the sea battle, Gylippus took them by surprise with a sudden attack at dawn on the forts. First he took the largest of the forts and then the two smaller ones, where the guards, who had seen how easily the largest fort had fallen, offered no resistance. [2] All the men from the first fort that was captured who retreated to the boats and a cargo vessel managed to return to the camp, but only with difficulty, because the Syracusan ships in the Great Harbor had the upper hand in the sea battle, and they sent a single trireme, a fast one, after them. But by the time the two smaller forts were threatened with capture, the Syracusans no longer had the upper hand, and the men who escaped from these forts found it easier to sail past them.

[3] What happened was that after the Syracusan ships fighting in front of the harbor mouth had overpowered the Athenian ships, they sailed in a disorganized fashion into the harbor and fell afoul of one another. Hence they gifted victory to the Athenians, who routed not only these ships but also those in the harbor, which had at first been getting the better of them. [4] They sank eleven Syracusan ships and killed most of the men, except that they took the crews of three of the ships into captivity. Three of their own ships were lost. They hauled the Syracusan wrecks onto the shore, and after setting up a trophy on the islet that lies off Plemyrium they returned to camp.

24. So the Syracusans came off worst in the sea battle, but they had the Plemyrium forts and erected three trophies for them. They demolished one of the two smaller forts that they had taken last, but repaired the other two and installed garrisons in them. [2] The Athenians sustained heavy losses during the taking of the forts, with men either killed or taken prisoner, and a large quantity of stores was captured as well, because they had been using the forts as a warehouse. There was a great deal of property in them: not just merchandise and grain, but also many of the trierarchs' effects, since the equipment for forty triremes, even including the sails, was kept there.* All of this was captured, along with three triremes that had been beached there. [3] So† the taking of Plemyrium was one of the most significant and pivotal causes of the degradation of the Athenian army. It meant that even sailing into the harbor to bring in supplies was now very hazardous, because the Syracusans had ships lying at anchor off Plemyrium to hinder any such incursions. Fighting was therefore required now to bring goods in, and in other respects, too, the capture of the forts dismayed and dispirited the Athenian soldiers.

25. Next the Syracusans sent out twelve ships under the command of Agatharchus, a Syracusan. One of these ships went to the Peloponnese with envoys on board charged with telling the Lacedaemonians that their situation seemed promising and urging them to step up the intensity of the war in Greece. The other eleven ships sailed to Italy, since they had learned that ships laden with money were on their way to the Athenians. [2] They met the ships and destroyed most of them, and also incinerated a cache of shipbuilding timber that was lying ready for the Athenians near Caulonia. [3] Then they went to Locri, and while they were moored there, one of the cargo ships from the Peloponnese, with Thespian hoplites on board, put in at the harbor. [4] The Syracusans took these hoplites on board their ships and sailed for home. The Athenians, who had posted a guard of twenty ships at Megara Hyblaea to watch for them, managed to capture one of the enemy ships with its crew, but failed with the rest, which made it safely back to Syracuse.

[5] Some skirmishing also occurred in the Great Harbor around the stakes that the Syracusans had driven into the seabed in front of

the old shipsheds so that their ships could lie safely at anchor inside this stockade, and the Athenians could not sail up and damage them with their rams. [6] The Athenians approached the stakes in a huge cargo ship fitted with wooden towers and screens, and men in small boats attached ropes to the stakes and began to winch them up with windlasses, or break them off, or dive down and saw them off. The Syracusans hurled missiles at them from the shipsheds, the Athenians returned fire from the cargo ship, and in the end the Athenians managed to remove most of the stakes. [7] The hidden part of the stockade was the most difficult for them to deal with. The Syracusans had driven some of the stakes in so that their tips did not show above the water, which made approaching the stockade dangerous; there was always the possibility of not spotting the stakes ahead and of a ship being impaled on them as on a submerged rock. But divers were hired to swim down and saw these off too—though the Syracusans later drove in new stakes. [8] Not surprisingly, given the proximity of the opposing armies to each other, each of them also came up with many other ways of making trouble for the other side; various forms of skirmishing took place and every kind of tactic was tried out.

[9] The Syracusans also sent Corinthian, Ambraciot, and Lacedaemonian envoys to the Sicilian cities to inform them about the taking of Plemyrium and to explain that they owed their defeat in the sea battle not to the Athenians' superior strength but to their own disorder. They told them that on the whole their situation was promising and asked for help against the Athenians in the form of ships and men, because another army was expected from Athens, and if they could destroy the one the Athenians currently had before the fresh one arrived, the war would be won. So that was how matters stood in Sicily.

26. Meanwhile, once the army of reinforcements that he was to take to Sicily had assembled, Demosthenes set out from Aegina and sailed to the Peloponnese, where he joined Charicles and his thirty Athenian ships. After taking the Argive hoplites on board they sailed to

Laconia, [2] where they first ravaged some farmland at Epidaurus Limera, and then landed on the Laconian coast opposite Cythera, at the site of the sanctuary of Apollo. They laid waste some of the land there and fortified a sort of isthmus, to create a place of refuge for helots to desert from the Lacedaemonians, and to act as a base, like the one at Pylos, from which to carry out plundering raids. [3] After helping to take the place, Demosthenes immediately set out for Corcyra, where he was to collect some allied soldiers, and then he was to sail to Sicily as quickly as possible. Charicles stayed where he was until the fortification of the place was complete, and then, after leaving a garrison there, he departed as well and returned home, as did the Argives.

27. This same summer there also arrived in Athens 1,300 peltasts from the Dii, a Thracian people whose weapon of choice is the short sword. They were supposed to be sailing to Sicily with Demosthenes, [2] but they arrived too late, so the Athenians proposed to send them back home to Thrace; in view of the war from Decelea it seemed expensive to keep them on, given that each of them was paid a drachma a day.

[3] Ever since Decelea had first been fortified in the course of the summer by the entire Peloponnesian army, and had subsequently been occupied by garrisons from the cities (which relieved one another at regular intervals) as a base for incursions into Attica, it had caused the Athenians a great deal of trouble, and in fact the devastation of property and the loss of life did as much as anything to bring the city to its knees. [4] The earlier invasions had been brief, and it had still been possible for them to make good use of the land for the rest of the year, but now the Peloponnesians were in continuous occupation. Sometimes an even larger force arrived, but at other times it was the regular garrison that had to meet its needs by making forays into the farmland and carrying out raids. Moreover, the Spartan king Agis was there and was devoting himself to prosecuting the war.

All this was injuring the Athenians gravely. [5] They had been deprived of the use of all their farmland; more than 20,000 slaves had deserted, most of them skilled workmen; and they had lost all their flocks and draft animals. Furthermore, since the cavalry was riding out every day to attack Decelea and protect the farmland, some of their horses were made lame by the rough ground and continuous hard work, and others were wounded. **28.** Another problem was that supplies from Euboea now had to be conveyed at considerable expense by sea around Sunium,* whereas previously they had been brought by a shorter route, overland from Oropus via Decelea. Everything Athens needed now had to be imported by sea, and it became more a fortress than a city. [2] By day the Athenians took turns to stand guard on the parapets, and at night, too, everyone except the cavalry did so,† some keeping watch close to where their weapons were stacked, others on the wall; this went on summer and winter, and it was wearing them down.

[3] But the heaviest burden was the result of their involvement in two wars, and of the fact that they had committed themselves to strive for victory with an intensity that no one would have believed possible if they had been told about it before it was actually a reality. For despite being besieged by the Peloponnesian forward operating base at Decelea, they did not withdraw from Sicily but in their turn tried to lay siege in the same manner to Syracuse (a city that in and of itself was just as great as Athens), and they so thoroughly astounded the Greeks with their strength and daring that, whereas at the beginning of the war people believed that they would hold out for a year or two, or three at the most, but certainly no more than that if the Peloponnesians were to invade Attica, in the seventeenth year after the first invasion, already utterly exhausted by the war, they went to Sicily and took on another war just as great as the one they were already waging with the Peloponnesians. [4] Because of all this, and now because of the serious damage caused by Decelea and the other heavy expenses they incurred, they found themselves seriously short of money. This was when they replaced the payment of tribute by their subjects with the 5 percent tax on goods carried by sea;* as the scale of the war

increased, their expenses exponentially increased while at the same time their income was decreasing, and they believed that this new tax would bring in more money.

29. To return to the Thracians who had arrived too late for Demosthenes: Because of their current financial straits, the Athenians did not want to incur the expense of their upkeep. They dismissed them and gave Dieitrephes the job of taking them home, ordering him also to use them in any way he could against the enemy in the course of his voyage, which would take him through the Euripus channel.* [2] He had them land and do some hasty plundering in Tanagran territory, and then in the evening he sailed from Chalcis in Euboea through the Euripus, disembarked the Thracians in Boeotia, and led them to Mycalessus.* [3] He was not spotted in the darkness and spent the night by the sanctuary of Hermes, which is about two miles from Mycalessus. He attacked the small town at daybreak and took it. The inhabitants had never expected anyone to come so far inland from the sea and attack them, so Dieitrephes took them by surprise and found them unprotected. Their wall was weak—in some places it had collapsed, and in others it had been built up to no great height—and the gates were not barred because they thought they had nothing to fear.

[4] The Thracians poured into Mycalessus, sacked the houses and the sanctuaries, and slaughtered the inhabitants. They spared neither old nor young but methodically set about killing everyone they came across, including women and children, and even draft animals and any other living creatures they found. Thracians, it should be said, are one of the most murderous of the uncivilized races when they have nothing to fear. [5] On this occasion, chaos was rife and death present in every form; they even attacked a school, the largest in the town, just after the boys had arrived, and cut them all down. The effect on the town of this particularly unexpected and horrific assault was nothing short of catastrophic.

30. When the Thebans heard about the sack of the town they sent help. They found the Thracians not far from the town, took their booty from them, panicked them into flight, and pursued them to the sea at the Euripus, where the ships that had brought them were lying at anchor. [2] Most of those who lost their lives did so trying to get back on board the ships; they did not know how to swim, and when the people in the ships saw what was happening onshore they moved out of range of bowshot. Overall in the course of the retreat, however, the Thracians were not doing badly against the Theban cavalry, who led the charge against them; employing the tactics of their country, the Thracians defended themselves by running forward out of the line and regrouping. Few of them lost their lives while doing this, but quite a large number who were caught looting in the town were killed. Altogether, 250 of the 1,300 Thracians died. [3] As for the Thebans and the others who joined them to defend the town, about 20 were killed, counting both cavalrymen and hoplites; Scirphondas, one of the Theban boeotarchs, was one of the casualties. [4] The Mycalessians lost a substantial portion of their population. So much for events in Mycalessus, a town that, relative to its size, suffered as tragic a fate as any in the war.

31. Demosthenes was by now sailing for Corcyra after the building of the fort in Laconia. On his way, as he passed Elis, he found moored at Pheia a cargo vessel that was about to transport a batch of Corinthian hoplites over to Sicily. He destroyed the ship, but the men escaped and later found another ship in which to continue their journey. [2] Demosthenes next went to Zacynthos and Cephallenia, where he picked up some hoplites and requested more from the Messenians at Naupactus. Then he sailed over to Acarnania, on the mainland opposite the islands, and went to Alyzea and Anactorium, which were in Athenian hands. [3] While he was there he met Eurymedon, who was on his way back from Sicily after completing the mission on which he had been sent during the winter, to take men and money there. Eurymedon told him, among other things, that while he was already on his way home he had learned of the capture of Plemyrium by the Syracusans. [4] Conon, the commander in Naupactus, came and joined them as well. He reported that, so far from backing down, the twenty-five Corinthian ships confronting his squadron were intending to fight, and he asked them to loan him ships, seeing that his eighteen were not enough to take on the Corinthians' twenty-five. [5] So Demosthenes and Eurymedon detached the ten best ships from their fleet and sent them off with Conon to join the squadron in Naupactus. Meanwhile, they continued to gather troops in preparation for their mission. Eurymedon also went to Corcyra, where he asked them to find crews for fifteen ships and enrolled hoplites. By now he had been deflected from returning to Athens by being appointed to a joint command with Demosthenes. And Demosthenes recruited slingers and javelineers from various places in Acarnania.

32. The envoys from Syracuse were by now traveling around the Sicilian cities after the capture of Plemyrium. They proved to be persuasive and assembled a sizable force. They were ready to bring these men to Syracuse, but Nicias had already learned what they were up to. He sent word to those of the Sicels who were his allies and who commanded the route this fresh army would take—they included the Centoripans and the Halicyaeans*—asking them not to let the enemy through but to join forces and block their passage. This was the only route available for them to attempt, he said, because the Acragantines had refused them passage through their land. [2] Obedient to the Athenians' request, when the Sicilian Greeks were on their way the Sicels set an ambush in three divisions and caught them off-guard with a sudden assault. They killed about 800 of the soldiers and all the envoys except one, a Corinthian,† who brought the 1,500 or so survivors to Syracuse.

33. Around the same time, reinforcements arrived in Syracuse from Camarina: 500 hoplites, 300 javelineers, and the same number of bowmen. The Geloans also sent help in the form of five ships, 400 javelineers, and 200 cavalrymen. [2] For by now all Sicily—not Acragas, which was neutral, but all the other cities that had previously been waiting to see what happened—had united with the Syracusans against the Athenians and were supporting them. [3] However, after the disastrous setback they had suffered at the hands of the Sicels, the Syracusans held off from attacking the Athenians right away.

Meanwhile, Demosthenes and Eurymedon set out from Corcyra and the mainland when their forces were ready and sailed over the Ionian Sea with all their troops to Cape Iapygia. [4] Next, after setting out from there, they put in at the Choerades islands off Iapygia, where they took on board about 150 Iapygian javelineers—Messapians, to be precise—and renewed an old friendship with Artas, the local ruler who had offered them these soldiers, before sailing on to Metapontium in Italy. [5] They persuaded the Metapontines to comply with the terms of their alliance and send along with them 300 javelineers and two triremes, and once they had added these to their fleet they sailed along the coast to Thurii, where they found that the members of the faction that opposed Athens had recently been expelled after a period of civil unrest. [6] They wanted to make Thurii the mustering point for the whole army and to carry out a review in case anyone had been left behind, and they wanted to persuade the Thurians to commit themselves with as much enthusiasm as was feasible to supporting the campaign, and even, given the favorable circumstances, to enter into an offensive and defensive alliance with Athens. So they waited there and opened negotiations to try to secure these objectives.

34. Meanwhile, the Peloponnesians in the twenty-five ships that were in position opposite the Athenians in Naupactus, to facilitate the passage of the cargo ships to Sicily, prepared for battle. They manned still more ships until they had almost the same number as the Athenians and moved to a new anchorage at Erineus in Achaea,* which is in the territory of Rhype. [2] The place where they were lying at anchor was a crescent-shaped bay, so the land forces of the Corinthians and their local allies who had come up in support had been posted on either side of the bay, on the horns of the crescent, while the ships were in position between them, blocking the entrance to the bay. The commander of the fleet was Polyanthes, a Corinthian. [3] The Athenians, commanded by Diphilus, left Naupactus and sailed into the attack with thirty-three ships.

[4] At first the Corinthians made no move, but then, at what seemed to be the opportune moment, the signal flag was raised and they set out against the Athenians. Battle was joined, and for a long while the two sides held out against each other. [5] Three Corinthian ships were destroyed, and although no Athenian ship was sunk outright, seven or so were put out of commission when they were rammed head-on and their outriggers were smashed by the Corinthian ships, the catheads of which had been strengthened for precisely this purpose. [6] After a battle that was indecisive and made it plausible for them both to claim victory, the two sides separated. (Actually, there were two things in favor of the Athenians' claim to victory: they took possession of their damaged ships when wind carried them into the open sea, and the Corinthians made no further attempt to launch an attack.) No pursuit took place, and no prisoners were taken either, because the Corinthians and Peloponnesians were fighting near the shore, so it was easy for them to save themselves, and none of the Athenians ships was sunk. [7] As soon as the Athenians returned to Naupactus, the Corinthians erected a trophy; they assumed that they had won the battle because they had disabled more of the enemy ships. Besides, they thought they had not lost for the same reason that the Athenians thought they had not won. That is, the Corinthians regarded a battle as won if they were not decisively beaten, and the Athenians considered a battle lost if they did not decisively win. [8] And after the Peloponnesians had sailed away and their land forces had disbanded, the Athenians, too, claimed victory by erecting a trophy; it was set up in Achaea about two miles from the Corinthian anchorage at Erineus. So that was the outcome of the battle.

35. Once the Thurians had been induced to contribute seven hundred hoplites and three hundred javelineers to the army, Demosthenes and

Eurymedon ordered the ships to sail along the coast toward Croton, while they reviewed all their land forces at the Sybaris river and then led them through Thurian territory. [2] When they reached the Hylias river, the Crotonians sent a messenger to tell them that their forces were not allowed to cross Crotonian land. So they went down to the coast, bivouacked for the night at the mouth of the Hylias, and were met there by the ships. The next day they embarked the troops and sailed along the coast, stopping at towns along the way (but bypassing Locri),* until they reached Petra, in the territory of Rhegium.

36. Meanwhile, when the Syracusans found out that the Athenians were on their way they wanted to try their luck once more with their fleet, and with their land forces as well, which they were assembling for this very purpose, as they wanted to be ready before the Athenians arrived. [2] They had modified their ships in ways they thought would afford them an advantage, given what they had learned by their experience of the earlier battle. In particular, they shortened the ships' prows to make them more robust, attached thicker catheads to the prows, and built long struts under the catheads that went through to the ships' sides, a distance of about nine feet, and projected outside the ships to about the same distance. These were the same modifications the Corinthians had made to their ships' prows for the fight against the Athenians at Naupactus. [3] The Syracusans thought this would give them an edge over the Athenian ships, which were not equipped for conflict in the same way but were light at the prow, made for outflanking a ship and ramming it in the side rather than for ramming head-on.

That the battle would take place in the Great Harbor was, in their opinion, another factor in their favor, because there would be a large number of ships in a relatively confined space, which meant they would be ramming the Athenians head-on. They would be striking weak, unreinforced rams with their sturdy, reinforced ones, and they were confident they would stave in the Athenians' prow sections. [4] They reckoned that the space would be too restricted for the Athenians to carry out either of their favored maneuvers—that they would not be able to either outflank the Syracusans or break through their line. They themselves would most probably be able to make it impossible for the Athenians to break through their line, and lack of space would prevent the outflanking maneuver.

[5] So the tactic of colliding head-on, which had previously been attributed to lack of skill on the part of the helmsman, was going to be the chief method employed by the Syracusans, and they were sure that it would serve them best. After all, any Athenian ship that was forced out of line would have nowhere to go by backing water except onto land, which was only a short distance away, and they would be restricted to the short stretch of land where their camp was; they themselves, on the other hand, would control the rest of the harbor. [6] Wherever the Athenians were forced back, they would be crowded into a small space—all of them into the same small space—and in the confusion they would fall foul of one another. (In fact, this lack of space was exactly what hurt the Athenians most in all these naval encounters, since, unlike the Syracusans, they did not have the whole harbor into which to back water.) And they were confident that the Athenians would not be able to sail around them into open water, not just because it was they themselves who would be controlling the ability to enter the harbor from the open sea or back out of it, but also, and especially, because Plemyrium was in their hands and the mouth of the harbor was not large.

37. Once they had compensated for their relative lack of skill and strength with these modifications—and their confidence had already been further raised by their performance in the earlier sea battle—the Syracusans launched a simultaneous attack by land and sea. [2] Shortly before the action began at sea, Gylippus brought out the land forces that were stationed in the city and set out with them toward the stretch of the Athenian wall that faced the city. Meanwhile, all the Syracusan hoplites, cavalrymen, and light infantry stationed in the sanctuary of Olympian Zeus were approaching the wall from the other direction. And as soon as these land forces were in place, the Syracusan and allied ships rowed out into the attack. [3] At first the Athenians thought the Syracusans were going to make an attempt with only their land forces; they were taken aback by the sight of the ships sailing into the attack as well, and they scrambled to respond. Some of them took up a position on and in front of the wall to oppose the Syracusans who were approaching there; some went out to meet the large cavalry force and the javelineers who were advancing rapidly from the sanctuary of Olympian Zeus and the outskirts of the city; others manned the ships or ran down to the beach to help launch them. When the ships had their crews, they put to sea to confront the Syracusans; the Athenians had seventy-five ships and the Syracusans about eighty. **38.** For much of the day they advanced and backed away, skirmishing with each other, but neither side was able to make any significant gain (except that the Syracusans sank one or two Athenian ships), so they separated, and at the same time the Syracusan land forces pulled back from the walls.

[2] The following day, the Syracusans rested and gave no indication of what they would do next. In view of the fact that the two sides had been evenly matched at sea in the previous day's fighting, Nicias expected the Syracusans to make another attempt. He therefore got the trierarchs to repair any of the ships that had been damaged, and had the merchantmen lie at anchor in front of the Athenian stockade that had been driven into the seabed in front of the ships to make up for their lack of a closed harbor. [3] He positioned the merchantmen with gaps of up to two hundred feet between them, so that if any of his ships was in trouble it would be able to escape safely and row back out again without being hindered. These preparations by the Athenians took the whole day, up to nightfall.

39. The next day, though at an earlier hour, the Syracusans employed exactly the same tactics on land and at sea to engage the Athenians as they had before. [2] At sea, the two sides confronted each other just as they had on the previous occasion and spent a long time skirmishing, but then a Corinthian called Ariston, son of Pyrrhichus, who was the best helmsman on the Syracusan side, prevailed upon the officers in command of the fleet to send word to those in charge in the city, telling them that the market stalls with provisions for sale should quickly be moved down to the shoreline, and everyone with any foodstuffs should be required to bring them down there and sell them. That way they could have the crews disembark and eat their midday meal right next to the ships, so that they could quickly renew their attack that same day, which the Athenians would not be expecting.

40. The commanders approved the idea; they dispatched a messenger to see to it, and the market was set up. All at once the Syracusans rowed astern back to the city, and the crews immediately disembarked and set about their meal there. [2] The Athenians, believing that the Syracusans had returned to the city because they considered themselves beaten, took their time over disembarking and seeing to various tasks, including their midday meal, because they supposed that there would be no more fighting that day. [3] But the Syracusans suddenly manned their ships and rowed into the attack once more. In considerable confusion, and with most of them unfed, the Athenians returned pell-mell to their ships and with some difficulty put to sea to meet the Syracusans. [4] For quite a while the two sides cautiously kept apart from each other, but then the Athenians decided to wait no longer, in case they brought about their own defeat through exhaustion. They decided to attack as quickly as possible and at the word of command they rowed into battle.

[5] The Syracusans met the Athenian attack and fought back. Since they were using their ships, as planned, for prow-to-prow ramming, the modifications to their rams enabled them to smash the Athenians' outriggers along much of the length of the ships. And the men who were hurling javelins from the decks were causing a great deal of harm to the Athenians, but not as much as the Syracusans in small boats, who sailed around the harbor, moved in close to the banks of enemy oars, and went along the sides of the ships, throwing javelins from

the boats at the oarsmen. **41.** Strenuous application of these tactics eventually gave the Syracusans victory in the battle, and the routed Athenians escaped through the line of merchantmen to their own anchorage. [2] The Syracusan ships pursued them as far as the merchantmen, until they were checked by the "dolphins" dangling from the ships' yardarms and overhanging the entrances.* [3] Two Syracusan ships, elated by victory, drew too close to the merchantmen and were destroyed, and one of them was captured along with its crew, [4] but the Syracusans had sunk seven Athenian ships and disabled many more, and they had also taken large numbers of prisoners and many lives. After withdrawing they erected a trophy for both sea battles. They were now extremely optimistic about their prospects at sea, where they felt that they were far superior to the Athenians, and they were sure that they would get the better of them on land as well.

42. So the Syracusans were getting ready to renew the attack on both land and sea. But at this juncture Demosthenes and Eurymedon arrived with the reinforcements from Athens: some seventy-three ships, including those contributed by non-Athenians; about five thousand Athenian and allied hoplites; a good number of Greek and barbarian javelineers; and a fair number of other kinds of troops, such as slingers and archers. [2] The immediate response among the Syracusans and their allies was no little consternation. When they saw that despite the fortification of Decelea a force had come that was as large or almost as large as the first one, and that there seemed to be no respect in which the Athenians were weak, they wondered whether there would ever come a time when they were finally free of the necessity of escaping from danger. But the immediate response among the Athenians of the original expeditionary force, given their previous troubles, was a considerable boost to their morale.

[3] Demosthenes could see how things stood; he was sure that if he wasted time he would have the same experience as Nicias, which was unthinkable. The enemy had been terrified of Nicias when he first arrived in Sicily, but then he spent the winter in Catana rather

than immediately attacking Syracuse, and as a result he stopped being perceived as a threat. And then Gylippus stole a march on him by coming with an army from the Peloponnese—an army that the Syracusans would not even have requested if Nicias had attacked right away, because they believed themselves strong enough and would only have discovered their misapprehension once they had been walled off, by which time it would have been too late: reinforcements, even if they had requested them, would no longer have done them as much good as before. Bearing all this in mind, then, and recognizing that he, too, was most formidable right now, on the first day, Demosthenes wanted to exploit the consternation caused by the arrival of his forces without delay. [4] The Syracusans' counter-wall, the one that had made it impossible for the Athenians to wall them in, was single, and it was clear to Demosthenes that if he gained control of the way up to Epipolae and then of the enemy camp there, he would meet no further resistance and would easily gain control of the wall. He was eager to make the attempt, which he considered the most direct way to end the war. [5] If the attempt was successful, Syracuse would fall to him, and if not he would take his forces back home and then the Athenians serving under him and the city as a whole would not be ground down with nothing to show for it.

[6] First, then, the Athenians took to the field and laid waste Syracusan farmland around the Anapus river. Apart from the cavalry and javelineers stationed in the sanctuary of Olympian Zeus, the Syracusans did not come out against them either on land or sea, and so the Athenian army and navy enjoyed the military dominance they had originally had. **43.** Next, Demosthenes decided to employ siege contraptions for his first attempt on the counter-wall, but when he brought them to bear they were set on fire by the enemy defenders on the wall. So he had the rest of his forces carry out a multipronged attack on the wall, but they were repulsed, and he decided not to waste any more time. He persuaded Nicias and his other fellow commanders to let him have his way, and then did as he had originally planned and made

an attempt on Epipolae.† [2] It was clearly impossible for his troops to make the approach and ascent in daylight without being seen, so he ordered them to gather five days' worth of provisions and, taking with him all the stonemasons and joiners and other essential personnel, such as archers, and whatever might be needed for wall-building if the attempt was successful, he set out early in the night with the infantry,† accompanied by Eurymedon and Menander (Nicias had been left behind in the fortifications), and advanced toward Epipolae.

[3] They reached Epipolae by way of Euryelus (the same route that the original army had first taken up to the plateau), passed the Syracusan pickets without being spotted, and approached the fort the Syracusans had built there. They took the fort, killing some of the garrison in the process, [4] but most of the men escaped and ran straight to the three camps the Syracusans had on Epipolae among their outworks—one for Syracusans, one for other Sicilian Greeks, and one for the allies—where they made the Athenian attack known and alerted the six hundred Syracusans who were the advance guards in that part of Epipolae. [5] The six hundred dashed off to put up a defense, but when they encountered Demosthenes and the Athenians they were routed, despite a spirited resistance. Wanting to take advantage of the momentum they had and to speedily finish what they had come to do, Demosthenes and his men carried straight on, while another detachment of their men turned to capturing the Syracusans' counter-wall. The men posted on guard at the walls ran away, and the Athenians began to tear down the battlements.

[6] The Syracusans and their allies, however, sallied from the outworks along with Gylippus and his men to resist the Athenians. They managed to mount an attack even though they were still dazed by the unexpectedness of this daring nighttime assault. At first the Athenians were too much for them and they fell back. [7] But as the Athenians advanced they lost much of their cohesion, because they thought they had already won, and they wanted to force their way as quickly as possible through all the enemy units they had not yet

engaged; if they slowed down, they thought, the enemy might rally. But the Boeotians first stood their ground against them and then attacked, routing the Athenians and turning them to flight.

44. At this point things became extremely confused and difficult for the Athenians, and finding out exactly what happened was not at all easy, even after consulting people from both sides.* After all, even in daylight, when the details of a battle are more certain, they are still not fully known by those taking part in the action; each person knows only what happened immediately around him, and then imperfectly. So in night combat—and this was the only such battle to take place between sizable armies in this war, at any rate—how would anyone know anything for certain? [2] The moon was shining brightly that night, but the soldiers' sight of one another was as one might expect in moonlight: they could see a figure in front of them but could not tell whether he was friend or foe. Both sides had a great many hoplites milling around in a limited space. [3] On the Athenian side, some were in the process of being beaten while others were still advancing unbeaten on their first approach. And most of the rest of the Athenians, who had either only just reached the plateau or were still on their way up, had no idea which body of men to head for, since, because of the rout, the soldiers in front of them were completely out of order, and it was not easy to tell people apart by the sound of their voices as they called out.

[4] The Syracusans and their allies seemed to be winning, and they urged one another forward with loud cries—there was no other way to communicate orders in the darkness—while at the same time resisting fresh waves of attackers. The Athenians were searching for their own men and judged everything that was coming straight at them to be hostile even if it was in fact a friend, one of those who had already turned to flight. They were constantly demanding the password, which was their only way of recognizing one another, and with all of them asking for it at the same time, not only were they causing a great deal of confusion among themselves, but they also revealed

it to their opponents. [5] But they did not similarly get to know the Syracusans' password because the Syracusans were winning and less scattered, and so they were less likely to fail to recognize one another. Consequently, when groups of men from both sides encountered each other, the Syracusans used their knowledge of the Athenian password to escape with their lives even if the Athenians were stronger, while any Athenians who failed to respond with the Syracusans' password were killed. [6] But what caused the Athenians the worst and most harm was the chanting of the paean:† because it scarcely differed from one side to the other, they had no way of knowing who was doing the chanting. So the use of the paean as a war-cry by the Dorians in their own army, such as the Argives and Corcyreans, alarmed the Athenians no less than when the enemy chanted it.*

[7] And so in the end, with most of the Athenian forces having lost cohesion once and for all, friends clashed with friends, citizens with fellow citizens, and they did not just panic one another but also came to blows, and it was not easy to separate them. [8] During the pursuit, the narrowness of the way back down from Epipolae meant that many men jumped down from the ridge and died. Most of those who made it safely down to level ground, especially if they were from the original army and better acquainted with the land, escaped to their camp, but some of the later arrivals became lost and wandered around the countryside until, at daybreak, the Syracusan cavalry rode around and killed them.

45. The next day, the Syracusans erected two trophies, one on Epipolae at the point of access to the plateau, and the other at the place where the Boeotians had first made a stand; meanwhile, the Athenians collected the bodies of their dead under a truce. [2] A large number of Athenian and allied lives had been lost, but the amount of weaponry that was captured was out of proportion to the number of the dead, because those who had been forced to jump off the ridge first shed their arms and armor, whether they died or survived.

46. Next, with their confidence restored once more to its former level by their unexpected success, the Syracusans sent Sicanus with fifteen ships to Acragas, which was racked by civil strife, to see if he could bring the place over to their side. And Gylippus again set off overland to the rest of Sicily to raise more troops; given the outcome of the battle on Epipolae he hoped to take the Athenians' walls by main force.

47. Meanwhile, the Athenian generals were trying to decide what to do in view of the defeat they had suffered and the utter despondency that now pervaded the camp. They were obviously not succeeding in their endeavors, and it was clear that the soldiers were resentful about remaining in Sicily. [2] Their discontent was due in part to ill health (of which there were two causes: it was the time of year when people are particularly liable to illness, and the place where they were encamped was marshy and insalubrious), and especially due to the apparent hopelessness of their situation. [3] Demosthenes, therefore, was of the opinion that they should stay no longer. Since his plan to risk the attempt on Epipolae had failed, he was in favor of leaving without spending any more time there, while it was still possible for them to cross the open sea, and while, thanks to the recently arrived ships, at any rate, they still had the upper hand over the enemy at sea. [4] And he said it would do Athens more good to fight those who were building a forward operating base in their own territory than to continue fighting the Syracusans, who would now prove difficult to defeat. And besides, it made no sense for them to be spending so much money on a pointless siege.

48. That was Demosthenes's view. Nicias agreed that the situation was dire but did not want their weakness to be mentioned openly; he did not want large numbers of others to be involved in voting publicly for withdrawal, because then the enemy would hear about it, and it would be more or less impossible for them to retreat stealthily when they wished to do so. [2] And another consideration was that, judging by the information he had about the enemy's situation—and he claimed to have better information than the other generals—there was still some reason to expect that it would be worse than their own if they persevered with the siege. They would wear them down by depriving them of supplies, especially since, with the ships now available to them, they had greater control of the sea than the Syracusans did. Besides, there was a faction inside Syracuse that wanted to surrender to the Athenians, and they were in communication with him and urging him not to leave.

[3] It was his awareness of these factors that made him behave as he did; although in actual fact he was still undecided—he was keeping both options open and continuing to consider what it was best for them to do—what he voiced out loud at the time was a refusal to lead the army away from Sicily. He was sure, he said, that in Athens the people would find it unacceptable for them to leave without their having voted for it, and the reason he was so sure was that they, the generals, would not have judgment passed on them by men with the firsthand experience of the situation that they themselves had. The vote would be cast, rather, by men who would make up their minds by listening to the fault-finding speeches of others; they would be persuaded by the slanders of some clever speaker or other. [4] Moreover, he said, even though the soldiers there in Sicily were currently complaining loudly about the dire straits they were in, many or even most of them would just as loudly voice the opposite complaint when they got back home, and claim that the generals had been bribed to turn traitor and withdraw. He knew the Athenian character, he said, and speaking for himself he had no wish to be taken to court on some dishonorable charge and to be unjustly put to death by the Athenians. No, if he had to die, he preferred to do so at a time and in a manner of his own choosing—to take his chances in Sicily and be killed by the enemy.

[5] However grim our situation, he went on, the Syracusans were even worse off. Paying their mercenaries, meeting the expenses of

their frontier posts, and moreover, maintaining a large fleet, as they had already for a year, had seriously depleted their treasury, and they would soon be desperate. They had already spent two thousand talents and owed even more, and if they lost even a small portion of their current forces as a result of not paying them they would be undone, because, unlike the Athenians, they were dependent on mercenaries rather than on conscripts. [6] So, he concluded, they should continue to wear the Syracusans down by besieging them, and not let their departure be determined by financial considerations when they were far better off financially than the enemy.

49. Nicias spoke forcefully, because he had good information about the situation in Syracuse; he knew they were short of money and that there was a substantial faction there that wanted to see the city under Athenian control, and in their messages they kept urging him not to leave. At the same time, he was more confident than before that they would win† at sea, at any rate. [2] But Demosthenes found the idea of continuing with the siege utterly unthinkable. If they could not withdraw the army without official permission from Athens and had to fight a war of attrition against the Syracusans, he said, they should move and make Thapsus or Catana their base for doing so. From either of these places they could use their land forces to overrun great swaths of countryside, they would be able to maintain themselves by plundering the enemy's property, and they would inflict real harm on them. And their ships would not be fighting in a restricted space, which favored the enemy, but in the open sea where their expertise would serve them well, and retreating and attacking would be easier because the ships would not be setting out from and putting into a small, circumscribed base. [3] In short, he said, there was no way he could approve the idea of remaining where they were; they should leave as soon as possible and not take their time about it. Eurymedon expressed his agreement with Demosthenes, [4] but Nicias's continued opposition gave them pause and they put off making a decision.

Besides, they thought Nicias might be so insistent because he had special knowledge of some kind. This is how the Athenians came to postpone their departure and stay where they were.

50. Meanwhile, Gylippus and Sicanus had returned to Syracuse. Sicanus had failed at Acragas because while he was still in Gela the members of the pro-Syracusan faction in Acragas had been banished from the city. But Gylippus brought a substantial fresh army with him from the rest of Sicily,† and also the hoplites sent in the spring from the Peloponnese in the cargo ships, who had ended up in Selinous, via Libya. [2] They were driven off course to Libya, where the people of Cyrene gave them two triremes and guides for their voyage; next, as they sailed along the coast, they fought alongside the people of Euesperides, which was being besieged by Libyans; then, after defeating the Libyans, they went from there to Neapolis, a Carthaginian trading post that is the closest place to Sicily—a voyage of only two days and a night—and sailed over to Selinous from there.

[3] As soon as these reinforcements arrived, the Syracusans began to get ready for another two-pronged assault on the Athenians, by land and sea. When the Athenian generals saw that an additional army had arrived in Syracuse, and that their own situation, so far from improving, was deteriorating daily in all respects—sickness in the camp was a particular problem—they regretted that they had not moved away earlier. Even Nicias stopped arguing against departure as he had before, except that he still insisted that the issue should not be voted on openly. So as discreetly as they could, the generals gave everyone notice that they would be quitting the camp by sea, and told them to be ready to leave when the order was given. [4] However, when all the arrangements had been made and their departure was imminent, there was an eclipse of the moon, which was full at the time.* Most of the Athenians took this seriously and asked the generals to wait, and Nicias, who was rather obsessive about divination and suchlike, said he would not even discuss the logistics of their move

until they had waited for the "thrice nine days" the seers were prescribing. And so the Athenians continued to postpone their departure and stayed where they were.

51. When the Syracusans found out about this they were even more motivated to keep the pressure up on the Athenians, whose plan to evacuate proved that even they had by now realized they were no longer dominant on sea or land. At the same time, the Syracusans did not want the Athenians to take up a position somewhere else in Sicily, where they would become more difficult opponents; they wanted to bring them to battle as soon as possible right there, where conditions favored themselves. [2] Accordingly, they set about enlisting crews for their ships. They trained the crews for as many days as they took to be sufficient, and then, when the time was right, on the first day they attacked the Athenian walls. Hoplites and cavalry came out through one of the gates to offer resistance, but it was not a large force and the Syracusans cut off some of the hoplites, routed them, and harried them back inside the fortifications. But the way back inside was narrow and the Athenians lost seventy horses and a few of these hoplites.

52. That day the Syracusan forces withdrew, but on the next day they sailed out with seventy-six ships and at the same time had their infantry advance against the Athenian walls. The Athenians launched eighty-six ships against them, engaged, and the naval battle began. [2] Eurymedon, who commanded the Athenian right wing, decided to try to outflank the enemy ships, but that brought him rather close to the shore; and after the Syracusans and their allies had defeated the center of the Athenian fleet, they turned to Eurymedon and pinned him in a bend of the inner bay of the harbor. Eurymedon was killed, and the ships that had accompanied him were destroyed. Then the Syracusans set out after the remaining Athenian ships and began to drive them onto land.

53. When Gylippus saw that the enemy ships were losing the battle and that the shoreline onto which they were being driven was not covered by the Athenian stockade and camp, he led a detachment of his men to the mole. He wanted to kill the Athenian sailors as they disembarked and to make it easier for the Syracusans to haul away the Athenian ships, once the shoreline was in friendly hands. [2] The Etruscans were on guard at that point for the Athenians, and when they saw Gylippus's men approaching out of formation, they fell on those in front, routed them, and drove them into the Lysimelea marsh. [3] Later, more Syracusan and allied troops arrived, and the Athenians, fearing for the safety of their ships, came up to confront them. The fight went the Athenians' way, and they pursued the enemy soldiers as they fled and killed a few hoplites. They saved most of their ships and gathered them in their camp, but the Syracusans and their allies captured eighteen of them and slaughtered the crews. [4] Seeing that the wind was blowing in the direction of the Athenian camp, they decided to try to set fire to the remaining Athenian ships, so they filled an old merchant ship with kindling and firewood, ignited the wood, and set the ship adrift. Fearing for the safety of their ships, the Athenians responded by devising fire-extinguishing countermeasures, and averted the danger by dousing the flames and preventing the merchantman from coming close.

54. Next, the Syracusans erected trophies for both the sea battle and their success up by the wall, when they cut off the hoplites and captured the horses, and the Athenians did likewise for the Etruscans' achievement in turning the infantry to flight and driving them into the marsh, and for their own similar success with the rest of their land forces.

55. Since the Syracusans had now won a brilliant victory at sea as well, despite their earlier fear of the ships that had come with Demosthenes, the Athenians were completely demoralized. They were greatly astonished at the turn of events, but even greater was their regret that they had undertaken the expedition in the first place. [2] These cities in Sicily were the only ones they had ever attacked that were of a similar character to their own: they had democratic constitutions just as they did, and ships, cavalry, and large-scale resources in general. The fact that they were democratic meant that the Athenians were unable to use their internal divisions as a kind of weapon against them by orchestrating a regime change, which might have worked as a way to bring them over.* And the fact that they had plentiful resources meant that they were unable to bring superiority in this respect to bear against them. The Athenians were largely failing, and if they had been in trouble before, they were in far worse trouble now that they had lost their superiority at sea, which they would never have thought possible.

56. The Syracusans, however, immediately took to sailing up and down the Great Harbor—there was nothing the Athenians could do about it—and they planned to close off its mouth, so that even if it was the Athenians' intention to slip quietly away by sea they could not do so. [2] The Syracusans were no longer concerned only with their own survival; they also wanted to deny it to the Athenians. It was their view, and they were right, that on the basis of each side's current resources they were far better off, and they felt that if they could defeat the Athenians and their allies on land and sea, the Greeks at large would judge this a glorious achievement. The rest of the Greeks would immediately gain either political freedom or freedom from fear, because the forces that remained to the Athenians would be insufficient to enable them to endure the war that would subsequently descend on them, and they themselves, the Syracusans, would be judged responsible for this and would win the sincere admiration of the rest of the world and future generations. [3] And indeed the contest was a worthy one, not just for these reasons but because they were prevailing over not only the Athenians but their many allies as well. Moreover, they had not acted alone, but had won the assistance of others; with the Corinthians and Lacedaemonians alongside them, they had made themselves one of the leading states of the Greek world. They had offered up their city to bear the brunt of the fighting, and they had greatly improved their proficiency in battles at sea.

[4] The importance of the contest is proved by the fact that no greater number of peoples had ever converged on a single city, except of course for the total number of peoples involved in the current

war against either Athens or Sparta. **57.** What follows is a list of the states that came and fought at Syracuse both for and against Sicily. They came either to help conquer the island or to help save it, and the side they chose was determined less by right or kinship than by what was expedient for each state or how it felt compelled to act given the circumstances.*

[2] As Ionians, the Athenians willingly went against the Dorian Syracusans, and they were joined for the expedition by peoples who spoke the same dialect as themselves and retained the same customs: the Lemnians, Imbrians, and Aeginetans (the people who occupied Aegina at the time), and also the Hestiaeans (the current inhabitants of Hestiaea in Euboea),* who were all Athenian colonists. [3] Others who fought alongside the Athenians were either their subjects or independent states in alliance with Athens, and there were some mercenary units as well.

[4] Among the tribute-paying subjects of Athens, troops were supplied by the Euboean states of Eretria, Chalcis, Styra, and Carystus; by the islands of Ceos, Andros, and Tenos; and by the Ionian states of Miletus, Samos, and Chios. Of these, the Chians joined the expedition as autonomous allies who paid no tribute but supplied ships.* Almost all these people are Ionians and of Athenian stock (with the exception of the Carystians, who are Dryopes). Although as subjects of Athens they had no choice in the matter, they, too, certainly joined the expedition as Ionians going against Dorians.

[5] There were also Aeolians: the people of Methymna, subjects of Athens who supplied ships rather than paying tribute, and the peoples of Tenedos and Aenus who paid tribute. These Aeolians were fighting under compulsion against fellow Aeolians from Boeotia, who were their original founders and fought for the Syracusans. The only Boeotians who fought on the opposite side were the Plataeans, as one would expect, given their hatred for their fellow Boeotians.

[6] The Rhodians and Cytherans were both Dorian peoples. Despite being colonists of Sparta, the people of Cythera sided with the

Athenians against Gylippus's Lacedaemonians; and the Rhodians, who are of Argive stock, were compelled to fight not only against the Syracusans, Dorians against Dorians, but also against their own colonists, the Geloans, who were on the Syracusan side.

[7] Among the inhabitants of islands off the Peloponnese, the Cephallenians and Zacynthians went along as members of independent states, but in fact Athenian mastery at sea left them, as islanders, with little choice in the matter. Corcyra was not just Dorian but unequivocally Corinthian, but the Corcyreans joined the expedition and fought against Corinthians and Syracusans, despite being colonists of Corinth and kinsmen of the Syracusans. On the face of it, the Corcyreans had no choice about joining the Athenians, but in fact they were just as glad as anyone to do so because of their hatred of Corinth.

[8] The Messenians, too—those we call by that name nowadays, the inhabitants of Naupactus and Pylos, which was in Athenian hands at the time—were recruited for the war, and there were also a few Megarian exiles who were compelled by the circumstances to fight against their fellow Megarians, the people of Selinous.

[9] The rest were those for whom fighting for the Athenians was more voluntary. The Dorian Argives were motivated to fight alongside the Ionian Athenians against their fellow Dorians more by their hatred of the Lacedaemonians than by their alliance with Athens—and by the hopes individuals entertained for immediate private gain. It was normal for the Mantineans and other Arcadian mercenaries to go up against anyone who was presented to them as the enemy, and on this occasion they were just as willing to regard fellow Arcadians who had come with the Corinthians as their enemies, because they were paid to do so. The Cretans and the Aetolians were also paid to take part, and the Cretans, who were cofounders of Gela with the Rhodians, found themselves fighting not alongside their colonists but against them, but they had no problem with that because they were being paid. [10] And some Acarnanians came, partly because they

were being paid to do so, but more because of their liking for Demosthenes and loyalty to Athens.

[11] All these peoples come from east of the Ionian Sea, but among the Italian Greek cities Thurii and Metapontium supplied contingents to fight for the Athenians; the state of the internal conflicts in which they were caught up at the time was such as to leave them little choice in the matter. Among the Sicilian Greek cities, Naxos and Catana supplied contingents, and among the non-Greek Sicilian communities so did the Egestans, the people who had requested Athenian intervention in the first place, and most of the Sicels. From outside Sicily some Etruscans fought on the Athenian side because of their hostility toward Syracuse, and there were also some Iapygian mercenaries. These were the peoples who took part in the expedition on the Athenian side.

58. On the opposite side, aiding the Syracusans, were Camarina (the neighbor of Syracuse), Gela (which is next to Camarina), and then Selinous (passing over neutral Acragas, which is the neighbor of Camarina). [2] These places are all on the coastline of Sicily that faces Libya, and from the coast that faces the Tyrrhenian Sea the people of Himera took the part of the Syracusans; the Himerans are in fact the only Greeks on this coast and the only people from there who supported the Syracusans. [3] These were the Sicilian Greek peoples who fought for Syracuse, all of them Dorians and independent; among the Sicilian barbarians, the Syracusans were supported only by the Sicels who had not defected from them to the Athenians.

From outside Sicily the Syracusans were aided by the Lacedaemonians, who provided a Spartiate commander and in addition a contingent of helots and freedmen;† by the Corinthians, who were the only ones to come with both ships and infantry; by the Leucadians and Ambraciots as kinsmen of the Syracusans; by Arcadian mercenaries who were sent over by the Corinthians; by Sicyonian conscripts; and from outside the Peloponnese by the Boeotians. [4] But compared with those who came from overseas, the Sicilian Greeks themselves provided more of every kind of resource, in keeping with the size of their cities and the fact that they were in the greatest danger; they collected a great many hoplites, ships, and horses, and a host of other kinds of fighters as well. And, again by comparison, it is hardly an exaggeration to say that because of the size of their city and because they were most at risk, the Syracusans themselves provided more than everyone else put together.

59. These were the forces that were assembled at Syracuse to support one side or the other. By now both sides had all these auxiliary contingents present with them, and neither side received reinforcements later.

[2] The Syracusans and their allies, then, understandably thought it would be a glorious achievement if they could follow up their victory in the sea battle by capturing the entire Athenian army, large as it was, and preventing them from escaping either by sea or overland. [3] So the first thing they did was set about closing the Great Harbor, the mouth of which is a little less than a mile wide, by having triremes and other vessels great and small lie at anchor there broadside on. They also got everything ready in case the Athenians dared to fight another battle at sea, and there was nothing small-scale about their plans in any respect.

60. When the Athenians saw the barrier forming across the mouth of the harbor and became aware of the Syracusans' general intentions, they realized they would have to act decisively. [2] Not the least of their current difficulties was the fact that not only did they now lack supplies for their immediate needs (because when they had assumed they would be sailing away they had sent word to Catana canceling any further consignments), but they would not have any in the future either unless they regained mastery at sea. So when the generals and the taxiarchs met to address their predicament, they decided to abandon the walls up on Epipolae and to wall off an area right by the ships, just large enough to accommodate their stores and those who were unfit for service. Soldiers would be detailed to guard this enclosure, but every other man from the rest of their land forces would embark and man all the ships that were sound, or even those that were far from seaworthy, and they would fight it out at sea. If they won they would go to Catana, and if they lost they would burn their ships, form a column, and retreat overland, taking whichever route would enable them to reach some friendly place as quickly as possible, whether it was barbarian or Greek.

[3] No sooner had this decision been taken than they put it into effect. They stole down gradually from the upper fortifications and enrolled crews for all their ships by ordering on board everyone of the right age who seemed capable of serving in some capacity. [4] In the end, a total of 110 ships had full complements of crews. They also embarked large numbers of Acarnanian and other mercenary archers and javelineers, and provided themselves with everything else they might need to carry out their plan—or at least everything they could, given their desperate situation. [5] When everything was just about ready, before putting to sea Nicias convened the entire army. He could see that they had been demoralized by their resounding defeat at sea—an experience to which they were unaccustomed—and that they wanted to risk all in battle as soon as possible because of the shortage of supplies, so before they went into action he attempted to lift their spirits by speaking in the following vein:

61. "In the coming battle, men, whether you're Athenians or allies, everyone alike will have the same goals: to save his life and to save his homeland. That goes for the enemy, too, no less than for each of you. Victory now at sea will make it possible for everyone to gaze once more upon the land of his birth, wherever that may be. [2] But we must not despair, and we must not behave like raw recruits who, if they lose their first battle, are ever afterward driven by fear to expect a similarly disastrous outcome. [3] No, you're Athenians, with plenty of experience of war, or you're Athenian allies, our constant comrades in arms, and so you're familiar with the unpredictability of much that happens in war. In the hope, then, that fortune may be with us, prepare yourselves to renew the fight in a manner worthy of the great army of which you are a part. Just see how many we are!

62. "After looking into the matter and consulting with the helmsmen, we've now put in place, as thoroughly as present circumstances allow, all the measures that in our view, given the restricted size of the harbor, will help us cope with the mass of enemy ships that we're going to face and the enemy's reliance on deck-based soldiers—factors that harmed us in previous engagements. [2] There will be many archers and javelineers on our decks—a mass of men that we wouldn't use if we were fighting a proper sea battle in open water, since the extra weight of the ships would impair our skill at maneuvering, but in this instance we're being forced to fight a land battle at sea, and they'll serve a useful purpose. [3] We've made all the structural changes that our ships were needing in response to the modifications the enemy made to theirs; and to counteract their reinforced catheads, which caused us particular harm, we now have grappling irons to be cast at any ship that has struck one of ours and to keep it from backing away again, provided the men on the decks follow this up by doing their duty. [4] As I say, we're forced to fight a land battle from our ships, and so it's obviously in our interest not to back water ourselves nor to let them do so—in our case, particularly, because all the land except the bit occupied by our infantry is in enemy hands.

63. "In view of this, what you have to do is fight as well as you can and avoid being driven ashore. And when ship strikes ship, don't let them separate until you've cleared the enemy deck of hoplites. [2] In saying this I'm addressing the hoplites as much as the crews, because what I've just said is more the work of those on deck than those below. Even now it's still possible for our infantry to come out on top most of the time. [3] But to turn to you crewmen,* I'm exhorting and at the same time begging you not to be too alarmed by the defeats we've suffered. We've enhanced the force on the decks and we have more ships now. Bear in mind that your knowledge of our dialect and imitation of our customs have led people to regard you for a while as

Athenians even though you aren't, and that this is a pleasure worth preserving. Your assimilation to our ways has impressed all Greece and you've also gained certain advantages: you enjoy the fruits of empire no less than we do, and far more than we do when it comes to inspiring fear in our subjects and to your being protected from ill treatment. [4] Because you're the only people who have freely opted to be partners in our imperial venture, it's only fair of you not to betray it now. Instead, with contempt for the Corinthians whom you've often defeated, and for the Sicilian Greeks, not one of whom chose to stand up to you while the fleet was at its best, beat them back and show that even when you're weak and have suffered setbacks your skill is perfectly able to cope with your adversaries' strength and run of good luck.

64. "As for those of you who are Athenians, I would remind you once more that you have no ships at home as good as those you have here, nor are there any more men of an age to serve as hoplites. If the outcome is anything other than victory, our enemies here will immediately sail there and the men we left over there will be incapable of successfully resisting the combination of their local enemies and these new attackers. And so you here will immediately find yourselves at the mercy of the Syracusans—and you know what your plans were for them when you came here—and our people there will find themselves at the mercy of the Lacedaemonians. [2] Accordingly, since you're in the position of facing a single battle for a dual purpose—the safety of both yourselves and those at home—now, if ever, is the time to be strong. Each and every one of you needs to remember that you who are about to embark are also, as far as the Athenians at home are concerned, all that remains of the state, its army and navy, and the great name of Athens. This is what's at stake, and so if any man is exceptionally skillful or courageous, there could be no better time for him to show his caliber than now, for his own good and for the safety of all."

65. Immediately after this address by Nicias, he ordered his men to board the ships. It was easy for Gylippus and the Syracusans to know that the Athenians were intending to fight at sea because they could see them in the very act of getting ready for it. They had been forewarned that the Athenians were planning to use grappling irons, and the meticulous measures they were taking before the battle included a means of defending against them. [2] They covered the prows and a considerable extent of the upper parts of each ship with hides, so that when thrown the grapnels would slip off without gaining a purchase. [3] When everything was ready, both the Syracusan generals and Gylippus addressed their men in the following terms:

66. "Syracusans and allies, we're sure that most of you are aware of the glory of what you've already achieved and know that future glory is at stake in the coming contest, because otherwise you wouldn't have applied yourselves so assiduously to your duties. But it may be that some of you don't see this as clearly as you should, so we'll spell it out. [2] The Athenians, who already had the largest empire of any Greeks, past or present, came to this country with the intention of enslaving Sicily first, and then, if things went well for them here, of doing the same to the Peloponnese and the rest of Greece. No one before you had ever offered resistance to their navy, the instrument with which they gained all their possessions, but by now you've won several battles against them at sea and you have every reason to think that you're going to defeat them again now. [3] For when men are humbled in a sphere in which they claim preeminence, their diminished self-respect is more fragile than if they hadn't held that opinion in the first place. Moreover, since their failure contradicts the expectations generated by their exalted opinion of themselves, they give in when giving in isn't warranted by the strength of which they're capable. This is likely to be the Athenians' experience at the moment. **67.** In our case, however, the preexistent feature of our character that enabled us to be bold despite our relative lack of skill has now been consolidated, and since we have now added to it the belief that, having defeated the strongest, we must be the strongest ourselves, the hopes and expectations of each and every one of us are doubled. And as a general rule the more realistic the hope of success, the greater the commitment a person brings to an endeavor.

[2] "The countermeasures they've put in place in response to and in imitation of our ships are familiar to us from our own style of fighting, so we won't be unprepared to deal with any of them. Contrary to established custom, they're going to have large numbers of hoplites on deck, and large numbers of javelineers too—embarked landlubbers, so to speak, from Acarnania and elsewhere, who won't even work out how to discharge their missiles from a sitting position.* They're bound to impair the efficiency of the ships, then, and they'll create complete chaos among themselves because of the unaccustomed demands they'll be making of their bodies. [3] Moreover—in case anyone here is worried by our lesser numbers in the coming battle—their numerical superiority will be no advantage to them, because in a restricted space their large numbers will make them too slow to be effective and will make them extremely vulnerable to the measures we've put in place. [4] I'll tell you the one thing that's quite certain, to judge by information we have that we think is indisputable: the reason they're risking battle in an attempt either to force their way out by sea or to retreat by land afterward is that their troubles are overwhelming and they've been reduced by the pressure of their current predicament to the desperate expedient of trusting to luck rather than their resources. There's nothing else for them to do, and they know they could hardly be worse off than they are at present.

68. "So we'll find them in disarray and with their luck turned against itself, but these men are our bitterest enemies and in fighting them we should be ruthless. We need to remember, first, that when dealing with enemies we are entirely within our rights to satisfy the anger in our hearts by punishing unjustified aggression, and, second, that we're going to be in a position to avenge ourselves on our enemies—and, as the saying goes, there's nothing sweeter than revenge. [2] That they're not just our enemies but our worst enemies you all know, because they came here with the intention of enslaving us. If they'd succeeded they'd have made our men suffer the worst of agonies, inflicted the grossest indignities on our children and womenfolk, and hung the most shameful of names on the city as a whole. [3] In view of this it would be quite wrong for anyone to treat them with mercy or to think it a gain if they free us from danger by departing. They'll do that anyway, in the unlikely event of their winning. But the prize for victory in this contest is a glorious one: if we do what we intend to do—and there's no reason to think we won't—they'll have been punished, and we'll bestow on the whole of Sicily in a more secure form the freedom whose fruits it formerly enjoyed. And ventures in which failure entails the least harm and success entails the greatest benefit are very rare indeed."

69. After this motivational address by the Syracusan generals and Gylippus to their men, they, too, began to man their ships, once they saw the Athenians doing so. [2] But the Athenians' situation made Nicias despondent. He could see the danger they were in, danger that was now fast approaching since they were on the point of putting to sea. As people do when great battles are imminent, he regarded all the practical measures they had taken as inadequate and all the words they had spoken as unsatisfactory. So once again he summoned every one of the trierarchs. Addressing each of them formally by his father's name, his own name, and the name of his tribe, he entreated any of them who already had some claim to distinction not to let themselves down and those whose ancestors were famous not to tarnish their families' virtues. He bade them call to mind their native country, the freest in the world, and how everyone there had the unrestricted right to live as they chose. He also said all the things that people tend to say at such critical moments when they are not worried about seeming to voice platitudes of the kind that do service for every occasion with their references to women, children, and ancestral gods; at such times of pervasive trepidation, people voice them out loud because they think they will help.

[3] Nicias stepped down after delivering this address, feeling with dissatisfaction that he had said only the bare minimum of what needed

to be said. He led his land forces to the sea, where he drew them up along the shoreline over as large an area as possible, so that they would be as effective as possible in encouraging their comrades in the ships. [4] Demosthenes, Menander, and Euthydemus, the Athenian generals on board the ships, launched the fleet from their camp and headed straight for the pontoon barrier at the mouth of the harbor, where a gap had been left in the barrier to allow ships in and out. Their intention was to force their way out into the open sea.

70. The Syracusans and their allies had already put to sea with almost the same number of ships as before, and had posted part of their fleet to guard the gap in the barrier. The rest of the ships were deployed all around the harbor so that they could fall on the Athenians from all directions, and their land forces were ready to move to wherever an Athenian ship came to shore. The Syracusan fleet was commanded by Sicanus and Agatharchus, each with overall responsibility for one wing, while Pythen and the Corinthians held the center. [2] When the Athenians reached the pontoon, in their initial impetus they overwhelmed the ships posted by it and began trying to undo the bindings that held it together. But then the Syracusans and their allies bore down on the Athenians from all directions and battle was joined at the barrier and throughout the harbor. The fierceness of the fighting—fiercer even than any of the other battles they had fought at sea—[3] was due to the determination with which the oarsmen responded whenever they were ordered into the attack, and to the great rivalry among the helmsmen as they tried to outskill one another. Moreover, the marines were doing their best to ensure that whenever their ship collided with one of the enemy's, they displayed the same level of skill as was being displayed by the rest of the crew. In short, every individual was eager to stand out from the rest in playing the part that had been assigned to him.

[4] With almost two hundred ships involved from both sides, this was, without a doubt, the largest number that had ever fought in such a small area. The limited space and the great number of ships involved

meant that little broadside ramming took place, because there was no room to back out after a ramming run or to break through the enemy's line. More frequent were clashes resulting from chance collisions between ships as one of them tried to attack or escape from another vessel. [5] While a ship was bearing down on another, it was liberally bombarded by the soldiers on the enemy's deck with javelins, arrows, and stones, and when it engaged, hand-to-hand fighting took place as the marines of each side tried to board the other's ship.

[6] The restricted space meant that in many places a ship might ram another and be rammed itself, and sometimes there were two or even more ships unavoidably jammed against one. The helmsmen found themselves in the position of having to think about defense here and attack there; instead of being able to give their attention to one point at a time, they had to deal with various emerging situations on all sides. And the din caused by so many ships colliding was loud enough not just to be terrifying, but to make it impossible to hear what the rowing-masters were saying. [7] On both sides they were constantly shouting encouragement and calling out orders prompted not just by their expertise but also, impulsively, by their striving for victory. On the Athenian side, they called on the crews to force their way out into the open sea and to commit themselves wholeheartedly to what might be their last chance of winning a safe return to their native land; on the side of the Syracusans and their allies, they reminded the crews how glorious it would be to prevent the Athenians from escaping and how victory would exalt their several states. [8] On both sides, the generals, too, if they saw anyone backing water when he was not compelled to do so, called out to the trierarch by name with a question. On the Athenian side they asked him if he was falling back because he now regarded the most hostile of lands as more congenial to him than the sea, which they had made their own at the cost of considerable effort; on the Syracusan side they asked whether men who, as they knew perfectly well, were focused entirely on finding some way to escape were putting them to flight even as they fled themselves.

71. On the shoreline, while the battle was evenly balanced the two armies were racked with anxiety and anguish, with the Sicilian forces yearning for yet more glory and the invaders afraid that their already dire position was about to get even worse. [2] Since the Athenians were absolutely dependent on their ships, their fear of the outcome was indescribable, and fluctuations in the battle at sea inevitably caused fluctuations also in how those on land reacted to what they saw.† [3] They were too close to the spectacle to see everything at once, so those who saw their side winning at some point were encouraged and began to implore the gods to grant them this chance of safety, while those who were looking in a direction where their side was coming off worse cried out in grief, more in thrall to the sight of what was going on than those who were actually involved in the action. From what others could see, the battle was evenly balanced, and they endured the harshest emotions: the continuous uncertainty of the struggle had even their bodies swaying back and forth in terrified sympathy with the impressions they were receiving, because all the time they were either just on the point of escaping or just on the point of losing their lives. [4] In short, within the single army of the Athenians, as long as the battle hung in the balance a whole range of responses could be heard at once, from cries of grief to cries of joy, from "We're winning!" to "We're losing!," and all the other various exclamations that might be heard from a great army under stress at a time of great danger.

[5] The men on the ships experienced much the same range of emotions—but then, after the fighting had gone on for a long while, the Syracusans and their allies routed the Athenians and, pressing home their advantage with decisive effect, harried them onto land with loud yells and triumphant cheering. [6] The Athenian crews—all those who were not captured while still on the water—were driven here and there onto the shore, and at that point they abandoned their ships and poured into the camp. The land forces were no longer divided in their reactions: in a single burst of emotion, unable to

stand the sight of what was happening, they cried out their grief and distress. Some of them ran to try to save the ships, while others went to the defense of what remained of the wall; but most of them now thought only about themselves and how they might save their lives. [7] The shock of the moment surpassed all previous shocks.† What had happened to them was almost exactly the same as what they themselves had done to others at Pylos, where, once the Lacedaemonians' ships had been destroyed, the men posted on the island were also lost. The same went on this occasion for the Athenians: nothing short of a miracle could save them.

72. The battle had been hard fought and both sides lost many ships and men. After their victory the Syracusans and their allies took possession of the wrecks and collected their dead, and then sailed back to the city and erected a trophy. [2] The Athenians were so overwhelmed by the enormity of their troubles that it did not even occur to them to recover their disabled ships or ask permission to collect the bodies of their dead, but they planned to leave right away, that night. [3] However, Demosthenes approached Nicias and, pointing out that they still had more seaworthy ships than the enemy, proposed that even now they should man the remaining ships and see if they could force their way out of the harbor at dawn. What he said was true: the Athenians still had about sixty ships, while their opponents had fewer than fifty. [4] Nicias liked Demosthenes's plan, but when they wanted to man the ships the oarsmen refused to go on board; the defeat had broken their spirits and they no longer believed they could win.

73. So all the Athenians now came round to the view that they should retreat overland. But on the Syracusan side, Hermocrates guessed that this was what they planned to do and foresaw danger if such a large army retreated overland, established itself somewhere in Sicily, and chose to renew the fight against them. He went to the authorities and proposed that they should not let the Athenians get away with retreating after dark—and he also explained his reasons for thinking this—but that the full levy of the Syracusans and their allies should go out immediately, barricade the roads, and guard the defiles through the hills before the Athenians reached them. [2] The authorities were fully in agreement with him over this and accepted that they should do as he suggested, but they doubted whether the men would be willing to obey. They were in a good mood, relaxing† after a tough battle, and enjoying a festival as well (it happened to be the day of the state sacrifice to Heracles). Overjoyed by their victory, most of them had turned to drinking during the festival, and the authorities thought the last thing they would do at the moment was obey an order to take up their weapons and go out into the field. [3] Accordingly, seeing that the authorities reckoned the plan unworkable and were refusing to endorse it, Hermocrates came up with the following ruse on his own. He was afraid that during the night the Athenians would get a head start and make it through the most difficult stretches of terrain without meeting any opposition, so he sent some of his friends with a cavalry escort to the Athenian camp just as it was getting dark. They approached close enough to be heard and, pretending to be Athenian sympathizers—there were, after all, certain people who had kept Nicias informed about events in the city—they called out to some of the soldiers and asked them to tell Nicias that he should not lead the army away that night because the Syracusans had the roads under guard, and instead to get ready and then retreat unopposed the next day.

[4] After delivering this message they left, and the men who had heard them reported what they had said to the Athenian generals. **74.** Not suspecting a trick, their response to the news was to make no move that night. And since they had in any case not set out immediately, they decided to stay where they were the following day as well, to give the troops time to pack as best they could what they might most need; they were to leave everything else behind and take with them when they set out only what they had that was essential to maintain life. [2] But the Syracusans and Gylippus had already left with their land forces. They barricaded the roads in the countryside that the Athenians were likely to take, stationed guards at the fords across the streams and rivers,

and deployed their men at what seemed the best places to confront the Athenian forces and stop them. Meanwhile, they had their ships row up to the Athenian ships and set about hauling them off the shore. The Athenians themselves had planned to burn the ships and had done so in a few cases, but no one stopped the Syracusans and they met with no interference as they rowed over to wherever any of them had run aground, attached ropes, and conveyed them to the city.

75. Next, once Nicias and Demosthenes decided that enough had been done by way of preparation, the army finally began to withdraw on the third day after the battle in the harbor. [2] What was so dreadful about their situation was not just that they were retreating after losing their entire fleet, and that their failure to achieve the success they had anticipated left both themselves and Athens at risk, but also that as they were leaving the camp every one of them encountered sights that tormented both eye and mind. [3] Since the dead remained unburied, whenever anyone saw the body of a friend lying on the ground he was overcome by a mixture of grief and dread. But the living were considerably more upset by the wounded and sick than by the dead, because they were being left behind alive and were far worse off than those who had perished. [4] Their pleading and their sobs made those who were leaving uncertain what to do. The invalids cried out to each and every friend or relative they saw and begged him to take them along. They clung to their tentmates as they passed on their way and followed them as far as they could, and when they gave up in despair or their strength failed them, they fell back, appealing for help in the name of the gods and crying out in their misery. In the end, the whole army was in tears, and they felt so torn that it was hard for them to set out, even though they were leaving a hostile land after tribulations that were too great for tears and in fear of what the future might hold for them.

[5] They were also overcome by a kind of shame and self-condemnation, because they resembled nothing so much as fugitives from a city that had been besieged into submission. And no small city

at that: the mass of people on the move totaled at least forty thousand.* Each of them was carrying whatever he could manage that might prove useful, and the hoplites and cavalrymen, contrary to their usual practice when under arms, were carrying their own food, either because they no longer had attendants or because they did not trust them; their attendants had been deserting for a long time, and most of them had seized the immediate opportunity to do so. But even what they were carrying with them was not enough, because the camp had no reserves of grain. [6] Moreover, even though, in spite of everything, it was some consolation that the burden of their troubles was distributed equally throughout the army, so that no one was suffering alone, at the time this did not make anyone regard his troubles as easy to bear, especially considering that he had reached this miserable end after such a splendid and confident beginning. [7] Surely no Greek army had ever experienced so thorough a reversal. They had come to enslave others, but instead they were now leaving in fear that this was the fate that was impending for them; instead of the prayers and paeans that had accompanied their departure from Athens, they were setting off with appeals to heaven of the opposite sort; and instead of traveling by ship they were on foot, reliant on their infantry rather than their navy. Nevertheless, the magnitude of the danger that still hung over them made all this seem bearable.

76. Nicias, aware of the army's gloom and how the troops felt about their changed circumstances, rode along the column, doing the best he could under the circumstances to raise their spirits and give them hope. He spoke louder and louder as he came up to each cluster of men, not just because of his eagerness to help, but because he wanted the good that his words might do to reach as far as possible.

77. "Athenians and allies," he said, "however grim our present circumstances seem, there's no need for despair. In the past, men have come safely through even worse than this. Nor should you condemn yourselves too much for either your defeats or your present undeserved hardships. [2] Look at me: my physical condition is as bad as any of yours—you can see what illness has done to me—and although I am, I suppose, considered as successful as anyone in both private and public life, I've been caught up in the same danger as the least of you. And yet I've spent my life scrupulously fulfilling my obligations to the gods and treating men with irreproachable justice. [3] In return for this piety of mine, my hopes for the future remain confident, and our misfortunes alarm me less than they might seem to warrant. They may even recede. After all, our enemies have enjoyed enough success, and if our expedition offended any of the gods, we've been punished enough by now. [4] We aren't the first to have attacked others; we aren't the first to have acted as fallible human beings and to have borne what fallible human beings have to bear.† So now it's reasonable for us to hope for more lenient treatment from the gods; we deserve their pity now, not their resentment. Just look at yourselves! Moderate your fears by recognizing your caliber and seeing how many comrades are arrayed beside you. The conclusion to be drawn from this is that as soon as you settle somewhere you constitute a city, and there's no other city in Sicily that would find it easy to resist an attack from you or uproot you once you're well established somewhere.

[5] "During our march, see that you take no risks and remain in good order, with each of you holding just one thought in his mind: that wherever we're brought to battle, victory will make that place ours, our homeland and our fortress.* [6] We shall be marching in haste, day and night, because we're short of supplies, and if we reach friendly territory belonging to one of the Sicel tribes—the Sicels are still firm friends of ours, owing to their fear of Syracuse—then you may consider yourselves safe. We've already been in touch with them, asking them to meet us and bring further provisions.†

[7] "In short, what it all comes down to, men, is this: you must appreciate that you have no choice but to be brave, because there's no place of refuge nearby to which you might flee if you turn cowardly. If you escape your enemies now, the non-Athenians among you will have a chance to gaze once more upon what you long to see, and the

Athenians will raise their city's power back up again from its fallen state to its former greatness. For it's men, not walls or unmanned ships, that constitute a city."

78. While offering these words of encouragement Nicias also reviewed the army as he passed by, tightening up and arranging the men wherever he found them disordered or tending to lose formation. Demosthenes did the same with his division and offered much the same advice as Nicias. [2] The army set out in square formation with Nicias's division leading the way and Demosthenes's following behind; the baggage-carriers and the general mass of people from the train were inside the hollow squares of hoplites. [3] At the ford across the Anapus river they found some of the Syracusans and their allies lined up and ready for battle. The Athenians turned the enemy to flight, gained control of the ford, and carried on, but they were harried by the Syracusan cavalry riding along their flanks, and came under javelin fire from light-armed troops.

[4] After covering about four and a half miles that day, the Athenians spent the night by a hill. They set out early the next day and, after marching half the distance of the day before, they came down to some level ground and made camp; the place being inhabited, they wanted to plunder the houses of anything edible and to collect water to take along with them. On their route there was very little water ahead of them for a long way. [5] Meanwhile, the Syracusans had overtaken them and were building a wall up ahead across the pass, which consisted of a steep-sided hill called the Acraean Rock, with precipitous ravines on either side. [6] The next day the Athenians carried on, and the Syracusan cavalry and javelineers came up in large numbers on both their flanks, hurling javelins at them and riding beside them in an attempt to make them halt. The Athenians fought them for a long time before retreating back to where they had made camp the night before. And they were even worse off for supplies now because the Syracusan cavalry was making it impossible for them to go out foraging.

79. They set out again early the next day and forced their way through to the hill where the pass had been walled off. There they found the Syracusan infantry waiting for them in front of the wall, marshaled many ranks deep because of the narrowness of the place. [2] The Athenians attacked in an attempt to take the wall, but came under heavy fire from the men who had been posted on the hill, the steepness of which made it easy for their missiles to reach their targets. Finding it impossible to take the wall by assault, they fell back again and rested. [3] It so happened that a rainstorm with occasional claps of thunder occurred during the fighting. This was not unusual for the time of year—it was getting close to autumn—but it further disheartened the Athenians, who saw the storm as another example of how everything was colluding for their destruction.* [4] While they were resting, Gylippus and the Syracusans sent a section of their forces to build another wall, this time behind the Athenians, to cut them off from the route by which they had come. But the Athenians sent some of their own men to counter the attempt and managed to stop them. [5] Then the whole Athenian army pulled back to more level ground, where they spent the night.

The next day, as they continued on their way, the Syracusans surrounded them and attacked from all directions. Many men were wounded. Whenever the Athenians attacked the Syracusans retreated, and whenever they retreated the Syracusans attacked, focusing especially on the rearmost lines in an attempt to sow panic in the army as a whole by inflicting gradual defeats on it. [6] The Athenians held out for a long time in this fashion but then halted while still on the plain—they had progressed less than a mile that day—and the Syracusans too disengaged and went to their camp.

80. That night, in view of the fact that their men were in a bad way (not only because by now they had no provisions left, but also because a lot of them had been wounded during the enemy's many assaults), Nicias and Demosthenes decided to have as many campfires lit as possible and then to lead the army away—not now by the route they had originally planned to take, but toward the sea, avoiding the route that was being watched by the Syracusans. [2] The general direction of this new route for the army was not toward Catana but the other part of Sicily, the part that goes down to Camarina, Gela, and the Greek and barbarian towns there. [3] So once a large number of campfires had been lit, they set out under cover of darkness. As tends to happen to all armies, and particularly very large ones, they were assailed by fears and alarms, especially because it was dark and they were marching through enemy territory with a hostile army close by, and they fell into disarray. [4] Nicias's division, which was leading the way, retained its cohesion and got a long way ahead, but Demosthenes's division, which was somewhat more than half of the army, lost touch with the others and was advancing in relative disorder. [5] Nevertheless, they all reached the coast at daybreak and took the Helorus road, as it is called. Their plan was to make their way to the Cacyparis river and follow it up from the coast through the interior, because they hoped to be met there by the Sicels whose help they had requested. [6] But when they reached the river, there, too, they found Syracusans: there was a guard-detail building a wall and a palisade to block the ford. They overwhelmed these guards, crossed the river, and carried on toward another river, the Erineus, on the advice of their guides.

81. Meanwhile, once it was daylight and the Syracusans and their allies became aware of the Athenians' departure, most of them blamed Gylippus, because they thought he had deliberately let the Athenians leave. They quickly set out after them—it was not difficult to tell which way they had gone—and caught up with them around midday. [2] As soon as they made contact with the rearguard—Demosthenes's troops, who were making slower progress and were in some disarray thanks to the confusion of the previous night—they attacked and brought them to battle. Since they had become separated from the rest of the army, the Syracusan cavalry had no difficulty in encircling them and confining them in one spot.

[3] Nicias's division was as much as six miles ahead because he had led his men on more quickly. To his mind, safety in a situation like theirs lay not in standing their ground and fighting, if they had any choice in the matter, but in retiring as quickly as they could, and fighting only when they were compelled to do so. [4] But Demosthenes had been in more continuous difficulty, as his was the last division in retreat, and so the first that the enemy attacked; and once he realized that the Syracusans were in pursuit, he stopped pushing forward and drew his men up for battle instead. However, this gave the Syracusans time to surround him, and then there was no way that he and his men could put up an organized defense. Pinned as they were in a large olive grove that was surrounded by a low wall, with farm tracts on either side of it, they were under fire on all sides from missiles. [5] The Syracusans had good reasons for employing this mode of attack rather than fighting at close quarters. Under the circumstances, taking that kind of risk against desperate men would favor the Athenians rather than themselves, and besides, now that their success was beyond doubt, they were reluctant to waste a single life beforehand. In any case, they were sure that these tactics would enable them to defeat and capture the Athenians.

82. After showering the Athenians and their allies with volleys of missiles from all sides throughout the day, Gylippus and the Syracusans and their allies could see that they had been ground down by their wounds and their general degradation. At first they issued a proclamation, inviting any of the islanders who so wished to come over to them on terms of freedom, and the contingents of a few cities did go over to them. [2] But then later they reached an agreement with Demosthenes for the surrender of his entire force: the men were to hand over their weapons, and none of them would suffer death by violence, incarceration, or starvation. [3] The whole army of six thousand men surrendered, and when they placed all the money they had in upturned shields, it filled only four shields. These men were immediately transported to the city. Nicias and his men, meanwhile, reached the Erineus that day, crossed it, and encamped on some high ground.

83. The next day the Syracusans caught up with Nicias, informed him of the surrender of Demosthenes and his men, and urged him to do the same. Nicias did not trust them and arranged a truce so that he could send a rider to investigate. [2] The man rode off and brought word back to Nicias that the others had indeed surrendered, so Nicias sent a herald to Gylippus and the Syracusans saying that he was ready to come to terms on behalf of the Athenians. He would repay the full amount of money that the Syracusans had spent on the war on the condition that they let him and his men go, and until the money reached them he would give the Syracusans some of his men as hostages, one man for every talent of money that was owed. [3] But these terms were unacceptable to the Syracusans and Gylippus, and they went on the offensive. They surrounded the Athenians and hurled volleys of missiles at them from all sides until late in the day. [4] This division of the Athenian army, like the other one, was suffering badly from lack of grain and other means of subsistence, but nevertheless they planned to wait for the dead of night and continue on their way. But as they collected their arms and armor, the Syracusans heard them and chanted a paean. [5] The Athenians, realizing that they were not going to get away with it, laid down their arms again, except that about three hundred men forced their way past the guards and set out as best they could under cover of darkness.

84. At daybreak Nicias led his men onward, but the Syracusans and their allies assailed them in the same way as before, with volleys of missiles and javelins thrown at them from all sides. [2] The Athenians continued to push on toward the Assinarus river. They thought that if they could get to the other side of the river, they would gain some relief from the pressure of being surrounded and attacked by both the Syracusans' numerous cavalry and the horde of light troops, and they were also eager to get there because of their wretched physical condition and their raging thirst. [3] But when they reached the river they lost all sense of discipline and plunged into it, with every one of them wanting to be the first to get across and the enemy now focusing their attacks on hampering the attempt. They forced the Athenians to crowd together as they tried to cross, so that they got in one another's way and trampled one another. Some died right there and then on the points of spears, while others became entangled in their equipment and were carried away by the current. [4] The Syracusans went and stood on the other bank, which was steep, and shot down at the Athenians, most of whom were gratefully quenching their thirst in a chaotic jumble in the deep bed of the river, [5] while the Peloponnesians went down into the riverbed and butchered them, especially those who were in the water. The water was immediately befouled, but it was still being drunk, bloody and muddy as it was, and even fought over by most of the Athenians.

85. Eventually Nicias surrendered to Gylippus, whom he trusted more than the Syracusans—but by then many bodies were heaped on top of one another in the riverbed and the army had been wiped out, either in the river or, if any of them escaped, by the cavalry. Nicias told Gylippus that he and the Syracusans could do whatever they liked with him, but asked him to call a halt to the massacre of his men. [2] So next Gylippus ordered his troops to start taking prisoners, and all the surviving Athenians, apart from the many who were hidden by their captors,* were rounded up alive. Men were also sent after the three hundred who had broken through the ring of guards in the night, and they were captured as well. [3] The number of soldiers who were rounded up as state property was not great, but more were spirited away—so many, in fact, that plenty of them were to be found all over Sicily—because they were not captured after a negotiated surrender, as Demosthenes's men had been. [4] And a significant number of lives were lost; this was, after all, slaughter on a large scale, the greatest massacre that occurred during the war. A great many men had also lost their lives in all the various assaults by the Syracusans during the retreat. Nevertheless, many managed to escape, either right away or in some cases later, when they absconded from their masters after being enslaved. The escapees found refuge in Catana.

86. The Syracusans and their allies reunited their forces, collected all the prisoners they had taken and the spoils, and returned to Syracuse. [2] All the ordinary soldiers they had captured, Athenians and their allies, they took down to the quarries, which was the most secure place to keep them under guard, but they cut the throats of Nicias and Demosthenes. This was not what Gylippus wanted; he thought that on top of all his other successes it would be a glorious achievement for him also to take the two enemy generals alive to Sparta. [3] One of them, Demosthenes, was in fact the Lacedaemonians' greatest enemy, because of what had happened at Sphacteria and Pylos, while the other, for the same reason, was considered their best friend in Athens, because he had devoted himself to the cause of the Lacedaemonians who had been captured on Sphacteria and, by persuading the Athenians to make peace, had secured their release. [4] This had won Nicias the friendship of the Lacedaemonians, and for his part this friendship was the main reason why he had trusted Gylippus and surrendered to him. But some of the Syracusans, or so it was said, those who had been in communication with him, were afraid that if he were tortured on that account he would spoil things for them when they had successfully got away with it. Others, above all the Corinthians, were afraid that, given how wealthy Nicias was, his money would buy him freedom and he would make fresh trouble for them later; so they prevailed on their allies and had him put to death. [5] This, or something very like it, was the reason why he was killed—a man who, of all the Greeks in my time at any rate, least deserved such a wretched end, seeing that throughout his life he had conducted himself with integrity.

87. For a while the men in the quarries were treated cruelly by the Syracusans. There were a great many of them crowded together without much room at the bottom of the quarries, and since the place afforded them no shelter they were plagued, even at this season, by sunny days of stifling heat—and then, by contrast, the nights that followed were autumnal and cold, and the varying temperatures played havoc with their health. [2] They were forced by the cramped conditions to do everything where they were, and moreover there were heaps of corpses piled up on top of one another, the bodies of men who had succumbed to their injuries or been killed by the changes in temperature or some other feature of their situation. The stench was unbearable, and they suffered badly from hunger and thirst, because for eight months each of them received only half a pint of water and one pint of grain a day. And of all the many other hardships that people thrust into such a place were likely to suffer there was not one that did not afflict them. [3] For about seventy days they lived all packed together in these terrible conditions, and then all of them except for the Athenians and the men from the Sicilian or Italian Greek cities who had taken part in the campaign were sold into slavery. [4] It is not easy to be precise, but altogether at least seven thousand men were taken prisoner.

[5] This turned out to be the most significant event of the current war, and it was also, in my opinion, more significant than any other event we hear about in Greek history; it was unique for the brilliance of the victors' success and the catastrophic nature of the consequences for the losers. [6] For the Athenians were completely and utterly defeated and their suffering was prodigious. It was nothing short of what people call annihilation: army, fleet, everything was destroyed, and few of the many made it back home. This is what happened in Sicily.

Book Eight

The nineteenth to twenty-first years of the war. **413/412:** *Reactions to the disaster in Sicily (8.1–6).* **412/411:** *Chios and Lesbos revolt from Athens (8.7–17); first treaty between Sparta and Persia (8.18); fighting in Ionia, and a democratic revolution in Samos (8.19–36.1); second treaty between Sparta and Persia (8.36.2–37); more fighting in Ionia and the eastern Aegean (8.38–44); Alcibiades changes sides again (8.45–47); Athenian oligarchs start to plan a coup (8.48–54); fighting in Rhodes and Chios (8.55); third treaty between Sparta and Persia (8.56–59); more fighting on Athens's northern border and in the eastern Aegean (8.60).* **411/410:** *conflict continues in the eastern Aegean and Asia Minor (8.61–63.2); oligarchic coup at Athens (8.63.3–71), and a democratic counter-coup among Athenian forces on Samos (8.72–77); more fighting in Ionia and the eastern Aegean (8.78–88); oligarchic regime at Athens is overthrown (8.89–98); further campaigns in the Aegean and Hellespont, including Athenian naval victory at Cynossema (8.99–109).*

1. When the news reached Athens, for a long time people refused to believe even the unequivocal reports they were receiving from soldiers who had actually been there and had escaped. It seemed incredible that the expeditionary force could have been so completely and utterly wiped out. When they finally accepted the truth of the reports, they became angry with the politicians who had played a role in pushing for the expedition, and also with the keepers of oracular archives, the professional diviners, and all those who at the time had raised their hopes by prophesying that Sicily would be theirs. [2] There was nothing but grief for them wherever they looked and they were filled with the utmost fear and dismay at what had happened. They were distressed not just by the personal losses that every one of them had sustained, but also by the loss to the city of so many hoplites, cavalrymen, and men of fighting age that it was impossible to see how they might be replaced. Moreover, since it was obvious that there were neither enough ships in the shipsheds, nor enough money in the state treasury, nor enough officers for the fleet, they could not at the moment see how they might survive. They expected their enemies in Sicily to launch a seaborne assault on Piraeus immediately, especially given the scale of their victory; their enemies in Greece, with their forces now doubled, to attack them in strength on land and at sea; and their allies, who would by then have rebelled, to join their enemies for these attacks. [3] Nevertheless, they decided to keep going as well as circumstances permitted—to build a new fleet, getting timber from wherever they could; to raise money; and to make sure of their allies, especially Euboea. And they decided to set limits on how much the city spent on its official functions and to create a board of senior men to hold preliminary discussions about the state of affairs as and when necessary. [4] In short, one way and another—and this is typical of a democracy—immediate fear made the masses ready to accept discipline. No sooner had these decisions been taken than they put them into effect; and so the summer ended.

2. The following winter, the immediate response all over Greece to the overwhelming catastrophe suffered by the Athenians in Sicily was a surge of excitement and elation. Neutral states felt that, even if their help was not requested by anyone, they should no longer remain aloof from the war but should attack the Athenians of their own accord; each of them believed that the Athenians would have targeted them if they had been successful in Sicily, and at the same time they did not expect the war to go on much longer, and thought that it would redound to their credit if they played a part in it. States that were allies of Sparta were united in their greatly increased eagerness to be rid of all the hardships they had suffered, and it seemed to be no distant prospect. [2] But the greatest elation was experienced by the subject states of the Athenian empire. Even those that lacked military strength were ready to rebel, because their judgment was being ruled by their emotions, and they could envisage no scenario in which the Athenians survived the next campaigning season. [3] As for the Lacedaemonians, all this boosted their confidence, and they were especially encouraged by the expectation that in the spring their allies in Sicily would come in strength, with their military capability now enhanced by the fleet that circumstances had compelled them to build. [4] In short, wherever they looked they could see nothing to dampen their hopes, and they planned to commit themselves wholeheartedly to the war, because they reckoned that bringing it to a satisfactory conclusion would put an end to the kinds of dangers that the Athenians would have posed for them if they had added the resources of Sicily to their own, and that if they destroyed the Athenians they themselves would then be the undisputed leaders of all Greece.

3. During the winter, then, Agis, the Spartan king, went straight into action. He set out with some of his forces from Decelea and raised money from his allies for the fleet, and then he headed for the Malian Gulf. Because of the long-standing enmity between Sparta and the Oetaeans,* he extracted money from them by stealing most of their livestock and selling it, and then, ignoring the complaints and protestations of the Thessalians, he forced the Phthiotic Achaeans and the other Thessalian subjects in the region to give him hostages and money—the hostages were deposited in Corinth—and tried to gain them for the Lacedaemonian alliance. [2] The total number of ships the Lacedaemonians required their allies to build was a hundred: twenty-five from themselves and the same number from the

Boeotians; fifteen from the Phocians and Locrians; fifteen from the Corinthians; ten from the Arcadians, Pellenians, and Sicyonians; and ten from Megara, Troezen, Epidaurus, and Hermione. In short, they were making thorough preparations to go to war right at the beginning of spring.

4. The Athenians, too, spent the winter putting their plans into effect. They acquired timber for the construction of ships and fortified Sunium to protect their grain-ships as they sailed around the coastline. They abandoned the fortress they had built in Laconia* when they were sailing around the Peloponnese on their way to Sicily, and in general they cut back on expenditure wherever they thought savings could be made. Their chief concern, however, was to keep an eye on their allies to forestall rebellion.

5. During the winter, while both sides were busy with all this, equipping themselves as though the war were only just beginning, the Euboeans, the first of the Athenian allies to do so, approached Agis with a view to rebelling from Athens. He welcomed their initiative and summoned Alcamenes, son of Sthenelaidas, and Melanthus from Sparta. They were to go to Euboea as its governors, and they came with a force of about three hundred freedmen. [2] At this point, however, the Lesbians arrived as well, also wanting to secede from the Athenian alliance. With the Boeotians acting as their advocates, Agis was persuaded to postpone his arrangements for Euboea. Instead he laid the groundwork for the Lesbian rebellion; he gave them as their governor Alcamenes, who had originally been destined for Euboea, and the Boeotians and Agis each promised them ten ships. [3] All these negotiations took place without the involvement of the Spartan state, because while Agis was at Decelea with an army under his command he had the authority to launch offensives wherever he wanted, to recruit troops, and to raise funds. At this point in time, in fact, it is hardly an exaggeration to say that Athens's allies were more prepared to submit to him than to the Lacedaemonians in Sparta, because with his army he was an immediate and fearsome presence wherever he went.

[4] So Agis was negotiating with the Lesbians. The Chians and Erythraeans* were also ready to rebel, but they went to Sparta instead of turning to Agis. They were accompanied by an envoy from Tissaphernes, who was the governor of western Asia Minor for King Darius, son of Artaxerxes.* [5] Tissaphernes too was trying to win over the Peloponnesians, and he was promising to provide maintenance funds. The King had recently required him to pay the tribute from his province because he had fallen into arrears thanks to the Athenians, who had made it impossible for him to exact the money from the Greek cities within his domain. He therefore thought he would be better placed to collect the tribute if he weakened the Athenians, and at the same time he would be gaining the Lacedaemonians as allies of the King and would be in a position to comply with the King's demand that he either capture or kill Amorges, the illegitimate son of Pissuthnes, who had raised a rebellion in Caria.*

6. So the Chians and Tissaphernes had a common purpose and were hoping for the same outcome from the negotiations, but just then Calligeitus, son of Laophon, and Timagoras, son of Athenagoras, arrived. They were both exiles from their cities—Megara and Cyzicus, respectively—who were living with Pharnabazus, son of Pharnaces,* and they had been sent to Sparta by Pharnabazus to request a fleet for the Hellespont. Pharnabazus had the same objectives as Tissaphernes: he wanted to see if he could get the cities in his province to defect from Athens in order to guarantee the tribute, and he wanted it to be him who was responsible for arranging the alliance between the King and the Lacedaemonians. [2] Given the different agendas that Pharnabazus's and Tissaphernes's delegations brought to the negotiations, a fierce competition arose among the envoys in Sparta, as one party tried to persuade the Lacedaemonians to send a fleet and an army first to Ionia and Chios, and the other tried to get them to give preference to the Hellespont. [3] But the Lacedaemonians were far more receptive to the petition of the Chians and Tissaphernes, because Alcibiades was supporting them, and thanks to their hereditary guest-friendship he had a particularly close connection with Endius, who was an ephor that year. In fact, it was owing to this guest-friendship that Alcibiades's family originally adopted a Lacedaemonian personal name, Endius's full name being Endius, son of Alcibiades.*

[4] Nevertheless, the Lacedaemonians first sent a non-Spartiate called Phrynis to Chios to assess the situation there—to see if they really had as many ships as they were claiming and whether, in general, the city had the capability it was reputed to have. He reported back that everything they had heard was true, and they immediately entered into an alliance with the Chians and Erythraeans and voted to send them a fleet. They decided to send only forty ships, because, according to the Chians, there were already at least sixty ships there. [5] They were going to send a first batch of ten ships commanded by Melanchridas, who was their navarch, but then there was an earthquake, and they appointed Chalcideus to replace Melanchridas and reduced the number of ships they were fitting out in Laconia from ten to five.* And so the winter came to an end and with it the nineteenth year of the current war, the history of which was written by Thucydides.

7. The next year, right at the beginning of spring, the Chians, who were worried that the Athenians might find out about the negotiations (all the delegations had managed to reach Sparta without the Athenians' knowledge), were pressing for the fleet to be sent, so the Lacedaemonians sent three Spartiates off to Corinth to convey the ships across the Isthmus from the Gulf of Corinth to the Saronic Gulf and to order the entire fleet—the thirty-nine ships at the Isthmus and the ships that Agis was fitting out for Lesbos—to sail to Chios. **8.** Pharnabazus's agents, Calligeitus and Timagoras, therefore refused to join the expedition to Chios or to release the money (twenty-five talents) that they had brought with them to contribute to the costs of the expedition; they planned instead to sail later with another expeditionary force raised on their own. [2] When Agis realized that the Lacedaemonians were intent on going first to Chios, he made no protest, but the allies met anyway in Corinth to decide what to do. Their decision was to send the fleet first to Chios under the command of Chalcideus, who was overseeing the fitting out of the five ships in Laconia, and then to Lesbos with Alcamenes in command, in keeping with Agis's intentions, and finally to the Hellespont, for which Clearchus, son of Ramphias, had already been assigned the command. [3] They also decided to bring half the ships across the Isthmus first and to send this flotilla on its way immediately, so that the Athenians would pay more attention to those that were leaving than to those that were brought across later. [4] They were setting out like this, with no attempt at concealment, because they considered the Athenians too weak to be a threat, since no substantial Athenian fleet had yet put in an appearance. And in keeping with this decision of theirs they immediately transported twenty-one ships across the Isthmus.

9. Although the allied states were impatient to get going, the Corinthians refused to commit themselves to joining the expedition until after they had celebrated the Isthmia, which fell at this time.* Agis, however, was perfectly ready to accept the Corinthians' refusal to break the Isthmian truce,* and to take on the expedition by himself as a private affair. [2] The Corinthians took issue with him over this and a delay ensued, during which the Athenians began to have a clearer idea of what was happening in Chios. They dispatched Aristocrates, one of the generals, but when he accused the Chians of planning to rebel they denied it. The Athenians therefore ordered them to demonstrate their good faith by sending ships back with Aristocrates to join the allied force, and they sent seven. [3] There were two reasons why they did so. First, the general Chian populace was unaware of all the wheelings and dealings, and the oligarchs, who were complicit, did not want to antagonize them yet, until they had acquired some strength; and, second, thanks to the delay, they had given up expecting the Peloponnesians to come in the foreseeable future.

10. Meanwhile, the Isthmia was being celebrated, and since the truce had already been proclaimed, the Athenians sent their delegates to it—and gained more reliable information about what was going on in Chios. As soon as the delegates returned, the Athenians set about making sure that the Peloponnesian ships would not set out from Cenchreae without their knowing about it. [2] But after the festival, the Peloponnesians set out for Chios with twenty-one ships under Alcamenes's command. At first the Athenians bore down on them with the same number of ships and tried to draw them out into the open sea. The Peloponnesians did not follow them far, however, and when they turned back to their harbor, the Athenians, too, withdrew and went back home; their flotilla included the seven Chian ships, and they were not sure they could rely on them. [3] But later they manned more ships, until they had thirty-seven in all, and as the Peloponnesians sailed along the coast, the Athenians chased them into Speiraeum, which is an uninhabited bay in Corinthia and the last one before the border between Corinth and Epidaurus. The Peloponnesians lost one ship out at sea, but the rest stayed close together and reached the anchorage. The Athenians launched a two-pronged attack, by sea with their ships and on land once they had put troops ashore. In the confusion and chaos that ensued, the Athenians disabled most of the ships that had been driven ashore and killed the commanding officer, Alcamenes. A few lives were lost on the Athenian side as well. **11.** After disengaging, the Athenians left enough ships to blockade the enemy in the bay, while they went and moored the rest at a small island nearby, where they made camp. They also sent to Athens for reinforcements, [2] because on the day after the battle Corinthian reinforcements reached the Peloponnesian ships, and soon after that more men came from nearby communities.

The Peloponnesians did not know what to do. They had no illusions about the difficulty of maintaining a guard in such a deserted spot, and they even considered burning the ships, but finally they decided to haul them ashore and have their infantry encamp there to keep them from harm, while they waited for a favorable opportunity to escape. Agis sent them help as well, once he became aware of the situation, in the form of a Spartiate called Thermon. [3] All the information the Lacedaemonians had for a while was that the ships had put to sea from the Isthmus; Alcamenes had been instructed by the ephors to send a messenger on horseback when this happened. Their immediate inclination was to dispatch five of their own ships with Chalcideus in charge and Alcibiades supporting him, but then this impetus was checked by the news that their ships had been forced to take refuge in Speiraeum. Faced with the failure of their first operation in the Ionian War, their morale plummeted and they changed their minds about sending the ships from Laconia. They even contemplated recalling some other ships as well, that were already at sea.

12. When this came to Alcibiades's attention he once again tried to convince Endius and the other ephors not to back out of the expedition. He told them they would reach Chios before the Chians heard about the naval disaster at Speiraeum, and that when he landed in Ionia he would easily persuade the cities to rebel by citing Athenian weakness and Lacedaemonian determination. After all, he said, they would be more likely to trust him on this than anyone else. [2] And privately, just to Endius, he argued that it would be a fine thing if the secession of the Ionians and winning the King as an ally of the Lacedaemonians were his doing, rather than the credit accruing to Agis, with whom Alcibiades had fallen out. [3] And after winning Endius and the other ephors over to his point of view, he set sail with the five ships under the command of the Lacedaemonian Chalcideus, and they sped on their way.

13. Meanwhile, the sixteen Peloponnesian ships that had served throughout the war with Gylippus were on their way back from Sicily. They were intercepted off Leucas and mauled by a fleet of twenty-seven Athenian ships commanded by Hippocles, son of Menippus, who was on the lookout for the ships from Sicily; all but one of them, however, escaped from the Athenians and sailed into Corinth.

14. In the course of their voyage, Chalcideus and Alcibiades seized anyone they met to prevent their movements from being reported. The first place they stopped on the Asian mainland was Corycus,* where they released these prisoners and had a preliminary meeting with some of the Chians who were in league with them. They agreed with their recommendation that they sail into the city unannounced, and their arrival there came as a complete surprise. [2] The general populace was dumbfounded and terrified, but the oligarchs had arranged for the council to be sitting at the time, and when Chalcideus and Alcibiades reported that many more ships were on their way—they refrained from mentioning the blockade of the ships in Speiraeum—the Chians, and then the Erythraeans, revolted from Athens. [3] Next Chalcideus and Alcibiades sailed to Clazomenae with three ships and induced the Clazomenaeans to revolt as well. The Clazomenaeans crossed over to the mainland and began to fortify Polichna, in case they ever needed to retreat from their island home. In fact, all the rebel cities were busy with fortifications and preparations for war.

15. It was not long before news of the Chian rebellion reached Athens, and they took certain steps not just in response to the extreme and undeniable danger they now found themselves in, but also because they doubted that their remaining allies would be willing to quell their restiveness now that the greatest of the allied cities had defected. First, although throughout the war they had adhered strictly to the policy of leaving the reserve fund of a thousand talents untouched,* their current fear was such that they immediately repealed the penalties for proposing that the fund be tapped or introducing a motion to that effect, and voted to put the money to use. And, second, they voted to man a large number of ships, and in the short term to send to Chios eight ships that had been withdrawn from guard duty at Speiraeum to go after Chalcideus's ships, but had returned after failing to catch up with them—they were commanded by Strombichides, son of Diotimus—and to follow these as soon as possible with another twelve under Thrasycles, which were also to be withdrawn from the blockade. [2] They recalled the seven Chian ships that were participating in the blockade of Speiraeum, freed the slaves among the crews, and imprisoned the non-slaves; they quickly found crews for another ten ships to replace all those that had been withdrawn and continue the blockade of the Peloponnesians; and they planned to man another thirty. In short, they were highly motivated and were doing all they could to dispatch an expeditionary force to Chios.

16. Meanwhile, Strombichides and the eight ships arrived in Samos town. He added one Samian ship to his flotilla and continued on to Teos, where he advised the citizenry against rebellion. But Chalcideus, too, was sailing to Teos from Chios, with twenty-three ships, while a land army of Clazomenaeans and Erythraeans was marching along the coast. [2] Strombichides had advance notice of their approach and put to sea, but when he was out in open water and saw how many ships there were from Chios, he turned and ran for Samos, with Chalcideus in pursuit. [3] For a while, the Teians refused the land forces entry into the town, but once the Athenians had taken flight they let them in. The land forces did nothing at first while waiting for Chalcideus to return from his pursuit, but he was taking his time, so on their own initiative they set about demolishing the fortifications the Athenians had built to protect Teos on the landward side. A small force of barbarians also arrived, with Stages, one of Tissaphernes's adjutants, in command, and helped them tear down the wall.

17. After pursuing Strombichides into Samos, Chalcideus and Alcibiades armed the crews of the Peloponnesian ships and left them in Chios. Then they replaced these ships with crews from Chios, and after manning twenty more ships they sailed to Miletus, intending to bring about rebellion there. [2] Alcibiades was on good terms with the leading men in Miletus, and he wanted to get the city to change sides before the Peloponnesian ships arrived. Then, seeing that he would have been jointly responsible, with the Chian forces and Chalcideus, for the defection of so many states, the credit would accrue to the

Chians and himself and Chalcideus—and, as he had promised, to Endius as the prime mover of the mission. [3] So they made sure that they remained unobserved for as much of the voyage as possible and reached Miletus shortly before Strombichides and Thrasycles, who had just arrived from Athens with twelve ships and had joined Strombichides in the race for Miletus. Alcibiades and Chalcideus succeeded in persuading the Milesians to revolt, and just then the Athenian fleet of nineteen ships sailed up to the city, but the Milesians refused to admit them, so they moored off the nearby island of Lade and put the city under blockade.

[4] Immediately after the revolt of Miletus, the first alliance was concluded between the Lacedaemonians and the King. Tissaphernes and Chalcideus were the chief negotiators, and the alliance read as follows:*

18. "The Lacedaemonians and their allies entered into a treaty of alliance with the King and Tissaphernes on the following terms: All the territory and cities that the King possesses and his forefathers used to possess are to belong to the King. The King, and the Lacedaemonians and their allies, acting in concert, are to forestall all the revenues and other goods from these states that used to go to the Athenians so that the Athenians receive neither the money nor anything else. [2] The King, and the Lacedaemonians and their allies, are jointly to prosecute the war against the Athenians. They are not to make peace with the Athenians except by the decision of both parties: the King, and the Lacedaemonians and their allies. [3] Any defectors from the King are to be the enemies of the Lacedaemonians and their allies, and any defectors from the Lacedaemonians and their allies are likewise to be the enemies of the King."

19. These were the terms of the alliance. Next the Chians manned another ten ships and sailed to Anaea, wanting to find out how things stood in Miletus and to raise more widespread rebellion among the cities. [2] But they received a message from Chalcideus ordering them to return and warning them that Amorges was coming overland with an army. On their way back they put in at Dios Hieron—and a fleet of sixteen ships hove into view, bearing down on them; this was a fresh batch of ships under the command of Diomedon, which had been dispatched from Athens even later than those commanded by Thrasycles. [3] The Chians' response to the sight was to flee: one ship went to Ephesus and the rest made for Teos. The Athenians seized four ships without their crews, who had managed to get ashore, but the rest found refuge in Teos. [4] The Athenians then sailed back to Samos, while the Chians put to sea again with their remaining ships and, joined by their land forces, persuaded Lebedus and then Haerae to revolt. After that, the troops and the crews returned to their various homes.

20. At much the same time, the twenty Peloponnesian ships in Speiraeum that had been driven there earlier, and were being blockaded by the same number of Athenian ships, made a sudden bid for the open sea. They came off best in the battle, captured four Athenian ships, and then sailed back to Cenchreae and began to get ready once again to sail to Chios and Ionia. And Astyochus, who was now to be responsible for the entire Peloponnesian fleet, arrived from Sparta as their navarch.

[2] The land forces withdrew from Teos, and then Tissaphernes went there in person with an army and completed the demolition of what remained of the Teian fortifications before leaving. Shortly after his departure, Diomedon arrived with ten Athenian ships and entered into a formal agreement with the Teians to the effect that they were to admit Athenians as well into their city. After this he sailed to Haerae and assaulted it, but he failed to take the town and left.

21. Meanwhile, on Samos the people rose up against the oligarchs; their insurrection was supported by the Athenians, who happened to have three ships there. The Samian people killed in total some two hundred of the most powerful aristocrats, punished four hundred others with exile, and distributed their land and houses among themselves. And from then on, once the Athenians, who now regarded them as reliable, had gone on to formally grant them their independence, the city had a democratic constitution. The democrats allowed the landowners no political role at all, and made it illegal for aristocrats to contract marriages with commoners and vice versa.

22. The Chians, who were just as determined as they had been at the start, wanted to get the Ionian cities to revolt even before the Peloponnesians arrived in force—or, in other words, they wanted to spread the risk as widely as possible. So later that same summer they sent thirteen ships to campaign against Lesbos, which had been designated by the Lacedaemonians as the next target (with the Hellespont to follow); and at the same time, a land army made up of the Peloponnesians who were already in the region and their local allies was marching along the coast toward Clazomenae and Cyme. The officer in command of this army was Evalas, a Spartiate, and the fleet was commanded by a non-Spartiate called Deiniadas. [2] The Chian fleet first put in at Methymna, which was persuaded to revolt, and after leaving four ships there the rest of them went to Mytilene and raised rebellion there.

23. Meanwhile, Astyochus, the Lacedaemonian navarch, sailed as intended with four ships from Cenchreae to Chios. Two days after his arrival, the twenty-five Athenian ships arrived at Lesbos with Leon and Diomedon in command—Leon having left Athens after Diomedon with reinforcements in the form of ten ships. [2] Astyochus too put to sea late that same day, with his fleet supplemented by one Chian ship, and sailed to Lesbos to do what he could to help. He arrived in Pyrrha and the next day went on to Eresus, where he learned that the Athenians had more or less effortlessly recovered Mytilene. [3] They had unexpectedly rowed right into the harbor, and after capturing the Chians' ships they landed troops, overcame the resistance, and gained possession of the city. [4] Astyochus heard the news not just from the Eresians, but also from the Chian ships commanded by Eubulus. These were the ships that had earlier been left in Methymna; they had fled when Mytilene had fallen and now joined him, but there were only three of them because one had been captured by the Athenians. After persuading the Eresians to revolt, Astyochus chose not to set out for Mytilene, and instead he armed the crews of his ships and sent them on foot along the coast to Antissa and Methymna under the command of Eteonicus. Meanwhile, he sailed on a parallel course with his own ships and the three from Chios, in the hope that, encouraged by their appearance, the Methymnaeans would persevere with their rebellion. [5] But he met with nothing but defiance on Lesbos, so he took his forces on board and sailed away to Chios. The allied land forces, originally destined for the Hellespont, were also recalled and dispersed to their various home towns. Later, six of the ships at Cenchreae supplied by the Peloponnesian allies joined them in Chios. [6] The Athenians restored the former status quo throughout Lesbos, which they used as a base for an expedition against Clazomenae. They captured Polichna on the mainland, which was still in the process of being fortified, and transported the Clazomenaeans back to their island town, except for those who had been responsible for the rebellion, who moved to Daphnous.* And so Clazomenae rejoined the Athenian alliance.

24. In the same summer, the Athenians who were blockading Miletus with their twenty ships off Lade made a landing at Panormus in Milesian territory. Chalcideus, the Lacedaemonian commander, came with a small force to offer resistance but lost his life. Two days later the Athenians sailed over to the mainland again and set up a trophy for their victory, but the Milesians tore it down on the grounds that they had no right to erect a trophy on land they had not occupied. [2] Meanwhile, Leon and Diomedon carried on the war against the Chians by sea with the fleet from Lesbos. They launched attacks from the Oenoussae islands off Chios, from Sidoussa and Pteleum (forts held by the Athenians in Erythraean territory), and from their base on Lesbos. Their marines were hoplites conscripted from the call-up lists, [3] and when they were put ashore at Cardamyle and Bolissus,* they fought and defeated the Chians who resisted them, taking many lives in the process, and laid waste the entire region. The Athenians were also victorious in two further battles, at Phanae and Leuconium.*

Following these setbacks, the Chians no longer dared to come out against them and the Athenians plundered the countryside, which was well stocked and had been unscathed ever since the Persian invasion. [4] After the Lacedaemonians, the Chians are the only people known to me who combine prosperity with prudence, and the greater the state grew the more securely they ordered it. [5] In rebelling they might seem to have acted with considerable recklessness, but even in this instance they held back until they had many good allies to share the risks and could see that not even the Athenians themselves were denying that after the Sicilian catastrophe their situation was extremely dire. And if they went somewhat astray in the midst of the unpredictable aspects of human life, they came to recognize their mistake along with many others who thought, like them, that it would not be long before the Athenians were utterly destroyed. [6] Given that the sea was closed to them and their land was being plundered, there was a move in some quarters to bring the city back over to the Athenians. When the authorities learned of this, they took no action themselves but called in Astyochus, the navarch, from Erythrae with four of the ships he had there, and set about considering ways in which they might put an end to the plot in the most temperate way possible, such as taking hostages. So that was the situation in Chios.

25. As summer was drawing to a close, a hoplite force of 1,000 Athenians, 1,500 Argives (the 500 light-armed troops sent by the Argives had been armed by the Athenians as hoplites), and 1,000 allies sailed from Athens in forty-eight ships—some of them doubling as troop-carriers—under the command of the generals Phrynichus, Onomacles, and Scironides. After putting in at Samos they crossed over to Miletus and encamped there. [2] The Milesians sallied out with a force consisting of 800 of their own hoplites, the Peloponnesians who had come with Chalcideus, and some of Tissaphernes's mercenaries—and Tissaphernes himself was there with his cavalry—and engaged the Athenians and their allies. [3] The Argives on their wing charged out ahead of the rest expecting no trouble, because they were going up against Ionians who they assumed would not even stand their ground; but they lost some cohesion as they went and were defeated by the Milesians, with almost 300 of them losing their lives. [4] The Athenians, however, first overcame the Peloponnesians and then drove back the barbarians and the general mass of their adversaries, but they were unable to engage the Milesians. After they had routed the Argives, they had withdrawn back into their city when they saw that the other contingents were coming off worse, and the Athenians brought their now victorious progress to a halt right by Miletus itself. [5] A particular feature of this battle was that on both sides Ionians overcame Dorians: the Athenians defeated the Peloponnesians facing them and the Milesians defeated the Argives. After erecting a trophy the Athenians set about walling off the city, which was on a kind of isthmus. Their thinking was that if they regained Miletus it would not be difficult for them to regain the other rebel states as well.

26. At this point, they were informed late in the day of the imminent arrival of a fleet of fifty-five Peloponnesian and Sicilian warships. Hermocrates, the Syracusan, had been prominent in urging the Sicilian Greeks to play a part in the final overthrow of Athens, and twenty of these ships came from Syracuse and two from Selinous, to join the ships that the Peloponnesians had been fitting out, which were now ready. A Lacedaemonian, Therimenes, was given the job of taking the combined fleet to Astyochus, the navarch, and they put in first at Leros, the island which lies off Miletus. [2] Then, when they learned that the Athenians were at Miletus, they sailed into the Gulf of Iasus,* because before taking any further action they wanted accurate information about the situation in Miletus. [3] Alcibiades—who had taken part in the battle, fighting alongside the Milesians and Tissaphernes—rode to Teichioussa, which lies in Milesia on the part of the gulf where they had bivouacked for the night after their voyage, and told them what had happened in the battle. He advised them that the success of the Ionian campaign, and indeed of the war as a whole, depended on their going immediately to the aid of Miletus and preventing it from being walled off.

27. They planned to go to the relief of Miletus at daybreak, but Phrynichus, the Athenian general, had received good information from Leros about the enemy ships, and although his fellow commanders wanted to stay and fight it out at sea, he said that not only would he not do that himself, but he would do his best to prevent them—or anyone else for that matter—from carrying out such a plan. [2] For in any situation, he said, if men can delay fighting until they know for sure how many enemy ships they will be going up against, and with how many of their own, they have the possibility of fighting at a time of their choosing after making unhurried and adequate preparations, and he would never take senseless risks just because he might be reproached for having acted shamefully. [3] In any case, there was nothing shameful in Athenians giving way to a naval force if that was the appropriate thing to do; regardless of the circumstances, there was more shame if they ended up being defeated. Moreover, defeat would not only bring shame on Athens but would also place it in the greatest danger, because after the disasters it had suffered it was hardly in a position to be proactive anywhere of its own free will, even if its preparations were sound, and should do so only if it had absolutely no choice in the matter. So much the less, then, should it be rushing into dangers of its own making when it was not being forced to do so. [4] He said they should speedily take on board those of their men who were wounded, and their land forces and the stores they came with, but leave behind what they had taken from the enemy so as to lighten the ships, and sail away to Samos. Then all their ships would be in one place, and they could use Samos as a base from which to launch offensives if any opportunities presented themselves.

[5] Phrynichus's fellow commanders agreed with him and he put his plan into effect; and the upshot was that, later no less than now—not only in this instance, that is, but whenever he held a position of

responsibility—he gained a reputation as a man of intelligence. [6] So in compliance with this plan the Athenians left Miletus in the early evening with their victory incomplete, and the Argives hurriedly sailed back home from Samos, riled by their disastrous losses.

28. At daybreak, the Peloponnesian ships set out from Teichioussa, and they put in at Miletus after the Athenians had left. They stayed there for one day, and then the next day they added the Chian ships to their fleet (these were the ships that had originally been under Chalcideus's command and had been driven into the bay at Speiraeum) and sailed back to Teichioussa, because they wanted to retrieve the equipment and stores they had unloaded there. [2] When they arrived, Tissaphernes came up with his land forces and persuaded them to sail against Iasus, where his enemy Amorges was in occupation. Their attack came as a complete surprise, because the Iasians assumed the ships were Athenian,* and the town fell to them. The Syracusans won special praise for their part in the action. [3] The Peloponnesians took Amorges prisoner—he was an illegitimate son of Pissuthnes and had rebelled against the King*—and handed him over to Tissaphernes, so that he could obey his instructions and deliver him to the King if it pleased him to do so. They also looted Iasus and the army gained a great deal of booty, because the place had long been prosperous. [4] They incorporated Amorges's mercenaries into their own forces without ill-treating them, because most of them were from the Peloponnese. The town they turned over to Tissaphernes along with all the people they had captured, both slave and free, and Tissaphernes agreed to give them one daric for each prisoner. Then they returned to Miletus. [5] Pedaritus, son of Leon, had been sent to Chios by the Lacedaemonians to take command there, and they now sent him off by land all the way to Erythrae with Amorges's former mercenaries; and they appointed Philippus to take charge of Miletus. And so the summer ended.

29. The following winter, once Tissaphernes had made sure that Iasus was in a position to defend itself, he went to Miletus and, as he had promised in Sparta, provided upkeep for all the ships for a month, at the rate of one Attic drachma a day for each man. But thereafter, he said, he would give half a drachma a day until he could consult the King, and if the King so ordered he would give the full drachma. [2] But when objections were raised by Hermocrates, the Syracusan general—not by Therimenes, who was not the navarch but was only accompanying the fleet in order to hand it over to Astyochus, and so was soft on the question of pay—an agreement was reached that more than half a drachma was to be paid to each man, the total sum being increased by the equivalent of five ships. That is, Tissaphernes offered thirty talents a month for fifty-five ships, and any ships over that number were paid according to the same formula.

30. That same winter, the Athenians at Samos were reinforced by an additional thirty-five ships from home along with the generals Charminus, Strombichides, and Euctemon. Once they had assembled the ships from Chios and all the others, they intended, after distributing their forces among the generals by lot, to mount a naval blockade of Miletus and dispatch both naval and land forces to Chios. [2] This was the plan they put into effect. Strombichides, Onomacles, and Euctemon were allotted the attack on Chios with thirty ships and troop-carriers for some of the thousand hoplites who had been at Miletus, while the other generals stayed at Samos with seventy-four ships, maintaining their mastery of the sea and mounting seaborne assaults on Miletus.

31. Astyochus happened to be in Chios at the time, rounding up hostages as a precaution against treachery. But when he saw that the arrival of Therimenes's ships had improved the position of the Peloponnesian alliance, he stopped selecting hostages and put to sea with a fleet consisting of the ten Peloponnesian ships and ten from Chios. [2] After an unsuccessful assault on Pteleum,* he sailed on to Clazomenae, where he set about trying to persuade the Clazomenaeans to banish the Athenian sympathizers to Daphnous and come over to the Peloponnesian side. He was supported in this attempt by Tamos,

Tissaphernes's adjutant governor of Ionia. [3] The Clazomenaeans refused to do as he demanded, so he attacked the town, but he failed to take it even though it was unwalled. So he sailed away on a strong wind, and while he went to Phocaea and Cyme the rest of the ships put in at Marathoussa, Pele, and Drymoussa, the islands that lie off Clazomenae. [4] The winds kept them there for eight days, which they spent plundering and consuming the stores that the Clazomenaeans had removed there for safekeeping, and then, after taking on board what was left, they sailed off to Phocaea and Cyme to join Astyochus.

32. While Astyochus was there envoys arrived from the Lesbians, who wanted to make another attempt at rebellion. They succeeded in persuading Astyochus, but the Corinthians and the rest of the allies were unenthusiastic because of the earlier failure, so Astyochus set out for Chios. The ships were driven here and there by a storm and ended up making land at various places on the island. [2] Next, Pedaritus, who had reached Erythrae with his land forces in the course of his march along the coast from Miletus, sailed over to Chios with his troops. Also available to Astyochus were approximately five hundred soldiers from the five ships who had been left behind, with their arms and armor, by Chalcideus. [3] Since some of the Lesbians were proclaiming their intention to revolt, Astyochus proposed to Pedaritus and the Chians that they should take their ships there and make sure that the rebellion went ahead. Either they would gain more allies, he said, or, even if the attempt was not entirely successful, they would at least weaken the Athenians. But Pedaritus and the Chians did not like the idea, and Pedaritus refused to turn the Chian ships over to him.

33. Astyochus therefore took the five Corinthian ships, along with one from Megara, one from Hermione, and the Lacedaemonian ships he had brought with him, and set out for Miletus to take up his navarchy. Before he left he repeatedly threatened the Chians, saying they should not expect any help from him if they ever needed it. [2] He made land in Erythraean territory, at Corycus, and spent the night there. Now, the Athenians from Samos, who were sailing in force to

Chios, also came to anchor there, but since they were on the far side of a ridge that separated them from the Peloponnesians, neither fleet was aware of the other. [3] That night a messenger came with a letter from Pedaritus informing Astyochus that some Erythraeans had been released from captivity on Samos in order to betray the city to the Athenians and had now arrived there, so Astyochus immediately put to sea and returned to Erythrae, not knowing how close he had come to a confrontation with the Athenians. [4] Pedaritus, too, sailed over and joined him, and the two of them held an inquiry into the supposed betrayal. They found that the men had made the whole thing up as a way of escaping from Samos, so they acquitted them of the charge and sailed away, Pedaritus to Chios and Astyochus to Miletus, his original destination.

34. Meanwhile, the Athenian forces too were on the move. They left Corycus and were sailing around the Arginum promontory when they encountered three Chian warships. As soon as they saw them they set out in pursuit, but a violent storm arose. The Chian ships only just reached safety in the bay there, but the three foremost Athenian ships were disabled and later washed ashore at Chios town. The men were either captured or killed, but the rest of the ships ran for the safety of the bay called Phoenicous under Mount Mimas.* Later they set out from there, came to anchor at Lesbos, and set about getting ready to build a fortified outpost.*

35. That same winter, a Lacedaemonian called Hippocrates left the Peloponnese with ten ships supplied by Thurii (which were captained by Dorieus, son of Diagoras, and two others), one Lacedaemonian ship, and one from Syracuse. He put in at Cnidus, which had by then been induced to revolt by Tissaphernes, [2] and when the Peloponnesians in Miletus heard of his arrival, they told him to guard Cnidus with half of his ships and to station the rest at Triopium, in order to seize the cargo ships from Egypt that put in there. Triopium is a headland in Cnidian territory with a sanctuary of Apollo. [3] But when the Athenians found out they were there, they set out from Samos and captured the six ships that were on lookout duty at Triopium, though the crews escaped. Then they sailed to Cnidus and put in there, and came very close to capturing the town, which was unwalled. [4] The next day they renewed the assault, but the Cnidians had improved their defenses overnight and had also been joined by the men who had escaped from the ships, so the Athenians were hardly in a position to do them harm and sailed away again. After ravaging Cnidian territory they returned to Samos.

36. Meanwhile, Astyochus arrived in Miletus to take charge of the fleet. The Peloponnesians were still well supplied with everything the army needed: they were receiving enough pay, the soldiers were able to avail themselves of the plentiful plunder from Iasus, and the Milesians were bearing the burden of the war with good spirits. [2] But the Peloponnesians had come to regard the first treaty with Tissaphernes, the one negotiated between him and Chalcideus, as flawed—and as less favorable to themselves than to Tissaphernes—so while Therimenes was still there they concluded a fresh treaty, as follows:

37. "Agreement between the Lacedaemonians and their allies, and King Darius and the sons of the King and Tissaphernes: There shall be peace and friendship between them on the following terms: [2] Regarding all the land and cities that are in the possession of King Darius or were in the possession of his father or forefathers, neither the Lacedaemonians nor the allies of the Lacedaemonians are to go against these with hostile or harmful intent, nor are the Lacedaemonians or the allies of the Lacedaemonians to exact tribute from these cities. Nor shall King Darius or any of his subjects go against the Lacedaemonians or their allies with hostile or harmful intent. [3] If the Lacedaemonians or their allies need the King's aid for any purpose, or the King needs the aid of the Lacedaemonians or their allies, whatever action they take by mutual agreement shall be the appropriate action. The wages of any military force of any size that is in the King's territory at the request of the King are to be paid by the King.† [4] Both parties are to prosecute the war against the Athenians and their allies together, and if they make peace they are to do so together. [5] If any city that is party to this agreement with the King proceeds against the King's territory, the others are to prevent it and defend the King as far as lies in their power; and if any city that is in the King's territory or is ruled by the King proceeds against the territory of the Lacedaemonians or their allies, the King is to prevent it and defend them as far as lies in his power."

38. After this pact had been concluded, Therimenes handed the fleet over to Astyochus and left in a small boat, never to be seen again.* [2] Meanwhile, the Athenians had already taken their troops over to Chios. They were the masters of land and sea, and they set about fortifying Delphinium, a village that in any case had a steep approach on the landward side; it also had harbors and was not far from Chios town. [3] The Chians made no response to the Athenian invasion. They had taken a beating in many of the earlier battles and in addition their internal situation was highly unstable. With Tydeus, son of Ion, and his faction already executed by Pedaritus for collaborating with the Athenians, and an oligarchy forcibly imposed on the general populace, the city was riven by mutual suspicion, and given their disunity they did not see themselves as a match for the Athenians in battle, nor did they think that Pedaritus's mercenaries were either. [4] They did, however, send word to Miletus asking Astyochus for help, and when he refused Pedaritus wrote a letter to Sparta accusing him of misconduct. [5] This was the state of affairs that the Athenians found on Chios. Meanwhile, they were launching seaborne attacks from Samos on the ships stationed at Miletus, but since the enemy refused to come out to meet them they withdrew back to Samos and remained inactive.

39. In the same winter, at about the time of the solstice, the twenty-seven ships that had been made ready for Pharnabazus by the Lacedaemonians, through the agency of Calligeitus of Megara and Timagoras of Cyzicus, set out for Ionia, with a Spartiate, Antisthenes, in command. [2] Along with this fleet the Lacedaemonians also sent eleven Spartiates, one of whom was Lichas, son of Arcesilas, to act as advisers to Astyochus. Their orders were to go to Miletus and work with the other authorities there to see that everything was in the best shape possible and, at their discretion, to send these ships—either just as they were, or a greater or smaller number—to Pharnabazus in the Hellespont under the command of Clearchus, son of Ramphias, who had accompanied them over to Ionia. It was also left to the discretion of these eleven commissioners to decide whether to remove Astyochus from his position as navarch—Pedaritus's letters had made them unsure of him—and appoint Antisthenes instead. [3] So the ships set out from Cape Malea across the open sea and were approaching the anchorage at Melos when they came across ten Athenian ships, three of which they captured—but without their crews—and burned. But then they became afraid that the Athenian ships that had escaped from Melos might inform the Athenians on Samos of their approach (which is exactly what happened), so in the interests of safety they lengthened their journey by sailing in the direction of Crete and then made land at Caunus in Caria. [4] Sure that they were now safe, they sent a message from there to the fleet in Miletus asking to be provided with a convoy.

40. During this same period of time the Chians and Pedaritus sent messengers to Astyochus, in spite of his reluctance, asking him to come with his entire fleet and help them survive the blockade. They said he should not let the greatest of the allied cities in Ionia be sealed off by sea and plundered by raiding parties on land. [2] Now, the Chians had a great many slaves—more than any other city except Sparta—and because of their large numbers they used to be punished with considerable severity for their offenses. So as soon as the Athenian forces seemed to be securely established in their outpost at Delphinium, the majority of the slaves deserted and joined them, and because they knew the countryside they were the ones who did the most damage. [3] So the Chians told Astyochus to come and help them while there was still hope and a chance of stopping the Athenians, given that they had not yet completed their fortification of Delphinium, and that they were building an additional, larger rampart around their camp and their ships. When Astyochus saw how enthusiastically the idea was greeted by the allies, he expressed his eagerness to help, even though, given his earlier threats, that had not been his original intention.

41. At this point Astyochus received a message from Caunus about the arrival of the twenty-seven ships and his Lacedaemonian advisers. Thinking that everything else was of lesser importance than providing a convoy for this many ships, which would give them a chance to achieve mastery of the sea, and ensuring that the Lacedaemonians who had come to supervise him traveled in safety, he abandoned the expedition to Chios and set sail for Caunus. [2] In the course of his voyage down the coast he made a landing at Cos Meropis,* and since the town was unwalled and had been left in ruins by an earthquake, the most severe within living memory, he set about ransacking it—the inhabitants having fled to the mountains—and plundering the countryside for its booty, except that he took only enslaved people, not those who were free. [3] On leaving Cos he reached Cnidus after dark. He felt the force of the Cnidians' advice that he should refuse his men shore leave and should sail right away, just as he was, against the twenty Athenian ships commanded by Charminus, one of the generals from Samos, which were watching out for the approach of the twenty-seven ships from the Peloponnese that Astyochus was sailing to join. [4] The Athenians on Samos had heard from Melos that these ships were on their way, and Charminus had posted lookouts on Syme, Chalce, and Rhodes as well as on the Lycian coast. By this time he had also found out that the ships were at Caunus.

42. So before his movements became known to the Athenians, Astyochus promptly sailed on toward Syme to see if he could catch the Athenian ships in the open sea. But heavy rain and foggy conditions caused his ships to become disoriented in the darkness and lose formation. [2] At daybreak his fleet was all scattered and his left wing was now visible to the Athenians, while the rest of his ships were still dispersed here and there around the island. So Charminus and the Athenians quickly put to sea with fewer than all their twenty ships, thinking that these were the ships from Caunus they had been looking for. [3] They fell on the enemy and immediately sunk three ships and severely damaged others. The battle was going their way, but then the bulk of Astyochus's fleet hove into view. The Athenians were not expecting this, and they were in danger of being surrounded and cut off. [4] Under the circumstances, they turned to flight. They lost six ships, but the rest reached the safety of the island of Teutloussa* and went on from there to Halicarnassus. After this, the Peloponnesians put in at Cnidus, where they were joined by the twenty-seven ships from Caunus. They set out with the combined fleet, set up a trophy on Syme, and returned to their anchorage at Cnidus. **43.** When the Athenians heard what had happened in the battle, they sailed to Syme with their entire fleet, but they made no move to attack the ships at Cnidus, nor did the Peloponnesians move against them. All the Athenians did was remove the naval equipment that had been stored on Syme and sail back to Samos, after putting in at Loryma on the mainland.

[2] The whole Peloponnesian fleet was now at Cnidus. Repairs were being carried out as necessary on the ships, and since Tissaphernes was there, the eleven Spartiates held discussions with him. They brought up their dissatisfaction with certain aspects of their earlier agreements and discussed how they should conduct the war from then on, so as to guarantee the best and most advantageous outcome for both themselves and Tissaphernes. [3] Lichas was especially critical of the way things were going. He pronounced both the treaty of Chalcideus and that of Therimenes unacceptable, and said he found it outrageous for the King to claim that all the land that he and his forefathers had ruled in the past was still his. This, he argued, would mean that the King would once again reduce all the islands to slavery, along with Thessaly, Locris, and everywhere north of Boeotia,* and that instead of liberating the Greeks the Lacedaemonians would be

imposing Persian rule on them. [4] He urged that a more acceptable treaty should be drawn up, or at least that the previous two should not be implemented, and he told Tissaphernes that they did not want his maintenance allowance on the existing terms. This irritated Tissaphernes, and he went away in an angry mood with nothing achieved.

44. The Lacedaemonians, however, had been approached by the leaders of the aristocrats in Rhodes and planned to sail there, expecting to gain for their side an island with plenty to offer in terms of both naval and land forces. They also hoped that, with the addition of Rhodes, they would be able to maintain their fleet from the resources of their existing alliance, without having to ask Tissaphernes for money. [2] So that same winter they immediately set out from Cnidus, and on Rhodes they put in first at Cameirus. Their fleet of ninety-four ships terrified the general populace, who did not know about the intrigue, and they fled, not least because the town was unwalled. But the Lacedaemonians convened a meeting of the Cameirans and the citizens of the other two towns, Lindus and Ialysus, and persuaded them to secede from the Athenian alliance. And so Rhodes went over to the Peloponnesians. [3] But the Athenians found out what was going on and sailed at this critical moment from Samos in an attempt to reach Rhodes before they defected. They came close enough to be visible out at sea, but they were just too late, and for the present they sailed away to Chalce and from there back to Samos. Later they made war on Rhodes by dispatching naval raiding parties from Chalce, Cos, and Samos. [4] As for the Peloponnesians, they collected the sum of thirty-two talents from the Rhodians, but otherwise rested for eighty days, with their ships drawn up on shore.

45. Meanwhile, and even before the Peloponnesians moved their quarters to Rhodes, intrigues were afoot. Alcibiades had become an object of Lacedaemonian suspicion, and after Chalcideus's death and the battle at Miletus, a letter arrived from Sparta for Astyochus ordering him to see to Alcibiades's death. It was not just that in general he did not strike the Lacedaemonians as trustworthy, but also that Agis had come to loathe him.* Frightened for his life, he first withdrew to Tissaphernes and then set about using his influence with him to harm the Peloponnesian cause. [2] Once he had made himself Tissaphernes's guide in all matters of policy, he got him to reduce the Peloponnesians' maintenance allowance, so that each man received not an Athenian drachma a day but half a drachma, and that irregularly. He told Tissaphernes to tell the Peloponnesians that half a drachma a day was all the Athenians, who had longer experience of seafaring than them, were giving their crews,* and that the reason for this was not so much that they could not afford more as that they did not want their men to become unruly as a result of feeling that they had surplus money. That is, they did not want to give their crews the opportunity either to undermine their fitness by spending money on unhealthy pursuits, or to desert their ships without worrying about leaving behind, as a hostage, the pay that was owing to them. [3] He also advised Tissaphernes to bribe the trierarchs and generals of the cities allied to Sparta and persuade them to concur with this policy. But he failed with the Syracusans, and their general, Hermocrates, was the only person who spoke for the alliance as a whole and opposed the policy.

[4] When representatives of the cities asked for money, Alcibiades on his own initiative dismissed them by arguing, as though he were speaking for Tissaphernes, that it was disgraceful for the Chians, who, despite being the wealthiest of the Greeks, were being saved by outside help, to demand that others risk their lives and money for their freedom, [5] and that it was unfair of the other cities, which before their rebellions had paid money into the Athenian treasury, to be reluctant now to contribute the same amount, or even more, when it was in their own interest to do so. [6] And he explained that Tissaphernes's thriftiness was perfectly reasonable, given that at present he was financing the war from his personal funds, but that if at some point in the future the King sent the maintenance money, he would pay the full amount and help the cities to a reasonable extent.

46. He also began to advise Tissaphernes not to be too eager to bring the war to an end—that is, not to give mastery of land and sea to just one side, either once he had received the ships that were being made ready in Phoenicia or by increasing the number of Greek crews on his payroll. What he should do, Alcibiades said, was allow each side to control one of these two elements, and leave the King the possibility of bringing in the other side against whichever of them was giving him trouble at any time. [2] If mastery of both land and sea were united in one side, he argued, the King would find it difficult to find anyone to help him destroy its supremacy, unless he were prepared, at great expense and risk, to enter the arena himself at some point and fight it out. It would be more economical—it would require only a fraction of the expense and at the same time it would be safer for him—to let the Greeks wear one another out. [3] And he said that Tissaphernes would find sharing power with the Athenians the more acceptable option, because they had fewer ambitions on land and the principles and practices they brought to the war were especially compatible with his interests. They would cooperate in a policy of enslavement, with the Aegean subject to themselves and all the Greeks who inhabited his kingdom subject to the King. The Lacedaemonians, on the other hand, were coming as liberators, and it was unlikely that they would liberate Greeks from other Greeks and yet not liberate them from Persians, unless the Persians at some time and in some way† eliminated them from the equation.

[4] So he advised Tissaphernes to wear down both sides at first and then, after reducing the Athenians as much as possible, to expel the Lacedaemonians from his land. [5] To judge by his actions, at any rate, by and large Tissaphernes found this plan to his liking, because the outcome was that he made Alcibiades one of his trusted advisers and regarded his guidance on these matters as sound. He was niggardly in providing the Peloponnesians with their maintenance allowance, making it impossible for them to fight at sea, and he kept promising that once the Phoenician ships had come they would fight

with the advantage of superior numbers. By these means he sabotaged the Peloponnesians and impaired the efficiency of their fleet, which had formerly been in excellent condition and a real force to be reckoned with. And in general he made it perfectly clear that he was not committed to helping them in the war.

47. Alcibiades had two reasons for offering this advice to Tissaphernes and the King while he was under their protection. He did consider it the best policy, but he was also working to secure his own restoration to Athens. He was sure that if he made it possible for the city to survive he would someday have the opportunity to prevail upon the Athenians to let him return, and he believed that this was most likely to happen if they could see that he was on good terms with Tissaphernes. And events proved him right. [2] The Athenian forces at Samos were aware of his influence with Tissaphernes, because he had already been in touch with the most important men there, asking them to let the best elements at home know that he was prepared to return, get Tissaphernes to support their side, and resume his duties as a citizen alongside them—provided that the city was an oligarchy and not the pernicious democracy that had driven him out. But knowing this about Alcibiades counted for less with the trierarchs and the most influential men among the Athenians on Samos than the fact that they had already resolved of their own accord to overthrow the democracy.

48. This subversive impetus started in the army and subsequently spread to Athens from there. A few people sailed over from Samos to meet with Alcibiades, and he held out the prospect of getting Tissaphernes to support their side, and then the King too, provided Athens was not a democracy (because if it was, the King would be unlikely to trust them, he said). At this, the leading Athenians began to entertain many hopes, not just for themselves personally—that they, the people for whom the war was proving to be the greatest burden,* would gain political control—but also that they would defeat the enemy. [2] After returning to Samos, they began to approach like-minded people and form them into a conspiratorial cabal, and they kept telling the mass of ordinary soldiers, when they spoke in public, that the friendship of the King and his provision of money to them depended on the restoration of Alcibiades and the abolition of the democracy. [3] And the ordinary soldiers did nothing; they may have been angry for a while at what was going on, but they kept quiet because it looked as though they could safely expect to be paid by the King.

Once they had briefed the troops, the oligarchic conspirators resumed considering Alcibiades's proposals among themselves and included more of their political allies in the discussion. [4] Most of them judged the scheme to be easily achievable and a sure thing, but Phrynichus, who was still one of the generals, saw no merit in it at all. In his opinion—and he was right—Alcibiades had as little desire for oligarchy as he had for democracy. Alcibiades, he said, was focusing solely on changing the existing constitution in Athens so that he could return at the invitation of the new regime, whereas their own chief consideration should be the avoidance of civil unrest. And where the King was concerned, now that the Peloponnesians were just as much a presence at sea as the Athenians and controlled some of the most important of the Greek cities in his empire, it would be impractical for him to court trouble by siding with the Athenians, whom he did not trust, when he could befriend the Peloponnesians, who had never done him any harm. [5] And as for the allied cities, to whom they would of course be promising† oligarchy, since Athens itself would no longer be a democracy, he said that he could not see that this would matter to them at all; it would not make the cities that had already revolted more likely to renew their allegiance, and it would not make the ones that remained more dependable. After all, their preference was for freedom, irrespective of whether it came with oligarchy or democracy, rather than enslavement under either system. [6] And as for the "men of honor and worth," as they were known, he said that the allied cities would not expect them to make life less difficult for them than the democracy had, since they were the facilitators and instigators of the crimes committed by the democracy, and the principal beneficiaries. In fact, if power was in the hands of these men, the allies would expect the death penalty to be imposed with more savagery than under the democracy, even on people who had never had a trial, and they would look to the commons to save them and restrain the excesses of the oligarchs. [7] He was absolutely certain that this was the view of the allied cities, Phrynichus said, because they had been taught it by experience; and so he, at any rate, could see no merit in Alcibiades's proposals or the current machinations.

49. The assembled conspirators, however, stuck to their original decision. They accepted the proposals before them and set about arranging to send Peisander* and others as envoys to Athens, tasked with negotiating for Alcibiades's restoration and overthrowing the democracy there, and thereby getting Tissaphernes on good terms with the Athenians. 50. But Phrynichus knew that when the matter of Alcibiades's return came up for discussion the Athenians would agree to it, and since in his speech he had made his opposition plain, he became afraid that, once recalled, Alcibiades would see him as an obstacle and do him harm. So he had recourse to the following stratagem: [2] He wrote secretly to Astyochus, the Lacedaemonian navarch, who was still at Miletus at the time. In the letter he said that Alcibiades was undermining the Lacedaemonian cause by brokering friendship between Tissaphernes and the Athenians, and he included a clear account of everything that was going on. Astyochus would forgive him, he wrote, for scheming to the detriment of a political enemy even when it might not be in his city's best interests.

[3] But Astyochus had no intention of punishing Alcibiades, not least because he was no longer within easy reach. Instead he traveled up to Alcibiades and Tissaphernes at Magnesia and told them about Phrynichus's letter from Samos—which is to say that he, too, became an informer. And it was also rumored that he was bribed to become Tissaphernes's ally and keep him informed about everything, not just this matter. That was taken to be the reason for the feebleness of his

response when the pay the Peloponnesians received was reduced to less than the full amount.

[4] Alcibiades immediately sent a letter to the Athenian authorities on Samos, denouncing Phrynichus for what he had done and demanding his death. [5] Phrynichus, disturbed and in danger of losing his life, wrote again to Astyochus. After reproaching him for his dishonorable disclosure of the contents of the first letter, he told him he was now ready to make it possible for the Lacedaemonians to destroy the Athenian forces on Samos, and he wrote detailed instructions on how they could do this, given the fact that Samos was unwalled. And he said that, since his life was now in danger, because he'd been betrayed by the Lacedaemonians, he could not be criticized for doing this or anything else, whatever it took to avoid being killed by his enemies. Astyochus revealed the contents of this letter, too, to Alcibiades.

51. But Phrynichus knew in advance that Astyochus would double-cross him. So when he found out that a pertinent letter was about to arrive from Alcibiades, he stole a march on Astyochus by informing the army himself that, since Samos was unwalled and not all the ships were at anchorage inside the harbor, the enemy intended to attack them there in their base. He said the information he had received about this was sound, and that they should go ahead with fortifying Samos as quickly as possible and generally remain alert. As general, he had the right to authorize this work. [2] So they set about the fortification, and one outcome of this whole affair was that, although Samos would have been fortified anyway, it happened sooner rather than later. Not long afterward, Alcibiades's letter arrived, accusing Phrynichus of betraying the army and warning them of an imminent attack by the enemy. [3] But Alcibiades was widely regarded as untrustworthy and it was thought that he was using his foreknowledge of the enemy's plans to attribute complicity in them to Phrynichus out of personal enmity, and so he did Phrynichus no harm and even confirmed what he had been saying by giving the same information.

52. Next Alcibiades continued to work on Tissaphernes and to try to persuade him to befriend the Athenians. Tissaphernes was afraid of the Peloponnesians because they had a larger fleet in the region than the Athenians, but he still wanted to comply with Alcibiades's recommendation if he could, especially when he bore in mind his quarrel with the Peloponnesians at Cnidus over the treaty of Therimenes.* (By now the Peloponnesians were on Rhodes and the quarrel had taken place.) In the course of this quarrel, Alcibiades's point, made previously, that the Peloponnesians were aiming to liberate all the cities was confirmed by Lichas, when he argued that it was intolerable for them to agree that the King should rule the cities that either he or his forefathers had ruled. With so much at stake, then, Alcibiades was resolutely grooming Tissaphernes and pressing his case.

53. Once the Athenian envoys who had been dispatched from Samos along with Peisander arrived in Athens, they delivered speeches in the popular assembly summarizing some of the many issues and stressing especially that it was possible for Athens to gain the King as an ally and get the better of the Peloponnesians; all they had to do was recall Alcibiades and make some modifications to the democracy. [2] But many people spoke out against this and in defense of democracy, while others, Alcibiades's enemies, loudly protested that it would be quite wrong for a criminal like him to be recalled. And the Eumolpidae and the Heralds* brought up the matter of the Mysteries, for which he had been banished, and urged the people in the name of the gods not to bring him back. In the face of all these objections and protestations, Peisander stepped up and had each of the objectors come forward one by one while he asked them whether they expected the city to survive when the Peloponnesians had at least as many ships at sea as they did and were ready for action; when the cities in the Peloponnesian alliance now outnumbered theirs; and when the Peloponnesians were being funded by the King and Tissaphernes, while they had run out of money. Their only hope, he said, was if someone could persuade the King to support them instead. [3] And when they replied that under these circumstances they could hardly expect the city to survive, Peisander then spoke plainly. "All right, then," he said. "We're never going to gain the King as an ally unless we have a less extreme form of government and unless, contrary to the current system, office-holding is restricted to just a few people. Then the King will trust us, and in the face of the current crisis we won't be spending more time discussing constitutional matters than on survival. We can always change the constitution later, if there are aspects of it that we don't like. And we'll never gain the King as an ally unless we bring Alcibiades back. He's uniquely placed to make all this happen."

54. While he was talking, the assembled people reacted unfavorably to his insistence on oligarchy, but once Peisander had explained that there was no other way for the city to survive, they gave in, swayed by a combination of fear and the thought that changes could be made later. [2] They voted to send Peisander and ten others to arrange matters at their own discretion with Tissaphernes and Alcibiades. [3] Moreover, as Peisander had also succeeded in blackening Phrynichus's name, the people relieved both him and his colleague Scironides of their generalships, and sent Diomedon and Leon off to the fleet as their replacements. Since Peisander believed that Phrynichus was still opposed to the deal with Alcibiades, he had accused him, falsely, of betraying Iasus and Amorges.* [4] Peisander also approached all the cabals that already existed in the city (their purpose being to influence lawsuits and elections)* and encouraged them to unite, put their heads together, and come up with a viable plan for overthrowing the democracy. Then, once he had made all the other arrangements that the plot required, so that they could get moving as soon as the time came, he and his ten colleagues set out by sea to go and meet with Tissaphernes.

55. In this same winter, after Leon and Diomedon reached the Athenian fleet they launched an attack on Rhodes. They seized some Peloponnesian ships that had been hauled ashore, made a landing, and defeated the Rhodians who came to offer resistance, and then withdrew to Chalce and carried on the war from there rather than from Cos. It was a better place from which to spot the Peloponnesian fleet on the move anywhere. [2] Xenophantidas, a Laconian, also arrived in Rhodes, sent there from Chios by Pedaritus. He told the Peloponnesians of the completion of the Athenian outpost on Chios and said that Chios would be lost unless they came to help with the entire fleet, and they agreed to do as he asked. [3] Meanwhile, Pedaritus himself took a force of his mercenaries and all the available Chian soldiers and attacked the rampart that the Athenians had built to protect their ships. Pedaritus managed to gain control of a stretch of this rampart and of some beached ships, but when the Athenians emerged from their camp and fought back, they first routed the Chians and then defeated the rest of Pedaritus's troops. Pedaritus himself lost his life, as did many of the Chians, and a great deal of weaponry was captured. **56.** After this the Chians were blockaded on land and sea even more closely than before, and a terrible famine began to afflict the city.

When Peisander and the other Athenian envoys reached Tissaphernes they discussed the terms of the proposed treaty. [2] But Alcibiades was far from sure of Tissaphernes; the satrap was more afraid of the Peloponnesians than the Athenians, and still wanted to put into effect the strategy he had been learning from Alcibiades, of wearing down both sides. So Alcibiades came up with a scheme whereby Tissaphernes would make such enormous demands of the Athenians that a treaty would be out of the question. [3] In my opinion, however, Tissaphernes, too, wanted the talks to fail, in his case because of his fear of the Peloponnesians, and when Alcibiades realized that Tissaphernes was not going to agree to the terms anyway, he did not want the Athenians to get the impression that he had no influence on Tissaphernes; so instead he decided to make it seem as though Tissaphernes was fully on board and eager to conclude an agreement, and that it was the Athenians who were not making enough concessions. [4] Speaking on Tissaphernes's behalf, with the satrap present at the meeting, he kept escalating his demands in order to bring it about that, even though for a long time the Athenians agreed to them, ultimately they were responsible for the failure of the talks. First he demanded that they give up all Ionia, and then he added the nearby islands and other tracts of land. In the end, when the Athenians continued to raise no objections and they were already meeting for the third time, out of fear that his lack of influence over Tissaphernes would be exposed for all to see, he demanded that the Athenians allow the King to have shipbuilding facilities in the region and sail along what would be his own coastline wherever he wanted and with as many ships as he wanted. [5] That was the end of it. The Athenians could not concede so much; they left for Samos in a rage, feeling that they had been deceived by Alcibiades.

57. Immediately after this, in the same winter, Tissaphernes went to Caunus. He wanted the Peloponnesians to make Miletus their base rather than Rhodes, and then, after concluding a fresh treaty with them, one that was as expedient as possible, he would give them their maintenance allowance and reduce the friction between them. He was concerned that a shortage of supplies for so many ships might force the Peloponnesians to fight the Athenians—a battle he thought they would lose—or that the crews would desert the ships, and in either case the Athenians would have gained their objectives without any help from him. But his main fear was still that in their quest for food the Peloponnesians would plunder the mainland. [2] So in view of all these considerations and possibilities, and in keeping with his policy of maintaining a balance of power among the Greeks, he summoned the Peloponnesians to a meeting, gave them their maintenance allowance, and concluded a third treaty with them, as follows:

58. "In the thirteenth year of the reign of King Darius, and in the year of the ephorate of Alexippidas in Sparta, a treaty was concluded on the Meander plain between the Lacedaemonians and their allies, and Tissaphernes and Hieramenes and the sons of Pharnaces,* pertaining to the concerns of the King and those of the Lacedaemonians and their allies. [2] All the territory of the King that is in Asia shall

belong to the King, and the King shall manage it as he pleases.* [3] The Lacedaemonians and their allies are never to enter the King's territory with harmful intent, nor is the King ever to enter the territory of the Lacedaemonians or of their allies with harmful intent. [4] If any Lacedaemonian or any ally of the Lacedaemonians enters the King's territory with harmful intent, the Lacedaemonians and their allies are to stop them. And if anyone from the King's territory proceeds against the Lacedaemonians or their allies with harmful intent, the King is to stop them. [5] Tissaphernes is to provide maintenance for the ships that are currently present in accordance with the agreed terms until the King's ships arrive. [6] Once the King's ships have arrived, it shall be up to the Lacedaemonians and their allies to maintain their ships if they so choose. However, if they want Tissaphernes to maintain the ships for them, Tissaphernes is to do so, but at the end of the war the Lacedaemonians and their allies are to reimburse Tissaphernes with the full amount of money they received. [7] Once the King's ships have arrived, the ships of the Lacedaemonians and their allies, and the King's ships, are to prosecute the war together, in whatever way seems best to Tissaphernes and to the Lacedaemonians and their allies. If they decide to make peace with the Athenians, they are to do so jointly."

59. These were the terms of the treaty. Tissaphernes next began to lay the groundwork for bringing up the Phoenician ships, as stipulated in the treaty, and for doing everything else he had undertaken to do. He was anxious to be seen making a start, at least, on these arrangements.

60. Meanwhile, as winter was coming to an end, the Boeotians took Oropus;* the Athenians had a garrison there, but the town was betrayed to them by sympathizers. They were helped by men from Eretria as well as from Oropus itself. They were planning to get Euboea to revolt, and Oropus lay threateningly close to Eretria, so as long as it was an Athenian possession it was bound to make things extremely difficult for Eretria and the rest of Euboea if they revolted. [2] With Oropus in their hands, the Eretrians went to Rhodes and invited the Peloponnesians into Euboea. But the Peloponnesians were more interested in going to the help of Chios, which was having a hard time of it, and they put to sea from Rhodes with their entire fleet. [3] When they were near Triopium they spotted the Athenian ships in open water on their way from Chalce. Neither fleet launched an attack on the other, and the Athenians went to Samos, while the Peloponnesians went to Miletus, since it was now clear that it was no longer possible for them to go to the help of Chios without fighting the Athenians at sea. And so the winter came to an end and with it the twentieth year of the current war, the history of which was written by Thucydides.

61. The following year, right at the very beginning of spring, a Spartiate called Dercylidas was sent with a relatively small army overland to the Hellespont in order to get Abydus (a Milesian foundation) to revolt, and the Chians, whom Astyochus at this time was still unable to help, were so oppressed by the blockade that they had no choice but to fight a battle at sea. [2] While Astyochus was still in Rhodes, Leon, a Spartiate, had been sent to Chios from Miletus to take charge there after the death of Pedaritus. He was in the region because he had come with Antisthenes as his second-in-command. He went to Chios with twelve ships that had been on guard duty at Miletus—five ships from Thurii, four from Syracuse, one each from Anaea and Miletus, and his own ship. [3] The Chians made a sortie out of the town with all their available land forces and seized a strongpoint, and at the same time their thirty-six ships put to sea and engaged the Athenians' thirty-two. A fierce battle ensued in which the Chians and their allies were having the best of it, but when it began to grow dark they returned home.

62. Immediately after this, once Dercylidas had completed his overland march along the coast from Miletus, Abydus in the Hellespont revolted and went over to him and Pharnabazus, and two days later Lampsacus did the same. [2] When the news reached Strombichides, he swiftly left Chios with twenty-four ships, some of which were troop-carriers with hoplites on board, to see what he could do about the situation. The Lampsacenes made a sortie out of the town, but Strombichides defeated them, and Lampsacus, which was unwalled, easily fell to him. He treated their stores and slaves as plunder, but allowed the free population to return to their homes. Then he went to Abydus, but since it refused to surrender and his assaults failed to gain him the town, he sailed away to Sestus, a town on the Chersonese opposite Abydus that had once been in Persian hands.* He installed a garrison there with the job of protecting the entire Hellespont.

63. Meanwhile, the Chians were more or less masters of the sea, and when Astyochus and the Peloponnesians at Miletus heard about the sea battle and found out that Strombichides and his fleet had left, they were greatly encouraged. [2] Astyochus went to Chios with two ships, collected the fleet from there, and then led all these ships in an attack on Samos. But the Athenians, riven by mutual suspicion, did not put to sea and offer battle, so he returned to Miletus.

[3] The Athenians were suspicious of one another because, at about this time or a little earlier, the democracy had been overthrown in Athens. When Peisander and the other envoys returned to Samos after their meeting with Tissaphernes, they not only consolidated their control of the army, but also encouraged the most powerful of the Samians to seize power as an oligarchy with their help—despite the fact that the recent civil uprising in Samos had been triggered by the desire to avoid oligarchy.* [4] At the same time, the Athenians in Samos, after talking things over among themselves, had decided not to include Alcibiades in their conspiracy, seeing that he did not want oligarchy and was in fact ill suited for it. They decided to go it alone, since they were the ones who were already running the risk, and to try to find a way to maintain their impetus and at the same time persevere with the war. And they committed themselves to financing the war

and supplying anything else that was needed from their own personal resources, seeing that now they would be bearing the burden for their own good, not that of others.

64. So once they had summoned up the courage to pursue this course of action, they immediately dispatched Peisander and half of the envoys to Athens to arrange matters there, with instructions also to establish oligarchies in the subject cities where they stopped en route. The remaining envoys they sent here and there to other subject states, [2] and they sent Dieitrephes, who was at Chios but had been appointed governor of the Thraceward region, to take up his post. So when he arrived in Thasos he overthrew the democracy, [3] but less than two months after his departure the Thasians began to fortify their city, thinking that they no longer needed their oligarchy to be supported by the Athenians because they were expecting to be liberated by the Lacedaemonians any day. [4] In fact, some Thasians who had been driven out by the Athenians were spending their exile in the Peloponnese, and with the help of their friends in the city they were working very hard to acquire ships and arrange the secession of Thasos from Athens. The situation was accordingly perfect for their plans: the city was in safe hands, and the democracy that would have opposed them had been overthrown. [5] So for the Athenians who established the oligarchy in Thasos the outcome was the opposite of what they had wanted, and I dare say that the same applies to many other of the subject states as well. They gained a prudent form of government* and freedom of action, and then set a course for outright freedom in preference to the specious "orderly government" offered by the Athenians.

65. In the course of their voyage, Peisander and his colleagues overthrew democracies in the cities, according to plan, and from some places they also gained hoplites as military support. When they arrived in Athens, [2] they found that most of the work had already been done by the cabals. For instance, some of the younger men had banded together and furtively killed Androcles, a prominent democrat who had been one of those chiefly responsible for Alcibiades's banishment. They had two reasons in particular for killing him: first, that he was a leader of the people, but second, because they thought it would please Alcibiades, whom they expected to be recalled and to get Tissaphernes on Athens's side. They also dealt in the same way with others who were unsympathetic to their cause, by surreptitiously doing away with them. [3] And they had already publicly proposed that the only people who were to receive a stipend from the state were those serving in the armed forces, and that no more than five thousand men, those who were best able to benefit the state with their money and their persons, were to have a share in government.*

66. In fact, however, this was no more than propaganda for the masses, because the people who were making these changes also intended to form the city's administration. It is true that the popular assembly and the council chosen by lot still continued to meet, but it was the conspirators who decided what issues they considered. Moreover, the only people to address these meetings were the conspirators, and the content of their speeches had previously been approved by their fellow conspirators. [2] No one else raised any objections; everyone was afraid and could see how widespread the conspiracy was. And anyone who did speak out against them rapidly met with some form of convenient death. The perpetrators never had to submit to an inquiry and suspects were never punished; the general populace just remained passive. People were so terrified that they considered themselves lucky not to suffer violence even if they had kept a low profile. [3] They were cowed by their assumption that the conspiracy was far more widespread than it actually was, and the size of the city and the impossibility of knowing everyone prevented them from discovering the truth. [4] By the same token, it was also impossible for anyone who chafed at the situation to complain to someone else and, with their help, devise countermeasures, because if he did he might find that he had misjudged the person to whom he was going to speak or that he was a faithless friend. [5] Suspicion governed the ways in which the general populace interacted with one another, in case the person they were dealing with was one of the revolutionaries. After all, some of the conspirators were people whose conversion to oligarchy had been wholly unforeseeable. In fact, it was these men above all who were responsible for the mistrust ordinary people felt for one another and who contributed the most toward the security of the oligarchs by embedding mutual suspicion in the general populace.

67. It was at this juncture that Peisander and his colleagues arrived and immediately set about what remained to be done. The first thing they did was convene the people and propose that ten commissioners be chosen with full powers to draft legislation, and that after a specified interval, once this board had finished its work, it should present the people with its recommendations as to how the city was best to be governed. [2] Then, when the specified day arrived, they confined the assembly to the Colonus hill (which is a little over a mile from the city and the location of a sanctuary of Poseidon),* and the only recommendation the commissioners made was that any Athenian citizen should be permitted to make any proposal he liked with impunity,* and that any kind of attempt to undermine the speaker, such as accusing him of making an unconstitutional proposal, should be liable to severe penalties. [3] And then, of course, dissimulation came to an end, and the proposal was made that the offices as presently established and the pay for officers should be abolished. Instead, a presiding board of five was to be created with the job of choosing a hundred men, who would each co-opt another three in addition to himself; then these four hundred men were to constitute the council, with full powers to govern as they judged best, and furthermore would convene the Five Thousand as and when they saw fit.*

68. It was Peisander who made this proposal, and overall it was he who was most conspicuously committed to the overthrow of the democracy. But the person who put the plan together in such a way that it led up to this point, and who had devoted the most thought to it, was Antiphon. There was no one in Athens at the time more accomplished than Antiphon, nor was there anyone better at coming up with ideas and arguing for them, and although he chose not to address the popular assembly or any other public arena, he had a reputation for artfulness that made him suspect to the people. However, if anyone asked for his services,* he was uniquely able to help them hold their own either in court or in the popular assembly. [2] And when he was on trial for his life for his part in the oligarchy and had to speak for himself—this was at a later time, when the measures taken by the Four Hundred had been rescinded by the democracy and were judged to have been bad for the city—the defense speech he delivered was without doubt better than any other before or since.

[3] Phrynichus too showed himself to be exceptionally committed to the oligarchy. He was afraid of Alcibiades because he knew that he knew of all his intrigues with Astyochus at Samos, but he was sure that Alcibiades was unlikely ever to be restored to Athens by an oligarchy, so once he had taken the project on he proved to be utterly reliable in the face of the risks. [4] Another leader of the antidemocratic revolutionaries was Theramenes, son of Hagnon, a man who was equally capable of delivering a speech and forming policy. So, with the involvement of many intelligent men, it was not surprising that the endeavor went well, despite its radical nature. After all, it was no easy task to deprive the Athenian people of the freedom they had enjoyed for almost a hundred years since the overthrow of the tyrants, during which time not only had they not been anyone's subjects, but for over half of it they had been accustomed to rule others.

69. No one raised any objections at the assembly meeting and these proposals were ratified. As soon as the meeting came to an end the Four Hundred were conducted to the council chamber. They had arranged things as follows. Because of the enemy outpost at Decelea, the Athenians were continually under arms, either guarding the walls or on patrol. [2] So that day the oligarchs allowed all the soldiers who were not in on the plot to stand down as usual, while their accomplices were told to wait quietly, not close to where the weapons were stacked, but not too far away either, and if anyone tried to resist what was going on they were to get their weapons and put a stop to it. [3] There were also in Athens soldiers from Andros and Tenos, 300 from Carystus, and some of the Aeginetan settlers (some of those the Athenians had sent to populate the island),* and these troops received the same instructions. This was in fact exactly the job for which they had been brought to Athens, equipped with their own arms and armor. [4] Once they had received their instructions, the Four Hundred, each of whom had a concealed dagger, went to the council chamber, accompanied by the 120 young men whose services they relied on if circumstances called for violent action. They interrupted the councilors chosen by lot,* who were in the council chamber, and told them to take their pay and leave. They themselves brought them their pay for what remained of their term of office and gave it to them as they were on their way out of the chamber.

70. So this was how the Four Hundred took over the council chamber; the councilors withdrew without making a fuss, and the rest of the citizens were quiescent and disinclined to make trouble. On this occasion the Four Hundred used the lottery system to appoint their own prytaneis, and they duly acknowledged the gods with prayers and sacrifices as they took up office, but later they made sweeping changes to the democratic system. One thing they did not do, however, was bring the exiles back home, because they would have had to bring Alcibiades back as well, but† otherwise they went about the management of the city's affairs with all the power at their command. [2] They also killed a few people, whose removal suited their purposes, and imprisoned or banished others. And they sent a herald to Decelea to tell Agis, the Spartan king, that they wanted to make peace, and that since he would no longer be dealing with the fickle people, there was no reason for him not to be more receptive to the idea of coming to terms with them.

71. But in Agis's opinion the city was not yet quiescent;† the people would not so readily give up their long-standing freedom, he thought, and the sight of a sizable army would spur them to action. Nor was he at all certain at the time that the turmoil in the city was over. So in his response to the envoys sent by the Four Hundred he said nothing that might lead them to expect an agreement, and he sent for a large number of reinforcements from the Peloponnese. Shortly after their arrival, he came down from the hills with the garrison from Decelea and the newly arrived troops and marched right up to the walls of Athens. His hope was that in the ensuing confusion the Athenians would be more ready to submit on terms of the Lacedaemonians' choosing, or even that the commotion that was likely to occur owing to the internal and external threats would enable him to take the city without meeting any opposition. He was sure that the Long Walls would be unguarded and that he could not fail to capture them.

[2] However, when he drew near the city, the Athenians responded with perfect composure. They sent out their cavalry and some of their hoplites, light-armed troops, and archers; shot down any of Agis's men who came close to the walls; and gained possession of some of the enemy corpses and their weapons. Realizing his mistake, Agis withdrew his forces. [3] He and his men stayed where they were in Decelea, but he sent the reinforcements back home to the Peloponnese after they had been in the area for a few days. Following this incident, the Four Hundred still continued to send envoys to Agis. They found him more receptive now to their approach, and they took his advice and sent envoys also to Sparta to negotiate the peace treaty they desired.

72. They also sent ten men to Samos to reassure the army and to explain that the oligarchy had been established not to harm the city or its citizens, but for the overall safety of the state, and that political affairs were in the hands of five thousand men, not only four hundred, even though, as a result of campaigns and overseas service, the Athenians had never so far been faced with an issue of such importance that five thousand people had assembled to debate it.* [2] These ten men were given further instructions as to what they should say and were sent off as soon as the oligarchs were in power, because they were frightened that the naval mob would not readily tolerate living under

an oligarchic system, and that if trouble arose in Samos, it would end in Athens with their overthrow.*

Events proved this fear well founded. **73.** In Samos there was already a move to overthrow the oligarchy. While the Four Hundred were consolidating their position in Athens, the following developments had taken place in Samos: [2] Under the influence of Peisander, once he arrived, and of the Athenians in Samos who were his accomplices, those of the Samians who had recently risen up against the aristocrats on behalf of democracy changed sides. These former democrats, numbering about three hundred, conspired together and intended to attack their former associates as being democrats.* [3] One of the Athenians in Samos was Hyperbolus, a disreputable individual who had been ostracized from Athens,* not because people were concerned about how powerful and influential he was, but because his fellow citizens despised him and were embarrassed by him. Aided and abetted by one of the generals, Charminus, and some of the Athenians in Samos, the former democrats assassinated him as a way of convincing the Athenians of their seriousness. This was not the only such action they took along with Charminus and his associates, and they were getting ready to launch an attack on the democracy. [4] But the democrats got wind of the plot and warned two of the generals, Leon and Diomedon, whose tolerance of the oligarchy was reluctant because they enjoyed the respect of the people. They also told Thrasybulus and Thrasyllus—the former a trierarch, the latter a hoplite—and others whom they judged to be constant and particular opponents of the conspirators. They should not stand idly by, they said, while they themselves were destroyed and Samos was alienated from the Athenians, when it was entirely due to Samos that their empire had endured for so long.

[5] After receiving this information, the democrats approached some of the soldiers one by one and asked for their help in making sure that this did not happen. Most importantly, they approached the crew of the *Paralus*, who were all free Athenian citizens and always hostile to oligarchy, even when it was not the current regime. And

whenever Leon and Diomedon were away on some expedition, they made sure to leave their comrades with some ships for their protection. [6] So when the three hundred launched their attack, they met with resistance from these people, too—above all, from the crew of the *Paralus*—and victory went to the democrats. They killed about thirty of the three hundred and punished the three ringleaders with exile, but they granted an amnesty to the rest and from then on lived as fellow citizens with them under a democratic constitution.

74. The Samians and the army had as yet no idea that the Four Hundred were in power, and they quickly sent the *Paralus* off to Athens with Chaereas, son of Archestratus, on board; he was an Athenian citizen who had been a fervent supporter of the democratic uprising in Samos, and he was to deliver a report about events in Samos. [2] On their arrival the Four Hundred immediately imprisoned two or three men from the *Paralus* crew, confiscated their ship, transferred the rest of them to another ship, a troop-carrier, and assigned them to guard duty off Euboea. [3] But as soon as Chaereas realized what was going on he somehow managed to escape. He made his way back to Samos and delivered an exaggerated report to the army about all the terrible things that were taking place in Athens. He claimed that flogging was being used as a punishment for everyone, slave or free;* that it was impossible for anyone to speak out against the government; that their wives and children were suffering abusive treatment; and that the Four Hundred intended to arrest and imprison all the relatives of men serving on Samos who were not sympathetic to their cause, so that they could put them to death if the troops refused to submit. And these were far from being the only lies he told.

75. On hearing what Chaereas said, the initial impulse of the troops was to stone to death those who had been foremost in forming the oligarchy and even anyone who had played any part in it. But then, when men who were partisans of neither faction restrained them, and pointed out that with the enemy fleet lying nearby, and ready to engage, there was a good chance that, if they went ahead, the outcome would be total

ruination, the soldiers simmered down. [2] After this incident, Thrasybulus, son of Lycus, and Thrasyllus (the two men who had been foremost in the democratic uprising), now openly wanting to bring about a permanent regime change in Samos, had all the soldiers, including those who had been most involved in the oligarchy, swear the most solemn oaths to the effect that they would espouse democracy and promote concord, wholeheartedly prosecute the war against the Peloponnesians, and treat the Four Hundred as enemies and break off diplomatic relations with them. [3] All the Samians of military age also swore the same oath, and the Athenian forces cooperated with the Samians in everything and shared the consequences of the risks they were running. For it was their view that there was no place of refuge for either them or the Samians, and that if they were defeated, either by the Four Hundred or by the Peloponnesians at Miletus, it would be all over for them.

76. So now they were locked in a duel, with one side wanting to impose democracy on Athens and the other to impose oligarchy on the army. [2] The soldiers immediately convened an assembly at which they sacked their former generals and any suspect trierarchs and replaced them with fresh trierarchs and generals, beginning with Thrasybulus and Thrasyllus. [3] Various people stood up and offered encouraging advice, saying, for instance, that the fact that Athens had revolted from them was no cause for pessimism; it was a smaller number of men who had broken away from them, and they themselves were not just the majority but were also better off in respect of providing themselves with whatever they might need.* [4] After all, since they had the entire navy, they would force the cities of the empire to pay them just as if they were based in Athens. Their city, Samos, was very strong, and they reminded the assembled troops that in the war against Athens it had come very close to depriving the Athenians of their mastery of the sea.* As far as resisting the Peloponnesians was concerned, they had the same base of operations as before. And given their possession of the fleet, it was easier for them to procure supplies for themselves than it was for the city Athenians.

[5] Moreover, they said, it was thanks to the fact that they were manning this forward position on Samos that the city had so far retained control of the sea-approaches to Piraeus, and in fact† they were now in such a strong position that if the city Athenians refused to restore democracy, they would be more capable of excluding them from the sea than vice versa. [6] Besides, any contribution the city could make toward helping them get the better of the enemy was worth little or nothing; in losing it, they had lost nothing, because the soldiers on Samos were providing for themselves, and the city no longer had money to send. Nor did they have good advice to offer, which is the justification for the control exercised by a state over its army. In this respect, too, they said, the city Athenians had made a mistake when they had abolished the ancestral constitution. They themselves, however, were upholding it, and they would try to force the city Athenians to do the same. This meant that they were no worse off even for people who could offer good advice. [7] And then there was Alcibiades; if they granted him immunity and recalled him, he would eagerly furnish them with an alliance with the King. Finally and most importantly, in the event of complete failure in the war, since they had such a large number of ships there were many places of refuge where they would find cities and land.

77. This is a sample of the issues they discussed among themselves in assembly and the ways in which they raised one another's spirits, and it was not all talk: they were also making practical arrangements for prosecuting the war. And when the envoys sent to Samos by the Four Hundred reached Delos and heard about all this, they stayed there and took no action.

78. Meanwhile, the Peloponnesian soldiers serving in the navy at Miletus were in full cry as well, claiming among themselves that their cause was being ruined by Astyochus and Tissaphernes. They were angry at Astyochus for refusing to engage the Athenians at sea—for having avoided battle not only earlier, during the time when they still had superior strength and the Athenian fleet was small, but also now, when the Athenians were said to be at odds with one another and had not yet concentrated their ships in one place. Instead, by awaiting the arrival of the Phoenician ships that were to be sent by Tissaphernes—though their arrival seemed to be more a promise than a reality—they were risking attrition. And then they were angry with Tissaphernes not just for his failure to bring up these ships, but also because he was undermining the efficiency of the fleet, by not giving them their maintenance allowance regularly or in full. They argued that they should fight it out at sea, with no further delay. The Syracusans were particularly insistent on this.

79. When Astyochus and the allies became aware of these mutterings, they met and decided to fight it out at sea, since they had been informed of the turmoil in Samos. They put to sea with all their 112 ships and headed for Mycale, having ordered the Milesians to make their way there overland.* [2] The Athenians' 82 ships from Samos happened to be moored at Glauce on the Mycale headland, at which point Samos is only a short distance away from the mainland, and when they saw the Peloponnesian ships bearing down on them they retreated to Samos. They did not think that with their numbers they were in a position to risk all in a battle. [3] Besides, they had received advance warning from Miletus that the enemy was eager to engage them, so they had already sent a messenger to Strombichides, and they were awaiting his arrival from the Hellespont with the ships from Chios that had gone to relieve Abydus. [4] So the Athenians retreated to Samos, and the Peloponnesians put in at Mycale and encamped there, along with their land force of Milesians and some of the local inhabitants. [5] The next day, as they were about to sail to Samos, they were informed that Strombichides had arrived with the ships from the Hellespont, and they immediately sailed back to Miletus. [6] With the addition of these ships to their fleet, it was the Athenians' turn to want to fight a decisive sea battle, and they launched an assault on Miletus with 108 ships. But no one put out to sea against them, so they returned to Samos.

80. The Peloponnesians refused to engage the Athenians because they doubted that they were a match for the full fleet, and they were also uncertain where they would find money to maintain their own sizable fleet, especially as Tissaphernes was proving to be a bad paymaster. So this same summer, immediately after this episode, they dispatched 40 ships to Pharnabazus under Clearchus, son of Ramphias, in accordance with the order he had originally been given in the Peloponnese.* [2] Pharnabazus had been inviting them to come and was expressing his willingness to pay for the maintenance of the fleet, and at the same time Byzantium had approached them with a view to rebellion from Athens. [3] So these 40 Peloponnesian ships set out across the open sea to avoid being seen by the Athenians during their voyage, but they were caught in a storm. Clearchus and most of the ships made land at Delos and later returned to Miletus—except that Clearchus went to the Hellespont overland to take up his command—while the rest, ten ships under the command of Helixus of Megara, made it safely to the Hellespont and enabled the revolt of Byzantium. [4] After this, once the Athenians at Samos found out about these developments, they sent ships to the Hellespont to supplement those they already had on guard there, and a minor engagement took place at sea off Byzantium, involving 8 ships on either side.

81. Thrasybulus still maintained—as he had done constantly since bringing about the regime change in Samos—that Alcibiades should be recalled, and he, along with the other Athenian leaders in Samos, eventually persuaded the army in an assembly to agree with him. Once they had voted for Alcibiades's restoration and had granted him immunity, Thrasybulus sailed to Tissaphernes and brought Alcibiades back with him to Samos. In his view, they would not survive unless Alcibiades could get Tissaphernes to change sides from the Peloponnesians to them. [2] An assembly was convened at which Alcibiades first complained about the disastrous effects on himself personally of his exile from Athens and moaned about all he had lost. Then, when he turned to public affairs, he spoke at length and made them very optimistic for the future. He greatly exaggerated the extent of his influence over Tissaphernes in an attempt to instill fear in the oligarchic leaders in Athens and to make it more likely that the cabals there would be disbanded. And he further intended his words to gain him more respectful treatment from the Athenians in Samos and boost their morale, and to make the enemy suspicious of Tissaphernes and crush any further hopes they might have of his help. [3] So Alcibiades boastfully promised the following huge benefits: He said Tissaphernes had assured him that as long as he had any property left—and provided that the Athenians earned his trust—they would not lack for maintenance, not even if he eventually had to turn his own bed into money.* He also said Tissaphernes had promised to deliver the Phoenician ships, which were already at Aspendus,* to the Athenians rather than to the Peloponnesians. But Tissaphernes, he said, would trust the Athenians only if he, Alcibiades, were safe and sound, restored to the Athenian fold, and acting as guarantor of his good behavior.

82. This was far from all that Alcibiades said, and when the assembled Athenian troops had heard him out they immediately elected him general alongside those already in office and put themselves entirely in his hands. Not one of them would have exchanged his immediate hopes of safety and revenge on the Four Hundred for anything, and they were now ready even to sail against Piraeus, owing to the contempt for the enemy with which Alcibiades's words had inspired them for the moment. [2] But, despite all the many people who were pressing for it, Alcibiades resolutely forbade them from sailing against Piraeus, which would entail leaving their nearer enemies in their rear. The war must be their priority, he said, and the first order of business was for him, now as their elected general, to sail to Tissaphernes and make arrangements for how to proceed with it. [3] And he set off straight after this assembly in order to make it seem that he and Tissaphernes consulted each other over everything, and also because he wanted Tissaphernes to give him more respect, once he knew that he had now been elected general and was in a position to do him both good and harm.

In other words, Alcibiades was using Tissaphernes to intimidate the Athenians and the Athenians to intimidate Tissaphernes.

83. When the Peloponnesians in Miletus learned of Alcibiades's restoration they became far more suspicious of Tissaphernes. This was not the first time they had come to doubt him: [2] at the time of the Athenian attack on Miletus (the one where they refused to put to sea and engage the Athenians),* Tissaphernes had become much more reluctant to give them money for the fleet, and now Alcibiades's elevation had intensified the hatred they had felt for the satrap even earlier. [3] As they had before, the soldiers—and not just the rank and file, but some of the others as well, important people—began to huddle together and consider the situation, given that they had never received their pay in full; it was always short, and irregular at that. Either a decisive battle should be fought at sea, they said, or they should be moved to a place where they would be given their maintenance allowance; otherwise the crews would desert. And they put all the blame on Astyochus, who, they said, was accommodating himself to Tissaphernes's whims for private gain.

84. While they were thinking along these lines, the following fracas took place involving Astyochus. [2] Insofar as the Syracusan and Thurian crews were largely made up of free men, they were also the most forthright in confronting Astyochus and demanding their pay. His response was more than a little obdurate, and he threatened even Dorieus as he was speaking on behalf of his men and raised his swagger stick against him. [3] When the massed troops saw this they did what naval types tend to do and furiously rushed at Astyochus, with the intention of stoning him. He avoided being stoned, however—he had seen them coming and sought refuge at an altar—and the mob broke up.

[4] Meanwhile, the Milesians launched a stealthy attack on the fortress that Tissaphernes had built at Miletus, captured it, and expelled his garrison. This met with the approval of the allies, and especially the Syracusans, [5] but Lichas was unhappy with it and said that all the inhabitants of the King's land, including the Milesians,

should up to a point accept their subservience to Tissaphernes and curry his favor until the war was well and truly over. This and other similar actions of his made the Milesians angry with him, and when later he fell ill and died they refused to let the Lacedaemonians who were there bury him where they wanted.

85. At the time of this clash of wills, with the Peloponnesians at odds with both Astyochus and Tissaphernes over the conduct of the war, Mindarus, Astyochus's successor as navarch, arrived from Sparta. He took over the command and Astyochus set out for home. [2] But Tissaphernes sent one of his agents, a bilingual Carian called Gaulites, along with him as an envoy. His job was to denounce the Milesian capture of the fortress and also to speak in defense of Tissaphernes. Milesians, as Tissaphernes knew, were on their way to Sparta specifically to complain about him, and they were accompanied by Hermocrates, who intended to prove that Tissaphernes was ruining the Lacedaemonian cause with Alcibiades's help and was playing a double game. [3] Tissaphernes and Hermocrates always quarreled bitterly whenever the issue of the payment of the crews came up, and eventually, after Hermocrates had been banished from Syracuse and other Syracusan generals had arrived at Miletus to take charge of their contingent of ships—these generals were Potamis, Myscon, and Demarchus— Tissaphernes inveighed against Hermocrates much more than before, now that he was stateless, and among other accusations he said that Hermocrates's hostility toward him dated from an occasion when Hermocrates had asked him for some money and been refused. [4] So Astyochus, the Milesians, and Hermocrates sailed off to Sparta; Alcibiades had already returned from Tissaphernes to Samos.

86. The Four Hundred's envoys, who had earlier been sent to reassure the troops in Samos and justify the oligarchy to them, arrived from Delos after Alcibiades's return. An assembly was convened and they tried to speak, [2] but at first the troops refused to let them and called for those who were trying to overthrow the democracy to be put to death. They eventually quieted down, however, and gave them a hearing. [3] And the envoys told them that the purpose of the revolution was Athens's preservation, not its destruction. Nor did the Four Hundred intend to surrender the city to the enemy; if they had wanted to do that, the invasion of Attica, which had taken place when they were already in power, would have been the perfect opportunity. They asserted that none of the Five Thousand would be debarred from a political role in his turn, and that their families were not being harmed in any way, let alone being treated abusively, as the liar Chaereas had claimed. There had been no disruption to people's lives, but every individual was still in possession of his own property. [4] That was far from all they said, but the assembled troops were in no mood to listen. They angrily expressed various opinions, but the dominant theme was that they should sail against Piraeus.

Alcibiades is widely regarded as having on this occasion, for the first time, done something that was of unparalleled benefit to Athens. If the Athenians in Samos had carried out their intention of sailing against their fellow citizens, there could be no doubt that the enemy would immediately have gained Ionia and the Hellespont—but he checked them. [5] No other single individual could have restrained the mob under these circumstances, but Alcibiades not only dissuaded them from sailing against Athens, but also rebuked those who were taking out their anger on the envoys for personal reasons and made them desist. [6] And it was he who responded to the envoys before sending them back home. He said that he had no objection to the Five Thousand wielding power, but that the Four Hundred should be deposed, and that the council should be reconstituted on its former lines, with five hundred members. And he said that if the measures that had been taken to curtail expenses meant that the armed forces were receiving more of their maintenance allowance, they had his wholehearted approval. [7] In general, he told them to persevere with the war and not make any concessions to the enemy. After all, he said, as long as Athens was safe they could reasonably hope to reach an agreement with their fellow citizens, but if either they in Samos or the city Athenians ever came to grief, there would be no one left with whom to be reconciled.

[8] A delegation from Argos was also present; they had come to assure the Athenian democracy in Samos of their support. Alcibiades thanked them and sent them back home with the request that the Argives make themselves available if called on. [9] These envoys had come with the crew of the *Paralus*, who had earlier been ordered by the Four Hundred to patrol Euboea in a troop-carrier. They had been given the job of taking some Athenian envoys (Laispodias, Aristophon, and Melesias) to Sparta on a mission for the Four Hundred. But when they put in at Argos in the course of their voyage, they seized the envoys, whom they regarded as ringleaders in the overthrowing of the democracy, and handed them over to the Argives. And then, instead of returning to Athens, they conveyed the envoys from Argos to Samos in the trireme they had been assigned.

87. This same summer, just when Peloponnesian anger with Tissaphernes was coming to a head for various reasons, but especially because of Alcibiades's restoration, which to their mind proved that he was collaborating with the Athenians, Tissaphernes, in an obvious attempt to allay their doubts about him, got ready to go to Aspendus and fetch the Phoenician fleet, and he asked Lichas to accompany him. The fleet would not be neglected, he said, because he would order his adjutant, Tamos, to maintain it while he was away. [2] Now, accounts vary, and it is not easy to be sure what he had in mind when he went to Aspendus or why, after going there, he did not bring the ships back with him. [3] There is no doubt that 147 Phoenician ships got as far as Aspendus, but there are all kinds of conjectures as to why they never arrived. Some say that Tissaphernes's purpose in leaving was to continue his planned attrition of the Peloponnesian fleet; at any rate, Tamos, whom he had left in charge, was considerably worse than him at providing the maintenance allowance. Others say that he had the Phoenicians come to Aspendus only in order to extract money from them for their discharge, because he never had any intention of making use of them in the first place. Yet others say he was prompted by the fact that the outcry against him had reached Sparta, and in order to clear his name he wanted to demonstrate that the ships really had been manned and made ready.

[4] To me, however, it seems transparently obvious that his reason for failing to bring the ships back with him was that he wanted to continue the attrition and curbing of the Greeks. He wanted them to grind each other down while he was making his way to Aspendus and wasting time, and he wanted to keep the two sides equal, rather than strengthening one of them over the other by providing it with reinforcements. After all, if he had wanted to, there can surely be no doubt that he could have brought the war to an end by turning up with the ships. In all probability he would have given the fleet and victory to the Lacedaemonians, who, even as things stood, were no longer inferior to the Athenians at sea but a match for them. [5] And he is especially convicted by the excuse he gave for not bringing the ships. He claimed that the fleet that had been assembled was not as large as the King had ordered—but in that case the King would surely have been all the more grateful to him for having spent less money and for achieving the same result with a lesser force. [6] Anyway, whatever his intentions were, Tissaphernes went to Aspendus and met up with the Phoenicians, and in response to his request for a colleague on his voyage to fetch the ships, the Peloponnesians sent Philippus, a Lacedaemonian, with two triremes.

88. When it came to Alcibiades's attention that Tissaphernes was on his way to Aspendus, he, too, set out for there, with thirteen ships. He promised the Athenians at Samos that his mission would serve them well and make them more secure, because he would either bring the Phoenician ships back for them or at least make sure that they did not go to the Peloponnesians. He had probably known for some time that Tissaphernes had no intention of bringing the ships back, and by giving the Peloponnesians the impression that Tissaphernes was his and the Athenians' friend, he wanted to drive as wide a wedge as possible between him and the Peloponnesians, to increase the pressure on him to come over to their side. So he put to sea and headed east straight for Phaselis and Caunus.

89. When the envoys sent by the Four Hundred arrived back in Athens from Samos and reported that Alcibiades had told them to stand firm and make no concessions to the enemy, and that he had also pronounced himself very optimistic about both reconciling them with the army on Samos and getting the better of the Peloponnesians, they considerably raised the spirits of a great many of the oligarchs, who had been discontented before and would gladly have abandoned the whole enterprise if they could have done so safely. [2] This majority now began to meet among themselves and to voice their many criticisms of the state of affairs. The leaders were people who were office-holders and centrally involved in the oligarchy, such as Theramenes, son of Hagnon, and Aristocrates, son of Scelias, and others who had gained preeminent positions in the administration. Now, however, since they were afraid (as they said) of what Alcibiades and the army in Samos might do, and were worried in case those who were making overtures to Sparta harmed the city in some way without the consent of the majority of their colleagues, they thought† they should get rid of the most extreme form of oligarchic government, demonstrate that the Five Thousand existed in reality and not merely in name, and establish a more equitable political system.

[3] This was the form of government for which they argued, but in pushing for the kind of conditions that are almost certain to bring down an oligarchy that has emerged from a democracy, most of them were motivated by personal ambition. For from the very first day when an oligarchy is established, every one of its members demands not just to be not equal to the others, but even by far their superior, whereas under the democratic system of filling offices it is easier for someone who loses out to accept the result, consoling himself with the thought that he lost out to people who were not his peers.* [4] However, what most obviously gave the dissidents their impetus was the strength of

Alcibiades's position in Samos, in combination with their belief that the oligarchy would not last, and so a competition arose among them, with each man striving to be the principal champion of the people.

90. A number of the leading members of the Four Hundred were among those most opposed to the kind of political system the dissidents were proposing. They included Phrynichus (the man who as general in Samos had earlier clashed with Alcibiades), Aristarchus (who had been an ardent opponent of democracy for longer than anyone else), Peisander, Antiphon, and others of the most influential men in the city. Earlier—as soon as they were in power, in fact, and then when Samos had seceded from them and become democratic—they had been sending some of their own people to Sparta and had been committed to making peace; they had also been fortifying the place called Eetionea. And now, when their envoys returned from Samos, they intensified their efforts, since they could see that people generally and some of their own number who had previously seemed reliable were turning against them. [2] They were worried not only about the situation in Athens, but about Samos, too, and so they hurriedly dispatched a twelve-man delegation, including Antiphon and Phrynichus, to Sparta with instructions to reach an accommodation with the Lacedaemonians on any terms as long as they were even somewhat tolerable.

[3] Meanwhile, they focused even more of their energy on the fortification of Eetionea. The purpose of the fortification—as admitted by Theramenes and his associates—was not so much to stop the Samos Athenians from entering Piraeus if they launched an attack by sea, but to allow the enemy to enter at will with ships and land their forces. [4] Eetionea is a breakwater projecting from Piraeus, situated right at the entrance to the harbor. So the purpose of the fortifications, which incorporated an already existing wall facing inland, was to enable the place to command the approach from the sea with only a few men stationed there. It could serve this purpose because both the old wall facing inland and the new wall that was being built facing the sea ended at the same point, at the northern tower of the pair

that guarded the narrow mouth of the harbor. [5] They also walled off a stoa—the largest one in Piraeus, which lay immediately adjacent to the new fortifications—and took it under their control. Then they made it illegal for anyone to sell grain from any other location; both existing stocks of grain and new imports were to be stored there and brought out for sale from there.

91. Theramenes had been decrying this fortification for quite some time, and after the envoys had returned from Sparta without having made any progress toward a peace agreement for the Athenian people as a whole, he even claimed that this fortification could well prove to be the ruination of Athens. [2] He based his argument on the coincidental fact that at just this time forty-two ships, which the Euboeans had been requesting from the Peloponnese, were already lying at anchor off Las in Laconia, being made ready for their voyage to Euboea. The fleet included Italian ships from Taras and Locri, and a few from Sicily, and was under the command of a Spartiate, Agesandridas, son of Agesandrus. Theramenes claimed that the mission of these ships was to help not Euboea but the men who were fortifying Eetionea, and that if the Athenians were not careful, they would be lost before they knew it. [3] And in fact something of this sort was being contemplated by the men he was denouncing; his claim was not mere slander. What the extreme oligarchs wanted above all was to retain power in Athens and rule the allies as well. Failing that, they wanted, while preserving their oligarchy, to be left in possession of the ships and fortifications that would allow them to be independent. And if that too was denied them, they wanted to avoid being the first in line for execution by a reconstituted democracy; rather than that, they would bring the enemy in and come to an agreement whereby they gave up their fortifications and ships and left Athens to the mercy of the enemy, as long as they were granted immunity and got away with their lives. **92.** That is why they pushed ahead so determinedly with the building of these fortifications, which had postern gates and entranceways for letting in the enemy, and why they wanted to complete the work in good time.

[2] Now, up to this point it had been a matter of people meeting secretly in small groups and talking among themselves, but then, after returning from his mission to Sparta, Phrynichus was struck down in a premeditated assault by one of the frontier guards; the attack took place in the agora, at its busy time in the late morning, not far from the council chamber, which he had just left. Phrynichus died instantly and his assassin escaped, but his accomplice, an Argive, was seized and tortured by the Four Hundred. However, he revealed the names of none of the originators of the plot; all he said was that a large number of people used to meet at the house of the commander of the frontier guards and in other houses. But no further disruption followed the incident, so at this point Theramenes, Aristocrates, and their sympathizers among the Four Hundred themselves and among outsiders grew more confident and began to act openly.

[3] The particular trigger was that the ships had left Las; they had sailed around to Epidaurus, and with that as their base they had overrun Aegina. In Theramenes's view, it was hardly likely that if they had been destined for Euboea they would have sailed across the gulf to Aegina and then back to anchor at Epidaurus unless they had come for precisely the purposes that he had constantly been denouncing. Inaction, he said, was no longer possible. [4] So after much rebellious talk and the voicing of suspicions, Theramenes and his associates finally turned to action. Aristocrates was at Eetionea, serving as a taxiarch in charge of his own tribe, and he and the hoplites who were working on the fortifications arrested Alexicles, a general appointed by the oligarchs who had been especially involved with the cabals, and imprisoned him in a safe house. [5] It is true that they were aided in arresting Alexicles by others, among them the commander of the frontier guards stationed on the Munychia hill, a man called Hermon; but the most significant aspect of the affair was that it was the will of the rank-and-file hoplites.

[6] When the arrest was reported to the Four Hundred, who happened to be in session in the council chamber, all those who deplored it

were immediately ready to arm themselves, and they threatened Theramenes and his associates. But Theramenes warded off their threats by declaring himself ready to go with them immediately and help to secure Alexicles's release. He took one of the generals who shared his views and set out for Piraeus, with Aristarchus and some of the young cavalrymen as an escort. [7] There was considerable uncertainty, of the kind guaranteed to cause fear, because those based in Athens thought that Piraeus was already in the hands of the hoplites and that Alexicles's arrest had been followed by his execution, while the men based in Piraeus were expecting an imminent attack from those in the city. [8] The older men were trying to stop people in the city from running around in search of weaponry, while Thucydides of Pharsalus, who represented Athenian interests there and happened to be in Athens, determinedly blocked the path of every individual he met and loudly warned them that they were in danger of destroying their city, given that the enemy was awaiting his opportunity nearby. And at last people did quiet down and refrained from doing violence to one another.

[9] When Theramenes, who was himself one of the generals, reached Piraeus, he expressed his anger at the hoplites, or at least he shouted at them, but Aristarchus and those who were in the opposite camp from Theramenes were genuinely angry. [10] Most of the hoplites, however, became actively confrontational and showed no signs of repenting. They demanded an answer from Theramenes as to whether he thought that Eetionea was being fortified for a good purpose or it would be better if the walls were demolished. And when he replied that if they wanted to tear down the walls, that was what he wanted too, the hoplites, joined by many people from Piraeus, promptly climbed up onto the walls and began to demolish them. [11] The call had gone out to people at large that anyone who wanted to see the Five Thousand in power rather than the Four Hundred should get to work. Even now they were still covering themselves by speaking of the Five Thousand; they did not dare to say outright "anyone who wants to see the people back in power," because if the Five Thousand

actually existed it might be dangerous for anyone to carelessly talk of "the people" within someone else's hearing. That was why the Four Hundred did not want the Five Thousand either to exist or to be exposed as nonexistent. If it existed, such a large number of participants in political processes would, in their view, be equivalent to outright democracy; and as long as people were uncertain whether or not it existed they would fear one another.

93. The next day, despite the fact that they had been unsettled by these events, the Four Hundred assembled in the council chamber. The hoplites in Piraeus released Alexicles, the man they had arrested, and finished demolishing the fortifications. Then they went to the Theater of Dionysus near Munychia, where they halted and held an assembly. Once they had decided on a course of action, they immediately marched into Athens, where they halted again, this time in the sanctuary of the Dioscuri.* [2] Some representatives of the Four Hundred came to them and spoke to them individually, trying to persuade those whom they judged to be reasonable people to take no action themselves and to restrain the others. They said they would publish a list of the names of the Five Thousand, and that the council of four hundred would be made up of men from this pool, serving in rotation and chosen in a manner to be decided by the Five Thousand. And they asked them in the meantime not to do anything that would seriously harm the city or drive it into the enemy's hands. [3] After many such arguments had been presented to not a few of their number, the crowd of hoplites became calmer than the day before, and they began to worry less about their own safety than that of the state as a whole.* So they agreed to convene an assembly on a specified day in the sanctuary of Dionysus to discuss how to restore concord in the city.

94. But when the day of the assembly arrived† and almost everyone had gathered there, it was reported that the forty-two ships commanded by Agesandridas had left Megara and were sailing past Salamis. There was not a man there in the crowd who did not think that the ships were heading for the Eetionea fortress, just as Theramenes and his associates had been saying all along, and it seemed a blessing that it had already been demolished. [2] Now, Agesandridas may have spent time in and around Epidaurus because of some prearranged agreement, but it is likely that he was also lingering there because of the conflict in Athens, hoping to be able to put in an appearance at a critical moment. [3] But as soon as the Athenians received the news, every available man ran down to Piraeus, thinking that their domestic conflict paled to insignificance beside the immediate threat of war launched by the enemy, who was now close to their harbor. Some embarked on the ships that were already afloat, others launched more ships, and yet others went to defend the walls and the mouth of the harbor.

95. The Peloponnesian ships bypassed Piraeus, however, and after rounding Sunium they anchored between Thoricus and Prasiae, and then later moved on to Oropus.* [2] The Athenians had no time to lose. They sent ships to Eretria under the command of the general Thymochares, but they were forced to make use of crews who had not had time to be welded into cohesive units, given the internal divisions in the city and their urgent need to go to the defense of a place of such critical importance—for Euboea meant everything to them now that they were excluded from Attica*—with as little delay as possible. [3] Once they arrived there and joined up with the ships that were already stationed at Euboea, there were thirty-six of them. They were compelled to fight right away, because Agesandridas led his fleet out to sea from Oropus after his men had breakfasted. There is only about seven miles of sea between Eretria and Oropus, [4] so as soon as Agesandridas set out against them, the Athenians began to organize the manning of their ships as well, in the belief that the crews were close to the ships. But in fact they were getting food for their breakfasts—and not from the marketplace (because the Eretrians had made sure that there was nothing for sale there), but from houses at the far edge of the town. The Eretrians had done this to increase the time it would take for the Athenian ships to be manned, which would allow the Peloponnesians to attack before the Athenians were ready and force them to put to sea whatever their state of preparedness. Moreover, it was the Eretrians who had signaled Oropus when it was time for the Peloponnesians to set out.

[5] So the Athenians were relatively unprepared when they put to sea and engaged the enemy just outside the harbor of Eretria. Nevertheless, for a short while they managed to hold their own, but then they turned to flight and were harried onto the shore. [6] The men who suffered worst were those who sought refuge in Eretria in the belief that it was a friendly town: they were slaughtered by the local inhabitants. But those who got inside the fortress that the Athenians held in Eretria survived, as did the ships that went to Chalcis. [7] The Peloponnesians captured twenty-two Athenian ships. The crews they either killed or took prisoner, and they set up a trophy. And before long they had induced all of Euboea to revolt except for Oreus,* which was securely in Athenian hands, and had established control over the island as a whole.

96. When the news of what had happened in Euboea reached the Athenians, their consternation was greater than ever before. Nothing— not even the Sicilian disaster, which had seemed so devastating at the time—had ever made them so afraid. [2] This was of course a perfectly reasonable reaction. The army in Samos had rebelled from them; they had no more ships or crews to man them; the city was riven by factional strife and there was no telling when civil war might break out; and now, on top of all that, this catastrophe had occurred and they had lost ships, but more crucially Euboea, which was of more practical importance to them than Attica.

[3] But what disturbed them more than anything else was what was closest to home—the possibility that the enemy might be bold enough to capitalize on their victory by immediately sailing against their port, Piraeus, which now had no ships to defend it. In fact, they expected the enemy at any moment. [4] And if the Peloponnesians had been bolder they could easily have done just that. Even the near presence of their ships would have considerably aggravated the divisions in the city, and if they had stayed and put Piraeus under a blockade they would have left the fleet in Ionia no choice but to come to the relief of their kinfolk and

their city, even though they considered the oligarchs their enemy. And in that case the Hellespont, Ionia, all the islands east of Euboea, and pretty much the entire Athenian empire would have been theirs. [5] This was by no means the only occasion when the Lacedaemonians proved to be the most convenient enemies for the Athenians to face.* The point is that the two peoples had entirely different characters—the one quick and the other slow, the one enterprising and the other risk-averse—and this benefited the Athenians a great deal, especially in the context of their possession of a naval empire. The point was proved by the Syracusans: they were most similar to the Athenians in character and were the most effective of their enemies.

97. Be that as it may, despite all their troubles, in response to the news the Athenians set about finding crews for twenty ships and convened an assembly, the first of which was held immediately on the hill known as the Pnyx, which had also been the regular meeting place earlier.* At this assembly, they deposed the Four Hundred and voted to hand executive power over to the Five Thousand, defined as those who could provide their own arms and armor,* and they decreed that no officeholders were to receive a salary from the state, on pain of being laid under a curse. [2] Other assemblies followed in quick succession, at which they voted for the institution of a board of legal commissioners and passed other constitutional measures. And this was the first time, at any rate in my lifetime, when the Athenians seem to have had a particularly fine political system. It was a judicious blend that took account of the interests of both the few and the many, and this was the chief factor that made it possible for the city to recover from the dire condition into which it had fallen.* [3] They also voted to recall Alcibiades and others of his associates, and they sent word to him and the army in Samos urging them to respond to his reinstatement by playing an active role in the new regime.

98. While all these changes were being put into effect, Peisander, Alexicles, and all the leading oligarchs withdrew to Decelea. Aristarchus was the exception. Since he was one of the generals, he quickly

Book Eight: 96–99

gathered some of the most barbarous of the archers and marched to Oenoe. [2] This was an Athenian fort on the border with Boeotia, and at the time a volunteer force of Corinthians had it under siege, along with a contingent of Boeotians whose help they had requested. The Corinthians were retaliating for a defeat they had suffered at the hands of the Oenoe garrison, when some of their men were killed as they were on their way home from Decelea. [3] After conferring with the Corinthians and Boeotians, Aristarchus tricked the Oenoe garrison by saying that the Athenian authorities had come to terms with the Lacedaemonians, and that they had to hand the place over to the Boeotians because that was one of the conditions of the treaty. They trusted him—he was a general, after all, and the siege had prevented them from finding out what was going on in Athens—so they left the fort with a guarantee of safe conduct. [4] So this was how Oenoe fell and the Boeotians gained it, and how in Athens the oligarchy came to an end and with it civil unrest.

99. This summer, at about the same time, the Peloponnesians at Miletus were roused into action. None of the men assigned by Tissaphernes when he went to Aspendus to give them their maintenance allowance were coming up with the money, nor so far was there any sign of the Phoenician ships or Tissaphernes—in fact, Philippus, the man who had been sent along with Tissaphernes, had written to Mindarus, the navarch, to tell him not only that the ships were not going to come, but also that Tissaphernes was playing the Lacedaemonians false. (The letter had been coauthored by Hippocrates, a Spartiate who had gone to Phaselis.) Moreover, Pharnabazus was inviting them to come; he was just as eager as Tissaphernes to gain the Peloponnesian fleet and get the rest of the Athenian cities in his domain to revolt, since he expected this to do him considerable good. So under these circumstances, Mindarus carefully made all the arrangements and then, withholding the order until the last minute, so that the Athenians in Samos would not get to hear about his plan, he set out from Miletus with seventy-three ships and headed for the Hellespont. Sixteen of his ships had gone there earlier in the summer and had been wreaking havoc in part of the Chersonese. However, a storm forced him to shelter at Icaros, where the unfavorable sailing conditions kept him for five or six days, and then he went to Chios.

100. When Thrasyllus found out that Mindarus had set out from Miletus, he, too, immediately put to sea, leaving from Samos with fifty-five ships and hastening to get to the Hellespont first. [2] On hearing that Mindarus was at Chios and likely to stay there for a while, he posted lookouts on both Lesbos and the opposite coast of the mainland, so that he would know if the ships moved in any direction. Meanwhile, he sailed to Methymna and told the inhabitants to be ready to supply him with barley and the other provisions he would need, because, if he was there long enough, he planned to attack Chios by sea from Lesbos. [3] Also, since Eresus on Lesbos had revolted, he wanted to sail there and see if he could take it. Some of the most influential aristocrats among the Methymnaeans, who had been banished, had brought over from Cyme about fifty hoplites who were sympathetic to their cause, and had hired a force of mercenaries from the mainland numbering about three hundred in all; they were commanded by Anaxarchus, a Theban, who was serving because of the kinship between Thebes and Lesbos. At first they had tried to gain Eresus by direct assault, but they were repulsed by the Athenian garrison from Mytilene, which had arrived in good time. But then, after they had lost a battle outside the town and been driven off, they returned through the mountains and got it to rebel.

[4] So Thrasyllus planned to sail against Eresus with all the available ships and assault the town. Thrasybulus was already there as well. He had sailed from Samos with five ships when news came that the exiles had crossed over from the mainland, but he arrived after the town had rebelled, and so he had gone and anchored nearby. [5] The Athenian forces were supplemented also by two ships that were on their way home from the Hellespont and by the Methymnaean fleet. In all they had sixty-seven ships, and they were getting

ready to try to capture Eresus with the troops from these ships, employing siege devices or whatever it took.

101. Meanwhile, after two days spent stocking up on provisions, and once his men had been paid three Chian fortieths* each by the Chians, Mindarus and the Peloponnesian ships left in a hurry on the third day of their stay on the island. They did not sail across the open sea, because they were worried about meeting the Athenian ships that were at Eresus, but set a course that would take them along the mainland coast east of Lesbos. [2] They put in at the harbor of the Carteria islands of Phocaea, and after eating their midday meal they sailed past the coastline of Cyme and reached Arginousae, on the mainland opposite Mytilene, in time for their evening meal. [3] From there, with much of the night still ahead, they sailed along the coast to Harmatous, on the mainland opposite Methymna, and after stopping for their morning meal they carried on past Cape Lectum, Larisa, Hamaxitus, and the other places thereabouts, and reached Rhoeteum—so they were now in the Hellespont—before midnight. Some of the ships also berthed at Sigeum and elsewhere on that stretch of coastline.

102. The Athenians had eighteen ships at Sestus, and when they were alerted by beacons and saw the many campfires that had suddenly blazed up on the enemy shore, they realized that the Peloponnesians were sailing in. They set out that same night, hugging the Chersonese shore, and sailed as fast as they could for Elaeous, in an attempt to get past the enemy ships and into open water. [2] They successfully eluded the sixteen ships at Abydus, even though these ships had received a message from their approaching friends telling them to watch out for an attempt by the Athenian ships to break out of the Hellespont. But not all of them managed to slip past Mindarus's ships; they became visible at first light and he immediately set out after them. Most of the Athenian ships made it safely to Imbros and Lemnos, but the four tailenders were overtaken near Elaeous. [3] One of these was captured with its crew after running aground at the sanctuary of Protesilaus,* and two others were captured without their crews. The fourth, which had been abandoned, was set on fire near Imbros.

103. Mindarus next added the ships from Abydus to his fleet, so that he had a total of eighty-six, and spent the day besieging Elaeous, but it held out and he sailed back to Abydus. [2] Meanwhile, the Athenians had been let down by their lookouts, and believing that no enemy ships could sail past them without their knowing about it, they were taking their time over their siege of Eresus. But when they found out what was going on they abandoned Eresus and hurriedly went to the defense of the Hellespont. They captured two Peloponnesian ships, which had earlier set out rather recklessly toward the open sea in the course of their pursuit of the Athenians, and later that day they reached the anchorage at Elaeous. They brought in all the ships from Imbros that had taken refuge there and spent five days getting the ships ready for battle.

104. The course of the battle that ensued was as follows: The Athenians were sailing hard by the coast in line-ahead formation in the direction of Sestus, and when this came to the attention of the Peloponnesians, they, too, put to sea from Abydus to confront them. [2] When the two sides realized that battle was imminent, the Athenians extended their line of seventy-six ships along the Chersonese from Idacus to Arriani, while the Peloponnesians extended theirs, of eighty-six ships, from Abydus to Dardanus.* [3] The Peloponnesians' right was held by the Syracusans, and the left by Mindarus himself with the fastest of the fleet's ships. On the Athenian side, Thrasyllus had the left wing and Thrasybulus the right; the other generals were posted individually here and there.

[4] The Peloponnesians were eager to initiate the fighting. Since their left wing overlapped the Athenian right, they wanted to cut them off from sailing out into the open sea, if they could, and to force the center onto land, which was not far distant. But the Athenians realized what they were trying to do, and at the point where the enemy wanted to block them off they set about extending their own line. They were getting the better of this maneuver, and their left wing had already been

extended past the headland called Cynossema, the Bitch's Tomb. [5] But the upshot of this was that they found themselves with only weak and scattered ships in their center, and their difficulties were greatly increased by the facts that they were outnumbered by the enemy ships facing them and that the pointed, angular shape of the Cynossema promontory made it impossible to see what was going on beyond it.

105. So in the center, when the Peloponnesians rowed into the attack, they had by far the best of the action: they drove the Athenian ships onto land and disembarked troops as well. [2] Thrasybulus on the right wing was unable to go and defend the center because of the number of ships that were attacking him, and Thrasyllus on the left wing could do nothing either; the Cynossema promontory made it impossible for him to see what was happening, and in any case he was hemmed in by the Syracusans and the others who were ranged against him in numbers more or less equal to his own. But eventually the Peloponnesian formation began partially to disintegrate, as some of their ships, made confident by the fact that they were winning, set out in pursuit of the Athenians. [3] When Thrasybulus saw this, he ceased maneuvering to extend the line of his wing; he had his ships suddenly turn and fight back against the enemy ships bearing down on them, and he turned them to flight. Then he caught up with the now disorganized Peloponnesian squadron in the center, where they had been winning, tore into them, and terrified most of them into panicked flight without having to fight them. And when the Syracusans, who had themselves begun to give way before Thrasyllus's ships, saw that the others had turned to flight, they did likewise.

106. After the rout most of the Peloponnesians fled for safety to the Meidius river and then later to Abydus. The Athenians captured no more than a few ships, because the narrowness of the Hellespont meant that the enemy did not have far to go to find places of safety, but there could have been no better time for them to achieve this victory at sea. [2] Previously, a series of lesser failures and the disaster in Sicily had made them afraid of the Peloponnesian fleet, but now they were freed from self-doubt and stopped regarding the enemy as a force to be reckoned with at sea. [3] However, they had captured no more than twenty-one ships—eight Chian, five Corinthian, two Ambraciot, two Boeotian, and one each from the Leucadians, Lacedaemonians, Syracusans, and Pellenians—while losing fifteen ships themselves. [4] They set up a trophy on the headland where the Cynossema is located, rounded up the wrecks, and returned the bodies of the dead to the enemy under a truce. Then they dispatched a trireme to Athens to deliver a report of their victory. [5] When the ship arrived and the Athenians heard about their unexpected success, they were much encouraged, coming as it did after the Euboean disaster and their internal conflicts, and they believed that Athens was still strong enough to win the war, if they went about it with determination.

107. On the fourth day after the sea battle, the Athenians in Sestus, who had rapidly repaired their ships, set off for Cyzicus, which had revolted. On the way, when they spotted the eight ships from Byzantium moored at Harpagium and Priapus, they rowed into the attack, defeated the enemy on land, and captured the ships. When they got to Cyzicus, an unwalled town, they brought it back over to their side and levied reparations on it. [2] Meanwhile, the Peloponnesians went to Elaeous from Abydus and recovered those of their captured ships that were still seaworthy—the Elaeousians had burned the rest—and they sent Hippocrates and Epicles to Euboea to collect the ships from there.

108. At much the same time, Alcibiades returned to Samos with thirteen ships from Caunus and Phaselis, claiming to have stopped the Phoenician ships from going to the Peloponnesians and to have improved relations between Tissaphernes and the Athenians. [2] He manned nine ships in addition to those he already had, levied a large sum of money from Halicarnassus, and fortified Cos Meropis. Then he appointed a governor for Cos and returned to Samos, since summer was now coming to an end.

[3] As for Tissaphernes, when he found out that the Peloponnesian ships had left Miletus and gone to the Hellespont, he broke camp and marched from Aspendus to Ionia. [4] While the Peloponnesians were in the Hellespont, the Antandrians, an Aeolian people, had brought hoplites overland across Mount Ida from Abydus and installed them in Antandrus,* because they were being mistreated by Arsaces, a Persian who was one of Tissaphernes's adjutants. The Antandrians had good reason to fear Arsaces. The Delians had settled in Atramyttium after the Athenians had evicted them from the island in order to purify it,* and Arsaces, claiming to have some enemies to attack (though he never said who they were), invited the best of them to play a part in his armed forces. He led them out on campaign, on the understanding that they were his friends and allies, but then he waited for them to be occupied with their midday meal, and at that point he surrounded them with his own men and shot them down. [5] With this example before them, the Antandrians were afraid he would treat them with equal savagery, and in addition he was inflicting other measures on them that they were finding intolerable, so they expelled his garrison from their acropolis.

109. When Tissaphernes found out about this latest act by the Peloponnesians on top of what they had done at Miletus and Cnidus (at Cnidus, too, they had expelled his garrison),* he realized that his relationship with them was close to the breaking point. But he was afraid of being further harmed by them in some way, and at the same time he was annoyed at finding that Pharnabazus had made them welcome and might prove to be more successful against the Athenians, despite having spent less time and money cultivating the Peloponnesians than he had. So he decided to go to the Peloponnesians on the Hellespont, in order to reproach them for what they had done in Antandrus, and to put up as plausible a defense as possible against the accusations that were being brought against him over not just the Phoenician ships but his conduct in general. First he went to Ephesus and sacrificed to Artemis . . .

The History of the Peloponnesian War

At this point Book Eight breaks off; Thucydides died (presumably) before finishing the book and before writing up the rest of the war. What follows is a short summary of the final years of the war, which ended in 404, taken from my general history of ancient Greece, Creators, Conquerors, and Citizens.

One of the first things the Five Thousand did was pardon Alcibiades. But he chose not to come home immediately: Athens was still in turmoil, with the trials going on of men whose conspiracy he had arguably instigated. So, despite lacking any official position, he continued to serve the Athenian cause, but as a maverick—as a kind of privateer who accepted orders from Athens, as Walter Raleigh did from Elizabethan England.

The years from 411 to 408 were the climax of Alcibiades's military career. Victories in the Hellespont, culminating with the annihilation of the Lacedaemonian fleet at Cyzicus, secured the grain route from the Black Sea for the foreseeable future. Money was hardly forthcoming from Athens these days, but Alcibiades proved good at extorting cash from Athenian allies, and his men plundered Pharnabazus's territory as well. They garrisoned Chrysopolis on the Bosporus and instituted a tax of 10 percent on freight. . . .

On the strength of these successes, Alcibiades at last returned to Athens in 408. The Athenian people had short memories: without a doubt his advice to the Lacedaemonians was partly responsible for their terminal condition, and he had fought well for the Lacedaemonians in Ionia. But he paved the way for his return by sending a large number of captured enemy ships to Piraeus, laden with prisoners and booty. The Athenians revoked all the charges against him, had the priests undo the curses they had pronounced after the affair of the Mysteries, elected him general with special powers, and sent him back to Samos to regain control of the Aegean as he had of the Hellespont. Before his departure, he stage-managed a great symbolic coup by providing a military escort that allowed the traditional procession from Athens to Eleusis for the Mysteries—the same Mysteries he had been accused in 415 of mocking—to take place for the first time in five years, since the Lacedaemonian occupation of Decelea.

Lack of resources, however, made it impossible for the Athenians to fight successfully on several fronts. They had to concentrate on the Hellespont and the Aegean, for the sake of their alliance and their grain—and on the mainland Nisaea, Cythera, and Pylos were all retaken. Then decisive disaster followed: the Lacedaemonians had bypassed the self-serving satraps and entered into an agreement with Darius himself. The King's younger son, Cyrus, was due to arrive in Anatolia with a mandate to support the Lacedaemonians with both men and money. Gone were the Athenians' last hopes of securing Persian funds for themselves, or even Persian neutrality. Ironically, the Athenians heard the news when their own ambassadors, on their way to Susa to try to negotiate some such deal for themselves, met the Lacedaemonian delegation on its way back.

Alcibiades found his match in the new Lacedaemonian commander in the Aegean. As bold as Brasidas, Lysander burned not just to see the Athenians crushed, but to see Sparta elevated to their position in the Mediterranean—with him at the helm. Lysander was the son of a Lacedaemonian "Inferior" (and so had been sponsored through the Lacedaemonian educational system by another family), and he seems to have longed to prove himself greater than true Spartiates. The young Persian prince Cyrus, aged fifteen, could have found no better shoulders on which to lay responsibility for the war in the Aegean.

Cyrus took up residence at Sardis in the spring of 407. Lysander spent much of the year based at Ephesus, training and preparing his men. He assiduously avoided battle with the Athenians; he built relationships with the Eastern Greek oligarchs (whether or not they were currently in power); and he flattered his way into Cyrus's favor and coffers, receiving over time as much as five thousand talents. The friendship between the two men was entirely self-serving on both sides: Lysander wanted Persian cash, and Cyrus knew that he would one day be in need of Lacedaemonian hoplites. His elder brother was the heir to the Persian throne, but Cyrus wanted it for himself.

Alcibiades's fall was sudden, burdened as he was with Athenian expectations. In the summer of 407, his fleet was defeated by Lysander off Notium, the port of Colophon, while Alcibiades himself was away, perhaps irresponsibly. The Athenians did not choose him as one of the generals for the following year. Rightly fearing prosecution back home, Alcibiades withdrew to a private fortress on the Thracian Chersonese. He never saw Athens again. Conon of the deme Anaphlistus, an experienced general, was dispatched to Samos to replace him as commander of the demoralized fleet.

In the campaigning season of 406, the Lacedaemonian fleet of 140 ships, led this year by Callicratidas, was more than twice as large as that of the Athenians and dominated the Aegean. Following a stunning victory at sea, in which thirty Athenian ships were lost, Callicratidas managed to trap Conon with forty remaining ships in the harbor of Mytilene. In a last desperate effort, the Athenians manned their ships with untrained men from every walk of life and stratum of society. In July this motley fleet of 110 ships set sail from Athens, under the command of no fewer than eight of the ten generals for that year. At Samos, they were joined by an allied flotilla and the remains of the Aegean fleet, and they sailed to relieve Conon. Callicratidas left ships to enforce the blockade and set out with the rest to intercept them. The battle, off the Arginusae islands, east of Lesbos, was long and hard, but in the end the Lacedaemonians were well and truly beaten, losing seventy-seven ships to the Athenians' twenty-five. The Lacedaemonian dead included Callicratidas.

In the emotional seesaw of these closing months of the war, Athenian hopes were again high. They had defeated a triumphant Lacedaemonian fleet and they stood a chance of regaining their Ionian losses. But they threw it all away. First, they condemned to death all the Arginusae generals, despite their great victory (and despite the misgivings of the assembly chairman for the first day of the trial, the philosopher Socrates), for having failed to pick up over two thousand of their own sailors who were floundering in the water and subsequently drowned. Two of the generals had disobeyed the summons home, but the other six, including the younger Pericles, were executed. The generals explained that a rising storm had made it impossible for them to rescue the men, but the Athenians wanted blood. The poor had borne the brunt of the fighting in the Ionian War; the battles had taken place at sea, so that losses among the hoplite rich had been negligible. They had had enough, and the generals were suitable scapegoats.

Cyrus was obliged to return east for a long while to attend the deathbed of his father and the accession of his brother as Artaxerxes II. Lysander's men saw some action on the coast of Anatolia in the summer of 405, and they even raided the coast of Attica, but his main target was again the Hellespont and the Athenian grain supply. The Athenians had no choice but to follow him there. They beached their ships at Aegospotami, so that they could keep an eye on the Lacedaemonians on the other side of the Hellespont at Lampsacus, but they had to forage widely for provisions. Coincidentally, Alcibiades was nearby, and he still felt sufficient loyalty to the Athenian cause to warn the three generals at Aegospotami of the weakness of their position. But they rudely sent him packing: "Others are in command now, not you" (Plutarch, *Alcibiades* 37.1). This was Alcibiades's last appearance on the public stage: he was assassinated in 403, seemingly by Pharnabazus, to gratify the Lacedaemonians.

When Lysander's attack came, the Athenians were entirely unprepared and he caught most of the ships still drawn up on the shore. All but ten or twelve ships were captured or destroyed, and thousands of men lost their lives, since Lysander had given the order to take no prisoners. Conon was one of those who escaped. In Athens, they prepared for siege. Lysander speeded up the process of starving them into submission by sending every Athenian he found in the Aegean back to Athens—all the thousands of cleruchs and garrisons, for example.

Within a very few weeks, the entire Athenian alliance had fallen apart. All over the Aegean, Lysander and his men were made welcome, democrats were cruelly massacred, and narrow oligarchies imposed instead, supported by a garrison under a Lacedaemonian governor. Democracy was truly under threat. These oligarchs were the men whose friendship Lysander had cultivated over the previous years; in effect, he was creating a personal empire. The towns, now subject to Sparta, were required to continue paying tribute, disguised as contributions to the war effort. Only the Samians held out for a while, and were rewarded with a grant of Athenian citizenship, should any of them choose to live in Athens—an empty gesture at the time, since Athens was staring defeat and possible destruction in the face. After settling affairs in the Aegean, the Lacedaemonians sailed for Athens in October 405.

Lysander ravaged Salamis and blockaded Piraeus with 150 ships, while Pausanias, who had come to the Agiad throne of Sparta in 408, invaded from the Peloponnese and camped right outside the city, and Agis's forces hovered nearby at Decelea. Starved of both food and allies, the Athenians were soon forced to negotiate. Remembering how they had slaughtered or expelled whole populations, they dejectedly expected the same treatment themselves. There was a division of opinion among the Lacedaemonian allies; Lysander wanted to destroy Athens, and some of the allies agreed with him. But the stated purpose of the war had been the ending of the Athenian alliance, not the destruction of Athens, and after prolonged negotiations, in 404 Athens surrendered not all its fortifications, but only the Long Walls and the Piraeus defenses. The war fleet was limited to twelve ships; the Delian League was formally dissolved, and Athens was effectively incorporated into the Peloponnesian League. The fortifications were demolished amid scenes of celebration: "People thought that this day marked the beginning of freedom for Greece" (Xenophon, *Hellenica* 2.2.23). They were wrong.

Glossary

Units of Currency

daric: a Persian unit of currency equivalent to about twenty drachmas.
drachma: the average daily wage for a skilled Athenian worker.
mina: one hundred drachmas.
obol: the smallest unit of currency in the Greek world. There were six obols in the Athenian drachma.
stater: a unit of variable value, though always worth more than one drachma. A Corinthian stater (3.70.4) equated to three drachmas; Phocaean staters (4.52.2) to twenty-four drachmas.
talent: six thousand drachmas (or sixty minas).

Other Technical Terms

acropolis: literally "high city"; i.e., the defensible, often fortified center of a Greek city. When used without any other qualification by Thucydides, it usually refers to the acropolis of Athens, home to the Athenians' most important sanctuaries as well as their treasuries.
agora: central square and/or marketplace. In Athens, the agora was also the location of several political institutions, especially the council (*q.v.*).
archon: magistrate or governor. In Athens, the "nine archons," who served a one-year term, were the most important of the city's magistrates; one of these nine, the "eponymous archon," acted as chief magistrate and gave his name to the year in which he held office (see, e.g., 2.2.1, 5.25.1).

Glossary

assembly: a meeting of the male citizens, or in some cases a subset of citizens, of a city-state, which discussed political matters. The exact powers of the assembly varied from city to city. In fifth-century Athens (and other democratic states) the assembly was the sovereign body and had wide powers to both create and authorize policy; in Sparta, the assembly seems to have had the power to ratify, but not to initiate, political decisions.

barbarian: non-Greek, as defined by (some combination of) language, ancestry (including mythical ancestry), and culture. By Thucydides's time, the word often carried a pejorative implication (because Greeks generally believed themselves to be more civilized than barbarians), but might sometimes be used more neutrally as a descriptive term.

boeotarch: chief official of the Boeotian Federation. Each division of the federation provided one boeotarch, and so their numbers fluctuated as the organization of the federation changed. There were eleven boeotarchs in 424/423 (4.91.1), but boards of seven or nine are also attested.

cleruch: an Athenian citizen who held an allotment of (usually agricultural) land in the territory of a subject state of the empire. This land (a *cleruchy*) had typically been confiscated by the Athenians from subject communities (often as a punishment for attempted rebellion, as in Mytilene at 3.50.2); it was then divided into portions and distributed to Athenians, who might either migrate to the territory and farm it themselves or rent it back to local inhabitants.

council: a political body, whose size, composition, and powers varied from state to state. In Athens, for most of the period covered in this work, the council had five hundred members, chosen by lot from among male citizens over the age of thirty and serving for one year. This council met daily and was responsible for much of the regular political business of the city, but it did not have any legislative authority. In other states (for example, Boeotia), the council appears to have had a more restricted membership and more extensive powers.

Glossary

deme: small settlements in Attica that also functioned as administrative subunits of the Athenian state (there were about 139 demes in this period). Membership of a deme was hereditary and was a requirement of Athenian citizenship. It was common practice (though not one habitually followed by Thucydides) to identify an Athenian by giving their name and the name of their deme.

ephor: a Spartan official that served on a board of five. Ephors were elected annually and were responsible for many aspects of Sparta's political and military administration.

guest-friend (*xenos*): a semiformal relationship between individuals and families, particularly high-status ones, that could persist across multiple generations, and that often operated across state boundaries. These relationships could facilitate economic and political interactions between individuals and states; they could also lead to suspicions about divided loyalties.

helots: the subordinated people of Laconia and Messenia, who made up most of the enslaved population of Sparta. Unlike the chattel slaves more characteristic of other parts of Greece, the helots were ethnically Greek, worked primarily as farmers (with obligations to provide agricultural produce to their masters), and could probably not be bought or sold; their status was perhaps therefore closer to serfdom than slavery. The helots significantly outnumbered (possibly by as much as 8:1) the citizen population of Sparta.

herm: a stone pillar topped with a bust (usually representing the god Hermes) and typically also decorated with a carved phallus. The phallus served an apotropaic function, to ward off evil from the place or area where the herm stood. In Athens, herms were located at the entrances to private houses as well as in public spaces (especially at road junctions).

hero: a semidivine figure, differentiated from the gods either because one parent was mortal or because, although born fully mortal, their actions in life caused them to be treated as semidivine after their death. Heroes were more likely than the Olympian gods to

Glossary

be thought to have close connections with a specific location, and in some contexts might be appealed to as protectors of that location. Because they were originally (wholly or partly) mortal, they might also be associated with relics or burial sites, and these could become the focus of religious activity.

hoplite: a heavily armed foot soldier. The hoplite took his name from his heavy shield (*hoplon*) and was also usually equipped with helmet, thrusting spear, and sword; he fought as part of a mass formation known as a phalanx. Hoplite service was typically restricted to those who met certain requirements of wealth (sometimes characterized as sufficient wealth to buy their own equipment) or property (there is often an equation between ownership of land and eligibility for hoplite service).

Lacedaemonian: an inhabitant of Sparta and the surrounding area. The label can be used of full Spartan citizens (Spartiates, *q.v.*) but is also applied to free, noncitizen inhabitants of the area (especially the perioeci, *q.v.*).

metic: a foreign resident, especially used of foreign residents in Athens. These residents did not have full citizenship rights, but did have some duties (e.g., payment of tax, military service) and some protections (e.g., access to some legal procedures).

navarch: a term used (especially in Sparta) for a naval commander. In Sparta, a sole navarch acted as supreme commander of the navy. In the early stages of the war, it appears that the Spartan navarch would be appointed as needed, to fulfill a specific mission, and would serve until the mission was completed; in the final phase of the war, the Spartan navarchy developed into a regular position, filled on an annual basis.

oligarchy: literally "rule of the few." The term could encompass quite a wide variety of constitutional forms, but a common feature was that political participation was more restricted than in democracies, usually on the basis of wealth.

Glossary

paean: a hymn, usually sung either to invoke assistance from a god or to offer thanks for divine protection or aid. The hymns were often (although not always) directed at Apollo ("Paean" is the name of a healing god, equated with Apollo). In Thucydides, we find paeans being sung before and after battles, and also being used as a battle cry.

Panathenaea: one of the most important Athenian religious festivals, held in honor of the goddess Athena. The festival took place annually in July or August; every four years it was celebrated as the "Great Panathenaea," an extended event involving greater participation from Greeks beyond Athens.

peltast: a light-armed soldier, named from his small, light shield (*peltē*). Unlike hoplites (*q.v.*), peltasts did not usually fight in formation, and were typically used as skirmishing or raiding forces. They would often be drawn from noncitizen, and sometimes non-Greek, groups.

penteconter: a fifty-oared ship, common in the archaic period, but superseded by the trireme (*q.v.*).

perioeci: literally "dwellers around." The best known are the perioeci of Sparta, members of dependent communities in Laconia and Messenia. They were not enslaved but did not have the same rights as Spartan citizens, and they regularly participated in Spartan military activities. Perioeci are also attested at Elis—these too seem to have been members of dependent, but not enslaved, communities.

prytany: the governing subcommittee of the Athenian council. Each tribal contingent in the council (fifty men, from the total council of five hundred) acted as the prytany for one month (there were ten tribes and ten months, so each tribe served as prytany once every year; specifying which tribe held the prytany can therefore be used as a dating formula). Members of the subcommittee were called prytaneis.

***Salaminia* and *Paralus*:** the two "state vessels" of the Athenian fleet. These triremes were manned exclusively by Athenian citizens (unlike other ships, whose crews also included noncitizens and enslaved people), and were often used for particularly important missions (e.g., in the attempt to bring Alcibiades back to Athens to face trial for his alleged crimes at 6.53.1).

satraps: high-ranking officials in the Achaemenid Persian empire who exercised authority over regions of the empire known by the Greeks as "satrapies," with particular responsibility for securing imperial revenues. Satraps answered to the Persian King, but in practice often operated with a high degree of autonomy.

Sicel: a non-Greek inhabitant of Sicily. Sicel habitation of the island significantly predates the Greeks' arrival.

Spartiate: a full citizen of Sparta and therefore a member of the ruling elite and able to attend the legislative citizen assembly. Spartiates were trained only for war and did no manual work; they were supported by helot agricultural laborers and perioeci businessmen. Thucydides is not consistent in identifying Spartiates with this label, and many of the men identified as Lacedaemonians were Spartiates.

stele: an inscribed stone, often used for the public display of treaties and other collective decisions.

stoa: a covered portico, usually open at the front. Stoas could be used as places of commerce, for administrative or political functions, or as storage spaces.

supplication: a formal request for protection and assistance, which might be directed to either a god or a human. The supplicated entity was required to respond to (but not necessarily to grant) the supplicant's request.

taxiarch: an Athenian military commander responsible to the general. There were ten taxiarchs, one for each tribe; each held office for one year.

tribe (Athenian): in Athens, one of ten civic subdivisions created as part of the democratic reforms of the late sixth century. Every Athenian citizen was a member of one of the tribes, and

Glossary

membership in a tribe in turn provided the basis for participation in many aspects of political and religious life and military service. Many boards of magistrates had one member from each tribe, for example, and the tribes functioned, in effect, as "regiments" of the Athenian army.

trierarch: a trireme commander. This office was assigned to the richest Athenians, who were given the responsibility for (and were expected to bear the expense of) equipping a trireme, as well as acting as its commander when it was deployed.

trireme: the standard warship of this period. The trireme had three banks of oars (requiring a rowing crew of about 170 men), which enabled it to reach high speeds but also necessitated a high degree of skill in its crew and commander. The principal tactic of trireme warfare was ramming.

trophy: a monument erected to mark victory in a battle, usually placed on or near the battlefield, and ideally as close as possible to the place where the critical moment of the battle occurred (the literal meaning of the term is, roughly, "turning point"). In this period, trophies were normally not stone structures, but consisted of offerings of captured armor (e.g., Brasidas's shield at 4.12.1) hung on a tree or sturdy post with outstretched arms.

tyrant: a sole ruler, often characterized as having acquired or exercising his power by illegitimate means. By Thucydides's time, "tyranny" was largely perceived as a negative phenomenon, although some writers of this period (including Thucydides at 6.54.5) suggest that at least some tyrannical rulers did not necessarily deserve their bad reputations.

Notes

Book One

1.1 *and the Athenians:* Thucydides's emphasis on the *History* as a written work is important (see Introduction).

2.1 *the majority of humankind was affected:* Even allowing for the Classical Greeks' restricted conception of the scope of the inhabited world, this is a significant exaggeration. The war seems to have had little or no impact on (for example) North Africa, the eastern part of the Achaemenid Persian empire, or the Iberian peninsula.

2.6 *Attica could not support them:* That many Greek settlements in Ionia (i.e., western Asia Minor) had been founded by Athens was a widely held belief in Thucydides's time, although it seems more likely that the link between Athens and these cities was in fact a later development, retrojected into an earlier period.

3.2 *son of Deucalion:* Deucalion was said to be the son of the god Prometheus. In many versions of his myth, he and his wife were the only survivors of the great flood inflicted on the earth by Zeus. It is worth noting that in this section of the *History* Thucydides is happy to use material that we would consider mythological in support of his historical analysis.

3.2 *Pelasgians:* The view that the Pelasgians were the earliest inhabitants of the region seems to have been widespread, although ancient sources disagree on whether they were early ancestors of the Greeks, or a non-Greek people displaced by or assimilated into migrating Greek communities. Thucydides's own position is unclear.

3.2 *Phthiotis:* A region of Thessaly.

4.1 *Minos:* This is the Minos of the Minotaur, the labyrinth, etc. Thucydides treats him as a historical figure.

4.1 *Carians:* This passage provides an origin story for the Carian communities in southern Asia Minor—which, like that of the Ionians to their north, might have a rather arm's-length relationship with what actually happened (see note on 1.2.6).

Notes to Book One

5.1 *mainland coast:* That is, the coast of Asia Minor.

5.3 *that part of the mainland in general:* Regions to the north of the Gulf of Corinth.

6.3 *Athenians are kin:* Since Athens was believed to have founded the Ionian cities (cf. 1.2.6), it followed that the inhabitants of those cities were thought to be "kin" (a concept understood both literally and metaphorically) of the Athenians.

8.1 *implicated in piracy:* For the claim that the Carians once lived in the Cycladic islands, see 1.4.1 (with its note). The claim that the Phoenicians (a Semitic people, originating in the Levant, who settled widely in North Africa and the western Mediterranean) also at some point had a significant presence in the Aegean is not now generally accepted.

8.1 *graves... were removed:* In 426/425 (see 3.104). "Purification" entailed removal of existing burials and a prohibition on births or deaths taking place on the island in the future.

8.3 *subordinates:* The theme of wealth being critical to both the pursuit and the maintenance of power will also be central to Thucydides's understanding of Athenian imperialism (particularly its rise, as described later in Book One, and the beginnings of its collapse, narrated in Book Seven).

8.4 *campaign against Troy:* The Trojan War is treated by Thucydides as a historical event (and, as we will see below, Homer's *Iliad* is treated as a historical source, albeit one that needs critical scrutiny). On Thucydides's chronology, the war took place around 1250 BCE.

9.1 *Agamemnon:* King of Mycenae. The abduction of his brother Menelaus's wife, Helen, by the Trojan Paris precipitated the Trojan War.

9.1 *Tyndareus:* King of Sparta and father of Helen. In some versions of the myth (although not the one recorded in the Homeric poems), Helen's suitors swore to defend whoever was chosen to become her husband.

9.2 *from Asia... poor people:* Thucydides alludes to a version of the myth in which Pelops, son of Tantalus and father of Atreus, came to Greece from Anatolia.

9.2 *Eurystheus:* The grandson of Perseus. His mother was Nikippe, sister of Atreus.

9.2 *Heracleidae:* The descendants of Heracles. They will later settle in the Peloponnese (1.12.3), becoming the legendary ancestors of the Spartans of Thucydides's own time.

9.2 *Chrysippus:* Half-brother of Atreus.

9.4 *all Argos: Iliad* 2.108.

12.3 *Arne:* A city in Thessaly (northern Greece). Its exact location is unknown.

Notes to Book One

12.3 *Cadmeïs:* Cadmus was the mythical founder of Thebes, the most important city in Boeotia. In the most common version of the myth, he left his native Phoenicia (modern Lebanon) in a failed quest to find his sister Europa, who had been abducted by Zeus.

13.3 *about 300 years before the end of the current war:* I.e., at the end of the eighth century. The generally accepted date for the invention of the trireme is the mid-seventh century, but it is possible that Thucydides is crediting Ameinocles with building another type of ship.

13.4 *before the same date:* Corcyra (modern Corfu) was a Corinthian colony. Tensions between the two states play a central role in Thucydides's explanation for the outbreak of the Peloponnesian War (see 1.32 ff.).

13.6 *Cyrus… Cambyses:* Ca. 600–530 and 530–522, respectively.

13.6 *Rhenea:* A small island adjacent to Delos (cf. 3.104.2).

13.6 *Massalia:* Modern Marseilles.

14.2 *Xerxes's expedition:* The Persian invasion of mainland Greece in 480.

14.3 *Themistocles:* The leading Athenian politician (and general) in and immediately after the Persian invasion. The final stages of his career and life are described by Thucydides in a digression at 1.135–138.

15.3 *one side or the other:* The "Lelantine War," probably to be dated to the late eighth century. Chalcis and Eretria were neighboring cities on the island of Euboea, fighting for control of the fertile plain that lay between them.

16.1 *Croesus:* The (in)famously rich ruler of the kingdom of Lydia in ca. 560–546. He expanded his territories to include the Greek communities in western Asia Minor. After Croesus's defeat by the Persians, the areas he had ruled (including these Greek communities) were incorporated into the Persian empire.

16.1 *islands as well with his Phoenician navy:* Thucydides is referring here to the islands closest to the coast of Asia Minor. Many of them came under Persian control soon after Darius's accession in 522.

18.1 *reckoning to the end of the current war:* This is the constitutional reform that, in Thucydides's time, was usually (albeit implausibly) attributed to the lawgiver Lycourgus, and dated to the ninth century.

18.1 *between the Persians and the Athenians:* The Battle of Marathon was fought in 490.

18.2 *the King:* Writing "the King" like this with a capital K reflects Greek usage. Throughout this book and ancient Greek literature in general it always refers to the king of the Persian empire.

19.1 *required to pay:* See 1.96–99 for a fuller explanation of the Athenian system of levying tribute from its subject allies.

Notes to Book One

20.2 *Harmodius and Aristogeiton:* In 514. Thucydides gives a fuller account of these events at 6.54–59.

20.2 *Panathenaic parade:* The central event of the Panathenaea (see the Glossary, p. 631), a procession that led from the edge of the city to the acropolis.

20.3 *never even existed:* These observations are generally taken to be a covert criticism of Herodotus, Thucydides's older contemporary, who mentions the double vote of Spartan kings at *Histories* 6.57.5 and the Pitanate division at 9.53.2.

22.1 *the speech as actually delivered:* The inclusion of speeches was a standard feature of ancient historical writing. Thucydides is unusual in attempting to provide an explicit statement of his approach to composing (and/or reporting) these speeches, although his comments here have been a subject of intense debate in modern scholarship (see Introduction).

22.4 *single hearing:* For discussion of this important and complex statement of methodology, see the Introduction.

23.1 *two battles at sea and two on land:* The two land battles are Thermopylae and Plataea. One of the naval battles must be Salamis; the other could be Artemisium (fought closer to the Greek mainland, but indecisive), or Mycale (fought off the coast of Asia Minor, but a clear victory for the Greeks).

23.3 *the plague:* Plague first struck Athens in the summer of 430. Thucydides describes the outbreak at 2.47–54.

23.4 *the fall of Euboea:* In 446, after the Athenian suppression of the attempted revolt of Euboean cities from the Athenian empire (cf. 1.114.1–115.1).

25.4 *Phaeacians... original inhabitants of the island:* In Homer's *Odyssey*, the Phaeacians inhabit an island called Scheria, depicted as a kind of utopia; the claim that Scheria was a real place (and that it was the same place as Corcyra) was a later development.

27.2 *Epidaurus... Hermione... Troezen:* These three states are located in the Argolid, in the northeastern Peloponnese.

30.3 *Actium and near Cheimerium in Thesprotis:* On the mainland coast, between Corcyra and Paxos.

35.1 *your treaty with the Lacedaemonians:* The "Thirty Years Peace" of 446.

40.2 *harm another state:* It is highly unlikely that the treaty included an explicit restriction of this sort.

40.5 *Samians' rebellion:* Samos attempted to secede from the Athenian empire in 440 (see 1.115.2 ff.).

42.2 *your treatment of the Megarians has already aroused:* This might be a reference to Megara's decision, in 461, to leave the Spartan alliance

Notes to Book One

and side instead with Athens, an act that, according to Thucydides (1.103.4), was the initial cause of Corinth's extreme hostility to Athens. An alternative possibility is that it is an allusion to the trade embargo imposed on Megara in the 430s (the so-called Megarian Decree, mentioned explicitly at 1.67.4).

47.1 *Sybota islands:* An island group just off the coast of Thesprotis, opposite Cape Leucimme on the southern tip of Corcyra.

50.1 *ships they had sunk:* Ancient ships, being made of wood, did not sink to the bottom of the sea, but when holed they soon foundered or sank until their gunwales were level with the surface of the sea, and if not towed away they would then finally sink to the ocean floor.

50.5 *too few to prevent their defeat:* Thucydides only here reveals that there must have been a further Athenian debate (after the one reported at 1.44) that resulted in a significantly increased commitment to supporting Corcyra (a trebling of the original Athenian force).

57.5 *Chalcidians... Bottiaeans:* The Chalcidians referred to here are those who inhabited the coastal area to the north of the three promontories of the Chalcidic peninsula (Potidaea was located on the isthmus of the southernmost promontory). The Bottiaeans were located in the same region.

61.2 *Therme... Pydna under siege:* Therme was in approximately the same place as modern Thessaloniki; Pydna is on the coast of the mainland, south of Therme and west of the Chalcidic peninsula.

61.4 *Strepsa via Brea:* Strepsa was a tribute-paying member of the Athenian empire; Brea was an Athenian colony. The exact location of both places is unknown.

61.5 *Gigonus:* On the west coast of the Chalcidic peninsula, north of Potidaea.

64.2 *Aphytis:* A city on the east coast of the Pallene promontory.

65.2 *Sermylians... near their town:* Another city on the coast of the Chalcidic peninsula, near the base of the central promontory.

67.5 *along the following lines:* The speeches that follow are important in establishing and elaborating the polarity between Sparta (slow, cautious, old-fashioned) and Athens (dynamic, innovative, ruthless) that underpins Thucydides's understanding of the conflict between them.

69.1 *Long Walls:* The walls connecting central Athens to its harbor at Piraeus (cf. 1.107.1 for their construction, in ca. 457).

73.4 *we stood alone against the barbarians:* This is factually incorrect (non-Athenian forces were also present on the Greek side at Marathon), but seems to have been a common Athenian misrepresentation.

Notes to Book One

77.6 *observed everywhere else in Greece:* An allusion to the (alleged) activities of the Spartan leader Pausanias, which will be described at 1.95 and 1.128–135.

81.6 *slaves to their land:* Archidamus's point is that the Athenians knew that the survival of Athens as a political entity was not conditional on their ability to control their own territory. In part, this is due to the practical consideration (which will be emphasised also by Pericles at 1.143.3–5) that Athens, because of its naval power and overseas possessions, did not have to rely on food grown in its own hinterland. In part, it is an acknowledgment of the fact that the Athenians had famously, in the Persian invasion of 480–479, demonstrated a willingness to abandon their own city in order to achieve victory. This idea—that it is people, not territory, that are the defining feature of Athens's power—is one that has already been introduced by Thucydides (at 1.10.2) and will recur in the work.

86.1 *I don't understand why:* The contrast between Athenian verbosity and Spartan brevity plays on a widespread stereotype. It also feeds into Thucydides's broader construction of the ideological and cultural differences between the two sides.

87.6 *lasted until then:* That is, until 433/432.

88.1 *already under their control:* A reiteration of Thucydides's claim at the start of this section (1.23.4–6) that it was fear of Athens's growing power, not the clashes over Epidamnus (etc.), that was the truest cause of the war.

89.1 *rise to greatness:* Thucydides here introduces a flashback (which ends at 1.117) outlining the growth of Athenian power in the period between the end of the Persian invasion (480) and the events he has just narrated. This is conventionally called the "Pentacontaetia" (fifty-year period), although in fact the summary ends at around 440, omitting discussion of Athens's continuing expansion in the first half of the 430s.

93.7 *make a stand… with their navy:* A foreshadowing of the strategy that the Athenians, on Pericles's advice, will adopt during the Peloponnesian War (cf. 1.143.5).

94.2 *Cyprus:* Cyprus was part of the Persian empire.

96.2 *on Delos:* In the mid-450s the treasury was moved from Delos to Athens, so by the outbreak of the war the Athenians had easier access to these accumulated funds (cf. 2.13.3).

97.2 *Hellanicus… got the chronology wrong:* Hellanicus of Lesbos (the only historian named in this work) was Thucydides's older contemporary. His work survives only in fragmentary quotations in other writers.

Notes to Book One

98.1 *Eion-on-Strymon:* In Thrace (northern Greece). This is an early example of Athens's desire to establish its power in this region, which was important both for strategic reasons (as a staging point on the route east) and because of its rich natural resources (particularly timber and precious metals).

100.2 *later the Thasian revolt took place:* Thucydides's chronology is vague (cf. his criticisms of Hellanicus at 1.97.2), but the revolt of Thasos can be dated to 465/464–463/462. Many other events narrated in this section are hard to date precisely.

100.3 *now known as Amphipolis:* Thucydides does not mention here the Athenians' second, successful, attempt to found a settlement at Amphipolis, which took place in 437/436 (see 4.102).

103.4 *supplied the garrisons themselves:* Pegae and Nisaea were the two harbor towns of Megara, with Pegae on the Corinthian Gulf and Nisaea on the Saronic Gulf.

104.1 *against Artaxerxes:* Artaxerxes I, King of Persia from 465–424.

105.1 *Halieis:* In the Argolid.

105.1 *Cecryphalea:* An island in the Saronic Gulf, about halfway between the Argolid and Aegina.

105.3 *Geranea mountains:* The mountain range north of the Isthmus of Corinth, which separated Corinthian and Megarian territory.

107.2 *motherland of the Lacedaemonians:* Doris is in central Greece (north of Boeotia and Phocis). For the belief that the Spartans had migrated from this region to the Peloponnese, see 1.12.3.

108.3 *Boeotia and Phocis:* Thucydides's brief report downplays the significance of this event: Boeotia was a major regional power, now effectively subordinated to Athens. Athenian control lasted for about ten years (cf. 1.113.3–4).

110.1 *after six years of warfare:* Ca. 455 or 454.

111.2 *general in command:* The first—understated—appearance of Pericles in the *History*.

112.1 *Three years later:* Probably 451.

114.1 *Not long after this:* Ca. 447/446.

114.2 *Eleusis and Thria:* Thria is just east of Eleusis; both are located in northwestern Attica.

115.1 *to last for thirty years:* This is the "Thirty-Year Peace" of 446. The violation (or avoidance of violation) of this treaty was a running theme in the prewar crises narrated by Thucydides earlier in Book One.

115.4 *governor in Sardis at the time:* Sardis was the administrative capital of this region of the Persian empire, and Pissuthnes was the highest-ranking Persian official.

Notes to Book One

116.1 *Tragia:* Just south of Samos.

116.2 *from Chios and Lesbos:* Chios and Lesbos were by this date the only two members of the Delian League that were still contributing to the alliance in ships rather than tribute (cf. 1.96.1, 1.99.3).

121.2 *equally responsive to orders*: The Corinthians idealistically contrast Peloponnesian cohesion with the diversity of the members of the Athenian alliance.

124.1 *Dorians...Ionians:* That the Greek world could be divided on ethnic lines between Dorians and Ionians was an important idea in this period, albeit not necessarily one to which Thucydides fully subscribed (see Introduction).

126.3 *Cylon:* Cylon's attempted coup is dated to the 630s or 620s.

126.12 *factions that supported him:* In 508/507. Cleomenes, king of Sparta, had invaded Athens in support of a faction opposed to the democratic reformer Cleisthenes, who was a member of this cursed family (the Alcmeonidae). According to Herodotus (*Histories* 5.72.1), Cleomenes ordered seven hundred Athenian families to go into exile on the grounds that they were also implicated in the curse.

128.1 *sanctuary of Poseidon at Taenarum:* At the southern tip of the Mani peninsula, in the Peloponnese.

128.1 *earthquake that struck Sparta:* See 1.101.2.

128.3 *acquitted of wrongdoing:* See 1.95.5.

128.6 *letter read as follows:* The authenticity of these letters is highly suspect; it is possible that they were forged in order to damage the reputation either of Pausanias or of Sparta.

132.5 *completely trusted by him:* The Greek term employed here (*paidika*) is used especially of the younger partner in the pederastic relationships that were characteristic of male homosexuality in this period. These relationships were formed between an older and a younger man, and (at least in theory) had an educational or tutelary aspect as well as a sexual one.

135.3 *ostracized:* A temporary (ten-year) banishment, decided by popular vote.

137.1 *Alexander's kingdom:* Alexander I, king of Macedon in the first half of the fifth century.

137.2 *besieging Naxos:* This is the attack on Naxos mentioned at 1.98.4, although the generally accepted date for that episode (early 460s) is not obviously compatible with the chronology of the rest of the Themistocles narrative (see next note).

137.3 *recently ascended to the throne:* This means that these events should be dated to the late 460s (Artaxerxes came to the throne in 465).

137.4 *failure to destroy the bridges at that time:* Themistocles claims that he had prevented the Greek forces from destroying the bridges that Xerxes had constructed across the Hellespont in his invasion of 480; this made it possible for the defeated Persian land forces to retreat back to Asia Minor. The episode is also reported by Herodotus (*Histories* 8.108–10), who adds the detail—alluded to by Thucydides—that the decision not to destroy the bridges was in fact championed by the Spartan admiral Eurybiades, not by Themistocles.

139.1 *decree that excluded the Megarians from the harbors of the Athenian empire and the Athenian agora:* This complaint was briefly mentioned (at 1.67.4) as one of the superficial causes of the war, and might also have been alluded to by the Corinthians at 1.42.2 (see note), but this is the most explicit indication so far that it was a significant matter. Other contemporary sources represent the Athenian measures against Megara as a primary cause of the outbreak of war; it seems that Thucydides, for reasons that remain debated, has chosen deliberately to de-emphasize this issue.

139.4 *the following advice:* Pericles's speech should be read as the counterpart to the speech of the Corinthians at 1.120–124. It responds directly (in content, though not in placement in the work) to several of their points about manpower, finance, and strategy.

Book Two

1.1 *heralds:* According to Greek convention, heralds, who were believed to be protected by the gods, could travel in safety even during wartime.

2.1 *at the start of spring:* The spring of 431. This elaborate formulation is in part an attempt to calibrate the date of the start of the war across the various chronological systems used in different parts of the Greek world, and in part a rhetorical gambit, emphasizing both the accuracy of Thucydides's knowledge and the point that *this* (and no other event) was the true start of the war.

2.1 *boeotarchs:* See the Glossary (p. 628).

2.3 *before war had actually broken out:* Almost every aspect of the attack that follows (its timing, the nature of the fighting, the involvement of women) violates the conventions of Greek warfare. Thucydides's decision to make this the first event of the war is unlikely to be accidental.

2.4 *halted:* The verb is literally "to ground arms," but this means "to halt" because the first thing hoplites did on halting was rest their heavy shields on the ground against their thighs.

5.6 *the Plataeans disagree:* This is a very rare example of Thucydides offering two versions of the same event and leaving his reader to decide

Notes to Book Two

- 9.2 *the Isthmus:* That is, the Isthmus of Corinth.
- 9.4 *the Messenians of Naupactus:* That is, the former inhabitants of Messenia in the Peloponnese, who had been resettled at Naupactus, on the north side of the Gulf of Corinth, after their failed attempt to revolt from Spartan control (cf. 1.103.1–3).
- 13.1 *guest-friend of his:* See the Glossary (p. 629).
- 13.1 *dispel the curse:* See 1.126–127.
- 13.3 *600 talents in tribute:* Note the increase from the original assessment of tribute, as reported at 1.96.2 (460 talents). The funds collected from allied tribute (as Thucydides noted at 1.96.2) were originally stored on the island of Delos, but had been transferred to Athens in the late 450s. Thucydides does not explicitly mention this development, although other sources suggest that it marked a significant stage in growth of Athenian imperial power.
- 13.5 *statue:* The monumental cult statue of Athena Parthenos—the creation of the sculptor Pheidias—which stood inside the Parthenon.
- 13.5 *replace them later with at least the same amount:* This qualification is important: taking money or precious objects from sanctuaries would be considered sacrilege (because these things belonged to the gods); "borrowing" them would be less problematic.
- 13.7 *Phaleric wall:* The wall that connected central Athens to the harbor at Phalerum, south of Piraeus.
- 13.7 *Munychia:* The southern area of Piraeus, consisting of a hill and a small harbor.
- 15.1 *Cecrops... Theseus:* In a common version of Athenian mythology, Cecrops was the first king of Athens. He is said to have been born from the soil of Attica. The mythical figure Theseus was believed to have ruled Athens in the Bronze Age, about ten generations later.
- 15.1 *Eumolpus... Erechtheus:* Erechtheus, according to Athenian mythology, was the sixth king of Athens (that is, about four generations before Theseus). Eumolpus was a son of the god Poseidon, from whom one of the two priestly clans of Eleusis (the Eumolpidae) claimed descent (in some other versions of the myth he is represented as a Thracian king).
- 15.2 *single council chamber and town hall:* It is quite possible that this process (known as *synoecism*) is indeed how the Athenian state of Thucydides's time came into being, though it was not, of course, carried out by Theseus. The date of the synoecism is debated, although current consensus places it somewhere in the tenth to eighth centuries BCE, rather than the thirteenth-century date implied by Thucydides's chronology.

Notes to Book Two

15.4 *Anthesterion:* Early March.
19.2 *Rheiti lakes:* Near the coast, just south of Eleusis.
19.2 *Cropia:* A settlement in northwest Attica, east of Eleusis.
20.4 *good portion of the Athenian population:* The total Athenian male citizen population in this period was in the region of thirty thousand to sixty thousand. The Athenians did not conduct a census, and any registers of citizens that did exist were held locally by the demes (for which, see the Glossary, p. 629). None of these, however, have survived. Any attempt to calculate the Athenian citizen population, and still more the total population, therefore relies on a high level of informed speculation and involves a very wide margin of error.
21.1 *and then retreated:* See 1.114.2.
22.1 *went astray:* Pericles, as one of the generals, did not have the formal power to prevent the Athenian assembly from meeting, and in any case the assembly was required to meet at least once a month. What he could have done, though, is persuade the relevant officials not to convene any additional meetings.
22.2 *Phrygia:* A short distance southeast of Acharnae.
22.3 *long-standing treaty:* The treaty of 462, mentioned at 1.102.4 (although Atheno-Thessalian relations had not been entirely smooth in the interim: see also 1.111.1).
23.1 *between Mount Parnes and Mount Brilessus:* That is, in northeastern Attica. Mount Brilessus is an alternative name for Mount Pendeli (the source of the Pentelic marble used for the Parthenon and other major monuments in Athens and beyond).
23.3 *Oropus:* In the far northeast of Attica, a region also claimed by Boeotia (and captured by them in 412/411; see 8.60.1).
25.2 *Brasidas, son of Tellis:* Like Pericles, Brasidas (who will go on to play a major role in the events of the war) is introduced into the narrative without fanfare.
26.2 *came to defend it:* Thronium and Alope are settlements near the coast of East Locris, roughly opposite the northern tip of Euboea.
27.2 *the earthquake and the helot rebellion:* In the mid-460s (see 1.101–103).
28.1 *and then it became full again:* The eclipse can be dated to August 3, 431.
29.3 *Pandion:* This mythological digression is uncharacteristic; its polemical tone suggests that Thucydides is reacting against some (now unknown) alternative version of the story.
29.3 *did what they did to Itys:* Procne and her sister Philomela killed Itys, the only son of Tereus and Procne, in revenge for Tereus's rape and mutilation of Philomela; they then cooked the child and fed him to

Tereus. The sisters transformed into birds (a nightingale and a swallow) in order to escape death at Tereus's hands.

29.6 *return Therme to him:* Perdiccas, king of Macedon, had broken off his alliance during the Potidaea campaign (1.62.1); the Athenians had attacked Therme (in Macedonia) in the same campaign (1.61.2).

30.1 *for their exclusive use:* Both of these communities were on the western coast of Acarnania, on a promontory opposite the northern end of Leucas.

34.7 *whenever it was needed:* This is a good example of a distinctive feature of Thucydides's historical practice: he provides one full description of recurring events and leaves the reader to fill in the details for subsequent iterations (or even, in the case of the public funeral, to remember that this event happened in every year of the war, as Thucydides does not mention it again). For further discussion, see the Introduction.

36.1 *right up to the present day:* This is a reference to the concept of *autochthony*—that is, the belief that the Athenians, unlike most other Greek peoples (cf. 1.12), had not migrated to their current home, but had always lived there: they were "born from the soil." This version of the Athenian origin story appears to have become particularly popular in the fifth century.

36.4 *both barbarian and Greek:* A historical survey of Athenian achievements was a characteristic feature of these speeches. Pericles's (or Thucydides's) decision to omit this survey and focus instead on praise of the contemporary city results in a speech quite unlike other examples of the genre.

48.3 *should it ever occur again:* There is an echo here (which is unlikely to be coincidental) of Thucydides's ambitions for his *History* as a whole, as set out at 1.22.4. On a medical rather than historiographical note: there is still no consensus on what the disease described in the following chapters actually was. Suggestions have included typhus, smallpox, measles, or a particularly virulent strain of influenza, but none of these exactly map on to Thucydides's account. It is quite likely, in fact, that this type of "plague" has either died out or mutated so significantly that it is no longer recognizable.

53.4 *before the sentence was carried out:* The contrast with the idealistic portrait of Athenian values set out by Pericles immediately before this account of the plague (at 2.35–46) is striking, and Thucydides must have intended it to be so.

54.5 *places elsewhere:* So the Athenians felt they had offended Apollo, who was the god of epidemics as well as prophecy.

55.1 *Laurium:* In the far south of Attica.

Notes to Book Two

58.1 *tried to take it in one way or another:* Siege tactics in this period were relatively unsophisticated. Artillery had not yet been developed, so the primary offensive weapon was the battering ram, although other, more experimental techniques were sometimes employed, such as the construction of a ramp to surmount a city wall (attempted at Plataea, 2.75) or the deployment of a kind of flamethrower (successfully used at Delium, 4.100). Starvation or betrayal were often more effective techniques than force.

63.2 *wrong...perilous:* An echo of how the Corinthians had characterized Athenian power in their speeches in Book One. It is perhaps unlikely that the Athenians themselves were willing to think of their rule as "tyranny."

65.4 *typical of the masses:* A characteristically negative assessment of the decision-making abilities of the Athenian democratic assembly. For further discussion of Thucydides's attitude to democracy, see the Introduction.

65.6 *even more widely recognized:* Here, Thucydides departs from his strict linear narration of the events of the war, effectively writing Pericles out of the story over a year before his actual death in the autumn of 429.

65.8 *totally incorruptible:* Other contemporary sources suggest that allegations of corruption were one of the most notable features of Pericles's political career.

65.11 *thrown into political turmoil:* Thucydides narrates these events in Books Six and Seven. Failures of leadership are indeed part of the story he relates there, but they are given less emphasis as the primary cause of the expedition's failure in the later section than they are here.

65.12 *brought about their own ruin:* Thucydides's *History* breaks off before these final events of the war, but they are recorded by Xenophon in the first two books of his *Hellenica*.

67.1 *Pharnaces...the King:* Pharnaces was the Persian satrap (regional governor) in Hellespontine Phrygia, the northwestern edge of the Persian empire.

67.4 *bodies into a ravine:* The equation is not quite as neat as Thucydides suggests, because ambassadors were generally held to be a protected group, and as such were supposed to be allowed to travel unhindered.

68.3 *in Peloponnesian Argos:* As in his account of early Greek history in Book One, Thucydides treats these mythical figures and events as if they were historical.

68.8 *first formally became allies:* The date of these events is unclear, but it is possible that they took place in the early 430s. If so, this would be another reason for Corinthian concern about Athenian expansionism in the run-up to the war (Ambracia was a Corinthian colony; see 2.80.3).

Notes to Book Two

69.1 *that coastline:* The western portion of the south coast of Asia Minor.

71.2 *battle that was fought in our territory:* The Battle of Plataea of 479, the final, decisive land battle between Greek and Persian forces in mainland Greece.

75.2 *Cithaeron:* The mountain range south of Plataea, which plays a role in several mythological tales. It is the place where the infant Oedipus was (unsuccessfully) exposed, where Heracles killed the lion of Cithaeron, and where Dionysus danced with the Bacchantes.

75.3 *[...]:* The transmitted text here reads "seventy," but this is an implausibly long time and it seems likely that the text is corrupt. Possible alternatives are "seven" or "seventeen," but there is no way of knowing which (if either) is correct.

78.2 *the time of the rising of Arcturus:* The middle of September.

79.2 *Spartolus in Bottice:* In the southern part of the Chalcidic peninsula.

79.4 *Crousis:* The exact location of this area is unknown. It might have been in the same immediate region as Spartolus, or farther north, at the top end of the Chalcidic peninsula.

80.6 *Oroedus's leadership:* All of these are tribal communities from this northwestern part of Greece.

80.7 *arrived too late:* Perdiccas had (in theory) reconciled with Athens in the previous year (see 2.29.6).

83.3 *Chalcis and the Evenus river:* Chalcis in southern Aetolia, not Chalcis in Euboea.

85.5 *Cydonia:* On the north coast of western Crete (modern Chania).

93.4 *Megara at night:* From the Isthmus to Megara is a distance of about twenty-five miles.

102.1 *Coronta:* A city in central Acarnania.

Book Three

2.1 *the whole of the island of Lesbos except for Methymna defected from the Athenians:* Methymna was one of five cities on the island (the others were Mytilene, Pyrrha, Eresus, and Antissa). Each city was an independent political unit.

7.4 *laid waste the farmland:* For the background to this campaign, see 2.102.

7.5 *Nericus:* A settlement either on or just adjacent to Leucas.

8.2 *spoke in this fashion:* Thucydides attributes to the Mytileneans a view of the growth of Athenian imperialism that is largely consistent with his own summary at 1.96–99, but that (for obvious reasons) places responsibility for the process more on the Athenians than the allies.

Notes to Book Three

15.1 *from Corinth to the sea on the Athenian side*: By means of the *diolkos*, a paved trackway, about five miles long, across the isthmus.

17.3 *a drachma a day as well:* A trireme had a total crew of around 200. About 170 of these were rowers and the remainder performed other tasks.

17.4 *more ships manned than ever before:* This chapter is problematic, above all because the figures it gives for the numbers and locations of ships deployed by Athens at this stage of the war are not obviously compatible with other things Thucydides tells us about Athenian military activity at this time (e.g., the reference in the previous chapter to the squadrons of 30 and 40 ships off the Peloponnese and Lesbos, respectively). It seems likely that the entire chapter is a later interpolation. An alternative possibility is that it has been mislocated in the text and actually relates to an earlier year (perhaps 430).

19.2 *hill of Sandius:* Probably about 20 miles northeast of Myous.

22.2 *sure footing in the mud:* It is likely that the decision to wear only one shoe had some religious significance (the practice is quite well attested in some rituals), which Thucydides prefers not to mention.

25.1 *without being spotted:* A walk of about 18 miles.

29.2 *Embatum, near Erythrae:* On the coast of Asia Minor, opposite Chios (i.e., just south of Lesbos).

31.1 *Pissuthnes:* The Persian governor of Ionia (see 1.115.4–5).

32.1 *Teos:* Southeast of Embatum, so Alcidas is now moving farther away from Lesbos. Ephesus and Clarus are in the same region.

32.2 *Samians from Anaea came to him:* Anaea, on the coast of Asia Minor opposite Samos, was where exiled (anti-Athenian) Samians had settled (as Thucydides will tell us at 4.75.1).

33.1 *the Salaminia and the Paralus:* See the Glossary (p. 631).

34.1 *Notium, the harbor of Colophon:* Alcidas is now traveling northwest, but is still in the same general area, the region of Asia Minor opposite the stretch of water between Chios and Samos.

37.2 *intrigue against you:* Here, and again at 38.1, Thucydides has Cleon echo sentiments voiced by Pericles at 2.60–64. The echoes are particularly striking given Thucydides's (apparent) admiration for Pericles and intense dislike of Cleon.

51.2 *as had happened before:* See 2.93–94.

52.1 *This is how it came about:* The near-juxtaposition of the descriptions of the fates of Mytilene and Plataea is often seen as deliberate, particularly since both episodes are framed around a debate over how each city should be treated. Whether Thucydides intended his reader

Notes to Book Three

- 54.3 *only Boeotians...freedom of Greece:* This is not true: contingents from Thespiae and Thebes were also present at Thermopylae (Herodotus, *Histories* 7.202), although (according to Herodotus) the Thebans were there against their will (7.222, 233).
- 54.5 *a third of our fighting men:* In the 460s (see 1.101.2–103.3).
- 55.1 *When the Thebans attacked us:* In 519 BCE.
- 56.2 *on a holy day:* The detail about the attack taking place on a holy day was not included in Thucydides's account of these events in Book Two.
- 57.2 *tripod at Delphi:* The monument set up by the Greeks to commemorate their victory over the Persians (which also features in the narrative of Pausanias's alleged misdeeds in 1.132.2–3).
- 58.1 *our alliance then:* The alliance is the one formed by many Greek states in 481 in response to the threat of Persian invasion. Among the issues at stake in this debate is the (very unclear) question of whether this agreement still held any force, or had been entirely superseded by the alliance created by Athens after the Persian withdrawal from mainland Greece (cf. 1.96).
- 58.5 *their murderers:* So called because the Thebans fought on the Persian side.
- 62.5 *subject to their rule:* In 457 (see 1.108).
- 62.5 *and defeated them:* In 447 (see 1.113).
- 63.2 *was already in place:* That is, the anti-Persian alliance of 481 (see 3.58.1, with the note).
- 63.3 *sworn agreement:* The reference is again to the alliance of 481 (see the previous note), although it is not the case that the "entire community of Greeks" was party to this agreement.
- 65.3 *a greater stake in the state than you did:* The logic of the Thebans' argument here is that the pro-Theban faction in Plataea was also an oligarchic faction (while the pro-Athenian faction was democratic); that oligarchs are wealthy; and that the wealthy have a greater stake in society. This last point seems to have been a fairly widely held tenet of oligarchic political ideology in this period.
- 68.1 *treaty...after the Persian invasion:* This must be a reference to the guarantee mentioned at 2.71.2, although what is described there is a promise of freedom and independence, not (as here) a requirement of neutrality.
- 68.3 *an internal political dispute:* We will find out more about the internal unrest in Megara at 4.66.

Notes to Book Three

68.5 *Plataea...alliance with Athens:* This is the alliance of 519, referred to by the Plataeans at 3.55.1. In emphasizing the length of the Athenian–Plataean alliance, Thucydides also implicitly draws attention to how ineffective it turned out to be (in spite of Athens's promise, at 2.73.3, that they would never abandon the Plataeans).

78.2 *what had happened at Naupactus:* See 2.84.

81.1 *isthmus of Leucas:* The isthmus connected the northern tip of Leucas to the mainland; at various points in antiquity (though not at this time) it was bisected by a canal, making Leucas a true island. By hauling their boats over the isthmus, the Peloponnesians avoided having to sail into the open waters west of Leucas, and could instead stick to the mainland coast.

82.1 *few or no precedents:* What follows is one of the most fully elaborated and explicitly presented examples of Thucydides's belief (set out as a theoretical position at 1.22.4) that the events of the period he narrated were at least in part determined by "human nature," and that certain patterns of behavior were therefore likely to recur. It is also a very good example of his habit (already visible in his narration of the plague in Book Two) of providing one detailed account of such recurrent events: the reader is surely expected to apply this model to the many other examples of civil strife that are mentioned, but not described in detail, in the work. Whether Thucydides also intended this template to be used to understand the Peloponnesian War as a whole is more open to debate, although at least some aspects of the behavior visible at Corcyra are seen (in fact, have already been seen) elsewhere in Thucydides's narrative.

84.3 *would be needed:* This chapter was recognized even in antiquity as an inauthentic interpolation, and almost all modern scholars concur. The problem is not that it is particularly un-Thucydidean in thought or expression, but that it was never mentioned or discussed by those ancient Thucydidean scholars whom we would have expected to discuss it; there is no trace of it until the second century CE. Could it be an early draft of a chapter that was excluded by Thucydides but somehow later found its way into the text?

86.2 *Chalcidian cities:* The Sicilian cities of Naxos and Catana. They are "Chalcidian" because they were colonies of the city of Chalcis on Euboea (cf. 6.3).

86.4 *bring Sicily under their control:* On Dorian and Ionian ethnicity, and Thucydides's attitude toward it, see the Introduction. Thucydides's comment here also foreshadows the Athenians' disastrous later attempt to conquer Sicily (which will be the focus of Books Six and Seven).

Notes to Book Three

88.1 *Islands of Aeolus, as they are called:* Off the north coast of Sicily. In Homer's *Odyssey* (10.1–79), Aeolus, the keeper of the winds, lived on a floating island in the far west. Odysseus visited the island and borrowed Aeolus's bag of winds in an (unsuccessful) attempt to ease his homeward journey. The volcano, known today as Stromboli, is still active.

89.1 *turned back:* It is possible that the Spartans withdrew for safety reasons, but earthquakes could also be seen as bad omens or as punishments for some transgression (cf. 1.128.1, where Thucydides reports the Spartan belief that the great earthquake of 464 was a punishment for their violation of the sanctity of the shrine at Taenarum). The Spartans had a reputation in this period for being particularly religious, and there are a number of occasions during the war when Thucydides is explicit that Spartan military activities were halted or amended because of a negative omen or other religious concern (e.g., 5.54.2, 5.55.3, 5.116.1).

89.3 *Athenian fortress:* The fortress had been established in the summer of 431/430 (see 2.32).

89.4 *Peparethos, too:* Modern Skopelos, off the coast of Thessaly.

91.3 *Oropus in Graea:* On the border of Attica and Boeotia.

92.1 *Heraclea in Trachis:* In the northern part of central Greece. At 3.92.6, Thucydides clarifies that this was not an entirely new foundation, but a rebuilding (and renaming) of an existing settlement (probably called Trachis).

92.3 *Doris, the motherland of the Lacedaemonians:* For the Lacedaemonians' "Dorian" heritage, see 1.12.3.

95.1 *then down into Phocis:* An ambitious plan, partly because of the length and difficulty of the overland march (from west to east across the challenging inland terrain of central Greece), and partly because the Phocians were at least in theory now allied with Sparta (cf. 2.9).

95.1 *Sollium:* A coastal city opposite Leucas, captured by the Athenians in the summer of 431/430 (see 2.30.1).

96.1 *Hesiod:* Hesiod lived in the eighth or seventh centuries BCE and was the most admired poet after Homer.

96.3 *Malian Gulf:* That is, to the eastern coast of central Greece.

97.2 *Aegitium:* After an initial advance northward (to Teichium), Demosthenes is now heading east.

102.5 *Proschium in Aetolia:* Farther west of Naupactus.

104.1 *purified Delos:* It is likely that this act of purification was at least in part a response to the plague. Such diseases were commonly seen as acts of god (and particularly of the god Apollo, to whom the island of

Delos was sacred), but it was also believed that the gods could provide protection from them.

104.4 *Hymn to Apollo:* This work is now generally thought not to be Homeric, but by a later (sixth-century BCE) poet. The version quoted by Thucydides is not quite the same as the transmitted text of the *Hymn to Apollo*. Homer himself, as soon becomes clear, was supposed to have been blind and was traditionally associated with the island of Chios.

104.6 *catastrophic events in Ionia:* The subjection of the Greek cities there to the Persian empire.

105.2 *Ambraciots:* Argos and Crenae are south of Olpae. Eurylochus and his army were, at this point, based farther south again, so would have to pass Argos and Crenae to link up with the Ambraciot forces.

112.1 *Idomene:* North of Metropolis, just beyond the southern borders of Ambracia.

Book Four

2.3 *Corcyra as they sailed past:* It was common practice in this period for ships to stay as close to land as possible, even when undertaking long voyages. Traveling from Athens to Sicily via Corcyra is therefore a more logical route than it might initially appear, because it allows for a shorter crossing of the Adriatic.

3.2 *formerly Messenia:* That is, territory that had been conquered and annexed by Sparta, probably in the eighth century BCE (events alluded to by Thucydides at 1.101.2).

3.3 *reliable garrison for the place:* The Messenians in Demosthenes's army are from the community in Naupactus, which was established when some (Peloponnesian) Messenians went into exile after their failed revolt from Spartan control (see 1.103.1–3). Forces from this community had been participating in Athenian operations since the start of the war, but this is the first time we see their Peloponnesian roots being exploited for tactical advantage.

7.1 *Eion (the one in the Thraceward region):* This is not the same place as the Eion (on the Strymon) of 1.98.1, 4.50, and 4.102. The site of this other Eion has not been identified.

16.1 *rations:* This is a relatively generous allocation of food. Herodotus reports, for example, that Spartan kings received a ration of two or four quarts of grain (*Histories* 6.57.3); later in the war, the prisoners in the stone quarries at Syracuse will receive only two cups of grain per day (7.87.2).

Notes to Book Four

17.2 *what needs to be done:* Spartan brevity of speech was already a stereotype in Thucydides's day. It has been alluded to already in the speech of the ephor Sthenelaidas at 1.86 (where he is represented as finding the Athenians' lengthy and complex speeches incomprehensible), and in the Spartans' (unsuccessful) attempt to avoid long speeches in making their decision about the fate of Plataea (3.52.4, 68.1).

21.3 *treaty:* The "Thirty-Year Peace" of 446 (cf. 1.115.1).

23.2 *seventy ships in all:* Presumably this total includes a few of the sixty-five Peloponnesian ships that the Athenians now had in their possession, but they had too few men to man such a large number of ships, and the rest were probably left unmanned and at anchor in the bay.

24.5 *supposed to have sailed:* The episode is related at *Odyssey* 12.234–259. In that telling of the story, Charybdis is represented as a whirlpool-generating sea monster, sitting opposite the equally monstrous Scylla—each capable of dragging sailors to their deaths. Thucydides, characteristically, prefers to explain the dangers of this stretch of water in more rational terms.

25.7 *Archias and his supporters:* Archias is otherwise unknown, and Thucydides provides no other information about his origins or motivations.

28.3 *called on Cleon to sail:* Thucydides's aside on the psychology of the crowd, and its capacity to undermine the intentions of political leaders, gives an insight into his (skeptical) views on democratic governance. We can compare his similar assessment of the dynamics of Athenian decision-making before the invasion of Sicily (6.24).

28.4 *Aenus and elsewhere:* The islands of Lemnos and Imbros, in the North Aegean, had been conquered and settled by the Athenians early in the fifth century. By the time of the Peloponnesian War, it appears that the inhabitants of those islands were no longer Athenian citizens but retained particularly close links with Athens. One sign of this is their frequent deployment (as here) in Athenian-led forces. Aenus, in Thrace, was a subject city in the Athenian empire. It is unclear, however, whether these men were serving under compulsion or were in Athens as a volunteer force.

30.1 *woods...his defeat:* The disastrous engagement described at 3.96–98 (in the summer of 426/425).

32.2 *oarsmen from the lowest level:* The rowers who manned the lowest bank of a trireme's three layers of oars appear (on the basis of jokes at their expense in Aristophanes's *Frogs*) to have had the lowest status in the crew, and might also have been paid less than other oarsmen. The decision to exclude them from the landing party might then reflect some lack of faith in their military ability.

36.3 *Thermopylae:* The famous battle of 480 BCE, in which a small Spartan force (along with some other Greeks) fought to the death against the Persian invaders.

40.2 *stones and arrows:* Key to understanding the shock caused by this event is the contrast with Thermopylae (a comparison Thucydides introduced at 4.36.3). The Spartans' refusal to surrender at the earlier battle, which had become a paradigmatic aspect of their identity, contrasts with their behavior here. The alleged exchange about arrows reinforces the comparison. In a famous anecdote told of the Battle of Thermopylae, the Spartan response to the threat that the Persian army was so huge that their arrows would block out the sun was, "If the Persians hide the sun the battle will be in shade rather than sunlight" (Herodotus, *Histories* 7.226).

42.4 *Cenchreae... Crommyon:* Cenchreae is the harbor of Corinth on the south side of the Isthmus; Crommyon lay on the coast between Corinth and Megara.

46.1 *[...]:* The number of ships is missing.

46.1 *a great deal of harm:* See 3.85.

50.2 *translated and read:* Thucydides is probably using "Assyrian" as a generic label for non-Greek writing. (It is more likely that the letter would have been written in Aramaic.) The reason for Persian frustration with Sparta's requests will become clearer in Book Eight, where Thucydides gives a more detailed account of later exchanges between Sparta and Persia and (especially) of their mutually incompatible diplomatic and political objectives.

52.1 *eclipse... earthquake:* This eclipse can be dated to March 21, 424.

52.2 *Rhoeteum:* In the Troad, close to the mouth of the Hellespont.

52.3 *Antandrus:* A coastal town on the mainland opposite Lesbos.

54.1 *two thousand:* The transmitted text here is not completely secure: it is possible that the correct figure should be "two hundred." Two thousand hoplites is a large force, but one which a city the size of Miletus would be capable of raising.

61.2 *Dorians... Ionians:* For Dorians and Ionians, see the Introduction.

66.1 *twice a year:* Thucydides had reported on Athens's annual invasions of Megara at 2.31.3, but it is only here that he reveals that they were in fact happening twice a year.

66.1 *Pegae their base:* Pegae was the northern harbor town of Megara.

68.5 *olive oil:* A puzzling tactic. There are no obvious military parallels for this practice, although oil was used in gymnastic and athletic contexts. As various commentators have noted, it is in any case not clear how oil would help to differentiate these men if they were also wearing body armor.

72.2 *first time... help from anywhere*: A glance at, say, 1.114.1 shows that this must mean that they had never received *uninvited* help, or perhaps "ever" means "ever in the current war."

73.2 *no dust were raised, as it were:* In athletic contests, if one wrestler ceded the bout to another without fighting, the winner was said to have won "without raising any dust."

74.4 *such a long time:* It is not clear how long this regime lasted, though it seems still to be in place in 421 (5.31.6). The fourth-century Athenian orator Demosthenes (18.96) describes Megara as being in Spartan hands in the early fourth century.

75.1 *fortifying Antandrus:* For this plan, see 4.52.3.

76.2 *Athenian-style democracy:* Cities in the region of Boeotia were grouped into a federation, which in this period was dominated by Thebes. The objective of the plotters seems to have been to create a more democratic constitution for the federation as well as for the individual cities within it.

76.3 *"Minyan" Orchomenus:* "Minyan" refers to an otherwise obscure mythical figure called "Minyas," who was said to have founded the city. Orchomenus is described in these terms in the Homeric poems. The epithet reflects an earlier, independent phase of the city's history, before it became part of the Boeotian Federation.

78.6 *Perdiccas's realm:* That is, Perdiccas, king of Macedon. In an earlier appearance in Thucydides's narrative (at 2.80 ff.), Perdiccas was allied with Athens but sending secret military assistance to Sparta.

80.1 *against their northern allies:* As long as the Spartans lacked superiority or even equality at sea, these were the only Athenian allies they could get to, because they could go by land.

81.3 *cut from the same cloth:* Thucydides's positive assessment of Brasidas is striking, and it is worth noting that this summary of his behavior (and responses to it) is not completely consistent with the detailed narrative of Brasidas's actions that follows. The fact that Brasidas was responsible for inflicting the defeat that led to Thucydides's exile from Athens (5.26) seems very likely to have influenced the historian's portrayal of the Spartan commander. In any case, however, the hope that Brasidas's successors might live up to this (possibly idealized) model of behavior was not fulfilled.

84.2 *along the following lines:* Once more (cf. 1.86, 4.17.2), Thucydides plays on the widespread perception that Spartans were either uninterested in rhetoric or incompetent in it. In this (as in other respects), Brasidas is represented as an atypical Spartan.

Notes to Book Four

88.2 *Stagirus:* On the northeastern coast of the Chalcidic peninsula. Stagirus is later famous as the birthplace of the philosopher Aristotle.

90.1 *fortifying Delium:* Delium was a sanctuary sacred to Apollo and other gods. As will emerge later in the narrative (4.98), the Athenians' use of this space for military purposes might have been more religiously problematic than this pragmatic description of their actions suggests.

92.4 *Euboeans across the water there:* Athens's harsh reaction to the attempted secession of several Euboean cities in 447/446 was described at 1.113–114.

92.6 *up until now:* The Battle of Coronea, fought in 447, was a major Boeotian victory over Athens (see 1.113).

95.3 *Oenophyta ... their land:* The Battle of Oenophyta, fought in 457, was an Athenian victory over Boeotian forces and gained them control of much of central Greece, but the gains achieved there were later reversed by Athenian defeat at the Battle of Coronea (see previous note).

97.2 *returned to Boeotia from Athens:* The usual conventions of Greek warfare allowed the victorious party in a battle to take the arms and armor of the enemy dead (which would be treated as battlefield booty), but it was generally expected that the enemy would then be permitted to retrieve the bodies of their fallen (a straightforward example of this principle in action comes shortly after this episode, at 4.101.4). The Boeotians' refusal to allow the Athenians to recover their dead was therefore a clear violation of Greek customs. Whether this is on a par with or more serious than the violations of Greek custom (allegedly) committed by the Athenians in their occupation of the sanctuary at Delium is open for debate—which is, of course, one reason why Thucydides devotes so much space to exploring the argument.

102.2 *Aristagoras ... by the Edones:* Aristagoras, tyrant of Miletus in the late sixth century, was a primary instigator of a significant revolt of the Greek cities of Asia Minor against Persian imperial rule. The rebellion (known as the Ionian Revolt) was a disaster, hence Aristagoras's withdrawal to Thrace to avoid Persian retributions (Darius was King of Persia at this time).

102.4 *visible from sea and land:* Thucydides has already mentioned the earlier, failed attempt to create a settlement in this region (at 1.100.2–3), but this is the first time we hear about the successful foundation of Amphipolis in 437. The event was not narrated in chronological sequence in Book One, even though it might be thought very relevant to the theme of the growth of Athenian power that Thucydides is exploring in that part of his work. It is possible that Thucydides avoided mentioning the city's foundation in Book One in order to downplay Athenian expansionism in the run-up to the war's outbreak; it is also possible that he chose to delay this information until it became directly relevant to his narrative of the war.

104.4 *come and help them:* Thucydides does not explain why he was on Thasos (or, perhaps more pertinently, whether he should have been at, or at least closer to, Amphipolis). The island was an important subject state in the Athenian empire, with a history of rebellion (cf. 1.100), but there is no evidence that it was considering secession at this point.

107.3 *Brauro:* Goaxis and Brauro are otherwise unknown. We might read Thucydides's decision to drop these apparently obscure names into his narrative as an attempt to signal his detailed knowledge of Thracian politics, perhaps especially given the unusual (to an Athenian) fact of a woman exercising agency in this sphere (contrast Pericles's advice to Athenian women at 2.45.2).

109.2 *King's canal:* The canal through the Athos peninsula created by Xerxes for his invasion of mainland Greece in 480. Its construction is described by Herodotus (*Histories* 7.22–24).

109.4 *Pelasgians:* On the Pelasgians in Athens, see 1.3.2, with the note.

118.1 *sanctuary and oracle of Pythian Apollo:* That is, the oracle at Delphi. It is not clear whether the Athenians had been formally barred from consulting the oracle in the first phase of the war, or (as perhaps is more likely) it had simply been impractical for them to access Delphi, because doing so would require crossing the hostile territory of the Boeotians and Phocians.

118.3 *god's valuables:* Dedications made at a sanctuary became the property of the god, with the result that many sanctuary sites became significant repositories of wealth (stored as either coined money or precious metals or a mixture of both). At 1.121.3, the Corinthians suggested that the Peloponnesian forces could draw on the resources of Delphi to fund their war effort, and this might be what is being alluded to here. It is also possible, though, that this clause relates to a less formal raid on the sanctuary's treasures, unreported by Thucydides.

118.4 *Coryphasium:* The Lacedaemonian name for Pylos.

118.4 *island they captured:* Minoa, off Megara.

118.5 *five hundred talents:* About fourteen tons (thirteen thousand kilograms).

118.11 *Resolved by the people:* The Athenian response is presented in the standard form of a decree of the assembly, including dating formula (for "prytany," see the Glossary, p. 631), names of officials, and decree proposer. This contrasts with Thucydides's more usual practice of

Notes to Book Five

presenting the business of the assembly in the form of speeches or debates rather than, as here, the outcome of those debates.

118.12 *fourteenth day of the month Elaphebolion:* Toward the end of March. The date is converted to its exact equivalent in the Spartan calendar in the final version of the truce (below, 4.119.1).

120.3 *forced upon them by others:* One strand of Athenian imperial ideology was that, as a naval power, Athens had a particular right to rule over island communities in the Aegean (or, in an alternative formulation, that the Aegean islanders were especially suited to being ruled over by Athens). This view emerges most clearly in the arguments of the "Melian Dialogue" (e.g., 5.84, 97). "Islander" can therefore at times become almost a synonym for "Athenian imperial subject"; it can also carry connotations of weakness or servility. Thus, the Scioneans' lack of timidity deserves particular comment, because islanders, and even quasi-islanders, might normally be expected to be more subservient to Athens.

121.2 *as though it were an island:* The significance of this point again lies in the implied equation between "islander" and "Athenian imperial subject" (see the previous note). That is, Brasidas's calculation is that the Athenians will treat these Thracian communities as their natural subjects and make particular efforts to reincorporate them into their empire (see also 4.122.5).

126.3 *who are Macedonians*: That is, the Lyncestians.

132.3 *illegally... so as not to leave such appointments to chance:* It is not clear why this was illegal. One possibility is that Brasidas was bypassing whatever official appointment process should have been used for these officials, instead ensuring that his own supporters were established as governors. Another is that the issue is the youth of these men: there might have been a Spartan law that made it illegal for men of military age to leave the city without permission.

133.1 *in the battle with the Athenians:* At Delium.

135.1 *returned to his post:* The bell was not part of an alarm system but was used to ensure that all of the sentries were at their post. Sentries would periodically pass a bell around the wall, and if it failed to complete its circuit, this would show that something was amiss. The flaw in this system (as revealed here) is that it required sentries to leave their position briefly so that they could pass the bell to the sentry at the neighboring post.

Book Five

1.1 *Pythian games:* The Pythian games, the second most prestigious of the panhellenic festivals (after the Olympic games), were celebrated

Notes to Book Five

sometime between late July and late August 422. The one-year truce (reported at 4.117.1) would otherwise have expired in the spring of 422.

1.1 *allowing the inhabitants to remain:* The earlier explanation came at 3.104.2. The description of the Delians as "consecrated" to Apollo probably means, in this context, that they were thought to have a particularly close relationship with the god (rather than being formally indentured to or owned by him). Their alleged "ancient crime" was (according to the fourth-century orator Hyperides) to have massacred some visiting Aeolians and stolen their gold.

1.1 *Pharnaces gave them:* Pharnaces was the governor of Hellespontine Phrygia, in northwestern Asia Minor. Atramyttium was a coastal settlement just south of the Troad, roughly opposite the island of Lesbos.

3.4 *treaty had been concluded:* The peace treaty of 421 (cf. 5.18–19).

4.2 *after the peace treaty:* The "Peace of Gela," the agreement made in the summer of 424 (see 4.65.1–2).

6.1 *Stagirus... Galepsus:* Stagirus, on the northeastern coast of the Chalcidic peninsula, had seceded from Athens in the summer of 424 (cf. 4.88.2). Galepsus was a coastal settlement east of Amphipolis; it had seceded from Athens in the winter of 424/423 (see 4.107.3). It is likely that Thucydides, who profoundly disliked Cleon (see, e.g., 3.36.6), downplayed the extent of his successes in the northern Aegean.

11.1 *honor Hagnon as they had before:* The Athenian general responsible for the foundation of Amphipolis in 437 (cf. 4.102.3–4).

13.1 *Pierium:* Also known as Cierium, in south-central Thessaly.

14.3 *Pylos and Cythera:* Raiding activity from these two locations was explicitly banned in the truce of 423 (4.118.4).

14.3 *as they had before:* In 465 (see 1.101–103).

14.4 *on the point of expiring:* Thucydides has not previously mentioned this peace agreement, which must have been made in 451. Argos was Sparta's main rival in the Peloponnese.

14.4 *Cynouria:* A disputed border region between Argos and Sparta, at this point controlled by Sparta (see 4.56.2).

16.1 *these things were happening to them:* Pleistoanax was exiled as a result of his actions in 446 (see 5.16.3 and the note) and recalled in the summer of 426. Thucydides mentions neither his exile nor his restoration in the correct (in terms of chronology) places in his narrative, reserving this information for the point where he has decided it is most relevant to his story. Pleistoanax's exile was briefly alluded to at 2.21.1.

16.2 *plow with a silver plowshare:* The "Zeus-born hero" is Heracles (from whom Sparta's kings were believed to be descended). The prophecy

Notes to Book Five

of "plowing with a silver plowshare" is, broadly, a threat that Sparta's undertakings would be unprofitable (perhaps because the expense of a silver plow would outweigh any profit from the harvest, or because a plow made of silver would be ineffective).

16.3 *dual kingship instituted:* Sparta's dual kingship, a distinctive feature of its constitution, persisted down to this period. There were two separate royal houses (Agiad and Eurypontid), each of which provided one king. Pleistoanax was an Agiad.

16.3 *bribed to withdraw from Attica:* In the invasion of 446 (see 1.114.2).

16.3 *Mount Lycaeum:* In Arcadia.

17.2 *the following terms:* This treaty is commonly referred to as the "Peace of Nicias." Thucydides's decision to report verbatim the text of the agreement (and of the alliances reported at 5.23, 47, 77, and 79) is somewhat unusual in the context of his work (though he does do the same for the terms of the truce, reported at 4.118–119). It has sometimes been seen as evidence of the unfinished state of Book Five (see Introduction).

18.5 *stipulated in the time of Aristeides:* According to the Aristotelian *Constitution of the Athenians* (24.3), Aristeides ("the Just") was responsible for the first assessment of tribute, made at the point of the Delian League's foundation in 478/477. Thucydides described this event at 1.96.2, but did not mention Areistides's role in it.

18.5 *Argilus... and Spartolus:* These were all cities that had seceded from Athens during Brasidas's Thracian campaign (although Stolus has not previously been mentioned).

18.6 *Mecyberna, Sane, and Singus:* Three tribute-paying members of the Athenian empire, located in the Thraceward region. At 4.109.3–4, Thucydides mentioned Sane's unwillingness to go over to Brasidas; the other two cities have not featured in the narrative until this point.

18.7 *Panactum:* An Athenian border fort, recently captured by the Boeotians (5.3.5).

18.7 *subject to the Athenians:* Athens's capture of Pteleum (whose location is unknown) has not previously been mentioned by Thucydides, but the other places listed here have all featured in his narrative of the preceding five years. ("Coryphasium" is an alternative name for Pylos.)

18.10 *Amyclaeum:* A sanctuary of Apollo, and one of the most important religious sites in Sparta.

19.1 *twenty-fifth day of the month Elaphebolion:* That is, the same date (at the beginning of the spring of 422/421) in both cities. For the coordination of local calendars, see 4.118.12, with the note.

22.2 *renew the treaty with them:* The Thirty-Year Peace between Argos and Sparta, which came into force in 451.

23.3 *enslaved population rises up in revolt:* That is, the helots. That the Spartans do not make an equivalent undertaking to the Athenians reflects the fact that slave rebellion was a much more realistic prospect in Sparta than in Athens. This in turn can be explained by the different slave systems employed by the two states: the heterogeneous, dispersed, and largely non-Greek slaves of Athens were less likely to revolt than the ethnically homogeneous helots of Sparta.

26.1 *captured the Long Walls and Piraeus:* In 404. Thucydides does not, in fact, extend his narrative up to this date (see Introduction), although this sentence is good evidence that he did intend to write an account of the entire war.

26.5 *calmly and collectedly:* A rare piece of autobiographical information. Thucydides did not mention his exile at the point when it happened, presumably during or shortly after his year of service as general in 424/423 (see 4.104.4–4.107.1).

28.2 *Athenian War:* See also 5.31.5. To the Athenians, the war was "the Peloponnesian War," but to the Peloponnesians it was "the Athenian War." It is only because of the hold that Classical Athens had and continues to have on European culture that it is nowadays called "the Peloponnesian War." Thucydides himself, at the very beginning of the work, calls it "the war between the Peloponnesians and the Athenians."

31.1 *Lepreum:* In the Peloponnese, on the border between Laconia and Elis (cf. 5.34.1).

35.8 *Crane in Cephallenia:* Captured by the Athenians in the summer of 431 (2.30.2).

38.2 *supreme authority in Boeotia:* The councils were made up of representatives from the member states of the Boeotian Federation. The four councils took turns in the leading role, and the leading council's proposals would be considered and (if approved) ratified by the other three.

39.1 *captured it:* Mecyberna's autonomy had, in theory, been guaranteed by the terms of the treaty of 421 (5.18.6).

39.3 *demolition of Panactum was immediately put in hand:* Thucydides delays the explanation for this act until 5.42, perhaps to emphasize how unexpected and provocative an event it was.

41.2 *each of them had claimed victory:* The so-called Battle of the Champions, which took place in the mid-sixth century. It is described by Herodotus at *Histories* 1.82.

Notes to Book Five

43.1 *Alcibiades, son of Cleinias:* The first appearance in the work of this figure, who was to become a central character in the second half of the war.

47.11 *stone stele on the acropolis:* This stele is partially preserved; the text inscribed on it is almost identical to that reported by Thucydides.

49.1 *Olympic truce:* A truce was announced for major panhellenic festivals to allow participants to travel safely to and from these events, as well as to enable the festivals themselves to take place without disruption. The pancratium was a brutal combination of boxing and wrestling, similar to what is today called mixed martial arts.

50.4 *crowned the charioteer:* Victory in the chariot race was credited to the owner of the chariot and horses, not to the chariot driver. The drivers were often enslaved people.

51.2 *threat to their lands:* For Sparta's foundation of Heraclea in Trachis, see 3.92–93.

53.1 *sailing around Scyllaeus:* Scyllaeus is at the southeastern tip of the Argolid peninsula. The sea route from Aegina to Argos would entail rounding this peninsula and then traveling north, up its western coast, to reach Argos. Access to Epidaurus, at the northeastern end of the peninsula, offered a shorter, land-based route to Argos.

54.1 *border in the direction of Mount Lycaeum:* That is, northwest of Sparta.

54.2 *Carneios:* August, approximately.

54.3 *laid it waste:* The Argives, that is, manipulated the calendar to avoid committing sacrilege by campaigning during a sacred month. This was not an uncommon practice in Greek warfare; it was made possible by the fact that a year, in all Greek calendars (which differed from city to city), fell short of 365 days, so that intercalation (the insertion of extra days) was always required.

55.3 *Caryae:* In northeastern Laconia (that is, in the general direction of Argive territory).

56.3 *from Crane:* These are the helots who had been settled in Crane (in Cephallenia) at the end of the summer of 421 (5.35.8).

57.2 *Phleious:* In the northeastern Peloponnese, roughly halfway between Corinth and Argos.

58.2 *Methydrium in Arcadia:* In the central Peloponnese. The Argives are attempting to prevent the Lacedaemonian forces from reaching Phleious.

63.4 *without their consent:* Normally, Spartan kings exercised sole command over their armies when on campaign, as Thucydides explains at

Notes to Book Five

5.66.2–4. However, they could be, and were, held to account for their actions on their return to Sparta.

64.2 *Orestheum in Maenalia:* In Arcadia, between Sparta and Tegea.

67.1 *reserved exclusively for these Lacedaemonians:* Sciritis was a region of Laconia (cf. 5.33.1). Other ancient sources describe the Sciritae as lightly armed soldiers, often used as scouts or watchmen. We only hear of their special claim to this position in a military formation from Thucydides.

68.2 *could not come up with a precise figure…overall:* An extremely unusual, albeit also very limited, admission of ignorance from Thucydides. See also 5.74.3 on Lacadaemonian casualty figures.

70.1 *armies when they advance into battle:* This is a nice example of Thucydides's preference for secular over religious explanations, though it's also unusual in that he acknowledges the possibility of a religious explanation.

71.1 *the better the protection:* Each hoplite carried a large shield on his left arm and his weapon in his right hand. This meant that the right-hand side of the body was exposed—unless, as Thucydides notes here, a hoplite could find some cover from the shield of the man to his right. Thus each hoplite—and therefore also the line as a whole—would tend to drift to the right.

72.4 *three hundred so-called Knights:* "So-called" because, by this period, these men fought as infantry rather than cavalry.

76.3 *agreement read as follows:* Thucydides again quotes the text of an agreement verbatim. In this case (and that of the agreement reported at 5.79), he quotes it in its original Doric dialect, rather than converting it into the Attic dialect in which the rest of the *History* is written.

77.4 *swear one themselves:* Argos's failure to provide this sacrificial victim was the alleged cause of the conflict (see 5.53.1). It is hard to decode exactly what this sentence means: either the phrasing is particularly opaque or the text is corrupt (or perhaps both). Presumably, though, one or both sides had to swear an oath either affirming that they were in the right in this religious dispute or conceding that they were wrong, and promising some sort of recompense.

80.2 *ancestrally Argive:* The claim that the Macedonian kings—the Argeads—had Argive ancestry was well established (the tale of their origins is alluded to by Thucydides at 2.99.3, and recorded in more detail by Herodotus, *Histories* 8.137).

84.2 *became openly hostile:* In the summer of 426 (3.91.1–3).

84.3 *ruling oligarchs:* The exchange that follows, known as the "Melian Dialogue," is Thucydides's only foray into the dialogue format (a style more usually associated with philosophical writing); however, the ideas he explores here (especially the problem of the competing claims of power, pragmatism, and morality) are of course recurring themes of the work as a whole.

105.2 *know it to be true of men:* There is a clear echo here of the view of power expressed by the Athenian ambassadors at 1.76.2.

Book Six

1.1 *gone with Laches and Eurymedon:* The expedition of 427–424 (cf. 3.86, 3.88, 3.90, 3.99, 3.103, 3.115, 4.1–2, 4.24–25, 4.58–65).

1.1 *hardly less demanding than the one against the Peloponnesians:* This is an important claim, both historically and historiographically. Thucydides will present the campaign in Sicily almost as a self-contained unit—a war within a war—and this is reflected in the structure of Books Six and Seven. We start, as in Book One, with a summary of Sicilian history, from the earliest times up to Thucydides's own day.

2.1 *the Cyclopes and the Laestrygonians:* The one-eyed (Cyclops) and man-eating (Laestrygonian) giants who appear in Homer's *Odyssey* (9.105–166 and 10.8–132, respectively).

2.3 *ended up in Sicily:* As in his account of early Greek history in Book One, Thucydides treats the Trojan War as a historical event (see note on 1.9.4).

2.6 *the part of the island that was the shortest distance from Carthage:* Carthage being a Phoenician city.

3.1 *mission to a sacred site:* In 734, according to the relative chronology that Thucydides uses in this section. The date of the foundation of Megara Hyblaea, described at 6.4.2 (see note below), provides the reference point from which the other foundation dates can be derived. The various origin stories that Thucydides goes on to provide probably do reflect what these communities believed about their pasts, and especially about their ties to cities elsewhere in the Greek world. However, they should not be taken at face value as accounts of what actually happened in the eighth and seventh centuries BCE.

4.2 *Gelon, the tyrant of Syracuse:* This event can be securely dated to 483, and thus provides the basis for the rest of Thucydides's chronological framework in this section.

6.1 *truest cause:* A deliberate repetition of the formulation used by Thucydides at 1.23.6 in his explanation of the causes of the war as a whole.

6.2 *earlier war:* The war of 427–424. Puzzlingly, Thucydides does not here mention (or make the Egestans mention) that there also existed a treaty between Athens and Egesta, probably to be dated to 418/417.

Notes to Book Six

We know about this treaty because an inscribed copy is partially preserved.

6.2 *expulsion of the Leontinians:* See 5.4.2–5.

7.1 *Orneae:* The exact location of this city is unknown, though it must have been somewhere between Argos and Nemea. At the Battle of Mantinea, the Orneatae had fought alongside the Argives (5.67.2).

10.2 *recent treaty:* The peace agreement of 421, which Nicias had played a major role in securing (cf. 5.43.2).

10.5 *before we've secured the one we have:* Nicias echoes here the advice which, according to Thucydides, Pericles had also given to the Athenians, and which they ignored after Pericles's death (2.65.7).

12.2 *certain person:* Nicias is referring to Alcibiades, as he did also at 6.10.2.

13.2 *get no help ourselves when we need it:* At 4.61.4, the Syracusan leader Hermocrates made a very similar observation about the asymmetric nature of Athens's interactions with Sicilian cities.

16.6 *Mantinea:* That is, in the battle of 418 (cf. 5.64–74).

20.4 *homegrown rather than imported:* Nicias's (or Thucydides's) insistence on the importance of cavalry is worth noting: this will be an important and recurring theme as the narrative of the Athenian invasion plays out.

27.1 *faces mutilated:* See the Glossary (p. 629) on herms. A joke in Aristophanes, *Lysistrata* 1094, suggests that not just the faces but also the phalluses of the herms were mutilated.

27.3 *bad omen for the expedition:* Hermes was, among other things, the god of travel and travelers, so an attack on objects associated with this god, at this precise moment, might be thought particularly inauspicious.

27.3 *overthrow the democracy:* The logic (or, in Thucydides's view, lack of logic) underpinning this assumption will become clearer later in the narrative (especially at 6.60), but a key reason for suspicion is the coordination of the attack: such widespread vandalism, in such a short time, could imply the existence of some sort of clandestine organization with both numbers and resources on its side. We know that there did exist in Athens secret or semi-secret groups that aimed to influence political affairs; such groups play a role in the coup of 411 (8.54.4, 8.65).

28.1 *Mysteries...in private houses:* The "Mysteries" are the Eleusinian Mysteries, one of the most important Athenian cults. Those who participated in the Mysteries were required to complete an initiation process, and noninitiates were not permitted to know any details of the rituals; performing the Mysteries outside their proper time and place was therefore

Notes to Book Six

particularly sacrilegious. The fact that the Eleusis cult was closely linked to the Athenian grain supply might have made this charge especially potent at this moment, given that access to grain appears to have been an important factor driving Athenian ambitions in Sicily.

31.2 *Pericles:* In 430 (see 2.56–58).

31.3 *upper bench of oarsmen and the officers:* The rowers on the top layer of the trireme were usually the most skilled, and they played an important role in setting the rhythm for rowers on the lower two banks. They had the best view of the oars hitting the water, and were best able to hear the commands of the rowing-master. They were also the most exposed to hostile fire, so their higher pay has sometimes been interpreted as a sort of danger money.

31.3 *call-up lists:* The board of ten generals was responsible for compiling call-up lists; there was one list for each of Athens's ten tribes (see the Glossary, p. 632). It is unlikely that the Athenians in this period maintained a central register of those eligible for hoplite service. Call-up lists would therefore need to be created from scratch for each campaign, a fairly significant administrative operation. The lists were probably constructed on the basis of information provided by officials in the demes (see the Glossary, p. 629): we know that each deme was required to keep a register of its male citizens, and the smaller size of the demes would also make it easier for local officials to know if a citizen should not be conscripted—if, for example, someone had been injured or was disabled.

33.5 *largely their own fault:* Hermocrates's assessment of the challenges the Athenians would face is notably similar to that set out by Nicias (at 6.21).

36.4 *another war just as great as the one in Greece:* Another echo of a point made by Nicias (at 6.10).

39.2 *always be thwarted:* It is striking that Thucydides places this defense of democratic ideology in the mouth of a non-Athenian, and within a speech in which the other core proposition (that the Athenians are not going to invade) is clearly incorrect. Should we conclude from this that Thucydides intended his reader to think that Athenagoras was also wrong about the merits of democracy? Or might it be that Thucydides can allow his "villains" to be right about some things? We might compare the speech he gives to Cleon in the debate over Mytilene in Book Three.

43.1 *thetes serving ... as marines:* Thetes were members of the poorest section of the Athenian citizen body. Since these men could not afford hoplite armor, they would usually serve as rowers in the Athenian fleet; their use (as here) as an infantry force is therefore atypical.

44.3 *Chalcidian Leontinians:* The Athenians' point is that both Rhegium and Leontini had been founded by settlers from Chalcis in Euboea, and should therefore take the same side. For the power of this sort of argument, see the Introduction.

49.4 *Megara Hyblaea . . . deserted:* It had apparently never recovered from its destruction by Gelon in 483, as reported by Thucydides at 6.4.2.

54.1 *ignorant about this incident:* The digression that follows is very uncharacteristic, in terms of the overall structure of Thucydides's work, but relates closely to two themes that he clearly thought important. First, it picks up on his observation (at 6.15.3–4) that the Athenians (mistakenly?) feared that Alcibiades was a tyrant in the making, allowing him to flesh out the reasons why tyranny still loomed so large in the Athenian consciousness, as well as to present his own, notably more positive, assessment of the nature of tyrannical rule. Second, it reinforces a central claim about the value of his own work, by reiterating his insistence on the importance (and difficulty) of acquiring accurate knowledge of past events. This was a point Thucydides made first and more fully in the methodological excursus at 1.20–22, and Athenian ignorance of the story of Harmodius and Aristogeiton was also invoked there.

56.1 *offered it to her:* The procession would have been part of a religious festival, and the position of "basket-carrier" a privileged role, usually given to girls or young women from elite families. The claim that Harmodius's sister was "unworthy" of the position is probably a veiled allegation of unchastity.

59.1 *reckless stroke:* Thucydides's conclusion differs dramatically from what seems to have been the established Athenian view of Harmodius and Aristogeiton: the two men were celebrated as "tyrant slayers," and were accorded unprecedented honors in Athens as the men who died to bring freedom to the city.

59.4 *the Lacedaemonians and the Alcmeonidae in exile:* These events, which took place in 511/510, are narrated in detail by Herodotus (*Histories* 5.62–65). The Alcmeonidae were an elite Athenian family; their descendants included Pericles and Alcibiades.

59.4 *Marathon:* In the unsuccessful Persian expedition of 490.

60.2 *whether or not what he said was true:* This was the Athenian orator Andocides, whose speech "On the Mysteries," defending himself against accusations of involvement in these events, is extant; the speech includes an account of this specific episode in the prison. Thucydides's decision not to name him must be deliberate, although the reason for it is unclear. Some commentators interpret it as an insult (denying Andocides the oxygen of publicity), while others see it as an attempt to shield him from further criticism.

70.1 *never been in battle before:* The less experienced soldiers, Thucydides implies, interpreted the storm in religious terms, and as a bad omen.

75.1 *Temenites sanctuary:* A sanctuary of Apollo, named simply for the precinct (*temenos*) surrounding it.

75.3 *in Laches's time:* Presumably in (or just after) 427, although Thucydides has not mentioned this alliance before.

76.2 *in Euboea in a state of servitude:* On Athenian treatment of Chalcis (and other Euboean cities) after their attempt to secede from the empire in 446, see 1.114.3.

82.4 *their mother city:* The suggestion that at least some of the Greek communities in Asia Minor collaborated more enthusiastically with the Persian invasion than was necessary (or that they were less enthusiastic than they could have been about seeking opportunities to rebel from Persia) is also visible in Herodotus's *Histories*. But the claim here that these communities should be seen as particularly culpable for those actions—as aggressors rather than victims—is unusual.

85.1 *a tyrant or an imperial state:* Euphemus follows the Corinthians (at 1.122.3), Pericles (at 2.63.2), and Cleon (at 3.37.2) in equating Athenian imperial power with that of a tyrant. The three Athenian speeches have broader thematic similarities, too, especially in their exploration of the motivations for and limitations on Athens's imperial ambitions. Euphemus's speech also picks up on some of the questions explored in the "Melian Dialogue" (5.84–113), particularly the relationship between justice and self-interest.

85.2 *around the Peloponnese:* The reference is to the Cephallenians, Zacynthians, and Corcyreans, who had joined the Athenian force in Sicily (although, in his catalog of forces at 7.57.7, Thucydides suggests that there was an element of compulsion in their participation).

86.1 *on that earlier occasion:* See 3.86.

88.9 *Mantinean business*: The Battle of Mantinea, described at 5.65–75.

89.4 *my family has always been opposed to tyranny:* A reference to Alcibiades's Alcmeonid ancestry. Herodotus (*Histories* 6.121, 123) describes the Alcmeonidae as "tyrant-haters," drawing attention in particular to their (alleged) bribery of the Delphic Oracle, which persuaded the Spartans to invade Athens and oust Hippias, the last of the Peisistratid tyrants.

90.2 *Carthage itself:* The idea of conquering Carthage was mentioned at 6.15.2 as one of Alcibiades's (unstated) goals, but it was not, as far as we know, settled Athenian policy. There is no evidence that any of the other extremely ambitious objectives that Alcibiades mentions in this speech formed any part of Athenian plans, though it is not absolutely impossible that some Athenians were nurturing such extravagantly expansionist goals.

91.6 *fortify Decelea in Attica:* A village in the foothills of Mount Parnes overlooking the fertile plain north of the city of Athens. Thucydides gives more information at 7.19.2.

91.7 *will come to you on its own:* In the form of runaway slaves.

91.7 *the lawcourts*: Jurors (some cases employed up to five hundred men) were paid for their duty and would lose income because the lawcourts would meet less frequently, given the dangers of travel from other towns in Attica to have cases heard, and the fact that many of the people who served as jurors would be occupied in the army or navy.

95.1 *returned home:* See also 3.89.1, with the note.

104.2 *citizenship that had once been granted his father:* Gylippus's father was Cleandridas (6.93.2), who had been one of King Pleistoanax's advisers in 446, and had therefore also been sent into exile (2.21). He spent at least some of his exile in Thurii on the east coast of Italy, a city founded by Athens in 444 with a mixed population. Thurii had remained neutral in the war but was now inclining to Athens (see 7.33.5). By the time of 8.35.1, however, it had gone over to the Peloponnesians.

105.2 *Epidaurus Limera:* Not the Epidaurus in the Argolid, but a settlement on the southeastern coast of Laconia, a little farther south than Prasiae.

Book Seven

9.1 *against Amphipolis:* Perdiccas, king of Macedon, appears to have switched allegiances again since his last appearance in the narrative (at 6.7.3, where the Athenians were raiding his territory).

13.2 *enslaved Hyccarans:* Hycarra was a Sicanian (i.e., non-Greek) settlement in Sicily, whose inhabitants had been enslaved after a raid in the summer of 415 (6.62.3).

18.1 *fortify Decelea:* Repeating the advice he had given in the previous winter (6.91.6), although Thucydides suggests that the idea of establishing a forward operating base in Attica had been mooted since before the start of the war (cf. 1.122.1).

18.2 *wrong side of the law:* There is an important shift here in the Spartan perspective, or perhaps in Thucydides's representation of the Spartan perspective, on who was to blame for the conflict. In his account of the preliminaries to the war, Thucydides reported that the Spartans

Notes to Book Seven

believed "the Athenians were culpable" (1.118.3) for the breach in the Thirty-Year Peace that led to the war.

18.2 *supposed to be peace:* See 2.2.3.

18.2 *if the other side was willing to go to arbitration:* An accusation levied by Pericles at 1.140.2.

24.2 *was kept there:* As Thucydides explains at 6.31.3, although the state provided the hulls and crews for the triremes, each trierarch (see the Glossary, p. 633) was responsible for providing his ship's equipment.

28.1 *Sunium:* Sunium is the southernmost point of Attica, famous for its temple of Poseidon. Euboea was one of Athens's most important sources of grain, and was also the place to which they had evacuated much of their livestock at the start of the war (2.14.1). The disruption of these trade routes will therefore have put considerable strain on Athens's food supply.

28.4 *5 percent tax on goods carried by sea:* Thucydides gives surprisingly little emphasis to this change, which represented a significant development in imperial administration (compare his more detailed analysis of the impact of tribute payment at 1.96, 99). We might, though, read the subsequent narrative of the terrible events at Mycalessus as an implicit comment on the consequences of Athenian financial mismanagement at this stage of the war.

29.1 *Euripus channel:* The narrow strait separating Euboea from the Greek mainland. The current in the channel changes direction several times each day. According to a (surely invented) anecdote, the philosopher Aristotle was so frustrated by his inability to explain this phenomenon that he hurled himself into the strait.

29.2 *Mycalessus:* A Boeotian town, located about twelve miles west of Thebes and about eight miles from the coast.

32.1 *the Centoripans and the Halicyaeans:* The Athenian pact with the Centoripans was reported at 6.94.3. The Halicyaeans have not been mentioned before by Thucydides, though an inscribed copy of a treaty between them and Athens survives, probably to be dated to 418/417.

34.1 *Erineus in Achaea:* On the southern side of the Gulf of Corinth, about sixteen miles east of Patras.

35.2 *bypassing Locri:* Locri and Athens had made a treaty in 422, but Thucydides suggests (5.5.2–3) that the Locrians, who had previously been allied with Syracuse (3.86.2), were not particularly committed to this agreement. The fact that they were willing to allow entry to a Syracusan fleet (7.25.3) implies that they had now changed sides again.

41.2 *"dolphins"... overhanging the entrances:* "Dolphins" were semicircular metal weights that could be dropped from above onto enemy ships.

44.1 *even after consulting people from both sides:* An unusual admission of the limitations of Thucydides's method of producing an accurate account by applying critical scrutiny to eyewitness records of events (see 1.22.2–3). We might note that the narrative that follows betrays little sign of this uncertainty (on Thucydides's part; the confusion experienced by participants in the battle is strongly emphasized).

44.6 *no less than when the enemy chanted it:* For paeans, see the Glossary (p. 631). Paeans are being used here as battle-hymns or chants. The confusion arises because the Athenians (and Ionians) either did not sing this type of battle-hymn at all, or sang a distinctly different type of hymn from that used by Dorian Greeks, so they perceived these Dorian paeans as something unfamiliar and (in this context) threatening. This, in turn, reflects what is (in Thucydides's view, at least) a more fundamental confusion of ethnic affiliations in this campaign (see note for 7.57.1 below).

50.4 *eclipse of the moon, which was full at the time:* The eclipse occurred on August 27, 413. Thucydides's comment about the phase of the moon reflects his knowledge that lunar eclipses occur only when the moon is full.

55.2 *regime change ... as a way to bring them over:* See Thucydides's observation at 3.82.1 that the usual pattern in this war was for democratic regimes or factions to seek Athenian support, and for oligarchs to turn to Sparta.

57.1 *given the circumstances:* The catalog is of course important in the information it conveys. But it also performs a rhetorical function: it allows Thucydides not only to emphasize the scale of this conflict, but also to delay, and therefore build up tension before, his narration of the decisive stages of the campaign. Finally, it enables him to continue to explore a key theme of his work: that political and military alliances in this period often failed to map onto the traditional, ethnically based divisions of the Greek world (see Introduction).

57.2 *Aegina ... Hestiaea in Euboea:* The qualifications in parentheses are needed because the original inhabitants of these communities had been expelled by the Athenians (the Aeginetans in 431 [2.27.2], the Hestiaeans in 446 [1.114.3]) and replaced with Athenian colonists.

57.4 *supplied ships:* Chios and Methymna (a city on the island of Lesbos) were by now the only two members of the Delian League that contributed ships rather than money (see 1.96.1, 99.3 for the original terms of and early developments in the alliance).

63.3 *to turn to you crewmen:* It seems that Nicias is here addressing the metic members of the Athenian fleet (for metics, see the Glossary, p. 630).

67.2 *sitting position:* The marines on the deck had to discharge their weapons from a sitting position so as not to stumble around and disturb the balance of the narrow trireme.

75.5 *at least forty thousand:* This figure seems implausibly high, since it is the same as the (approximate) maximum size of Athenian and allied forces in Sicily; that is, it makes no allowance for the extensive casualties suffered during the campaign.

77.5 *our homeland and our fortress:* Here Nicias repeats his own advice (or warning?) to the Athenians before they embarked on the expedition: they would be attempting to create a new homeland in hostile territory (6.23.3). We are presumably expected to remember that Nicias thought such a task was likely to be very difficult even when the Athenian army was at full strength.

79.3 *everything was colluding for their destruction:* That is, they interpreted the thunder as a negative portent (cf. 6.70.1).

85.2 *hidden by their captors:* Their captors were presumably hoping to be able to sell or ransom these men for their own private gain. At the end of the war, the Athenians recorded thanks and honors for a citizen of Cyrene who had spent one hundred minas ransoming Athenian prisoners from Syracuse. Prisoners of war could be a lucrative asset, whether for individuals or for the state.

Book Eight

3.1 *Oetaeans:* A people who occupied territory near the Spartan colony at Heraclea in Trachis (cf. 3.92.2).

4.1 *fortress they had built in Laconia:* The fort was in southern Laconia, opposite Cythera (see 7.26.2).

5.4 *Erythraeans:* This is the Erythrae in Asia Minor, on the mainland opposite Chios.

5.4 *Darius, son of Artaxerxes:* Darius II, who had acceded to the Persian throne in 423.

5.5 *Amorges...rebellion in Caria:* Pissuthnes had been Persian governor of western Asia Minor (see 1.115.4–5, 3.31.1) until his unsuccessful rebellion and execution in 415. Tissaphernes was his successor in the role.

6.1 *Pharnabazus, son of Pharnaces:* Pharnabazus, son of the Pharnaces who appeared at 2.67.1, had succeeded his father as Persian governor of Hellespontine Phrygia, the province to the north of the one controlled by Tissaphernes.

6.3 *Endius, son of Alcibiades:* Endius had also been one of the Spartan envoys to Athens in the summer of 420 (cf. 5.44.3) and was involved in

Notes to Book Eight

Alcibiades's machinations then, although Thucydides did not, at that point, mention the connection between the two men.

6.5 *reduced... from ten to five:* The earthquake, interpreted as a portent, seems to have prompted the Spartans to reformulate and scale down their expedition (rather than abandoning it entirely; cf. 3.89.1, 6.95.1).

9.1 *Isthmia... which fell at this time:* The Isthmian Games, a panhellenic festival celebrated at about the time of the summer solstice. The festival honored Poseidon, god of (among other things) earthquakes; it has been suggested that the recent earthquake might have increased the Corinthians' reluctance to disrupt the event.

9.1 *Isthmian truce:* This truce, like the Olympic truce (5.49.1), entailed a temporary suspension of warfare, intended to allow safe travel to and participation in this panhellenic festival.

14.1 *Corycus:* Just south of Erythrae.

15.1 *reserve fund of a thousand talents untouched:* Established in the summer of 431 (see 2.24.1).

17.4 *alliance read as follows:* In Book Eight, as in Book Five, Thucydides reports several treaties verbatim. This, as well as the absence of any set-piece speeches in this book (as also in Book Five), has led many commentators to see both books as at least partially unfinished, on the grounds that, if Thucydides had had more time, he would have converted this "raw material" into his own words. This view also assumes that the speeches, which are typically among the most complex parts of the work, would have been among the last things to be added. For more discussion of the unfinished state of the text, see the Introduction.

23.6 *Daphnous:* Another mainland settlement, presumably close to Clazomenae, but its exact location is unknown.

24.3 *Cardamyle and Bolissus:* On the northeast and northwest coasts of Chios, respectively.

24.3 *Phanae and Leuconium:* Phanae is in the southwest of the island; the location of Leuconium is unknown, although it is sometimes placed (by inference from the apparent trajectory of the Athenians' campaign, moving counterclockwise round the coast) in the eastern or southeastern part of the island.

26.2 *Gulf of Iasus:* South of Miletus. The description of Leros as "off Miletus" is not very accurate.

28.2 *assumed the ships were Athenian:* This is because (as Thucydides never quite explicitly says, but we know from other sources) the Athenians were backing Amorges's revolt.

28.3 *Amorges... rebelled against the King:* See 8.5.5, with the note.

Notes to Book Eight

31.2 *Pteleum:* The Athenian fort in Erythraean territory (see 8.24.2).

34.1 *Mount Mimas:* The promontory on the north of the Erythrae peninsula.

34.1 *fortified outpost:* This was not built on Lesbos, but on Chios (see 8.38.2).

38.1 *never to be seen again:* There is no particular reason to suspect foul play in Therimenes's disappearance; travel by sea, particularly in winter and in a small boat, always carried some risk.

41.2 *Cos Meropis:* At the northeast end of the island of Cos.

42.4 *Teutloussa:* A small island immediately south of Syme.

43.3 *islands... Thessaly, Locris... north of Boeotia:* These were the regions of Greece that had (briefly) come under Persian control in the invasion of 480–479.

45.1 *Agis had come to loathe him:* According to Plutarch (*Life of Alcibiades* 23.7), the rift occurred because Alcibiades had slept with Agis's wife, Timaea, and claimed to be the father of her son Leotychidas.

45.2 *half a drachma a day... their crews:* The usual rate of pay for Athenian sailors was one drachma a day (3.17.3, 6.31.3). It is possible that the disaster in Sicily had forced the Athenians to impose a pay cut, but it is also possible that we should see this claim as an example of Alcibiades's willingness to be economical with the truth.

48.1 *greatest burden:* This belief was probably based on the fact that at least some of the richest Athenians were required to spend their own resources on Athenian naval expeditions (through the trierarchic system; see the Glossary, p. 633). It is likely, too (though not absolutely certain), that the richest Athenians paid higher contributions to the emergency war tax (the *eisphora*, first levied in 428/427 [3.19.1]; see also 8.63.4, for voluntary contributions toward war expenses).

49.1 *Peisander:* A prominent Athenian politician. This is his first appearance in the work, although we know from other sources that he was involved in the inquiry into the affair of the herms and the Mysteries (cf. 6.53–61): that is, he was previously a pro-democratic (or at least anti-oligarchic) figure, but has now changed sides.

52.1 *treaty of Therimenes:* The second treaty between Sparta and Persia, reported at 8.37; the quarrel over its terms is the one reported at 8.43.2–4.

53.2 *the Eumolpidae and the Heralds:* Two hereditary groups who provided the most important priests and officials for the cult at Eleusis.

54.3 *betraying Iasus and Amorges:* In the events described at 8.28.2–4.

54.4 *cabals... influence lawsuits and elections:* This information about the existence of secretive political groups in Athens can help us understand (belatedly) why the Athenians might have thought that the groups involved in the mutilation of the herms also had a political goal in mind (see 6.27).

Notes to Book Eight

- 58.1 *sons of Pharnaces:* Including Pharnabazus, the Persian governor of Hellespontine Phrygia (see 8.6.1, with the note). Hieramenes was a Persian official, perhaps acting here as a representative of the king.
- 58.2 *the King shall manage it as he pleases:* This clause addresses one of Lichas's concerns about the previous treaty—that it potentially conceded to the Persians the right to rule over parts of mainland Greece and the Aegean islands (8.43.3)—but still represents a significant concession, ceding to Persia the regions of western Asia Minor that had been outside Persian control (but part of the Athenian empire) for much of the fifth century. It is possible, though, that the Spartans hoped to be able to claim that the reference here to "territory" rather than "cities" meant that the Greek cities in Asia Minor were not covered by the agreement.
- 60.1 *Boeotians took Oropus:* On the border between Attica and Boeotia, and a frequent bone of contention between the two states.
- 62.2 *Sestus... that had once been in Persian hands:* The Persians had abandoned Sestus shortly after the end of the Persian Wars, after a siege led by the Athenians and their allies (1.89.2).
- 63.3 *recent civil uprising... the desire to avoid oligarchy:* The democratic revolution of 412, described at 8.21.1.
- 64.5 *prudent form of government:* "Prudence" is a quality often attributed to more oligarchic forms of government, in contrast to the (alleged) recklessness of democratic regimes. As Thucydides notes at 3.82.8, however (in his account of the civil war at Corcyra), this language could also be used insincerely, to conceal more self-interested motivations.
- 65.3 *no more than five thousand men... were to have a share in government:* If implemented, this would still have been a significant change from the existing democratic regime, in which all those who served as civic officials, sat in the council, or performed jury service received pay (thus making it possible, at least in theory, for the poor to perform these roles), and in which all male citizens, regardless of wealth, were entitled to participate in the assembly. This was somewhere in the region of thirty thousand to sixty thousand men, although actual attendance at assembly meetings would have been much lower (see 8.72.1, with the note).
- 67.2 *Colonus hill... sanctuary of Poseidon:* This choice of location, outside the city walls, might have been intended to deter many Athenians (and perhaps particularly the poorest Athenians, who were less likely to have armor) from attending the meeting, especially given that a Spartan army was still present in Attica.
- 67.2 *with impunity:* The Athenians usually enforced a system in which it was illegal to make proposals that were considered "contrary to the

Notes to Book Eight

law"; any politician who did so could be prosecuted. Since there was no formal or unified code of Athenian law at this date, this rule provided considerable scope for delaying, or even blocking, controversial legislation, because it meant that, in theory, any Athenian could challenge a proposal they thought problematic and require it to be considered in a court of law. Suspension of this rule enabled a swifter and less scrutinized approach to legislation than was usually the case.

67.3 *council...as and when they saw fit:* By creating a Council of Four Hundred, the conspirators were reviving an institution that had existed before the late sixth-century democratic reforms of Cleisthenes.

68.1 *his services:* As a speechwriter.

69.3 *Aeginetan settlers...populate the island:* These Athenians had settled in Aegina after the expulsion of the Aeginetans in 431 (2.27.1). Presumably they had now returned to Athens because Aegina was considered too dangerous (see 8.92.3).

69.4 *councilors chosen by lot:* That is, the members of the democratic Council of Five Hundred, the body responsible for the day-to-day running of the state. Councilors were drawn from across Attica; each member served for a year, and could serve only twice in his lifetime.

72.1 *five thousand people had assembled to debate it:* We do not have exact figures for attendance at the Athenian assembly, but five thousand is likely to be an underestimate. The capacity of the assembly-place in this period was somewhere between six thousand and ten thousand, and some votes had a quorum of six thousand.

72.2 *their overthrow:* Athenian triremes were rowed (at least partly) by the poorest Athenians, who could not afford armor or a horse. Those who served in the navy were thus especially likely to be affected by the new restrictions on political participation.

73.2 *attack their former associates as being democrats:* These "former associates" must be those who had participated in the democratic revolution of 412 (8.21.1), but who (unlike these three hundred) had not changed sides and were still pro-democracy.

73.3 *ostracized from Athens:* Ostracism was a ten-year sentence of exile, decided by popular vote. The date of Hyperbolus's ostracism is uncertain, but it took place sometime between 418 and 415.

74.3 *slave or free:* One of the principles of Athenian democracy was that citizens could not usually be subjected to corporal punishment.

76.3 *whatever they might need:* This is another variation on a theme that has cropped up throughout the work (see, e.g., 1.81.6, 7.64.2, and 7.77.7). Is "Athens" defined by its physical form and location—it is, and can only be, the city in Attica—or does it consist of "the people

Notes to Book Eight

of Athens" (or even a subset of the people of Athens), wherever those people happen to be? Here, the argument is that it is the democratic Athenians who constitute the "real" Athens, even though they are physically located in Samos.

76.4 *in the war against Athens... mastery of the sea:* That is, in the Samian rebellion of 440 (see 1.115–117).

79.1 *make their way there overland:* The Mycale headland is about twenty-five miles northwest of Miletus.

80.1 *order he had originally been given in the Peloponnese:* In the summer of 412 (see 8.8.2).

81.3 *turn his own bed into money:* This plays on a widespread Greek perception that Persians lived lives of great luxury, manifested especially in the expense of their household furnishings.

81.3 *Aspendus:* A city in Pamphylia, in southeast Asia Minor.

83.2 *refused to put to sea and engage the Athenians:* See 8.79.6.

89.3 *people who were not his peers:* Most democratic offices in Athens were assigned by random lottery rather than by election.

93.1 *sanctuary of the Dioscuri:* In the center of Athens, on the north slope of the acropolis.

93.3 *the state as a whole:* Athenians who served as hoplites had a moderate level of wealth, and many (or even all) of them might have expected to be included in a government of "Five Thousand," as indeed turns out to be the case (see 8.97.1).

95.1 *moved on to Oropus:* A circumnavigation of Attica, down the west coast and then back up the east coast.

95.2 *excluded from Attica:* See 7.28.1, with the note.

95.7 *Oreus:* Formerly known as Hestiaea, it was taken over by the Athenians in 446 (see 1.114.3).

96.5 *convenient enemies for the Athenians to face:* Thucydides here makes explicit a contrast he has been hinting at, or putting in the mouths of various speakers in the *History*, throughout the work (see the note on 1.67.3).

97.1 *regular meeting place earlier:* The Pnyx hill was the regular meeting place when the democracy was in power.

97.1 *the Five Thousand,... their own arms and armor:* That is, in effect, the hoplite class. There had been sixteen thousand Athenian hoplites at the start of war, according to 2.13.6; their numbers must by now have been significantly smaller.

97.2 *dire condition into which it had fallen:* This is the most explicit statement in the work of Thucydides's own political views. See the Introduction for further discussion.

Notes to Book Eight

101.1 *Chian fortieths:* Presumably a small denomination of the local currency; its exact value is unknown.

102.3 *Protesilaus:* Protesilaus was the first Greek to be killed at Troy. His sanctuary is the setting for the final episode in Herodotus's *Histories* (an episode that also involves the Athenians [9.116–121]), though this might be pure coincidence rather than deliberate historiographical allusion.

104.2 *from Abydus to Dardanus:* The Athenians are mustering along the north side of the Hellespont, and the Peloponnesians along the south side.

108.4 *Antandrus:* Antandrus was a city on the western coast of Asia Minor, opposite Lesbos. For its strategic importance, see 4.52.3.

108.4 *in order to purify it:* In the summer of 422 (see 5.1).

109.1 *Miletus and Cnidus (at Cnidus, too, they had expelled his garrison):* The episode at Miletus was described at 8.84.4; the information that there had been a similar incident at Cnidus is new. Presumably, to judge by Tissaphernes's reaction, the Peloponnesians had helped the Antandrians acquire their hoplites.

Textual Notes

I have translated the recension of the Greek text by G. B. Alberti. This was published in three volumes: *Thucydidis Historiae* (Istituto Poligrafico dello Stato, 1972, 1992, 2000). However, Thucydides's Greek is often difficult, and as all editors and translators do, I differ from Alberti's text at a number of points, as follows. These places are indicated in the translation by an obelus (†). An asterisk in the text refers the reader to a note in the "Notes" section of the book on pp. 635–679.

1.36.3	Reading ἐν for ἄν with Thompson ap. Gomme ad loc.
1.107.3	Reading ν′ ναυσὶ with Lewis.
1.126.6	Retaining the received MSS text—i.e., reading πολλοὶ and omitting <ἁγνὰ>.
1.142.3	Reading πρὸς πόλιν ἀντίπαλον with Gomme.
2.10.3	Reading ἀξιωτάτους (with some MSS) παρεῖναι (with all MSS), and therefore retaining ἔλεξεν.
2.20.4	Reading πολῖται with Polle.
2.42.4	Retaining the MSS μᾶλλον.
2.44.1	Reading ἐπίστασθε with Herwerden.
2.44.1	Omitting Gomme's added εὖ.
2.65.12	Following Hornblower, we read "eight" here in place of the "three" of the MSS. That is, 411–404, counting inclusively, in the Greek way.
2.93.3	Reading τολμῆσαι ἄν, καθ' ἡσυχίαν δ' εἰ with Hude.
3.9.2	Reading ἐπινοίᾳ with Hude.
3.11.3	Reading ἑκόντας with a scholiast on the passage and recent editors.
3.16.1	Omitting τῆς Πελοποννήσου.
3.38.1	Deleting ὄν with Haase.
3.38.3	Reading τοῖς ῥήτορσι with MS C.
3.44.2	Reading οὐδ' ἐᾶν, following suggestions by Gomme and Lindau.

Textual Notes

3.58.1	Reading τότε.
3.62.5	Reading ἵππον with Cobet.
3.89.5	Retaining ἐπισπωμένην with the MSS.
3.112.1	Reading, with Smith, a comma after προκαταλαβόντες and no brackets.
4.4.1	Retaining τοὺς στρατιώτας.
4.8.6	Reading, with Burrows, κέ (25 stades) for ιέ (15).
4.9.2	Reading ἐσβιάσασθαι with Van Leeuwen.
4.30.3	Reading αὐτόσε with Krüger.
4.44.2	Reading τοιούτῳ τρόπῳ with de Romilly.
4.45.2	Reading ἐν ᾗ with Classen.
4.67.3	Reading ἐκδρομή for φυλακή, with Gomme.
4.73.2	In addition to Gomme's correction of γε to τε, I move καὶ to before ὥσπερ ἀκονιτί.
4.73.4	The Greek of these last two clauses is irredeemably corrupt and all translators employ some guesswork.
4.80.3	Reading θρασύτητα, suggested to me by A. J. Woodman.
4.108.5	Reading ἐπιόντι with Gomme.
4.117.2	There is a lacuna in the text that I have filled with what must be the sense, following Hornblower and Rhodes.
4.118.14	There is a gap in the text.
4.120.1	There appears to be a gap in the text.
4.129.3	A comparison with 4.123.4 suggests this emendation (see Hornblower), with the number of hoplites lost.
5.7.3	Reading περιμένειν with Marshall.
5.16.2	Reading τοῦ Δελφοῦ with Cobet.
5.18.5	Reading τάσδε δὲ πόλεις with Steup.
5.20.1	In all the MSS this last clause is given as "since the first invasion of Attica and the beginning of the current war." But at 2.19.1, Thucydides says that the first invasion of Attica took place eighty days after "the business at Plataea," which was the first event of the war, so along with many editors and translators I have deleted "the first invasion of Attica."
5.36.2	Reading the Greek without a lacuna.
5.47.6	Reading ἐπειδὰν with Kirchhoff.
5.49.3	Reading παρ' αὐτοῖς with Andrewes.
5.50.2	Omitting θυσίας καὶ ἀγώνων with Krüger.
5.63.4	Reading ἐκ τῆς πολεμίας with Haase.
5.79.4	Retaining the received δὲ and omitting Dover's added ἄδε.
5.83.4	Reading ἀποστάντος with Poppo.
5.99	Reading τοὺς for που with Krüger.

Textual Notes

5.105.2 Retaining κειμένῳ with good manuscript support.
5.110.2 Omitting ξυμμαχίδος τε καὶ γῆς with Stahl.
5.113 Omitting καὶ with Classen.
5.116.3 Moving the comma to after ἑαυτῶν, with Smith.
6.4.1 Reading παραδόντος with Classen.
6.4.2 Reading μεταπέμψαντες with Marchant, and therefore retaining the MSS τῆς for Alberti's τις.
6.5.3 Reading Γελῴων with Dodwell.
6.6.1 Reading προσγεγενημένοις with a number of good MSS.
6.10.1 Reading ὑμᾶς with some MSS and recent editors.
6.15.4 Reading διαθέντος with Herwerden.
6.21.2 Reading [ἐν] τοῖς, with Badham.
6.31.3 Reading κενὰς with most MSS.
6.87.5 Retaining τοῖς ἄλλοις with the MSS, and reading τοὺς Συρακοσίους with Camps.
6.100.1 Reading, with two good MSS, πυραμίδα, "of which πυλίδα in the other MSS seems to be a banal corruption; there is no more difficulty in a passing reference to 'the pyramid' than in the reference (6.98.2) to 'the fig tree'" (Dover).
7.5.3 Omitting μὲν with the majority of the MSS.
7.6.1 Reading μάχεσθαι with the majority of the MSS.
7.24.3 Reading τε with MSS BH.
7.28.2 The text of this clause is somewhat corrupt, but this must be the sense.
7.32.2 Reading του with Herwerden.
7.43.1 Omitting καὶ with some MSS.
7.43.2 Reading πεζὴν with Wölfflin (cf. Plutarch, *Nicias* 21.5).
7.44.6 Omitting καὶ with some MSS.
7.49.1 Reading, with Linwood, μᾶλλον ἢ πρότερον ἐθάρσησε κρατήσειν.
7.50.1 Reading τῆς ἄλλης Σικελίας, suggested to me by A. J. Woodman.
7.58.3 Omitting δύναται... εἶναι with recent editors, as a gloss that has crept into the text.
7.71.2 Reading διὰ τὸ ἀνώμαλον τῆς ναυμαχίας ἀνώμαλον καὶ τὴν ἔποψιν with Bauer, Wölfflin, and recent editors.
7.71.7 Reading ξυμπασῶν with Dionysius of Halicarnassus.
7.73.2 Reading ἀναπεπαυμένους with the majority of the MSS.
7.77.4 Reading ἀνεκτέα.
7.77.6 Reading ἄλλα with the MSS.
8.37.3 I have transferred this sentence here, where it seems to belong, from the end of §4.
8.46.3 Reading πῃ with Goodhart and Tucker.
8.48.5 Reading ὑποσχήσεσθαι with Böhme.

Textual Notes

8.70.1	Retaining the δὲ of the MSS.
8.71.1	Retaining the MSS text: τὴν πόλιν οὐχ ἡσυχάζειν οὐδ' εὐθὺς...
8.76.5	Reading ἔσπλου, οἳ with Tucker.
8.89.2	Reading ᾤοντο with Delebecque.
8.94.1	Omitting ἐν Διονύσου with Steup.

Index of Proper Names

This index omits names that are merely addenda to main personal names, such as patronymics; so, for "Phalius, son of Eratocleides," Phalius is listed but not Eratocleides. Also omitted are a certain number of one-off names, such as those of witnesses that append the verbatim transcripts of treaties. A bold letter by a place name indicates that it features in the maps with the corresponding number (see the List of Maps on p. xi). A bold number is a book number: thus "**2**.29" means "Book 2, chapter 29," and "**2**.29, 95" means "Book 2, chapters 29 and 95."

Abdera, Abderites, **B, F, 2**.29, 97
Abydus, **B, D, 8**.61–62, 79, 102–108
Acanthus, **4**.84–88, 114, 120, 124, **5**.18
Acarnan, **2**.102
Acarnania, -ians, **A, E, 1**.5, 111, **2**.7, 9, 30, 33, 68, 80–83, 102–103, **3**.7, 94–95, 102, 105–114, **4**.2, 49, 77, 89, 101, **7**.31, 57, 60, 67
Acesines (river), **4**.25
Achaea, -ans, **A, B, 1**.111, 115, **2**.66, 83–84, 86, 92, **3**.92, **4**.21, **5**.82, **7**.34
Achaea Phthiotis, **1**.3, **4**.78, **8**.3
Acharnae, -ians, **2**.19–21, 23
Achelous (river), **E, 2**.102, **3**.106
Acheron (river), **1**.46
Acrae, **C, 6**.5
Acraean Rock (hill), **7**.78
Acragas (river), **6**.4

Acragas, Acragantines, **C, 5**.4, **6**.4, **7**.32–33, 46, 50, 58
Acrothoi, **J, 4**.109
Acte (peninsula), **J, 4**.109
Actium, **1**.29, 30
Admetus, **1**.136
Aeantides, **6**.59
Aegaleos (mountain), **2**.19
Aegina (island), -etans, **A, B, 1**.14, 41, 67, 105, 108, 139–140, **2**.27, 31, **4**.56–57, **5**.53, 74, **7**.20, 26, 57, **8**.69, 92
Aegitium, **G, 3**.97
Aenesias, **2**.2
Aenianians, **5**.51
Aenus, **D, 4**.28, **7**.57
Aeolis (Aetolia), **3**.102
Aeolis (Asia), Aeolians, **D, 3**.31, **4**.42, **7**.57, **8**.108
Aeolus, Islands of, **C, 3**.88, 115

Index of Proper Names

Aesimides, **1.**47
Aeson, **5.**40
Aethaea, **1.**101
Aetolia, -ians, **A, G, 1.**5, **3.**94–98, 100, 102, 105, 114, **4.**30, **7.**57
Agamemnon, **1.**9
Agatharchidas, **2.**83
Agatharchus, **7.**25, 70
Agesander, **1.**139
Agesandridas, **8.**91, 94–95
Agesippidas, **5.**52, 56
Agis, **3.**89, **4.**2, 6, **5.**54, 57–60, 63, 65–66, 71–73, 83, **7.**19, 27, **8.**3, 5, 7–9, 11–12, 45, 70–71
Agraei, Agraeis, **2.**102, **3.**106, 111, 113–114, **4.**77, 101
Agrianes, **F, 2.**96
Alcaeus, **5.**19, 25
Alcamenes, **8.**5, 8, 10
Alcibiades, **5.**43–46, 52–56, 61, 76, 84, **6.**8, 15, 28–29, 48–53, 61, 74, 88–93, **7.**18, **8.**6, 11–14, 17, 26, 45–54, 56, 63, 65, 68, 70, 76, 81–83, 85–90, 97, 108
Alcidas, **3.**16, 26, 30–33, 69, 76, 79–80, 92
Alcinous, **3.**70
Alciphron, **5.**59
Alcmeon, **2.**102
Alcmeonidae, **6.**59
Alexander, **1.**137, **2.**99
Alexarchus, **7.**19
Alexicles, **8.**92–93, 98
Alexippidas, **8.**57
Almopia, Almopes, **2.**99
Alope, **2.**26
Alpaeans, **3.**101
Alyzea, **7.**31
Ambracia, Ambraciots, **A, E, 1.**26–27, 46–48, **2.**9, 68, 80–81,
3.69, 102, 105–114, **4.**42, **6.**104, **7.**7, 25, 58, **8.**106
Ameiniades, **2.**67
Ameinias, **4.**132
Ameinocles, **1.**13
Ammeas, **3.**22
Amorges, **8.**5, 19, 28, 54
Ampelidas, **5.**22
Amphilochia, -ians, **2.**68, 102, **3.**102, 105, 107, 110, 112–114
Amphilochus, **2.**68
Amphipolis, **A, B, J, 1.**100, **4.**102–109, 132, **5.**3, 6–11, 14, 16, 18, 21, 26, 35, 46, 83, **7.**9
Amphissa, **G, 3.**101
Amyclaeum, **5.**18, 23
Amyntas, **2.**95, 100
Amyrtaeus, **1.**110, 112
Anactorium, -ians, **B, E, 1.**29, 46, 55, **2.**9, 80–81, **3.**114, **4.**49, **5.**30, **7.**31
Anaea, -ans, **D, 3.**19, 32, **4.**75, **8.**19, 61
Anapus (river; Aetolia), **2.**82
Anapus (river; Syracuse), **K, 6.**66, 96, **7.**42, 78
Anaxarchus, **8.**100
Anaxilas, **6.**4
Androcles, **8.**65
Androcrates (hero), **3.**24
Andromedes, **5.**42
Andros (island), **B, 2.**55, **4.**42, 84, 88, 103, 109, **5.**6, **6.**96, **7.**57, **8.**69
Androsthenes, **5.**49
Aneristus, **2.**67
Antandrus, -ians, **D, 4.**52, 75, **8.**108–109
Anthemus, **2.**99–100
Anthene, **5.**41
Anticles, **1.**117
Antimenidas, **5.**42
Antiochus, **2.**80

Index of Proper Names

Antiphemus, **6.**4
Antiphon, **8.**68, 90
Antissa, **D**, **3.**18, 28, **8.**23
Antisthenes, **8.**39, 61
Aphrodite (goddess), **6.**46
Aphroditia, **4.**56
Aphytis, **1.**64
Apidanus (river), **4.**78
Apodoti, **3.**94, 100
Apollo (god), **1.**13, 29, 118, 123, 132, **2.**15, 91, 102, **3.**3, 94, 104, **4.**76, 97, 118, **5.**18, 23, 47, 53, **6.**3, 54, 75, **7.**26, **8.**35
Apollonia, **1.**26
Arcadia, -ians, **A**, **1.**2, 9, **3.**34, **5.**29, 31, 33, 57–58, 60–61, 64, 67, **7.**19, 57–58, **8.**3
Archedice, **6.**59
Archelaus, **2.**100
Archestratus, **1.**57
Archetimus, **1.**29
Archias (Camarinaean), **4.**25
Archias (Corinthian), **6.**3
Archidamus, **1.**79–85, **2.**10–13, 18–20, 47, 71–75, **3.**1
Archonides, **7.**1
Argilus, **J**, **1.**132, **4.**103, **5.**6, 18
Arginousae, **8.**101
Arginum, **8.**34
Argos (Amphilochia), Argolis, Argives, **E**, **2.**68, 80, **3.**102, 105–108, 112
Argos (Argolis), Argives, **A**, **B**, **1.**9, 102, 107, 135–137, **2.**2, 27, 68, 99, **4.**42, 133, **5.**14, 22, 27–32, 36–38, 40–48, 50, 52, 53–84, 115–116, **6.**7, 29, 43, 61, 67–70, 89, 95, 100–101, 105, **7.**18, 20, 26, 44, 57, **8.**25, 27, 86, 92
Arianthidas, **4.**91

Aristagoras, **4.**102
Aristarchus, **8.**90, 92, 98
Aristeides (general), **4.**50, 75
Aristeides (the Just), **1.**91, **5.**18
Aristeus (Corinthian), **1.**29
Aristeus (another Corinthian), **1.**60–65, **2.**67
Aristeus (Spartan), **4.**132
Aristocles (Delphian), **5.**16
Aristocles (Spartan), **5.**71–72
Aristocrates, **8.**9, 89, 92
Aristogeiton, **1.**20, **6.**54, 56–57, 59; *see also* Harmodius
Ariston, **7.**39
Aristonous (of Acragas), **6.**4
Aristonous (of Larisa), **2.**22
Aristonymus, **4.**122
Aristophon, **8.**86
Aristoteles, **3.**105
Arnae, **4.**103
Arne, **1.**12
Arrhabaeus, **4.**79, 83, 124–125, 127
Arriani, **8.**104
Arsaces, **8.**108
Artabazus, **1.**129, 132
Artaphernes, **4.**50
Artas, **7.**33
Artaxerxes, **1.**104, 109, 137, **4.**50
Artemis (goddess), **3.**104, **6.**44, **8.**109
Artemisium, **3.**54
Asia, **1.**6, 9, 16, 109, **2.**67, 97, **4.**75, **5.**1, **8.**58
Asine (Laconia), **4.**54
Asine (Messenia), **4.**13, **6.**93
Asopius, **3.**7
Asopus (river), **2.**5
Aspendus, **8.**81, 87–88, 99, 108
Assinarus (river), **7.**84
Astacus, **E**, **2.**30, 33, 102
Astymachus, **3.**52

687

Index of Proper Names

Astyochus, **8.**20, 23–24, 26, 29, 31–33, 36, 38–42, 45, 50–51, 61, 63, 68, 78–79, 83–85
Atalante (island), **2.**32, **3.**89, **5.**18
Atalante (Macedon), **2.**100
Athena (goddess), **1.**126, **2.**13, 15, **4.**116, **5.**10, 23
Athenaeus, **4.**122
Athenagoras, **6.**35–41
Athens, Athenians, **A**, **B**, **I**, *passim*
Athos, Mount, **J**, **4.**109, **5.**3, 35, 82
Atintanians, **E**, **2.**80
Atramyttium, **5.**1, **8.**108
Atreus, **1.**9
Attica, **A**, **B**, **1.**2, 9, 58, 101, 109, 114, 125, 138, 143, **2.**6, 10–23, 32, 47, 56–57, 70, 71, **3.**1, 13, 15, 17, 25–26, 89, **4.**2, 5–6, 8, **5.**16, 17, **6.**17, 91–92, **7.**18–19, 28, **8.**86, 95–96
Aulon, **4.**103
Autocharidas, **5.**12
Autocles, **4.**53
Axius (river), **F**, **2.**99

Battus, **4.**43
Bisaltia, -ians, **J**, **2.**99, **4.**109
Bithynia, **D**, **4.**75
Boeotia, -ians, **A**, **G**, **I**, **1.**2, 10, 12, 107–108, 111, 113, **2.**2, 6, 9, 12, 18, 22–23, 78, **3.**2, 13, 20, 54, 61–62, 66–67, 87, 91, 95, **4.**70, 72, 76–77, 89–101, 108, 118, **5.**3, 16, 26, 32, 35, 36–40, 42, 44, 46, 50, 52, 57–60, 64, **6.**61, **7.**19, 29, 43, 45, 57–58, **8.**3, 5, 43, 60, 98, 106
Boeum, **1.**107
Bolbe, Lake, **J**, **1.**58, **4.**103
Bolissus, **8.**24

Bomians, **3.**96
Boriades, **3.**100
Bormiscus, **4.**103
Bottiaea, **2.**99–100
Bottice, Bottiaeans, **1.**57–58, 65, **2.**79, 99, 101, **4.**7
Brasidas, **2.**25, 85–86, 93, **3.**69, 76, 79, **4.**11–12, 70–74, 78–88, 102–117, 120–129, 132, 135, **5.**2–3, 6–11, 13, 16, 18, 34, 110
Brasideans (regiment), **5.**67, 71–72
Brauro, **4.**107
Brea, **1.**61
Bricinniae, **5.**4
Brilessus, Mount, **2.**23
Bronze House, the, **1.**128, 134
Bucolion, **4.**134
Budorum, **2.**94, **3.**51
Byzantium, Byzantines, **B**, **D**, **F**, **1.**94, 115, 117, 128–131, **2.**97, **8.**80, 107

Cacyparis (river), **7.**80
Cadmeïs (= Boeotia), **1.**12
Caicinus (river), **3.**103
Calchedon, **D**, **4.**75
Cales (river), **4.**75
Callians, **3.**96
Callias (Athenian), **1.**61–63
Callias (another), **6.**55
Callicrates, **1.**29
Calligeitus, **8.**6, 8, 39
Calydon, **3.**102
Camarina, -aeans, **C**, **3.**86, **4.**25, 58, 65, **5.**4, **6.**5, 52, 67, 75–81, **7.**33, 58, 80
Cambyses, **1.**13–14
Cameirus, -ans, **D**, **8.**44
Canastraeum (cape), **J**, **4.**110
Carcinus, **2.**23

Index of Proper Names

Cardamyle, **8.**24
Caria, -ians, **B**, **1.**4, 8, 116, **2.**9, 69, **3.**19, **8.**5, 39, 85
Carneia (festival), **5.**75–76
Carteria (islands), **8.**101
Carthage, -inians, **C**, **1.**13, **6.**2, 15–19, 34, 46, 88, 90, **7.**50
Caryae, **5.**55
Carystus, -ians, **1.**98, **4.**42–43, **7.**57, **8.**69
Casmenae, **6.**5
Catana, -aeans, **C**, **3.**116, **5.**4, **6.**3, 20, 50–53, 62–65, 71–75, 88, 94, 97–98, **7.**14, 42, 57, 60, 80
Caulonia, **C**, **7.**25
Caunus, **D**, **1.**116, **8.**39, 41–42, 57, 88, 108
Ceädas, the, **1.**134
Cecrops, **2.**15
Cecryphalea (island), **1.**105
Cenaeum (cape), **3.**93
Cenchreae, **4.**42, 44, **8.**10, 20, 23
Centoripa, -ans, **C**, **6.**94, **7.**32
Ceos (island), **7.**57
Cephallenia (island), **A**, **B**, **E**, **1.**27, **2.**7, 30, 33, 80, **3.**94–95, **5.**35, **7.**31, 57
Cercina (mountain), **F**, **2.**98
Cerdylium, **5.**6, 8, 10
Cestrine, **1.**46
Chaereas, **8.**74–75, 86
Chaeronea, **I**, **1.**113, **4.**76, 89
Chalce, **D**, **8.**41, 44, 55, 60
Chalcideus, **8.**6, 8, 11–12, 14–17, 19, 24–25, 28, 32, 36, 43, 45
Chalcidians (Sicily), **3.**86, **4.**25, 61, 64, **6.**3–5, 44, 76, 79; *see also* Ionians
Chalcidice, Chalcidians (Thraceward region), **A**, **B**, **F**, **J**, **1.**57–58, 62, 65, **2.**29, 58, 70, 79, 95, 99, 101, **4.**7, 78–79, 81–84, 102–103, 109–110, 114, 123–124, **5.**3, 10, 21, 80, 82–83, **6.**7, 10
Chalcis (Aetolia), **E**, **1.**108, **2.**83
Chalcis, Chalcidians (Euboea), **1.**15, **6.**3–5, 76, 79, 84, **7.**29, 57, **8.**95
Chaleians, **3.**101
Chaonians, **E**, **2.**68, 80–81
Charicles, **7.**20, 26
Charminus, **8.**30, 41–42, 73
Charoeades, **3.**86, 90
Charybdis, **4.**24
Cheimerium, **1.**30, 46, 48
Chersonese (Corinthian), **4.**42–43
Chersonese (Thracian), **B**, **1.**10, **8.**62, 99, 102, 104
Chios (island), Chians, **B**, **D**, **1.**19, 116–117, **2.**9, 56, **3.**10, 32, 104, **4.**13, 51, 129, **5.**84, **6.**31, 43, 85, **7.**20, 57, **8.**5–12, 14–17, 19–20, 22–24, 28, 30–34, 38, 40–41, 45, 55–56, 60–64, 79, 99–101, 106
Choerades (islands), **7.**33
Chromon, **3.**98
Chrysippus, **1.**9
Chrysis, **2.**2, **4.**133
Cilicians, **1.**112
Cimon, **1.**98, 100, 102, 112
Cithaeron (mountain range), **2.**75, **3.**24
Citium, **1.**112
Clarus, **3.**33
Clazomenae, **D**, **8.**14, 16, 22–23, 31
Clearchus, **8.**8, 39, 80
Clearidas, **4.**132, **5.**6, 8–11, 21, 34
Cleippides, **3.**3
Cleoboulus, **5.**36–38
Cleomedes, **5.**84
Cleomenes (Spartan), **3.**26

Index of Proper Names

Cleomenes (Spartan king), **1.**126
Cleon, **3.**36–41, 44, 47–50, **4.**21–22, 27–30, 36–39, 122, **5.**2–3, 6–7, 10, 16
Cleonae (Acte peninsula), **J**, **4.**109
Cleonae (Argolis), **5.**67, 72, 74, **6.**95
Cleopompus, **2.**26, 58
Cnemus, **2.**66, 80–86, 93
Cnidus, **D**, **3.**88, **8.**35, 41–44, 52, 109
Colonae, **1.**131
Colonus (hill), **8.**67
Colophon, **D**, **3.**34
Conon, **7.**31
Copae, **4.**93
Cophus (bay), **5.**2
Corcyra (island), -eans, **A**, **B**, **E**, **1.**13–14, 24–57, 68, 118, 136, 146, **2.**7, 9, 25, **3.**69–81, 84–85, 94–95, **4.**2–3, 5, 8, 46–48, **6.**30, 32, 42–44, **7.**26, 31, 33, 57
Corinth, Corinthia, -ians, **A**, **B**, **G**, **I**, **1.**13, 24–60, 66–72, 103, 105–106, 114, 119–125, **2.**9, 30, 33, 69, 80–81, 83, 92–94, **3.**15, 70, 72, 85, 102, 114, **4.**42–45, 49, 70, 74, 100, **5.**16, 25–38 *passim*, 48, 52–53, 57–60, 64, 75, 83, 115, **6.**34, 73, 88, 93, 104, **7.**2, 4, 7, 17–19, 25, 31–32, 34, 36, 39, 44, 56–58, 63, 70, 86, **8.**3, 7–11, 13, 32–33, 98, 106
Coronea, **I**, **1.**113, **3.**62, 67, **4.**92–93
Coronta, **2.**102
Corycus, **8.**14, 33–34
Coryphasium (= Pylos), **4.**3, 118, **5.**18
Cos (island), **B**, **D**, **8.**41, 44, 55, 108
Cos Meropis, **8.**41, 108
Cotyrta, **4.**56
Crane, -ians, **2.**30, 33, **5.**35, 56

Crannon, **2.**22
Crataemenes, **6.**4
Crenae, **3.**105–106
Crestonia, -ians, **J**, **2.**99–100, **4.**109
Crete, Cretans, **B**, **2.**9, 85–86, 92, **3.**69, **6.**25, 43, **7.**57, **8.**39
Crocyleum, **3.**96
Croesus, **1.**16
Crommyon, **4.**42, 44–45
Cropia, **2.**19
Croton, -ians, **C**, **7.**35
Crousis, **2.**79
Cumae, **C**, **6.**4
Cyclades (islands), **1.**4
Cyclopes, **6.**2
Cydonia, **2.**85
Cyllene, **E**, **1.**30, **2.**84, 86, **3.**69, 76, **6.**88
Cylon, **1.**126
Cyme, **D**, **3.**31, **8.**22, 31, 100–101
Cynes, **2.**102
Cynossema, **8.**104–106
Cynouria, **4.**56, **5.**14, 41
Cyprus, **1.**94, 104, 112, 128
Cypsela, **5.**33
Cyrene, **1.**110, **7.**50
Cyrrhus, **2.**100
Cyrus the Great, **1.**13, 16
Cyrus the Younger, **2.**65
Cythera (island), **A**, **4.**53–57, 118, **5.**14, 18, **7.**26, 57
Cytinium, **G**, **1.**107, **3.**95, 102
Cyzicus, **D**, **8.**107

Damagon, **3.**92
Danube (river), **F**, **2.**96–97
Daphnous, **8.**23, 31
Dardanus, **8.**104
Darius I, **1.**14, 16, **4.**102, **6.**59
Darius II, **8.**5, 37, 58
Dascon (person), **6.**5

690

Index of Proper Names

Dascon (place), **K**, **6**.66
Dascyleum, **1**.129
Daulia, **2**.29
Decelea, **6**.91, 93, **7**.18–20, 27–28, 42, **8**.3, 5, 69–71, 98
Deiniadas, **8**.22
Delia (festival), **3**.104
Delium, **I**, **4**.76, 89–90, 93, 96–97, 100–101, **5**.14–15
Delos (island), Delians, **B**, **1**.8, 13, 96, **2**.8, **3**.29, 104, **5**.1, 32, **8**.77, 80, 86, 108
Delphi, -ians, **A**, **G**, **I**, **1**.25, 28, 103, 112, 118, 121, 126, 132, 134, 143, **2**.17, **3**.57, 92, 101, **4**.118, 134, **5**.16, 18, 32, **6**.54
  Pythian games at, **5**.1
Delphinium, **8**.38, 40
Demaratus, **6**.105
Demarchus, **8**.85
Demodocus, **4**.75
Demosthenes, **3**.91, 94–98, 102, 105, 107–114, **4**.2–4, 8–11, 29–32, 36–38, 66–67, 76–77, 89, 101, **5**.80, **7**.16–17, 7.20, 26–27, 29, 31, 33, 35, 42–43, 47–49, 55, 57, 69, 72, 75, 78–83, 85–86
Demoteles, **4**.25
Dercylidas, **8**.61–62
Derdas, **1**.57, 59
Dersaei, **2**.101
Deucalion, **1**.3
Diasia (festival), **1**.126
Didyme (island), **3**.88
Dieitrephes, **7**.29, **8**.64
Diemporus, **2**.2
Dii, **F**, **2**.96, **7**.27
Diodotus, **3**.41–49
Diomedon, **8**.19–20, 23–24, 54–55, 73
Diomilus, **6**.96–97

Dionysia (Anthesteria; festival), **2**.15
Dionysia, City (festival), **5**.20, 23
Dionysus (god), **2**.15, **3**.81, **8**.93–94
Dioscuri (gods), **3**.75, **4**.110, **8**.93
Dios Hieron, **8**.19
Diotimus, **1**.45
Diphilus, **7**.34
Dium (Acte), **J**, **4**.109, **5**.35, 82
Dium (Macedon), **4**.78
Doberus, **F**, **2**.98–100
Dolopia, -ians, **1**.98, **2**.102, **5**.51
Dorcis, **1**.95
Dorians, **1**.12, 18, 24, 124, **2**.9, 54, **3**.86, 112, **4**.42, 61, 64, **5**.9, 54, **6**.4–6, 77, 80, 82, **7**.5, 44, 57–58, **8**.25
Dorieus, **3**.8, **8**.35, 84
Doris, -ians, **G**, **1**.107, **3**.92, 95
Dorus, **4**.78
Drabescus, **J**, **1**.100, **4**.102
Dracontides, **1**.51
Droi, **2**.101
Drymoussa, **8**.31
Dryopes, **7**.57
Dryoscephalae, **3**.24
Dyme, **2**.84

Earth (goddess), **2**.15
Eccritus, **7**.19
Echecratidas, **1**.110
Echinades (islands), **2**.102
Edonia, Edones, **1**.100, **2**.99, **4**.102, 107, 109, **5**.6
Eetionea, **8**.90–92, 94
Egesta, **C**, **6**.2, 6, 8, 10–13, 19, 21, 33, 44, 46–48, 62, 77, 88, 98, **7**.57
Egypt, -ians, **1**.104, 109–110, 112, 130, **2**.48, **4**.53, **8**.35
Eidomene, **2**.100
Eion (Chalcidice), **J**, **4**.7

Index of Proper Names

Eion (on the Strymon), **A**, **1**.98, **4**.50, 102, 104–108, **5**.6, 10
Elaeatis, **1**.46
Elaeous, -ians, **D**, **8**.102–103, 107
Eleusinium, the, **2**.17
Eleusis, Eleusinians, **I**, **1**.114, **2**.15, 19–21, **4**.68
Elimiotae, **2**.99
Elis, Eleans, **A**, **E**, **1**.27, 30, 46, **2**.9, 25, 66, 84, **5**.16, 31, 34, 37, 43–50, 58, 61–62, 75, 78, **7**.31
Ellomenus, **3**.94
Elymians, **6**.2
Embatum, **3**.29, 32
Endius, **5**.44, **8**.6, 12, 17
Enipeus (river), **4**.78
Entimus, **6**.4
Enyalius (god), **4**.67
Eordia, Eordi, **2**.99
Ephesia (festival), **3**.104
Ephesus, **D**, **1**.137, **3**.32–33, **4**.50, **8**.19, 109
Ephyra, **1**.46
Epicles, **8**.107
Epicydidas, **5**.12
Epidamnus, -ians, **A**, **1**.24–29, 38, 146, **3**.70
Epidaurus, -ians, **1**.27, 105, 114, **2**.56, **4**.45, **5**.26, 53–58, 75, 77, 80, **6**.31, **8**.3, 10, 92, 94
Epidaurus Limera, **4**.56, **6**.105, **7**.18, 26
Epipolae, **K**, **6**.75, 96–97, 101–103, **7**.1–5, 42–47, 60
Epitadas, **4**.8, 33, 38–39
Erechtheus, **2**.15
Eresus, -ians, **3**.18, 35, **8**.23, 100–101, 103
Eretria, **1**.15, **4**.123, **7**.57, **8**.60, 95
Erineus (Achaea), **7**.34
Erineus (Doris), **1**.107

Erineus (river; Sicily), **7**.80, 82
Erythrae (Boeotia), **3**.24
Erythrae (Ionia), **D**, **3**.29, 33, **8**.5, 14, 16, 24, 28, 32–33
Eryx, **C**, **6**.2, 46
Eteonicus, **8**.23
Ethiopia, **2**.48
Etna, Mount, **C**, **3**.116
Etruria, Etruscans, **4**.109, **6**.88, 103, **7**.53–54, 57
Euboea (island), -ans, **A**, **B**, **I**, **1**.23, 98, 113, 114–115, **2**.2, 14, 26, 32, 55, **3**.3, 17, 87, 89, 92–93, **4**.76, 92, 109, **6**.4, 84, **7**.28, 57, **8**.1, 5, 60, 74, 86, 91, 95–96, 106–107
Eubulus, **8**.23
Eucleides, **6**.5
Eucles (Athenian), **4**.104
Eucles (Syracusan), **6**.103
Euctemon, **8**.30
Euesperides, **7**.50
Euetion, **7**.9
Eumachus, **2**.33
Eumolpidae, **8**.53
Eumolpus, **2**.15
Eupalium, **G**, **3**.96, 102
Euphamidas, **2**.33, **5**.55
Euphemus, **6**.75, 81–88
Eupompides, **3**.20
Euripus (strait), **7**.29–30
Europe, **1**.89, **2**.97, **4**.75
Europus, **2**.100
Eurybatus, **1**.47
Euryelus, **K**, **6**.97, **7**.2, 43
Eurylochus, **3**.100–102, 105–109
Eurymachus, **2**.2, 5
Eurymedon (person), **3**.80–81, 85, 91, 115, **4**.2–3, 8–9, 46, 65, **6**.1, **7**.16, 31, 33, 35, 42–43, 49, 52
Eurymedon (river), **1**.100

Index of Proper Names

Eurystheus, **1.**9
Eurytanes, **3.**94, 100
Eustrophus, **5.**40
Euthydemus, **7.**16, 69
Evalas, **8.**22
Evarchus (of Astacus), **2.**30, 33
Evarchus (of Catana), **6.**3
Evenus (river), **2.**83

Fish Point, **2.**25

Galepsus, **J**, **4.**107, **5.**6
Gaulites, **8.**85
Gela, Geloans, **C**, **4.**58, **5.**4, **6.**4–5, 67, **7.**1, 33, 50, 57–58, 80
Gelas (river), **6.**4
Gelon, **6.**4, 94
Geraestus, **3.**3
Geranea (mountain range), **1.**105, 107, **4.**70
Getae, **F**, **2.**96, 98
Gigonus, **1.**61
Glauce, **8.**79
Glaucon, **1.**51
Goaxis, **4.**107
Gongylus (Corinthian), **7.**2
Gongylus (Eretrian), **1.**128
Gortyn, **2.**85
Gortynia, **2.**100
Graea, **2.**23, **3.**91
Greece, Greeks, *passim*
Gulf
  Ambracian, **1.**29, 55, **2.**68, **3.**107, **4.**49
  Corinthian, **A**, **1.**107, **2.**69, 83, 86, 92–93, **4.**76, **8.**7
  Iasian, **8.**26
  Malian, **G**, **3.**96, **4.**100, **8.**3
  Pierian, **2.**99
  Saronic, **8.**7
  Terinan, **6.**104

Gylippus, **6.**93, 104, **7.**1–7, 11–12, 21–23, 37, 42–43, 46, 50, 53, 57, 65–69, 74, 79, 81–83, 85–86, **8.**13
Gymnopaediae (festival), **5.**82
Gyrtone, **2.**22

Haerae, **8.**19–20
Habronichus, **1.**91
Haemus (mountain), **F**, **2.**96
Hagnon, **1.**117, **2.**58, 95, **4.**102, **5.**11, **6.**31
Halex (river), **3.**99
Haliartus, **I**, **4.**93
Halicarnassus, **D**, **8.**42, 108
Halicyaeans, **7.**32
Halieis, **1.**105, **2.**56, **4.**45
Halys (river), **1.**16
Hamaxitus, **8.**101
Harmatous, **8.**101
Harmodius, **1.**20, **6.**53–54, 56–57, 59; *see also* Aristogeiton
Harpagium, **8.**107
Harpine, **5.**50
Hebrus (river), **F**, **2.**96
Hegesander, **7.**19
Helen (of Troy), **1.**9
Helixus, **8.**80
Hellanicus (historian), **1.**97
Hellen, **1.**3
Hellespont, the, **B**, **F**, **1.**89, 128, **2.**9, 67, 96, **4.**75, **6.**77, **8.**6, 8, 22, 39, 61–62, 79–80, 86, 96, 99–106, 108–109
Helos, **4.**54
Hephaestus (god), **3.**88
Hera (goddess), **1.**24, **3.**68, 79, 81, **4.**133
Heraclea (Black Sea), **4.**75
Heraclea (Trachis), **G**, **3.**92–93, 100, **4.**78, **5.**12, 51–52

Index of Proper Names

Heracleidae, **1**.9, 12
Heracleides (Syracusan), **6**.73
Heracleides (another Syracusan), **6**.103
Heracles (god), **5**.64, 66, **7**.73
Heraeans, **5**.67
Heraeum (headland), **5**.75
Heralds, **8**.53
Hermaeondas, **3**.5
Hermes (god), **7**.29
Hermione, **1**.27, 128, 131, **2**.56, **8**.3, 33
Hermocrates, **4**.58–65, **6**.32–35, 72–73, 75–81, 96, 99, **7**.21, 73, **8**.26, 29, 45, 85
Hermon, **8**.92
Hesiod, **3**.96
Hestiaea, -ans, **1**.114, **7**.57
Hestiodorus, **2**.70
Hiera (island), **3**.88
Hieramenes, **8**.58
Hierophon, **3**.105
Himera, -ans, **3**.115, **6**.5, 62, **7**.1, 58
Himeraeum, **7**.9
Hippagretas, **4**.38
Hipparchus, **1**.20, **6**.54–57
Hippias (Arcadian), **3**.34
Hippias (Athenian tyrant), **1**.20, **6**.54–59
Hippocles, **8**.13
Hippoclus, **6**.59
Hippocrates (Athenian), **4**.66–67, 76–77, 89–90, 93–96, 101
Hippocrates (Geloan), **6**.5
Hippocrates (Spartan), **8**.35, 99, 107
Hippolochidas, **4**.78
Hipponicus, **3**.91
Hipponium, **C**, **5**.5
Hipponoidas, **5**.71–72

Homer, **1**.3, 9–10, **2**.41, **3**.104
Hyacinthia (festival), **5**.23, 41
Hyaei, **3**.101
Hybla Geleatis, **6**.62–63, 94
Hyblon, **6**.4
Hyccara, -ans, **C**, **6**.62, **7**.13
Hylias (river), **7**.35
Hyperbolus, **8**.73
Hypnians, **3**.101
Hysiae (Argolis), **5**.83
Hysiae (Boeotia), **3**.24

Ialysus, **D**, **8**.44
Iapygia (cape), -ians, **C**, **6**.30, 34, 44, **7**.33, 57
Iasus, **D**, **8**.28–29, 36, 54
Iberia, -ians, **6**.2, 90
Icaros (island), **D**, **3**.29, **8**.99
Ida, Mount, **D**, **4**.52, **8**.108
Idacus, **8**.104
Idomene (hills), **3**.112–113
Ietae, **7**.2
Illyrians, **1**.24, **4**.124–125
Imbros (island), -ians, **D**, **3**.5, **4**.28, **5**.8, **7**.57, **8**.102–103
Inaros, **1**.104, 110
Inessa, **3**.103, **6**.94
Iolaus, **1**.62
Ionia, -ians, **B**, **D**, **1**.6, 12, 16, 89, 124, 137, **2**.9, 15, **3**.31, 33, 86, 92, 104, **4**.61, **5**.9, **6**.4, 76–77, 80, 82–83, **7**.5, 57, **8**.6, 11–12, 20, 25–26, 31, 39, 56, 86, 96, 108
Irians, **3**.92
Isarchidas, **1**.29
Ischagoras, **4**.132, **5**.21
Isians, **3**.101
Isocrates, **2**.83
Isthmia (festival), **8**.9–10

694

Index of Proper Names

Isthmus, the, **1**.13, 108, **2**.9, 10, 18, **3**.15, 18, 89, **4**.42, **5**.18, 75, **6**.61, **8**.7–8, 11
Istone, Mount, **3**.85, **4**.46
Italus, **6**.2
Italy, **C**, **1**.12, 36, 44, **2**.7, **4**.24, **5**.4–5, **6**.2, 34, 42, 44, 88, 90–91, 103–104, **7**.25, 57, 87, **8**.91
Itamenes, **3**.34
Ithome, Mount, **1**.101–103, **3**.54
Itys, **2**.29

Labdalum, **K**, **6**.97–98, **7**.3
Lacedaemonians (i.e., Spartans), *passim*
Lacedaemonius, **1**.45
Laches, **3**.86, 90, 103, 115, **4**.118, **5**.43, 61, **6**.1, 6, 75
Lacon, **3**.52
Laconia, -ians, **A**, **2**.25, 27, 56, **3**.7, **4**.3, 16, 41, 53, **5**.14, 33–35, 115, **6**.105, **7**.19–20, 26, 31, **8**.4, 6, 8, 11, 91
Lade (island), **8**.17, 24
Laeaei, **F**, **2**.96–97
Laestrygonians, **6**.2
Laispodias, **6**.105, **8**.86
Lamachus, **4**.75, **6**.8, 49–50, 101, 103
Lamis, **6**.4
Lampsacus, -enes, **D**, **1**.138, **6**.59, **8**.62
Laodoceum, **4**.134
Larisa (Aeolis), **8**.101
Larisa (Thessaly), **A**, **2**.22
Las, **8**.91–92
Laurium, **2**.55, **6**.91
Learchus, **2**.67
Lebedus, **D**, **8**.19
Lectum (cape), **8**.101

Lecythus, **4**.113–116
Lemnos (island), -ians, **B**, **D**, **1**.115, **2**.47, **3**.5, **4**.28, 109, **5**.8, **7**.57, **8**.102
Leocoreum, **1**.20, **6**.57
Leocrates, **1**.105
Leon (Athenian), **8**.23–24, 54–55, 73
Leon (Spartan), **3**.92, **5**.44
Leon (another Spartan), **8**.61
Leon (place), **K**, **6**.97
Leontini, -ians, **C**, **3**.86, **4**.25, **5**.4, **6**.3–4, 6, 8, 19–20, 33, 44, 46–47, 50, 63, 65, 76–77, 79, 84, 86
Leotychidas, **1**.89
Lepreum, Lepreates, **5**.31, 34, 49–50, 62
Leros (island), **D**, **8**.26–27
Lesbos (island), -ians, **B**, **D**, **1**.19, 116–117, **2**.9, 56, **3**.2–6, 8–16, 26–31, 35–50, 69, **4**.52, 75, **5**.84, **6**.31, **8**.5, 7–8, 22–24, 32, 34, 100–101
Leucas (island), Leucadians, **A**, **B**, **E**, **1**.26–27, 30, 46, **2**.9, 30, 80–81, 91–92, **3**.7, 69, 80–81, 94–95, 102, **4**.8, 42, **6**.104, **7**.2, 7, 58, **8**.13, 106
Leucimme (cape), **1**.30, 47, 51, **3**.79
Leuconium, **8**.24
Leuctra, **5**.54
Libya, -ans, **1**.104, 110, **2**.48, **4**.53, **6**.2, **7**.50, 58
Lichas, **5**.22, 50, 76, **8**.39, 43, 84, 87
Ligurians, **6**.2
Limnaea, **E**, **2**.80, **3**.106
Lindii, **6**.4
Lindus, **D**, **8**.44
Lipara (island), -ians, **3**.88

Index of Proper Names

Locri, Locrians (Italy), **C**, **3**.86, 99, 103, 115, **4**.1, 24–25, **5**.5, **6**.44, **7**.1, 4, 25, 35, **8**.91
Locris, Locrians (Greece), **A, F, I**, **1**.5, 103, 108, 113, **2**.9, 26, 32, **3**.89, 91, 95–97, 101–102, **4**.96, **5**.32, 64, **8**.3, 43
Long Walls
  at Argos, **5**.82–83
  at Athens, **1**.69, 107–108, **2**.13, 17, **5**.26
  at Megara, **1**.103, **4**.66–70, 73, 109
Loryma, **D**, **8**.43
Lycaeum, Mount, **5**.16, 54
Lycia, **2**.69, **8**.41
Lycophron (Corinthian), **4**.43–44
Lycophron (Spartan), **2**.85
Lyncus, Lyncestians, **2**.99, **4**.79, 83, 124, 129, 132
Lysicles, **3**.19
Lysimelea (marsh), **K**, **7**.53
Lysistratus, **4**.110

Macarius, **3**.100, 109
Macedon, -ians, **A, F**, **1**.58–61, 63, **2**.80, 98–101, **4**.124–128, **5**.83, **6**.7
Machaon, **2**.83
Maedi, **2**.98
Maenalia, -ians, **5**.64, 67, 77
Magnesia (Asia), **D**, **1**.138, **8**.50
Magnesia (Thessaly), **2**.101
Malea, **D**, **3**.4, 6
Malea (cape), **4**.53–54, 56, **8**.39
Malis, Malians, **A, B**, **3**.92, **5**.51
Mantinea, -eans, **3**.107–111, 113, **4**.134, **5**.26, 29, 33, 37, 43–45, 47–48, 50, 55–81 *passim*, **6**.16, 29, 43, 61, 67–68, 88–89, 105, **7**.57
Marathon, **1**.18, 73, **2**.34, **6**.59
Marathoussa (island), **8**.31

Marea, **1**.104
Massalia, **1**.13
Meander (river), **D**, **3**.19, **8**.58
Mecyberna, **J**, **5**.18, 39
Medeon, **3**.106
Medes, **1**.104, 130
Medma, **5**.5
Megabates, **1**.129
Megabazus, **1**.109
Megabyxus, **1**.109
Megara, -ians, Megarid, **A, I**, **1**.27, 42, 46, 48, 67, 103, 105, 107–108, 114, 126, 139–140, **2**.9, 31, 93, **3**.51, 68, **4**.66–74, 75, 76, 109, 118, **5**.16, 38, 58–60, **6**.4, 43, **7**.57, **8**.3, 33, 94
Megara Hyblaea, **C**, **6**.4, 49, 75, 94, 97, **7**.25
Meidius (river), **8**.106
Melanchridas, **8**.6
Melanthus, **8**.5
Meleas, **3**.5
Melesander, **2**.69
Melesias, **8**.86
Melesippus, **1**.139, **2**.12
Melitea, **4**.78
Melos (island), -ians, **B**, **2**.9, **3**.91, 94, **5**.84–116, **8**.39, 41
Memphis, **1**.104, 109
Menander, **7**.16, 43, 69
Menas, **5**.21
Mende, -eans, **J**, **4**.7, 121–124, 129–131
Menecolus, **6**.5
Menedaius, **3**.100, 109
Meno, **2**.22
Messapians, **3**.101, **7**.33
Messenia, -ians, **A**, **1**.101, **2**.9, 25, 90, 102, **3**.75, 80, 94–95, 97, 100, 107–108, 112, **4**.3, 9, 32, 36, 41, **5**.35, 56, **6**.4, **7**.31, 57

696

Index of Proper Names

Messina, -ians, **C**, **3**.88, 90, **4**.1, 24–25, **5**.5, **6**.4, 48, 50, 74, **7**.1
Metapontium, -ines, **C**, **7**.33, 57
Methana, **4**.45, **5**.18
Methone (Macedon), **4**.129, **6**.7
Methone (Messenia), **2**.25
Methydrium, **5**.58
Methymna, -aeans, **D**, **3**.2, 5, 18, 50, **6**.85, **7**.57, **8**.22–23, 100–101
Metropolis, **3**.107
Miciades, **1**.47
Miletus, Milesia, -ians, **B, D**, **1**.115–116, **4**.42, 53–54, **7**.57, **8**.17, 19, 24–30, 32–33, 36, 38–39, 45, 50, 57, 60–63, 75, 78–80, 83–85, 99–100, 108–109
Mimas, Mount, **8**.34
Mindarus, **8**.85, 99–104
Minoa (island), **3**.51, **4**.67, 118
Minos, **1**.4, 8
Molossians, **E**, **1**.136, **2**.80
Molycreum, **G**, **2**.84, **3**.102
Morgantina, **4**.65
Motya, **C**, **6**.2
Munychia, **2**.13, **8**.92–93
Mycale, **1**.89, **8**.79
Mycalessus, -ians, **7**.29–30
Mycenae, **1**.9, 10
Myconos (island), **3**.29
Mygdonia, **1**.58, **2**.99–100
Mylae, **C**, **3**.90
Myletidae, **6**.5
Myoneans, **3**.101
Myonnesus, **3**.32
Myous, **1**.138, **3**.19
Myrcinus, **J**, **4**.107, **5**.6, 10
Myronides, **1**.105, 108, **4**.95
Myrrhine, **6**.55
Myscon, **8**.85
Mysteries, Eleusinian, **6**.28, 53, 60–61, **8**.53

Mytilene, -eans, **B, D**, **3**.2–6, 8–15, 18–19, 25–31, 33, 35–50, **4**.52, 75, **8**.22–23, 100–101; *see also* Lesbos

Naucleides, **2**.2
Naupactus, **A, B, E, G**, **1**.103, **2**.9, 69, 80–81, 83–84, 90–92, 102–103, **3**.7, 69, 75, 78, 94–102 *passim*, 114, **4**.13, 41, 49, 76–77, **7**.17, 19, 31, 34, 36, 57
Naxos (island), -ians, **B, D**, **1**.98, 137
Naxos (Sicilian town), **C**, **4**.25, **6**.3, 20, 50, 72, 74–75, 88, 98, **7**.14, 57
Neapolis, **C**, **7**.50
Nemea (Aetolia), **3**.96
Nemea (Peloponnese), **5**.58–60
Nericus, **3**.7
Nestus (river), **F**, **2**.96
Nicanor, **2**.80
Niciades, **4**.118
Nicias (Athenian), **3**.51, 91, **4**.27–28, 42, 53–54, 129–132, **5**.16, 43, 45–46, 83, **6**.8–25, 46–47, 62, 67–69, 102–104, **7**.1, 3–8, 10–16, 32, 38, 42–43, 48–50, 60–65, 69, 72–86
Nicias (Cretan), **2**.85
Nicolaus, **2**.67
Nicomachus, **4**.89
Nicomedes, **1**.107
Nicon, **7**.19
Niconidas, **4**.78
Nicostratus, **3**.75, **4**.53, 129–130, **5**.61
Nile (river), **1**.104, 110
Nine Springs, **2**.15
Nine Ways, **1**.100, **4**.102; *see also* Amphipolis

Index of Proper Names

Nisaea, **I**, **1**.103, 114–115, **2**.31, 93–94, **3**.51, **4**.21, 66–70, 72–73, 85, 100, 108, 118, **5**.16
Notium, **3**.34
Nymphodorus, **2**.29

Odomantes, **2**.101, **5**.6
Odrysians, **2**.29, 95–98, **4**.101
Odysseus, **4**.24
Oeanthians, **3**.101
Oeneum, **G**, **3**.95, 98, 102
Oeniadae, **E**, **1**.111, **2**.82, 102, **3**.7, 94, **4**.77
Oenoe, **2**.18–19, **8**.98
Oenophyta, **I**, **1**.108, **4**.95
Oenoussae (islands), **8**.24
Oesyme, **J**, **4**.107
Oetaeans, **3**.92, **8**.3
Olophyxus, **J**, **4**.109
Olpae, **3**.105–111, 113
Olympia, **A**, **1**.121, 143, **3**.8, **5**.18
Olympic games, **1**.6, 126, **3**.8, **5**.47, 49–50, **6**.16
Olympus, Mount, **A**, **4**.78
Olynthus, -ians, **J**, **1**.58, 62–63, **2**.79, **4**.110, 123, **5**.3, 6, 10, 18, 39
Oneum, Mount, **4**.44
Onomacles, **8**.25, 30
Ophiones, **3**.94, 96, 100
Opicia, Opici, **6**.2, 4
Opus, **2**.32
Orchomenus (Arcadia), -ians, **5**.61–63, 77
Orchomenus (Boeotia), **I**, **1**.113, **3**.87, **4**.76, 93
Orestes, **1**.111
Orestheum, **5**.64
Oresthis, **4**.134
Orestians, **E**, **2**.80

Oreus, **8**.95
Orneae, Orneatae, **5**.67, 72, 74, **6**.7
Orobiae, **3**.89
Oroedus, **2**.80
Oropus, -ians, **I**, **2**.23, **3**.91, **4**.91, 96, 99, **7**.28, **8**.60, 95
Oscius (river), **F**, **2**.96

Paches, **3**.18, 28, 33–36, 48–50
Paeonia, -ians, **F**, **2**.96, 98–99
Pagondas, **4**.91–93, 96
Palaerus, **2**.30
Palarians, **3**.92
Pale, **1**.27, **2**.30
Pallene (peninsula), **J**, **1**.56, 62, 64, **4**.116, 120, 123, 129
Pammilus, **6**.4
Pamphylia, **1**.100
Panactum, **I**, **5**.3, 18, 35–36, 39–40, 42, 44, 46
Panaei, **2**.101
Panaerus, **4**.78
Panathenaea (festival), **1**.20, **5**.47, **6**.56
Pandion, **2**.29
Pangaeum (mountain), **2**.99
Panormus (Achaea), **2**.86, 92
Panormus (Miletus), **8**.24
Panormus (Sicily), **C**, **6**.2
Pantacyas (river), **6**.4
Paralus, **2**.55
Paravaeans, **E**, **2**.80
Parnassus (mountain), **G**, **3**.95
Parnes, Mount, **I**, **2**.23, **4**.96
Paros (island), **B**, **4**.104
Parrasians, **5**.33
Pasitelidas, **4**.132, **5**.3
Patmos (island), **3**.33
Patrae, **2**.83–84, **5**.52
Pausanias (Macedonian), **1**.61

Index of Proper Names

Pausanias (Spartan king), **3**.26
Pausanias (Spartan regent), **1**.94–96, 128–135, 139, **2**.71–72, **3**.54, 58, 68
Pedaritus, **8**.28, 32–33, 38–40, 55, 61
Pegae, **1**.103, 107, 111, 115, **4**.21, 66, 74
Peirasus, **2**.22
Peisander, **8**.49, 53–54, 56, 63–65, 67–68, 73, 90, 98
Peisistratus, **1**.20, **3**.104, **6**.53–54
Peisistratus (grandson), **6**.54
Peithias, **3**.70
Pelargicum, **2**.17
Pelasgians, **1**.3, **4**.109
Pele (island), **8**.31
Pella, **F**, **2**.99–100
Pellene, -ians, **2**.9, **4**.120, **5**.58–60, **8**.3, 106
Peloponnese, -ians, **A**, **B**, **G**, **I**, *passim*
Pelops, **1**.9
Pelorus (cape), **4**.25
Peparethos (island), **3**.89
Perdiccas, **1**.56–59, 61–62, **2**.29, 80, 95, 99–101, **4**.78–79, 82–83, 103, 107, 124, 128, 132, **5**.6, 80, 83, **6**.7, **7**.9
Pericles, **1**.111, 114, 116–117, 127, 139–145, **2**.12–13, 21–22, 31, 34–46, 55, 58–65, **6**.31
Perieres, **6**.4
Perrhaebia, **4**.78
Perseus, **1**.9
Persia, Persians, **1**.13–18 *passim*, 23, 41, 69, 73–77, 86–104 *passim*, 131, 132, 142, 144, **2**.13, 16, 21, 48, 71, 74, 97, **3**.10, 34, 54–65 *passim*, **4**.36, **6**.4, 17, 33, 76, 82–83, **7**.21, **8**.24, 43, 46, 62

Petra, **7**.35
Phacium, **4**.78
Phaeacians, **1**.25
Phaeax, **5**.4–5
Phaedimus, **5**.42
Phäeinis, **4**.133
Phaenippus, **4**.118
Phagres, **2**.99
Phalerum, **1**.107, **2**.13
Phalius, **1**.24
Phanae, **8**.24
Phanomachus, **2**.70
Phanotis, **I**, **4**.76, 89
Pharnabazus, **8**.6, 39, 62, 80, 99, 109
Pharnaces, **2**.67, **5**.1
Pharos (island), **1**.104
Pharsalus, **A**, **1**.111, **2**.22, **4**.78
Phaselis, **2**.69, **8**.88, 99, 108
Pheia, **2**.25, **7**.31
Pherae, **2**.22
Philip, **1**.57, 59, 61, **2**.95, 100
Philippus, **8**.28, 87, 99
Philocharidas, **5**.21, 44
Philocrates, **5**.116
Philoctetes, **1**.10
Phleious, Phleiasians, **1**.27, **4**.70, 133, **5**.57–60, 83, 115, **6**.105
Phocaea, -ans, **D**, **1**.13, **8**.31, 101
Phoceae, **5**.4
Phocis, -ians, **A**, **G**, **I**, **1**.107–108, 111, 112, **2**.9, 29, **3**.95, 101, **4**.76, 118, **5**.32, 64, **6**.2, **8**.3
Phoenice, **2**.69
Phoenicia, -ians, **1**.8, 16, 100, 110, 112, 116, **6**.2, **8**.46, 59, 78, 81, 87–88, 99, 108–109
Phoenicous, **8**.34
Phormio, **1**.64–65, 117, **2**.29, 58, 68, 69, 80–81, 83–85, 88–92, 102–103, **3**.7, 17

Index of Proper Names

Photyus, **2**.80
Phrygia, **2**.22
Phrynichus, **8**.25, 27, 48–51, 54, 68, 90, 92
Phrynis, **8**.6
Phthiotis, *see* Achaea Phthiotis
Phyrcus, **5**.49
Physca, **2**.99
Phytia, **3**.106
Pieria, -ians, **2**.99–100
Pierium, **5**.13
Pindus (mountains), **2**.102
Piraeus, **1**.93, 107, **2**.13, 17, 48, 93–94, **5**.26, **6**.30, **8**.1, 76, 82, 86, 90–96
Pissuthnes, **1**.115, **3**.31, 34, **8**.5, 28
Pittacus, **4**.107
Plataea, -ans, **B**, **I**, **1**.130, **2**.2–6, 9, 10, 12, 19, 71–78, **3**.20–24, 36, 52–68, **4**.67, 72, **5**.16, 32, **7**.18, 57
Pleistarchus, **1**.132
Pleistoanax, **1**.107, 114, **2**.21, **5**.16, 33, 75
Pleistolas, **5**.19, 25
Plemyrium, **K**, **7**.4, 22–25, 31–32
Pleuron, **3**.102
Pnyx, the, **8**.97
Polichna (Clazomenae), **8**.14, 23
Polichna (Crete), **2**.85
Polis, **3**.101
Polles, **5**.6
Pollis, **2**.67
Polyanthes, **7**.34
Polycrates, **1**.13, **3**.104
Polydamidas, **4**.123, 129–130
Polymedes, **2**.22
Poseidon (god), **1**.128, **2**.84, **4**.129, **8**.67
Potamis, **8**.85
Potidaea, -ans, **A**, **B**, **F**, **J**, **1**.56–68, 85, 118–119, 124, 139–140, **2**.2, 13, 31, 58, 67, 70, 79, **3**.17, **4**.120–122, 129–130, 135, **5**.30, **6**.31
Potidania, **3**.96
Prasiae (Attica), **8**.95
Prasiae (Laconia), **2**.56, **6**.105, **7**.18
Pratodamus, **2**.67
Priapus, **D**, **8**.107
Priene, **1**.115
Procles, **3**.91, 98
Procne, **2**.29
Pronni, **2**.30
Propylaea, **2**.13
Proschium, **3**.102, 106
Prosopitis (island), **1**.109
Prote (island), **4**.13
Proteas, **1**.45, **2**.23
Protesilaus, **8**.102
Proxenus, **3**.103
Pteleum (Erythrae), **8**.24, 31
Pteleum (Greece), **5**.18
Ptoeodorus, **4**.76
Ptychia (island), **4**.46
Pydna, **1**.61, 137
Pylos, **H**, **4**.3, 6, 8–16, 23, 24, 26–41, 46, 55, 80, **5**.7, 14, 35–36, 39, 44–45, 56, 115, **6**.89, 105, **7**.18, 57, 71, 86
Pyrrha, **D**, **3**.18, 25, 35, **8**.23
Pystilus, **6**.4
Pythangelus, **2**.2
Pythen, **6**.104, **7**.1, 70
Pythodorus (Athenian), **2**.1, **3**.115, **4**.2, 65
Pythodorus (another Athenian), **6**.105

Ramphias, **1**.139, **5**.12–14
Rhegium, **C**, **3**.86, 88, 115, **4**.1, 24–25, **6**.4, 44–46, 49–51, 79, **7**.1, 4, 35
Rheiti lakes, **2**.19
Rheitus (stream), **4**.42

Index of Proper Names

Rhenea (island), **1**.13, **3**.104
Rhium, **2**.84, 87, 92, **5**.52
Rhodes (island), -ians, **B, D, 6**.43, **7**.57, **8**.41, 44–45, 52, 55, 57, 60–61
Rhodope (mountain), **F, 2**.96, 98
Rhoeteum, **4**.52, **8**.101
Rhype, **7**.34

Sabylinthus, **2**.80
Sacon, **6**.5
Sadocus, **2**.29, 67
Sagreus, **7**.19
Salaethus, **3**.25, 27, 35–36
Salamis (Cyprus), **1**.112
Salamis (island; Greece), **A, 1**.73, 137, **2**.93–94, **3**.17, 51, **8**.94
Salynthius, **3**.111, 114, **4**.77
Same, **2**.30
Saminthus, **5**.58
Samos (island), -ians, **B, D, 1**.13, 40–41, 115–117, **3**.32, 104, **4**.75, **6**.4, **7**.57, **8**.16–100 *passim*, 108; *see also* Anaea
Sandius (hill), **3**.19
Sane, **J, 4**.109, **5**.18
Sardis, **D, 1**.115
Scandea, **4**.54
Scione, **J, 4**.120–123, 129–133, **5**.2, 18, 32
Sciritis, Sciritae, **5**.33, 67–68, 71–72
Scironides, **8**.25, 54
Scirphondas, **7**.30
Scombrus (mountain), **F, 2**.96
Scyllaeus, **5**.53
Scyros (island), **1**.98
Scythians, **2**.96–97
Sea
  Adriatic, **A, C, 1**.24, **2**.97
  Aegean, **F, I, J, 1**.98, **3**.32, **4**.46, 57, 109, 129
  Black, **D, F, 2**.96–97, **3**.2, **4**.75
  Cretan, **4**.53, **5**.110
  Ionian, **A, C, G, 6**.13, 30, 34, 44, 104, **7**.33, 57
  Sicilian, **4**.24, 53, **6**.13
  Tyrrhenian, **C, 4**.24, **6**.62, **7**.58
Selinous, -ountians, **C, 6**.4, 6, 8, 13, 20, 47–48, 62, 65, 67, **7**.1, 50, 57–58, **8**.26
Sermylia, -ians, **1**.65, **5**.18
Sestus, **D, 1**.89, **8**.62, 102, 104, 107
Seuthes, **2**.97, 101, **4**.101
Sicania (= Sicily), Sicanians, **6**.2
Sicanus (river), **6**.2
Sicanus (Syracusan), **6**.73, **7**.46, 50, 70
Sicels, **3**.88, 103, 115, **4**.25, **5**.4, **6**.2, 4, 34, 45, 48, 62, 65, 88, 94, 98, 103, **7**.1–2, 32–33, 57–58, 77, 80
Sicily, -ians, **C, 1**.12, 14, 17–18, 36, 44, **2**.7, 65, **3**.86, 88, 90, 99, 103, 115–116, **4**.1, 2, 5, 24, 46, 48, 58–65, 81, **5**.4–5, **6**.1–53, 61–94, 96–104, **7**.1–18, 21–28, 31–34, **8**.2, 4, 13, 24, 26, 91, 96, 106
Sicyon, -ians, **I, 1**.28, 108, 111, 114, **2**.9, 80, **4**.70, 101, **5**.52, 58–60, 81, **7**.19, 58, **8**.3
Sidoussa, **8**.24
Sigeum, **D, 6**.59, **8**.101
Simaethus (river), **6**.65
Simonides, **4**.7
Simus, **6**.5
Singus, **J, 5**.18
Sinti, **F, 2**.98
Siphae, **I, 4**.76–77, 89–90, 101
Sitalces, **2**.29, 67, 95–101, **4**.101
Socrates, **2**.23, **8**.109
Sollium, **2**.30, **3**.95, **5**.30
Soloeis, **C, 6**.2
Solygea, **4**.42–43

Index of Proper Names

Sophocles, **3.**115, **4.**2–3, 46, 65
Sparta, **A, B,** *passim*
Spartiates, **1.**128, 131–132, **2.**12, 25, 66, **3.**92, 100, **4.**8, 11, 38, **5.**9, 15, 63, **6.**91, **7.**19, 58, **8.**7, 11, 22, 39, 43, 61, 91, 99
Spartolus, **2.**79, **5.**18
Speiraeum, **8.**10–12, 14–15, 20, 28
Sphacteria (island), **H, 4.**8, 55, 57, 108, 117, **5.**14–15, 34, 35, 43, 75, **7.**86
Stages, **8.**16
Stagirus, **4.**88, **5.**6, 18
Stesagoras, **1.**116
Sthenelaidas, **1.**85–87
Stolus, **5.**18
Stratonice, **2.**101
Stratus, -ians, **E, 2.**80–84, 102, **3.**106
Strepsa, **1.**61
Strombichides, **8.**15–17, 30, 62–63, 79
Strongyle (island), **3.**88
Strophacus, **4.**78
Strymon (river), **A, F, J, 1.**100, **2.**96–97, 99, 101, **4.**102, 108, **5.**7, **7.**9
Styphon, **4.**38
Styra, **7.**57
Sunium, **7.**28, **8.**4, 95
Sybaris (river), **7.**35
Sybota (bay), **1.**50, 52, 54, **3.**76
Sybota (islands), **1.**47, 54
Syme (island), **D, 8.**41–43
Syracuse, -ans, **3.**86, 88, 90, 103, 115, **4.**1, 24–25, 65, **5.**4, **6.**3–6, 11, 17, 20, 32, 35, 37–38, 41, 45, 48–52, 63–88, 91, 93–94, 96–104, **7.**1–8, 11–15, 18, 21–25, 28, 32–33, 36–87, **8.**26, 28, 35, 61, 78, 84, 85, 96, 104–106

Taenarum, **A, 1.**128, 133, **7.**19
Tamos, **8.**31, 87
Tanagra, **I, 1.**108, **3.**91, **4.**76, 91, 93, 97, **7.**29
Tantalus, **4.**57
Taras, **C, 6.**34, 44, 104, **7.**1, **8.**91
Taulantians, **1.**24
Tegea, -eans, **4.**134, **5.**32, 40, 57, 62, 64–67, 71–76, 78, 82
Teichioussa, **8.**26, 28
Teichium, **3.**96
Teisamenus, **3.**92
Teisander, **3.**100
Teisias, **5.**84
Tellias, **6.**103
Temenitis, **7.**3
Temenus, **2.**99
Tenedos (island), **3.**2, 28, 35, **7.**57
Tenos (island), **7.**57, **8.**69
Teos, Teians, **D, 3.**32, **8.**16, 19–20
Teres, **2.**29
Tereus, **2.**29
Terias (river), **6.**50, 94
Teutiaplus, **3.**29–31
Teutloussa (island), **8.**42
Thapsus, **C, 6.**4, 97, 99, 101–102
Tharyps, **2.**80
Thasos (island), -ians, **B, J, 1.**100–101, **4.**104–105, 107, **5.**6, **8.**64
Theaenetus, **3.**20
Theagenes (Athenian), **4.**27
Theagenes (Megarian), **1.**126
Thebes, Thebans, **A, B, I, 1.**27, 90, **2.**2–6, 71–72, **3.**22, 24, 54–68, 91, **4.**76, 93, 96, 133, **5.**16, **6.**95, **7.**18, 30, **8.**100
Themistocles, **1.**14, 74, 90–93, 135–138
Thera (island), **B, 2.**9
Theramenes, **8.**68, 89–92, 94

Index of Proper Names

Therimenes, **8**.26, 29, 31, 36, 38, 43, 52
Therme, **1**.61, **2**.29
Thermon, **8**.11
Thermopylae, **2**.101, **3**.92, **4**.36
Theseus, **2**.15, **6**.61
Thespiae, -ians, **I**, **4**.76, 93, 96, 133, **6**.95, **7**.25
Thesprotis, -ians, **E**, **1**.30, 46, 50, **2**.80
Thessalus, **1**.20, **6**.55
Thessaly, -ians, **A**, **B**, **1**.2, 12, 102, 107, 111, **2**.22, 101, **3**.93, **4**.78–79, 108, 132, **5**.13–14, 51, **8**.3, 43
Thoricus, **8**.95
Thoucles, **6**.3
Thouria, **1**.101
Thrace, -ians, **D**, **F**, **1**.100, 130, **2**.29, 67, 96–101, **4**.75, 101, 102, 105, 129, **5**.6–7, 34–35, 38, 67, **7**.9, 27, 29–30
Thraceward region, **1**.56–60, 68, **2**.9, 67, **3**.92, **4**.70, 74, 79, 82, 102–123, **5**.2–3, 6–12, 21, 26, 31, 35, 80, **8**.64
Thrasonides, **7**.7
Thrasybulus, **8**.73, 75–76, 81, 100, 104–105
Thrasycles, **8**.15, 17, 19
Thrasyllus (Argive), **5**.59–60
Thrasyllus (Athenian), **8**.73, 75–76, 100, 104–105
Thrasymelidas, **4**.11
Thria, **1**.114, **2**.21
Thriasian Plain, **2**.19–21
Thronium, **2**.26
Thucydides (the historian), **1**.1, **2**.70, 103, **3**.25, 88, 116, **4**.51, 104–107, 135, **5**.26, **6**.7, 93, **7**.18, **8**.6, 60

Thucydides (another Athenian), **1**.117
Thucydides of Pharsalus, **8**.92
Thurii, -ians, **C**, **6**.61, 88, 104, **7**.33, 35, 57, **8**.35, 61, 84
Thyamis (river), **1**.46
Thyamus, Mount, **3**.106
Thymochares, **8**.95
Thyreatis, **2**.27, **4**.56–57, **5**.41, **6**.95
Thyssus, **J**, **4**.109, **5**.35
Tilataei, **2**.96
Timagoras (Cyzicene), **8**.6, 8, 39
Timagoras (Tegean), **2**.67
Timanor, **1**.29
Timocrates, **2**.85, 92
Timoxenus, **2**.33
Tissaphernes, **8**.5–6, 16–31 *passim*, 35–37, 43–49, 52–54, 56–59, 63, 65, 78, 80–85, 87–88, 99, 108–109
Tlepolemus, **1**.117
Tolmides, **1**.108, 113
Tolophonians, **3**.101
Tolophus, **3**.100
Torone, **A, J**, **4**.110–116, 120–122, 129, 132, **5**.2–3, 6, 18
Torylaus, **4**.78
Trachis, Trachinians, **3**.92, 100, **4**.78, **5**.12, 51
Tragia (island), **1**.116
Treres, **2**.96
Triballi, **F**, **2**.96, **4**.101
Trinacria (= Sicily), **6**.2
Triopium, **8**.35, 60
Tripodiscus, **4**.70, 72
Triteans, **3**.101
Troezen, **A**, **1**.27, 115, **2**.56, **4**.21, 45, 118, **8**.3
Trogilus, **K**, **6**.99, **7**.2
Trotilus, **6**.4

Index of Proper Names

Troy, **1**.3, 8–11, **2**.68, **4**.120, **6**.2
Twelve Gods, the, **6**.54
Tydeus, **8**.38
Tyndareus, **1**.9

Venerable Goddesses, the, **1**.126

White Fort, **1**.104

Xenares, **5**.36–38, 46, 51
Xenocleides, **1**.46, **3**.114
Xenon, **7**.19

Xenophantidas, **8**.55
Xenophon, **2**.70, 79
Xerxes, **1**.14, 118, 128–129, **3**.56

Zacynthos (island), -ians, **A**, **B**, **E**, **1**.47, **2**.7, 9, 66, 80, **3**.94–95, **4**.8, 13, **7**.31, 57
Zancle, **6**.4–5
Zeus (god), **1**.103, 126, **2**.15, 71, **3**.14, 70, 96, **5**.16, 31, 47, 50, **6**.64–65, 70, 75, **7**.4, 37, 42

RAISING READERS
Books Build Bright Futures

Dear Reader,

We'd love your attention for one more page to tell you about the crisis in children's reading, and what we can all do.

Studies have shown that reading for fun is the **single biggest predictor of a child's future life chances** – more than family circumstance, parents' educational background or income. It improves academic results, mental health, wealth, communication skills, ambition and happiness.[1]

The number of children reading for fun is in rapid decline. Young people have a lot of competition for their time. In 2024, 1 in 10 children and young people in the UK aged 5 to 18 did not own a single book at home.[2]

Hachette works extensively with schools, libraries and literacy charities, but here are some ways we can all raise more readers:

- Reading to children for just 10 minutes a day makes a difference
- Don't give up if children aren't regular readers – there will be books for them!
- Visit bookshops and libraries to get recommendations
- Encourage them to listen to audiobooks
- Support school libraries
- Give books as gifts

There's a lot more information about how to encourage children to read on our website: **www.RaisingReaders.co.uk**

Thank you for reading.

---

[1] OECD, '21st-Century Readers: Developing Literacy Skills in a Digital World', 2021, https://www.oecd.org/en/publications/21st-century-readers_a83d84cb-en.html

[2] National Literacy Trust, 'Book Ownership in 2024', November 2024, https://literacytrust.org.uk/research-services/research-reports/book-ownership-in-2024